# Understanding the Bird of Prey

# Understanding the Bird of Prey

*Nick Fox*

hancock

house

ISBN 0-88839-317-2
Copyright © 1995 Dr. Nick Fox

**Cataloging in Publication Data**
Fox, Nick, 1949-
    Understanding the bird of prey

    Includes bibliographical references and index.
    ISBN 0-88839-317-2

    1. Birds of prey.   2. Falconry.   3. Aviculture.
I. Title.
QL696.F3F69 1995    598.9'1    C95-910637-5

Production: Lorna Brown and Nancy Kerr
Cover photo: Dr. and Mrs. N. C. Fox

Published simultaneously in Canada and the United States by

**HANCOCK HOUSE PUBLISHERS LTD.**
**19313 Zero Avenue, Surrey, B.C. V4P 1M7**
**(604) 538-1114    Fax (604) 538-2262**

**HANCOCK HOUSE PUBLISHERS**
**1431 Harrison Avenue, Blaine, WA 98230-5005**
**(604) 538-1114    Fax (604) 538-2262**

# Contents

# Illustrations

# Preface

This book was started in 1968 with hand-written notes, and finished in 1994 on a laptop. What a lot has happened in that time! We've had the pesticide crisis resulting in a change in public attitude toward birds of prey, a blossoming of international research and conservation work on raptors, a long and successful struggle to breed raptors in captivity resulting in a major increase in supply of birds for falconry, and we've had a technological revolution in telemetry, computers, and genetic research.

My main reason for writing this book has been to teach myself. Whenever I have dug into a subject, I've written it up as a way of summarizing my thoughts. Sometimes I had to leave an aspect for a few years until I've had time to do more research or investigation into it, or until the subject itself has matured. For example, it is only in the last few years that domestic breeding has become routine.

The result is a very unbalanced pile of material. I have tried to level it out, but now I console myself with the thought that, just as it has been written in bits and pieces, so it will probably be read in the same way. It is a book to be dipped into.

Although it is based on science, in fact on over 2,000 papers, and each part has been subject to scientific peer review, it is not written in a scientific style. This is because most of the people reading it, who have hands on experience with hawks, are not scientists and prefer an easier read. And it is because I have no illusions that scientific style increases objectivity. So, as a compromise, I have listed at the end of the book in order of chapter, key texts which are readily available and which will open the door to the subjects for the serious student.

I am a lucky fellow. After hawking my way through a zoology degree at the University of St. Andrews in Scotland, and through teacher training at Dundee, I had four years in the Southern Alps of New Zealand doing my doctorate on all aspects of the biology of the New Zealand falcon. This species was at that time, to all intents and purposes, unapproached by modern science. I had a whole undocumented falcon species to go at! Not only that, the species was an extremely intriguing one, a falcon with accipiter tendencies. What a privilege it was to enter this uncharted territory and

what a good all-round training for a young biologist!

After New Zealand, I taught wildlife illustration for some years, which gave me an insight into the right side of the brain and the frustrations young artists have in trying to use it. A completely different approach to that of the scientists.

Through all this time I continued with research and breeding of hawks, and with farming, horses and dogs. Then, six years ago, I met a remarkable man called Mohamed al Bowardi. He led me by the hand into the fascinating world of Arabian falconry. I agreed to undertake the breeding and research of falcons for the newly forming National Avian Research Center in Abu Dhabi, a project set up by the Al Nayhan family. These people have flown passage and haggard sakers for many centuries. They represent a strong, unbroken train of tradition and knowledge of falconry. Among various other tasks I agreed to breed, hack, train and enter twenty falcons a year able to compare with their best passage birds. To do this by October each year, without using bagged game, crystallizes the thoughts wonderfully. It gave me a chance to temper this book in the fire of experience. Each year I have to bring on as many fine falcons as most people fly in a lifetime; I can't do it alone, I have to teach my staff and working pupils as we go along. They have been guinea pigs for this book and over the years have given me their comments and feedback (not all of them printable!).

Many have contributed to this book. First and foremost are the birds themselves. They motivated me, inspired me and trapped me more surely than I did them. I hope that as a result of this book they will be handled with more understanding and that this will be their reward.

Many people have helped with the final production. My peer reviewers were Neil Forbes MRCVS, Greg Simpson MRCVS and Nigel Harcourt-Brown MRCVS (Structure and function), Prof. Colin Pennycuick (Flight), Prof. David Bird and Mr. Bob Berry (Breeding), Dr. Frederic Launay and Mr. Steve Layman BSc (Development and behavior), Mr. Steve Layman BSc (Training and conditioning), Dr. Ian Newton (Hunting strategies of wild raptors and sections 8.3–6), Prof. Tom Cade, Dr. Mike Nicholls, Dr. Ken Felix, Mr. Hal

Webster, Mrs. Jemima Parry-Jones, Dr. Walter Bednarek, Mr. Paul Llewelyn and Dr. Cecilia Lindberg (Ethics), and Ms. Renatta Platenberg MSc (Rehabilitation). Earlier drafts have been commented on by Mr. Tom Bailey MRCVS, Dr. Steve Sherrod, Dr. Nigel Barton, Mr. David Hancock, Miss Katie O'Neal, and Mr. Seth Layman. Mr. Chris Eastham undertook some of the last-minute data processing to ensure the data are as recent as we could make them.

Many other people have helped with information, material, discussions, comments on "bad practices," photographs and so on, probably wondering if this book would ever see the light of day. I thank them all for their support and patience, and apologize for not being able to name everyone.

The Department of the Environment in Britain has been very helpful with statistics on raptors in captivity, and the National Avian Research Center in Abu Dhabi has provided financial support enabling the book to be completed. I am very grateful to both these organizations.

I have tried to avoid falconry jargon and for the sake of clarity have called the falconer "he" and his bird "she." I have used the words "hawk" and "raptor" interchangeably whereas if I need to specify a particular group I have used accipiter, buteo, accipitrid hawks, falcons, etc. To my colleagues in Britain, I apologize for the American spelling. Sacrifices had to be made.

I must take responsibility for all opinions and for any errors. I hope you will be able to distinguish between factual material, interpretation and opinion and make the necessary allowances.

Finally I would like to thank my wife Barbro for her support through this long project, and my young son Benjamin, who came hawking for the first time this season, and who constantly makes me think about the legacy we are leaving for the next generation to cope with.

Adult white gyr 'Icicle.'

# Foreword

Birds of prey have stirred human emotions since time immemorial because of their fierce beauty, great strength, commanding presence, and superlative skill as hunters. Who knows when the first primitive man looked skyward and decided to adopt the eagle as his totem? Who first saw a peregrine stoop and thought to take her for his hunting companion? Surely it happened well before recorded history.

Today, birds of prey are arguably the most popular group of birds. Certainly they attract the most ardent and zealous devotees, whether they be falconers, rehabilitators, breeders, banders, scientists, or birdwatchers. There is something about these winged predators that evokes the strongest possible feelings in the breasts of their admirers and causes such people to do all kinds of strange things in order to maintain a closeness with their feathered idols, as Bil Gilbert detailed in a most revealing account for *Audubon* some years ago. To have such a magnificent creature as a hawk, falcon, or eagle accept you as its companion and to allow you to enter its space is to gain a rare perspective on life.

At a time in our social and cultural development when most human beings have lost direct contact with nature and living things and are separated more and more from the natural world, there is a great need for nurturing avocations that give people the opportunity for intimate, eye-to-eye relationships with other kinds of animals. Deep in the human psyche there is a longing to know "other bloods." It is a part of what the Harvard biologist, E. O. Wilson, has termed "biophilia"— the love of life that stems from the ancestral and mystical connectedness that human beings have and feel for other forms of life. For many it is mainly a subconscious yearning, but it becomes a vibrant, overt passion for a few, special people. An opportunity to experience this kinship with other animals and with nature helps people to understand their dependence on the earth's natural processes and on the web of interconnected relationships among all living things.

Unfortunately, all too many of us now receive most of our information and knowledge of animals and the living world from television or the glossy pages of magazines and coffee table books. More and more human attitudes about nature are shaped by these representational, often distorted pictures rather than by real-life experiences.

It was not always so. When I was a boy growing up in the 1930s and 1940s in Texas, and later in California, I had a constant succession of wild pets ranging from jars full of red ants to "horny toads," ground squirrels, deer mice, opossums, crows, owls, and my first hawk when I was nine years old. This venerable tradition of pet-keeping no doubt goes back to the very origins of humanity and was the basis for the domestication of animals. The list of great naturalists and biologists whose careers sprang from such simple pursuits is too long to enumerate but includes such names as Aristotle, Frederick II of Hohenstaufen, John James Audubon, Louis Agassiz, Theodore Roosevelt, William Beebe, Aldo Leopold, Roger Tory Peterson, Fran Hamerstrom, and at least two Nobel prize winners, Niko Tinbergen and Konrad Lorenz, whose classic 1935 paper, *Der Kumpan in der Umwelt des Vogels*, was based largely on his personal experiences with hand-tamed birds.

One wonders how many potentially great biologists are being lost to society now because opportunities for hands-on experiences with wild animals are so limited. Gone are the days when a young boy or girl could go freely into the woods or field and bring back a wild pet as a companion. It is now against the law to do so in most places. There are international treaties, national laws, state and provincial laws, municipal laws, and societal disapprobation of all sorts. It is, of course, true, and we all know that many of these wild creatures that used to be taken so lovingly into childhood embrace ended up either dead or leading miserable lives in confinement. That is part of the reason for the laws and social disapproval. Still, on balance, there is much to be said in favor of keeping wild animals as companions, and today the grosser forms of unintended mistreatment can be avoided with modern knowledge of veterinary practices, husbandry, and caretaking.

It is of more than passing interest that falconry, raptor rehabilitation, and captive breeding are among the few legal and acceptable ways in which people can still have personal relationships with nondomesticated animals. The practitioners of these pursuits are privileged members of society, and because birds of prey are so highly esteemed and basically rare creatures, they have a special responsibility to make certain that the birds which come into their ken and care receive the most enlightened and humane treatment possible. Many new innovations in the care and handling of birds of prey have come about in the last 30 years: captive breeding, telemetry, greatly increased knowledge of nutrition and treatment of diseases and injuries, understanding of behavior and how it can be modified, especially by imprinting, and new equipment such as Aylmeri jesses, loop leashes, shelf perches, and other things.

As a practicing falconer and raptor biologist, Nick Fox has been in the thick of many of these developments. He received his Ph.D. degree from the University of Canterbury for original research on the little known New Zealand falcon, he has propagated raptors for many years, done pioneering telemetry studies on the home range and movements of the once endangered Mauritius kestrel, worked on the reintroduction of the red kite in Great Britain, and most recently been involved with the National Avian Research Center of Abu Dhabi raising and training captive-bred falcons for Arab falconry. This book is a distillation of the knowledge and understanding of raptors that he has acquired through these diverse activities over the span of time in which the practices involved in handling birds of prey have undergone such radical and improved change.

*Understanding the Bird of Prey* will serve as an advanced primer for the many devotees of raptors coming on the scene as the twenty-first century approaches and as a stimulating refresher for the old hands, who always need to be challenged by new ideas and methods. Together with an up-to-date manual on avian veterinary practices, the reader of this book has all the basic scientific and managerial underpinnings needed to keep birds of prey physically and psychologically fit in the captive environment and the means to gain entry into that very special and inexhaustibly fascinating world of the eagle, the hawk, and the falcon.

TOM J. CADE
The Peregrine Fund, Inc.

New Zealand falcon.

# 1

# Structure

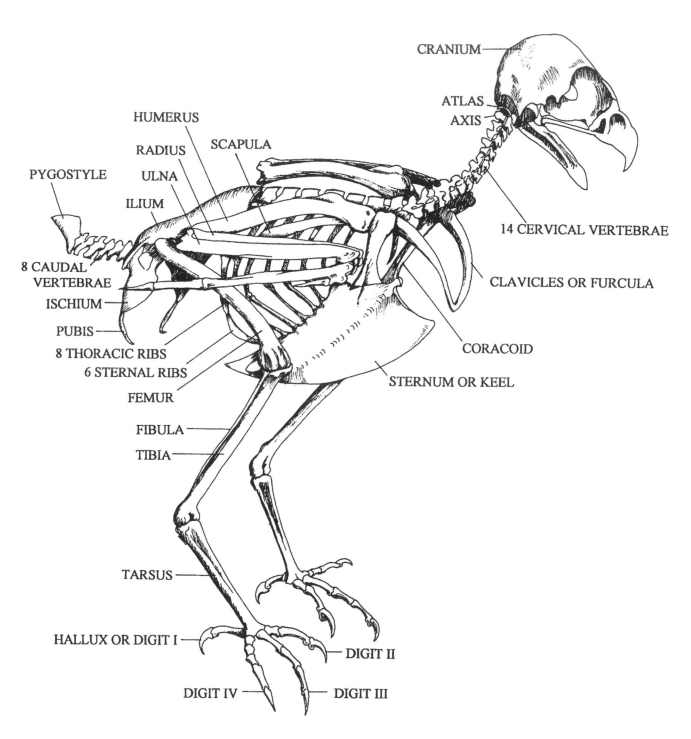

Figure 1.2.1 The skeleton of the common buzzard.

# and Function

## 1.1    Introduction

Science owes to hawking the first scientific study of bird structure. This is Frederick II's thirteenth-century manuscript *The Art of Falconry*. His work stood virtually alone for 300 years until 1572 when Coitier, the Dutch father of avian anatomy, published his studies. Unlike Aristotle before him, Frederick insisted on seeing the evidence for himself. He reared children in isolation to investigate speech and he cut men open to observe the process of digestion. He wasn't always right; he thought birds had diaphragms, but his approach to falconry through natural science was a sound one which we can only update. Nowadays there are a lot of useful books on anatomy available, some of which are listed in chapter 9, Further Reading.

The aim here is to describe structure in relation to function, particularly those aspects of interest to falconers, breeders, and rehabilitators. It is based primarily on dissections of the common buzzard *Buteo buteo,* which are available here as road casualties, but also on various other raptor species which are mentioned where they differ.

Raptors rely on flight for their survival and their skeleton, feathers, skin, and flight muscles make up about 60 percent of the payload (figure 1.1.1). The contribution of each part of the body toward survival is balanced against the cost of carrying it. As you work through this book, you will see how everything about a raptor, its structure, flying ability, and behavior patterns, are honed to a peak of refinement by that moment of truth when a hawk actually hunts its prey. Most raptor populations are controlled through mortality, mainly at the stage when juveniles are trying to survive on their own. Those which survive to breed have come through an uncompromising test of their structure and function.

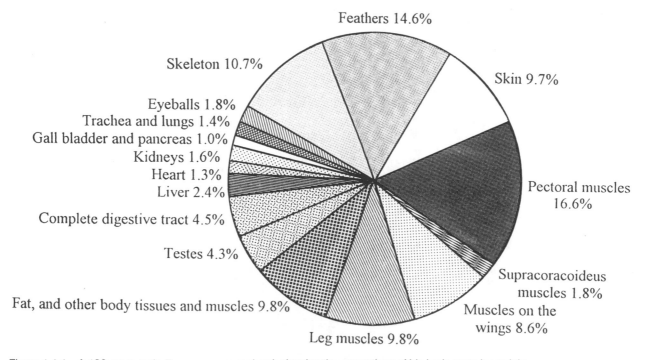

Figure 1.1.1   A 129 gram male European sparrowhawk showing the proportions of his body parts by weight.

## 1.2    The skeleton

The demands of flight have stripped down the hawk skeleton to combine lightness with strength. Most of the bones are hollow and filled with light spongy bone or internal cross-braces and marrow. The general layout of the common buzzard skeleton is shown in figure 1.2.1 see page 16. The pelvis, or synsacrum, and the back, or notarium, are both fused structures separated by one free vertebra in the midback. This helps give rigidity to the bird's body. The neck is very flexible allowing free movement for the head and compensating for the rigidity of the body and the relative immobility of the eyeballs.

The lower part of the body is made up of the large, shieldlike breastbone or sternum. This, with its deep keel and the fused clavicles or wishbone below the crop supports the powerful pectoral muscles which drive the wings. To prevent the sternum from pulling up and crushing the head there are two stout braces, the coracoids, which run up to the shoulders. Being so exposed to impact, the clavicles can often be broken in head-on collisions. When this happens the hawk droops the wing on the injured side and the pectoral muscles may waste slightly on that side.

A young New Zealand falcon displays a rounded nostril with central tubercle and a tomial tooth behind the tip of his beak.

Not only are some of the bones air filled, but many of them are pneumatic or connected to the system of air sacs (see section 1.5). Should the hawk break its upper wing or leg it can actually breath through the broken bone. The lower leg bones contain bone marrow which makes red blood corpuscles.

The limb bones are thin-walled tubes and there is some evidence that the delicate cross-braces which give them their girder-like rigidity are

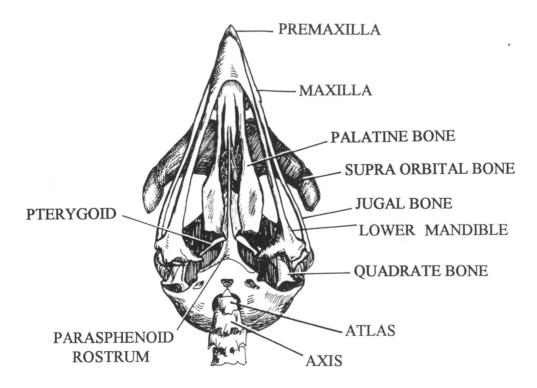

Figure 1.2.2 The skull of the common buzzard from below.

aligned with the forces exerted on the bone in response to the forces on the whole animal. Thus if a growing hawk is not given the opportunity to exercise adequately in its first months of life the cross-braces will be randomly oriented and the limb bones will be weak. Details of the wing and leg bones are given in 1.8 and 1.17.

The raptor skull (figures 1.2.2 and 1.2.3) is highly adapted and is much lighter than those of the archosaurian reptiles from which it evolved. The beak is light and covered with horny keratin. In the falcons and falconets there is an extra notch called the tomial tooth just behind the tip of the beak. This is thought to aid in breaking the necks of prey, the normal falcon method of killing. The beak grows down from the waxy cere which is usually gray or yellow and is sensitive to the touch. Inside the outer horny layer of the beak is the main growing zone which is well-supplied with blood vessels. Below this is the bony core, the premaxilla. Should the beak become overgrown or damaged (figure 1.2.4) it is a relatively simple matter to clip the tip and reshape the sides with a sharp knife, rattail file, or emery board. Splitting or flaking at the side of the beak is best treated by trimming back any loose snags and then cutting back the tip of the beak as far as is safe. This reduces the leverage on the split. If the hawk is provided with plenty of bony joints or tirings to pull at, and some abrasive surfaces to feak or wipe its beak on, it will stay in good order. The beak should never be allowed to get too overgrown otherwise the "quick" or soft interior will extend, preventing reshaping.

The nostrils or nares are circular in the falcons, with a central pin or tubercle (see 1.3). The rear portion of the aperture is shielded by a thin plate of bone. In accipiters, buteos, eagles, and owls, the nostrils are oval with a much reduced tubercle.

The eyes are large, occupying about two thirds of the skull and almost touching each other inside the head. They are protected and supported by a ring of bony sclerotic plates embedded around the rim of each eyeball and by a supraorbital ridge forming a tough bone and cartilage eyebrow, shading the eye and giving the hawk its fierce appearance. Behind this ridge, toward the center of the skull, the eyeball lies unprotected immediately below the skin and is vulnerable to damage by thorns or barbed wire.

The jaws are double hinged like those of snakes. When the hawk opens its mouth, two small quadrate bones, one in each angle of the jaw,

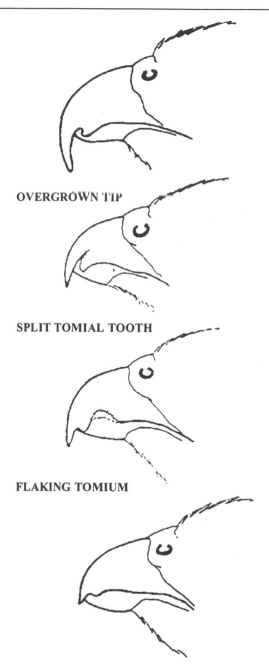

**OVERGROWN TIP**

**SPLIT TOMIAL TOOTH**

**FLAKING TOMIUM**

**BEAK TRIMMED HARD BACK TO REDUCE STRAIN ON A DAMAGED AREA**
Figure 1.2.4 Coping falcon beaks.

swing forward two or three millimeters (figure 1.2.3). The lower jaw hinges down from the quadrate bones and the upper jaw has a flexible bony hinge behind the cere. As the quadrate bones swing forward, they push the jugal arch or cheek bones forward and these push the beak upward. At the same time, two small rodlike pterygoid bones inside the throat are also pushed forward by the quadrate bones and they in turn push forward the

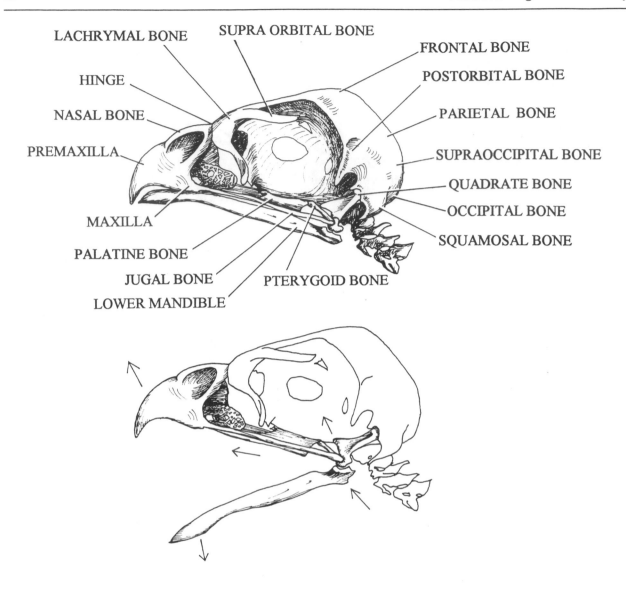

LACHRYMAL BONE       SUPRA ORBITAL BONE

FRONTAL BONE

HINGE                                            POSTORBITAL BONE

NASAL BONE                                      PARIETAL  BONE

PREMAXILLA                                     SUPRAOCCIPITAL BONE

QUADRATE BONE

OCCIPITAL BONE

MAXILLA                                          SQUAMOSAL BONE

PALATINE BONE

JUGAL BONE          PTERYGOID BONE

LOWER MANDIBLE

Figure 1.2.3 The skull of the common buzzard, side view, showing the movement of the lower mandible.

palatine bones lining the roof of the mouth. The palatines are fused to the interior of the beak. Thus, when the hawk opens its mouth, the beak, the cheeks, entire palate, and lower jaw move forward and outward. In some of the owls, such as the barn owl, opening the mouth also extends the jaw outward on each side so that the gape increases by about six millimeters, enabling prey to be swallowed whole.

For the falconer the significance of these bone movements can be seen when fitting the hood. As the cheek bones and lower jaw move forward when the mouth opens, they act as wedges. A leather mouthpiece which crosses them will inevitably either rub the delicate skin that covers them or will let in light. The only way to fit the hood so that the hawk can open its mouth sufficiently to cast, and which is light tight and nonabrasive, is to cut the mouthpiece so that it seals the eyes at the lores (the soft skin in front of the eyes) and then follows just above the jugals to the rictus or corners of the mouth (see figure 3.8.1). Meanwhile, the bulge in the back of the hood caused by the braces, fits snugly under the occiput at the back of the skull, preventing the hood from being hooked off. At the sides, the hood also curves inward sufficiently under the quadrates to prevent removal. In this way the hood can be locked on and yet gives very little restriction to the gape.

## 1.3    The senses

"He has eyes like a hawk." We all know that hawks can see well, but what are their eyes really like and do they even live in the same visual world as us?

Birds of prey have the most highly evolved eyesight of all living organisms. Like humans and related species, but unlike most mammals, birds see in color as well as in black and white. The light-sensitive retina at the back of the eye contains color-sensitive cones as well as tone-sensitive rods for vision in poor light. They also have a wider spectrum of colors than ours. Recent research has shown many birds can see into the ultraviolet range, just as insects can, and therefore some plumage patterns which to us appear drab, to birds may appear quite colorful. Kestrels can detect areas of vole trails by the ultraviolet urine stains.

In the common buzzard, these cones are packed much more densely than in humans and it can probably resolve details eight times better than us. While we have only one part of the visual field in focus, the buzzard has two focal spots or foveas in each eye and these are joined by a horizontal strip of extra sensitive area (figure 1.3.1). One of these foveas, the central fovea, faces outward and is adapted for detecting small movements. When a hawk cocks its head slightly to examine the sky, it is using one of its central foveas (figure 1.3.2). The other, temporal fovea, faces forward and is best at resolving detail, in conjunction with binocular vision. The horizontal strip is used for scanning. Even outside the foveas the buzzard has visual

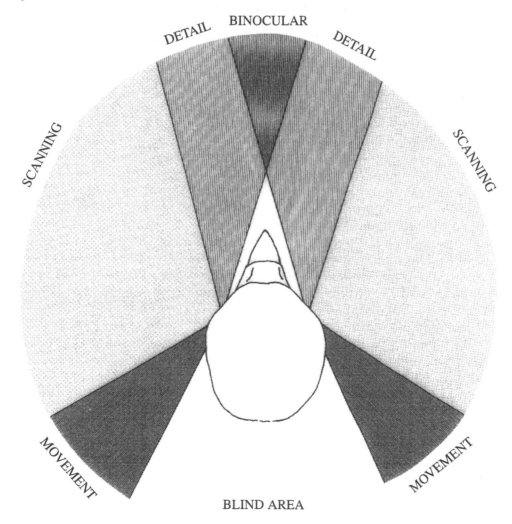

Figure 1.3.1 The field of vision of a common buzzard.

Figure 1.3.2 This saker has noticed an eagle. She cocks her head to use her central fovea.

acuity about twice ours. Using its temporal foveas and binocular vision, together with head-bobbing, the buzzard can build up a detailed stereoscopic image and a good perception of distance.

The common buzzard and most diurnal raptors, have about 45–55 degrees of binocular vision and a total field for each eye of about 170 degrees. There is a blind area behind the head of about 70 degrees. Owls, which have primarily binocular vision and immobile tubular bony eyeballs, have little lateral vision and no central foveas.

At the top of each cone cell is an oil droplet—usually red, orange, yellow, clear, or green. These heighten the contrast of colored objects and also act as haze filters. Protruding into the eye from the retina is the pecten, a large, elongated body well-supplied with blood vessels. It is thought to supply nutrients to and remove waste from the retina by diffusion across the eye fluids. It also appears to act as a movement detector bycasting a shadow across the retina.

In contrast to mammals, most of the muscles controlling the hawk's lens and pupil are striated muscle and can be contracted voluntarily. Thus a peregrine, unhooded into bright sunlight, can promptly adjust its pupils to avoid being dazzled. Similarly, it can fly well toward the sun. To accommodate close focusing, the pupil and the Crampton's muscle around it, are able to squeeze

the lens and cornea and this can be seen in accipiters. When they examine very near objects, such as food in their feet, their pupils shrink noticeably.

The third eyelid or nictitating membrane is translucent or transparent (some waterbirds use them as spectacles for focusing under water). The membrane cleans and protects the eye and the hawk seldom uses its other eyelids during the daytime. When it grapples with prey, its third eyelids constantly flick across to protect the eyes from sharp feathers or thorns. The hawk cleans its eyes by rubbing them on its scapulars; it would be too risky to use claws for this, as it does for scratching its head.

Although examination of a hawk's eye shows relatively few rods and indicates a poor ability to see at dusk, field experience does not support this. Many wild falcons hunt well after dusk, and some hunt in moonlight. One radio-tracked goshawk flew 13 kilometers (8 mi) during the night and trained birds will come in long after it is too dark to see them until they actually arrive. Curiously, gyrfalcons, which one would expect to have good night vision because of the long dark winters, seem to have very poor discrimination in low light.

Pigeons can detect the polarization plane of light and use this for navigation. It is likely that raptors too can detect the polarization of light and thus sunlight, the sky, and reflections to them show polarization patterns.

Raptors can see things which are much closer together in time than we can. For example, the television is designed for human vision. It doesn't show a whole picture; it is just a fast-moving dot which tricks the human eye into thinking it is a picture. The television flickers 25 pictures a second which the human eye translates as one moving picture because it can only see up to 20 events per second. This is called the Flicker Fusion Frequency or FFF. Studies by Dr. Andrew Allen and his students indicate that hawks have an FFF of about 70–80 events per second and thus have difficulty in interpreting television as pictures. Raptors which rely on high speed chases and have to avoid branches or catch agile prey need a high FFF. A dragonfly, for example, has an FFF of up to 300 events per second with a high-speed brain and reactions to match. A Hobby trying to catch one needs similar fast reactions otherwise it would have no chance. These very fast sensory systems need very fast nervous systems to work them and in accipiters, for example, it is likely that some of these nerve pathways from the eyes and ears, via sensory neurons, to the motor neurons which control the muscles, have only minor links with association neurons in the brain. Given the time taken for impulses to traverse the nervous system and the latency periods between impulses, the accipiter would not have much time to "think" consciously about its reaction to ensure that it does the appropriate thing. We thus say that the bird is "nervous;" it seems to overreact in the wrong way to harmless stimuli. We can train out some of this nervousness but we cannot reconstruct the bird's entire sensory and nervous systems. It is these fast reactions which make it such an efficient predator. Thus it is actually living in a world moving about ten times faster than ours and it is important to remember that although physically we may be standing side by side, mentally we are in different worlds.

The same high-speed nervous system, with fast impulses, and short refractory times, which serves the hawk's eyes, also supports its hearing. The hearing of birds is better than ours. They can hear a wider range of sounds and discriminate between closer frequencies than we can. They have only one ear ossicle, the c. A thick tegmentum or fold of tissue rapidly dampens vibrations in the eardrum enabling birds to detect sounds only

0.6–2.5 milliseconds apart. Their FFF for hearing is thus 2,500–6,000. Hawks can easily recognize one another by their individual voices even though they may look the same. Parent falcons can pick out their offspring and their mates from among similar falcons even after some weeks separation, and show it in no uncertain terms! Hawks can readily discriminate between different footfalls and different car engines. Just as with eyesight, raptors live in a completely different sound world to us. Forest and nocturnal raptors are particularly receptive to sounds, as are the harriers. The soft, silent plumage of owls is probably as much an adaptation to enable the owl to hear the prey as it is to prevent the prey hearing the owl.

It is likely that the nervous system actually works at different speeds, according to hormonal influence. The drowsy animal reacts only slowly, whereas when the animal is under the influence of adrenalin, its reactions speed up and its FFF for both vision and hearing markedly increase, as if it is experiencing events in slow motion. This neuro-hormonal response curve would enable the hawk to match the high metabolic cost of achieving a high FFF, with its immediate needs.

The ability of a hawk to hold its head still when on a moving perch or hovering is not just done through eyesight. If a hawk is hooded and placed on a rotating perch it is capable of holding its head stationary. The organs of balance are well-developed in birds; imagine standing on one foot on a waving branch at night in a storm with your head tucked under your shoulder, fast asleep!

It used to be thought that most birds, with a few notable exceptions such as the kiwis and the turkey vulture, cannot smell. But this is probably an oversimplification. It is true that few can detect airborne scents and the olfactory lobes of the brain which deal with smell are small, but examination of the nostrils does show scent-detecting cells in many species. Each nostril has three cavities or conchae separated by delicate bony baffles similar to the interior of a small snail shell. The first cavity acts as a baffle and thermoregulator. The second is covered with mucus-producing ciliated cells and warms and moistens the air. Only the third cavity contains scent-detecting cells. This cavity opens directly into the roof of the mouth and it is thus possible the bird is able to smell, as well as taste the food actually in its mouth. I have not investigated this more thoroughly in raptors, but I have noticed on several occasions various hawks pick up and reject meat while holding it only by the horny tips of the beak where it seems no taste buds could be functioning.

The third cavity also opens into the infraorbital sinus. This sinus, which lies in front of and slightly below the eye, links up with the sinus on the opposite side and also with various small cavities throughout the skull. An infection here of sinusitis may infect one or both sides and can be difficult to eradicate.

The nasal glands are a flattened ovoid in falcons and lie half in the orbit and half extending into the orbital sinuses. In accipiters they are thinner and more elongated, lying tightly against the front of the orbit. In kites and buteos the glands lie in a depression in the frontal bone.

Birds of prey produce a salty solution from the nares thought to be secreted by the nasal glands in much the same way that some marine birds use salt glands. This is an extra-renal route for the excretion of excess sodium and chlorine ions. Although there is some experimental evidence supporting this, it does not explain why the nasal secretions should coincide with eating.

In my experience, the nasal secretions appear to be more of an overflow of fluids from the buccal cavity which are sneezed away when they block the nares. Females feeding young chicks drool large quantities of liquid onto the food for the chick to ingest and it is not clear if this fluid is salivary or nasal, or both, in origin. Research by Claus Fentzloff has revealed high levels of calcium in this liquid, which presumably is of benefit to young chicks.

The central tubercle in the nostril of falcons remains a puzzle. The theory that they act as baffles during high speed flight is not very convincing. Falcons which have had them removed with a hot needle, as was the practice of some eastern falconers, apparently performed well enough. Also other species which lack them, such as eagles, are capable of traveling just as fast. In the dynamic gliders such as the albatrosses, petrels, and fulmars, part of the nostril is thought to act as air velocity sense organs; these species are also able to smell air scent. In the falcons, the second nasal chambers on each side interconnect. Should air strike one nostril with more pressure than the other, then air should pass between the nostrils through the passageway. Whether or not this passageway is lined with sensory cells awaits further investigation.

## 1.4   The digestive system

The back of the tongue and the palate have backward-pointing spines, or papillae, which help the hawk gulp down food. As the beak closes, the entire upper palate moves backward, pushing the food before it. The esophagus (figure 1.4.1) is slightly muscular and opens into the crop which is extremely elastic. It lies to the right side of the windpipe, or trachea, and is therefore asymmetrical, although this does not become obvious until the crop is almost full. No digestion, apart from that caused by saliva, occurs in the crop; it is mainly a storage organ. Bit by bit the food is "put over" into the proventriculus or glandular stomach. To do this the hawk first stretches up its head and then pushes it down chin first in a flattening movement, often wriggling its head far to one side (figure 1.4.2). It all looks a little alarming but the hawk is perfectly well. Owls have no crop; instead the food passes directly to the stomach.

In birds of prey the muscular stomach, or gizzard, is relatively thin walled. Unlike chickens, hawks do not need to grind up hard seeds. The proventriculus and the gizzard thus merge together into a pear-shaped organ. The walls of the proventriculus are lined with epithelial cells which secrete strong peptic enzymes and hydrochloric acid, making a pH of 2.0–3.5. Diurnal raptors can digest most of the bones of their prey although keratinous structures, such as beaks, claws, and feathers, tend not to be affected. Owls are less able to dissolve bones and their pellets often contain near-complete skeletons.

The gizzard is lined with a one millimeter thick, slightly cheesy, yellow layer called the cuticle or koilin which is secreted by a layer of mucus cells. The cuticle protects the gizzard from the acid secretions of the proventriculus and provided that the bird has a natural diet the cuticle is constantly worn away, or sometimes is shed completely (see section 5.11). The outlet of the gizzard contains a grooved valve which prevents indigestible food going further. The soft parts of the prey are leached out by the chemical secretions and travel on down the intestine for further digestion and absorption. The feathers and fur are slowly compacted by the contractions of the gizzard to form a pellet. These contractions occur every 20–30 seconds and in the common buzzard have a pressure of 8–26 millimeters of mercury. When the gizzard is almost full of unwanted matter the pellet or

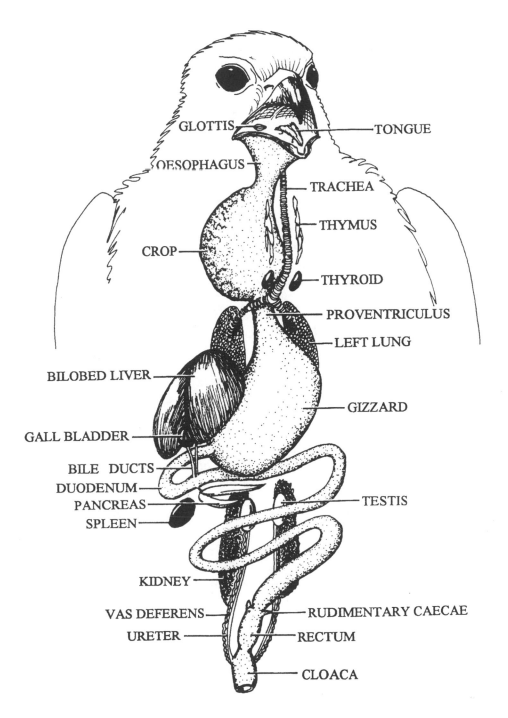

Figure 1.4.1 The digestive system of the common buzzard.

pellets are regurgitated. Normally this occurs before midmorning, either at the night perch or sometimes after killing, but usually before feeding on the first kill of the day. Captive hawks can often be induced to cast an hour or two early by offering them food.

The liver is large in birds of prey. The liver and

gall bladder of a buzzard together weigh about 20 grams—2.5 percent of its total body weight. It is in two lobes overlying the gizzard, protected by the pectoral muscles and sternum and cushioned from impact by the thoracic airsacs which surround it. The liver stores excess sugars, fats, and vitamins (especially vitamin A), synthesizes certain pro-

Figure 1.4.2 "Putting over" the crop.

teins, makes bile which is stored in the gall bladder, and excretes waste products from the blood, detoxifying it.

The gall bladder has two ducts which empty into the duodenum about 20 centimeters beyond the gizzard, about one-sixth of the way along the intestine. bile is normally secreted continuously at about 0.5–1 milliliters per hour and its job is to emulsify fats. Although normally important in carnivorous birds, the gall bladder was absent in several peregrines recorded by Gorham and Ivy in 1938. The bile pigment, biliverdin, stains the mutes green when the gut is empty; it can also pass back up, staining the castings of an empty hawk.

The pancreas lies in a loop of the duodenum and has one to three ducts into the intestine. Its enzymes digest fats, proteins, and carbohydrates which are then absorbed in the intestine. The pancreatic secretions are alkaline to neutralize the stomach acids.

Digestion and absorption are the chief functions of the intestine and the food is carried along by peristaltic waves. The walls are lined with tiny finger-like villi to increase the surface area for absorption. The intestine is often host to parasitic infections such as coccidia, roundworms, and tapeworms which although relatively harmless at low levels can, at higher densities, ulcerate the delicate lining and lead to anemia and expose the bird to secondary infections. During the first few days of life the yolk sac feeds via a duct into the small intestine between the jejunum and the ileum. Once the yolk is used up, the duct atrophies, leaving a small papilla, the vitelline diverticulum.

Gamebirds have a pair of large blind-ended tubes, the caeca, coming off the lower portion of the intestine at the sphincter with the rectum. These are used for the bacterial decomposition of crude fibrous foods, but raptors, which have a high protein diet, have only rudimentary caeca about four millimeters long. These usually contain lymphoid tissue.

Unlike mammals, birds have only one urino-

genital opening, the cloaca. The upper part of the cloaca, the coprodeum, receives feces from the intestine; this fecal material is black or brown. The middle part of the cloaca, the urodeum, receives semisolid urine from the kidneys via the two ureters which constantly move the urine down by peristalsis; the urine is extremely concentrated and also contains insoluble white uric acid crystals. Urine in the urodeum is moved by retroperistalsis back up into the rectum where more water is reabsorbed. Urine and feces are then excreted from the cloaca together, the coprodeum being semieverted so that feces do not come into contact with the urodeum and the proctodeum. On the dorsal or upper surface of the proctodeum is a small lymphatic pocket, the cloacal bursa or Bursa of Fabricius. This helps to combat infections, particularly when the bird is young.

The length of the gut, from mouth to cloaca, is about 135 centimeters in the buzzard. The rates at which food travels along it are discussed in section 5.9. Work by Dr. Nigel Barton has shown how the "attacking hawks" (see section 6), which rely mostly on agile prey, have shorter, lightweight, less efficient guts than the "searching hawks," such as the buzzards, which are more efficient at digesting their food. Thus some accipiters have guts only half as long as buteos of the same size, and need more food, but digest it more quickly.

## 1.5    The respiratory system

The respiratory system in birds has two main functions—to exchange carbon dioxide for oxygen and to regulate body temperature. Whereas we humans have a rather inefficient tidal flow of air in and out of our bag-like lungs, resulting in a permanent stagnant residue, birds have a unique circular flow system so that air goes in at one end of the lungs and through to the other, rather like a radiator. In addition, birds have a complex system of airsacs which extend throughout the body cavity and, in many birds, even into the hollows of the main bones and vertebrae (figure 1.5.1). Birds do not have a large moveable diaphragm. Instead, the intercostal muscles between the ribs raise and lower the sternum, pumping the airsacs like bellows. This is often synchronized with wing beats during flight. In many species, breathing and wing beating are in time during cruising flight. The action of the wings beating helps the movement of pulling air through the lungs. As the bird needs more oxygen, it doesn't necessarily breath faster, it breathes more deeply.

The airsacs themselves are very like flimsy polythene bags, they cannot be used for gas exchange (the lungs have to do this) but as they ramify so widely throughout the bird's body they are extremely effective in the transfer of heat, particularly in cooling the bird during hard exertion.

As the bird expands its thorax by lowering the sternum, air is first drawn into the lower airsacs, the posterior thoracic, and the abdominal airsacs. When the sternum is raised, the air is then squeezed forward into the lungs. The next time the chest is expanded, air is drawn out of the lungs into the forward airsacs. Then, when the sternum is raised for the second time, the air is expelled back up the trachea and out. So it takes two complete breathing movements of the chest for any given "piece" of air to go through the whole system and thus two "pieces" are in transit at any one time. Because of this, when the bird is expanding its chest, it is in fact emptying its lungs, unlike us. Only when it lowers its chest again is air pushed forward into the lungs. However, because the airsacs buffer the sharp differences in air pressure, the overall effect is that air suffuses more or less continuously through the lungs.

Birds live life at a faster pace than we do. Flight requires a higher body temperature and a faster metabolism. So birds require proportionately more oxygen. But because bird blood haemoglobin is about twice as efficient as ours at shuttling oxygen and carbon dioxide, and because of their free-flowing breathing system, a buzzard needs to breathe at only 15–30 breaths per minute; half the rate of a mammal of the same weight.

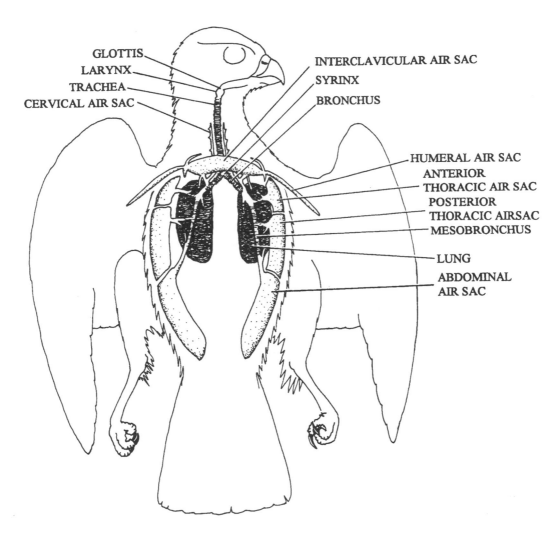

Figure 1.5.1 The respiratory system of the common buzzard.

Birds cannot sweat because they have no sweat glands. A peregrine dripping with sweat after a hard flight would not only look dreadful but would scarcely be able to fly at all, just like one that has bathed. Despite this, birds do lose some water by passive evaporation from the skin. When they get too hot, they mainly lose heat by the evaporation of water from the internal surfaces of the airsacs and panting, or in owls, gular fluttering, further increases the rate of evaporation. Overheating is one of the main limiting factors on flight performance for many birds. In temperate climates, an exercising falcon, such as a peregrine, will start panting to cool itself long before it needs to pant for increased gas exchange.

The voice of birds of prey is reasonably simple although piercing. It is produced in the syrinx where the trachea divides to go to the lungs.

The airsacs and lungs are the seat of various illnesses including aspergillosis and air sacculitis or inflamed airsacs. Aspergillosis is a fungal infection and looks like bread mold growing in the airsacs. Should the interclavicular airsac become inflamed, or infected, the hawk may cast its food or refuse a large crop. This is because the weight of the crop pinches the airsac against the clavicles and causes discomfort.

The airsacs of free-living raptors often become choked with long, thin *Serratospiculum* nematode worms. These can be relatively harmless unless there are too many or if they cause a secondary infection. It can be tricky to treat these because they must be physically removed.

Sometimes, especially in young raptors, an airsac will leak air under the skin and the bird blows up like a balloon. Although alarming, it can usually be treated by pricking the skin with a sterilized needle, deflating the skin, and holding in the hand for a while, maintaining a light pressure over the skin. The leak usually seals spontaneously in the fast-growing bird.

## 1.6   The urinogenital system

The kidneys lie in the renal fossa of the pelvis (figure 1.6.1). The ureters carry waste products from the kidneys to the urodeum, the middle chamber of the cloaca. Birds' kidneys are much more efficient at conserving water than are those of most mammals, about 75–80 percent of the urine is in the form of insoluble uric acid which forms the white part of the mutes. This is probably

an adaptation for survival during the time the chick is confined inside the eggshell.

The reproductive system of birds is extraordinary in that, when not in use, it shrivels away almost to nothing. This gives the bird less weight to carry around all winter. With the lengthening days of early spring the pituitary gland in the brain releases hormones—follicle stimulating hormone, luteinizing hormone, and prolactin—which stimulate the sex organs to grow. Soon they have grown to 200–300 times their dormant size and start to produce hormones of their own. Some of these feedback and control the hormone secretions of the pituitary and sex organs and stimulate further development, courtship, and nesting behavior.

Males have two functional testes just above the kidneys (figure 1.6.1). These enlarge in early spring and start to produce spermatozoa which pass down into the ductus deferens where they are stored. After insemination the semen is stored in the oviduct of the female and may fertilize eggs for several days afterward. Although spermatozoa can swim using their long tails, their progress is slow and erratic. The main movement of the semen is accomplished by the oviduct itself undergoing a reverse peristalsis. During copulation oxytocin released from the female's pituitary gland induces waves of contractions which transport the semen high up the oviduct within about three minutes of copulation. In the wild, falcons frequently maintain the copulatory position for two or three minutes after the male has left and, if well placed, one can see the cloaca contracting and expanding rhythmically. Often the female wails softly at this time.

In the female, often only half of the reproductive system, the left side, is functional. However, in birds of prey, the right side is often present and may be partially active. Early in the breeding season the ovaries enlarge and start to produce small, yellow, yolklike ova. When mature, an ovum leaves the follicle in the ovary and is swept into the funnel-like infundibulum which has also enlarged. This is called ovulation and in chickens occurs 15–75 minutes after the preceding egg has been laid. In raptors this interval is usually longer. Fertilization must take place at this point before the outer layers of the egg are laid down during the egg's progression down the oviduct. Curiously, unlike mammals, in birds it is the female which decides the sex of the offspring. Some of the eggs contain a male chromosome and some do not. All

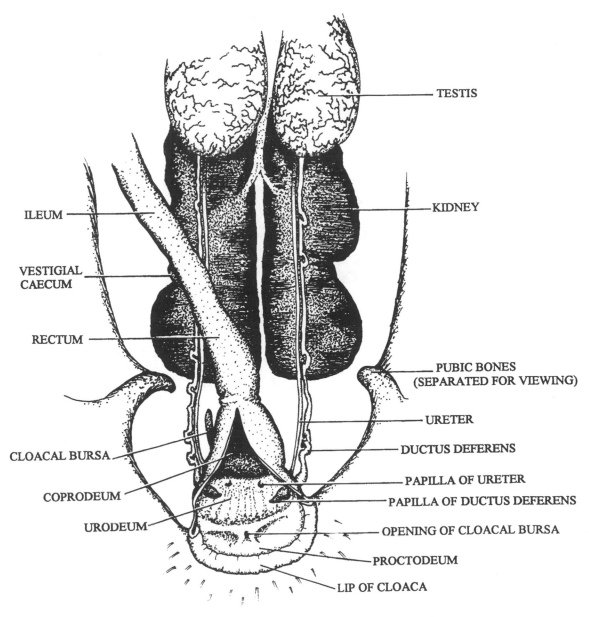

ILEUM

VESTIGIAL
CAECUM

RECTUM

CLOACAL BURSA

COPRODEUM

URODEUM

TESTIS

KIDNEY

PUBIC BONES
(SEPARATED FOR VIEWING)

URETER

DUCTUS DEFERENS

PAPILLA OF URETER

PAPILLA OF DUCTUS DEFERENS

OPENING OF CLOACAL BURSA

PROCTODEUM

LIP OF CLOACA

Figure 1.6.1 The urinogenital system of the male New Zealand falcon in breeding condition.

of the sperm cells contain a male chromosome.

The detail of reproduction and development of the egg is discussed in chapter 2.

## 1.7    The blood system, the lymphatic system, and the nervous system

The heart in the common buzzard has four chambers and lies immediately inside the sternum. It weighs about seven grams, 0.9 percent of the total body weight. The heart rate increases from a resting rate of 80–100 up to 250 beats per minute during exercise. Tests on the blood are a useful diagnostic tool. They can reveal systemic infections, high cholesterol levels, parasitic diseases, pesticide levels, the DNA profile, and so on. A variety of tests evaluate the red blood cells or erythrocytes (packed cell volume and total count, hemoglobin concentration, mean corpuscular values, reticulocyte count, and erythrocyte morphology), the white blood cells or leucocytes (total count, differential, and morphology), the thrombocytes, and the coagulation rate.

The lymphatic system is difficult to identify

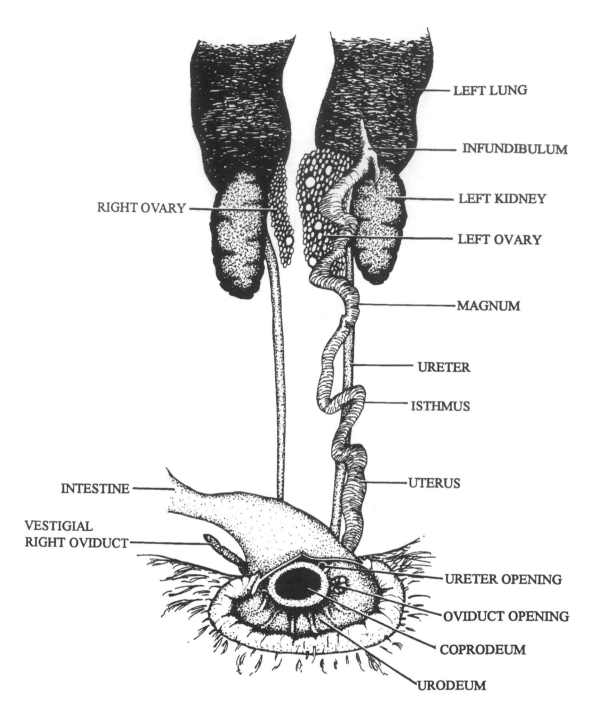

Figure 1.6.2 The urinogenital system of the common female buzzard in winter.

with the naked eye. Only one organ, the spleen, is clearly visible (see figure 1.4.1). This is a dark red, oval body 10–15 millimeters in diameter lying beside the gizzard. It is concerned with the antibody response to infection and produces white blood cells. It also dismantles old red blood cells.

The nervous system of birds is similar to that of mammals. The cerebral cortex which probably controls conditioned behavior and learning is large but not as well developed as in mammals, and the corpus striatum controlling perception, locomotion, and instinctive behavior is dominant. Birds probably have less direct conscious control of body movements than do mammals. Portmann in

1950 found that a falcon whose cerebral hemispheres had been removed was able to capture and hold a mouse but did not know what to do with it next. Bird behavior thus tends to be more instinctive and stereotyped than in mammals.

In some ways they can be thought of as going from one sequence of behavior to the next, each sequence being controlled by the corpus striatum and the overall picture set by the bird's physiological state as governed by its hormones. Thus when a bird is "ready" it starts to build a nest. The nest building is mainly instinctive; first timers usually build almost as good a structure as experienced ones. The same urge drives the bird to collect the nest material and to achieve this it may need to show some intelligence and learning—for example in finding out where suitable material is and how to bring it back when one of the items is unwieldy. The sight of a clutch of eggs in the nest is the signal for the next sequence—incubation—and so on. Many actions which are quite complicated and appear to be intelligent, including as far as I can tell, most of the search and attack strategies (see chapter 6), seem to be instinctive and appear for the first time in a complete and near-perfect form, rather than being developed through many learned stages.

Although when things go wrong, such as a chick falling out of the nest, birds often behave stupidly because their instinct program is not set up to cover such a contingency, the system by and large works well. For a sparrowhawk which may live for only two breeding seasons there is more survival value in doing it all by instinct than by learning. It might otherwise take several seasons before it succeeded in building an adequate nest.

Raptors probably rank among the more intelligent birds and are certainly brighter than chickens, but they are not as clever as the opportunists such as the crow family. In general, the more specialized a hawk is, the less it is able to adjust to different circumstances and the less intelligent it appears to be. Those with a wide repertoire of hunting techniques (see section 7.3) are able to survive in a variety of habitats and are all-rounders, with intelligence to match. Where the specialist relies on superior physical ability and suitable habitat, the all-rounder is more able to adapt and to use its brain to outsmart the prey.

## 1.8    The wing structure

The wings are based on the pectoral girdle which consists of the shoulder blades or scapulars, the coracoids, the fused clavicles or wishbone, the humerus, and the wing bones (figure 1.8.1). The main tendons which control wing movements are powered by the strong pectoral muscles which attach to the keel and to the clavicles. This system keeps weight off the wings and below the bird's

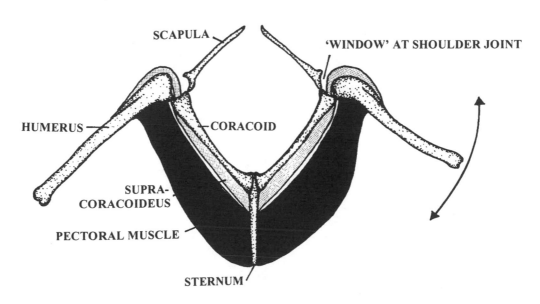

Figure 1.8.1 The pectorals pull the wings down. The supracoracoideus muscles pull them up via a pulley through the shoulder to the top of the humerus.

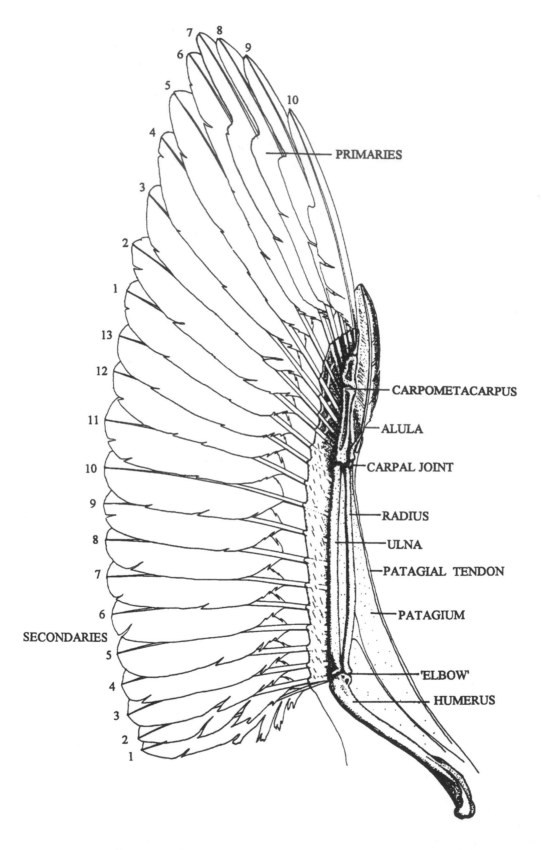

Figure 1.8.2 The structure of the wing of the common buzzard.

center of gravity, thus making the bird less unstable. The breast muscles immediately under the skin are the massive pectorals which pull the wing downward and provide thrust. Between these and the sternum are the supracoracoideus muscles which raise the wings using tendons which run through a pulley hole in each shoulder, the triosseal canal. As raising the wings is easier than the downstroke the supracoracoideus muscles are only 5–10 percent of the size of the pectorals.

The pectoral muscles are made up of red muscle fibers and white muscle fibers. These are discussed more fully in 5.15. The pectorals have about twice as many mitochondria as the supracoracoideus, and about 1.5 times the oxidative activity. My data on a sparrowhawk, a merlin, a common kestrel, five New Zealand falcons, two common buzzards, a red kite, a saker, a Harris, and a Griffon vulture, show pectorals of 11.3–17.6 percent of the total body weight, and supracoracoideus of 0.9–1.5 percent of the total body weight. The Griffon had proportionately the heaviest pectorals, reflecting the scaling effects of such a large (9.25 kilograms) bird, but it also had proportionately the smallest supracoracoideus (see 1.16).

The accipiters, as well as having red fibers for general flying, also have white fibers for sprinting. This enables them to explode from the fist with the same vigor as a rocketing pheasant. During acceleration, and when climbing, accipiters develop propulsion on the upstroke as well as on the downstroke (see 1.16). The shoulders rotate, producing a backward flick of the slotted primaries which store energy in them and straighten during the upstroke. The supracoracoideus muscles which raise the wings have a high proportion of white fibers and are noticeably paler. They give some power to the upstroke during the sprint.

The contractions of the breast muscles lower the upper wing bone or humerus (figure 1.8.2). This is air filled and connected to the airsac system. It is strengthened by small cross-bracing structures inside the cavity. The humerus carries the small tertiary feathers, but no flight feathers. From the humerus, the radius and ulna carry the secondaries, each feather being attached by two ligaments to small bony knobs on the ulna. The secondaries provide lift and they number from ten in accipiters to thirteen in the common buzzard and as many as twenty-five in the Bateleur eagle. Between secondaries 4 and 5 is an extra tectrix or

covert feather which makes it appear as if a secondary is missing. The radius, a long, slim bone along the leading edge of the wing, acts as a brace and, should the hawk hit an obstacle, is first in line for damage.

Between the humerus and the radius (figure 1.9) is a large flap of skin called the propatagium which makes an aerodynamically "clean" edge to the airfoil shape of the wing. It is held in place by two elastic tendons which run up to small muscles at the shoulder. Should these slacken, the propatagium fails to contract fully when the wing shuts and a fold remains visible. This condition is prevalent in some bloodlines of peregrines. It does not noticeably affect the bird's flight, but nonetheless, birds with this defect should not be used for breeding. If the elastic tendon is severed completely in an accident it needs very careful repair if the bird is to regain full powers of flight with a proper airfoil.

The radius and ulna connect to the wrist or carpal joint which, like our wrist, is complex both in structure and in movement. A blow or injury to the joint can cause the joint capsule to swell in a condition known as the "blaine," a bursitis similar to tennis elbow or housemaid's knee. Like so many joint problems it may, with rest and warmth, clear up entirely, or it may reappear under stress and persist, in which case the hawk will have to be retired from strenuous flying.

Two structures arise from the carpal joint: the alula and the manus or hand. The alula is the remains of the thumb and supports three small stiff features called the bastard wing. As air speed over the wing falls below a certain level, the alula erects and acts as a Handley Page slot, smoothing the airflow over the wing and, by putting off turbulence a little longer, enables the bird to fly more slowly without stalling. This can be clearly seen when the bird lands or brakes.

The manus consists of the fused remnants of the fingers and supports ten primary or flight feathers. The primaries are the source of power in flight and they fold away like scissors under the secondaries when the wing closes. The way in which they work is complex, as is the whole action of the wing. One should be very skeptical of the claims of some rehabilitators that a bird's flight is normal just because it can stay in the air for a few hundred meters. A rehabilitated accipiter or large falcon may be capable of apparently normal cruising flight and yet be significantly impaired in power, agility, and endurance during an attack. Whereas many species of birds which rely on their wings mainly just for transport can survive quite drastic wing injuries, raptors, particularly the rapacious species which rely on their attacking ability, cannot.

## 1.9    The tail structure

The tail is made up of two rows of five feathers placed each side of the pygostyle or tailbone. Two additional feathers, the deck feathers, lie centrally, just above the others (figure 1.9.1). The pygostyle has a raised keel to support the tail feathers embedded 17 millimeters into their sockets. Above the root of the deck feathers is the preen gland with a small wick supplying oil for preening.

The tail is used for steering and braking, particularly by those species which hunt in forests. The long-tailed hawk *Urotriorchis macrourus* and the *Micrastur* forest falcons show the most extreme development. Because the tail creates drag it is dis-

pensed with as far as possible by the high speed aerial species. Some species which fly fast and accurately, such as swallows and swifts, have taken up both options—long outer tail feathers for steering and the rest of the tail shortened to reduce drag. These V-shaped tails help to smooth the two vortices which spill off the edges of the tail during flight.

The small amount of extra lift provided by the tail is offset by the extra drag and only when soaring in rising air is the tail opened for added lift. The tail also tends to stabilize pitching; the up and down movement like a boat heading into waves. But a long tail, with its extra drag, induces turbulence more easily and thus large birds tend to have short tails. This reduces stalling speed and makes it easier for them to land.

## 1.10    Feather structure

Raptors have five main types of feathers, the flight feathers, the contour feathers covering the body (some of which have after-feathers), down feath-

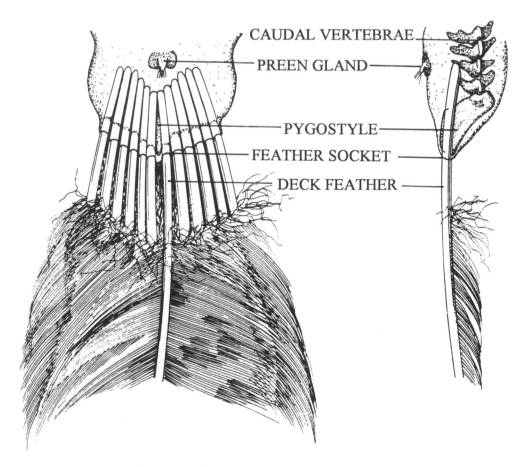

CAUDAL VERTEBRAE

PREEN GLAND

PYGOSTYLE

FEATHER SOCKET

DECK FEATHER

Figure 1.9.1 The structure of the tail of the common buzzard.

ers for insulation (especially in the chick), small hairlike filoplumes scattered over the body, and tiny hairlike crine feathers around the beak and nostrils which shed off dried blood. Some raptors, particularly the harriers, have powder-down feath-ers which flake into talclike powder giving a fine bloom to the feathers and perhaps a degree of waterproofing.

Feathers are made of keratin, the same protein as hair, horn, and fingernails. They are dead once

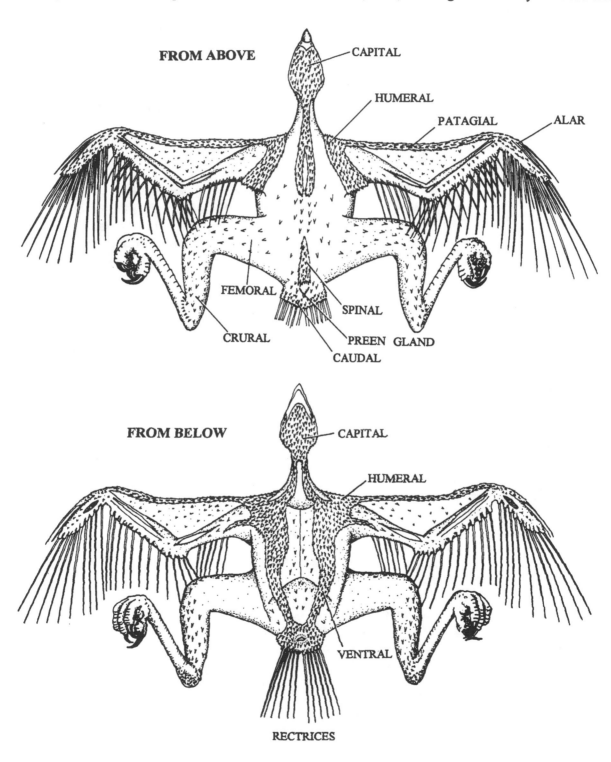

Figure 1.10.1 The feather tracts of the common buzzard.

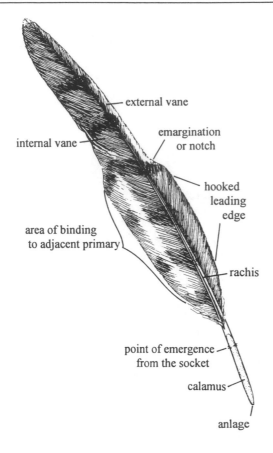

Figure 1.10.2 A primary feather from the right wing of a European sparrowhawk, viewed from below.

complete and can thus be trimmed or repaired without the bird feeling anything; only the sockets are alive. They are not distributed all over the body but grow mainly in well-defined zones (figure 1.10.1). The body feathers are erectile and are each controlled by four muscles. On a cold day the bird fluffs out for extra insulation; if warm or stressed, it sleeks its feathers down. Birds such as gyrfalcons have more down on the feather-free areas for better insulation in cold climates. Some of this down can easily be removed when flying them in hot climates, to prevent undue heat build up. Overheating is the main performance limiting factor for gyrs in warm climates.

The flight feathers consist of a hollow quill or calamus and a central shaft or rachis with vanes on each side made up of hundreds of barbs (figures 1.10.2 and 3). The barbs are held together by millions of barbules which have hooks on the lower leading edge locking the whole structure together. When the bird preens these are settled back in place like a zip fastener.

Different feathers have different degrees of stiffness and elasticity. For example, the leading primaries are stiffer than the trailing ones and the primaries of an adult peregrine are stiffer than those of a juvenile. Across the species we have measured using the Pennycuick and Lock technique, we found that the peregrine had the stiffest primaries, followed by the northern goshawk, gyrfalcon, saker, Harris, and common buzzard. There is more work to be done on this.

## 1.11 Feather maintenance

The hawk looks after its feathers by preening using light waterproofing oil from the preen gland at the base of the tail, and by bathing in water or dust. Many species also sunbathe; the ultraviolet light acting on the provitamin S in the oil on the skin produces vitamin $D^3$ which is essential for calcium absorption and without which growing chicks may

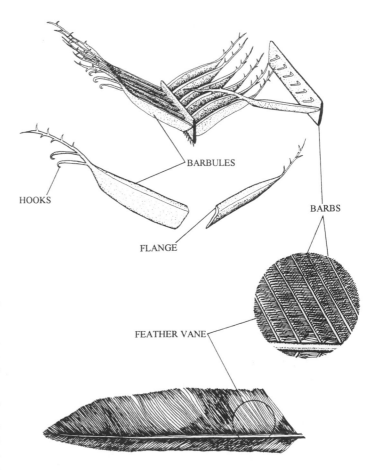

Figure 1.10.3 The structure of a European sparrowhawk primary feather.

develop rickets. Since 1972, I have regularly used silicon fabric waterproofing spray on hunting falcons during periods of wet weather with beneficial effects. In one disastrously wet grouse-hawking season we used a whole can on three falcons in three weeks. The desert falcons particularly, are quickly drenched in our British climate, and hawks taking ground game soon get sodden by the wet grass.

Raptors are susceptible to feather parasites especially in the summer in warm climates, or when taking prey such as rooks and crows which harbor a lot of parasites. A heavy infestation may indicate a concurrent disease or injury and may also be implicated in the spread of avian pox and avian malaria. The commonest parasites are the pale gray lice which crawl on the feathers and are often visible when the hawk is hot. Tiny feather mites can damage the feathers by stripping the barbules and the repulsive large, flat, sideways-scuttling, hippoboscid flies are often seen on young birds. Some of these black hippoboscids are capable of short flights, usually up one's sleeve. All these parasites can be swiftly eradicated using Johnsons' Antimite, Duramitek, or other similar preparations specifically produced for birds. It is wise not to offer a bath for a day or two after application and to keep the hawk hooded and head shielded during spraying or dusting.

If a feather is slightly bent, it can be restored to shape by warming it up. Vultures use the same method; after many hours of soaring, their primaries become set in a curve, rather like a bow that has been left strung. By sunbathing on a perch for awhile the vulture uses the heat to straighten out the feathers.

Broken feathers can be repaired by splinting, imping, plugging or sewing in depending on where they are damaged. Flight feathers must be able to twist and bend naturally and therefore repairs on the outer two thirds of the feather are seldom successful for long. Proper flexion is reduced and this puts extra strain on the ends of the reinforcement which breaks after a while. We use very fine piano wire, filed square in section, tapering finely at both ends. A flexible glue keeps the two butts together. Repairs to the inner third are better, assuming an exactly matching replacement is available. Bamboo plugs in the hollow quill are probably the easiest way of achieving this and it should be borne in mind that the hollow shaft of the feather continues for some distance inside the skin socket.

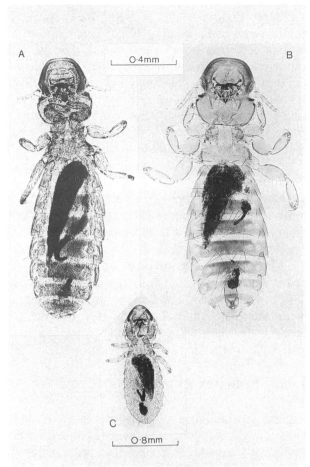

Falcon lice—*Degeeriella rufa*. A: Adult female. B: Adult male. C: Nymph.

In buzzard-size hawks this distance varies from 15–30 millimeters according to the feather concerned. About one half of this distance can safely be used for plugging and therefore even if only a small stump of feather is showing, it is repairable. Broken feathers should always be repaired promptly otherwise neighboring feathers will break under the extra strain. Therefore when putting the bird away to molt it is important to ensure that all feathers are complete even if the replacements are from the wrong species, otherwise the newly growing feathers, lacking support, may break off in the blood. Rehabilitators should become skilled at feather repairs to ensure that birds can be released back to the wild, with a good serviceable set of feathers, rather than be held for a protracted period to molt, which raises further complications.

Falconers' birds tend to break their feathers much more than do wild raptors and most of this is traceable to bad management. Of course, genuine accidents do occur in the field. Inexperienced hawks often catch quarry so that they fall into a tree rather than on to the ground. The hawk, sprawled or wedged in the branches, is unable to kill the quarry and yet is unwilling to let it go. One is lucky if feather damage is the only result. Fortunately, hawks soon learn not to do this. Ground game such as hares are also a fruitful source of broken feathers. If your goshawk by the end of the season looks as if it has survived a trip through a jet engine then you have been over-facing it and are lucky it hasn't ruptured an airsac. Although it is always tempting to try for the largest quarry that the hawk can catch, it is much harder to take the smaller, more agile species.

Most feathers are broken or weakened through bad management. Poor handling on the fist, badly designed equipment, and general carelessness and incompetence all take their toll. If your hawk is breaking feathers while in captivity than a stringent review of technique is called for.

## 1.12   Feather growth

Raptors go through a series of plumages in their lives. They hatch with a short natal down. After about 7–14 days their second, thicker, down coat grows through. This allows them to control their own temperature to a large extent, thus freeing up the female to go hunting to meet their high food demands. As the growing chicks approaches full body weight, the juvenile plumage grows through. For a time, the chicks are harlequins of feathers and down before emerging in full juvenile plumage. Many juveniles undergo some body molt in their first autumn, but their main molt starts in their next spring. Then they gradually grow their adult plumage, being clean molted by the autumn. Flight feathers are replaced gradually over the easier summer months, to minimize any impairment to the bird's hunting ability. Many larger species, such as eagles, are unable to complete the molt in one year and it drags on so that the bird always has a mix of at least two plumages.

Molting is triggered by a variety of environmental and hormonal factors. An increasing day length triggers the molt via the pituitary gland, and starvation or illness can retard it, delay it, or stop it altogether. Females usually molt heavily while they are incubating whereas the males, which are busy hunting, delay their molt until the females are ready to hunt too. Migratory species tend to stop molting during the migratory period, the migratory tundra peregrine, for example, starts its molt in the summer in Alaska or northern Canada then interrupts it until it reaches South America in September or October. Once on the wintering grounds the molt is resumed.

Birds that have developed with a minimal fear response (see section 4.10), such as hand-raised birds, are better adapted to captivity and do not suffer from the persistent low-level stress that wild-caught or some parent-reared individuals do. Low-level stress entails constant secretion of adrenalin which is antagonistic to the sex hormones; such birds are therefore harder to bring into breeding condition and do not usually molt rapidly or well.

At higher levels, adrenalin causes constriction of the peripheral blood vessels such as those to the skin and to the feather buds or papilli. A human being, when badly frightened, goes "white as a sheet." So too does a bird, but the skin cannot be seen through the feathers. Any feathers which were growing when the bird was frightened have their blood supply restricted and hence receive less nutrients for a period. Adrenalin also reduces the nutrient levels in the blood because it reduces the blood supply to the intestine. The tail feather of a peregrine grows at about 0.2 millimeters per hour. When frightened, the bird secretes adrenalin in seconds and the effects may take one to two hours to subside. During this time, the rapidly growing epidermal cells in the follicle may be starved of nutrients and a stress mark or fault bar may grow down about 0.5 millimeters wide.

Similarly, if the bird is starved or ill for a period, the blood-sugar levels and nutrients fall and again the deprived follicles produce a "hunger trace" or, in extreme instances, the whole growing shaft may be pinched off. Similar weaknesses develop in the horns and hooves of cows when calving or in human hair or fingernails when you are seriously ill. All these structures are made of keratin and all depend on a good blood supply for normal growth.

Reduction in blood pressure to the follicles resulting in reduced nutrients and oxygen reaching the feather germ also occurs naturally. The metabolism of birds is lowest during sleep (see also section 5.9). The normal temperature of about 41.6 to 41.9 degrees centigrade drops to around 41.1 degrees centigrade and the metabolic rate, and hence circulation rate, is reduced. If the bird is in poor condition, or if its metabolic demands are high, as in winter or during illness, this can result in fault bars every night, or in owls, every day. If the bird is starved or debilitated, as well as fault bars forming, after three to four days the growth rate of the feather slows down too. Because of the way the feather germ is positioned in the follicle, the barbule forming region is the first to suffer when nutrients are reduced.

Although feathers have an extremely high strength to weight ratio they are still quite heavy. A bald eagle *Haliaeetus leucocephalus* measured by Brodkorb had feathers and down weighing 677 grams—16.6 percent of its total body weight, whereas its skeleton weighed only 272 gram—6.7 percent. Pigmented feathers, such as black areas containing melanins, tend to be tougher because more pigments are secreted in the black areas. Thus pale feather tips usually wear off rapidly until a dark area is reached. Pale marks in the middle of a dark feather can wear away differentially or be more susceptible to the nibblings of feather mites or lice. Some falcon species, such as the gyrfalcon, sooty falcon, and Eleonora's falcon are genetically dichromatic; that is they have a dark phase caused by a preponderance of eumelanin, a true black pigment. Other genera, such as the buteos, also show melanistic phases, some of which probably involve phaeomelanins which give dark browns and red browns.

Feathers are dead once complete and, when molted, do not drop loose but are pushed out by the growing new feathers. If a feather follicle is damaged by injury, it may grow twisted or stunted feathers. Or, if the follicle is normal but the blood supply is reduced, for example by scarring or infection, it may grow normal feathers which, once they reach a certain length, make heavier demands on the follicle than the blood supply can cope with; feather growth continues for a little longer but the vanes do not unfurl and finally the shaft pinches off. Repeated feathers attempt to grow but suffer the same fate. The rest of the feathers on the bird grow normally. This may be due to an infection. One way to treat it is to cut off the unfurled feather every two weeks just beyond the sheath. This reduces the physical strain on the injured socket while the feather is growing. After six or eight weeks the quill forms, the feather hardens off and the socket is less delicate. A replacement feather can then be fitted into this quill and with any luck the socket will take the strain. If the socket has

It is quite common to see follicular damage to the tail of wild Australasian harriers and the replacement feathers grown back deformed.

healed completely, the bird should molt normally next time. If the dermal papilla or the blood supply is affected, the prognosis is less cheerful.

Prey species, such as pigeons and gamebirds, have very loose feathers which come out in bunches when a hawk tries to grab one (see 7.4). Such feathers are regrown and pigeon racing enthusiasts therefore pull out a broken feather rather than repair it. Raptors, on the other hand, have much tougher follicles and if a feather is forcibly wrenched out, the socket may be permanently damaged, particularly if the feather was in the blood. Some falconers plug the empty socket with wax or short length of quill to prevent it closing up and distorting the new feather.

Very rarely, raptors show a continual molt; as soon as the feathers are grown or half grown they all drop out again. This appears similar to French molt in budgerigars which is caused by a virus but in raptors may be due to a malfunction of the thyroid, pituitary, pineal gland, or gonads. Stress on a feather, such as caused by an overheavy tail-mount, can also stimulate follicle development, causing the feather to be shed. If a juvenile feather is shed prematurely, it is replaced by an adult feather and this can be used to sex some species, such as merlins, by pulling out a body feather from a bird that cannot be sexed on the basis of measurements.

All falconers hope for a clean and rapid molt

and great is the gnashing of teeth in late summer when a few lingering old feathers stubbornly refuse to budge. On the first hawking trip of the season they oblige you by dropping out in the cadge. So what can be done to ensure a smooth molt?

First of all it is essential to reduce stress as much as possible, especially for any nervous birds. Personally, I dislike having any hawk tied up when it is not being flown and from January until July all my birds are in breeding pens or, if juvenile, in molting pens. There they can get a little exercise, bath, sunbathe, play, and watch the world go by, up out of the way of damp and mutes.

Other than a good varied diet, including additional vitamins and essential amino acids, and perhaps some honey, it is best not to use any molting agents unless you know you have a real problem bird. Injections of the female sex hormone progesterone can cause early molting, as can thyroxine, but further research on these is needed, especially as thyroxine can be toxic close to therapeutic levels. The nearer to the normal date that treatment is given, the less hormone is required to trigger the molt. They may thus be useful to make the molt start early but they do not make the molt period itself substantially shorter. The activities of the thyroid appear to affect molting the most, then the sex hormones, then the pituitary.

Another approach is to alter the photoperiod by bringing the apparent year forward a month or two. One regime used successfully in America is a twenty-hour day length in very early spring until the first feathers drop, then eight hours winter photoperiod. This has resulted in all the primaries being molted at once and the birds unable to fly. I tried a regime similar to this, but slightly less drastic, and one of the four falcons was unable to fly for three weeks while molting. Essentially, you are bringing the summer equinox forward and getting the bird as quickly as possible onto a shortening autumn photoperiod.

Raptors show two main patterns of molt. The accipitridae, which include all the accipiters and buteos, have a descending molt. The primaries are dropped one by one, starting in the angle of the wing and working outward so that the outermost primary (P10) is the last to drop. The secondaries also start from the angle of the wing and work in toward the body.

In contrast, falcons start their wing molt from the center of the primaries, usually P4, outward in both directions, and from the center of the secondaries, usually S5, in both directions outward.

Both groups of birds normally drop the center (deck) feathers first from the tail, the remaining tail feathers being shed in a wide variety of sequences. Usually no feather is dropped until its neighbor is three-quarter to half grown although occasionally a falcon will drop all its remaining ten tail feathers as soon as its new deck feathers are complete. Because feathers are dead, the body has no way of detecting if they are broken. Broken feathers are molted no sooner or later than whole ones.

The whole process of molting in birds of prey is spread out over the summer months avoiding stress periods such as rearing young or migrating. A first-year bird which drops its first feather in mid-March is doing quite well to be clean molted by mid-August.

## 1.13 Wing shape, aspect ratio, dihedral, and tail variations

Above all else, the shape and structure of a raptor's wings and tail are a reflection of its potential as a flying machine, and in turn a reflection of the ways it searches for and catches its prey (see chapter 6). When you consider that a majority of young raptors die in their first year, primarily because they cannot catch enough food, then you appreciate the massive selection pressure finely tuning individuals for their habitats. This applies not just to the individual but also to the splitting up of each species into two groups, male and female, each adapted by size to exploit subniches within the same ecosystem.

This fine tuning can be seen in many features

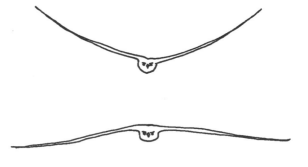

Figure 1.13.1 Top: A red kite has a large dihedral angle which gives lateral stability against rolling. Below: An accipiter has a negative dihedral angle, making it laterally unstable.

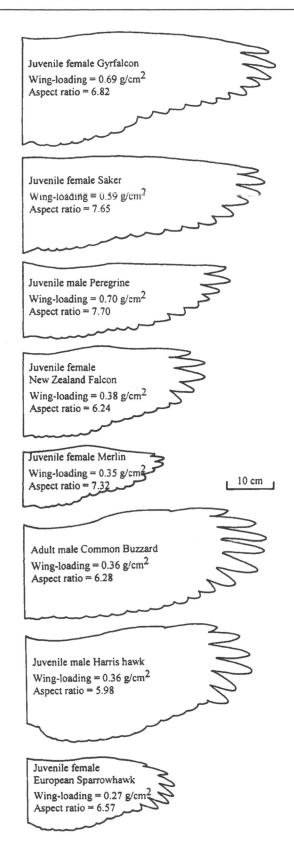

Juvenile female Gyrfalcon
Wing-loading = 0.69 g/cm$^2$
Aspect ratio = 6.82

Juvenile female Saker
Wing-loading = 0.59 g/cm$^2$
Aspect ratio = 7.65

Juvenile male Peregrine
Wing-loading = 0.70 g/cm$^2$
Aspect ratio = 7.70

Juvenile female
New Zealand Falcon
Wing-loading = 0.38 g/cm$^2$
Aspect ratio = 6.24

Juvenile female Merlin
Wing-loading = 0.35 g/cm$^2$
Aspect ratio = 7.32

10 cm

Adult male Common Buzzard
Wing-loading = 0.36 g/cm$^2$
Aspect ratio = 6.28

Juvenile male Harris hawk
Wing-loading = 0.36 g/cm$^2$
Aspect ratio = 5.98

Juvenile female
European Sparrowhawk
Wing-loading = 0.27 g/cm$^2$
Aspect ratio = 6.57

Figure 1.13.2 Tracings of some raptor wings showing the different aspect ratios.

related to flight. Many hawks, such as buzzards, rely on searching for easy prey so that the main selection pressure is on their searching ability (see 6.1). The attack, when it comes, is just a simple one. These birds tend to have low wing loadings, and are specialists at gliding and soaring. They are usually fairly stable in the air, with a large dihedral and medium to high aspect ratio.

The dihedral angle measures how high the wings are held above horizontal, making the bird selfrighting and less prone to rolling (figure 1.13.1). The soaring birds tend to be relatively stable so that they can almost fall asleep and yet still remain level. The attacking hawks, on the other hand, are selected during the attacking phase of the hunt and need to be fast and agile. They tend to have a negative dihedral, or anhedral, making them prone to roll easily and be very unstable. A mere flick sends them over. It is the difference between a white-water canoe and a punt. Of course birds can change their wing configuration at will and can increase stability, not only by changing the dihedral, but also by sweeping back the wings.

The searchers, while soaring, have open, slotted wing tips which are ranged from the front of the wing tip to the back at decreasing angles of attack (figure 1.15.4). During fast airspeeds the tips bend up further and twist, increasing the angle of attack into lift. The bird soars up, but slows down. The primaries straighten a little, maintaining an optimum angle of attack for the airspeed. This appears to be a passive mechanism, but nerves in the feather bases presumably indicate the extent of bend on the primaries and tell the bird when the airspeed is so low that it must resume flapping. The effect of the slotting is to maintain adhesion of the air passing over the top of the wing, and thus reducing the stall speed. This effect is much less developed in the attacking hawks which, because of their higher wing loadings, glide at higher speeds. They achieve it by altering their whole wing profile (see figure 1.15.3).

The aspect ratio is the ratio between the wingspan and the average wing width. Because birds wings are not exact rectangles, we calculate this as Span$^2$/Wing area. The high-speed gliders, such as the peregrine, have long, narrow high aspect ratio wings of about 7.7 (figure 1.13.2). This reduces the induced drag, but makes it harder for them to maneuver, especially at high speeds when the strain on the open wing is at its greatest. The slow speed soarers, such as the buzzards, vultures, kites,

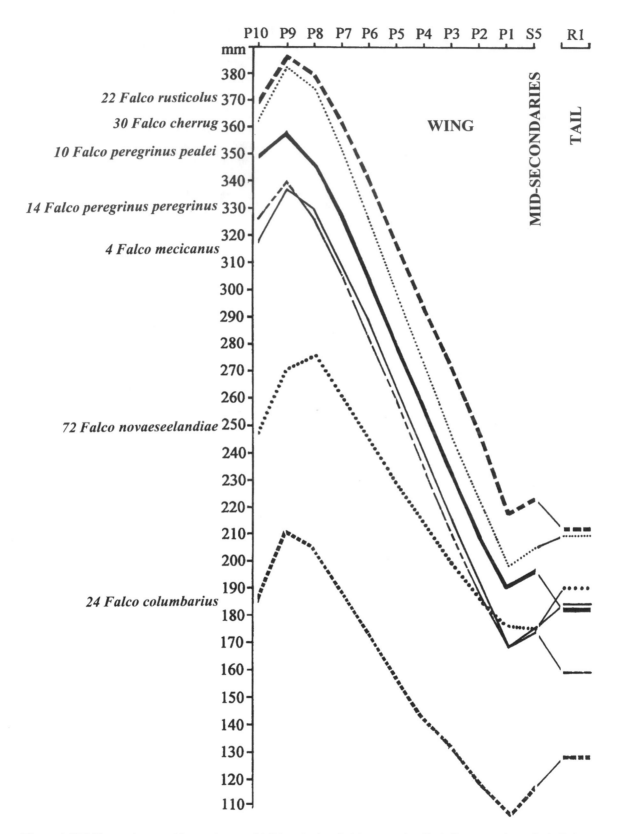

Figure. 1.13.3 Mean primary, midsecondary, and tail lengths for six falcon species (including two subspecies). Both sexes and all ages are combined. Sample sizes as shown.

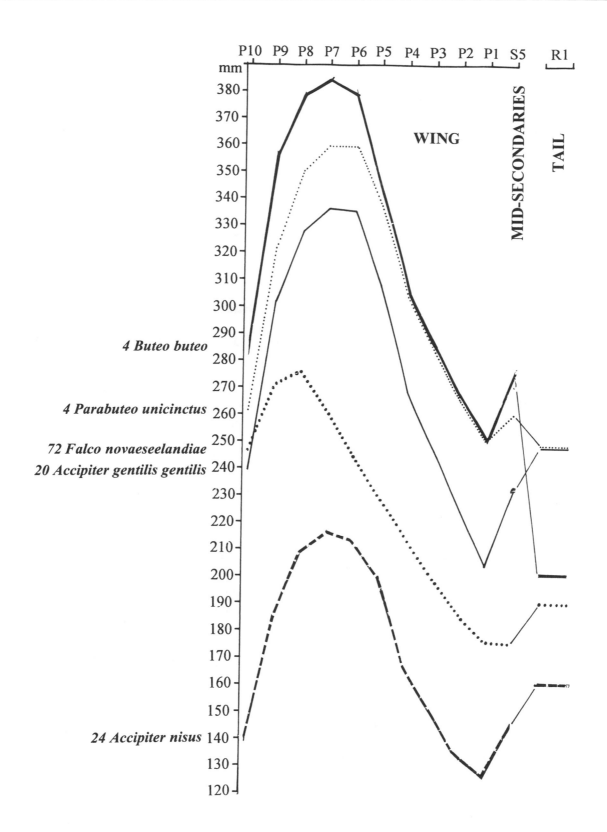

Figure. 1.13.4 Mean primary, midsecondary, and tail lengths for five raptor species, both sexes and all ages combined. Sample sizes as shown.

The female aplomado falcon (left) has short wings and a long tail and flies at 335 grams. The male peregrine (right) flies at 450 grams. Was the aplomado the "Aletho" of old Spain?

*Photo: Harry McElroy*

and some eagles, have a medium aspect ratio of about 6.3, and quite a cambered wing. They do not attempt agile maneuvers at any speed. The accipiters, traditionally known as "shortwings" also have a medium aspect ratio, but their wings are a different shape. Their wings are not primarily adapted for gliding and soaring, but for supplying thrust. The key to the accipiter wing is acceleration, and this is discussed more fully in 1.16. Thus it is possible for two wings to have the same wing area, but have different functions. For example, the female New Zealand falcon wing and the male peregrine wing are the same area, but they have different aspect ratios.

By measuring raptors (see 2.4) it is possible to see the specialist differences in the shape of the wing and tail (figures 1.13.3 and 4). The peregrines have the most pointed, narrow wings and short tails. They are the high speed gliders. The desert falcons, such as the gyr, saker, and prairie have less pointed, wider wings and longer tails. They have a more general-purpose format, switching from bird to mammal prey as the need arises. The New Zealand falcon has a more accipitrine shape and I have shown it again among the accipiters for a comparison. The merlin too, is somewhat accipitrine, chasing small agile birds and needing to be very maneuverable.

The common buzzard (figure 1.13.4) has a long, broad wing and a short tail. The goshawk has a shorter, narrower wing tip and a long tail. The Harris wing lies between the two but also it has a long tail. The sparrowhawk is a shorter-winged version of the goshawk. From figure 1.13.2, you can also see that the secondaries are enlarged in the accipiters, the Harris hawk, the New Zealand falcon and the gyrfalcon, or, putting it another way, the inner primaries are reduced.

There is plenty of room for more research on these topics. The important thing to understand is that there are many physical differences between the species, often small, but normally significant. To appreciate them, they have to be viewed within the whole lifestyle of the bird: its skeletal and muscle systems, its physiology, its psychology, and the details of the way it hunts. Everything is interrelated.

## 1.14   Variations between juveniles and adults

Young birds are afraid of flying fast. This is very sensible of them. Have you ever driven your car as fast as it can possibly go? Speed kills! Every year we watch the hack falcons develop their flying skills and it is quite obvious that, to start with, they are not happy about flying fast because they cannot handle the landings. Fortunately, at this stage their feathers are still in sheath and they tend to flop without any real damage. But if you confine a hawk, such as a saker, in a breeding pen and don't let it fly until it is hardpenned, it may well have a panic attack. It takes off, develops quite an airspeed before it realizes what is happening, and unable to brake, land, or even turn, it may fly a kilometer or two before crashing. If it crashes into a tree and scrabbles onto a branch it may refuse to try flying again for one or two days. As you sit below the tree during this time, you can reflect on why it has happened.

The wild young raptors which develop naturally learn over their first four weeks to cope with the maneuvers of normal flight. They play together and snatch leaves off trees, gradually developing their coordination. But their parents are still supplying the food, so that they do not have to attempt hazardous flight maneuvers chasing prey. This is when the selection pressure starts. One way around the problem is not to try to catch fast agile prey. Many juvenile raptors, such as red-tailed hawks, sakers, and prairie falcons, in their first autumn behave more like "searchers" than "attackers" ( see chapter 6). They catch easy things like worms, insects, voles, and other small prey.

When winter comes, many of these prey disappear. They get locked into the frozen ground, hidden by snow, or just die back. The juveniles have to turn to more difficult prey and become more like "at-tackers." Many don't make it. Those which do can handle higher-speed attacks and are able to survive on lower prey numbers. By the next spring, when prey is plentiful, they have proven themselves as hunters and are able to provide not only for their own needs but for a family too.

All this is reflected in the wings. The juveniles tend to have longer wing and tail feathers than the adults. This gives them a lower wing loading and a lower stall speed. They can fly more slowly than their parents, more like "searchers." Their feath-ers also tend to be softer, less easily broken, but not as efficient for fast flight.

We have a lot of data on this but it is very complicated because the different genera change in different ways. The peregrine and merlin, for example, have shorter narrower wings and shorter tails in their adult plumage. Accipiters shorten their tails but get longer, more pointed, wings. They become more falconlike. The only way to study this is to obtain data on both juvenile and adult plumages for the same individuals, rather than single plumages for random individuals. This is another rich area for someone looking for a research project.

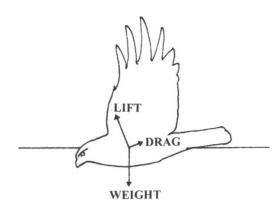

Figure 1.15.1 The forces acting on a soaring buzzard.

## 1.15 Gliding and soaring

Gliding and soaring are forms of unpowered, fixed-wing, flying dependent on three forces: lift, weight, and drag ( figure 1.15.1). The bird moves forward through the air under the influence of gravity, in a sinking, angled descent. The forward movement generates lift through the airfoil of the wing, but the climb rate is less than the sink rate through the surrounding air. If the whole mass of air rises faster than the bird sinks, then the bird can still gain altitude; this is soaring. In gliding, the bird sinks through the air in order to travel, it trades height for distance, whereas in soaring the

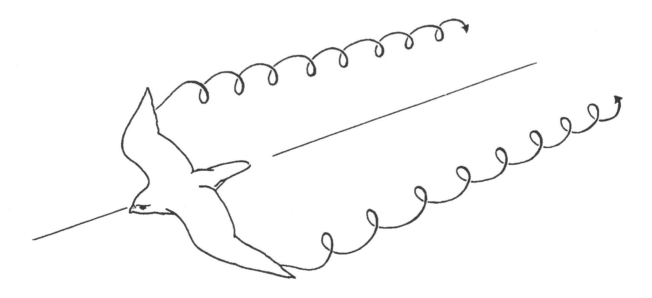

Figure 1.15.2 Vortices spiral off the wing tips of a peregrine as it glides on fixed wings.

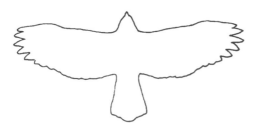

HARRIS GLIDING AT 6.0° AT 7.0 METERS PER SECOND

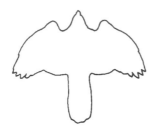

HARRIS GLIDING AT 8.5° AT 16.2 METERS PER SECOND
(AFTER TUCKER AND HEINE, 1990)

Figure 1.15.3 The profile of a Harris hawk alters as the glide becomes steeper and faster.

bird is raised up by the air going up faster than the bird is sinking. Thus soaring is a form of gliding which uses rising air to gain altitude. When gliding, the hawk slowly loses height as it gains distance and the ratio of height to distance traveled is called the glide angle. A reasonably capable gliding bird with long narrow wings, such as an adult peregrine, achieves a glide angle of 6 degrees or less, a ratio of about 1 in 10, which means that from a height of 300 meters (1000 ft) it reaches a horizontal distance in still air of 3 kilometers (about 2 mi), or even better. This is achieved by reducing drag through having a hard, streamlined

contour, long, narrow wings and a short tail, not by reducing weight. Adjustments in weight alone alter the speed of descent but do not affect the glide angle. A heavy peregrine still achieves the same glide angle as a light one, but travels faster during the glide. The smooth contours minimize the disturbance to the surrounding air. The air rolls smoothly over the wings, spinning off the trailing edge of the wing tips as vortices (figure 1.15.2).

As the glide angle gets steeper, the bird folds its wings in closer to the body (figure 1.15.3) and travels faster. This reduces the leverage strain on the pectoral muscles but increases drag slightly.

It is very common to see a wild falcon, in its home area, circle up on open wings with tail fanned in a column of rising air, perhaps near a hill face, until it is a speck in the sky, and then glide in a straight line toward its chosen hunting area. Using these two flying techniques very little energy is needed to cover its whole home range. Once you get used to being with the falcons, you can "see" these invisible lifts, almost as clearly as an elevator in a department store.

Soaring is a form of gliding in that the bird is sinking through the air all the time. When soaring, the bird is not necessarily trying to cover a big horizontal distance but rather to stay in the same locality gaining height, cooling off, displaying or searching for prey. The emphasis therefore is not so much on travel but on staying up. This means the bird's airspeed can be sacrificed so that for any given glide angle it sinks less per minute. Therefore, the specialist soarers have reduced weight as much as possible. At normal flight speeds, drag is proportional to airspeed, so at lower airspeeds it is less important, and therefore the bird can have big lifting surfaces—big wings, deep secondaries, big

Figure 1.15.4 The airflow over a buzzard's wing tip before the stall.

fanned tail. The extra drag these give is more than compensated for, at low speeds, by the extra lift they give.

Also in soarers, the outer primaries are emarginated so that the wing tips are deeply slotted or "fingered." Each primary tip thus acts as a separate narrow airfoil giving lift with minimum drag and also lowering the stalling speed. To achieve this, the primaries are progressively stiffer toward the leading edge of the wing. The wing stalls when the air flow over the top of the wing, instead of being smooth and sucking the wing up, becomes turbulent. Slotting redirects air over the top of the

Figure 1.15.5 Adult buzzard soaring.

Figure 1.15.6 Adult peregrine in fast glide.

Figure 1.15.7 Adult buzzard gliding.

Figure 1.15.8 Juvenile northern goshawk gliding.

Figure 1.15.9 Juvenile northern goshawk soaring.

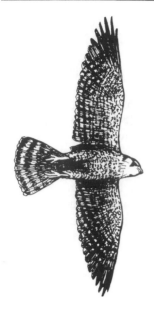

Figure 1.15.10 Peregrine soaring.

Figure 1.15.11 Peregrine gliding.

wing, reducing the turbulence, lowering the stalling speed so that the bird can stay airborne at lower forward speeds (1.15.4).

Other species, such as accipiters and game birds, have slotted wings for an entirely different reason. Pheasants do not soar! These birds use their slotted wings for a power sprint and this is discussed in 1.16.

The specialist soarer, having reduced its sink rate to a minimum, needs a source of air which is rising faster than the hawk is sinking. This is supplied either by forced updrafts at hill slopes or by air warming up to form thermals. Obviously in flat areas the hawk must rely on thermals alone. In cool climates these are unreliable and specialist soarers, and some eagles and buteos, cannot survive there. Their range is restricted to places where lifting air is available often enough for them to find food. They usually have to wait each morning until the air heats sufficiently to rise. Frederick II forbade his falconers to fly their falcons after 9 A.M. because of the risk from eagles which start to soar then.

Although most raptors can glide and soar, the most rapacious species, such as the large falcons and accipiters, are primarily adapted for the attacking phase of the hunt (see 6.1), and this is usually a powered flapping flight. But, unlike airplanes, birds are alive and are able to alter their flight profiles from moment to moment. Thus a peregrine, by adjusting her wings and feathers, can optimize herself for high-speed gliding and then

change to a soaring profile. You can read her intentions by her shape: narrow, slightly flexed wings and closed tail indicate that she is gliding and is intent on covering a big horizontal distance—perhaps she has seen some distant prey (see 6.13). Fanned wings and tail show that she is striving for height rather than distance. She may have found a column of rising air which will take her right up to the cloud base (figures 1.15.5–11).

Species with low wing loadings, such as the buteos, mainly search for quarry which is easy to catch. They are masters of soaring and gliding. They cannot manage a fast agile sprint and their favorite attack is the glide attack (6.13).

## 1.16  Powered flight

Ignoring for a moment all aerial maneuvers such as turns, take offs and landings, powered flight, in which the hawk propels itself by flapping its wings, has several recognizable gaits. First is steady flight, more or less equivalent to our walking. Studies by Spedding, Pennycuick, and Rayner have shown that when a falcon, such as a kestrel or peregrine, is flying very slowly, at less than three meters per second, the upstroke is passive, gives no lift, and no longer generates a vortex. The result is a doughnut-shaped vortex ring caused by the thrust of the downstroke (figure 1.16.1). During the upstroke the wing is flexed quite closely into the body, and, as it were, draws in and then shrugs off the trailing vortex of air.

The buzzards and eagles fly in a similar way except that their wingbeat is deeper, slower, and

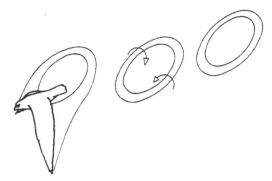

Figure 1.16.1 A vortex ring is formed by each downstroke of the wing. The upstroke is passive.

folds up more. Their upstroke is faster than the downstroke. During strenuous flight it is likely that the upstroke is active, giving some lift, but in slower flight it is probably passive.

As the falcon speeds up to above seven meters per second, the airspeed is sufficient to raise the wings, reducing the workload of the supracoracoideus muscles. Now the upstroke is active and generates trailing vortices (figure 1.16.2). Instead of folding closely to the body, the wing is held stiffer and straighter in the upstroke, resulting in the typical flickering flight of the cruising peregrine (figure 1.16.3).

When the raptor wants to go faster than cruising speed it has three choices: the buzzards and big eagles can't really sprint, so to make a faster attack they must come in from a height in a fast glide (see 6.13). The falcons and the accipiters can actually fly faster but they do it in two different ways. At this point I seem to have reached the edge of known science, so I can only tell you what I think is happening. The problem of course is that it is not easy to study a sprinting raptor in detail, with or without a wind tunnel.

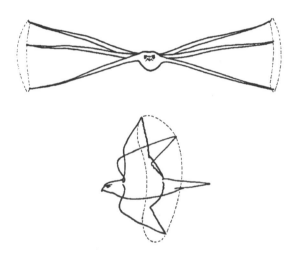

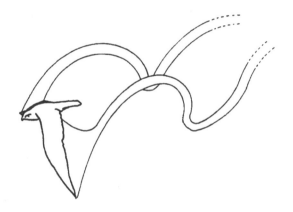

Figure 1.16.2 The falcon in normal flapping flight with continuous trailing vortices.

Figure 1.16.3 The stiff, shallow wingbeat of the cruising peregrine.

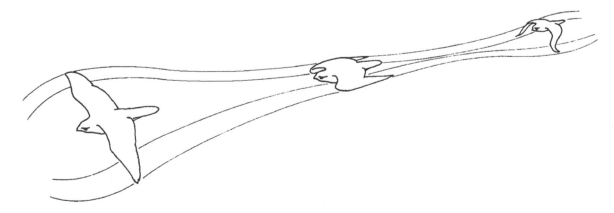

Figure 1.16.4 A peregrine with pumping, high speed wingbeat.

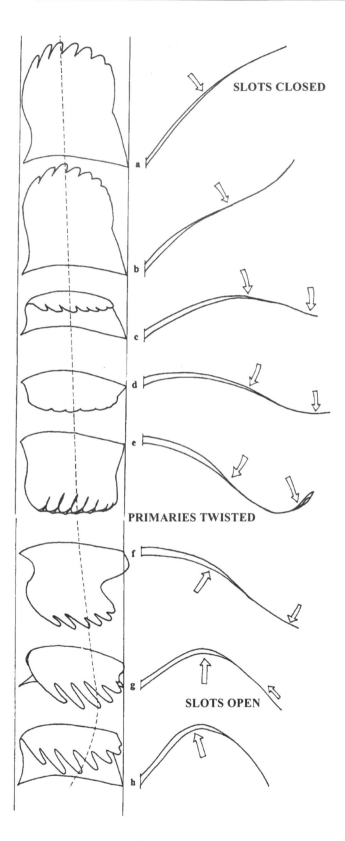

SLOTS CLOSED

PRIMARIES TWISTED

SLOTS OPEN

Figure 1.16.5 (a–e) The downstroke of a sprinting goshawk, (f–g) the upstroke of a sprinting goshawk.

The falcon, already traveling very fast, at such a speed that its normal cruising wingbeats would slow it down, is like a cyclist who cannot pedal fast enough for it to make much difference. So the falcon glides with wings half shut, the secondaries providing lift, but otherwise minimizing leverage strain on the pectorals. The vortices trail smoothly behind (center, figure 1.16.4) as in a steep glide (compare figures 1.15.2 and 3). Then the falcon makes a series of deep pumping wingbeats in which it puts as much power as it can into some big fast downstrokes, faster even than the speed at which it is traveling, and angled to provide thrust, rather than lift. The result, which is very noticeable in a sprinting gyrfalcon, is that each wingbeat visibly pushes the bird forward in the air with a spurt of speed. It is almost as if it is being kicked from behind by an invisible boot. Only a short burst of these pumping beats is needed for the falcon to reach such a speed that further flapping can no longer help. By then something will have happened.

The accipiter also sprints but has a slightly different problem to solve. Whereas the big falcon needs to travel very fast over long distances, the accipiter needs to travel very fast over short ones. Its battles are won or lost in seconds. Therefore its problems are not so much one of top speed, but of acceleration. At the start of its sprint effort, the accipiter is either still, or moving slowly. So its sprint has to start from near zero. Whereas the gyrfalcon is like a cyclist who is winning a long race by sheer top speed, the accipiter is like a cyclist waiting at the starting line to win a race which finishes after 50 meters. At the finish it may not have even reached its top speed, but may still be accelerating. Therefore it has to cram as much effort as it can into a short period of time, and it cannot waste half of that time on a useless upstroke which does not contribute toward the thrust. It gets round this by using a slotted elastic wing which not only stores energy, but also reduces drag in the upstroke.

During the down stroke (figure 1.16.5 a-e), thrust and lift are generated, but, because the wing is so short and the pectorals have such a mechanical advantage, the primary tips are bent backward to the point where their tips twist 90 degrees from the plane of the wing, in both vertical and horizontal planes (figure 1.16.5 e). The bird then starts to draw in its wings, actively using its supracoracoideus muscles (1.16.5 f). The elastic primaries

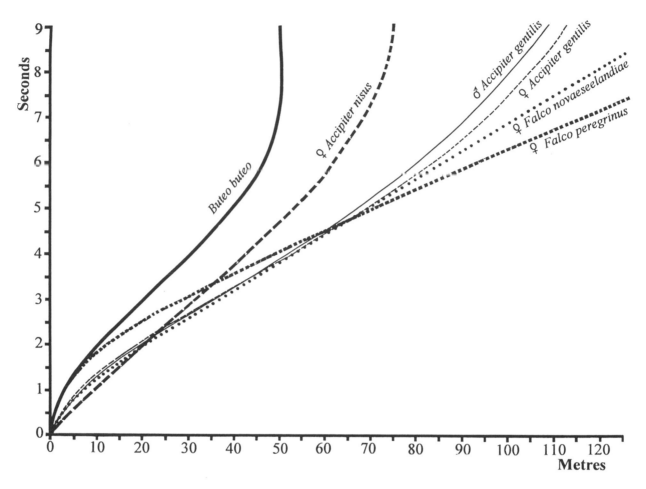

Figure 1.16.6 Acceleration curves for common buzzard, female European sparrowhawk, male goshawk, female goshawk, female New Zealand falcon, and female peregrine in a level sprint.

start to recover their normal shape, thrusting the air both downward and backward. This provides lift and thrust and also helps the supracoracoideus muscles. The wing is now half way back up and semifolded. The blades of the primaries are now edgeways on, in line with the angle of incidence. At the top of the upstroke they all come together, seal up and start to provide thrust again as the wing comes down.

Assuming still air and level, powered flight we can plot approximate acceleration curves for a variety of raptors. Lacking directly comparable data from fit hawks, I have compiled these curves from several sources, particularly from works by H. J. Slijper and T. A. M. Jack and from my own observations. While they may not be very accurate for absolute speeds, they give an idea of the differences between the species, although of course individual birds vary considerably.

Common Buzzards (figure 1.16.6) are rela-

tively weak at powered flight; slow to accelerate and with a slow top speed, they soon burn out. One seldom sees a buzzard sprint more than 100 meters and rarely 200 meters. It quickly starts to rest by gliding between beats, shown in the graph at 40 meters. During level flight it can manage about 10 meters per second, beating its wings at about 5.0–6.5 beats per second. There is very little quarry that travels slowly enough to tempt a buzzard into much more than an 80 meter effort. Most prey is either caught quickly (for example a vole) or quickly outdistances the buzzard in a tailchase (for example, a partridge). Then the buzzard will tail off and perch, in this case at 45 meters.

On the other hand, small accipiters, such as the sparrowhawk, develop full speed in under one second, within the first few meters. This explosive sprint gives them the edge over all other raptors in cover. But few will maintain a flat out sprint after 100 meters; normally the flight has been concluded by then one way or the other, and if unsuccessful, the sparrowhawk will probably perch after 150 meters or so.

Slijper's work on goshawks showed that the male starts off faster but is overtaken by the female at around 70 meters. Once she gets going, the female is slightly faster. After about 130 meters or so goshawks usually slacken off somewhat; having failed to kill in the initial sprint, they either give up or cruise along gaining height to mark where the quarry puts in.

Over the first 20 meters the peregrine is not much faster than the buzzard but by 50 meters it is building up speed, overtaking the goshawks by about 130 meters and keeping up a good pace for several hundred meters. Over a long distance it is probably outdistanced in level flapping flight only by the gyrfalcon.

The New Zealand falcon, with its accipitrine flight profile but falconine physiology, starts off much like a small male goshawk. By the time a female sparrowhawk has covered 80 meters the falcon has reached 100 meters. By about 130 meters, as the goshawks start to fade, she is going strongly but is overtaken by the peregrine which has got into her stride. By the time the peregrine has gone 280 meters the New Zealand falcon lags about 40 meters behind and both disappear over the horizon with no slackening.

The acceleration and top speed of the predator must parallel those of the prey in a tail-chase attack. Quail have similar flight patterns to sparrowhawks, pheasants to goshawks, and pigeons (with a slightly faster take off) to peregrines. Strong, long-flying prey are soon ignored by accipiters unless they can be caught in a sprint or ambush.

The effect of the rocketing ability of accipiters can be seen in their acceleration over the first 40 meters. Cooper's hawks, for example, normally beats their wings at 4.0–5.5 beats per second, but during take off fly at 7–8 beats per second, using pectoral muscles which are about 17 percent of total body weight. They cover this distance when the buzzards and most falcons have barely gone 20 meters. Their performance over this distance is critical in making direct flying attacks (see 6.10), and in estimating the maximum distance at which it is feasible to attack a particular quarry species and have some hope of overhauling it. Large falcons tend not to attempt short direct attacks but prefer more calculated long ones. Buzzards do not

sprint at all if they can possibly avoid it; instead they use height to give them an impetus for a glide attack, or a dive.

Apart from the infinite permutations of acceleration curves and attack distances, there is the question of agility. Here the accipiters, the merlins, and the New Zealand falcon score highest, the larger falcons and Harris hawks are somewhat less able, and finally, lumbering at the rear, come the buzzards. The quarry too vary a great deal in their agility (see section 7.4). Agility tends to be bought at the expense of top speed; a long tail gives agility but creates drag.

## 1.17  The foot structure

The leg and foot of a raptor has seven functions: to support the weight of the body, to act as a rudder during some flight maneuvers, to cushion the impact of landing, to catch, to hold and in some species, to kill prey, to help regulate body temperature, to preen those parts of the body inaccessible to the beak, and, in some species, to act as courtship signals. To perform some of these tasks effectively the foot must be light in weight for maximum agility and with a surface that is easy to keep clean of blood, dirt, and bacteria. To meet these requirements the foot has evolved so closely to the physical limitations of living tissues that there is very little margin for error and it is not surprising therefore that the foot is so prone to disorders.

The foot basically is a series of bones and sheathed tendons (figure 1.17.1). Behind the tibiotarsus and tarsometatarsus run the very strong flexor tendons. Muscles higher up in the thigh control these. The flexor tendons run right down through the ball of the foot along the underside of each toe to the furthest pads. When the muscles contract, the foot closes tightly. The tendons slide in grooves in the underside of the toe bones and are held in place by toughsheaths. Thesheaths are lined with fine ridges rather like the grooves of a fingerprint and engage with rough ridges on the tendons themselves (figure 1.17.2). When the foot tightens, these ridges lock together like a ratchet mechanism on a handbrake. Possibly you will have noticed a stiff, jerky, creaky effect when loosening the grip of a live hawk; this is the ratchet being forcibly overridden. The ratchet has two useful purposes for the hawk: it enables it to "lock" its foot closed on a branch while sleeping,

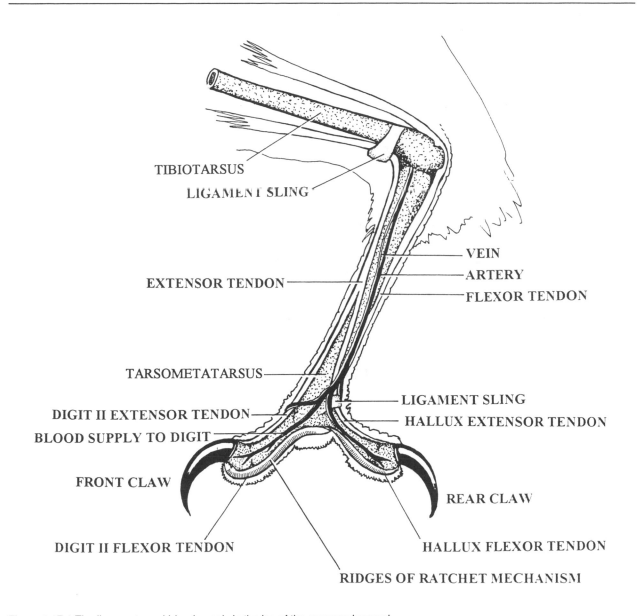

TIBIOTARSUS

LIGAMENT SLING

VEIN
ARTERY
EXTENSOR TENDON
FLEXOR TENDON

TARSOMETATARSUS

LIGAMENT SLING
DIGIT II EXTENSOR TENDON
HALLUX EXTENSOR TENDON
BLOOD SUPPLY TO DIGIT

FRONT CLAW
REAR CLAW

DIGIT II FLEXOR TENDON
HALLUX FLEXOR TENDON

RIDGES OF RATCHET MECHANISM

Figure 1.17.1 The ligaments and blood supply in the leg of the common buzzard.

and it means that once it has got a tight grip on its prey it does not require much muscular effort to maintain the grip. A human attempting to grip hard with his hand can only do so for a few seconds before the muscles lose power; if the victim stays quiet at first and then suddenly jerks away he finds the grip has relaxed. Of course the ratchet, like so many devices, is subject to technical hitches; not a few ospreys have drowned by being unable to unlock from an oversize fish. The use of a thin glove can encourage a falconry hawk, especially an excitable one, to lock onto the fist. These birds are known as "sticky-footed."

The flexor tendons run through a groove at the top of the tarsometatarsus in such a way that as the weight of the sleeping bird tends to buckle the legs, so the flexors tighten the grip on the perch. Conversely a goshawk, whose tendons are set at a fairly tight adjustment, is uncomfortable on a flat surface. It cannot open its feet completely without straightening its upper legs into a position which is tiring to maintain and, if kept on a flat surface for several weeks, the flexor tendons may collapse.

The extensor tendons run down the front of the tibiotarsus and the tarsometatarsus, one of them branching back through a ligament sling, or retinaculum, to a rear toe. Their effect is to extend the toes and of course they are weaker than the flexors.

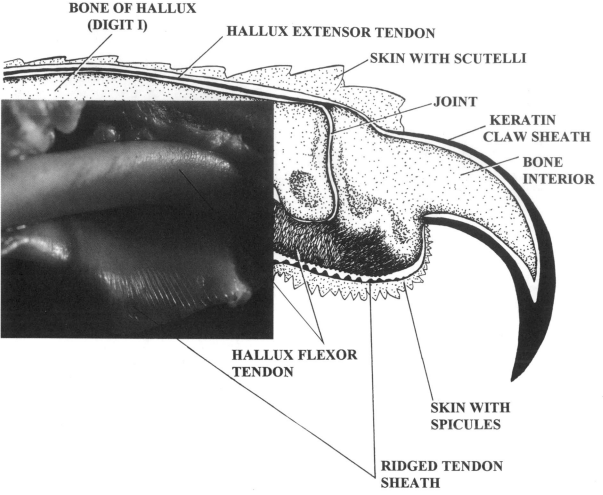

BONE OF HALLUX
(DIGIT I)

HALLUX EXTENSOR TENDON

SKIN WITH SCUTELLI

JOINT

KERATIN
CLAW SHEATH

BONE
INTERIOR

HALLUX FLEXOR
TENDON

SKIN WITH
SPICULES

RIDGED TENDON
SHEATH

Figure 1.17.2 The ratchet mechanism in the foot of the common buzzard.

The two ligament slings act like pulleys and keep the tendons in place, otherwise they would pull away from the bone like a bowstring.

The blood vessels lie just under the skin thus avoiding being pinched by the tendons. Both artery and vein run alongside each other for most of their course. This means that the warm outgoing blood in the artery is cooled by the returning blood in the vein which is itself warmed by the artery. This conserves heat in cold weather and during exertion or hot weather the vessels dilate allowing the bird to lose quite a lot of heat this way. Some vultures even excrete urine onto their feet to increase evaporative cooling. Fortunately, falconers' birds are usually better behaved!

As the foot consists mostly of bone and tendon, the blood circulation within it is meager, especially during long periods of inactivity. This means that any injury—a sprain, torn ligament, bite, thorn, or scratch, can take a long time to heal.

An infection is hard to overcome. Prolonged pressure can lead to degeneration of the underlying tissues or the formation of a core of dead tissue like a corn. The undersides of the feet have lump-like grips. If the hawk is kept on a smooth surface these become the pressure points. First they become polished and often pink, then they slowly die, allowing bacteria to enter. The surrounding tissue reacts by building up layers of cells, resulting in a type of bumblefoot.

Some falconry species, such as peregrines, are very heavy for their size and so their feet have to carry more weight than usual. The large falcons are often very phlegmatic in captivity, increasing their risk of corns. A beef diet seems to make raptors more prone to foot trouble and if the bird is kept fat and fed in the evening an extra 25 percent weight is on the feet all night, just when the bird is inactive and with one foot up.

Preventive husbandry can reduce these risks.

Birds are best kept on perches with sufficient curvature to prevent undue tension of the flexor tendons but of sufficient width to spread the weight evenly over the whole foot area. A rippled surface, such as astroturf, prevents pressure points without causing abrasion and a drained surface stops the soles of the feet being continually damp and soft and reduces bacteria. A balanced diet with tirings encourages good foot tissues and a good circulation, discouraging "filled" legs, and reduces the likelihood of the hawk picking at its feet in boredom. The pen should be designed to prevent the bird landing heavily and bruising its feet. Feeding in the morning and a careful watch on the bird's weight reduces the constant pressure on the feet because the food is digested more rapidly during the daytime (see section 5.9). Careful coping of the claws, combined with proper handling to prevent selfinflicted injuries, and prompt attention to bites and thorns will reduce the risks of infection. Al-

The bumblefoot on this Australasian harrier was started by a thorn.

though treatments for foot conditions are constantly being improved, prevention is still better than cure.

The claws are of different sizes and shapes. The hind claw and inner claw are primarily used for killing and gripping prey and are therefore the largest. The claw on the center toe (digit III) is short with a lateral flange on the inner side. The hawk uses this to preen and scratch the delicate areas of the head which could be damaged if scratched with the point of a sharp claw (figure 1.17.3). The outer toe's claw is also short. These two toes give the hawk stability when perched and increased reach for catching prey.

The skin of healthy adults of most raptor species is bright yellow due to carotene pigments. In the large falcons the breeding adult males have noticeably deeper yellow feet than their mates, whose feet have lost color, possibly owing to the uptake of carotene for the developing eggs. The males show their bright legs during the tippytoed walk of courtship display (figure 2.6.2).

The proportions of the feet vary according to the prey normally taken. Raptors which catch birds in the air, such as sparrowhawks, peregrines, merlins, orange-breasted falcons, and New Zealand falcons, have long toes with pronounced grips underneath. The peregrines have short tarsi to withstand the impact of the stoop, whereas the sparrowhawks and New Zealand falcon have long tarsi to enable them to snatch birds from cover and during a twisting tail chase.

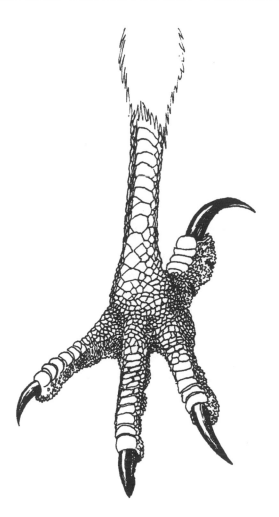

Figure 1.17.3 The right foot of the common buzzard.

Mammal specialists, such as the kestrels and many species of buteos, have shorter stronger toes; often these mammals are killed by the strength of the grip rather than by a bite.

Intermediate forms, which catch both birds and mammals, such as the goshawks and the desert falcons, have an intermediate foot, reflecting the dual-purpose role. Others are specialists, such as the secretary bird, which has very long legs and small, strong feet for dealing with snakes. Careful examination of the feet shows that they are just as finely tuned for their lifestyle as are the wings.

## 1.18 Sexual dimorphism and variations with lifestyle

Although size differences are very noticeable to the casual observer, size is just one of many parameters which should be looked at together to understand what is going on. Sexual dimorphism is when the sexes are of different sizes or shapes. In raptors the females are usually larger and some people call this Reverse Sexual Dimorphism (RSD). Sexual dichromatism on the other hand, is when the two sexes are of different colors. This is usually in the adults. Juveniles often also have a different color plumage...you can see that the water is already getting muddy!

Colors are usually to do with the way hawks react with each other, for example in courtship. Many species, such as the saker and the common buzzard, are very variable but are hard to differentiate as juvenile or adult, male or female, by color. So dichromatism is more of an evolutionary luxury rather than a necessity in raptors.

Sexual dimorphism is most pronounced in "attackers" and least in the "searchers" (see chapter 6 and Tom Cade's *Falcons of the World*). Many other characteristics come in the same package. The attackers tend to have high wing loadings, an unstable, anhedral profile, and catch agile prey in an active attack. They have a lower hunting success but usually one kill is sufficient for the day and they have short, lightweight, less efficient guts. The main selection pressure acts on them during the attacking phase of the hunt.

Searchers tend toward the opposite on all these features. In between are a host of intermediate species making up a spectrum. So it seems likely that sexual dimorphism is selected for most strongly during the attacking phase of hunting agile prey. Raptors try to evade this selection pres-

sure in two ways. As juveniles, some behave temporarily more as searchers, as discussed in 1.14. As adults they can reduce the selection pressure by widening their prey base. This is achieved by one sex taking the smaller prey and the other taking the larger ones. In this way one species can virtually fill the niches of two species. Doing this may trespass on the niche of another species above or below in the size scale. This can be seen in the North American accipiters: the sharpshin, the Cooper's hawk, and the goshawk, partitioning six niches between them. This could limit the extent to which one of them can diversify up or down the size scale. If you take away close competitors, the species could be more dimorphic, and this is seen in the New Zealand falcon, until a point is reached at which the female is so large that she might too easily intimidate the male.

Why should the female be the sex which is larger? Why not the male? The female is the one which lays the eggs and has to stay at the nest for six or seven weeks. She is dependent on the hunting ability of the male, and later, her brood is also dependent on him. This period is timed to coincide with the young prey animals leaving their nests. The male has access to the young of all his normal prey species, plus the young of the female's prey species, which at that time are smaller. He has to find prey which is worth the energy cost of ferrying back to the nest (he is better off consuming any insects he may catch because they are not worth taking home). He also has to find prey within the size range which he can easily carry. In the absence of neighbors, his hunting range is thus limited by how far away it is worth going to catch something and bring it back. By the time his chicks are getting large enough to be safely left alone for a while so that the female can also hunt, the prey have also grown larger. She can cash in on this more easily and economically than can the male. Thus it is all a balance between the method of attack, the size of the prey, and the timing of the development of young raptors and young prey.

There are other factors which arise from this situation. Theoretically the large female can more easily produce eggs, but on the other hand a female sparrowhawk is just as effective an egg producer as a female goshawk four times her size. A big female may be better at defending the nest. She may also be aggressive toward or dominate the male. I believe these are all outcomes of sexual dimorphism, rather than causes of it. There are plenty of predators in which the male is larger than the female. If the male was really such a rapacious fiend as he is painted, why doesn't he just kill his defenseless young? In reality, raptors are strongly inhibited against killing anything at the nest and there are many instances in which raptors have brought young prey back to the nest still alive and then adopted them and reared them.

The most severe selection pressure and attri-tion in raptors operates during searching for, and most particularly during attacking prey. This is the moment of truth in a raptor's life and the time when poor performers are weeded out. The driver for sexual dimorphism operates through mortality of poor hunters, and the driver for the female being larger operates through productivity during nesting. That's what I think.

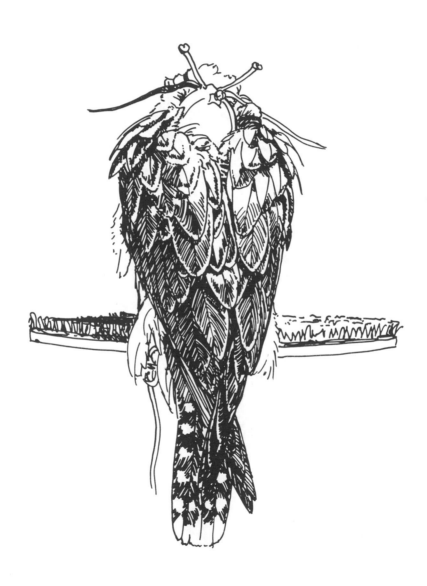

Saker asleep.

# 2 Managing a

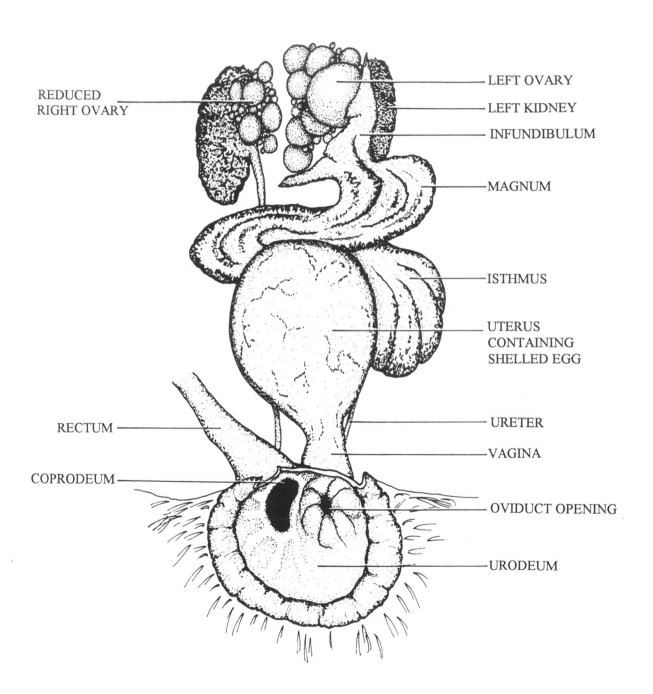

REDUCED
RIGHT OVARY

LEFT OVARY

LEFT KIDNEY

INFUNDIBULUM

MAGNUM

ISTHMUS

UTERUS
CONTAINING
SHELLED EGG

URETER

VAGINA

RECTUM

COPRODEUM

OVIDUCT OPENING

URODEUM

Figure 2.17.2 The reproductive tract of a female saker during laying.

# Breeding Program

## 2.1   The process of domestication

The remarkable progress of domesticating many raptor species in the 1970s and 1980s is a process which will continue to unfold (see 8.5). Currently, in the mid-1990s, most breeders are quite happy to breed what they can. Some state-run projects are deliberately breeding only indigenous subspecies or populations because the offspring are wanted for release to the wild. Some breeders are content to breed what they have; the offspring are only wanted for falconry and, once a particular pair are breeding, it is a pity to split them up. Other breeders are selecting for particular traits. For example, certain lines of peregrine which are renowned for waiting-on are selected for game hawking. Physically and genetically they appear standard, but when flown they have a marked tendency to go up. Some breeders are looking for size; they put together large Aleutian Peale's peregrines or big Finnish goshawks. Others are selecting for speedy bloodlines. This process is bound to continue and in the next twenty years certain bloodlines will come to prominence for these reasons.

Some breeders are taking matters one step further by making intersubspecies hybrids, interspecies hybrids and, in some cases even intergeneric hybrids, such as a Cooper's hawk crossed with a Harris hawk (see 8.4). Most of the wider outcrosses are very different genetically and in the long-term will be sterile. Others, such as the gyr/saker, are very closely related, appear perfectly fertile and perhaps throw new light on our understanding of the taxonomy of these groups. Among falcons, second generation hybrids are now common. For example we fly a lot of gyr/saker X sakers. We also fly a gyr/peregrine X New Zealand falcon. The Domestic Falcon *Falco domesticus* is just around the corner. This is falconry's equivalent of the racing pigeon and the domestic poultry breeds.

Many purists will hold up their hands in horror at all this, but the story is far from finished. Once the "breed" stage is reached, there is then the question of open and closed stud books. This stage happened in Europe over the last two centuries with many of our horse and dog breeds. It was a somewhat haphazard and very interesting process developing, for example, the thoroughbred horse and the English pointer. Our forebears added a little of this and a bit of that to the recipe until they reached the type they wanted, then they closed the stud book and started breeding "true" lines. Nowadays one can only alter the English pointer by selecting from registered animals. If one decided to add some setter blood for example, the offspring would be classed as mongrels and would not be registerable. Insofar as this maintains the genetic integrity of the breed, the closed stud book is a good thing. On the other hand it means that the main evolutionary development of the breed is now over and that the breed is restricted now to the limited gene pool it originally started with. If this was large, well and good. But if it was small, the breed will gradually become more inbred through the generations.

It will be some time before this stage is reached with raptors. It has been exciting meeting the challenge of domesticating birds of prey and it will certainly be interesting to watch the bloodlines emerge. For this to happen there has to be selection pressure. In race horses this is competitive racing. In hunting dogs this is fieldwork and competitive Field Trials. In show animals it is Show Standards (some of which are really grim). Field Trials are in many ways a good idea but they suffer from two problems; one is that they measure the training of the dog more than its genes. The other is that they have closed down the uses of the dogs into very tight stereotyped patterns, such as retrieving, based largely on shooting (they are now called "gun dogs"). This neglects other aspects of the dog such as how long their potential working lives are, how easy they are to train, how good they are with children, how easy they are to live with, and so on.

In raptors, the selection pressures are a little different. The first one is whether or not they will breed at all. For example we have a pair of gyr/sakers here which laid twelve eggs this year and produced twelve chicks. Every fertile egg this female has ever laid has hatched. We have other pairs which have never laid at all. Once the chick has been reared, it then has to be evaluated in various ways before the decision is made to breed from it. We measure it, we train it and evaluate its hunting performance for the type of flight it is intended for, we assess its mental suitability for breeding, we look at its pedigree, and sometimes its DNA profile, then we look for a suitable mate for it and calculate the coefficients of relatedness to see if they will maximize the genes we are selecting for. Most breeders are unable to do this because of the economies of scale. They will be led to some extent by market forces. What sells well is obviously desirable. Unfortunately it is also sold and therefore out of the breeder's hands and not available for breeding. We get round this in two ways: one is that we train and hawk with a lot of our own birds each year, sometimes twenty or more. The other is that we lend out birds to other falconers and then call them back in once sexually mature. In America, and now in Spain, there are competitive Sky trials which to some extent test the ability of the birds. I am against Sky trials because they degrade the sport of falconry into a competition between raptors and between their owners, and because it gives the public and young falconers the idea that falconry is all about releasing bagged game (see 8.9).

At present we don't have Breed Societies. Falconry clubs tend to be based on geographical area rather than breed. But a Harris Hawk Society may not be far away. Harris hawkers tend to be a sociable lot. There will probably never be a Goshawk Society. People who fly goshawks end up antisocial, introverted, stubborn, sensitive, and have generally used up all their patience on their birds....

Having looked at breeding from an overall perspective, we are now in a position to look at evaluating the bird, breeding from it and raising good youngsters.

## 2.2    The genetic assessment of pairs

From the start you should have a clear idea of your general breeding plan, based on factors discussed in 8.5. and 8.6. You will know whether you are trying to maintain the widest variety of genes or whether you plan to intensify certain genomes by line-breeding. Therefore you need some information about the genes which your birds carry.

The traditional way to do this is to use a pedigree (figure 2.2.1). This will show the ancestry back several generations, perhaps even to founder stock. It may also give additional information which is useful, such as how the bird was reared and who bred it. The pedigree may also link up to a computer stud book such as SPARKS. Pedigrees are simple and basic to a breeding plan. Surprisingly few people buying a hawk show the remotest interest in its pedigree. This will change in time as purchasers become more discerning.

Fewer people still know how to use a pedigree. It is not enough just to look at the pedigree of your new hawk and say, "Oh look! Her grandmother was The Galloping Gourmet—she must be good!" What if you are planning to put two birds together as a pair, and you can see that they have one or two shared ancestors in their pedigrees? How do you calculate how related they are?

Genetics unfortunately tends to be 90 percent theory and only 10 percent reality. Let's look first of all at what relatedness means. Let's start with two gyrfalcons, one from Alaska and one from Greenland. So they must be unrelated. Wrong. Of course they are related or they wouldn't both be gyrfalcons. The question is: how related are they? Human beings and chimpanzees for example share 95 percent of their genetic material. They are almost the same! We are all related to some extent and so we need to assess what this background level of relatedness is.

When two parents breed together, each donates half its genes. We can say therefore that, on average, the relatedness between parent and child is half (or 0.5 or 50 percent). The same applies to siblings: a brother and sister are 50 percent related, (except identical twins, which are 100 percent related.). The background level of relatedness lies somewhere between this close relationship of 50 percent and zero. In a genetically diverse population the background level of relatedness may be as low as 15 percent, but in a bottlenecked population it could be over 40 percent. Therefore we cannot say that our founder birds are unrelated, that they have a coefficient of relatedness of zero.

For the sake of simplicity, SPARKS, and similar studbooks assume that founder birds are unrelated. The only way to find out what the background level of relatedness is, is to profile the DNA and calculate it. This is what we had to do with our New Zealand falcon program. We had to trap wild falcons from all over the breeding range,

## CERTIFICATE OF PEDIGREE

SPECIES : GYRFALCON

SEX
RING NO.
HATCH DATE :

BREEDING METHOD :
☐ Natural
☐ Artificial Insemination

HATCHING METHOD :
☐ Parents Full-Term
☐ Parents Part-Term
☐ Incubator Full-Term
☐ Incubator Part-Term
☐ Foster Hen

REARING METHOD :
☐ Parents
☐ Foster Parents
☐ Group
☐ Hand

A PROPOSED PAIRING

Certified as a True Record

Name : ...........................

Signature : ...........................

MALE: PANG
SPECIES GYRFALCON
RING NO 7812 W
HATCH DATE
BREEDER:

MALE: WHISPER
SPECIES GYRFALCON
RING NO 3279 W
HATCH DATE
BREEDER:

MALE: SHADE
SPECIES GYRFALCON
RING NO. 10976
FOUNDER FROM CANADA

FEMALE: GEM
SPECIES GYRFALCON
RING NO. 10803
FOUNDER FROM GREENLAND.

FEMALE: JESSICA
SPECIES GYRFALCON
RING NO 10594
HATCH DATE
BREEDER:
FOUNDER BIRD FROM ALASKA

MALE:
SPECIES
RING NO.

FEMALE:
SPECIES
RING NO.

FEMALE: OLIVIA
SPECIES GYRFALCON
RING NO 0255 X
HATCH DATE
BREEDER:

MALE: VENOM
SPECIES GYRFALCON
RING NO 0384W
HATCH DATE
BREEDER:

MALE: SHADE
SPECIES GYRFALCON
RING NO 10976
FOUNDER FROM CANADA

FEMALE: GEM
SPECIES GYRFALCON
RING NO. 10803
FOUNDER FROM GREENLAND

FEMALE: ISOBEL
SPECIES GYRFALCON
RING NO 0210 X
HATCH DATE
BREEDER:

MALE: SHADE
SPECIES GYRFALCON
RING NO. 10976
FOUNDER FROM CANADA

FEMALE: JESSICA
SPECIES GYRFALCON
RING NO. 10594
FOUNDER FROM ALASKA

SPECIES:
RING NO.

Fox 1995

Figure 2.2.1 A pedigree form showing the proposed pairing calculated in the text.

take blood and look at the DNA. This gave us a starting point. We discovered that some individuals trapped over 300 kilometers apart were related by up to 50 percent. This means they were as close as brother and sister! So much for founders being unrelated! What this meant was, not that they were brothers and sisters, but the population as a whole was closely related, having at some point dwindled to low numbers and then made it back up again. This is not necessarily a bad thing. A severe bottleneck weeds out the bad genes and thus further inbreeding is less likely to be harmful. Inbreeding in a more varied population is more likely to reveal "genetic skeletons in the closet."

A species, such as the ferruginous hawk, might have a very varied population in the wild but when imported to another country for breeding, maybe only ten individuals might come in. Of these maybe only six birds breed. Of these maybe one pair produces 50 percent of the total young. This is not too drastic at first, but go a decade and a few generations down the line, as we are now with

some of our species, and problems can arise.

Calculations of coefficients of relatedness, and covariance charts, get very difficult. But it is not hard to follow relatedness in a simple three or four generation pedigree. This is what you do:

Take the pedigrees of the two birds you are planning to mate and put them side by side. If they have no common ancestors then you can assume that for practical purposes that they are "unrelated" or more properly, their relatedness is close to background level. Let's choose a pairing with three common ancestors, Jessica, Gem, and Shade which are wild founder birds:

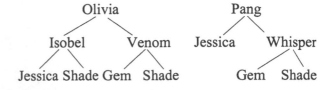

Each generation is related by 50 percent to the next. So first we trace Jessica up to Olivia. They

DNA profiles of "fingerprints" of a family of gyrfalcons run by Dr. David Parkin at the University of Nottingham. can you tell which are related and which aren't.

*Photo: David G. Fox*

Measuring instruments: sliding calipers and steel rules.

The quail are reared in purpose-built quail cages in flocks of about 25 birds.

are 0.5 × 0.5 = 0.25 related. Pang is also 0.5 related to Jessica. So for this one common ancestor, Olivia and Pang are related by 0.25 × 0.5 = 0.125.

For Gem, their relatedness is 0.5 × 0.5 × 0.5 × 0.5 = 0.0625.

For Shade it is more difficult. Both Olivia's grandfathers are Shade. This doubles the genetic contribution for that generation level. So for Olivia, Shade is 0.5 × 0.5 + 0.5 × 0.5 = 0.5. Pang's complement is 0.5 × 0.5 = 0.25, thus 0.5 × 0.25 = 0.125 for Shade in total.

Then we add together all the coefficients of relatedness for all the common ancestors:

Jessica = 0.125
Gem = 0.0625
Shade = 0.125
Total = 0.3125

What does this mean? A pairing which shows a coefficient higher than 0.125 is likely to show signs of inbreeding. This could be a genetic defect, such as a crossed beak, or it could be inbreeding depression, such as reduced hatchability. It depends too, on the proportion of "bad" genes in the populations. But as a general rule of thumb, try not to pair birds related more closely than 0.125. Olivia and Pang are destined for unrequited love, and we must look for alternatives. This is how the pedigree acts as a working tool for the breeder. Similarly, if the breeder is attempting to concentrate a particular characteristic, such as waiting-on ability, he might decide to line breed, building up the genetic contribution from the ancestors which performed best.

## 2.3   The genetic compatibility of pairings

Whatever care you may take to ensure that your pairings are the optimum genetically, there are still some aspects outside the ken of man. Some pairs are just not very compatible genetically.

They may lay fertile eggs without problems, but then some of the eggs fade out and die during development. You try every trick in the book to hatch the eggs, but still some die. We have a female saker now age seven. She is paired to a white gyr × saker. We have hatched every single fertile egg she has ever laid. And yet another saker, unrelated, paired to another white gyr × saker, lays eggs of which 50 percent always fade out during incubation.

Genetic compatibility also affects thriftiness.

Some pairings "nick" together well. They produce a high proportion of really good progeny. Others fare less well. If this is the case, the problem can often be solved by rematching the birds.

Harris hawks in Britain and North America often show leg defects which have been attributed to inbreeding. Actually, most of these birds are well outcrossed and the defects are preventable by adjusting the diet of the female in the preegg laying period (see 2.10).

## 2.4   Selection of breeding stock: physical assessment

Once you are satisfied that a certain bloodline is genetically suited for your plans, how do you pick out the individual bird you want? Some falconers go on weight, but as we shall see in 5.8, weight is very variable, and as a selling point can be made to say whatever you want. We sold two sister Harris hawks last year, same age and size. One recipient rang back and complained that his bird flew at only 36 ounces (1008 g) and the other rang and said his was taking hares at 45 ounces (1260 g).

So we don't rely too much on weights!

Color is another common criterion. Arab falconers especially often have marked preferences for different colors. Some of these can be predicted early on. For example a white gyr has very white claws at hatching whereas a good black gyr has black claws, a black beak, gray fluff, and cere. Fully feathered youngsters can also be selected on plumage and we take photos of each from above and from below with the wing and tail fanned. However, many raptors have an unremarkable juvenile plumage and you don't know what the adult plumage will be like until later, when the bird has already been sold and paired up. Also colors are just colors; they do not tell you much about the bird as a hunter.

Therefore we take a number of measurements which help to define the bird as a flying machine (see 1.13–1.16). These measurements are kept on a computer database and by comparing the new bird against mean values for previous records we can make some fairly exact quantitative statements about the bird. To do that, it is essential that we all take the same measurements in the same way as otherwise the results are not comparable. Trolling the literature for data is haphazard for this reason.

The measurements we take are designed in such a way that most of them can also be taken

Wing length and wing width

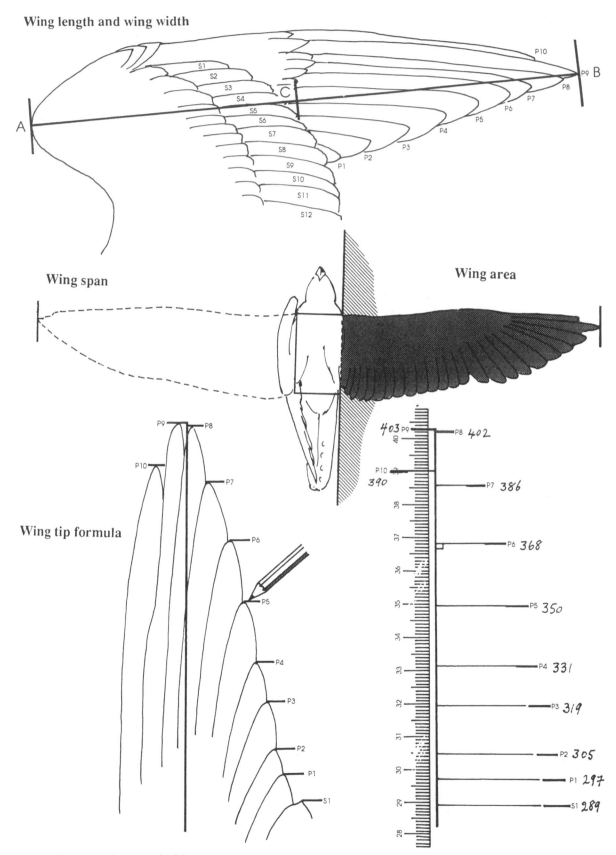

Wing span

Wing area

Wing tip formula

Figure 2.4.1 Measuring the wing of a falcon.

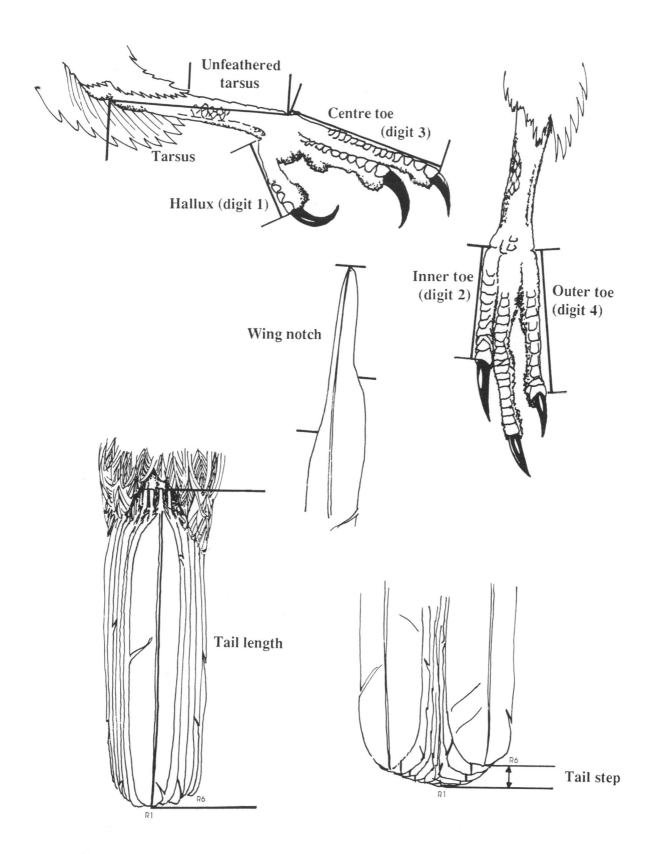

Figure 2.4.2 Measuring the foot and tail of a falcon.

# NATIONAL AVIAN RESEARCH CENTER
# FALCON DATA SHEET

| Species: *SAKER* | Microchip No: *002-552-309* |
| Sex: *♀* | Leg ring No: *UK 86262 / 271-91W* |
| Hatch date: *UNKNOWN 1990* | Geographic origin: *UNKNOWN* |

Date measured: *1/12/93*          Measured by: *M.J. PATERSON*

| Wing | P10 | P9 | P8 | P7 | P6 | P5 | P4 | P3 | P2 | P1 |
|---|---|---|---|---|---|---|---|---|---|---|
| Length (mm) *390* | *376* | *390* | *385* | *368* | *347* | *313* | *287* | *267* | *239* | *213* |
| Notch leading vane (mm) | | *96* | *70* | *50* | | | | | | |
| Notch trailing vane (mm) | *85·* | *67* | | | | | | | | |

| Wing width to S5 *225 mm* | Both wings area (cm²) *1835 cm²* |
| Wing width ratio *57·7 %* | Wing loading (g/cm²) *0·65* |
| Wing span *1240 mm* | |

| Tail Length (mm) *225* | Tail step (mm) *MOULTING* |

| Leg Tarsus (mm) *61* | Unfeathered tarsus (mm) *36* |
| Hallux digit 1 (mm) *33* | Inner digit 2 (mm) *35* |
| Centre digit 3 (mm) *56* | Outer digit 4 (mm) *36* |
| Diameter of tarsus at midpoint: | |

**Weight** with estimated empty crop and no equipment          *1190*          g.

**Condition** : ~~Fat/~~ ~~Average~~/Lean/~~Thin~~.

**Photos dorsal and ventral enclosed:**          *YES*

**Source of specimen:**
**Samples taken:**
Blood for DNA sent to:          *KEPT*
Blood for pesticide analysis sent to:
Faeces sent to:
Swabs sent to:
Feathers sent to:
Carcase sent to:
Other material:

Fox 1995

**Veterinary treatment:**

Figure 2.4.3 Falcon data sheet.

from museum study skins. This has the advantage of immediate access to large quantities of data, many more than most breeders would see in a life time. The measurements we take are shown in figures 2.4.1 and 2.4.2 and they are recorded on a data sheet as shown in 2.4.3.

WING LENGTH (A-B) is the straight distance from the carpus to the tip of the longest primary on the flattened wing. WING WIDTH (A-C) is the distance from the carpus to the tip of secondary 5. WING WIDTH RATIO is AC /AB X 100 percent.

To obtain the Wing area, lay the open wing across the edge of a table with the leading edge straight and trace the outline onto a sheet of paper. Label the outline with the bird's identification. This will be used for further measurements and for the calculation of TOTAL WING AREA. To calculate the total wing area we take the area of both wings, together with the area of the wing root box (the area of the body between the wings). The quickest and most accurate way to calculate the area in square centimeters from the tracing is to count the squares on squared paper. The total wing area is then used in the calculations for WING-LOADING. The WINGSPAN is wing tip to wing tip in millimeters. Unfortunately, only the most modern museums store open wings.

To obtain the WING TIP FORMULA lay the closed wing tip onto some flat paper and carefully mark down all the primary tips with a pencil. Remove the wing and draw in a center line following the wing chord. Using a set square, mark off all the marks onto the center line. Knowing that in this example the overall wing length was 403 millimeters, place the edge of a ruler along the center line with 403 aligned with the longest primary. Read off the measurements for the other feathers in millimeters. This is used to provide the wing tip profile.

The NOTCH or emargination is measured from the tip of the wing to the center point of the notch.

The TARSUS is measured from the groove in the tibiotarsal joint diagonally along the tarsometatarsus bone to the groove in the joint with the center toe. The TOES and HALLUX are measured with the digits extended straight and exclude the claws.

The TAIL LENGTH is measured from the tip of a center (deck) feather (rectrix 1) to the point at which the feather emerges from the skin.

The TAIL STEP is the difference between the tip of the outermost tail feather (rectrix 6) and the tip of the center tail feather (rectrix 1) on the same side. Where the two sides do not match, take the mean value.

The WEIGHT, measured in grams, is taken either by perching the bird on some scales and subtracting the weight of all equipment, or by placing the bird in a cotton bag and suspending it from the scales. The condition of the bird should be noted and an estimate made of the weight of crop contents.

At this time we also make a note if blood has been taken for storage for DNA profiling, and if any other treatment is undertaken.

## 2.5 Performance assessment

On the back of the physical assessment form we keep records of the bird's performance (figure 2.5.1). Although we are experimenting with quantifying performance in terms of top speed in level flight, endurance, and so on, we are still working on this and so at the moment we record performance based on a subjective assessment. Because we train and hunt quite a lot of falcons every year, it is possible to judge them and to make comparisons. But you need to do a dozen or so individuals of each species before you can reach any conclusions.

We also keep records of training and hawking. All of these records are kept on the bird's file and help us to assess its merits. Of course many birds are reared specifically for breeding and are not flown at all. The likely performance of these birds has to be assessed by the achievements of siblings, parents, or progeny, bearing in mind that these relationships share on average 50 percent of their genes.

## 2.6 Mental suitability for breeding

Whether or not two birds will pair up depends on what they think of each other. Love is the same the world over! We tend to have an image of our ideal future partner, based on our experiences in childhood. It is the same for raptors. The raptor's image of its future sexual partner is formed partly by instinct and partly by its parents. If it imprinted on its natural parents (see 4.8 and 4.11) then all is plain sailing but if it has been hand-reared for part of its development it may be imprinted on two types of parents, hawks and humans. This puts it in

Date left hack box:    $28-06-91$   $(46\ days\ old)$
Date finished hack:   $15-07-91$
Number of days flying at hack: $17$
Date started training:   $16-07-91$
Date flying free:     $30-07-91$
Date completed training:
Name of trainer:    NcF.

**GENERAL COMMENTS:**

Temperament: (hot) average, placid, steady, nervous, erratic.
Intelligence: (clever) average, stupid.
Voice:   silent, (screams occasionally,) frequently, persistently.
Hooding: excellent, average, (difficult occasionally,) often.
Footing: (good) average, poor.
Turning: (tight) average, wide.
End-on speed :   Very fast (fast) average, slow.
Acceleration : Good, (average,) slow.
Powered climb : (Good) average, slow.
Unpowered climb : Good (average,) slow.
General flying ability and precision: (Good) average, poor.
Persistence in pursuit: (Excellent) good, average, poor.
Ability to kill in cover : (good,) average, poor.
Confidence with large strong prey: (Good) average, poor.
Appetite: large (average,) small.
Heat resistance: good (average,) poor.
Other comments:

Hunting performance:

Hawking sheets enclosed.
Took 5 crows in 7 flights in Northumberland.
11 houbara in Pakistan.

Figure 2.5.1 Performance assessment chart.

Figure 2.6.1 The male (right) approaches with a confident, "fronting" posture. The female is not intimidated—she wants to play.

Figure 2.6.3 This is the "Angel" threat posture. Don't come any closer!

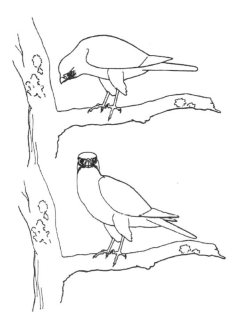

Figure 2.6.2 This male is sleek and alert, bowing and bobbing and staring with wide eyes at the female. He wants to copulate.

Figure 2.6.4 Warbling or the two-wing stretch.

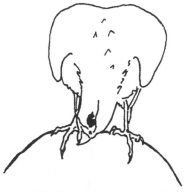

Figure 2.6.5 Feaking or cleaning the beak using an up-and-down movement of the side of the beak.

conflict. A frequent outcome of this is that the bird may pair up with another of the same species but be frigid and refuse to copulate. Therefore it is important to rear future breeding stock carefully.

There are two ways round this problem. One is to rear the youngsters using an imprint female. It will grow up identifying itself as a hawk but used to breeding enclosures and treating humans like passing sheep or clouds—moving but harmless and irrelevant. The other way is to rear groups of youngsters together. This is called "social rear-

ing" in America or "creche rearing" in Europe.

This identification of future partner is not just about hawks and humans. It also occurs between different species and colors. If you rear a peregrine with a peregrine and then in adulthood put it in a

Figure 2.6.6 The one-wing, one-leg stretch.

Figure 2.6.9 Mantling over food.

Figure 2.6.7 Scratching the face with the center toe. Raptors scratch with their foot in front of the wing, not behind it.

Figure 2.6.10 Rousing.

Figure 2.6.8 Winnowing or wing exercising.

Figure 2.6.11 Sunbathing with back to the sun.

pen with a saker, it may refuse to have anything to do with it. A few motivated birds may pair up but many go year after year without much sign of breeding. If you want to make a hybrid by natural pairing then it is best to rear the two species together or cross foster them. This is the mechanism which prevents species all getting mixed up in the wild. It is not that breeding is prevented because the birds are genetically incompatible (many *are* genetically compatible), it is because the birds tend to pair up only with what they consider to be their own species.

This effect is not just at species level; it also

occurs between different color phase birds of the same species. If you take a baby falcon and rear it for a few days with a black gyrfalcon and then remove it and place it in the nest of a white gyrfalcon, it shows every sign of terror and retreats from the new parent. If you had left it all the time with the black gyrfalcon and then in later life tried to pair it with a white gyrfalcon, it would have a major sexual turn off. You can easily imagine the effects of different color siblings and differently programmed partners. Some combinations will thus do well, others will always be inhibited.

Some breeders set great store by "compatibility." In my experience this is rather a myth. If the birds have been reared in the right way, are settled in captivity, and internally are coming into breeding condition, then they should pair up and go some way toward breeding. The problems arise when birds are obtained from a variety of backgrounds of unknown history. Such motley birds may be inhibited for various reasons outlined above and this is interpreted as "incompatibility" as if it was on a personal level. The reasons lie deeper.

If the conditions are right, personal likes and dislikes don't come into it. For example, tundra peregrines migrate back to their breeding grounds in the spring. Males arrive first and wait for passing females. If one comes past they may have a brief greeting ceremony and then copulate within just an hour or two. Also, DNA profiling shows that many birds, including raptors, indulge in extramarital sex when the opportunity arises. Similarly, if one of the parents is killed, a new partner may take up residence and nesting duties within hours. It has even be known for chicks to start life with one set of parents, for one parent to be shot and replaced, then the other, so that the chicks fledge with completely different parents!

Another aspect of mental suitability for breeding is the extent to which a raptor is stressed in captivity. Domestic raptors, properly reared, are completely at ease in breeding pens. I have a white jerkin here called Icicle whose pen covers one of my office windows. If I come in soon after dawn he chups to me for a while in greeting, then goes back to sleep, a headless white fir-cone on my windowsill.

But wild caught raptors, especially rehabilitated ones additionally stressed by injuries, may not adjust well to captivity. They may appear not too bad, but breeding is the acid test and many fail to come into breeding condition. It is particularly important for these birds to have quiet, roomy, natural-type secluded pens. If such a bird is paired with a nice randy, relaxed partner, it might overcome its inhibitions and breed. Some stressed birds appear nervous and show no sign of courtship. Others are even more high strung and may kill their mate. More often though, a female kills her mate through frustration and tension in their relationship (domestic violence) than through captivity-induced stress.

When you watch your hawks in their pen, how do you know if they are happy and are getting along with each other? You have to learn to read their behavior and understand what it means. The figures 2.6.1–11 are of New Zealand falcons and are fairly typical for falcons in general. Harris hawks on the other hand have a completely different behavioral repertoire and even if you understand falcon language you have to go back to school to learn Harris language. Even within a genus there are differences, so when I go down a row of mixed imprints of different falcons, I have to remember to talk in saker language, then in gyr, then in peregrine, and so on. Sometimes I get in a muddle! Some play behavior is very close to aggression and some birds can switch, cat-like, from pussyfooting to daggers drawn. It is important to understand their basic behavior to interpret how they are getting on and what, if anything, can be done to remedy a problem.

## 2.7   Breeding facilities for natural pairs

When I first started breeding I had to catch my own falcons and start from scratch. I figured that the nearest I could get to Mother Nature, the happier they would be. So I built a pen 50 feet long, full of trees, with ten nest sites. You could sit in one of the two hides for hours and not see a bird. And they bred!

Then I started to get clever. The next time I had to build pens, this time in Britain, I started to eliminate all those features which I thought were superfluous. I aimed for the minimalist, cost-effective aviary. Some of these worked well too, depending on the birds. A typical minimalist aviary of this design is shown in *Falcon Propagation* and in figure 2.7.1. These pens work quite well for medium-sized raptors which do not require much stimulation to breed and we use them for most "commercial" production.

Trickier species have special needs. Females of species which are strongly dimorphic, such as the accipiters and the New Zealand falcon, often kill their mates, so it is useful for these to have double pens connected by windows. These windows can be solid, or meshed, or open, or barred so that only the males can pass through. To find the spacing of the bars, we place the male in a box with temporary bars covering one end and leave him there for some hours to see if he can get out. We adjust the bars until he can just get through. We do the same for the female. Then we design the real bars at a distance halfway between the two measurements. Many pairs do better if they do not see each other all the time. Absence makes the heart grow fonder. Gyrs have a lovely clamorous greeting ceremony but get bored with each other when present all the time. They need stimulation. Nervous male accipiters are happier if there are bushes in the pen for them to escape behind.

The skylight and seclusion pen, designed by Dr. Leonard Hurrell, works well for nervous raptors. But even the scattiest ones like a window; it steadies them down and is an endless source of interest for them. Of course a window need not be the same as our idea of a window; it can be a very small hole. For example a window 5 centimeters in diameter with a perch next to it is enough for the hawk to look out comfortably and yet feel itself unseen. It can easily retreat into the peace of the pen if people come near.

A few features need to be incorporated when building a pen. The first of these is strength. A pen should be built to last 10–20 years without major work done on it. This is how long the pair may be in it and building activity will disrupt them. Lapboard and cheap timber are not suitable. They soon deteriorate and either hawks escape or predators get in; the result is expensive. We build our pens of concrete block rendered smooth. Various steel profiles on a timber frame are good too, but actually are not much cheaper. Flat galvanized steel is fine for interior walls but can be noisy in a storm. We have one block like this called "The Thunderbox." All timbers and roofs should be bolted on with steel straps and all plastic or fiberglass sheeting should be covered with mesh because plastic at

least will shatter in time. Jemima Parry-Jones recommends "Onduline" roofing; this material seems to have a lot of advantages.

The pen should be completely vermin proof, which means something substantial up to waist height. Rats may move in the autumn and we kill them with a poisoning campaign before they can get into the pens. Cats get onto the pen roofs and can keep an incubating bird off the eggs all night, resulting in mysterious failed hatches. An electric wire around the roof usually keeps them off, but persistent offenders may need sterner measures.

The pens should be built so that every part of it can be viewed from one place or another. Each bird should be seen and checked every day for signs of illness. To view the birds we use peepholes, one way glass windows, and close circuit televisions. The materials, especially the perches, floor and food trays, should be properly disinfectable with a comprehensive disinfectant such as "Virkon," otherwise the pen will become "sick" over the years. We mainly use concrete floors which are cleanable. They can have pea gravel or sand in heavy use areas and an astroturf mat in any places where birds habitually thump onto the ground. Deep gravel is cheaper but tends to build up bacteria and can then be a major chore to change. Larger pens can be grass but it is important to keep the vegetation under control either by blitzing it or with sheep. Tall nettles restrict the available flying space and are a hazard. If a bird lands in them it may be unable to get out. No cut vegetation should be allowed to mold in a pen.

All our perches are covered with coarse astroturf, even for the merlins. We have never had a

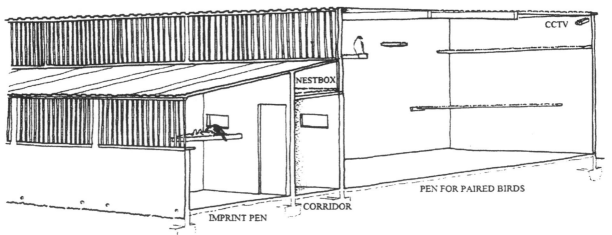

Figure 2.7.1 A section through our breeding pens with imprints along the front and natural pairs behind the central corridor.

case of bumblefoot here, not even in retired Arab hunting birds which have previously had bilateral foot operations in the Middle East. The main perches are removable for cleaning and all are pressure-washed before disinfecting. Any objects or surfaces near a perch are covered with a smooth material so that feathers will not be abraded. Harris hawks and other species which suffer from the cold have heating tape wrapped around their perch under the astroturf; this prevents frost bite and dry gangrene. Some of the perches are big and wide, giving plenty of room for two hawks. Then they can adjust their personal distances gradually, as they get better acquainted. The perches vary from very low to quite high so that the hawk can gain height by hopping up from perch to perch. This is essential for some of the big falcons; when a female is molting and laying, she cannot fly up steeply and could otherwise be unable to regain the nest to lay. Some of the perches, usually near the nest, have a moulded concrete area. The hawks feak on this and it helps keep their beaks in trim. Food trays, baths, and so on should be sited to avoid mutes from overhead perches.

Our pens face south over a quiet valley so the birds get plenty of sun through big high windows. Each pair thinks they own the valley and remonstrate strongly if a fox comes into view 300 meters away. The gyrs flirt outrageously with passing buzzards and herons.

The nest boxes are large and roomy to accommodate large broods. The substrate is fine pea gravel for all species including stick nesters. No peat, hay, or straw is used. Since we moved our hay barn 100 meters away from the hawks we have stamped out aspergillosis completely. Stick nesters have their nest over the pea gravel so that if inexperienced birds make a poor nest the eggs will still be properly supported. Each pair have at least two nests to allow for recycling. They almost always use the alternative site for the second clutch. There are peep-holes to each nest; some of these are covered with black sticky tape and only opened or pin-pricked as needed. Sitting birds are very sensitive. When we have a female which has to be checked through the night for egg laying so that we can inseminate her, we install a small night-light on a dimmer. It is used only for two or three nights when actually needed.

We use a variety of food hatches and trays. The main thing is that they can easily be checked and cleaned and that all feeding points are kept clear of mutes. This stops an infection cycle. Baths are refillable from an outside hose connection and are removed and sterilized as necessary.

For medium-sized raptors like peregrines we aim for a minimum floor area of about 250 square feet (23 sq m) and a height of about 12 feet (3.6 m). A greater height than this tends to cause more problems than it solves. All windows should be as high as possible and unapproachable from the outside. Of course, if the pens will be on show to the public then it has to be possible to see the birds easily. This raises a lot of further considerations and one is then not designing a breeding pen for the birds so much as an exhibit for the people.

You may have noticed that I haven't said anything about security against thieves. The first rule with security is not to discuss it. So I won't.

## 2.8 Breeding facilities for imprints

Our facilities for imprinted raptors are very straightforward. Each has an individual chamber about 2.4 meters (8 ft) by 3.0 meters (10 ft) with access through a door to a central corridor or double door system. This size is large enough for the bird to get some exercise but small enough so that the handler is all the time inside the bird's individual space (figure 2.8.1). This means the bird does not have to nerve itself up to approach the handler to interact. It will not flit around the pen trying to avoid the handler because there is no space to go into.

There is a large, barred front window with a wide astroturfed windowsill perch at waist height overlooking an area where the birds can see things going on without being threatened or spooked. A bath and low perch are placed under the nest to keep them free from mutes. The floor is concrete with a thin layer of sand. Each pen has a corner nest at chest height with a window directly at the nest into the corridor. The nest is the central focus for imprints and it should be designed so that both bird and handler can use it together conveniently. The window glass is clear so that it is possible to interact both ways through the window. This is particularly useful with some females which can turn crabby suddenly and grab your face. Later it is useful for monitoring eggs and chicks in the nest and, if the female is sensitive, we cover the window temporarily with cardboard and make a peep-hole.

Imprint pens have covered roofs with one of

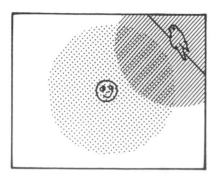

Figure 2.8.1 Left: Man and imprint. They cannot avoid being in each other's space so they stand their ground. Right: Unmated pairs need room to avoid each other until they pair up.

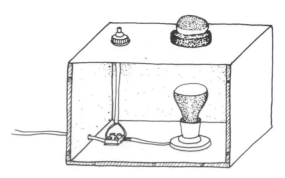

2.9.1 A simple egg candler (cut away view).

the sheets clear. With males especially, it is important to have some control over their environment. Cold or wet days will lower their semen production and they need to be kept dry and in even temperature conditions for maximum steady production.

## 2.9    Incubator and broody rooms.

The first consideration for incubator and brooder rooms is hygiene. The floors, walls, ceiling and all surfaces should be sterilizable by light spraying with Virkon. Nothing is kept in the rooms except what is actually needed. All the rooms and equipment are thoroughly fumigated at the start of the season after cleaning. No unnecessary staff are allowed in the rooms and child bolts are fitted to

the tops of the doors to prevent access.

The air in the rooms is maintained at a steady temperature of about 18 degrees centigrade and there are extractor fans to change the air as needed. In extreme climates it is also necessary to control the humidity in the rooms. The rooms are placed internally in the building, with no windows, to avoid fluctuations in temperature and to allow complete darkness for egg candling during the day.

The electricity circuits are fitted with antisurge devices and with power-off alarms and there are petrol driven and battery-powered standby generators. Any experienced breeder knows that if there is a chink in the system, fate will sooner or later find it.

There are a variety of small incubators on the market, some of which are not really good enough for raptor eggs and are designed for the small poultry breeder or for schools. Still-air incubators are gentle on the eggs, cheap, and good for hatching and early brooding, but they can be tricky for taking eggs right through, especially if the room temperature varies.

A few basic points to look for in incubators are:
  a) simple design with nonabsorbent easy to clean parts,
  b) good electronic thermostat with back-up,
  c) electronic humidity control,
  d) adjustable turning mechanism with adjustable rollers,
  e) even temperature spread throughout the machine, and
  f) all windows double glazed and able to maintain heat for at least an hour during a power failure.

We use Grumbach forced-air incubators run at 37.3 degrees centigrade: three smaller units for

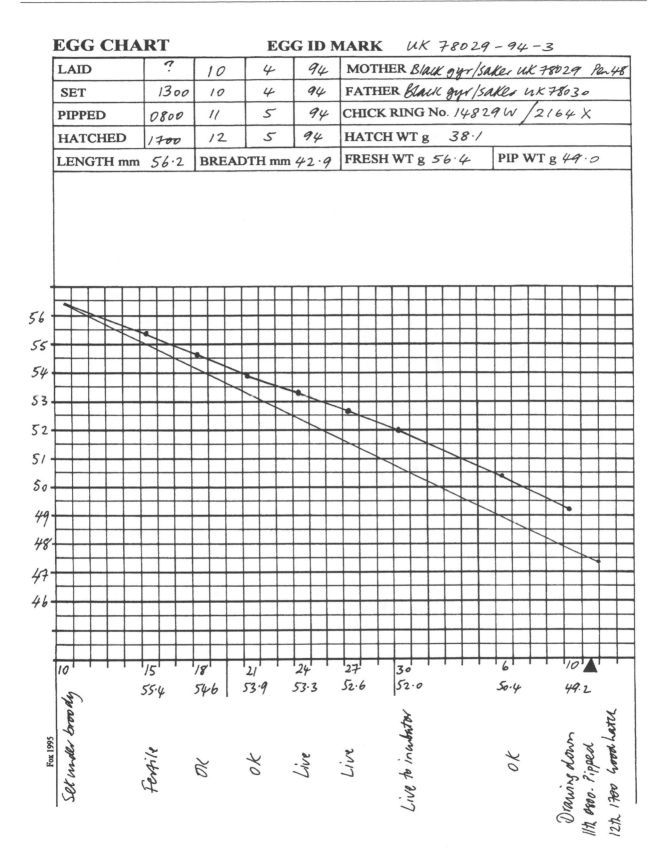

**EGG CHART**   **EGG ID MARK**   *UK 78029 - 94 - 3*

| LAID | ? | 10 | 4 | 94 | MOTHER *Black gyr/saker UK 78029 Pen 48* |
| SET | 1300 | 10 | 4 | 94 | FATHER *Black gyr/saker UK 78030* |
| PIPPED | 0800 | 11 | 5 | 94 | CHICK RING No. *14829W / 2164 X* |
| HATCHED | 1700 | 12 | 5 | 94 | HATCH WT g  *38.1* |
| LENGTH mm  *56.2* | BREADTH mm *42.9* | FRESH WT g *56.4* | | PIP WT g *49.0* | |

Figure 2.9.2 An egg chart.

Grumbach incubators in the incubator room.

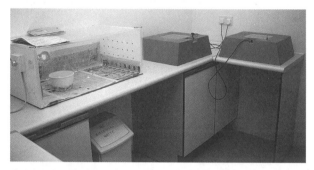

Polyhatch still-air incubator lids for brooding baby raptors, and a twin-lamps brooder box.

A polyhatch incubator lid on a damp towel used for hatching quail eggs. After the hatch, the shells are thrown away, the towel is washed, and there is very little cleaning to do.

raptor eggs, a hatcher, and a large unit used all the year round for quail eggs. Raptor eggs are incubated in a separate room away from poultry eggs.

The eggs are weighed about twice a week on an electronic balance and candled using a simple candler (figure 2.9.1). This illuminates the egg with a 60-watt silvered bulb from below. It is switched off and on just for the few seconds nec-

essary to check the egg. It is made of aluminum sheet bent over two plywood sides and a base, and has vents in the side walls to release any heat. Records are kept on a simple egg chart (figure 2.9.2). Normally the eggs are incubated at 20 percent relative humidity, less if they are overweight and more if they are too dry.

The best incubators are broody bantams and we keep different sizes according to the size of eggs to be incubated. *Falcon Propagation* covers the main points about managing broodies. Their hygiene and management need careful attention and the flocks need to be managed so there will be sufficient proven sitters throughout the spring. Our best results have been with broodies and we leave all the raptor eggs with them until close to pipping, except for problem eggs. An embryo that has been well-incubated by a bantam is strong enough to overcome most minor problems at hatching and early rearing. For the small breeder, some bantams for incubation, together with a Polyhatch lid for hatching and early brooding (see figure 2.28.1) will give the best, most reliable results most cheaply. Broodies are particularly good for the breeder who has to be away at work during the day time and can't be continually hovering over incubators. No hay, straw, or peat should be used in broody nests because they will transmit *Aspergillus* spores into the eggs and kill them. We use pea gravel and sand as a base and heat reservoir with sterilized chemical-free wood shavings, shredded paper, or cat litter for the cup.

## 2.10   Food supply, storage, vitamins, and food-borne diseases

What food to feed the breeding stock is a balance between cost, palatability, nutritional quality, availability, and health risk. It also depends on the different stages of the breeding cycle.

Quail, pigeons, rats, and mice are the most expensive and most complete diets. Chickens are cheaper. Hares, rabbits, and day-old cockerels are the cheapest. We don't use large mammal meat, such as beef, because we don't keep any really large raptors. Hawks find all these diets palatable except, sometimes, rats and mice. Some buteos and owls eat these with relish but many of the falcons refuse to touch them. All fresh-killed food is more palatable than frozen food. We breed our own quail and this is a major performance in itself because through the spring and summer we use about 500 quail per week. One can also purchase frozen quail. Hawks find these less exciting than twitching fresh quail, also one has no control over vitamin levels and fat content. Ex-layer quail are usually very obese and should be fed very sparingly.

Chickens in the form of your own grown-on poults are fine, ex-layers and chicken heads less so, primarily because of health risk. If you visit some of the poultry farms the last thing you want your precious hawks to eat is something that has come from there. We have a lot of large falcons here which can be prone to obesity and a proportion of light, low-fat food such as rabbit and hare is good for them. These have been hawked, netted, dogged, or rifle shot and most of the diseases they are prone to are not transmittable to birds. They are not nutritious enough for merlins and small accipiters.

Frozen day-old cockerels from hatcheries are available in many countries and are very commonly fed to hawks. They are a whole animal diet, cheap, palatable and easy to use. We use them in the nonbreeding months but never for young hawks. Of course there are hawks and hawks. A diet that would rear healthy buzzards would kill an adult merlin. The yolks of day-old chicks are high in cholesterol and so many people remove them. The hawks themselves like the yolk.

Pigeons and wild-source birds are a health risk. All should be frozen for at least two weeks to kill off the trichomonads but freezing will not destroy any viruses or bacteria. Shot wood pigeons are a good diet provided they have been shot with steel shot, not lead shot, and are carefully inspected before use. They should be in good, well-muscled condition, with a clean liver. Any diet with suspected shot or shattered bone fragments should also include plenty of casting material.

One can never provide a completely pathogen-free diet, nor is this desirable. Low levels of suitable potentially pathogenic organisms are needed in the diet so that the hawk can build up a resistance. Otherwise when eventually a young hawk gets to eat its own wild-caught prey it could become ill. But pathogen levels in the diet should be at planned low levels; it is not an excuse for poor hygiene.

For a week before killing, the quail are fed a diet free of coccidiostats and antibiotics; they are also given a vitamin boost. They are not fed for 24 hours before killing. Then we pull their necks and

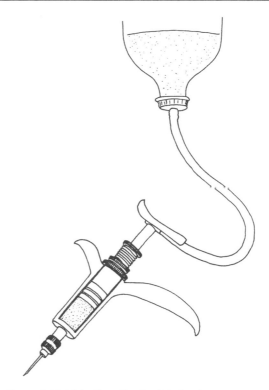

Figure 2.10.1 Injecting vitamins into food.

feed fresh, or lay them out to cool off before being placed in the freezer room on open trays to freeze quickly. The next day they are packed in sealed and dated bags for storage. Before feeding, the wings and feet are removed. With frozen birds and when feeding young hawks, we remove the intestinal tract but always leave the liver, heart, skin, and feathers. In some countries, particularly the Middle East, it is common practice to skin and eviscerate the quail. Although this keeps the falcons tidy, it deprives them of most of the benefit of a whole animal diet and predisposes them to bumblefoot. Falcons need the skin, liver, and a little bird fat; it improves their skin and feather quality. As a preventive treatment for bumblefoot in the Middle East we are using a regime as follows for the molting birds:

1. Feed food with the skin on and liver in.
2. Sprinkle one pinch of vitamin supplement onto each falcon's food every day. Damp the food first to make the mix stick to it.
3. Put one drop of cod liver oil on each falcon's food every day.
4. Give each falcon a fresh egg yolk three times a week.

This supplement is prepared to our own formula of vitamins, minerals, and amino acids and is designed to maintain a healthy structure of the skin to reduce the tendency to bumblefoot. It is also used to make a quick and complete molt with strong new feather growth. When fed this supplement last molting season in the Middle East, not a single falcon needed attention for bumblefoot.

Freezing and storing the food tends to destroy the fat-soluble vitamins. Artificial and monotonous diets can also lead to nutritional deficiencies which, while not being apparent in nonbreeding adult raptors, can lead to problems in breeders, especially in egg quality and hatchability and in the health of young raptors. A deficiency in the mother leads to a deficient egg which can lead to irreversible problems in the small chicks. Supplementing a chick under five days old is risky and still cannot compensate for an earlier deficiency because the internal organs and metabolism have already been based on the egg contents and because for the first 3-4 days of life the chick's nutrition is from its own yolk.

Captive birds, especially in the wet British climate, tend not to receive as much sunshine as wild ones, and they need this to help make their vitamin $D^3$. This is also one of the fat-soluble vitamins and therefore we provide extra in the form of cod liver oil. Many of the vitamins cannot be stored in the body and are needed every day. The basic supplement we use is Nekton-S at 0.5 g/kg of hawk daily. To this we add 2 drops of cod liver oil per kg of hawk and make the mixture up as an emulsion in water, fresh each day. This is placed in an inverted bottle tubed to a sheep injector which gives premeasured injections of vitamins into each item of food (figure 2.10.1). The food is thawed in trays overnight and the water base to the supplements helps to counteract the effects of dehydration from freezing.

During the breeding season we also feed carophyll orange at 0.1 g/kg. These carotene pigments are normally available to raptors in wild bird fat and are responsible for the orange color of the soft parts of adult raptors. An orange cere and feet are courtship signals for raptors and even if not entirely essential for health, they certainly look more natural and healthy to me.

About a month before egg laying we also feed Nekton-E at 0.5 g/kg to promote courtship behavior, semen production, and breeding especially in first timers or difficult birds. It is discontinued once the last egg has been laid or, in the case of males, when semen is no longer needed.

We have not arrived at these doses of supplements by scientific method. There have been no quantitative controlled nutritional studies of diet in breeding raptors that I know of. In addition there is a bewildering variety of different species, climates and basic diets. But for our birds, in our conditions, we have reached these decisions, using hatchability and survivability as the key criteria. This subject does not stand still.

Our annual regime for large falcons works out like this:

Throughout the year   - Nekton-S at 0.5 g/kg of hawk.
                               - Cod liver oil at 2 drops/kg of hawk.
From 1 Jan include     - Carophyll orange at 0.1 g/kg of hawk.
1 March or 4 weeks before laying, add
                                 - Nekton-E at 0.5 g/kg of hawk.
Feed                            - quail 4 days per week.
                                 - day old chicks 2 days per week.
                                 - rabbit or hare 1 day per week.
Discontinue Nekton-E and carophyll at the end of egg and semen production.
During laying           - fresh-killed quail/rats.
During incubation    - day old chicks and rabbit.
During rearing         - quail until young can fly, then wean in chicks and rabbit.
Rest of the year      - chicks and rabbit.

## 2.11   The program in winter

Once the young birds have all gone it is time to clean out all the pens, disinfect them, make any repairs before the winter and check birds for parasites. All CCTV cameras are removed as they are not needed in the winter months and will only deteriorate. All equipment is cleaned and repaired, spare parts ordered and fitted, and stored away properly. The birds should have just about completed molting and are now on a low-protein maintenance diet. Some of them will go through an autumn courtship or *herbstbalz* at the equinox when they are on the same day length as in the spring. This is a good time to match up new pairs. Staff take their holidays at this time and it is a convenient moment for a nervous breakdown, or a busman's holiday, a hawking trip.

As far as possible it is good to keep the birds lean and fit. They should fly down promptly when food is put in and can spend time tiring on joints of rabbit and hare. This continues until after the shortest day. From then on it is time to prepare for spring.

## 2.12 The program in spring

Soon after the shortest day is the time to get the bantam flocks sorted out and settled in. They are best run in groups of about a dozen birds in each bantam house and should have about 16 lock boxes for each 12 birds. We keep ours normally without a cockerel but when we want new birds we either put a cockerel in early, during January to March, and set those eggs, or late, in June when the bantams have finished sitting. However, most molt and have a refractory period before coming back into lay in the summer.

Just before the first raptor eggs are expected, we give the bantams a definitive clean. The whole room, lock boxes, feeders, and drinkers are pressure-washed and disinfected. The birds are treated for external and internal parasites and color-ringed. Nest material is put in and clean dry wood shavings are spread on the floor. From then on they are a no-go area and are monitored closely. Each bird must be solidly broody for at least a week before being given raptor eggs.

Similar treatment is being meted out to the falcons and their pens, so that they are clean and settled about a month before the first egg. Sensitive ones are done earlier, "regulars" are done late. The falcons have their beaks and talons coped (see figure 1.2.4 page 19) and the clumsy ones are crutched; the fluffy feathers around the vent are trimmed so that they do not impede copulation. All nest material is changed, everything is checked and CCTVs are installed and aligned using two people with walkie-talkies. The food ration is gradually improved (see 2.10) and they are fed 4–8 times per day to stimulate courtship.

How do you know how the birds are getting on? The problem is first of all to properly understand the elements of courtship behavior in the wild, and then to recognize it in a more condensed form in the aviary birds. For example, many male falcons in spring swoop at the female repeatedly and then zoom around the nest cliff (figure 2.12.1). This is known as mock attacking and cliff racing. When you see this in the pens you might conclude that the male is freaking out and attacking the female. So either by studying the wild birds, or by watching films, or reading books, you need to establish clearly in your own mind, what calls and behavior you would expect of your birds, and you should be able to put it all together into a simple chart as in figure 2.12.2. Of course not all pairs follow exactly the same sequence, some get stuck early on, others who are more experienced, may skip most of it and go straight into copulation without many preliminaries. But once you are clear of the roles of each sex, and how everything is condensed in an aviary, you should be able to diagnose problems and come up with some solutions. And you *will* have problems.

Once the first egg arrives it is rather like white-water rafting. There is no going back, you just

Figure 2.12.1 Male New Zealand falcon cliff racing and mock attacking the female.

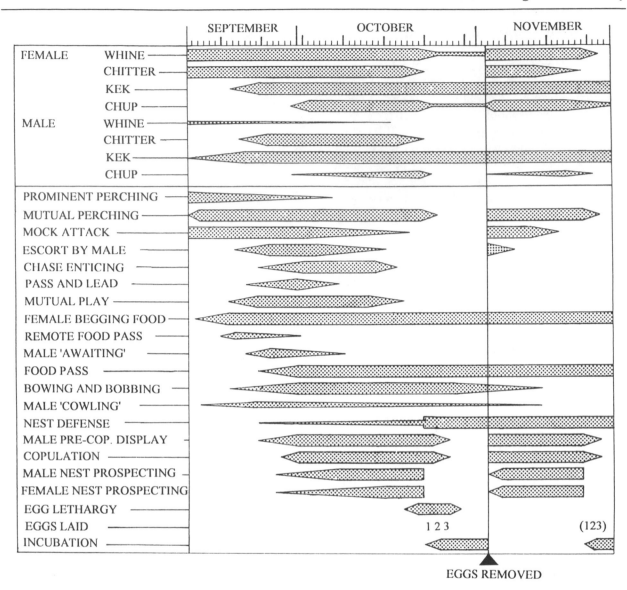

Figure 2.12.2 The courtship behavior of wild New Zealand falcons as a chart. Spring starts in September.

have to take each problem as it comes and try to come out the right way up.

## 2.13   Obtaining semen: voluntary donors, stripping, electro-ejaculation

The best semen is given voluntarily, either by natural copulation or by copulation with another object. Natural copulation takes ten to twenty seconds, sometimes more, and at the height of courtship some pairs copulate every half an hour or so. Others may copulate only a few times each day but still show good fertility. Birds copulate at any time but most commonly in the early morning and during sunny, mild weather.

Just because the pair copulates does not mean that the eggs will be fertile. Life is not that simple. Young or early season birds often "fire blanks" and even when semen is ejaculated a lot of it will miss the female's cloaca, and of that which does reach the semieverted cloaca, only a proportion gets drawn up into the oviduct.

Generally, it is easier for a male to produce semen than it is for a female to lay eggs. Many males have mature semen even though they have shown little or no sign of breeding condition. Many gyrs and peregrines produce semen for a short period in their second season, they do better in their third season and reach full production by their fourth season. The testes enlarge greatly in the early spring before producing mature semen (figure 2.13.1).

The other way to obtain "voluntary" semen is to use an imprint male and condition him to copulate on a hat (a method pioneered by Boyd Les), or on your knee, glove, or a cushion. All this takes a lot of man hours of conditioning, which, being operant conditioning, is dependent very much on the bird. Some birds never become voluntary donors; many do not become sufficiently motivated until they are five or six years old. Once the bird copulates voluntarily then its mate (you) has to be there in person three times a day right through the breeding season. A substitute person or your absence is liable to make him shut down either for a few days or even for the remainder of the season. So the bird is a major commitment. On the other hand he can produce three or more good samples a day, sufficient to cover four laying females. One thus comes to rely on him. When he eventually drops dead, never at a convenient time, his absence can knock a big hole in a breeding program. Also, from so much use, he can rapidly genetically dominate a breeding program. After three or four years his daughters come on stream and then one is looking for different semen. Voluntary donors are thus a real asset but one should not be tempted to rely too heavily on one individual.

In order to train a male to copulate with a hat, we are asking him to cross quite a big behavioral gap. Copulating with hats is not part of his natural repertoire! It is possible to make the whole sequence more natural by teaching him to copulate with a stuffed or dummy female which he has been introduced to at an early age. A tape recording of female precopulatory whining can be played from a box on which the stuffed bird is perched. In other words, the biological signals are as close as possible to those programmed into his instincts. A great advantage of this method is that the stuffed female can be introduced into the male's pen via a sliding door by anybody, not just a specific person. This frees up the handler and allows the male to stay in a good settled regime. Once the male is starting to tread the female, it is possible to substitute a pad or cushion which is more convenient for collecting semen. For some reason many imprints have a foot fetish and may start to copulate with your boot.

If semen cannot be obtained voluntarily, then the male can be stripped. Anyone contemplating stripping a male should be thoroughly and three-dimensionally familiar with the anatomy of the male urino-genital tract. The best way to achieve

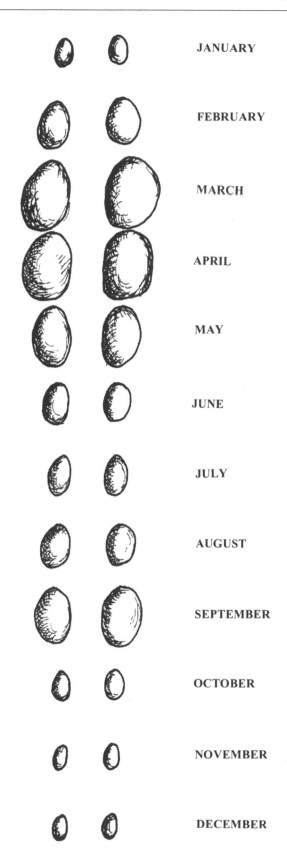

Figure 2.13.1 Monthly changes in testicular development for northern raptors.

this is by dissection of an adult male of the same species. Although stripping is a nonintrusive technique and is simple once one can do it, it is not something to be recommended to untrained people. A great deal can be learned by watching someone doing it, followed by practicing on chickens, but after that there is no substitute for hands-on experience and few breeders will be happy to let you use their precious birds. Stripping should involve only gentle, controlled pressure used in a full knowledge of what you are doing. Rough or ignorant handling, apart from being inhumane, could injure the bird.

A good imprint male, properly treated, will provide semen every day or every other day for six or more weeks. To do this he needs to be carefully hand-raised and made well to the hood. Preferably he should be flown to the lure in his first season. By his third season, sometimes sooner, it should be possible to go into his pen and he should court strongly. Either he can be free in his pen, with nonremovable jesses and a chest high nest, or he can be tethered to a block with a car tire nest filled with pea gravel adjacent to the block. The nest is an important focus for him. He should not be fed for at least twelve hours prior to stripping otherwise the semen may be contaminated with mutes. One therefore needs to be able to predict when semen will be needed and diet the male accordingly. When you go into the pen, even though he is fat, you should be able to take him onto the fist and hood him without any fuss or alarm.

We normally take him then to a special room which is cool and very well lit. His claws should already be well trimmed to prevent selfinjury. While I hold him by the jesses an assistant then holds him across the body with both hands. We then wrap a cloth quickly and fairly tightly round him. The cloth is 30 centimeters (12 in) wide and about 2.4 meters (8 ft) long. The material is fairly

heavy, like thick curtain material. It is wrapped around the chest of the bird with the trailing edge in line with the tip of the allula on each wing, just in line with the point where the legs emerge from the body. The other edge loosely forms a hollow tube over his head to prevent him biting the underside of my right arm. I monitor his breathing and heart rate throughout using my right hand. See photos on page 138.

I sit on a chair holding him on my left thigh on his back so that his head is in the middle of my lap and his tail projects out across my left leg. I place my right hand lightly over his chest and hold his right leg between my little finger and ring finger and his left leg between my longest finger and my index finger. In gyrs, the left leg is held between my index finger and thumb. The legs are held at the "hock" joint, between the tibia and the tarsus. With my two middle finger tips and thumb I draw up the vent feathers to expose the cloaca. Meanwhile I lay my left hand along the length of the tail which is pressed gently down until it is at an angle of 45 degree to the floor. My left little finger and ring finger curl under the pygostyle, supporting the tail and creating a bed of positive light pressure from below. My left index finger and my thumb exert gentle pressure in the area between the vent and the pubic bones.

The first time this is done each season I carefully "crutch" him by trimming all the fluffy feathers for a radius of about 2 centimeters all around the vent. Then the area is damped down with cotton wool soaked in warm water. The vent is blotted dry by dabbing with a tissue, rather than by wiping which makes him sore.

Meanwhile my assistant has made preparations to receive the semen. He has a warm glass plate with a series of hollows, each containing a small droplet of semen extender. Microscope slides, cover slips and a set-up microscope stand warm and

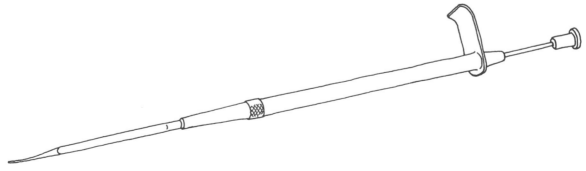

Figure 2.13.2 Ultipette semen collector with disposable tips.

ready. He holds an ultipipette with a new disposable tip ready to collect the semen (figure 2.13.2).

We are now ready to obtain the semen. There is no preparatory massage, no abdominal pressure, no force of any kind. Even if mutes are present, the pressure will usually be insufficient to draw them into the cloaca. First, using the finger tips and end knuckles of my two middle fingers of my right hand, I slightly catch the surface skin above the urodeum and draw it very slightly toward the bird's head without exerting any pressure at all. This slightly opens the vent. Then, continuing this movement, I exert a little pressure with the knuckle of my right long finger over the junction between the coprodeum and the urodeum. This exerts an inward pressure on any mutes in the coprodeum and and outward pressure on any semen in the seminal papilli in the urodeum. Some semen may appear and is collected from the semiopen vent. Then I draw my left index finger and thumb along the vent side of the pubic bones back to the cloaca, keeping pressure against the underside of the pygostyle. This milks semen down the lower reaches of the ducti deferentia. There are no semen storage organs present there in raptors but even so, semen standing in the tubes of the ducti deferentia is drawn down. I then maintain the pressure on the gathered semen using the end knuckles of my right ring and long fingers. This enables me to slacken with my left hand and reposition my fingers. This time, using my left index finger and thumb, I place them either side of the vent and, without pushing downwards (which would drive the semen away) I stretch the vent outward slightly in a side-to-side direction. This causes the cloaca to be somewhat exposed and the semen is available for collection held in a well of the vent. Once this is collected, or if none appears, I then press downwards slightly with my left finger and thumb and pinch them in again toward the cloaca, thus driving semen toward the vent. I continue with this movement, everting the vent and exposing the lips of the urodeum. Inside these lips are the two papilli of the ducti deferentia. My finger and thumb gently push the semen up from the ducts, through the papilli and out through the lips of the urodeum where it wells up and is promptly collected in one or two seconds with the ultipipette. None of this pressure has been on the rectum or coprodeum.

All of this procedure takes about ten or fifteen seconds. We repeat it four or five times. While my assistant unloads the collected semen I relax my hold on the bird slightly and he will usually give a little kick which exerts some abdominal pressure. When this happens, semen in the testicular end of the ducti deferentia flows down into the cloacal end which has just been emptied. You can often actually hear it move. This semen is then in a position to be stripped out. After the four or five attempts the whole length of the two ducts have thus been drained. Sufficient semen should thus be collected for one or two inseminations. If not much semen was collected, it is because it was not there. There is no point in further handling of the bird; reasons need to be sought elsewhere. Checking that the vent is once more inverted, we unwrap the cloth and let the bird stand up on the fist. He is then returned to his pen, unhooded and a few moments are spent talking to him and giving him some quail. Males will normally immediately revert to displaying in the nest and it is important to overcome any negative effects of handling.

If necessary, the same procedure can be followed with a male which is paired up with a female. In this case it is important to catch him before he has fed in the morning. The rest of the procedure is the same. Many males which do not copulate still have good semen and can thus become fathers, if not proud ones.

In pairs which lay infertile eggs the breeder will usually inseminate immediately after the first egg, and perhaps again after the second, using semen from the male or from another male. Many pairs, once they have reared young, settle down and copulate normally in subsequent years. Others are hardy wallflowers and require intervention every year.

Another method which has met with varying success is electro-ejaculation. This conjures up visions of birds being given an electrical thump rather like treating a cardiac arrest victim. In reality the voltage is so low that you cannot feel it, in fact we sent our machine back after the first season, thinking it was not working. Most of the work has been done with psittacines and we are still experimenting with raptors. Two electrodes are used, each lubricated with KY jelly. One is shaped like a .22 bullet and is placed in the coprodeum. The other is placed in good electrical contact with the skin in the lower kidney region. The object is to provide a small electrical stimulation from the testes to the papilli of the ducti deferentia. The ducts should then briefly contract, ejaculating the semen.

In small raptors, such as merlins, the cloacal electrode is 15 millimeters long by 3.2 millimeters diameter. The voltage is about 3–5-volts AC, current 3–10 mA. This will not damage the rectal mucosa. In gyrs and peregrines the cloacal electrode is about 20 X 5 millimeters. The voltage is about 15-20-volts AC, current 10-20 mA.

The object of electro-ejaculation is not just to obtain semen; this can be achieved more quickly and easily by stripping, but to obtain semen with the quality and viability of voluntarily ejaculated semen. We'll look at these aspects next.

## 2.14  Handling and assessing semen quality

With semen, it is often a question of using what little one has, and being grateful for it. Also, once familiar with a certain semen donor, a quick glance under the microscope is usually sufficient to assess the semen before using it. However, anyone undertaking an insemination program should have a clear understanding of the different factors, not only because a poor sample stands little chance of fertilizing the egg, but because a contaminated sample could infect the female and cause fatal peritonitis or sterility. It has even been known for people to inseminate with mutes, thinking it was semen.

Semen consists of live unprotected cells in suspension. They must not be subjected to temperature shock, chemical insult, or changes in pH or osmolarity, otherwise they quickly die.

So the first step in handling semen is to warm all utensils which will be in contact with it. This is best achieved by placing glass plates, microscope slides, cover slips, and extender in an incubator for fifteen minutes before use. Immediately before taking the semen we then place a small drop of

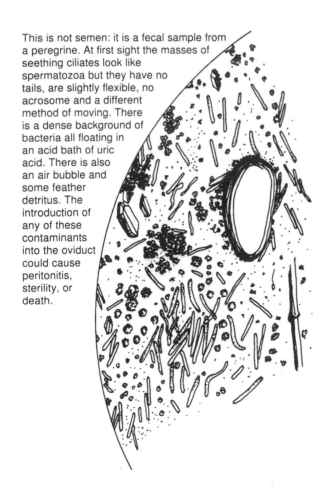

This is not semen: it is a fecal sample from a peregrine. At first sight the masses of seething ciliates look like spermatozoa but they have no tails, are slightly flexible, no acrosome and a different method of moving. There is a dense background of bacteria all floating in an acid bath of uric acid. There is also an air bubble and some feather detritus. The introduction of any of these contaminants into the oviduct could cause peritonitis, sterility, or death.

 Ciliate protozoans from the feces. They can propel themselves directly forward and directly backward. They can also wriggle slightly, like an eel.

 Small uric acid crystals from the kidneys and detritus from fecal contamination.

 Larger uric acid crystals.

 Bacterial contamination constantly jostling in one place through Brownian movement may also contain small flagellates.

 Budding yeasts. Relatively harmless in small numbers.

 Spermatozoon. Note circular acrosome at tip, tubular or slightly barrel-shaped body which is not flexible, circular mitochondrion at base of long whip-like flagellum or tail.

 Out of focus spermatozoa should be present. These indicate that the preparation is sufficiently deep for sperm to swim freely and hence indicate motility. A compressed preparation will make the sperm look dead.

Figure 2.14.1 A fecal sample from a peregrine.

Figure 2.14.2 Key to objects seen in samples.

extender into each small well of a hollowed glass plate using a 250 microliter ultipipette with disposable tips. As the semen is collected it is pipetted and rinsed into one of the drops of extender. When a concentration of 1:1 has been reached we start a new well, or, if it appears that a particular sample may be contaminated or of a different quality to the rest, we place this in a separate well. The extender we use is Beltsville chicken extender; it may be possible to design a better one for falcon semen but we have found this to produce good results. Thus the semen goes straight into warm extender and is kept isolated from contaminants.

The normal procedure at this stage is to examine a small amount of semen under 400X magnification, quickly assess it and then load up the remainder and use it on a female. But in order to make a quick assessment you still need a broader understanding of what to look for. Additionally, there are times when it is desirable to assess more fully one or more semen samples in order to assess

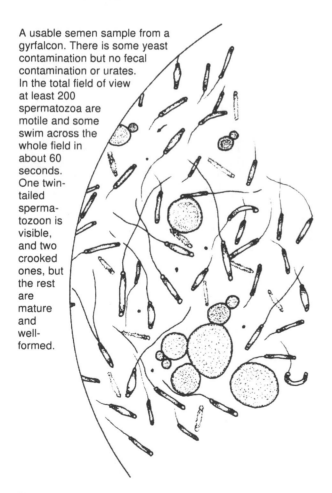

A usable semen sample from a gyrfalcon. There is some yeast contamination but no fecal contamination or urates. In the total field of view at least 200 spermatozoa are motile and some swim across the whole field in about 60 seconds. One twin-tailed spermatozoon is visible, and two crooked ones, but the rest are mature and well-formed.

Figure 2.14.3 A semen sample from a gyrfalcon.

the production of a particular male and its likely effect on the various females. So let's look at semen more closely, step by step.

The first factor is quantity. As little as 10 microliters can be used successfully but a normal useable sample will be 50 microliters, which extends to 100 microliters. This is about one drop from a dripping tap. There is not much point in using more than this because the excess is liable to bubble out of the everted oviduct and be wasted. It is often better to use the surplus for another insemination.

The next factor is contamination. Normal semen appears slightly milky, often with a slightly yellowish tinge. Sometimes it is almost clear, sometimes straw-colored. To the naked eye, it can often be confused with watery mutes and hence it is essential to examine all samples under the microscope before use. Sometimes a small swirl of solid white urates contaminates the sample. If the semen is valuable it may still be possible to decant off the semen from the more solid contaminant and obtain a useable sample. Contamination is dangerous for three reasons: Urates are strongly acidic; they appear as sharp sugar-like crystals of uric acid. Sperm which are swimming strongly now, are in fact swimming in a lethal acid bath and will be dead in a few minutes. Certainly they won't survive long enough in the oviduct to do their work. Secondly, irrigating the oviduct with acid is at best introducing an unwanted irritant, at worst it could provoke a bad reaction resulting, for example, in a soft-shelled egg. Thirdly, examination of semen contaminated with mutes will also reveal myriads of hostile organisms, ranging from bacteriaincessantly jogging about with Brownian motion, to flagellates almost as large as the sperm themselves (figure 2.14.1 and 2.14.2). Putting these into the oviduct can infect the oviduct, or they can get right up into the body cavity causing peritonitis, or they can sit in the oviduct alongside the waiting sperm cells and infect the ovum at fertilization causing early death of the embryo. Thus contaminated semen can cause sexually transmitted infections possibly killing the egg, or the female, or rendering her temporarily or permanently sterile. The message is: if in doubt, do not use it.

Semen can show other contaminants which are less deadly. Many samples contain yeasts which appear as spherical bodies. These are usually benign and do not cause a problem. Red blood cells

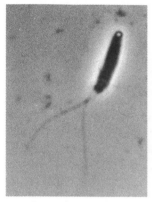

A

A) White gyr semen—a spermatozoon with two tails.
B) White gyr semen at the edge of an air bubble.

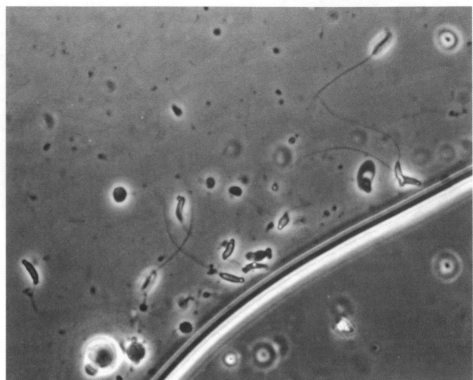

B

C) White gyr semen in a hypotonic diluent which causes the spermatozoa to inflate.
D) White gyr semen showing contamination.

D

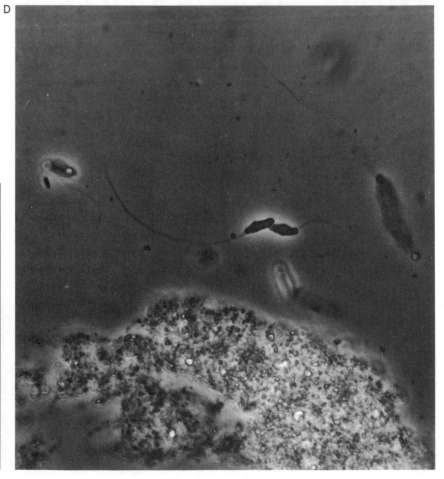

C

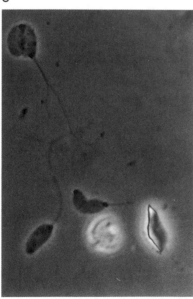

also are not a problem but should not be there. They indicate some tissue damage to the male which may point to a poor stripping technique. You should never see them in the semen. If they occur, the male should be rested for some days to allow the injury to heal.

Having obtained a useable quantity of clean semen, the next step is to look at sperm count. This of course depends on how much you have diluted it with extender. As a rough guide, a sample which is ready to use should have about 100 sperm cells visible in a 400X magnification field (2.14.3). There might be several times this amount, but less than about fifty may be too diluted. If you wish accurately to assess the actual sperm count of a particular male then the semen must be undiluted and a volumetric analysis made with a hemocytometer.

Perhaps more important than actual sperm count is the assessment of progressive motility. At least ten sperm should be moving in a 400X field and preferably this should be vigorous movement with individuals moving rapidly right across the field of view within about 60 seconds. This is the best measure of fertilizing capacity. A good sample will have hundreds of sperm moving in all directions. Motility is very temperature dependent. A sample stored in the fridge will appear inactive but as it warms up to body temperature the sperm should become fully active. Also a low volume of liquid on the slide may cramp the sperm under the cover slip and prevent them moving; it is important to have enough volume to assess motility.

If the male has not been stripped for three or four days, semen will have been waiting in the ductus deferens and some of the sperm cells will be aged or even dead. This is why it is better to strip every second day so that the semen is fresh. If you have a sample which looks relatively inactive it is sometimes possible to differentiate between live and dead sperm cells using nigrosin stain. Dead sperm are stained pink whereas live ones remain transparent. To do this, place five small drops of stain on a slide and warm to body temperature. Add one drop of semen to the stain and mix well with a fine needle. Leave for one minute for the stain to penetrate. Taking another slide, smear the sample out across the slide in the same way as a blood smear. Dry this out quickly over a heat source and examine carefully under the microscope, preferably under oil immersion. Semen from different species take up stain variably

and there seem to be no completely reliable stains at present for determining sperm survival. Obviously, if it turns out that most of the sperm are dead, then do not use the sample and review your procedure with the male.

Another aspect of the sperm to consider is whether they appear normal or are deformed. There are always some abnormal sperm cells, possibly because the male is a hybrid or is not in full production or is in poor health. Surprisingly, it is often the misshapen sperm which are most motile. Some have Y-shaped bodies, some are long and thin, and some have two tails (see page 86). Provided there are still plenty of motile normal sperm, the semen is useable because fertilizing ability is dependent only on the acrosome and the head itself. So do not worry; you will not end up with a falcon with two tails!

In the course of all this handling you may have altered the osmolarity of your sample. If the precious drop of semen has dried up a little, then the concentration of the fluid medium will have increased. The osmolarity around the membrane of the sperm cell will tend to pull water out of the cell and desiccate it. Conversely, if the extender is too dilute for the sperm, the cells start to swell up like lemons. None of this is good for them.

Semen may look the same but behave differently. The best semen results from frequent voluntary copulation either in a natural pair or with a voluntary imprint donor. Such semen can fertilize a falcon egg 12 days after insemination. There are probably several reasons for this. The semen will be fresh and of the right maturity; the sperm are ready but have not been stored in the male for too long. Second, the seminal fluid is of the optimal proportions of life-supporting electrolytes. Third, it will have been ejaculated cleanly without contamination. Such semen can frequently be stored for 60–72 hours in the fridge and still have a good chance of fertilizing an egg. Stripped semen is much more variable. It may be stale, it may be immature, it may have the wrong proportions of seminal fluid, and it may be contaminated. These all affect its storage potential outside the female and within the oviduct, as well as its fertilizing capacity. Stripped semen thus can vary from as good as voluntary semen to downright dangerous. The semen quality is heavily dependent on the way the breeder manages the males and it is essential to take great care in this, otherwise the whole project will be unproductive.

## 2.15  Storing and transporting semen

A raptor sperm cell has a life of up to two weeks between maturation and death. It is still immature when shed from the epididymis and then matures in the upper portion of the ductus deferens. From there, it may be stored in the ductus deferens of the male, it may be stored outside the bird in a container, or it may be stored in the female. Judging from experience of various permutations, rather than from any rigorous experimentation, it appears semen does not live long in the male. If a male is stripped right out, after one day he may have a moderate volume of lively semen with a low sperm count. If untouched for two days he should have a good volume of lively semen with a good sperm count. If untouched for three days the result is much the same, but after this the volume and sperm count stay up but the ratio of live sperm goes down. Five days after stripping he may give a sample which has plenty of volume and a high sperm count, but very little motility. One assumes therefore that sperm survives only for a few days when stored in the distal portion of the ductus. But to complicate matters, some males which have not been stripped and have not copulated seem to empty out the ductus and hence maintain stores of lively semen all the time. Natural pairs, of course, copulate several times a day so there is a rapid turnover of semen and the sample will be fresh and active. A carefully managed insemination program aims to obtain semen from the male while it is still young. Depending on the individual male this usually means stripping every second day, ie. not more often because the volume could be reduced, and not less often because the semen could be aged; it might appear good initially but would have just a short life left ahead of it.

Once out of the male, if not used immediately, it can be stored diluted 50:50 with extender, in a fridge at 4 degrees centigrade, rewarming again gently before use. This procedure has been used by many breeders for a long time, the aim being to reduce the metabolic rate of the semen without subjecting it to temperature shock. In the chilled state, semen can be transported to distant females by storing it in small centrifuge tubes in a container in a mix of ice and salt in a thermos flask. Each sample should be labelled with the time and date it was taken and the band number of the male. Voluntary semen stored like this for up to 72 hours

can successfully fertilize eggs. Stripped semen on the other hand, depending on its history, tends not to store well out of the body and is best used fresh.

Experiments with freezing bird semen have had some success. The equipment and expertise necessary for cryogenics, together with the low resultant fertility, prevent it being a viable proposition at this time, except for endangered species. However recent studies using 8 percent dimethyl sulfoxide as a cryoprotectant look promising because it does not have to be removed from the semen before inseminating. The frozen semen can be stored in liquid nitrogen for several years and fertility rates of 40–57 percent have been achieved with American Kestrels.

Once in the female, the sperm is stored in grooves or crypts in the wall of the lower oviduct and in the infundibulum. A single good shot of fresh voluntary semen can remain viable there for up to twelve days and can also fertilize two or three eggs in a row. The environment in the oviduct must therefore be more congenial to it than in the male. When using mixed semen from males of different species, the species which is most closely related to the female tends to take precedence in fertilizing the egg. Also, if there is semen still present and viable in the oviduct from a previous insemination and the female is then inseminated with fresh semen, the new semen tends to take precedence over the old. The best plan is thus to take the semen from the male early in its life and get it into the female where it will live longer and has the best chance to do some good.

## 2.16  When to inseminate

Having obtained the semen, the next hurdle to cross is when and how to get it into the female. The solutions to these questions are dictated by the characteristics of the female reproductive system (1.6). Normally a single egg is released from the left ovary as an exposed yolk. After ovulation it floats free and then enters the funnel-like infundibulum at the start of the oviduct. Once it proceeds down the oviduct to the magnum, the albumen and shell membranes are added and it is then impossible for a spermatozoon to fertilize it. Thus, to be successful, the spermatozoa need to be in position at the top of the oviduct ready to make contact with the yolk in its brief transitory period between ovulation and further development.

Once the egg is beginning to plump up, and

particularly once the shell is on, it is not safe to evert the female. She can only be inseminated safely by this method within twelve hours of laying a previous egg. An insemination carried out within about two hours, occasionally up to four hours, of an egg being laid has a good chance of catching the next egg before the membranes are added. On the other hand, if the female is everted at this time, the newly ovulated egg may be expelled out of the infundibulum away into the abdominal cavity. There it will usually be harmlessly reabsorbed. As another egg will not be ripe for ovulation for at least another 48 hours or so, the timing of the sequence will show that an egg is "missing." Thus one is gambling on the benefits of catching the next egg against the possibility of losing the egg altogether. This is a risk worth taking immediately after the first egg is laid, but not necessarily after subsequent eggs. It is also worth taking if using stripped semen with only a short life span.

On the other hand, if good voluntary semen is available, it is easier and safer to go for the window of about 3–10 hours after the egg is laid. This will miss the egg already in the system but will be held over in the oviduct and to cover the next egg to be released. We call this a "leapfrog" insemination. Either type of insemination may cover two or even three eggs, or they may not. With good semen and steady females I prefer to inseminate after every egg. On the other hand, if the female is a little put off by the handling, it is often better to inseminate after every second egg and hope for the best.

If we have a natural pair which has started to lay but no copulation has been seen, I prefer to obtain semen from another male and evert and inseminate the female after the first egg. Then I leave them alone, if possible secretly pulling the first egg early on. If she has had a good shot of semen she could lay 2–3 more eggs of which maybe two might be fertile. She can then incubate these, or dummies, and then be encouraged to rear young. This may well bring the male into full working order next year.

With a natural pair which never copulate but lay and rear well, then I usually inseminate every egg or every other egg, much as for imprints.

## 2.17  How to inseminate

If the female will stand voluntarily for copulation, she can be inseminated several times a day by placing the semen with an inseminator onto her partially everted cloaca (figure 2.17.1). This mimics natural copulation. Because the semen is not introduced directly into the oviduct, a lot is wasted and it is better to make many small inseminations to achieve high fertility. Therefore, one must have plenty of semen "on tap," which in practice means a voluntary donor. The advantage of this method is that it is not physically or mentally stressful for the female. It can thus be undertaken at any point in the ovulatory cycle, even before any eggs have been laid and even when a shelled egg is almost ready for laying (figure 2.17.2). It is thus the only safe artificial way to inseminate the first egg of a series.

The more effective, but more stressful method, is to evert the lower portion of the uterus and place the semen directly into it using an inseminator. The inseminator we use is a commercial turkey or chicken inseminator which uses disposable plastic straws. It is quick, efficient, and ideal. There is virtually no risk of injury or infection to the female and there is good control of small semen samples.

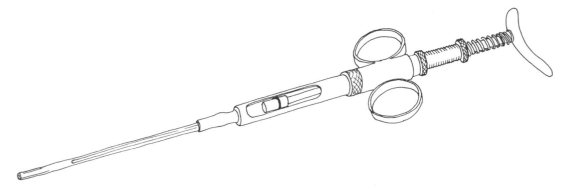

Figure 2.17.1 Artificial inseminator with disposable semen straw.

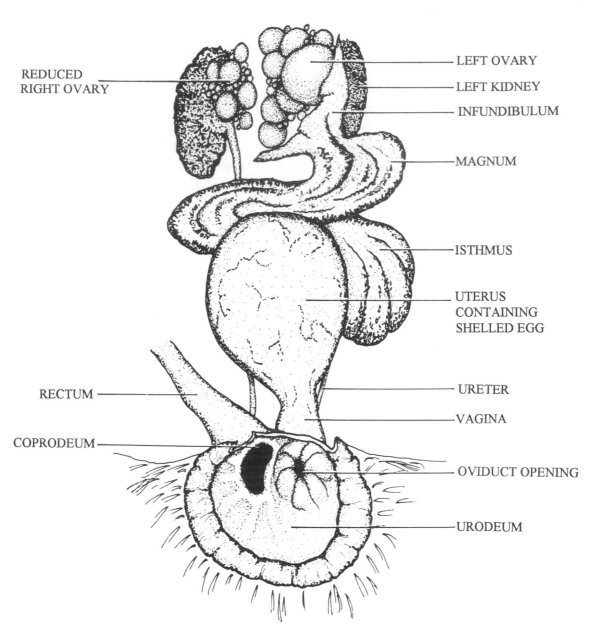

REDUCED
RIGHT OVARY

LEFT OVARY

LEFT KIDNEY

INFUNDIBULUM

MAGNUM

ISTHMUS

UTERUS
CONTAINING
SHELLED EGG

RECTUM

COPRODEUM

URETER

VAGINA

OVIDUCT OPENING

URODEUM

Figure 2.17.2 The reproductive tract of a female saker during laying.

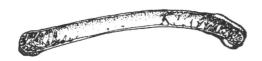

Figure 2.17.3

Figure 2.17.4

To inseminate the bird, I go into the pen and catch her; with an imprint this usually just entails picking her up like a broody bantam. Naturally paired females may need to be caught with a net. More often they refuse to vacate the nest and stand over

Figure 2.17.3 Section through right femur of a juvenile female northern goshawk in September, showing normal trabeculae.

Figure 2.17.4 Section through right femur of an adult female northern goshawk in March, showing the store of medullary bone prior to egg laying.

their precious new-laid egg glowering at me. One then has the task of collecting either the bird or the egg without damaging the egg. Usually I extend my gloved fist and the female will grab it. I then gently flip her out of the nest onto the floor, remove the egg and then net her. Alternatively, if she backs off a little, I extend my gloved fist toward the female but to one side of the nest, then quietly move my whole arm sideways over the egg. Then I slip my right hand along under my left arm to remove the egg.

Remember the hormones of the female at this stage are on a roller-coaster ride. She has just achieved a massive mobilization of skeletal calcium to produce the eggshell in a few hours (figures 2.17.3 and 4). Now everything is suddenly in reverse and she is trying rapidly to restore her calcium levels using dietary calcium. She is in a very fragile state and should be handled with extreme care, but with speed and assurance. It is not a time for dithering. Everting a fat, sassy female gyr at 2 A.M. in your pajamas with a torch held under your chin is a wonderful test of one's nerve and not conducive to regaining sleep.

The female is cast in the same way as done for the male. Again, with my long finger of my right hand I ease back the skin from the abdominal side of the vent. Then with the end knuckles of my right hand I gently exert some very controlled abdominal pressure, supported by my left hand. Usually this causes the coprodeum to evacuate its mutes which flow over my left hand. Then, if the female just pushes a little herself, the oviduct everts on her left side of the urodeum, clear of the area of mutes. If any urates get onto the exposed oviduct they are removed with a dab of cottonwool. The oviduct needs to be everted for no more than two or three seconds, and only far enough out to recognize the opening and insert the straw. The inseminator straw is then winkled gently only one centimeter into the oviduct, assuming a bird the size of a peregrine. The moment the straw is in position, I relax all abdominal pressure so that the straw is now 4–5 centimeters inside the normal relaxed oviduct. The plunger is gently pressed, withdrawing the straw slowly at the same time. Then the straw is removed completely. I usually hold the female calmly for a few moments while the assistant removes any equipment, such as nets, ladders, egg boxes, etc. from the pen. Then, holding her by the legs, tail-base, and wing tips, I quickly unwrap the cloth and strike the hood braces. Then I place

her back on the nest, remove the hood, and leave. If she is an imprint, I give her some quail and make a fuss of her. Imprints normally carry straight on with a full nest ledge display, quite unperturbed.

The main sperm storage site is near the junction of the oviduct and the cloaca. In most birds there is a secondary one in the infundibulum. At ovulation sperm travel rapidly up the oviduct for fertilization. This is the only time when live sperm are found free-swimming in the lumen of the oviduct. If the egg is swamped with live sperm at ovulation by an enthusiastic deep insemination, then more than one sperm may fertilize it. The egg may develop for a few days and then die early as a result of polyspermy. This can often be detected by examining tissue under the microscope. Divided cells present in a failed egg normally indicate fertility.

## 2.18  Variations in fertility

The fertility rate using artificial insemination is not usually as good as through natural copulation, although the results depend on many different factors. Also, if the outcross is a wide one, then there is a higher embryo mortality. Usually it is easier to fertilize the early eggs than the tail-enders.

We keep records of all insemination details on a female insemination chart (figure 2.18.1). We also record the details of semen production for each stud male. These records are essential in order to learn and progress, and in decision-making in subsequent years. Each bird is different and there is no blanket solution. Rather, it is a question of working out the best plan for each bird based on its individual characteristics.

It is not always easy to tell whether or not an egg is fertile. Just because an egg has gone rotten or addled does not mean it had been fertile; it just means bacteria have got in. When an egg has been diagnosed as not developing normally and all hope has been abandoned, then it is best to open it and examine the blastodisc carefully for cell development. If you leave the egg until after the breeding season, bacteria will get in and you will never know whether it was fertile, or at what stage it died, let alone have any idea of cause of death. If, on the other hand, you know that an egg is definitely infertile because the female had not been inseminated, it is often useful to incubate it for two or three weeks. This will tell you its weight loss characteristics which is useful information when making plans next year (see 2.26).

## FEMALE INSEMINATION CHART

| Female: *1982 PEREGRINE . TRACER'S MOTHER . UK 82261* | | | | | | | *PEN 29* |
|---|---|---|---|---|---|---|---|

| Egg No. | Date & time laid | Laying interval | Date & time inseminated | Lay - insem interval | Fertility | Semen quality | Stud male |
|---|---|---|---|---|---|---|---|
| 1 | 26/3  0330 | | 26/3  0500 | 1½ hrs | | Large Good | White gyr Icicle UK 79979 |
| 2 | 28/3  1330 | 60 hrs | 28/3  1415 | ¾ hr | Fert | Large Good | Grey gyr Reiver UK 79981 |
| 3 | 30/3  2300 | 59½ hrs | 31/3  0045 | 1¾ hr | Fert | Large Good | "          " |
| 4 | 4/4  1530 | 124½ hrs | 4/4  1800 | 2½ hr | Fert | Large Good | Icicle UK 79979 |
| 5 | 7/4  0030 | 57 hrs | 7/4  0130 | 1 hr | Fert | Large Moderate | Reiver UK 79981 |
| 6 | 9/4  1130 | 59 hrs | 9/4  1220 | 50 mins | Fert | Large Moderate | "          " |
| 7 | 11/4  1530 | 52 hrs | 11/4  1610 | 40 mins | Clear | Large Good | "          " |
| 8 | 13/4  2130 | 54 hrs | 13/4  2245 | 1¼ hrs | Clear | Large Good | "          " |

*1994* (to the left of row 1)

Fox 1995

Figure 2.18.1 The female insemination chart.

## 2.19  Laying

The onset of breeding is brought about by a number of factors such as temperature, rainfall, diet, and the presence of a nest site and a suitable mate. But the key factor is the photoperiod or day length. This is what tells the birds' biological clocks what time of year it is. Of course not all birds breed in the spring. Some, such as the Eleonora's falcon, delay breeding to coincide with the autumn migration of passerines through the Mediterranean. Other species, in hot climates, time their breeding to coincide with the rainy season and to avoid the dry season.

Birds are sensitive to periods of daylight, even of low intensity. One 40-watt bulb in a large room is sufficient to register with the bird as "daylight" and one breeder had merlins laying in January owing to extra day length provided by a nearby streetlight! Red light is the most important wavelength and is registered by the bird both through the eyes and through the top of the head where it stimulates the hypothalamus.

Although the intensity of the light above a

minimum level is not important, the duration of the light and the way it is administered is critical. Do not think that by leaving a light on all night that the hawks will come into breeding condition. British raptors normally need 14–16 hours light per day to come into breeding condition and this is best worked up to in stages over a period of time. It is thus possible to bring them into condition earlier or even give them an extra breeding season. With New Zealand falcons I have put them through an extra winter so that they scraped a year earlier than normal. However, playing around with photoperiods needs a thorough understanding of the subject, otherwise it can have unforeseen effects. Once birds have come into breeding condition on an increasing day length, they go through a long refractory period in which day length does not affect them. It can happen, for example, that one gives a pair extra lighting early in the season, attempting to bring them on, but they fail due to other factors, such as temperature, holding them back. Then, as real spring progresses, the birds are on a static day length and do not have the increasing day length to bring them on. They may anyway have gone into a refractory period and even perhaps started to molt. On the other hand, if one is attempting to breed birds from a different latitude, emulating the annual changes in day length in its country of origin may well swing the balance. Generally speaking, photoperiods are best left natural unless the breeder has a specific reason for changing them.

The presence of a suitable mate is also important for breeding especially in nonmigratory species. For those working with imprinted raptors for artificial insemination and who therefore have to do the "courting" themselves, the work of Barfield on ringdoves may be of interest. He found that solitary females exposed to a male for 15 minutes each day showed oviducts of 1.1 grams, for one hour a day 2.1 grams, and on continual exposure 3.6 grams, after seven days. One cannot therefore shirk one's duties as a mate!

Most raptors are semideterminate layers apart from those species which only lay one egg. Most falcons, for example, lay about four eggs. If the first egg is removed as soon as it is laid, that is to say pulled sequentially, the falcon may lay 6–10 eggs, occasionally up to twenty. This is very taxing for her health and often the last eggs are thin-shelled. On the other hand, if a dummy egg is added to the first so that she feels two in the nest,

she may start to shut down and lay only two more eggs, making her total three. Some females are determinate layers, laying their standard quota of three or four eggs regardless of what manipulations are attempted. We have a 15-year-old imprint buzzard called "Beast-that-lurks." Every year BTL lays two infertile eggs, no more, no less, before going on to foster-rear up to 12 chicks on a "conveyor belt" system. We also have an imprint buzzard which, without pulling, lays a setting of 11 eggs. She's called "Omelette."

Females of small species usually first lay in their second season. Some peregrines and gyrs also can lay at two but many do not lay until they are four or five. Some of course don't lay at all. Domestic raptors, thoroughly at home in breeding pens, always lay better than wild-caught birds. The first clutch is often small; once birds have reared young they lay and recycle better.

Should a first clutch fail or be removed, many females will recycle and lay a second clutch, occasionally even a third. During the first half of incubation the balance of hormones in the body of the female is changing in order to prepare her for the next stages in the breeding cycle and for the molt. Only if the balance has not swung too far will she be able to ovulate a second clutch of eggs and this will take two to three weeks after the eggs are removed before she is ready to lay again.

Females have a limited number of ova predetermined before they are themselves hatched. Some people think that therefore if you pull too many eggs early in a falcon's life she will "run dry." In reality falcons may run dry in old age but not for this reason. Many can lay 12 or even 20 eggs a year for ten or more years. There are two other aspects to consider: "saving" a female for the future by only single clutching her will not necessarily result in more of her genes being passed on. She might die prematurely. Secondly, the more young she produces early in life, the quicker they will mature and themselves breed.

The oviduct is the original production line. The ripe ovum, on its release from the ovary, is briefly unrestrained at the mouth of the infundibulum where it is fertilized by semen which has either newly traveled up the oviduct or which has been stored in grooves in the oviduct wall awaiting ovulation.

Once fertilized, the egg travels quite quickly through the infundibulum to the magnum where the albumen or egg-white is added. In chickens this takes 3–4 hours. The next region, the isthmus, takes $1\frac{1}{4}$ hours to add the two shell membranes. The final portion of the oviduct, the uterus or shell gland, takes about 6–7 hours to "plump" up the egg with fluid and the female drinks frequently at this time. A further 13–14 hours are required to add the shell and pigmentation. In raptors, most of which are on a 50 hour egg-laying cycle compared to the chicken's 24 hour cycle, these stages take considerably longer and it is not known if this extra time is spent proportionately at each stage or whether the egg is delayed for longer at some point in the cycle; at least 24 hours is spent in the shell gland.

In the common buzzard, the shell weighs about 5 grams and is about 98 percent calcium carbonate, the remainder being structural protein. About 70 percent of this calcium is obtained directly from the diet and 30 percent is endosteal calcium which has been stored in the female's bones prior to egg laying. About 12 percent of the bone substance in the female's body may be mobilized in this way, and, if too many eggs are pulled from her, apart from the eggs being thin-shelled, she may show symptoms of bone weakness. No calcium is stored in the shell gland itself; it is all transported there and removed directly from the bloodstream.

Later, a considerable amount of the eggshell calcium will be reabsorbed by the developing embryo for bone formation. This makes the shell weaker at hatching time. Weight measurements of shells for shell-thinning analysis in pesticide studies should take embryonic development into account.

A female common buzzard weighing 900 grams (32 oz) lays an egg weighing about 70 grams ($2\frac{1}{2}$ oz). If she lays four eggs in seven days this represents a considerable investment of nutrients. Particularly if eggs are being pulled from captive raptors it is essential that the layers are fed on an adequate balanced diet, otherwise the hatchability of the egg suffers and the health of the female may be endangered, or she will go off the lay. Some Harris hawks lay readily on a quail diet but stop if changed to day-old chicks. Unfortunately, we know very little about the reproductive or nutritional physiology of birds of prey, which are themselves a variable group. One has to rely on and extrapolate from studies of other species, especially poultry, and these may not be truly representational.

Two or three days before laying, the female goes into "egg lethargy." She may appear slightly ill, feathers loosely ruffled, weight on both feet and with large, slow mutes. Her appetite becomes poor and she may tend to tear at the food and then flick it about and discard it. Some, on the other hand, show little sign. Often if the weather turns cold in the spring, or if the female is unfit, she may retain the egg in the oviduct and have difficulty laying it. This can become serious very quickly. The problem can be diagnosed by feeling the shelled egg in the abdomen, but there is a grave risk in catching and handling her that you may break the egg inside her. This could rapidly lead to peritonitis and death. Neglect her and the risk is the same. To induce egg laying, we give an intramuscular injection of oxytocin together with 5 milliliters of warm 10 percent calcium borogluconate subcutaneously. She may lay down before or after laying but stands during the actual laying, which takes only a few seconds.

## 2.20  Incubation

Once the egg has been laid, it can remain unincubated for several days and yet still hatch. About 86 percent of fertile eggs should hatch under optimum conditions and storage for three or four days has little noticeable effect. After about a week, hatchability falls rapidly and after two weeks few will survive. Before incubation proper starts, the parents turn the eggs periodically and brood them lightly at night to prevent them freezing. In the day they may shelter them from the hot sun. At temperatures above 21 degrees centigrade (70°F) the egg starts to develop. Unlike chickens and ducks, which lay a lot of eggs, birds of prey lay small clutches and few eggs wait more than four or five days before they are incubated. Also once incubation starts, the parents sit on the eggs very steadily indeed and do not leave them exposed for long periods. Mean periods off the eggs for raptors in cold or temperate climates are usually less than two minutes; frequently the male, having brought food in for the female, will replace her on the eggs immediately after she comes off them. Even in tropical climates the eggs are seldom exposed for more than ten minutes. In general therefore, raptor eggs are not preadapted to tolerate erratic incubation to the same extent that game bird or waterfowl eggs can. Although eggs might survive several hours of exposure once, if they have been properly incubated otherwise (indeed I have hatched one with frost on it), frequent $\frac{1}{2}$–1 hour exposures weaken the embryos and reduce eventual hatchability.

Particularly if cooled rapidly to below 21 degrees centigrade, both eggs and chicks can go into suspended animation. Chilled chicks can appear completely dead with no signs of breathing and yet, if warmed up again to about 36 degrees centigrade, may revive. Accidentally chilled chicks should always be warmed up before being discarded for dead. Once I had a friend telephone about a brooder failure he'd had the night before. I told him to retrieve the dead chicks from the bin and warm them up. A few of them came back to life and my reputation as a miracle worker was well-established!

With eggs, the problems arise when they are partially cooled to between 21–35 degrees centigrade. Development still continues but at a slower pace and so abnormal cell divisions occur. The eggs may die soon or may survive and die later in development. Embryos die quickly if their temperature rises above body temperature (41 degrees centigrade); they have no temperature regulating mechanism.

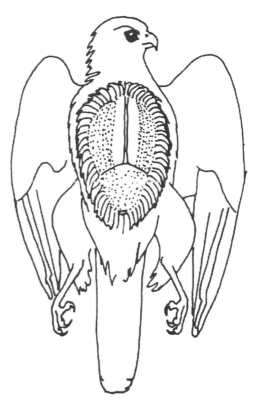

Figure 2.20.2 The brood patch of a wild female Mauritius kestrel while brooding 7–10-day-old chicks.

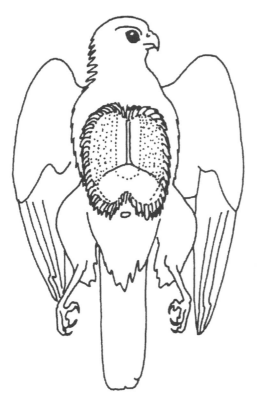

Figure 2.20.1 The brood patch of a wild female Mauritius kestrel after one week of incubation.

Once incubation begins, the eggs slowly warm up over several days by heating applied through an incubation or brood patch which has developed in the female in response to oestrogen and prolactin (figure 2.20.1 and 2). The feathers on the breast and belly drop out leaving a large area of naked skin fringed by quite long feathers of the ventral tract which act as a heat seal. The skin itself becomes swollen with jellylike fluid like a large blister and the blood supply increases. The effect is rather like laying a soft hot-water bottle on top of the eggs. Full development of the brood patch is reached about one third through the incubation period. The breast feathers start to regrow again at about the same stage as the chicks are growing their own body feathers.

## 2.21 The structure of the egg

The structure of the egg is shown in figure 2.21.1. The shell is made primarily of calcite on an organic matrix laid down in layers but with thousands of tiny pores. These pores allow oxygen to enter the egg and water and carbon dioxide to escape. The shell and some of the pores are cov-

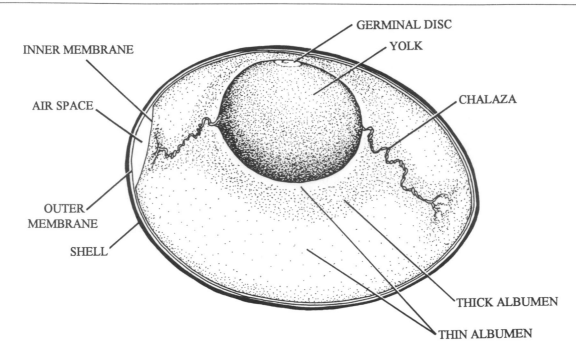

INNER MEMBRANE

AIR SPACE

OUTER
MEMBRANE

SHELL

GERMINAL DISC

YOLK

CHALAZA

THICK ALBUMEN

THIN ALBUMEN

Figure 2.21.1 The structure of the egg.

ered with a thin cuticle which is water-repellent and hinders the entry of bacteria. Any pigmentation is laid down on the outer layer of the shell.

Inside the shell are two fibrous membranes. One lines the shell and the other encloses the contents. The two membranes separate at the blunt end to form an aircell. Occasionally these membranes fail to adhere and the aircell then moves anywhere within the egg. This condition is fatal.

Within the membranes is the egg albumen composed of a protein and water. The albumen forms a thick envelope surrounding the yolk, floating freely in thin albumen. The yolk itself is suspended at each end by the chalazae, which are twisted strands of protein fibers.

The yolk is contained by porous membranes and consists of lipoproteins which nourish the growing embryo. Floating on the top is the germinal disc 3–4 millimeters in diameter. If fertile, this develops into the embryo which lies on the yolk just under the upper surface of the shell, in contact with the source of heat.

In medium-sized raptors, the shell comprises 8.8–11.9 percent of the fresh weight. In falcons, the yolk makes up about 23–25 percent of the fresh weight, although individual birds sometimes produce yolks of only 16 percent. Red kites, Harris hawks and common buzzards produce yolks in the range 15.5–21 percent of fresh weight. It seems

that the desert species, such as the Saker falcon and Harris hawk, have smaller yolks and more albumen than temperate species, and perhaps could tolerate greater weight loss during incubation. We need more data to reach firm conclusions on this.

## 2.22 The development of the embryo

As the egg progresses through the various stages of development its appearance as seen through a candler, changes as in figures 2.22.1–8.

A fresh falcon egg, viewed from above, appears relatively transparent (figure 2.22.1). There is a small air cell, but it is hard to see it. The yolk

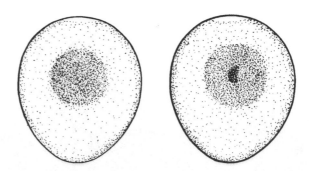

Figure 2.22.1 The undeveloped egg, from above.

Figure 2.22.2 The egg at five days, from above.

is visible as a vague dark mass which floats to the upper surface. Both fertile and infertile eggs appear the same but after a week an infertile egg will remain looking like this, apart from the air cell which enlarges slightly.

After five to seven days, in the fertile egg a small dark blob is visible on top of the yolk, which is still free-floating (figure 2.22.2). A day or two later it becomes noticeably elongated and kidney-shaped with the embryo lying on its left side. In eggs with a strongly mottled shell the embryo will not be easily seen this early; instead, the most noticeable change is that the outline of the yolk becomes harder and slightly larger than before.

By the eighth to tenth day the yolk itself is no longer visible but the embryo has become larger and darker (figure 2.22.3). An area of shading daily enlarges around the embryo gradually spreading around the whole egg. Blood vessels may be visible radiating from the embryo.

Viewed from the side, the half-shading first covers the upper half of the egg and is free-floating (figure 2.22.4). Seen against the half shading, the air cell is clearly visible. The shading itself is made up of the growing chorioallantoic membrane. This is the life support system for the growing embryo.

Figure 2.22.7 The egg at 31 days, from above.    Figure 2.22.8 The egg at pip.

Its fine capillary system is responsible for the uptake of oxygen through the shell and the discharge of carbon dioxide.

At about midterm, the shading has spread around the entire egg although some clear albumen may remain visible at the pointed end (figure 2.22.5). The air cell is easily seen and has enlarged considerably. The embryo appears as a large, irregular, poorly defined dark mass which swoops around spontaneously under the shell propelled by the amnion.

Soon after midterm the contents of the egg "black-out" and remain too dense to see anything throughout the rest of incubation (figure 2.22.6). Eggs which are overweight may still show some clear areas. The aircell is clear and continues to enlarge slowly.

One to two days before pipping, the aircell increases in size rapidly and draws down on the upper surface of the egg along the equilibrium line (figure 2.22.7). Seen here from the side, the asymmetry is very noticeable and careful candling may show a moving shadow when the embryo presses against the air cell membrane.

Soon after the initial pip, extensive shading can be seen in the aircell (Figure 2.22.8). The chick has successfully split part of the aircell membrane and now occupies some of the aircell. This gives it additional space so that it can rotate to cut out.

## 2.23 The temperature of the egg

Inevitably during incubation, the top of the egg warms up most while the underside remains close to ground temperature. The heating power of the parent is not very great; Drent found, for example, that if herring gull eggs were left uncovered for 60 minutes at 11 degrees centigrade air temperature it took a further 110 minutes of incubation to bring them back up to temperature. Effectively this total

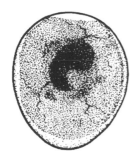

Figure 2.22.3 The egg at 8 days, from above.    Figure 2.22.4 The egg at 8 days from the side, showing half shading.

Figure 2.22.5 The egg at 20 days, from above.    Figure 2.22.6 The egg at 28 days, from above.

time of 170 minutes is time with reduced development and the eggs will take that much longer in total to hatch. After 100 minutes uncovered, the eggs cool almost to ambient air temperature. Raptors overcome this by having only short and infrequent change-over periods. In very cold temperatures the egg may be exposed for only a few seconds as the parents change over. Merlins will even occasionally incubate side by side, sharing the eggs between them.

During the first half of incubation, whatever the position of the egg, the embryo floats to the top and lies just under the shell where it is maintained at a temperature close to that of the brood patch. Initially the temperature of the egg is cooler than that of the surrounding air in the nest but after a few days, owing to contact with the brood patch and then later to the heat produced by the embryo itself, it rises above the inter-egg air temperature. Once the female is sitting steadily, the embryo

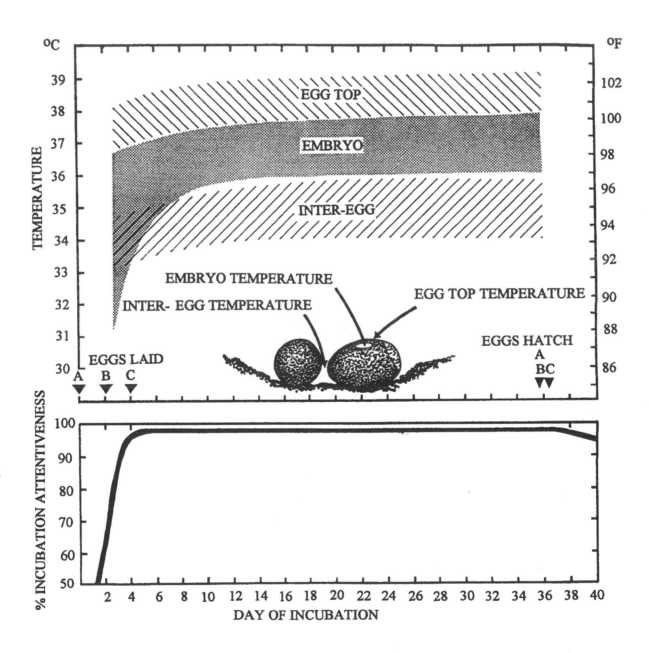

Figure 2.23.1 Variations in falcon egg temperatures in relation to parental attentiveness during incubation. Based on Drent (1970), Schwartz, Weaver, Scott and Cade (1977), Smith and Fox (1988), and our own data on merlins, Mauritius kestrels, New Zealand falcons, prairie falcons, sakers, gyrfalcons, and peregrines.

temperature remains within the range 34–39 degrees centigrade, the average value depending on species. The temperature of the bottom half of the egg tends to be about ten degrees lower, depending on ground temperature.

During the second half of incubation and especially during the last third, the embryo is growing and metabolizing rapidly and thus creating some heat itself. This heat is not sufficient for the embryo to maintain its own temperature, but it does contribute significantly to heat production in the nest. The still-air incubator, by simulating the temperature gradient experienced by the egg and by having a low heating capacity which warms the eggs gently, allows the growing embryo to develop its own microclimate. This mimics more closely the situation in the wild than does the forced-air incubator.

Using the very detailed data of Drent (1970) on gulls, together with studies of other species, and our own data (Smith and Fox 1988) on incubation attentiveness and characteristics, I have constructed temperature curves for the eggs of a typical medium-sized raptor such as a peregrine, goshawk or buzzard. Obviously these vary slightly from species to species and according to climate, nest type, and ambient temperature but figure 2.23.1 shows the general trends in temperature throughout a clutch of eggs during natural incubation.

After about the tenth day, the embryo, although still very small, is now fully formed and the remainder of the cell divisions mainly involve growth rather than differentiation. A small proportion of incorrect cell divisions are therefore less likely to prove fatal and eggs are easier to incubate artificially from this point on.

## 2.24 The turning of the egg

During the first half of incubation, the yolk, with the germinal disc on its upper surface, is free-floating within the albumen and only loosely anchored in place by the chalazae. The high (30 percent) fat content is distributed in the yolk so that it is lighter than the surrounding albumen and always maintains the embryo uppermost. The chalazae are two light cords of protein both twisted in the same direction so that the yolk is held in place like someone twisted up in a hammock. Further rotation in one direction would tighten the twist and in the other direction unwind the twist. If the egg is

rotated, the yolk gently settles back at the top, cushioned from jarring and abrasion by a layer of thick albumen.

If the egg is placed on a smooth flat surface it will be found to be evenly weighted, with no tendency for any one part of the shell to remain uppermost. The effect of the parent's beak movements at this stage is to turn the egg randomly, thus reducing premature adhesions of the extra-embryonic membranes; adhesions which could flaw subsequent development and positioning. Another effect is that the yolk, on turning, comes into contact with fresh albumen and the nutrient supply contained in it. A third effect, important in species with large clutches, is to bring eggs at the edge of the nest into the center. A difference of about 5–6 degrees centigrade exists in Mallard nests between central and peripheral eggs but this is less extreme in raptors, most of which are able, in the females at least, to keep all the eggs in contact with the brood patch at the same time.

In a joint project with Dr. Ken Smith in 1988 we investigated temperature and turning rates of eggs for bantams, a captive common buzzard and a wild common buzzard. We embedded 17 mercury tilt switches into a balanced dummy egg containing a transmitter which sent signals to a receiver and data logger, which was periodically downloaded to a computer. This egg reported the angle at which it was lying to the nearest ten degrees. The results for all parents were fairly similar. The birds moved the eggs every 15–16 minutes or so. Most of the turns were in the range 5–60 degrees with occasional turns in the range of 60–180 degrees. Usually the eggs had little, bit-by-bit turns, rather than complete rollovers, although gradually during the course of the day each egg would turn over completely.

During this first half of incubation the fine capillary network of the chorioallantoic membrane is growing. It gradually lines the entire interior of the shell. If an egg is unturned, it does not form properly. Tullett and Deeming found that if the membrane covered only 95 percent of the shell, hatchability fell to 46 percent. If it covered only 90 percent of the shell, hatchability dropped to 14 percent. Thus turning is essential until the chorioallantoic membrane is complete. Of course the embryo may not die immediately. Only later, when the embryo's metabolic demand is higher, is the defective chorioallantois unable to keep up.

By about 55 percent of the way through incubation the situation changes. The membrane surrounding the embryo and the shell membranes fuse and the embryo, no longer free-floating, becomes fixed inside the shell. The egg is now unevenly weighted and if placed on a smooth surface or floated in warm water will tend to roll back to a fixed alignment. Thus the turning movements of the parent at this stage do not rotate the egg but simply free it from the friction of the neighboring eggs for a moment so that it can roll back toward its equilibrium position. In other words the turning tends to maintain the eggs in relatively fixed orientations, not to rotate them randomly as in the first half of incubation. This is important for the attainment of the correct hatching position.

As incubation progresses further, this equilibrium position becomes more obvious and if the upper surface is marked it can be seen on candling to coincide with the furthest drawn down part of the aircell. The first slight pip of the shell normally takes place a little to the left of this line at the edge of the aircell and it is possible to predict and mark the exact spot where the pip will occur several days beforehand. A well-positioned pip is a good indicator that the chick itself is positioned correctly. As the pip progresses and the egg-tooth is raised higher, the first actual complete hole will tend to be further to the right, on the equilibrium line itself. When the chick starts to hatch properly the break up will continue right-handed around the blunt end of the egg.

The parent sits assiduously but lightly on the eggs at this time and is very attentive. This reduces the chances of the egg membranes drying up and yet guards against crushing the eggs. If the hatching egg is turned hole downwards, the chick will start cheeping in distress. This call stimulates the parent to poke the eggs around until the egg rolls back upright, otherwise the chick risks suffocation.

Thus between days seventeen and the pip, depending on species, the embryo is getting itself into the right position which it must adopt in order to hatch successfully. A number of malpositions can occur which may prevent the chick pipping through the shell, or rotating to cut its way out, or may cause it to pip at the pointed end. Many of these malpositions are lethal and are traceable to the ways in which the egg has been turned throughout incubation. A malpositioned chick may not be able to pip into air and thus may drown when it tries to use its lungs. Only very prompt detection in this case will save it.

## 2.25  The gas exchange of the egg

As incubation progresses, the embryo exchanges carbon dioxide for oxygen by diffusion through the pores of the shell into the fine capillaries of the chorioallantois which acts rather like a placenta. Gas exchange is proportional to embryonic development, slow at first but increasing rapidly during the second half of incubation. By the time the aircell draws down, the demand on the chorioallantois reaches its peak. The embryo is metabolizing rapidly and the lungs have not yet come into use. This is when any defect is fatal. The embryo just dies.

If the eggshell is highly porous it allows a good exchange of gases to the chorioallantois. It also allows a lot of water out and the egg may dry up too quickly. Water lost by evaporation during incubation is replaced by metabolic water during the development of the embryo. An early embryo is about 90–92 percent water, whereas an adult bird is about 60 percent water. About half the initial fat in the egg is metabolized during incubation. Any efforts to block the pores to reduce water loss through the shell also affect gas exchange with possibly lethal results. Therefore it is better to control the weight loss of a very thin-shelled egg, not by sealing the shell with wax, but by covering a proportion of it with removable cling film. This reduces water loss during the first part of incubation and helps to maintain the weight, then, later on, the cling film area can be reduced to allow for the increasing gas exchange.

The developing embryo absorbs about 6–7 percent of the calcium from the shell but this does not appreciably alter its porosity to gases. Permeability to gases does increase by about 25 percent suddenly around day seven due to the formation of the aircell and the drying of the inner membrane. Removal of the cuticle by sanding or bleaching also increases porosity.

If the shell is too impervious, not only will the embryo lose too little water, with all the problems that that entails, but also it is likely to suffocate. Any embryos which hatch are slow to thrive.

## 2.26  The weight loss of the egg

During incubation the egg loses weight at a steady rate through evaporation and through metabolizing fat. Depending on species, about 16 percent of fresh egg weight is lost between setting and pipping and 4 percent between pip and hatch. Once the shell has a hole in it at pip and the chick is breathing through its lungs, water loss is quite rapid and the membranes quickly dry up if humidity is not maintained. If the chick fails to lose sufficient weight it is too cramped to turn inside the shell and may drown in its own fluids at pip. Infertile eggs tend to lose weight at about the same rate as fertile eggs. Species adapted to arid conditions have less permeable shells than damp-climate species and do not lose weight as easily. Some of them compensate by having a higher proportion of albumen.

Eggs which have lost less than 10 percent by pipping are in grave danger of suffocation, drowning, or malpositioning. Eggs which lose more than 20 percent tend to be too weak and sticky. Occasionally we have hatched eggs at 8 percent and 22 percent but usually eggs fail at these limits.

There are several ways to control weight loss during artificial incubation. If an egg is losing too much weight, the first step is to raise the humidity conditions. One can also spray the egg all over every two hours with warm sterile water.

Some eggs react dramatically to this while others show no difference. The procedure effectively lowers incubation temperature and probably slows down the metabolism somewhat. It should not be used in the first half of incubation to any drastic extent.

If this is insufficient it is possible to seal part of the shell area to reduce porosity. This is a dangerous undertaking because alterations to shell porosity also affect gas exchange and it is easy to suffocate the embryo by rendering a proportion of its chorioallantois inoperative. The cling-film method is safest because it is adjustable. If the desiccation really is critical I sterilize the shell over the air cell with alcohol. Then I very carefully pierce the shell with a fine sterile needle taking care not to damage the egg contents. Then I inject about 1 milliliter of warm sterile water into the aircell and seal the hole, either with some nail varnish, or, if I plan to repeat the performance, with a small patch of tape. The weight of the egg is recorded before and after the procedure. After about three hours, the water in the aircell has been absorbed by the embryo. I have repeated the procedure several times without problems, but of course it must not be done too close to pipping otherwise the chick may drown.

The more common problem in a damp climate

is getting sufficient weight off the egg, particularly in desert species. Eggs dry out slowly even when infertile or when in store. So if you have eggs from a mother whose eggs always have a weight loss problem, first weigh the egg as soon as it is laid. Then place it on its side in some blue selfindicating silica gel at about 12 degrees centigrade. Store it like this, turning it two or three times a day and changing the gel if it starts to go pink. When it has lost sufficient weight or after four days, whichever comes first, then set it. Some eggs refuse to lose weight with this treatment but then lose weight more rapidly once incubation temperature is reached.

If the female is stressed in some way during egg formation, perhaps some cold weather brings on a touch of egg-binding, the egg may remain too long in the shell gland and receive too thick a shell. These rogue eggs can be difficult. Silica gel is not very effective in a forced air incubator unless all the vents are completely sealed. Sanding an egg, particularly during the first ten days, risks damaging the fragile embryo through vibration or jerkiness while rubbing. The real danger comes to the embryo during the second half of incubation when it risks being suffocated as its metabolic demand increases. Sanding in the second half is less risky. It is best to use a medium to coarse paper. Just sand over the aircell. Sand right down to the shell membrane which should flex over a 5–10 millimeter circle. When the weight has been corrected, a dab of nail varnish will stop further loss.

Spraying the egg over the aircell with sterile water also tends to pull weight off. For some reason it does tend to strengthen the embryos. But it must not be overdone or the eggs will gain weight.

We always maintain an egg chart for each egg, showing its weight loss. We also candle the eggs once or twice a week. This only takes one or two seconds. We do not make density calculations and we do not try to control weight by any drastic means unless the situation is serious. Weight loss is important but should not be an over-riding consideration. It is better to concentrate on giving the egg a good quality of incubation. Strong embryos overcome small weight loss variables.

## 2.27 The hatch

About 72 hours before hatching, the egg starts an ordered sequence of events which are critical (figure 2.27.1). The chick must progress from allantoic respiration to lung breathing, retract its yolk sac and hatch and it is necessary to understand what is going on, especially if intending to help an egg with a problem.

At the time when the air cell is beginning the "draw down" the complexis hatching muscle at the nape of the chick's neck becomes swollen with lymph and twitches spasmodically. The twitching movement extends throughout the whole body of the chick causing it to straighten briefly. These unbending movements press the chick tight against the eggshell and force the beak upwards. On the upper ridge of the beak is the small egg tooth which eventually penetrates the inner shell membrane into the air cell. Once the beak is into the air cell, the chick is able to start breathing air into its lungs although it is still dependent on allantoic gas exchange. With its lungs in operation it is able to cheep and this is a sure sign that breathing has started. The beak piercing the air cell membrane may also be visible on careful candling (figure 2.27.2).

With continuous rebreathing, the air in the air cell becomes high in carbon dioxide and this stimulates the hatching muscle to further activity. With more faint tapping and pressure from the chick, the shell wall gives way and a slight lifting of a fragment of shell becomes visible. This is called "starring." This allows a small amount of fresh air into the air space and the chick usually becomes quiet for some hours. Working sporadically, the chick then begins to break up an area around the pip and also splits the air cell membrane much further so that, on candling, it can be seen to occupy most of the air cell and is much looser inside the shell. Gradually the chick enlarges an opening and the beak and egg tooth come into view.

The chick may rest at this point for a further twenty-four hours. During this time the lungs and airsac system are becoming fully functional and gradually take over total responsibility for gas exchange. The blood circulation in the allantois slowly shuts down and the large allantoic artery and vein, which act as an umbilical cord, gradually change color from red to white or pale blue. These vessels cross the wing and head on the right side of the pip and can often be seen through the aperture. Gentle squeezing with blunt forceps will determine if blood is still flowing. If the supply has shut down, the squeezed portion does not refill.

Once the allantois has shut down, the chick

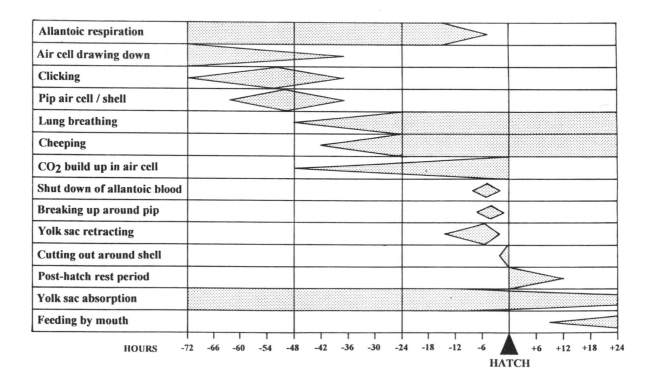

Figure 2.27.1 Events in the egg at hatching time.

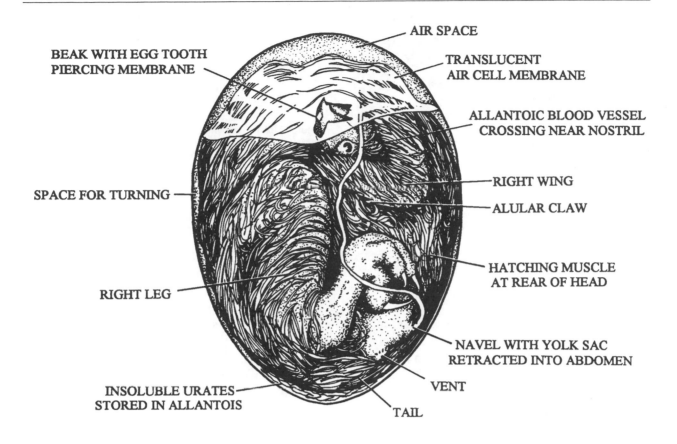

BEAK WITH EGG TOOTH
PIERCING MEMBRANE

AIR SPACE

TRANSLUCENT
AIR CELL MEMBRANE

ALLANTOIC BLOOD VESSEL
CROSSING NEAR NOSTRIL

SPACE FOR TURNING

RIGHT WING

ALULAR CLAW

HATCHING MUSCLE
AT REAR OF HEAD

RIGHT LEG

NAVEL WITH YOLK SAC
RETRACTED INTO ABDOMEN

VENT

INSOLUBLE URATES
STORED IN ALLANTOIS

TAIL

Figure 2.27.2 The position of a peregrine chick at hatching.

starts to rotate inside the shell. Some species, such as most falcons, have small vestigial claws on the tips of the alula, and also sometimes, the manus, which may help during rotation. Within about fifteen minutes the chick circles about half to two-thirds around the egg, industriously cutting out the shell as it goes. Soon it is able to push up the cap with its shoulders and kick itself free of the shell, leaving the membranes and excreted uric acid waste behind. The allantoic blood vessels quickly fall away from the navel. By one or two days after hatching the hatching muscle has reduced in size and is no longer swollen with lymph. The total time from pip to hatch in birds of prey varies considerably from about 30–70 hours but is usually complete within 50 hours.

Falcons tend to pip right at the edge of the aircell so that they puncture the aircell membrane and the shell more or less together. Accipitrid hawks on the other hand, more commonly puncture the aircell membrane first and enter the aircell. They may stay quietly in this position for 24 hours before starring the shell and then fairly quickly

move on to hatch within another 24 hours or so.

Especially with opaque hawk eggshells, it can be hard to determine if the hatching egg is still alive. Everything is black, quiet and ominous. It is easy to panic at this stage and cause irreparable damage. A quick simple test can determine the best course of action to take. First cut a piece of cling film like a handkerchief. Place the egg on it pointed end down and wrap the egg up in it so that the corners twist together to form a little wick 10 centimeters or so long. Then take a bowl of water at blood heat and let it stand until it is perfectly still. Gently lower the egg into the water using the wick. It will stay dry because of the cling film. If the embryo is alive the egg will twitch and the slightest movement is magnified by the lever effect of the wick. This movement will show from about the second half of incubation. If the embryo is near hatching and shows no movement after one minute, it is almost certainly dead.

In precocial birds, such as chickens and ducks, whose young leave the nest as a group together soon after hatching, it is important that they all

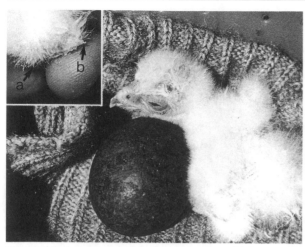

The small claw on the alula (a) and manus (b) in a newly hatched New Zealand falcon. This was the first chick ever bred in captivity, in 1976.

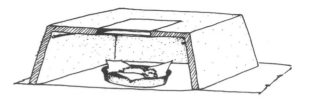

Figure 2.28.1 A polyhatch incubator lid used for brooding chicks age 1–3 days. The heating element is above, there is a double thermostat and a double-glazed window.

emerge within a short space of time, even though the eggs had originally been laid over a number of days. They behave a bit like trade unionists; it is a question of "one out, everybody out." This synchronization process is achieved in two ways. First, the parents tend not to start proper incubation until the clutch nears completion and, second, the cheeping of the chicks inside the eggs stimulates adjacent slower neighbors to speed up their hatch. Birds of prey tend not to show this mechanism. Often they start incubation when the clutch is only half complete. Leaving a "clicking" egg touching a younger hatching egg does not, from my data at least, shorten the second egg's pip to hatch interval. It is not necessarily an advantage for birds of prey to have a synchronized hatch. Indeed, in harriers and owls, the chicks may hatch over several days and the survival of the late hatchlings will depend on food availability at the time. This seemingly cruel mechanism of controlling brood size enhances the survival of the early hatchlings and maximizes ultimate productivity.

## 2.28   Rearing to seven days

However experienced the parents, things can easily go wrong at hatching time and chicks may disappear. Therefore, in almost all cases, we hatch the eggs ourselves in a hatcher, rear them for a few days until they are strong, and then mother them on to parents before the imprinting process is too far on.

Once the chick has hatched it will be tired and misshapen from being cramped inside the egg. It

needs several hours of rest. During this time its natal down will dry and become fluffed out and the chick will lose some weight. As water is withdrawn from the muscle tissues over the first three days, the muscles get more tone and the chick, at first floppy and helpless, will soon be alert and able to sit up and beg. The hatching muscle will disappear after a couple of days.

Once dry, the chick is removed from the hatcher and marked with a colored pen before being placed with other youngster in a brooder. This is simply the lid of a Polyhatch still-air incubator placed on some clean newspaper on a work top (figure 2.28.1). The chicks are in tissue lined plastic bowls and the temperature is a few degrees less than incubation temperature. The chicks themselves are the best thermometers; if too hot they sprawl apart, if too cold they huddle. A solitary chick obviously needs a hotter brooder than a group which can snuggle together for warmth.

After two or three days in the still-air brooder the chicks are removed to a brooder box (2.28.2). This is a plastic bin box or water tank with a thin wedge-shaped layer of clean pea gravel on the floor. Over this is placed a thin flat heating element like an electric blanket. These are used for reptile cages and home-brewing. We obtain ours

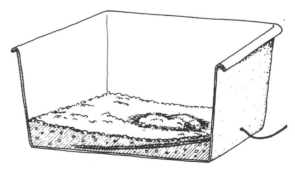

Figure 2.28.2 A brooding box for chicks over three days. A towel-covered electric heating pad is embedded in pea gravel at an angle to give a temperature gradient.

from AB incubators. It is covered with a towel to protect it and laid on the bed of pea gravel so that it is near the surface at one end and buried at the other. This creates a temperature gradient. More pea gravel is placed on top so there is a flat bed of gravel warm at one end and cool at the other. The chicks are placed on this and crawl about until they find their most comfortable position. If the room is cold or if the chicks are being trained to accept a brooding parent, we place a light hand towel over the box secured loosely with clothes pegs. The aim is to keep the chicks as cool and fresh as possible consistent with comfort; this is how they thrive best. We do not used forced air brooders; the chicks should be encouraged to control their own temperature and not forced into a programmed regime. The pea gravel surface encourages strong and well-aligned leg bones and is hygienic, being replaced after each batch of chicks.

For the first two days or so the chicks are using up their yolk sacs and do not need much nourishment. Their feeds are mainly just gently to get the digestive tract working properly without over loading it. They are weighed before and after each feed and records are kept. These are essential to identify a problem quickly and as a source of reference for future chicks, and are important when more than one person is doing the feeds. Small raptors, such as merlins, are fed five times a day to start with, the others four times a day. Falcon chicks sit up and beg. It is only necessary to chup once or twice to encourage them to gape and the food can be put in with blunt forceps. Accipitrid chicks, such as accipiters, buzzards, kites, harriers, and eagles, do not gape. Instead the food must be held in front of them. They will ignore it, then just as you are about to give up, they make a wild snatch and miss. But soon they get more coordinated and feeding goes smoothly. Of course if you mother baby falcons onto an accipitrid raptor the chick will gape and the mother will dangle but nothing gets fed. Also accipitrid raptor chicks will fight each other in "Cain and Abel" battles. These have to be separated and kept covered so that they sleep. An accipitrid chick will beat up a falcon chick who is completely bewildered by such behavior and does not fight back. This is how you get falcons called "Scarface."

For the first two days we feed quail muscle, liver, and heart. These are stripped off the fresh-killed quails and ground up very finely in a sterilized mincer. We do about 50 quail at a time. A scoop of the resulting mix is then placed in a polythene bag on a table and smoothed out flat, about 5 millimeters thick. A ruler is pressed into it so that the result looks like a thin chocolate bar. This is labelled "baby food," dated, and placed in the freezer. In a few minutes it has frozen solid. At feeding time, the required number of segments are broken off and thawed in a glass tub in a saucepan of warm water. A whisper of Nekton-S is dusted onto the ration and a few drops of water are sprinkled on to moisten it. We no longer use saline or probiotics because we have seen no improvements. If the egg quality and incubation was good, the chicks will not be a problem.

On the third day we merge in "junior food." This is whole, skinned quail with the intestinal tract removed but heart and liver left in. A little fat is good too. This is ground up twice to make an even mix. It is frozen in the same way. Again, it is thawed and fed with some Nekton-S and water. In this way, food for the raptor chicks has to be prepared only once or twice a season. The food quality is better and it is easier on the staff. Of course only fresh-killed food can be treated thus; it is not safe to refreeze frozen food. We never feed day-old chicks to young raptors; they are a false economy.

Between day 5–7 it is time to mother chicks

Figure 2.28.3 The mothering-on cage.

Figure 2.28.4 The "born-again" method.

back on to parents. We prefer to mother them first to imprints. It is easy to check them properly three times per day and the mothers do a better job of rearing than we do. Our data consistently show that the chicks grow faster and stronger than hand-raised ones however dedicated we are. One reason may be that the imprints stuff more food into the chicks than we would ever dare. Around day 9–12 it is time to fit closed rings (see 2.29) and then the chicks can go onto natural paired parents. The chicks will be accustomed to being brooded and fed by a mother and quickly accept a different mother.

Meanwhile, the natural pairs have been kept incubating dummy eggs. These are either plaster-filled ones or hard-boiled ones. Inexperienced birds are not allowed to sit real eggs for long because they often break an egg. When the time comes for mothering on a chick the parents should have been incubating for at least half the incubation period. Experienced birds will usually accept a chick without too much problem. If there is some doubt, we use the mothering-on cage (figure 2.28.3). This is a little domed cage which protects the chick if the parents attack it. The chick should then beg and trigger the mother's parental instincts. When she tries to brood the chick in the cage you know she is prepared to accept it and you

can then remove the cage and leave the chick unprotected.

Inexperienced or wild-caught mothers may be totally upset by the chick or put off by the cage. The problem is to make a gradual transition from inert egg to chick. When the parents sit on a pipping egg the parental bond is strengthened and a shy mother suddenly becomes a defensive tiger. It is best to try to make this happen before introducing a precious raptor chick. One way is to give her a chicken egg to hatch. As soon as the chick has hatched, replace it with a raptor chick. If a chicken chick is not available then we get two chicken eggshells fitted telescopically to make one big egg. Inside is a young quail. When both parents have incubated this they are then prepared for hatching. It is important to pay attention to the male as well as the female. Then you can put in your chick. The most dangerous moment is when the mother comes back on to the nest, sees something moving and just grabs it and flies off with it. I once saw this happening, nipped in and caught the chick from the female just before it hit the ground! The way we get over this is to use a goose egg. This is the "born-again" method (figure 2.28.4). The goose egg is cleaned and painted to look like the raptor's eggs. A hole is made, removing about a third of the shell. A five-day-old raptor chick is then placed in

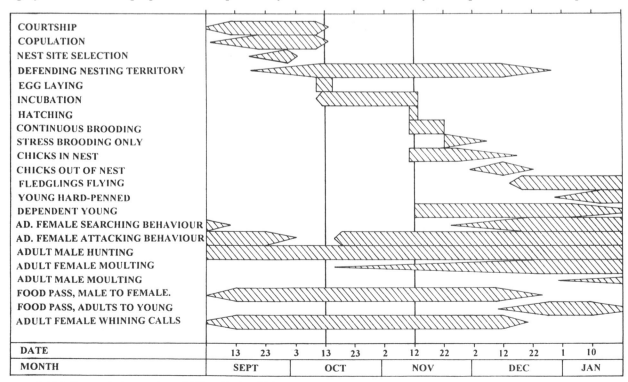

Figure 2.28.5 Events during rearing wild New Zealand falcons.

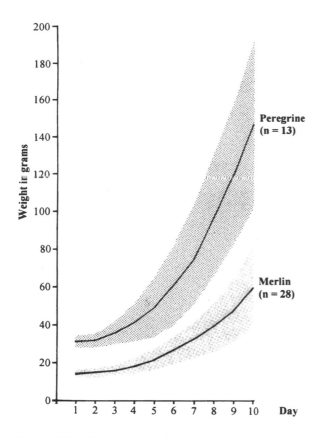

Figure 2.28.6 Growth rates of peregrine and merlin chicks showing averages and ranges of weights.

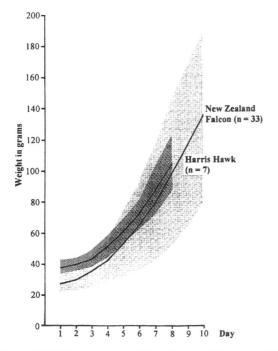

Figure 2.28.7 Growth rates of New Zealand falcons and Harris hawks showing averages and ranges of weights. Harris hawks may scream if hand-reared beyond day 7.

the goose egg and the egg placed in the nest with a couple of dummies, so that the chick is invisible. The female comes back on and sits on this super-stimulus egg. The egg wriggles and cheeps! The female is thrilled. She broods it and after a while the chick "hatches." Soon the parents are feeding it. The next day the eggs are removed and some more chicks added and there is seldom a problem.

It is worth going to all this risk and effort. If the parents rear a brood it reinforces their pair-bonding and pen-bonding. This means they will breed better next year. Noncopulators may copulate, single clutch pairs can be recycled. You have established a good breeding pair. The youngsters too will grow up being imprinted on parents and will thus be suitable for falconry and future breeding.

Again, what happens in the aviary is a condensed version of events in the wild (figure 2.28.5). You should be familiar with the normal sequence of events through the season.

## 2.29  Methods of identification

When the chick is about nine days old it is time to fit a closed identification ring on its leg (figure 2.29.1). In America, Britain and parts of Europe this is an aluminum ring stamped with a serial number. Government rings also carry a government mark and in Britain at least are recorded on the central database. The ring may also carry the year of hatch and the breeder's name.

Closed rings come in various sizes from P and S for merlins to V for male peregrines, W for female peregrines and X for female gyrs (see Appendix 2). Of course at nine days it is not easy to sex a chick and therefore it is best to put on the female ring above the male ring. They can be held loosely in place for a couple of days using Elastoplast, until the foot has grown enough to stop the ring coming off (figure 2.29.2).

These close rings are as near as you'll get to showing that the bird is aviary-bred. It will be sold as "ABCR" (Aviary-Bred Closed-Ringed). Once the chick is older it can be ringed for identification purposes with another type of ring. A popular open ring in Europe is the "Hess" ring (2.29.1). This is put on and closed, then a small steel pin is fitted through a hole linking it up. The metal part of the join is then crushed, and the barbs on the pin prevent removal without damaging the ring.

In America and Britain, the government cable

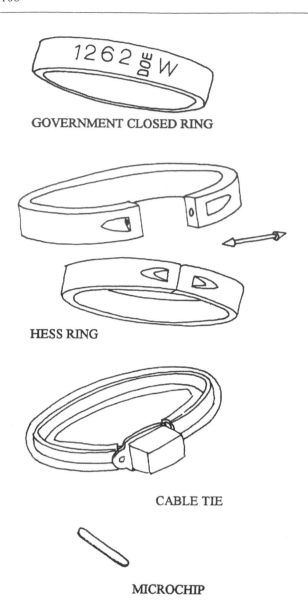

GOVERNMENT CLOSED RING

HESS RING

CABLE TIE

MICROCHIP

Figure 2.29.1 Closed ring, Hess ring, cable tie, and a microchip.

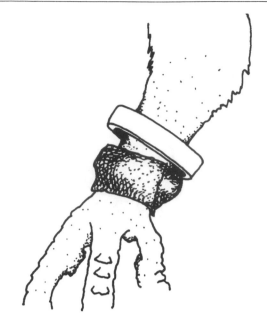

Figure 2.29.2 The female ring is placed above the male ring, which is temporarily held in place with loosely bound Elastoplast.

tie ring has been frequently used but is not popular. Hawks easily remove it and thieves easily fiddle it. It is gradually being phased out.

A modern way of marking is the PIT tag or microchip, about 8 millimeters long by 2 millimeters wide. It can be implanted under the skin or into muscle and will give a coded number readout when scanned from 5–10 centimeters away by a scanner. It is a bit like the scanner of a bar code. It is a very effective system of marking but does have some drawbacks. One is that it cannot be seen by eye and so there is no immediate visual evidence supporting the bird's legality. Another is that it is

only as good as the central database supporting it. These databases, and the systems themselves, are still in competition and duplication at the moment. Thus, if your bird is stolen, there is not yet a very good chance that you will get to hear of it being found. Also of course this method does not authenticate the bird's previous history in any way; it doesn't prove captive breeding or parentage. We are using it at the moment in wild sakers in our field projects in Kazakhstan, Pakistan, and Mongolia. The young sakers disperse and are trapped on migration, sold in Pakistan and find their way to the Middle East. There our biologists and vets in the Falcon Hospitals find them with scanners and report them to our computer in Abu Dhabi. Later when these birds are released again we can detect them back on the nesting grounds. In this way we can determine the harvest and sustainability of sakers in Arab falconry.

Another way to identify a chick is to take blood from it for a DNA profile. We take one drop from the brachial vein and store it indefinitely in 95 percent ethanol. It can be profiled at any time. Using this we can identify our birds again if stolen and also we can prove the parentage. Thus a drop of blood can be considerable protection and no cost is incurred unless the DNA is actually profiled. This is probably the best way to detect and deter criminal activity.

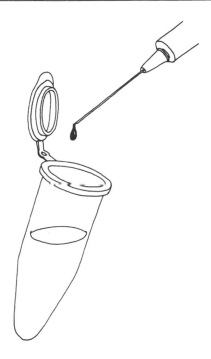

Figure 2.29.3 Blood for DNA profiling.

## 2.30  Systems of rearing the older chick

Once the ring stays on and the chick is being reared by parents, there is a short respite in which to plan ahead. If the chick is to be hacked, either for falconry or for release, it can stay with parents until about a week before it is due to fly. Then it is transferred to the hack box (see 5.2). If it is not scheduled for hacking it is best to leave it with the parents for at least one month after its first flight. The first two weeks are spent completing feather growth. After that, although fully feathered, the youngster's joints are still hardening and are very fragile, especially in long-legged or violent species. Also, in the wild, the youngster would still be dependent on its parents at this age. If you take it in hand then, it will start to react to you as a parent. This may include screaming and looking toward you for food, rather than getting out and catching its own. This period should be extended in species with a long dependency period, such as Harris hawks. If possible they should be left with their parents, or in sibling groups untouched by man, until at least two months after first flight. This reduces the risk of screaming and makes the bird easier to enter. Further delay tends to be counterproductive: the bird needs the flying experience and the exercise to develop its physical perform-

ance fully and learns a great deal at this age.

If the bird is intended for natural breeding, it can either be left with its parents until removed for pairing, or it can be reared away from its parents. Some parent-reared birds, particularly gyrfalcons, can be a little nervous and as a result, very slow to come into breeding condition. If reared in sibling groups, they tend to be steadier, but creche- or socially reared raptors tend to be noisy for falconry. An alternative which is perhaps the ideal, is to use a tame imprint parent to rear the birds. This leaves them properly imprinted but also well-adusted to life around humans.

## 2.31  Finding the right homes for the young stock

This is always the worst part about breeding raptors. Having spent so much trouble producing them it is important that they go to good homes and it is always distressing to hear that one has been badly treated. It is almost impossible to gauge the abilities of a prospective purchaser. Many falconers of twenty or thirty years experience didn't learn properly in the first place, have developed plenty of bad habits since, and have closed their minds to any further progress. Some beginners, on the other hand, although short on practical experience, will bend over backwards to do the best for their birds.

Many falconers who do not breed hawks have no real idea of the work and uncertainty involved. They ring up wanting birds as if you are a grocery store and do not appreciate that there is a lot of attrition between a new-laid egg and a finished, hacked female falcon. Usually, the more experienced they are, the less used they are to paying, and they almost expect you to give them a bird as a favor! Having been used to obtaining wild birds for free, they find it disagreeable having to buy one. Younger buyers on the other hand often go to the other extreme, buying and selling birds like changing shoes, and never sticking with one long enough to get the best out of it. Almost without exception, if there is a problem, falconers blame it on the breeder rather than on themselves. If it goes well, then the falconer claims the glory! Most experienced breeders keep a blacklist of problem people.

The Middle East market is particularly difficult and fickle. It is essential that breeders fully understand what type of bird is wanted and how to prepare it so that it is suitable for Arab falconry. At present there are only a very few Arab falconers able to bring out the best in an aviary-bred falcon and adapt their methods to the birds. Therefore it is important that the birds fit the method, which has evolved primarily for the passage saker.

To the person planning on buying a young raptor, I suggest you follow the advice in Jemima Parry-Jones' book on obtaining one, and also examine yourself carefully. Do you have all the necessary factors to make a success of the bird? Have all your birds turned out reliable, successful hunters? If they didn't, in what way did you fail? Have you sought help? Are you likely to improve this time? Now that raptors are more easily available it is even more important to realize the responsibility that the trainer has for each bird. If your bird was a healthy youngster when you got it, and now it has a problem or is a poor hunter, it is almost 100 percent certain that it is YOUR fault. Face it, analyze it, and do something about it.

## 2.32  Maintaining breeding records

There are so many small, but vital, items of information in breeding that it is impossible to progress on any scale without good records. They are essential as a guide for the future, a basis for learning and of course for legal reasons. Unused copies of our data sheets shown in this part of the book are provided in Appendix 3. You are welcome to copy them.

In addition to our data sheets and databases, and to legal and veterinary documents, we keep a Day book. On the front of this is a schematic plan of all the pens with the occupants labelled to age, sex, species, and ring number. The book itself is then divided up with two or three pages for each pen. Any events happening in any pen are recorded each day as they happen. A new book is started each year, but the previous year's book is always close at hand for quick reference on laying dates and so on.

The other overall document is the Stocklist. This again lists all the birds broken down by age and sex (aren't we all?), species, ring number, both parents, and owner. The secondary stocklist covers all birds out on loan. The stocklists are dated and up-dated periodically, being in frequent use for CITES applications and so on.

However small your operation, careful records are the key to making progress.

Old female golden eagle.

Young New Zealand falcons at hack.

# 3 Equipment

Figure 3.12.2. Gyr on shelf perch.

# and Facilities

## 3.1   Obtaining good equipment

Facilities for breeding raptors have already been described in part two. When raptors are being held using falconry techniques, either for falconry itself, or displays, or rehabilitation, then specialist equipment is needed. Now that so much falconry equipment is available commercially there is little need to make it yourself.

If you are going to buy your equipment you do at least need to know how to recognize good workmanship and good design. Unfortunately, although some furniture for sale is excellent, some is absolute rubbish. If you wish to make your own equipment Beebe and Webster, Glasier, Upton, Ford and Kimsey, and Hodge provide useful descriptions.

There is very little margin for error in managing captive raptors. All the small details must be attended to carefully or a hawk could be quickly injured or dead. Destroy all faulty or old equipment so that you wont be tempted to use it again, and if you hear yourself saying words like "that will do for now," go back to square one.

## 3.2   Anklets and jesses

The Aylmeri anklet is the best way to attach jesses. Traditional jesses are now obsolete and in America they are illegal and rightly so. There are various ways of putting on the anklets but this one is very simple:

a) Cut a strap of light, tough, prestretched leather of the required width and in the center, at what will be the bottom edge, make about 15 small cuts so that the edge curls outward and will not chafe (figure 3.2.1). We use a white, chrome-tanned leather. Our telephone number is written on the front of one anklet and the hawk's name on the other. We use Indian ink protected by leather shellac for long-lasting legibility. Put rubber contact glue, such as Evostick, on the inside at each end.

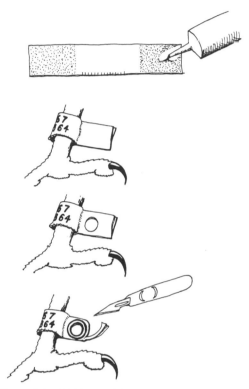

Figure 3.2.1 Making and fitting anklets.

b) Place the anklet around the hawk's leg and bond the glue tightly with a pair of pliers. Then punch a hole through using a scrap piece of leather under the punch to get a clear cut.

c) Place the eyelet in position from the outside of the leg with the eyelet washer on the inside. Crimp the eyelet with an eyelet punch. If the eyelet is too large for the pliertype handpunch weld or fit the eyelet punch parts onto a big pair of pliers or mole grips to make a sturdy hand-held eyelet punch.

d) Trim off excess leather to a rounded shape.

e) Apply a light coat of leather oil such as Neats foot oil, Saturol, or Mars oil. The complete operation can be done in two or three minutes with the hawk hooded on the fist.

If the hawk is a young one, this is also a good time to snip of any unwanted closed rings.

Anklets can cause a number of problems.

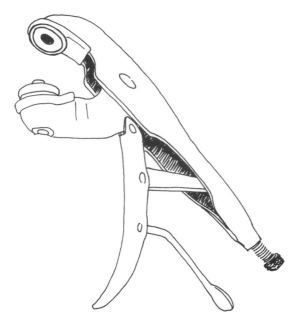

Figure 3.2.2 Mole grips for fitting eyelets.

Over-greasing may cause sand to stick inside, which can abrade the hawk's legs, as can prolonged bating. In small accipiters a common problem is an awkward sore at the back of the leg.

There are three ways to reduce these problems. Man the hawk so that it seldom bates, use a shock absorber in the leash, or manage the hawk in such a way that it is never tethered but kept in a flight pen when not in use. In hot climates a few ventilation holes in the anklet may help.

Mews jesses are easily constructed, always in pairs, from prestretched leather (figure 3.2.3). Take care not to weaken the leather when making the slits. There is no need for a hole punched at the inner end of the slit. There is no magic leather for jesses; the tannage is as important as the species. Badly tanned kangaroo is just as bad as sheepskin. If in doubt, make a cut in the leather and pull to see how easily it tears. There is no point in using a stainless steel swivel that could tow a car if the jesses couldn't pull a chicken off its nest. Last year

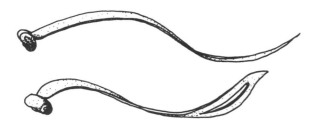

Figure 3.2.3 Top: Field or flying jess. Below: Mews jess.

I recovered a lanner somebody had lost and I could tear the jess slits with one hand. No wonder it had escaped!

Mews jesses should just be long enough to go down through the palm of the hand and out between the fingers, exposing the swivel. Any longer than this and the bird is in danger of straddling the block or of getting the jesses wrapped around her upper tarsus. As these jesses are not used when hawking there is no need to make them any longer. For a peregrine, the jesses are about 15 centimeters (6 inches) from the button to the far end of the slit. If the hawk bites at its jesses an application of antinail-biting fluid, mustard, or curry powder often solves the problem.

Never fly a hawk with slitted jesses. Sooner or later it will get hung up. If you have seen, as I have done, somebody's hawk caught by one leg hanging from a live electricity crossbar, or another in the top of an unclimbable tree, or another thrashing amongst the strands of a barbed-wire fence, you

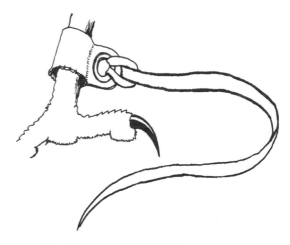

Figure 3.2.4 "Nonremovable" flying jess.

will swear never to use such things in the field. Nor should you be tempted to commit even worse a sin: turning the mews jesses round so that they are held to the anklets by the slits and the button end is left dangling, waiting to get caught in the fork of a branch (figure 5.24.6).

Normally it is best to fly falcons with no jesses at all. But sometimes, particularly if hawks are being flown, more control is needed and field jesses are one solution. They can be like lightweight slitless mews jesses (figure 3.2.3), or, if the hawk is in the habit of promptly removing button jesses, slit jesses of the type shown in figure 3.2.4 can be used.

## 3.3 Swivels

Provided that a good quality swivel is used this item should cause no problems at all. The difficulties start with cheap swivels. Remember that although an item of equipment may be temporary, the resulting accident could be permanent. The swivel should be welded stainless steel or at least phosphor bronze or brass, brazed, or silver-soldered. The joints should be well fitted and the shank head threaded and welded on. The shank itself should be visible to check for wear. Of the 13 types of swivel or clip shown in figure 3.3.1 and 2, only A-C are safe for tethering birds.

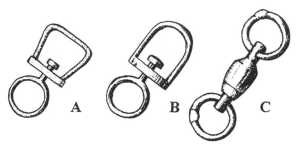

Figure 3.3.1 Swivels A–C are safe.

The Sampo range of game fishing swivels are strong and work well. They should be replaced after a year or so as wear cannot be detected. The jesses are attached to the fixed end. The cheap Japanese imitations of Sampo swivels do not rotate

so easily and need proper steel rings put on them. Key rings should never be used as they have very little strength. Try doing a load test on one and you will be shocked. The old Mollen type swivel (J) was unsafe but the modern steel ones of this pattern are fine.

The quickest and most trouble-free way of attaching the swivel to the jesses is to thread both jesses through together. Avoid any kind of spring swivel or clip, especially type E. The jess has only to cross the outside of the spring for them to fail.

Within a day of writing this I heard of someone who has just lost his peregrine. It freed itself from a springclip on a screen perch, flew out of the mews door which had been left open and was found later hanging dead in a tree. The falconer has now attached his goshawk to the springclip!

## 3.4 Leashes

Leather leashes are not safe and have been the cause of many deaths and losses. A good terylene leash can be easily made for a trivial sum and will not break without showing wear. Take some round woven terylene cord, preferably of the closely woven soft variety. Cut it to the length required and pull out the central core leaving a flat hollow tube which will hold a good knot. Tie a neat overhand knot in one end and slide on a leather washer. Heat seal both ends and cover the knot in a thin

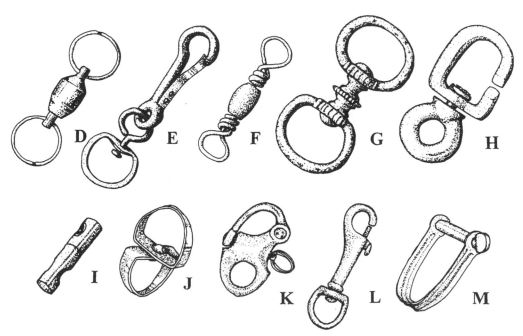

Figure 3.3.2 Swivels D–M are unsafe.

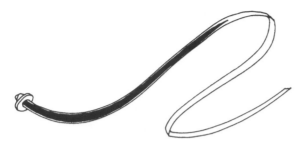

Figure 3.4.1 Traditional jess with rubber insert.

coat of epoxy resin so that it cannot loosen. A few minutes work will last for years.

If you wish to incorporate a shock absorber into the leash cut a length of inner tube from a car tire one third of the length of the leash and tapered so that it slides up inside the hollow tube and through the leather washer into the knot (figure 3.4.1). Leave the lower two thirds of the leash for tying the falconer's knot. Having tried many types of clip-on and parallel shock absorbers, I have found nothing to beat the inserted absorber. Young accipiters are especially prone to leg injury if no absorber is used because the terylene has little or no elasticity. The inserted absorber is very convenient and discreet. Nobody will even notice that you are using it—except your hawk.

The traditional leash has two design faults which have caused injuries to many hawks and, in

some cases, death. One problem is that the button rides up between the jesses, the hawk turns round a few times and is soon completely trapped, its legs abraded, sprained, or even broken (figure 3.4.2).

The second problem is the falconer's knot which can be undone or can work loose through the activities of the hawk. The hawk then escapes with its leash trailing and you can count yourself lucky if she doesn't kill any of the other hawks out weathering before she flies off and hangs herself. This is an unnecessary disaster.

To overcome this I have since 1979 used the loop leash with completely satisfactory results. It is made of woven terylene with the core removed (figure 3.4.3). A 75 centimeter length is folded back inside itself leaving a 5–8 centimeter loop. A rubber insert can be fitted as a shock absorber. A small extra tab of light terylene is tied and epoxied onto the loop to aid threading. The other end has a button in the usual way.

The perch ring has a small steel loop with an internal diameter of about 15 millimeters ($^5/_8$ inches). The leash is threaded through this and is left there with the perch when the hawk is taken away. When you approach with the hawk, first thread the leash up through the hawk's swivel, then double the leash back down through the perch ring (figure 3.4.4). Slip the leash button through

Figure 3.4.2 Tangling caused by the traditional leash.

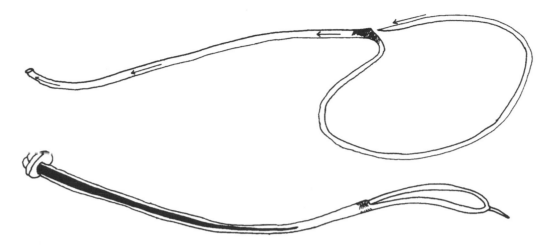

Figure 3.4.3 Top: Making a loop leash. Below: Loop leash with rubber insert.

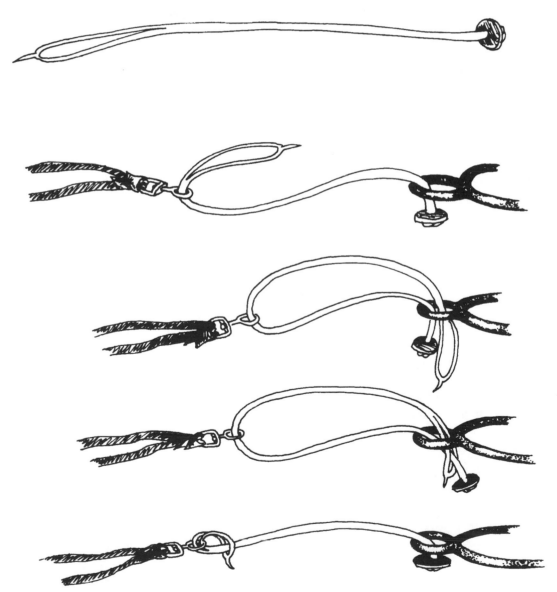

Figure 3.4.4 Tying a loop leash.

Figure 3.4.5 A short loop leash on an indoor perch.

the loop, pull and the loop will slide up and lock on the swivel. All this takes just a moment and the leash cannot come undone or jam the swivel. In addition, there is now an extra swivel point at the perch end of the leash so that tangles are eliminated with no extra weight, clips, or other devices. A similar but shorter leash is used in the mews (figure 3.4.5).

## 3.5    Bells

The size of the bell and the way it is mounted is more important than its weight. For example, medium-size bells for a male peregrine weigh 3.8 grams (Lahore type), 5.5 grams (Asborno type), and 7.3 grams (typical British handmade brass bells). A large size Lahore bell weighs about 7.0 grams. The weight differences between them are not even equivalent to a good mute! It follows then that we are looking for bells which are small for the sound that they give; transmitters are the ultimate conclusion and we'll look at them later. Assuming that one has obtained a suitable conventional bell, how then to put it on the hawk?

The last place to put a bell is on the hawk's leg. It may be convenient for you, but look at it from the hawk's point of view. As was shown in section 1.17, the raptor foot is a very highly evolved instrument finely tuned by the rigors of survival through hunting success. Already we are obliged to use some sort of anklet and a closed registration ring. These can be designed to be reasonably neat but it is sheer folly to clutter a bird up with a bell or a transmitter on its leg. Can you imagine trying to play a game of football with a football strapped to each ankle? The problem is that falconers are so used to seeing cluttered up legs and so rarely have a chance to see the nimbleness of wild hawks that they take their hawk's poor performance for granted. Leg bells can be dangerous too. I have twice seen goshawks trapped in forked branches by their leg bells.

We do use leg bells during hacking because the tail is not hard-penned then. If you have to use a legbell look out for the following: first make sure that the bewit is double looped so that no bell metal comes into contact with the hawk's legs where it can cause sores. Second, make sure that the metal strap on the bell has been flattened and will hold the bell up at right angles to the tarsus. Lahore bells are made with rounded loops which require altering. Third, use prestretched leather for the bewit and put it on with sufficient tension to hold the bell clear of the leg without restricting blood flow. Slack bewits and cumbersome bells are extremely irritating for a hawk. Plastic cable ties should not be used directly on the tarsus because of the risk of overtightening and because they can be abrasive. The alternative of attaching the bell with a cable tie to part of the anklet is also a clumsy arrangement; better to get the bell off the leg altogether.

The other two sites for bells are on the neck and the tail. I have used neck bell, necks on rubber bands on a variety of species and found them the most effective of all if used properly (figure 3.5.1). Although commonly used in America and India,

loose neckstrap is a hazard, hawks can get a claw or beak caught in it while preening (3.5.3 and 3.5.4) and the bell dangling in flight hangs below the hawk's profile and will catch on objects such

Figure 3.5.3 Neck bell caught by a claw while scratching.

Figure 3.5.1 Neck bell on a wide rubber band.

European falconers are unfamiliar with them, which is a pity. A hawk cannot feed without loudly ringing its neck bell, neck which is a considerable consolation if you have a hawk down on a kill somewhere at dusk. The bell should be well fitted, not so tightly that it is muffled by feathers (figure 3.5.2) and not so loose that the strap is visible. A

Figure 3.5.4 Neck bell in normal position over crop.

Figure 3.5.2 Neck bell caught in the mouth while preening.

as strands of wire in a fence. I only use neckbells on species which strike from the feet first position (see 6.14), not on those, such as the large falcons, which often strike with the head passing before the feet. Having myself been struck many times by wild falcons stooping I can see how liable a neck-bell is to be knocked into the falcon's clavicles although in fairness I have never heard of neck-bells causing this injury. For goshawks I use a heavy duty rubber band as a neckstrap. It is 7 millimeters wide and when laid flat, 80 millimeters long. When the bell is attached, the remaining loop is 60 millimeters. I stretch the band over the hawk's head while it is hooded and it is left in place all the time. Depending on how active the hawk is the band needs replacing about every three weeks. Some hawks will rip off such a band immediately in which case something much stronger might be needed until the hawk settles. However, I am not speaking from experience here as all my hawks have accepted the neckbell well.

The other site for a bell is on the tail. This is by far the best place. It is out of the hawk's way, it rings well and is held clear of debris, snow, etc. However, many falconers do not use it because they cannot put one on securely. The tailmount problem is first to attach the mount securely and second to ensure that the tailfeathers do not get damaged or fall out.

A system which has survived the acid test over a good number of seasons is as follows:

a) Prepare an oval sounding board of shatter-proof plastic such as nylon, preferably a bright or white color (figure 3.5.5). This is to prevent the bell dangling under the tail and to show strangers that the hawk is not a wild one. Punch out two holes for the loop and one long hole for the bell loop and stamp on any wording required for identification. Smear black paint into the lettering and wipe off excess.

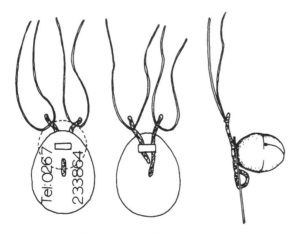

Figure 3.5.5 The "plectrum" tail bell mount from above, below, and from the side.

b) Using 2.5 millimeter diameter braided terylene as used in a creance, thread up the bell onto the tailmount. Before tightening, soak the terylene in epoxy apart from the two ends which should stay flexible so that the hawk can fan its tail. The rigid loop below

the bell is to take the transmitter.

c) Heat seal the ends of the two tags to stop them unraveling and attach a rot proof terylene thread to each by passing it through on a needle and knotting it. This is to prevent it sliding off the tag.

d) cast the hawk and expose the base of the tail. Some people advocate giving the hawk tranquilizers but if the situation is that traumatic it is probably better to take the tranquilizers yourself! It is easier if you mask off the rest of the tail from the feathers you are working on by sliding in a big white sticky label and pressing it down lightly so that it stays in position if the hawk moves.

e) The mount will be attached as near to the body as possible; there is seldom any need for trimming but you may need to clear some fluff away. Being so close to the preen gland the shafts of the tailfeathers are often oily and repel glue so you may need to roughen them a little at the attachment sites. The two tags are bound by the threads to the two feathers each side of the central deck feathers. This distributes the weight of the mount over four feathers, not just two. This reduces the risk of the follicles being damaged and of the feathers being dropped prematurely, or pulled out. Place some rubber-based glue such as Evostick (not epoxy which will eventually flake away) onto the tags, the threads, and the feather shafts. Pass the threads around each shaft three times, ensuring that the glue is all round the shaft, then tie off tightly with a reef knot. Put a dab of glue on the knot and trim off the surplus ends. Do the same for the other tag and for very active hawks repeat the bindings. A sprinkling of talc stops the feathers sticking to the wet glue. Leave the hawk hooded quietly until the glue is dry.

I do not actually pierce the feather shaft with a needle because of the risk of weakening it. With small hawks, such as merlins, care must be taken not to pinch the shaft when tightening the thread. If necessary the shaft can be reinforced with a sleeve made from 1 centimeter of shaft from a slightly larger feather, well glued of course.

Such a tailmount will last all season and from the hawk's point of view is the least uncomfortable site for a bell. It irritates far less than leg bells and the transmitter is safer there because the hawk cannot get a good pull at it. Should it so wish a

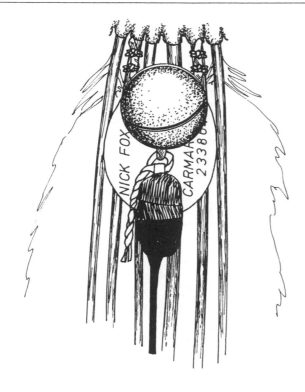

Figure 3.5.6 The "plectrum" tail mount in position.

Figure 3.5.7 Tail bell clipped directly to deck feather.

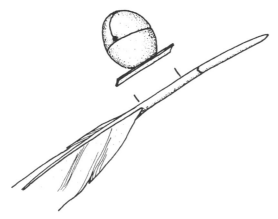

Figure 3.5.8 Tail bell bound directly to tail feather.

falcon can destroy a leg-mounted transmitter in a few moments.

In recent years we have experimented with attaching bells directly to the tail feather, either by adapting the bell (figure 3.5.7) or by opening the loop and binding it on (figure 3.5.8). Alternatively one can pass a small leather tag through the bell loop and bind it to the feather.

Nowadays telemetry has virtually outmoded bells as a means of finding the hawk but I still use one bell on the tail. This is mainly to protect the hawk from shooters when out of my sight and also it is useful at home to know what the hawk is doing by the sound of her bell.

## 3.6    The tail sheath and taping

Tail sheaths are useful when training an accipiter or any bird with a vulnerable tail. It is a light tube which wraps around or slides on to the tail, preventing the tail opening and thus protecting it. This is preferable to taping because it can easily be removed for flying and then be replaced for traveling. Although hawks occasionally break feathers in the field, for example by falling into a tree when holding struggling prey, most feathers are broken through mismanagement at home. The general attrition of bad handling causes the feathers to weaken and eventually to break.

There are various designs of tail sheath including wrap-around ones with velcro attachments. A really violent hawk may need a sheath reinforced with piano wire or nylon bristles from a yard brush. The following design, if adjusted for the size of the hawk, has stood the test of time and is easily made:

a)   Take a square of heavy-duty polythene sheet such as is used in fertilizer bags (figure 3.6.1). With sandpaper, roughen a 25 millimeter strip along one edge, apply a flexible contact rubber adhesive such as Evostick and allow to dry. When dry, warm the glued area to activate the glue, fold over, and stick down. This makes a strong rounded top rim to the sheath.

b)   Measure the width of the hawk's tail at the tail mount and at the tip and mark out this tapered shape down the center of the polythene. The two sides will now fold over inward with a 15 millimeter overlap for gluing. Mark and cut these accordingly, roughen and glue. Note that the top rim folds outward

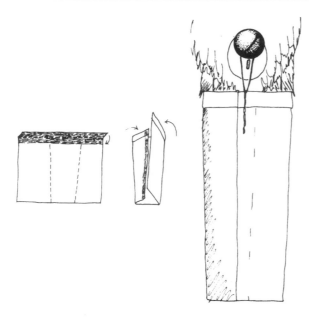

Figure 3.6.1. A plastic removable tail guard.

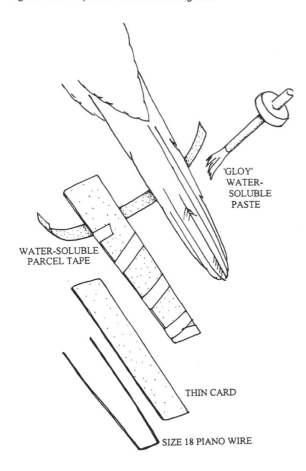

Figure 3.6.2 Taping a tail.

leaving a smooth surface inside the sheath.

c) Using the finest 1 millimeter braided terylene sew about six stitches down the center leaving a loop 4 centimeters long which is used to loop over the tailbell to hold the sheath up. Glue the knots.

d) Trim off the end of the sheath so that when it is in position it is 5 millimeters longer than the tail. For a goshawk such a sheath should weigh no more than 5 grams.

During rehabilitation, air travel, and for fresh-caught hacked birds, we tape the tail (figure 3.6.2). We tape a hoop of piano wire under a thin card and tape this under the tail. If the wire rusts, it will not mark the tail. All the tape is based on water-soluble glue which dissolves away in warm water. Tails should not be taped for more than two weeks unless really necessary, otherwise the feather vanes start to disintegrate.

The same method is used to support the first five primaries when a falcon is boxed by air.

## 3.7   Gloves

There are various gloves available, from buckskin falconry gloves to goatskin rodeo gloves. Mostly it is a matter of personal taste and depends on the type of hawk being carried. Gloves should be looked after properly and kept clean, otherwise they are a major source of bacterial infection.

The glove should have some means of attaching the hawk to it. Wrapping or draping the leash around the fingers may be traditional but it is just not good enough. It is so easy for a sudden bate to pull it out and in cold weather or on rough ground the falconer can easily stumble and let go. I have seen somebody let go of a sparrowhawk, leash and all, and watched it disappear into the sky to certain death. Each summer when we ran course at least one person each week, sometimes more, let go of the hawk by mistake, only to realize with a sigh of relief that he had been made to tie the hawk to the glove.

When using a traditional leash the simple solution is to tie it with a falconer's knot to the tassel loop which should be a proper continuous loop of braided terylene not some light or ornamental strap. The system I use with the loop leash is similar to that described by Jack Mavrogordato in *A Falcon in the Field*. Below the wrist of the glove is a brass eyelet to which is attached two lengths of braided terylene about 35 centimeters long (figure

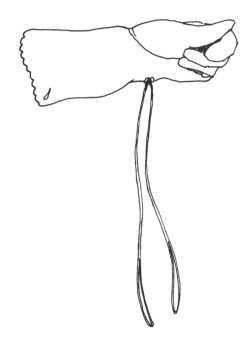

Figure 3.7.1 Glove with field leashes.

3.7.1). Each length ends in a loop. On picking up the hawk, the bird is first called onto the fist and one of the hanging cords is tied to the swivel with a falconer's knot. The loop leash is then undone and left on the perch. At no stage is the hawk unsecured. When ready to fly, the jesses are removed and a cord is threaded through each anklet and looped over a finger, prior to unhooding (figure 3.7.2). If the slip is not imminent the cord is tied with a falconer's knot in the interim. When

Figure 3.7.2 Falcon held by field leashes.

ready, the hood is removed and the cord slips easily away leaving the hawk free and unfettered.

## 3.8    Hoods

Raptors live in a visual world and by temporarily blind-folding them with a hood they can be shielded from visual stimuli which would otherwise stress them. Instead of being frightened or bating wildly and risking injury, the hawk stands quietly and many will often go to sleep. Thus hoods have an important role in managing raptors in captivity, not just for falconry but for veterinary and rehabilitation work as well. If you have raptors on the premises, you should have well-fitting hoods to hand for each species and sex.

There are plenty of books on how to make hoods and they are easily available commercially. Over the years I have used almost every design of hood made, including replicas of medieval hoods, rufters, several types of spring-loaded ones, gutta-percha ones, even stitchless hoods made of lamb scrota! But I keep coming back to the one-piece blocked design shown, with Dutch braces which can be closed with one hand (figure 5.22.1). Soaking it in silicone solution used for waterproofing walls makes it waterproof but still allows the leather to breath.

A good hood should meet a number of criteria: the hawk should not be able to get it off. It should be easy to put on and take off. The hawk should be able to feed andcast through it safely. It should be light in weight, sit comfortably on the hawk's head without causing condensation, irritation or trailing braces which annoy the hawk. It should be light-tight. It should not cause sores around the gape or pinch the nape feathers. It should be easy to make and to duplicate. It should be tough, durable, weather-proof, and easily cleaned or renovated. It should be elegant.

We make all our hawks of all species to the hood. Hooding makes training easier because it enables you to "switch off" the hawk when necessary, protecting her from undesirable sights which not only might upset her but also might be linked in the hawk's mind, to her handler. Some hawks are more difficult to hood than others and this is something which requires skill. There are a lot of little tricks and wrinkles according to circumstances, and not many short cuts. In some ways it is like jumping a horse over a fence, first you throw your heart over; the rest follows. Hooding is

Figure 3.8.1 Fitting the hood.

discussed in section 5.22.

A well-fitting hood should not cross the rictus, the angle of the mouth, because it will either chafe or let in light, owing to the way the mouth opens (see figure 1.2.3). At the back it should fit snugly under the occiput (figure 3.8.1) so that it cannot come off. It should not extend any further than this otherwise it will impede neck movements and press on the crop. During early training we usually use a hood that is too large. It slips on and off easily and the hawk can see through it like blinkers on a harness horse. Often they start to feed on the fist this way without being distracted. After a few days, a closer-fitting hood is used.

To measure a hawk for a hood, take the width of the head behind the eyes, in millimeters (figure 3.8.2). Some common sizes and patterns are shown in Appendix 2.

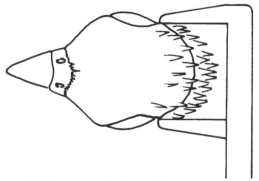

Figure 3.8.2 Measuring the head of the hawk for hood fitting.

## 3.9   Telemetry

I am no electronics whiz so I will not burden you with the latest circuit diagram. But I have used telemetry quite a lot in the course of raptor research and falconry and there are one or two points worth mentioning.

The most important thing about telemetry is not range, nor portability but *reliability*. Purchase a good outfit from a well-established firm and don't get involved with fly-by-night traders and home-made sets. When the moment comes when you need telemetry it must work.

Following on from that, make yourself thoroughly familiar with the gear under field conditions, especially around hills and pylons. Carry it with you out hawking. Don't leave it at home or in the car or, most frustrating of all, distribute it in bits for your companions to carry. When you need it, you need it. The first few minutes of loss are critical, as many have found to their cost.

Check your gear before leaving home. Co-ax cable easily breaks undetected so keep a spare. The antenna should be firmly attached to the transmitter and fully electrically insulated. The transmitter batteries, if not already sealed, should be firmly held in place with insulating tape and sealed against damp and rain, otherwise they will drain rapidly. Always check your transmitter signal and tuning immediately prior to flying. There are various ways of attaching the transmitter. I have used double plastic-coated wire bag ties twisted on to the tailmount loop and have been pleased with the result (figure 3.5.4). Alligator clips and electrical cable ties fail in normal use. The whole system should have the minimal electrical conductivity from the antenna to the hawk to reduce the risk of electrocution on power lines.

Transmitter design is changing constantly. Everybody wants more range. In open desert, this is useful, but in Britain a transmitter operating further than about 10–15 kilometers is usually wasted output because you cannot often get a line of sight signal that far away; there is usually something in the way. Better to translate the extra power into longer battery life. If your transmitter has a life of five days and you have already used it for three, if you then lose your hawk you have only 48 hours to get her back. Of course the battery could last longer. Or not...

Many hawks will quickly damage or remove a leg-mounted antenna. There is no point in using a transmitter with a battery life of two weeks if the hawk removes it ten minutes after you lose her. If you have to use a dummy transmitter to condition your hawk to accept it then stop and ask yourself if she really likes what you are doing. Better to mount it on the tail where it will not annoy or hamper her so much. Leg mounts (figures 3.9.1–3) are the only real option for hack-hawks while their tails are growing, but we are experimenting with back packs (figures 3.9.4–7). Back packs are use-

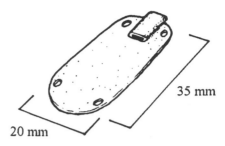

Figure 3.9.4 Back pack mounting for removable transmitter.

Figure 3.9.1 Clip-on removable leg transmitter for tame hacking imprints.

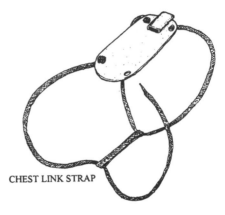

CHEST LINK STRAP

Figure 3.9.5 Back·pack with harness ready for fitting. The straps are of tubular teflon tape with a thin rubber core.

Figure 3.9.2 Wild hack transmitter—leg mount assembly.

Figure 3.9.6 Back pack harness connected.

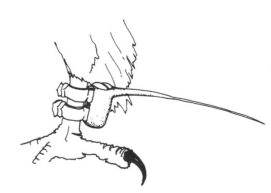

Figure 3.9.3 Wild hack transmitter on the leg.

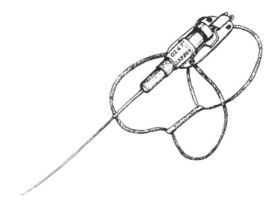

Figure 3.9.7 Back pack with transmitter clipped on.

ful for mounting on free-living research birds; an
alternative is to tie it onto the tail (figure 3.9.8) so
that the transmitter is jettisoned when the deck
feathers molt. Another popular format for falcon-

Figure 3.9.8 Research transmitter attached to deck feathers of
Mauritius kestrel.

ers is the French spring clip (figure 3.9.9) shown
here with a short, base-loaded antenna. I remove
the transmitter when not in use because this reduces wear and tear and enables me to check it. On
removing the transmitter, leave the battery in until
you put the transmitter away properly in its or-
dained place at home, out of the reach of kids.
Nothing is more easily lost than a transmitter with
the battery out! New batteries should be checked
with a voltmeter and used batteries should be dis-
posed of so that you don't get mixed up.

At the start of each season, usually when the
first birds go out at hack in mid-June, all our transmitters are carefully checked over, refurbished and
color-coded, then retuned, taking care to recheck
the tuning at a distance to ensure that it is tuned to
the strongest peak of the signal. Lists of the transmitter colors and their tuning are then stuck on
each receiver, in the car, and in the staff room of
our main building which acts as "air traffic control" for the hack birds. The name of each hack

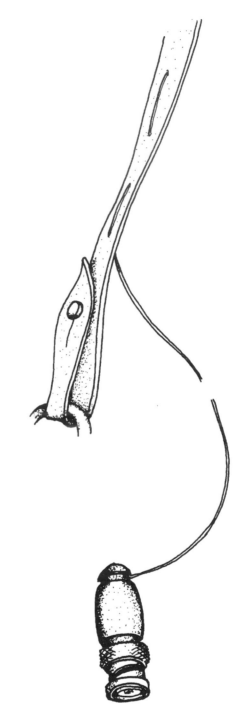

Figure 3.9.10 Bag strap aerial attachment.

Figure 3.9.9 French clip tail transmitter.

bird is listed against its signal. In the varying temperature of a British summer there can be considerable temperature drift on the transmitter signals and it is best to select well-separated signals, preferably of a variety of pulse lengths.

The receiver should be properly maintained and protected. Plastic models will not survive hard use. Apart from the yaggi I also use a small single wire aerial (figure 3.9.10). It runs from the receiver in my hawking bag up the front shoulder strap to my opposite shoulder and is made of plastic-coated steel trace wire. At the flick of a switch I can then tell if the hawk is within 500 meters or so and approximately in which direction. Another easily made device for yaggi-phobes is shown in figure 3.9.11. A small piece of spiral piano wire is

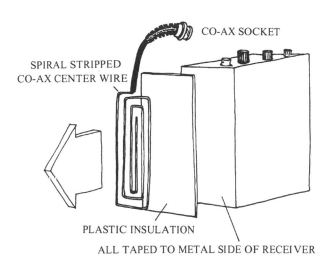

Figure 3.9.12 An aerial on the receiver for total yaggi-phobes.

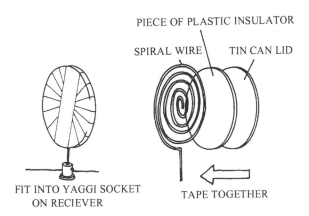

Figure 3.9.11 A simple aerial for local tracking.

fitted into the yaggi socket on the receiver. On one side of it is a metal tin lid separated by a piece of plastic as insulation. This shields it from incoming radio signals from behind, thus making it directional. It is excellent for ranges of about 500 meters and handy for locating hack hawks in woods, or hawks on kills in farm crops. It is all you need for flying Harris hawks or accipiters. A progression from this is shown in figure 3.9.12 and makes the receiver directional over local distances; it is extremely convenient.

I carry the receiver in a central pocket of the hawking bag so that it is cushioned from shock and protected from rain. It is in its own bag with a flap top fixed by velcro. In a pocket inside the flap is an earphone. This is indispensable in stormy weather, effectively doubling the range of the receiver.

The yaggi is a piece of equipment which is easy to learn to hate. There are more user-friendly

designs with arms made of flexible tape for use in woodland, or which fold down completely to a 30 centimeter pack which fits in the hawking bag. I prefer this model because it is less of a hazard in the event of a fall when riding.

Car aerials are useful for the more desperate situations, together with large scale maps. I always carry a small flashlight in my hawking bag. In winter one is usually racing against the fading light and it is all too frequent to kill at dusk. With telemetry one can search all night but you need a flashlight with you. One evening I crawled within an arm's length of my New Zealander on a crow inside a thick hedge bottom before I could see her. A hawk left out overnight on a kill can cause a whole bundle of trouble.

Some of the more traditional falconers regard telemetry as "last-resort" equipment, to be used at most only once or twice a season. This is a perfectly valid approach, but I don't subscribe to it. Having been in the habit of using telemetry for long periods on wild falcons and on hack falcons one comes to regard telemetry as an extra sense, particularly useful in my case because I'm deaf in one ear and cannot tell the direction of sounds. One comes to look at a landscape from the viewpoint of radio waves, very much in the same way that flying teaches you to "see" air. I flew falcons for fourteen years prior to telemetry and being used to the discipline which that demanded, I appreciate all the more the possibilities and opportunities in hawking which have been opened by telemetry. A great deal of the hawking which I enjoy now would be folly to attempt without telemetry. Certainly, to obtain "classical" flights with big falcons, open country is always necessary, but there is a wide variety of hawking to be had in other terrain, and this is described in part seven. Most of the really spectacular hawking is to be had in hilly country with powerful air currents, the sky's answer to white water. To hawk such country requires control, trust—and reliable telemetry. Paradoxically, the person who is using telemetry on a daily basis and constantly checking and becoming familiar with his equipment, tends to be less likely to lose a bird than the person who only uses it in a crisis.

We have young people here every year who learn basic radio-tracking at hacking time. They get into difficulties for a number of reasons, for example they don't properly understand what all the different knobs on the receiver do, such as gain, volume, headphone socket, diminutor, and different frequency settings. They don't understand about peaks and nulls, about bounce and interference. Most of all, they fail to think carefully and deduce as much as they can from the signal. They don't know what a falcon soaring up and down just over a horizon sounds like, what signal to expect from a hawk down in a ditch or gully, what a faulty battery connection does to the signal, or a faulty antenna connection, how to sort out several signals all on close frequencies, and so on. All these things only come with experience, and one can either wait until it happens for real, or you can experiment first without risking your bird. The technology is really only as good as the person operating it.

## 3.10   Field equipment

It is a good idea to get together all the field gear you need in one bag or coat so that when you pick it up, you know it's all there. Alternatively stick a checklist on the dashboard of your car.

I take a radio receiver, earphone, and yaggi, a creance, a small flashlight, a lure, a pick-up or feed-up piece of meat, a killing knife, and a washable bag for quarry. Spare batteries and maps are kept in the car. The hawking bag has no buttons which might snag a lure-line and is high and secure so that I can run fast. Some "traditional" bags are a liability in this respect. When we are on horses I also take pliers and a walkie-talkie and equip each member of the Field with a hood and lure in their saddlebags. These lures are simple recall lures

with a 1.5 meter cord either wrapped round them or used as a loop over the shoulder (figure 3.10.1).

Figure 3.10.1 A simple recall lure of rubber inner tube. It is sometimes garnished with wings or meat.

During training we take thrown lures or exercise lures (figure 3.10.2 and 3). The use of these is explained in section 5.16.

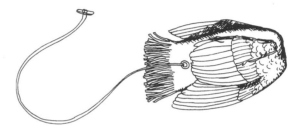

Figure 3.10.2 A thrown lure to teach waiting-on.

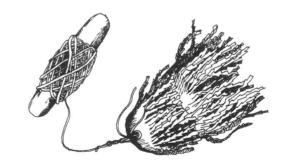

Figure 3.10.3 An exercise lure.

Figure 3.10.4 A clockwork pigeon lure.

A

B

C

A Red-tailed hawk *(Buteo jamaicensis)* adult female, North America.　　　　*Photo: David G. Fox*

B Snowy owl *(Nyctea scandiaca).*　　*Photo: David Hancock*

C Short-eared owl *(Asio flammeus).*　　*Photo: Miles Ertman*

D Ornate hawk-eagle *(Spizaetus ornatus).*
　　　　　　　　　　　　　　*Photo: D. Mancini*

E Bald eagle *(Haliaeetus leucocephalus).*
　　　　　　　　　　　　　　*Photo: David Hancock*

F Andean condor *(Vultur gryphus).*　　*Photo: David Hancock*

Preceding page: Juvenile male black gyrfalcon *(Falco rusticolus).*　　　　　　　　*Photo: Seth Anthony*

D

E

F

A

B

A Juvenile male hybrid Cooper/Harris *(Accipiter cooperii x Parabuteo unicinctus)*.

B Red kite *(Milvus milvus)*.

C Bicolored hawk *(Accipiter bicolor)* the females have short wings and extremely long tails. From the back they look like the micrasters.

*Photo: Harry McElroy*

D A fine adult female northern goshawk *(Accipiter gentilis)*.

*Photo: Dr. Walter Bednarek*

E Juvenile female northern goshawk *(Accipiter gentilis)*.

*Photo: Dr. Walter Bednarek*

C

D

E

A

B

C

D

E

Opposite page: Young female gyr/saker x saker.
*Photo: Seth Anthony*

A Female prairie falcon *(Falco mexicanus)*.      *Photo: Miles Ertman*

B Female African pygmy falcon *(Polihierix semitorquatus)*.      *Photo: David Hancock*

C Male New Zealand falcon *(Falco novaeseelandiae)*, Maclaren Bay, Adams Island, Auckland.
     *Photo: N. Hyde.*

D A designer falcon 'Cocktail' half New Zealand falcon, quarter gyr, quarter Peale's peregrine, flying
at 520 g (18.6 oz.) he took over 70 corvids in his first season.      *Photo: Martyn Paterson.*

E Young female peregrine *(Falco peregrinus)*.      *Photo: Seth Anthony*

F Adult female altai falcon *(Falco cherrug altaicus)*.

F

A

B

C

A  Stud birds should be selected carefully. This gyrkin 'Reiver' is well proportioned and has sired many good hunting birds.

B-E  In addition to being measured, each new potential breeder is photographed.

D

E

Weathering and imprint pens are along the front. The top window opens to pens at the back for natural pairs.

The facilities at Patuxent for breeding large numbers of American kestrels for research.

Pens for female imprint falcons.

A  A female peregrine bows and eechips prior to copulation.

B  This gyr/peregrine chups in his nest whenever I am in earshot.

A

B

C  This gyrkin is stimulated by the stuffed female posing for copulation.

C

D  Soon he begins to mount the pad, which is easier for semen collection.

D

A Bob Berry's young gryfalcons being socially reared in Wyoming. Sometimes an older chick will be treated as a parent by the younger ones.

B These are minimalist pens for big falcons. There are two nest ledges with access doors to the hide and mirrored one-way glass for viewing. The pen number '17' is for the CCTV.

C When you are stuck indoors writing a book the least you can do is have a falcon nesting on your office windowsill.

A

B

C

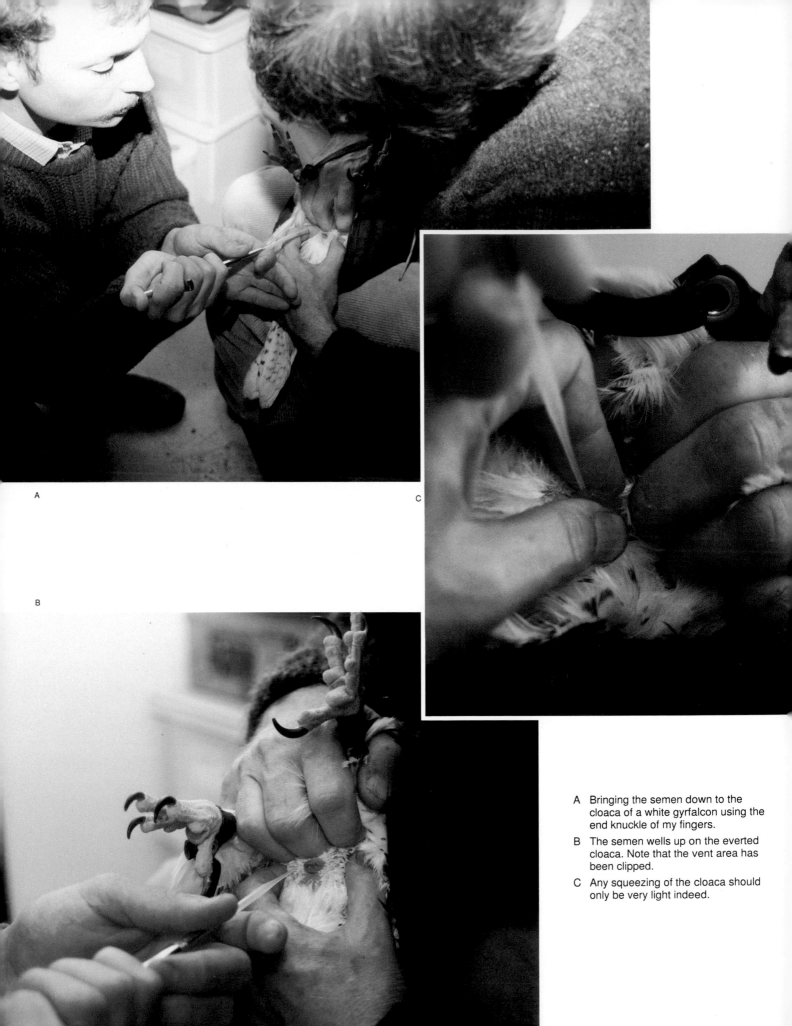

A  Bringing the semen down to the
   cloaca of a white gyrfalcon using the
   end knuckle of my fingers.

B  The semen wells up on the everted
   cloaca. Note that the vent area has
   been clipped.

C  Any squeezing of the cloaca should
   only be very light indeed.

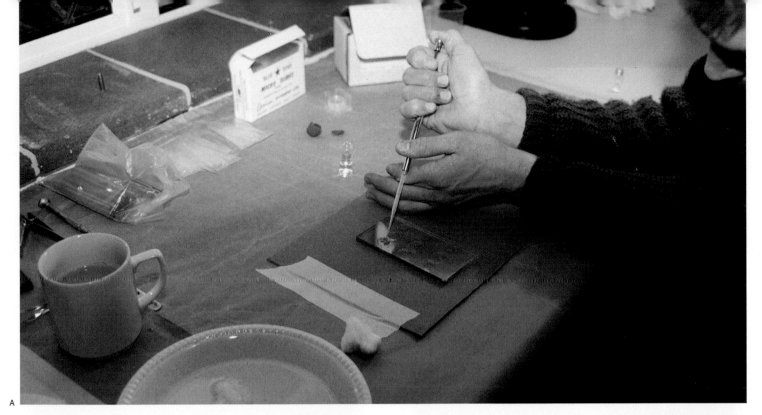

A

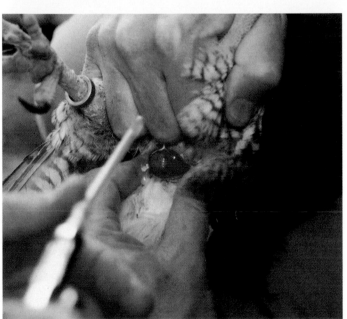

B

C

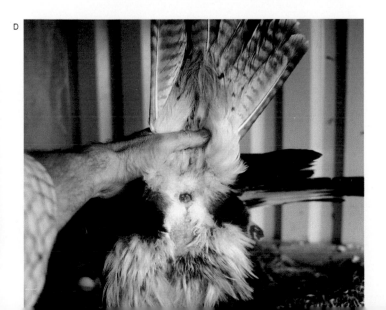

D

A  Mixing the semen with extender on a glass plate.
B  Everting a female peregrine to locate the oviduct.
C  Inseminating a female peregrine.
D  An imprint common buzzard stands for copulation, exposing her cloaca and brood patch.

A    A fresh undeveloped falcon egg on the candler.

B    This falcon egg is about 10 days old. The chorioallantois is spreading around the shell giving characteristic half shading.

C    This 15 day old falcon egg is now completely covered inside by the chorioallantois and has a nice rosy glow.

D    This falcon egg has died. It has been 25 days in the incubator and has an air cell but died about ten days earlier. It has soft blotched and clear areas which drift slowly when the egg is turned.

E    This Harris egg is about to pip. The air cell is drawing down.

F    This falcon chick was overweight and failed to hatch. The yolk sac is still unretracted.

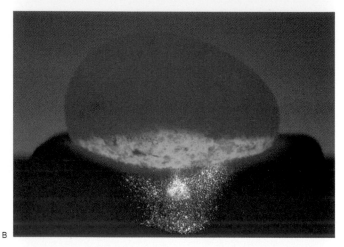

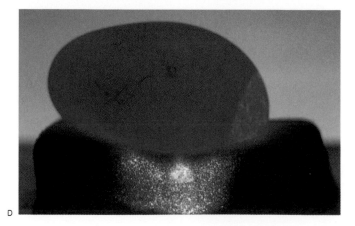

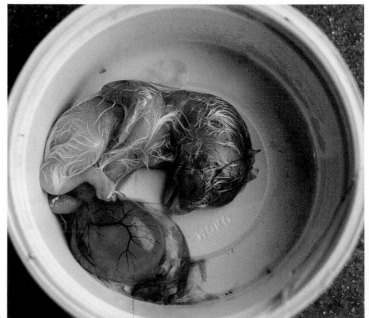

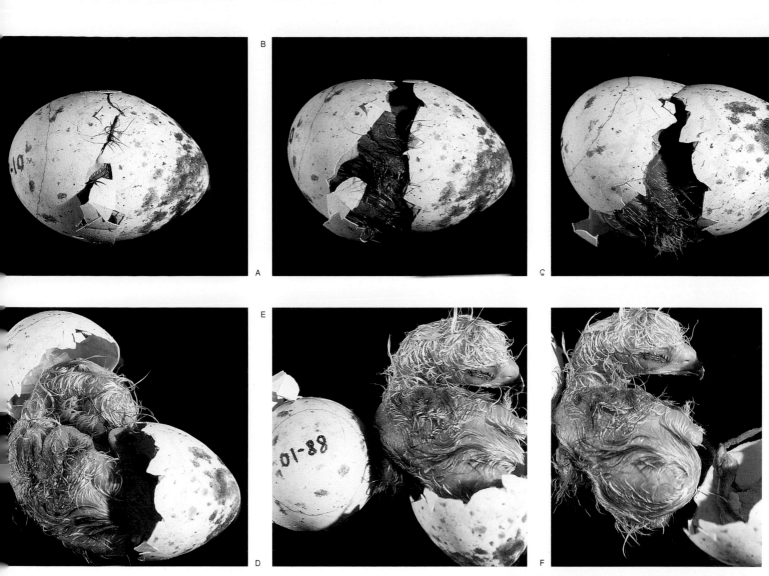

A - F  A Welsh red kite chick cuts around the shell and kicks itself free.  *Photos: Seth Anthony*

G  This young chick is one of 47 chicks returned to the wild in Wales and England as part of the program to help kites.

A  This old imprint saker 'Destiny' is ideal for rearing groups of chicks until they can be fostered onto natural pairs.
*Photo: Martyn Paterson*

B  A common buzzard foster-rearing young red kites.

C  Bob Berry socially rearing his gyrfalcons.

D  Accipitrid hawks, such as this common buzzard, hold the food in their beaks, waiting for it to be snatched by the chicks. Falcons, on the other hand, actually place the food into the chicks' mouths.

Opposite page: This peregrine has hatched one chick and the other eggs have pipped.
*Photo: David Hancock*

A

A  The hood should just clear the angle of the beak.
*Photo: Seth Anthony*

B  These chicks have been fostered on to a pair of white gyr/altai sakers who do not like being photographed.  *Photo: Martyn Paterson*

C  A bunch of baby gyr hybrids and kites. What will their futures be?

D  Fledgling sakers in Kazakhstan have been fitted with back pack radio tags to monitor their dispersal, behavior, and return from migration.
*Photo: Dr. R. E. Kenward*

B

C

D

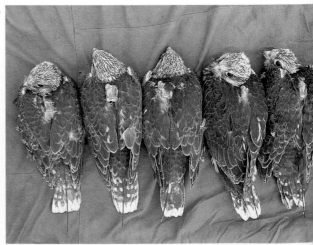

Young sakers at hack in Wales in a landscape very reminiscent of Kazakhstan.

Young gyr/altai sakers at hack in Wales, wearing leg mounted radio tags.

*Martyn Paterson*

A

B

A  Imprinted falcons use a windowsill as an eyrie while at tame hack.

B  The youngsters spend much of the time asleep.

C  This young gry/saker and my wife's horse 'Henry' get acquainted.

C

A

B

C

D

E

A  Harris hawks learn from each other.
*Photo: R. Lowery*

B  A New Zealand falcon teaches its young to chase by releasing prey for it.

C  Our hack box in Northumberland.
*Photo: Martyn Paterson*

D  This young falcon was electrocuted. Man-made hazards are increasing all the time.
*Photo: Seth Anthony*

E  The falcons soon gain strength on the wing.
*Photo: Seth Anthony*

A

B

A Small boys are very good at jumping into rushes to flush rabbits
for Harris hawks. *Photo: Seth Anthony*

B This red-tail must quickly take the rabbit by the head.
*Photo: W. Wübken*

C This experienced goshawk has quickly seized the rabbit by the
head and killed it. *Photo: Dr. Walter Bednarek*

C

B

A  Seth Layman exercises a young falcon to a swung lure.

B  The falcon learns to turn sharply.

C  Once the falcons have gone to Arabia, Khamiz calls them for exercise at our hunting camp.

D  Martyn Paterson exercises a peregrine/saker to the pole lure.

C

D

HAWKING IN INDIA

A  Sakers being manned in the streets of Bharnagar in pre-partition India.

B  High-jumping several sakers at a time in India.           *Photos: Drs. F. and J. Craighead.*

C  Exercising a saker to the lure in India.

A

B

C

A  Tracking hares in the Empty Quarter. Insert: The saker, her shadow, and the hare all converge.
B  Mohamed Al Bowardi picks up his falcon by covering the hare with sand.
C  Khalifa Saif al Qumzi and I take a hare after a lot of running.

A

B

A  Picking up a young New Zealand falcon from a red grouse, Kinlochewe, Scotland.

*Photo: Tom Bailey*

B  A male peregrine plucks his grouse at Kinlochewe. I get a sandwich and a young dog gets a good sniff.

*Photo: Tom Bailey*

C  Martin Jones' old grouse-hawking cottage on the North York moors.

D  A hacked male gyr/peregrine (right) sold to Geoffrey Pollard. A good solid falcon with broad shoulders and a wide chest.

*Photo: Geoffrey Pollard*

C

D

A

A Base camp for sage-grouse hawking in Nevada.
B An old gyrkin takes his sage grouse.
C Steve Baptiste with young white gyrfalcon hawking in Nevada.

C

B

A

C

D

A  A New Zealand falcon hawking Gordon Robinson's gray partridges
   in Devon.                                              *Photo: Barbro Fox*

B  Peregrine with guinea fowl in South Africa.      *Photo: Dr. E. E. Oettlé*

C  Hungarian partridges in North Idaho.            *Photo: Alison Meyer*

D  Lorenzo Machin hawking red-legged partridges in Spain. They will
   not lie to the point in this open ground.

E  Partridge hawking in Spain. Hawks which can reach each other
   must never be left unattended. Game hawks may sit quietly but
   crow hawks certainly don't. Our team is three female *brookei*
   peregrines, a male gyr/saker/peregrine and a male gyr/saker.

F  After hawking in Spain—little snacks!

B

E

F

A

A A falconer in Kazakhstan with his eagle. She is a beerkut *(Aquila chrysaetos)*.

B Members of the Japanese Falconers Association hawking pheasants and Chinese bamboo partridges near Tokyo, using passage and home-bred goshawks. Center is Mr. Kaoni Hanami, 16th Headmaster of the Suwa Hawking School. He attended the Emperor of Japan from 1924 for almost half a century. *Photo: Mitsuharu Tanaka and Zenjiro Tagomori*

C The weathering ground at the 1993 NAFA Meet at Kearney, Nebraska.

D A passage female sparrowhawk in Turkey fitted with a halsband and used for catching quail. *Photo: Ali Baycin*

B

C

D

Some of our crow falcons weathering in Northumberland.

*Photos: Seth Anthony*

A hawking meet in Northumberland. Mounted (left to right): Peter Owens, Steve Layman, Tony Owens, the author, Dr. Cecilia Lindberg, Barbro Fox. Standing: Seth Layman and Martyn Paterson. Pony trap: Jeremy Smith, Katie O'Neal.

A  Waiting for crows on passage.  *Photo: Laurie Campbell*

B  Replacing the jesses on a peregrine/saker which has killed a crow. The field is Barbro Fox, Tony and Peter Owens and Dr. Jeremy Scratcherd. This flight was two kilometers (1½ miles).  *Photo: David Taylor*

C  Preparing to slip a black gyr/altai saker 'Black Jack.'  *Photo: Seth Anthony*

D  A flight in progress.  *Photo: Seth Anthony*

E  A crow is knocked down by a falcon.  *Photo: Seth Anthony*

F  A cast of gyr/sakers has brought a crow down to a wall.  *Photo: Seth Anthony*

G  Hot horses and a full crop.  *Photo: Seth Anthony*

Both photos are of hawking in Abu Dhabi where houbara are still occasionally hawked from camels.

A

B

C

A Sometimes we follow a track for a kilometer or more.
B On hard sand the hare leaves little trace.
C Hare tracks in soft sand are easy to follow.

A

B

A   A pause for rest.
B   Tracking houbara on foot.
C   Mr. Mohammed Al Bowardi takes a hare with his passage saker.

C

A

A  Coming back into camp.

B  Manning falcons in camp.

C  At the end of the day, endless cups of gower and time for stories and companionship.

D  Salukis with the camel boy, Abu Dhabi.

B

D

C

D

A As soon as it gets light we prepare to go hawking.

B Khameez trains a newly molted gyrfalcon.

C Khalifa Saif mans his saker which is attached to a mangala. The passage falcons of Arabia are among the best manned birds in the world.

D A saker at exercise.

B

C

A  After two months crow hawking our falcons adjust to a new life in the desert.

B  One of our gyr/saker/sakers 'Nahar.' Now in her fourth season, she has taken houbara, stone curlew, and many hares.

C  Most passage sakers in Arabia are purchased through dealers, such as these in Peshawar.

D  At the end of the season many of the wild-caught sakers are released to the wild. Khalifa Saif has cut the jesses from this falcon at the Straits of Hormuz, where she can make her way back to Afghanistan and her breeding grounds.

A

D

B

A  Peter Walters Davies collects young kite chicks from us for return to nests in the wild. Forty-seven chicks have now been hatched from threatened eggs and released in Wales and England. Many are now breeding.

B  Owls are not very suitable for tethering and displaying at shows. They are better displayed at home in their breeding aviaries.

C  ICONA's breeding program for the Spanish imperial eagle near Toledo, relies on technical support from falconer/breeders.

D  A baby kite about to be given to a foster parent so that it will be naturally imprinted.

E  The notorious animal souk in Sharjah. I have seen many kestrels, harriers, and kites caged here, as well as hunting falcons.

C

E

A Flying a peregrine, a New Zealand falcon, and a merlin during a course in Wales.

B Dr. Ken Riddle and Dr. Robert Kenward attach a back pack to a saker at the Abu Dhabi Falcon Research Hospital. The tag allows the falcon to be tracked after its return to the wild at the end of the hawking season.

C Oscar Mitumbili hawking guinea fowl in Zimbabwe.
*Photo: Ron Hartley*

Following page: Nine-year-old Ahmed Al Qumzi with one of our domestic falcons. The future lies with our children.

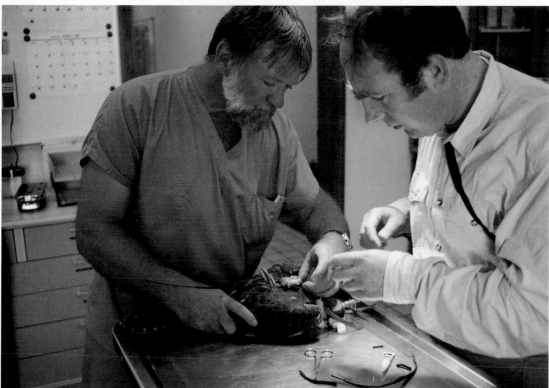

The clockwork pigeon lure has two uses: it can either be used instead of a live pigeon to get back a reluctant falcon, or it can be made in the form of quarry, such as a crow, and used for entering. The mechanism inside flaps two stubby arms to which are bound real wings. The head is wobbly with glass eyes. The mechanism is embedded inside a foam body which is covered in feathers stuck onto wet latex or Copydex in the way described by Frank Beebe. We are experimenting with various forms at the moment. It has to be strong enough to survive repeated attacks and yet be soft enough not to harm the falcon. In practice one can usually hide the pigeon once the falcon returns and throw out the normal lure as a substitute.

I always carry a lightweight pair of field-glasses from the day the first hawk is on a creance. It amazes me how many people manage without them. Often they don't. During exercise and when crow-hawking I take a good pair of Zeiss glasses which are invaluable for assessing the falcons' fitness and for spotting crows.

A good horn or bone whistle is handy for the dogs or for the hawks. Metal ones stick to your lips in winter. A light crook stick is good for beating and hooks over my left arm when I need my right hand free. Sometimes I loft the hawk over the pointing dog so that she has a good start. When I am training her to do this I put my hawking glove on the handle.

## 3.11  Perches

During intensive handling, such as during training, it is often necessary to tether a raptor on a perch. This should be regarded as a necessary evil; as soon as it is no longer necessary, the bird should be free-lofted. It will stay healthier and fitter un-tethered.

Perches are the source of an unending catalogue of disasters, some of which are described in 5.24. Birds either escape from them, or get injured by them or develop foot complaints from them. A well-designed and made perch costs little more than a bad one so it makes sense to use the best equipment from the start.

In 1974, I sent a falcon to an acquaintance who placed her on a brand-new lathe-turned block "just like in the books." I advised him to change the polished flat top for something more domed and rough. Human nature being what it is, he didn't want to ruin his smart new block, so he left it. Six

weeks later I had a phone call: the bird couldn't stand properly, could she be sent down to me for treatment? The flexor tendons to the hind toes had collapsed. I hacked her free for three months and the condition stabilized, but there was no cure. Foolishly perhaps, I sent her back, and she was dead in a few more months. Her brother, which we kept, lived to be 16 and a great-great-grandfather.

Traditionally, falcons are kept on cylindrical blocks which supposedly equate to a rock, while accipiters and buteos are given a narrower perch similar to a branch. There is no real anatomical or ecological basis for this; if an accipiter prefers a block then use one. Have you asked your bird what she prefers?

I was a teenager in the sixties and rarely wore shoes. To this day I go barefoot all through the summer months when I can. I can really sympathize with a falcon on a block, and appreciate how comfortable or uncomfortable different surfaces are. We use astroturf on all the falcon perches, for over a hundred raptors, most of them large falcons, and we have never had a bird develop bumblefoot. Some of these birds have had bilateral surgery for bumblefoot in the Middle East before being retired for breeding and they are fine. Bumblefoot is 99 percent preventable, and it's all to do with perches, diet, and hygiene.

The best descriptions of perches and their construction are given by Kimsey and Hodge. We opt for the very simplest designs with the minimum of moving parts. When the climate is variable, wood tends to split and iron rusts, so it is worth using more permanent materials.

The falcon block we use is made of resin-coated reinforced concrete with stainless steel fittings (figures 3.11.1 and 2). We also have some hardwood or nylon ones. The top is at least 20 centimeters (8 ins) to prevent the risk of straddling. The astroturf is held in position by a sleeve of rubber inner tube. If a drumskin of rubber is placed over the top under the astroturf, it is possible to irrigate the top with disinfectant solution, like a paddling pool, for treating foot injuries. The block is tapered to stop the leash binding and has a very loose ring which cannot jam. The attachment ring for the loop leash protrudes slightly to make the ring swivel better. The tie point is at least 20 centimeters (8 ins) above the ground to reduce the risk of breaking a leg during a bate, and the leash is 40 centimeters (16 ins).

The only other type which is fairly safe is a

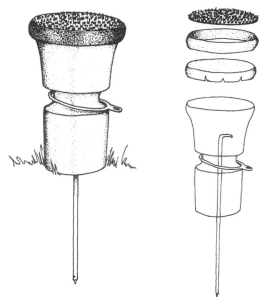

Figure 3.11.1 A falcon block.      Figure 3.11.2 A falcon block, construction details.

block with a loose sleeve around the center pin to reduce the risk of tangling. This has a low ring point which is less desirable. There are various other types of falcon blocks which can cause injuries, such as the ones in figures 3.11.3 and 4. The

Figure 3.11.3 When jesses straddle a block.

3.11.4 When the leash wraps round the block.

arab block, or Wakr, is good in desert conditions and very portable. They are not designed for hawks to be left unattended for long, as is common in western falconry.

For accipiters the bow perch shown in figure 3.11.5 takes some beating. I have never known it to tangle or snag. The area where the hawk stands is covered in rough, coarse leather. If rope is used it should be thin so that the ring does not catch on the grooves. I have seen a sparrowhawk break off a claw on a rope-bound perch. Other materials, such as alkathene, can also be used; in this case grooves can be cut in it longitudinally to give the hawk an uneven surface without hindering the ring. If the hawk is liable to bate violently, she may fracture a leg owing to the low tie-down point. One way to reduce the risk of this is to stretch a short "bowstring" of rubber at each end of the bow as shown in figure 3.11.6. There should be nothing

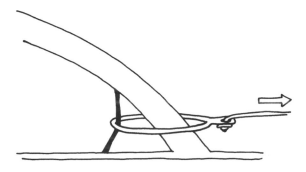

Figure 3.11.6 A rubber shock absorber on a bowperch.

preventing the ring from pulling freely over the perch (figure 3.11.7).

An alternative which is popular in America, is the Meng tail-saver perch which has a high tie point and causes less stress on the legs.

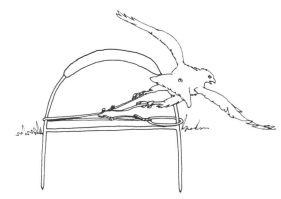

Figure 3.11.7 What happens when the ring does not slide easily over the perch.

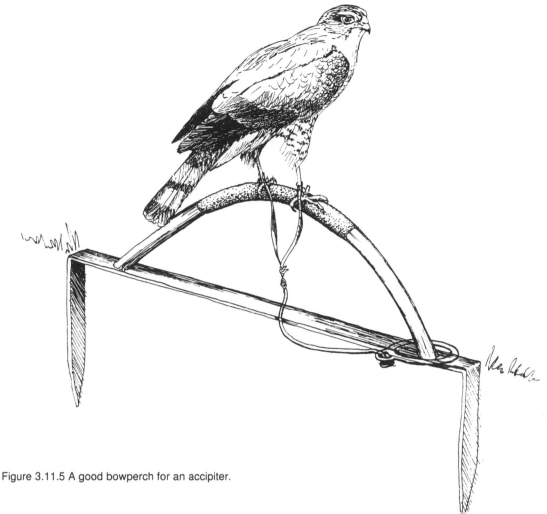

Figure 3.11.5 A good bowperch for an accipiter.

When placed out to weather on a day perch the hawk is very vulnerable to the weather, predators and humans. Eagles, buzzards, harriers, goshawks, owls, crows, magpies, polecats, mink, ferrets, cats, foxes, dogs, badgers, raccoons, and snakes have all killed hawks out weathering. Cattle may break in over the fence. A trained hawk flying nearby may attack a tethered one, and humans may injure, frighten, or steal a hawk. Two people I know, who leave their hawks out all night in open porches, have both lost four in one night to foxes and yet both still leave their (remaining) hawks out. Designs for safe weathering areas are given by Kimsey and Hodge and they are essential for the person who has to leave his hawk unattended while tethered.

During the day, depending on the weather, the hawk should be offered a bath and drinking water. Most baths are too small. Wild hawks often bath in water out of their depth and many is the time I have trotted downstream as my goshawk has had a thorough ten-minute bath floating down a river. The bath water should come halfway up her chest. Shy or stressed hawks will not bath except in natural type conditions in privacy and it is quite easy for a rehabilitating hawk to become dehydrated standing right next to a pan of water. The desert falcons and kestrels often like a dust bath and some fine dry sand can be offered in a tray. A handful of pea gravel as rangle (see 5.11) is often appreciated by tethered raptors.

## 3.12 Night quarters and temporary quarters

While raptors are being kept tethered, they need somewhere absolutely safe as night-quarters. In moderate climates they can stay out in secure sheltered weatherings, but in cold or wet weather they must be brought in otherwise they could suffer illnesses caused by damp or frost. In the wild, most raptors, except harriers and some owls, roost high

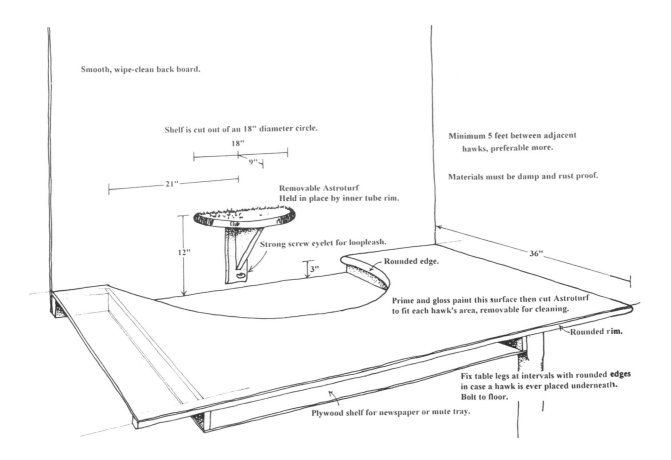

Smooth, wipe-clean back board.

Shelf is cut out of an 18" diameter circle.

18"

9"

21"

Minimum 5 feet between adjacent hawks, preferable more.

Materials must be damp and rust proof.

Removable Astroturf
Held in place by inner tube rim.

12"

Strong screw eyelet for loopleash.

36"

Rounded edge.

3"

Prime and gloss paint this surface then cut Astroturf to fit each hawk's area, removable for cleaning.

Rounded rim.

Fix table legs at intervals with rounded **edges** in case a hawk is ever placed underneath. Bolt to floor.

Plywood shelf for newspaper or mute tray.

Figure 3.12.1 The individual shelf perch, construction detail.

off the ground in an airy place sheltered from the prevailing wind and from ground predators.

The screen perch (figure 5.24.2) has killed many hawks, including my old hawk-eagle "Gorgon" who was killed within two days when I lent him to a friend with a screen perch. The best alternative for falcons is the individual shelf-perch (figure 3.12.1 and 2). It is important that all the measurements are exactly right. The measurements in 3.12.1 are for any species of falcon on a loop leash 16 inches long and jesses 6 inches long. For the first few days of training, while the falcon is still jumpy, she is kept hooded at night.

Accipiters can also be placed on the shelf perch but tend to be decorative with their mutes when facing the wall. For them we use a long perch (figure 3.12.3 and 4). The perch is covered in astroturf on a batten wrapped in rubber inner tube so that it is all sterilizable. A removable polythene sheet runs down the back wall and across the shelf. Newspaper soaks up the mutes and is changed daily.

Figure 3.12.2 Gyr on shelf perch.

Figure 3.12.3 The long shelf perch.

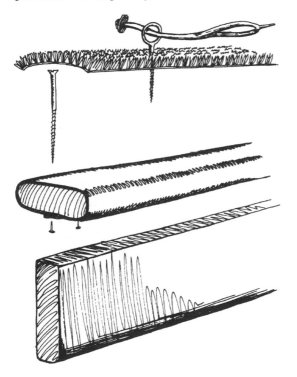

Figure 3.12.4 The long shelf perch, construction detail.

Both the shelf perch and the long perch can be designed to fold down against the wall. A garage can thus accommodate several birds during the season but returned to normal use for the rest of the year. Alternatively, when space is short, a junior falconer can be provided with a bunk bed under-

neath as a sort of human guard dog. In this case he or she is called an under-falconer.

When away from home, it is often necessary to use various sheds as temporary night quarters. This is when accidents happen. The commonest is that one hawk kills another. Figure 3.12.5 shows a temporary arrangement which is fairly safe, provided that no predator can enter the room. Two

Figure 3.12.5 A temporary indoor night perch for two falcons.

squared blocks of wood are nailed from below onto the underside of a pole. This stops it rolling and raises it off the ground so that newspaper can be slid underneath. The bark and any soft wood is blazed off with an ax so that a staple can be hammered in securely. The best staples are the large barbed ones. The staple attaches a Sampo swivel to which the hawk is attached by a short loop leash.

It is never a wise move to tether a hungry accipiter in the same room as other hawks. She will be bating to kill them and they will be uneasy. During trips, accipiters are best kept in boxes during the night. In Britain it is illegal to keep a hawk in a box too small for it to spread its wings except when transporting it. Car hawk boxes are a very sensible arrangement and the hawks love them. Most will bate to get into their box and often will rouse and tuck a foot up before you have finished securing them. These traveling boxes should be well-ventilated and cleaned out daily.

Traveling boxes are especially useful in that hawks can be left unattended in them for several hours provided the weather is cool, and that inquisitive people can't see in. Falcons normally travel hooded on long-perches, in which case they must be attended at all times. A variety of designs are given in Kimsey and Hodge which is worth obtaining before you start. Traveling boxes should always be darkened with no mesh or sharp objects inside. Many welfare or rehabilitation organizations still transport injured wild raptors in weld mesh cat cages, which is at best disgraceful. The approved airline (IATA) design for raptor traveling boxes is not much better, with drinking and food troughs and various access holes. I normally

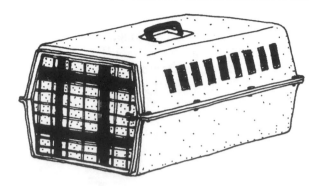

Figure 3.12.6 A portable kennel. The mesh door has cardboard taped on the interior.

avoid shipping raptors with airlines which insist on these unsuitable boxes. One of the handiest items of equipment to have is a large plastic portable kennel, designed for shipping dogs and cats by air (figure 3.12.6). With a mat of astroturf on the floor, they can be used for air-freighting raptors, they can be used to move injured or sick raptors and they can be used as overnight observation boxes for sick raptors needing quiet and warmth. They take down into two halves for cleaning and storage.

## 3.13   Daily records, routine, and hygiene

While a hawk is tethered, it is normally either in training or being flown daily. A record chart is important to monitor progress from day to day and from year to year. I sometimes refer back 15 or more years. An example of a simple basic chart is given in figure 3.14.1 and a blank is in the appendix. Charts are invaluable when you are flying several hawks at once, or when more than one person is flying a bird, or when teaching a young

falconer. On hawking trips I keep a hawking diary with names of visitors and descriptions of flights, but this is all icing on the cake. Your daily chart is a working tool.

You should also have a daily and weekly routine to keep everything clean and tidy. Saturday or Sunday morning is a good time to have the weekly thorough clean out, removing all soiled material, disinfecting perches, checking for faulty equipment and generally setting everything fair. Young handlers of any animals should learn this basic discipline right from the start, before they actually take responsibility for a bird themselves. As you sit and read this, would you be happy to show me round your birds right now, or would you need to do a quick clean up before I came?

Routine cleaning will help prevent disease and keep birds healthy into old age. As part of your equipment you need proper poultry grade disinfectants, hoses, scrubbing brushes, possibly a pressure washer, fumigation materials, and a basic first aid box for both raptors and humans. You also need proper facilities for storing and preparing food. There is no veterinary section to this book because the emphasis is strongly on prevention, rather than cure. Statistically we find that with proper husbandry we need to call a vet approximately once every hundred raptor years. Your job is to prevent illness and check the birds carefully so that when something does look worrying you can contact a specialist vet promptly and with good back-up information.

So far in the book we have looked at the bird itself, breeding a youngster, and assembling the equipment you need before you can start any hands on training. We still need to look at how the bird's mind works before we are ready to take a raptor on the fist.

Sparrowhawk chasing blackbird.

# 4 Development

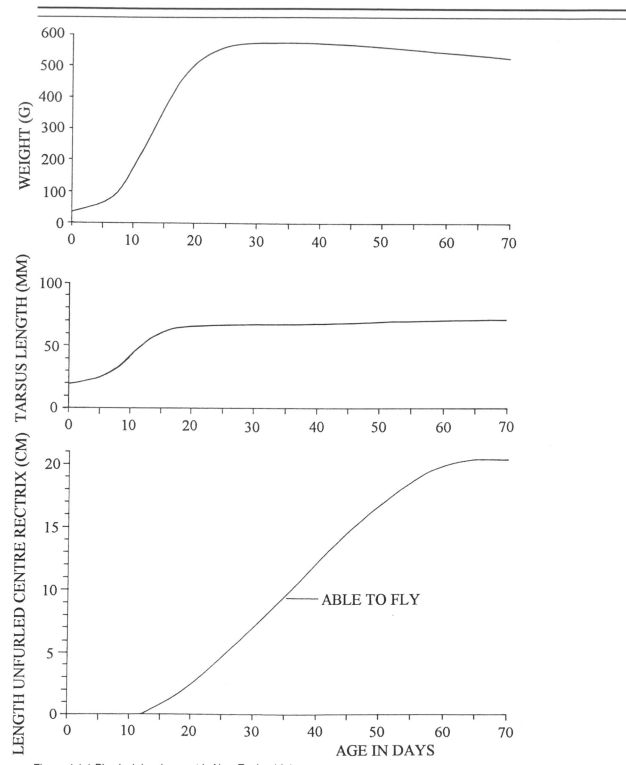

Figure 4.1.1 Physical development in New Zealand falcons.

# and Behavior

## 4.1   Physical development

Growth follows two stages. First the chick's energy is devoted to bodily growth and then, as it nears the full size, its energy is directed into growing its feathers.

Newly hatched raptor chicks are covered with a fine coat of natal down, dense in species from cold climates and sparser in the hot desert species. The occipital muscles at the back of the head which are used for pipping the shell are still swollen and the chick barely has strength to lift its head. Often the eyes are closed. The chick responds to the soft calls of its mother by raising its head briefly and gaping for food.

During the first week the chick rapidly gains weight. Although the yolk sac is used up after about three or four days, the abdomen grows tremendously to cope with the food intake and the chick is virtually a living gut, a food processing machine.

After 7–8 days for small hawks, and 12–14 days in large hawks and falcons, the second, woollier down coat grows through the natal down and enables the chick to control its own temperature and survive comfortably for short spells without brooding. This frees the mother for hunting and she is able to assist the male in catering for their almost insatiable appetites. The parents spend

Figure 4.1.3 New Zealand falcons at 8 days old.

Figure 4.1.4 New Zealand falcons at 14 days old.

Figure 4.1.2 A New Zealand falcon at one day old.

most of their time obtaining sufficient food. During this period the long bones of the body are growing rapidly, as is the whole skeleton. By about 18 days for small hawks, and 22–26 days for larger species, the chick has reached full adult weight. Any deficiency in the quantity or quality of the diet during this growth stage will result in a slowing or stunting of growth and may also result in porosis, rickets, or other deficiencies, some of which are lethal or irreversible.

As the long bones begin to harden, the bird begins to look more hawklike and may be able to shuffle about or take a few faltering steps. Now its efforts are put into feather growth and the prima-ries and tail feathers are sprouting well. In a few more days the chick is a harlequin of feathers and down and then, quite soon, it appears fully feath-ered. Any dietary deficiency at this stage will cause stress marks on the growing plumage. Al-though the chick may appear fully feathered, the flight feathers are still short and heavy with the sheaths still in blood. Much time is spent in preen-ing, playing, and wing exercising with bouts of snoozing in between.

At this time of bone and feather growth, the chick's senses and brain are also developing. It can see and hear well and recognizes its parents. This is the most sensitive period for the various aspects of imprinting (see section 4.7). How it is treated both physically and mentally during these brief weeks will profoundly affect it for the rest of its life.

By four weeks old, small hawks are starting to fly. Larger species follow at 5–6 weeks. But it is some further time before they are hard-penned. Feathers which appear to have lost their sheaths may still have soft shafts inside the feather sockets and it is best to keep the youngsters well fed for a week or so beyond this point. The skeleton too is still calcifying and the joints firming up. The heads of the long bones are still not properly fused to the shafts. Newly fledged hawks should be handled very carefully to avoid excessive strains or vio-lence. Young accipiters, if tethered, may not only sprain a limb but also may damage their leg scales which are still soft at this time.

Modern methods of domestic breeding and rearing chicks have resulted in a high success rate in the physical side of development. Most of the problems which arise are on the mental side and therefore most of this part will be devoted to be-havior and its origins. It is much easier to diagnose a physical problem than a mental one. Before we

Figure 4.1.6 New Zealand falcons at 45 days old begging for food from a parent.

can go on and train a hawk, we have first to under-stand the bird's natural behavior and the factors influencing it.

## 4.2    The components of behavior

The behavior of a bird of prey is the product of three components and their interactions. The first component is innate or inherited and as such is virtually unalterable. The second is imprinted on the bird in early life and is largely unalterable thereafter, but the third, learned behavior, can be modified during the life of the bird. For those rearing or handling captive raptors, who may wish to rear a bird suitable for release to the wild, or one that is optimal for falconry or for breeding, it is essential to understand what can, and what cannot, be done.

These components can be listed as follows:
Inherited or innate behavior.
   – Specific instincts.
   – Individual temperament.
   – Biological urges and drives.
   – Memory.
Imprinted behavior.
   – Imprinting on parents.
   – Imprinting on siblings.
   – The fear response.
   – Imprinting on future sexual partner.
   – Imprinting on nest type, site, and habitat.
Learned behavior.
   Involuntary learning.
   – Habituation.
   – Classical conditioning.
   – Operant conditioning.
   – Association.
   – Trauma learning.

Figure 4.1.5 New Zealand falcons at 22 days old.

Voluntary learning.
- Insight learning.
- Experience.

## 4.3 Inherited behavior

Every raptor is hatched with its own individual "biological program," a legacy from its forebears who themselves, generation after generation, have been among the elitist percentage which has survived long enough to breed. Their program has three separate but interacting components: specific instincts, individual temperaments, and biological drives. Each bird too has a different capacity for storing information in its memory.

This genetic or inherited component has the potential to make the bird behave in certain ways, if and when the appropriate circumstances arise during the bird's lifetime. In captivity, these circumstances may not happen and so the bird may never express that particular behavior, or, alternatively, it may express it in a different or displaced way which may be puzzling to the handler who does not understand the origin of the behavior.

### Specific instincts

These are instincts which are characteristic of the species and they center primarily on the corpus striatum (section 1.7). The buzzard, for example, quite apart from differences in structure and physiology, is quite different from a goshawk. Its temperament matches its anatomy and is geared toward catching small, slow-moving prey. Similarly, although the peregrine and the goshawk are both rapacious in that they are exclusively predators of vertebrates, their temperaments and their approaches to the problems of hunting are quite different. Their courtship and nesting behaviors differ too.

In general, those species which attack active quarry, such as birds, over short distances, tend to live in or near woodland and to have very fast reactions and an impulsive nature. To our eyes they seem to over react to stimuli and appear fearful. Their nervous systems are so finely tuned that, as a group, they are the most prone to fits and nervous disorders. It seems as if the reaction from stimulus to response is so fast that it cuts out the conscious part of the brain which therefore gets small chance to identify and make a decision about the stimulus. Thus the goshawk may see a small movement and impulsively launch an almost im-

mediate attack. Only when the bird is actually in flight does its brain process the signal, identify it as a piece of uninteresting thistledown, and abort the attack. As well as the accipiters, the forest-dependent hawk-eagles and the Micrastur forest-falcons show similar behavior. In a wooded habitat, events happen suddenly and the successful raptor is the one which can react in time to exploit the fleeting chance before the prey can reach the safety of nearby cover.

Species which attack active quarry over long distances live in the open and their attacks are often premeditated, tactical, and unspontaneous. These species, such as the falcons, tend to have more equable temperaments. Of the large falcons, the peregrine is probably the most specialized predator and tends to have a fairly consistent and uninquiring temperament. This can make them rather dull birds in captivity but reliable performers in the field. The merlin, the gyrfalcon, and the New Zealand falcon, even when several years old, will often spend an hour at a time playing like cats with a twig or a prey item, catching it again and again. It is as if their mental energy is overflowing and needs an outlet.

More of bird behavior is instinctive than appears at first sight. In many situations, especially those which occur only once or twice in a bird's life and for which it is important that it is done correctly, it is more advantageous for the bird to do them instinctively than to have to learn them. For example, courtship behavior, copulation, nest-building, incubation, and rearing of young are all stereotyped instinctive behaviors. There is a small learning component—parents do learn to improve their feeding of small chicks for example—but by and large, first time breeders have almost as good a chance of producing young as experienced birds have.

It is not always advantageous for the whole program to be instinctive. Some elements may need to be learned, and learned rapidly. This is where imprinting (see 4.7) comes in. Birds learn to identify their parents quickly and certainly through imprinting and then their instinctive behavior patterns—food-begging and so on—can take over and make the bird act appropriately. Otherwise the chick could waste its energy begging at a tussock of grass or a passing seagull.

Some aspects of a bird's life rely entirely on instinct. It cannot be learned because the bird has no chance to learn it; it has to get it right first time.

Apart from breeding behavior, migration is a good example. The hawk may migrate along quite a complicated route navigating instinctively without help from its parents. Some of these traditional migration routes are programmed in a bird's genes and passed on from generation to generation.

Other aspects of a bird's life cannot be covered by instinct because they are much too variable. It appears for example that the various search and attack behavior patterns described in Part 6 are basically instinctive. They appear in a variety of genera in recognizable forms and when they are used by a young hawk for the first time they occur as complete sequences, such as the glide attack (6.13) or the ground-skimming indirect flying attack (6.11). Although the young hawk is equipped, according to its species, with its own repertoire of instinctive attack patterns, instinct cannot properly prepare it for the wide variety of prey it is likely to encounter, the prey's evasion tactics and the problems imposed by terrain. The hawk has to learn these by experience and use whichever attack styles are appropriate. It also learns of course, to improve its flying skills, its footing ability and its basic attack strategies. These are based on instinct but are improved by learning. The more specialized the hawk species is, the more its hunting behavior is governed by instinct. The more of a generalist or opportunist a species is, the more its behavior is shaped through learning.

It takes time for a hawk to gain this experience and develop hunting skills. Often two thirds die before succeeding (see 8.3). Only when a hawk has gained sufficient hunting skills to support not only itself, but also its family (an extra hunting load of perhaps 4–6 times), is it fit to breed. There is no point in a hawk becoming sexually mature before its hunting skills are adequate. Large falcons take two or more years to become sexually mature and they are also slow to peak in their hunting skills. Small hawks, such as merlins, kestrels, and sparrowhawks, not only become sexually mature sooner, but also become proficient at hunting more quickly. This may be because for them the direct flying attack (see 6.10) and, in the case of the merlin and sparrowhawks, the tail chase (see 6.12), are the most important attacks. These are the basic instinctive attack strategies. The more advanced strategies, such as the glide attack and indirect flying attack require detailed experience of the prey's reactions in order to be developed and this requires a maturation process.

This underlines the evolutionary balance between stupidity and intelligence. A hawk which can live by stereotyped innate hunting behavior is ready to breed before one with a long learning period. The latter may well die before breeding at all. The smaller hawks tend to have a shorter generation interval, breeding early and dying early. The strategists have a high juvenile mortality but are often long-lived.

Skilled adult strategists can exist in areas where there are perhaps only one tenth of the prey numbers which unskilled juveniles would need. Most of the attacks launched by experienced strategists are at opportunities which the naive youngster doesn't even recognize as opportunities. It is like the country boy coming to the big city looking for work. There are opportunities all around him but he doesn't realize where to look.

Nesting is timed so that at the period of peak food demand, when there are big chicks in the nest, there is also a maximum food supply. This timing is most obvious in species such as the Eleonora's falcon which depends on migrant passerines. But it is equally important that this supply of naive young prey continues long enough for the young raptors to develop their hunting skills, otherwise they will "miss the boat" and many will die.

Thus breeding, which has all the major components stereotyped or easily learned through imprinting, is mainly instinctive, whereas hunting behavior, although basically structured through instinct, has a large learning element so that the hawk adapts to the wide variety of contingencies it has to face to catch prey. The differences in emphasis of these two aspects of a hawk's life— breeding and hunting—are reflected in the failure rate; first time breeders are only marginally less successful than experienced ones whereas inexperienced hunters have a much higher risk of starving than have adults.

## 4.4　Individual temperaments

Individual birds of the same species have different temperaments, just as humans do. Some are placid, some are excitable, some are easy to teach, some are withdrawn. Except in cases involving changes in body chemistry there is little scope for altering temperament; this is beyond the frontiers of avian science at the moment. So the falconer has to rely on luck or good judgement in choosing a bird with a good temperament. Variety is the spice of life!

## 4.5   Biological urges and drives

Raptors are not static machines. Changes are going on in their body chemistry as they grow up and as the seasons go by. For example, young hawks chase their parents for food. The parent, rather than live quarry, is the stimulus for them to chase. Quite suddenly, perhaps triggered by a small loss in body weight, or by the parent releasing live prey, the youngsters' programs switch to prey seeking.

Once fully grown, other stages in the biological program occur. Some species are migratory. Abruptly one autumn day the otherwise trained and responsive hawk may fly away, completely over-riding all you have taught it.

Later in life raptors come into breeding condition. The two sexes diverging into different roles, females tending not to hunt but to beg her partner for food, males hunting in excess of their own requirements and tempting the female with food and by courtship displays (see 2.12).

Certain species, particularly falcons, have a strong drive to store food. One female New Zealand falcon of mine caught five small birds in a row, caching each one before chasing another. Sometimes this urge to chase and then hide the food seems totally to overcome the desire to eat, and the two activities, hunting and eating, become entirely dissociated. This happens too in house cats which hunt assiduously and bring home countless dead prey but which then refuse to eat them and eat only from their food bowl.

Thus these urges and drives, triggered by environmental stimuli such as increasing spring day length, together with internal maturation processes, unleash instinctive programs so that the birds relate properly and attempt to breed in a way that is appropriate and adapted to their situation.

## 4.6   Memory

Generally the memory of raptors is good and once the bird has been trained very little is forgotten. Fortunately their sensory world is similar to ours and this is reflected in their memories. Their main senses cover sights (in color), then sounds, then to a lesser extent taste, touch, and, very little, scent (see 1.3). As in most humans, their comprehension and recall is better for sights than for sounds. Even after more than a year of absence, hawks recognize previous owners and recall the significance of the lure and hood. As predators, their visual acuity and recognition are much better than ours and it takes an inexperienced falconer some years to realize just how much a hawk recognizes. Usually of course the bird does not demonstrate this recognition and it is only occasionally that one gets an insight into it. For example, my old goshawk sitting silently on the lawn on her bow perch, surrounded by my students, used to call to me immediately when I showed just part of my head at the laboratory window. Similarly, hawks recognize places where in the past they have caught prey and will sometimes divert in order to check out the place.

Memory should not be confused with intelligence. You can be very bright, but have a poor memory, or be quite stupid and have a good one. Don't forget that!

## 4.7   Imprinted behavior

I define imprinting as: a distinct genetically programmed learning mechanism in which there is a permanent attachment, during a specific sensitive period, of an innate behavior pattern to specific objects which thereafter become important elicitors of that behavior pattern. Rather a wordy definition, I know, but it is important to be clear what we are talking about. As almost all birds, wild or captive, are imprinted on *something* it is obviously very misleading to refer to hawks which are imprinted on man as "imprints." Instead I use the term "malimprint" to indicate a bird that is not completely naturally imprinted, or alternatively, one must state the objects which it is imprinted on.

In precocial birds, such as chickens and ducks, which leave the nest soon after hatching, imprinting takes place during a critical sensitive period—usually between 13 and 16 hours of age. This rapid identification of mother, siblings, and danger is of obvious survival value to precocial chicks, so that they all stick together when they leave the nest.

Altricial birds, on the other hand, stay in the nest for some time while they develop physically. Most raptor chicks keep their eyes shut for the first day or two and their imprinting is much more protracted—weeks rather than days or hours—and therefore are regarded as having "susceptible sensitive periods" rather than "critical periods" for imprinting.

These longer sensitive periods in altricial birds mean there is much more of a chance for things to

## DEVELOPMENTAL STAGES

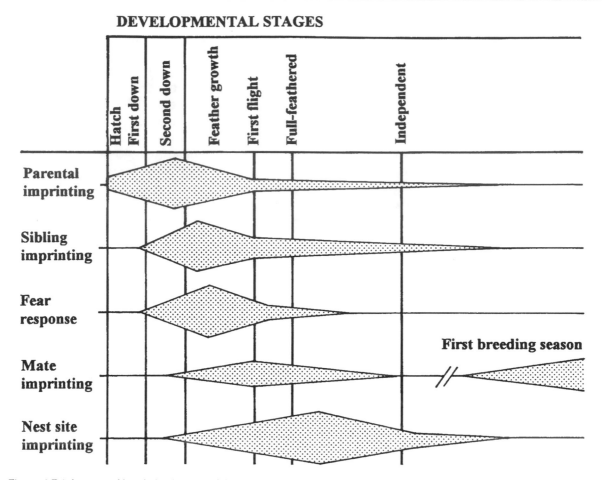

Figure 4.7.1 Aspects of imprinting in young falcons.

go wrong and, as this is also the age at which raptors are taken for falconry, various forms of malimprinting are common.

There are five main parts to imprinting in raptors and these overlap chronologically:

— Imprinting on parent.
— Imprinting on siblings.
— Development of fear response.
— Imprinting on future sexual partner.
— Imprinting on nest type, site, and habitat.

Scientific work on imprinting has mostly centered on easily bred precocial species such as ducks and chickens. These give much neater scientific results than hard-to-breed, solitary, altricial predators such as birds of prey. So most of the information given here is based on uncontrolled experiences of my own and other workers on young raptors, together with scientific information on some other altricial species. This is a very poorly understood aspect of raptors which would repay further study.

The susceptible periods for the five aspects of

imprinting in birds of prey can be shown diagrammatically. It should be emphasized that these vary from species to species and under different conditions and the exact plotting of them, if feasible, has yet to be clarified.

## 4.8    Imprinting on parent

Newly hatched raptors, being poor sighted, at first respond to the call of the mother; this in falcons is the "chup" or "eechip" call. The chick responds by gaping for food. By the time the second down coat has replaced the natal down, the chick is much more aware of its surroundings. This is a very rapid period in its mental development. At this stage it begins to imprint on the parent as the provider of food; food begging is directed specifically at the parent and not at any random shadowy movement. This imprinting continues during the whole period in the nest. Once the parent has been identified, the chick develops fear of "nonparent" objects and if it is switched from natural to human parents or vice-versa will show initial fear of the new strange parent. But, provided that the new parent persists, the chick soon settles down and continues its imprinting period, this time on the new parent. Peregrines start to imprint on their parents from about the fifth day.

Although chicks will imprint on objects quite dissimilar to their natural parents—humans for example—they imprint more strongly and more rapidly on objects which closely approximate their natural parents. In other words there is a genetically programmed parent image, albeit a hazy one. Please don't talk to me about cuckoos, let's keep it simple.

How does the hawk develop its own selfimage? If the hawk is reared by a human, it may identify that human as a parent, and later, a human as a sexual partner. But does the hawk think that it looks like a human too, or does it think that it looks like a hawk? If it can't understand a mirror, how does it know what it, itself, looks like? I'm still working on this little problem. For example, some years ago I fostered some New Zealand falcons to some gyrs. Then I trained one of the young females. She had been used to bossing her "mother" around in the breeding pen and was certainly not intimidated by a bird of gyrfalcon size. Out hawking (at 550 grams) she would happily attack any common buzzards that came near, even though they weighed around 900 grams. (This is not for falconers with poor nerves or slow legs.) As far as I could see, she "believed" that she was at least as big as the buzzards. When she got older, she bred a lot of nice youngsters, paired naturally with a male New Zealand falcon. But of course she had imprinted on them as siblings. Did she think she was a gyr, or a New Zealand falcon? Or did she think she was a gyr and that a New Zealand falcon male was an appropriate mate? Although this subject is complicated by ethological problems of observation and interpretation, it is important because of applications to management of rehabilitated birds (see 8.2) and of hybrids (see 8.4).

## 4.9 Imprinting on siblings

As the chick becomes aware of its mother, so too does it realize the presence of its siblings. These brothers and sisters are a mixed blessing. At first they are a source of warmth, but as the chick becomes older they represent competition for food and then, later, positive dangers as robbers of food.

The chick responds by mantling over and defending the food, or by carrying it away, but at the same time the siblings are reasonably inhibited against injuring one another. Some of the accipitrid hawks, such as buzzards, kites, and some eagles, are prone to Cain and abel battles in which the oldest chick attacks a younger one. To some extent this behavior is genetically programmed, but is also dependent on food. During fieldwork on Welsh red kites, video cameras revealed this going on at most nests, often with fatal results. We also noticed it when hand-rearing baby kites. However, when we put these kites under an old common buzzard as a foster mother, the behavior stopped within hours and never recurred. This buzzard was such a good mother that even with seven kite chicks she would keep them constantly fed. Whenever one so much as opened one eye, she was there with food in her beak, waiting to feed it. Also, during the early days at least, she would sit firmly on the chicks. The only time she "raised the lid" was to feed them, so the chicks had no daylight time in which to attack each other.

## 4.10 Development of the fear response

Once the chick has imprinted on its parents and siblings, then the fear response develops. The imprinted objects are now familiar and any new objects are henceforward experienced as unfamiliar and to be feared. Chicks first show fear of an intruder to the nest just as they grow their second down coat, before feathers begin to show. They respond by crouching down and huddling, or by sitting up and kekking or screaming. Females tend to be sullen and crouch, whereas males tend to be more active and vociferous. Sometimes when checking nests of wild New Zealand falcons in the Southern Alps I would be attacked by nestlings scarcely more than ten days old and hardly able to move out of the nest bowl. They would still sally out valiantly and try to grab some part of my anatomy!

## 4.11 Imprinting on future sexual partner

The way in which raptors imprint on sexual partners is complex and poorly understood. It seems to start after the initiation of the fear response, and is independent of the presence or absence of siblings.

Hand-rearing chicks together with their siblings certainly does not prevent them imprinting on humans as sexual partners. The chick seems to identify primarily with the food source (normally the parent) as the future sexual partner, but a hand-reared bird, reared in a group, if isolated from humans, may pair with another of the same species. Raptors that have been foster-reared by other, related species both in the wild and in captivity appear to be able to pick the right partner when the time comes, but ecological requirements and courtship differences are probably important in preventing hybrid pairs from forming in the wild. Many of the experiments on reintroductions by cross-fostering, are inconclusive because of the presence of synchronous dual imprinting which we will discuss in 4.14.

Some birds, such as cuckoos, are not reared by their natural parents and so their future sexual partner must be selected through instinct and not through imprinting, although the foster species they select for egg laying may be determined by imprinting. In raptors it seems that both factors contribute.

In some species, and this sometimes happens with captive raptors, a male and a female reared together often fail to form a sexual pair bond with each other. This is because they maintain their sibling relationship. If placed with other members of the opposite sex, or if separated for a couple of months during their first winter, they usually pair up normally.

## 4.12  Environmental imprinting

Once the active participants (parents, siblings, and intruders) have been identified by the growing chick, the static factors make an impression. At first these are the immediate surroundings—the type of nest, whether a stick nest, rock cavity or on the ground. Then, once the chick can fly, it imprints on larger aspects of the nest—the tree, cliff, or man-made structure—and the surrounding habitat. There is a strong correlation between the type of nest in which chicks grow up and the type they will subsequently choose as adults. It is even possible for two populations of a species to exist in one area in a state of virtual genetic isolation; the ones which use stick nests seldom breeding with others which use cliff nests.

As well as this site imprinting, which is fairly well documented in raptors, there are examples of

continuity of attempted use of nest sites over many years which, owing to parents and young being killed every year, must have been chosen through factors other than imprinting. In these cases the aerodynamic properties of the nest site and area (see 1.16) and other geophysical factors may be the lure for continuity. Thus, although a falcon may cruise a cliff looking for a ledge, because that's its idea of "home," the decision on exactly which ledge to use may be based on the fact that a little upcurrent of air just there makes take offs and landings much easier than on a neighboring ledge which although a better shape, is in a bad downdraft.

## 4.13  Practical aspects of imprinting

As imprinting in raptors is so drawn out, rather than compressed into a tightly scheduled sensitive period as it is in ducks or sheep, and as there are at least five different aspects which overlap, so there can be various combinations of ways in which hawks become imprinted, depending on their treatment during development. The two common extremes are shown in figure 4.13.1. Naturally imprinted, wild-caught birds are usually fairly suitable for falconry. Their main disadvantages are their well-developed fear response (which makes accipiters particularly difficult to use), and their nest site imprinting which can make aviaries appear so alien that the bird is too stressed to come into full breeding condition. Their hunting ability is usually good, although sometimes they range too independently of the falconer to be of much practical use.

The opposite extreme is the raptor that has been openly hand-reared by man on its own. It incessantly screams at its human "parent" for food, it treats humans as siblings and mantles over its food, it is aggressive on kills and may even fly at and attack the handler. Because falconry demands that the hawk comes to the falconer for food, and that the falconer must rob the hawk of its kill, the falconer acts as both parent and sibling and reinforces this jealous behavior, unless he works his handling system out very carefully. The natural process of independence from the parent does not take place and the raptor's behavior is arrested at a juvenile dependent stage. Such birds, if continually taken hunting without a proper chance at prey, may vent their frustrations on the escorting "parent" (the falconer) or other provid-

|  | Wild-caught bird | Bird reared openly by human from day one. | Domestic falconry bird |
|---|---|---|---|
| Parental imprinting | Begs for food from own species. | Begs for food from humans, rejects own species. | Begs from own species, doesn't scream at humans, ignores them. |
| Sibling imprinting | Shows competitive aggression/ jealousy, mantling, etc. with own species. | Treats humans as siblings. Instinctive predator response on kill, to own species. | No aggression or jealousy over food toward humans. |
| Fear response | Fearful of other predators, particularly man. | No fear of humans, especially of handler. May fear own species. | No fear of humans, own species, dogs, etc. |
| Mate imprinting | When mature, female begs from male of own species. Male courts female. | Female screams at human "husband" for food in spring. Male courts human "wife." | Responds sexually to own species only. |
| Nest site imprinting | Responsive to natural nest sites. | Prefers artificial nest type in which it was reared. | Prefers artificial nest and is relaxed in aviaries. |

Figure 4.13.1 Different ways of imprinting.

ers of quarry, such as the dogs. If it kills, it may leave the prey to drive off any competitive "siblings" (the falconer and his dogs).

There are several antidotes to these problems, all based on minimizing the falconer-parent-sibling image and maximizing independent game-catching attitudes and these are examined in section 5.3.

Changing the falconer often produces an immediate change, especially in accipiters which seem to identify individuals more specifically than falcons do. But the new relationship that the hawk builds with the falconer is usually based on the old imprinted images of falconer-parent and before too long it is screaming again, this time at its new "parent."

When human-imprinted raptors come into breeding condition the females tend to refuse to hunt but beg to the falconer "husband," while males make courtship overtures to the faloner "wife." A wide variety of unnatural objects can stimulate them into copulation. These birds are well-adjusted to artificial environments and readily come into breeding condition in captivity. But although they are adjusted to humans, they show varying unnatural responses to their own species and often kill each other if placed together in pens.

In recent years, imprinting techniques on humans have become more refined, either to prevent the bird from pairing naturally so that, if a hybrid is lost it would not pair up with a wild bird, or to produce a bird for breeding, either as a semen donor or egg layer, which will be used for artificial insemination. Such imprints are hand-reared from day one in isolation. As soon as the bird can feed itself, hand-rearing is stopped and instead the bird is fed finely chopped whole animal diet in a feed bowl. Food is never brought openly to the bird. Either the youngster is hooded and then the food bowl placed beside it, or the chick is itself placed next to the bowl. Hooding practice continues several times a day from the start of the second down coat until the bird is at least hard-penned. Throughout the youngster's entire growth period it is kept constantly in sight of humans going about their daily business. Once it can walk, it can be outside for part of the day. It can be flown at tame hack (see 5.4), although this is not necessary for birds intended solely for breeding. Such birds progress naturally and quickly to hunting and should not scream. But if the method is done half-heartedly, it is disastrous and also these birds must not have their weight reduced much at all in their first season. For this reason they are better suited to waiting-on flights at game rather than pursuit flights requiring more weight control.

In between these two extremes of natural and unnatural imprinting is a wide variety of possible combinations of malimprinting depending on the treatment the bird receives at each stage of its development. The label "imprint" or "malimprint" is a very general term which doesn't mean a lot unless more detail of the condition is given. Unless the developmental history of the bird is known, it takes quite a lot of time and skill to identify in what ways a bird's imprinting is unnatural and what the objects of the imprinting are.

Many falconers advocate keeping the young raptors together in a pen without seeing humans until the birds are fully fledged. They have then been horrified that the birds have started screaming. This is because the chicks have imprinted on one another as siblings but have had no parent object on which to imprint. In these circumstances of deprivation it seems the susceptible period is drawn out until after the birds have fledged. Thus they may imprint on the falconer, being the first object with which they have a parent relationship, and of course respond by screaming for food. This bond is normally not as strong as the natural parent imprinting but it is permanent and is reinforced by subsequent calling to the fist in falconry training. If the birds are almost fully fledged (branchers) when first put into the pen they will already be imprinted on their natural mother and, provided this is not overlaid by human interference, they will remain naturally imprinted. Some falconers like a young hawk to come out of the rearing pen "good and wild." The wildness is an indication that the fear response has not been overwhelmed by human interference and thus that other aspects of imprinting have not been interfered with. But the fear response itself is not a desirable thing in a falconry or potentially breeding bird and it can be selectively removed during development without affecting other aspects of imprinting.

The third column in figure 4.13.1 shows the domestic falconry/breeding bird. While being a fearless falconry bird it has no imprinted ties with the falconer and is suitable for normal pairing in breeding pens. Rather than attempt to avoid malimprinting by isolation, the developing chick can be offered a definite, recognizable parent object on which to imprint. There is then no problem with late malimprinting. Probably the best way to do this is to have the chick raised by a human-imprinted female of its own species. This has two distinct advantages; first it means that the chick becomes naturally imprinted on its own species— it identifies its adopted mother as food provider and will not scream at the falconer. Second, because the adopting parent is not afraid of humans, it is possible for the rearing process to be done where there is plenty of human activity in the

immediate area. The adult female does not show fear reactions to humans and in the absence of these signals the chick grows up not fearing man, or any other objects which are present, such as dogs or machines. This of course is provided that the chick starts before its fear response has developed. It is important that the humans show absolutely no interest in the chick, or in the food supplying process, otherwise the chick may imprint on them either as food providers or as siblings. Instead the chick must identify humans as being harmless parts of the scenery, similar to trees, bushes or clouds. Once a number of chicks have been raised by foster mothers, they themselves usually breed satisfactorily in aviaries. If these pens are exposed to human comings and goings (but not interference or feeding) the parents will rear the next generation with no fear of man, in other words your birds will then be truly domesticated.

Skylight and seclusion aviaries which are good for nervous breeders such as accipiters because they prevent the birds seeing things outside which might disturb them, are bad for rearing youngsters. Ideally the pen should have a window, high up. This window need not be large; it is solely for the bird to see out, not for you to see in. Thus one window per bird with a perch below it, the window being the size of the palm of your hand, is sufficient. Whenever it is quiet, even the nervous birds will be up at the window watching out, retreating to the rear of the pen when disturbed. If necessary the windows can be blocked during the early breeding season. But once the youngsters start to feather, it is important that they are able to see the big outside world. Otherwise, when they are drawn out for training the whole experience is too traumatic and stressful, and the bird may be "highly strung" to the point of being impossible to handle.

Another way of obtaining natural imprinting but no fear response, is inferior to the first and uses a replica parent, usually a hand dummy. The first method is followed as closely as possible but the role of the mother is played using a hand dummy resembling the natural parent. It has the advantage of not requiring a possibly erratic foster mother but it is harder to prevent the chick associating humans with the food supplying process. It has to be done scrupulously carefully, otherwise the chick will realize the whole thing is a cunning plot. I regard it as a last resort.

This female New Zealand falcon is an asynchronous dual imprint. She nested and laid eggs while at hack but would not copulate.

A third method of rearing is "creche" rearing, in which groups of chicks are reared together by human foster-parents. This produces very steady birds which are suitable for breeding in natural pairs. But some species, especially Harris hawks, tend to get too familiar and if cut down a little for falconry, quickly degenerate into nasty screamers.

If you are buying a bird, this very important stage in its development will be out of your control. One breeder's definition of "parent-reared" may actually entail hand-rearing until 10–14 days old. This is usually done to improve the chick's chances of survival and to wait until the closed ring stays on. But falcons start to recognize and imprint on their feeder from day five and, if put out at day ten to natural parents, these early few days are often still recognizable in the subsequent behavior of the youngster, even after a wild hack. If you value your bird, you should inquire closely into exactly how it was reared, and you should also inquire as to the integrity of the breeder beforehand.

## 4.14 De-imprinting

Imprinting, as I have defined it, is irreversible. However, examples do occur in which it appears to have been reversed. Examples spring to mind of passage hawks, sometimes even wild-caught adults, which have become "screamers." Others, of birds imprinted on man that have gone on to breed naturally in the wild or in captivity. In the naturally imprinted wild birds that appear malimprinted this is caused by conditioned learning (see section 4.17) and is often associated with injury; the injured bird is even more dependent on the handler and may revert to juvenile begging behavior. Being conditioned rather than imprinted, this is easily reversed.

In examples of malimprints subsequently breeding naturally it can be seen from the imprinting chart that many varieties of malimprinting can occur, including dual-imprinting. Dual-imprinting can occur when both imprint objects are present at the same time (synchronous), or when one is present after another (asynchronous), as when a bird is taken half-developed from the nest (and thus "half-imprinted" naturally) and completes the remainder of the imprinting period being hand-raised. When this happens the bird usually appears fully imprinted on humans (depending of course on the proportions and extent of exposure), but on reaching sexual maturity, if presented with only a natural mate, may breed successfully, or at least show some natural pairing behavior. Synchronous dual-imprints on the other hand, those which had both natural and artificial parent\mate objects present at the same time during the entire imprinting period, may well breed naturally and be additionally stimulated by the artificial "mate."

Asynchronous dual-imprinting is usually at the root of most problems and misunderstandings in domestic raptors.

Accipiters, unlike falcons, might have a reversible fear response. Certainly some accipiters which are aggressively tame malimprints go quite spooky when molting out without human contact. They seem to become very tame again when handling recommences. Human imprinted falcons and buteos, however fat and unattended, usually stay relatively fearless (although they may become highly territorial!). The way in which fear, imprinting, physical condition, mental conditioning, and stress are interlinked in accipiters needs more study; we are hardly beginning to understand it. Perhaps the fear response in accipiters is less strongly cross-linked with the other imprinted behaviors than it is in falcons and buteos. Perhaps accipiters are just plain incomprehensible.

Only birds that are completely naturally imprinted in all five aspects are potentially suitable for release to the wild. If you take on the responsibility of rehabilitating an orphaned raptor and fail to rear it so that it is naturally imprinted, then do not release it to the wild. You are not doing anybody any favors by releasing such a bird and you must examine yourself as a rehabilitator and see what can be done to prevent further failures (see 8.2).

## 4.15   Learned behavior

This section is a hard one to write because it brings together the fields of ethology, animal psychology, and empirical training methods. Each has its own followers with their own terminology and a skepticism of other approaches. Each has a contribution to make to the total problem and yet each on its own is too narrow or too shallow an outlook. I will give just a simplified resumé of what is an extremely complex, interrelated, partially understood subject which is not really susceptible to scientific investigation.

To me, there are two facets to learning: invol-

untary and voluntary. Involuntary learning creates an involuntary response or lack of response through the autonomic, nonconscious part of the nervous system. The trained behavior is prompt, automatic, and unthinking. It includes habituation, classical conditioning or reinforcement, operant conditioning, association, and trauma learning.

Voluntary learning produces conscious, voluntary responses which are not automatic and not necessarily immediate. It includes insight learning and experience. Intelligence may be regarded, in a simple way, as the ability to learn; the product of intelligence and experience being wisdom.

In chapters 5 we will be getting down to the practical nitty-gritty of training and motivating raptors. Here in chapters 4 we are looking at the theory and principles behind behavior and learning. Once these principles are understood, not only do the solutions to practical problems become fairly obvious, the whole process of training can become effective and streamlined, taking a lot less effort than before.

## 4.16   Habituation

Habituation entails exposing the hawk to a stimulus so often that it ceases to respond. It "gets used" to things. This was traditional "manning." The hawk was simply tied to somebody's fist day and night until it was too tired, physically and mentally, to react. And so the wild accipiter sat quietly on the fist despite all the nearby stimuli which formerly alarmed it.

There is one big problem with habituation: like conditioning, it wears off. This means that the habituator's work is never done. The Elizabethan austringer used to man his goshawk in the morning until it had roused three times, before flying it. Most of the hard work in training a wild-caught accipiter is habituation. Basically the hawk is exposed to unpleasant stimuli such as people, machinery, hoods, and so on, and this is repeated frequently until the hawk gives no response. Because there is no response there is no reward.

One of the main reasons for weathering hawks is "maintenance manning" or habituation, but careful positioning of pen windows will often keep a hawk sufficiently tame without the risks and disadvantages attendant on conventional weathering.

A good use of habituation is in teaching a goshawk to ignore white ferrets. After a few days of seeing the ferret in its hutch, the hawk pays no further attention. Similar habituation can be used to overcome "hang-ups." My old goshawk used to have a neurotic dislike of plastic containers such as buckets, hawk baths, and ferret boxes. Leaving these in her mews over the molt, especially hanging on elastic so that they moved and bobbed in the breeze, totally cured her. Often when a neurosis is originated by trauma learning (see section 4.18), habituation seems to make a long-lasting, almost permanent cure. Certainly the effect lasts longer than when habituation is used against everyday stress stimuli.

Here is an example of unintentional misuse of habituation: a friend telephoned to ask why his falcon persistently ignored the lure. He had introduced the lure to the falcon by garnishing it with food and throwing it down beside the falcon on her block. This was what his books recommended. The falcon had jumped down onto the lure and eaten the food, checked the lure for any other food and hopped back onto her block. The falconer left the lure there all day while he was at work. Next day, and thereafter, the falcon ignored the lure and would only come to the fist. The falconer had successfully habituated her to ignore the lure. The remedy was to start again with a new lure of different appearance and to pick the falcon up with a tidbit on the fist as soon as she had eaten the lure food.

In general, habituation is more effective and more persistent in young birds than in old ones. Young hawks are still developing their habits. Old hawks, like dogs, horses, and humans, often get too set in their ways to do much with. If habituation is stopped, such as at the end of the season when the hawk is put down to molt, the process is achieved more easily the next time. Each season the hawk needs a little less manning to reclaim it.

Habituation to one type of stimulus often deadens the response to other similar stimuli too. For example, a goshawk which refuses white ferrets may refuse white rabbits as well. On the other hand goshawks can be very discriminating and may work amicably with one dog and yet be totally stressed in the presence of another, even one of the same breed.

To speed and accentuate the effects of habituation it is often possible to introduce some positive reinforcement, for example, by placing food in the hood for a hood-shy hawk, or feeding the hawk while carrying during manning. Great care must be taken that the hawk does not bate too much from the fist or it will begin to associate the fist with an unpleasant experience and thus train itself to become even more wild. This is where the sensitivity of the falconer is paramount; it is not a question of patience.

## 4.17 Conditioned learning

Conditioned reflexes work through the nonconscious autonomic part of the nervous system and the response is rapid and automatic. An example is when you see a person or animal yawn and even before they've finished yawning you find yourself yawning. Try it out next time you are in the train or on a bus after a long day. In the same way the sound of water trickling onto tin evokes a very rapid and embarrassing reflex! The reflex starts less than a second after the stimulus and requires no thought at all. Frequently it is only one's own reflex response that draws one's conscious attention to the original stimulus.

Classical or Pavlovian conditioning follows this order: stimulus or cue (eg whistle), response (eg flying to the fist), reward (eg eating food), all occurring rapidly one after the other. This is positive conditioning or reinforcement.

Cues can be very small indeed. Given that raptors have better sight and hearing than us, they are capable of noticing cues even beyond our perception. Cues can be very brief and very slight and if you find the hawk is doing something puzzling, look carefully at the situation; she may be reacting to a cue you haven't noticed. I remember once bringing my female goshawk into the living room one evening in early spring to dry out after a day's rabbiting. I perched her on the back of a chair in an alcove. She preened and settled down and then did something odd: she glanced at a piece of electrical flex dangling against the wall. I thought "She wants that flex. She must think it's a branch. Maybe she wants to nest." So I went out and got some twigs and dumped them on the chair. Sure enough, down she jumped and spent a happy evening building herself a nest in the chair! Similarly, if you watch Steve Martin's videos, you can see how his parrots react promptly to small cues which we normally wouldn't even notice. During falconry we use lots of cues, such as a whistle or call, hand-signals and swinging the lure. We actually give out a lot more cues than we really intend, and often hawks react to these without us realizing it.

Usually this is no problem, the hawk is getting to know our personal ways of doing things. When it becomes inappropriate, it is called *superstitious behavior.* We have a male Harris here at the moment. He has only been trained a couple of weeks, by someone using a dark brown glove. We took him out hawking in the rushes and found that he would come to anyone who held up a dark brown glove, but not to anyone with a light-colored glove. So we will have to sort out that little bit of unintended superstitious behavior!

Once the animal has noticed the cue and done the required behavior, then the act can be reinforced. As Karen Pryor or Steve Martin would say: *Positive reinforcement is anything that occurs in conjunction with an act that tends to increase the likelihood that the act will occur again.* Positive reinforcement is the best way to train raptors. The reward is usually food or quarry but there are many other, more subtle rewards. Once you have worked out what motivates the hawk in any given situation, what it really wants, then you can give an appropriate reward.

*Negative reinforcement is something the subject wants to avoid. It occurs in conjunction with an act and tends to decrease the likelihood that the act will occur again.* For example, if you wave a hood around in a hawk's face and then proceed to hood it in a rough and ready manner, the hawk will soon associate just the sight of the hood with the forthcoming nasty experience and will bate as soon as she sees the hood. Notice that the action and the reinforcement occur close together so that the animal is able, by its actions or inactions, to change the reinforcement. Raptors are quite capable of learning by negative reinforcement (see trauma learning) and by more subtle negative conditioning such as when a falcon starts to refuse a prey she finds unpalatable. But the falconer must take infinite care that the negative experience is not linked to him. Otherwise it will undo the tenuous bond he has worked so hard to build up. Also, training by negative reinforcement is selflimiting because the animal will only do enough to make the negative reinforcement stop, whereas with positive reinforcement it will make bigger and bigger efforts in order to get more reward.

*Operant* conditioning is when the behavior comes first, without a stimulus, and is then reinforced. It is a tricky part of training because you are dependent on the animal doing the behavior before you can reinforce it. It may do so accidently

or you may have contrived the situation as best you can so that the behavior is likely to happen. This is where natural bred-in instincts are so important. For example, when a peregrine waits on just a little, you try to give positive reinforcement by serving quarry under her. Day by day she waits on higher, longer, and steadier. The trainer should always be looking for ways to motivate his hawk to *do* things so that they can then be positively reinforced. Often this means trying to break down the behavior into a lot of small intermediate steps, rather than trying to get there in one big jump.

An example of operant negative reinforcement is when a dog jumps on to the best sofa and is given a prompt slap. After a few performances the undesired behavior ceases. It needed the dog to do the undesired behavior first before you could train it not to do it.

Whatever the nature of the reinforcement—positive, negative, real, or implied—it must be given *as close to the behavior as possible,* otherwise it is not linked with the behavior. So if you beat a dog for running off only when it gets back, the dog links the *punishment* to coming back. Thus this is punishment, rather than negative reinforcement. Intelligence can in some measure be taken as the extent to which a person or animal can stretch these links between the cause and effect, in time, in space, and in abstraction. In general, the shorter the link the more effective the lesson. Contrast this with a game of chess in which you are trying to think through a whole series of potential consequences to the reward or punishment of a move.

While you are actually training or shaping the behavior you want, it is best to give a positive reward every time the act occurs. But from then on, if the behavior is not reinforced, it may fade away. If you don't reward the hawk for coming to you it will, after a while, become slow to come and eventually stop coming at all. On the other hand, if you reward it every time, it will start to take the reward for granted and become complacent. It is better from then on, to reinforce using a variable schedule which in practice means rewarding about every fifth time. But the schedule of reward should be random, not regular. In other words in ten calls you might give two or three rewards in total, scattered randomly among the ten calls. You might reward twice in a row and then nothing for seven or eight times. You are in control of the reward system, not the hawk. This is similar to what happens when the hawk chases prey. You might think that this would be more discouraging than if you rewarded the hawk every time, but this is not so. Imagine a light switch. Every time you switch it the light comes on. Then one day nothing happens. You try it a couple of times more. Still nothing. So you give up. Try the same thing with a flashlight. You switch it on, nothing happens. Not an unusual occurrence with the average flashlight! So you try several times more and eventually start checking the connections, the batteries, the bulb, and so on, convinced that you'll get it going.

I was out with a friend hawking some time ago and I noticed that he always offered a tidbit when he called the hawk. If there was no tidbit, the hawk wouldn't come; he had trained latency into the procedure. So I said "Why don't you call her *without* food?" So he tried it and the hawk refused. I thought to myself "That's odd, if it had been one of my hawks she would have come. How would I have made her come? I would just sort of *willed* her into coming." But, on analyzing it more carefully, I realized that I have always trained using a variable schedule (probably because I can't be bothered to mess around with all those tidbits!). Similarly, once the hawk is trained, I don't put food on the lure at all. Food on the lure is a health hazard, it encourages possessiveness, and there is always the risk of the hawk getting it off.

The most effective training is when the reward is as close as possible to the act, preferably only milliseconds. But it may not be physically possible to achieve this and any delay risks disassociating in the hawk's mind the link between act and reward. This gap can be bridged with a token reward, such as a word of praise, a pat or a smile. This works best with social animals but it can also be used successfully for birds, and perhaps this is one area where falconers are lacking. Steve Martin says the word "Good" to his parrots, as a bridge before actually rewarding them. We use a bridge in the form of an ungarnished lure. We whistle and swing the lure (cue), the hawk takes the lure (bridge) we come up with the pick-up piece rewarding the hawk for coming and positively reinforcing our own approach. This also gets around the problem of the hawk associating our approach with stealing her prey (negative reinforcement).

As well as training the hawk to come, and reinforcing the behavior, there is a further aspect to consider: timing. When you train her, she must come *immediately*. She is perfectly capable of this,

Figure 4.17.1 When you call your young buzzard, do you read her mind correctly?

after all, if the cue was a rabbit or other prey, she'd be after it in a flash. The way to do this is, right from the start, never to call her for more than three seconds. If she hasn't come by then, put your fist or lure away and do nothing. Don't call her again. Turn away from her, close the incident, go to a different position. Don't walk toward her (who's training who?). If you want to get nearer, then go in at a tangent. Make her realize that she had her chance and she missed it. The mistake was yours because you lacked judgement. The experienced trainer can read his hawk and, knowing her history, can predict her behavior. So he takes care always to be successful in what he asks. So the training goes quickly, rather like somebody running across a river on stepping stones. He's marked his route, checked his stones, and goes confidently and quickly from rock to rock. The less experienced trainer gets halfway across and either falls in or finds that the gap between rocks is too wide and has to spend time figuring out another route.

Thus although a hawk may be "trained," there is a world of difference between one that will only come for food, is sulky or moody, and has established patterns of refusal, and one that comes when called immediately. A hawk which has been trained properly, first time and at its own speed, and kept up to it, will be better than one on which hours and weeks of somewhat confused, repetitive training has been lavished by an inexperienced person. It is important to be able to "read" a hawk

Figure 4.17.2 Did she come to you or did you come to her?

so that you are able to anticipate. Thus when a falcon is flying you "know" what she is "thinking" from her little signs and act accordingly so that the lesson goes smoothly without a hitch. Being half a second late in realizing something is all that it takes to ruin a lesson, or even to lose a bird. As you get better at communicating with the hawk, she will seem more intelligent. Some people are better at reading these little signs than others; curiously, a high proportion of our falconers are mildly dyslexic, they seem better with the animals than with the written word. The problem is that although these people are "natural" handlers, they cannot verbalize or analyze what they are doing.

Punishment is the point at which the training of raptors, excepting perhaps some eagles, differs from that of social animals such as dogs and horses. *Punishment happens after the action, is not directly associated with the action, and the animal has no control; it cannot stop doing the action to avoid the punishment, because it already stopped doing it some time earlier. Punishment is inflicted personally by the trainer.* Punishment does not work on raptors because most falconry birds are nonsocial. They do not belong to a structured society and it is only in a structured society that agreed morals, a moral conscience, and dominance (the means of applying morals) can exist.

A dog, for example, is a social animal with all the biologically inherited programs for social behavior. We say it has a "willingness to please," that is to say it is willing to have its behavior modified by more dominant individuals in its own society. We can thus introduce to it the concept of "sin." If we decide that stealing from the rubbish bin is a "sin" for our dog, then the first time it does it, we grab it by the scruff of the neck, give it a

shake, stare it in the face and growl "NO!" (negative operant reinforcement). We link the word "No!" by association to our actively disapproving dominating shake. Quite soon just the bridging word "No!" is enough negative reinforcement to keep the dog away from the bin. Because the dog is a social animal it is prepared to accept our commands without rejecting us—the leaders of his pack. As the dog grows up he considers, as we do, that stealing from the bin is a sin and he can be trusted to leave it alone. If occasionally a scrap of food proves too tempting for him, he shows every sign of guilt when caught.

The hawk, quite simply does not have a conscience because it does not have a society. It cannot therefore be given a concept of sin and so punishment to this end is fruitless. Not only this, because the hawk does not accept our dominance, any punishment we give it just alienates it. It links the punishment with us rather than with the hypothetical sin or undesired behavior. We have to take care therefore that our treatment of the hawk is consistently good and positive in order to maintain the bond, which in a hawk not imprinted on man, is flimsy. A dog will very rarely abandon its owner however cruel he may be, but a hawk, unless imprinted that way, has no social bond and will soon show its disapproval in a very practical way.

This wild freedom from a social conscience is one aspect of raptors that has fascinated man over the centuries. Perhaps it is a way for the falconer to escape by proxy from the bonds that hold him to his position in life, secure but at times, constrained.

Being territorial, raptors do have signals of dominance and submission, but these are usually brief before fight or flight. Also, as man is so different in size and movement, it is difficult for him to mimic these signals. Nevertheless the falconer should know them, if only to avoid them. Flying or perching in a prominent way over a hawk is a sign of dominance. So if you stand towering over a hawk which is on a low perch or on a kill, it feels threatened. A direct stare held for more than a second is a threat. Entering the personal territory of an unbonded bird that does not regard you as a mate, parent, or sibling is threatening; this distance varies from about 10 meters to about ½ meter, depending on many factors. Obviously to train a hawk you have to get this close and it is a sign that the bird is beginning to accept you as less of a threat once it stands on your fist eyeing things other than you.

Because raptors can't really be trained by punishment, then further whole areas of training are not possible. For example, when earlier you trained the dog not to jump onto the sofa, first you used operant negative reinforcement. This developed his conscience and reinforced your position as pack leader. From then on, if you saw the dog so much as looking at the sofa, you could growl "No!" and the dog would know that you disapproved of what he was contemplating. Then we go into the bedroom. This time there is no need to start from scratch and let the dog jump onto the bed and so on. You just look at the bed, the dog understands what you mean, you growl "No!" and the dog has learnt without more being said. He has extended his area of guilt. Soon you have a dog which "understands your every word." He is in marked contrast to a street stray which owes you no allegiance and doesn't understand you.

## 4.18 Trauma learning

This is learning which needs only one lesson or experience and which occurs under traumatic or stress conditions. Usually the lesson is a negative one, and it can often be the start of a neurosis or phobia. For some reason, when an animal is in severe stress or crisis state, input stimuli are perceived very clearly and, as it were, flash to the brain so violently that they fuse together regardless of whether or not there is a logical or meaningful connection. The whole conglomeration of a split second's input becomes deeply etched on the memory. Thus humans may remember every inconsequential detail of the moment before a car crash, right down to the tune on the car radio. Just hearing this tune subsequently may be sufficient to induce an automatic and unpleasant reaction. Thus trauma achieves in one lesson what would have taken many repeats by classical conditioning.

Trauma learning takes place both intentionally and unintentionally in falconry. It can be used intentionally when teaching a young dog to keep away from hawks. The puppy is allowed to sniff at a big hawk such as a redtail and the hawk promptly gives him an experience he never forgets and never needs to learn again.

Unintentional trauma learning can take place when a hawk is subjected to a violent but necessary treatment such as beingcast to have equipment changed. Many falconers hood the hawk or

get someone else to do thecasting to avoid themselves being associated in the hawk's mind with the experience. Or the hawk may have a bad experience with quarry, or with the vet. For the wild-caught hawk, her first experience of man may be traumatic, as she is trapped and handled. Unless care is taken at this stage, she can associate this trauma, not just with mankind in general, but with you in particular. As a result of this, many wild-caught hawks can be very sensitive when approached on the kill.

Undesirable behavior picked up in association with trauma can be very hard to eradicate. Habituation linked with positive reinforcement are the best methods to use.

## 4.19 Insight learning

Insight learning assumes that, at some level, the bird has knowledge or understanding of a situation, through its consciousness. Conditioning, on the other hand, bypasses the conscious mind. It is easy enough to teach the hawk the significance of the lure as a possible food source. You show the hawk the garnished lure and after one or two meals the hawk has learned the lesson. Then, in the field, the process which is going on at some level in the hawk's brain is something like this: "I feel hungry. That lure means food. I will fly down and feed on it."

Under ideal conditions flying a hawk which has been taught rather than trained (ie conditioned), works reasonably well. The problems come when other signals also reach the hawk's consciousness and over-ride the decision. For example: "I feel hungry. That lure means food. When it stops raining I might fly down and feed on it. It won't fly away." Result: one very soggy frustrated falconer.

The falconer who has conditioned his bird to respond immediately has much better control over the hawk because the bird's response is automatic. But it takes skill to develop conditioned reflexes in a bird when negative reinforcement cannot be used and when the bird is free to move rapidly in three dimensions. Attempting to condition the bird when it is not motivated, or giving sloppy, unclear, or protracted signals, can ruin the conditioning of the bird and one is then left at the mercy of the bird's conscious decisions.

One aspect of insight learning is that it is relatively permanent. Once a hawk has learned the significance of something, it seldom forgets it. Conditioned responses wear off but knowledge is permanent. You can't unknow something. Once innocence is lost, it cannot be recovered. Once a hawk knows what the lure means, it will remember even years later. It may not do anything about it, but it will know all the same. If you inadvertently let your hawk into a secret, for example if she discovers that farmyard hens are hot dinners, you cannot then whisper in her ear and say "Please forget that little secret." All you can do is keep her well away from hens and perhaps try some negative conditioning. But she will always know about hens; she has learned by insight and her innocence has been lost.

Insight learning tends not to be used so much by modern falconers, which is a shame because it is very quick and effective. The best way is the natural way, that is to use another hawk to "show" the youngster what to do. Normally it learns a lot by insight learning, watching its parents and siblings and joining in. The single falconer's bird on the other hand often has to learn every single thing on its own, without any example to follow. This can lead to problems with entering or with going up to wait on. If the bird is imprinted in such a way that it can safely be flown free with a make-hawk, then this is a great advantage. The hawk can learn from example. Care has to be taken that the bird learns just enough to appreciate the situation without becoming dependent on the make-hawk.

## 4.20  Experience

Behavior learned from experience is basically a mixture of the types of learning already discussed, but occurring in an uncontrolled fashion. Imitation can be a short cut to experience. Also by exposing the bird to a range of stimuli, such as different species of prey, experience teaches the hawk to discriminate. Hawks learn that ducks start off slowly, then speed up and keep going, whereas pheasants start off fast, then slow down and stop. By experiencing these differences, the hawk learns to adapt accordingly.

The developmental age of the bird affects its ability to learn. As the imprinting process is completed, so the age of learning blooms. When the hawk can fly, it is at its most impressionable and remains so for the first year of life. The old saying "You can't teach an old dog new tricks" has some foundation in truth. It has been shown experimen-

tally with chaffinches, for example, that if they fail to learn their song repertoire through being isolated during the first few months of life, then they never pick it up.

Exactly how much this affects birds of prey is not known, but individual raptors do show various marked preferences, such as becoming wedded to certain favorite quarry species. Also hawks which have been kept in aviaries for their first twelve months of life are markedly harder to prepare for hunting wild quarry, not just physically but mentally also. Whereas the young hawk may learn something after just one exposure, the older bird may need several repeats to pick it up. Conversely, some old hawks which have been trapped in the wild never fully adjust to being in captivity.

All of the points mentioned about hawks learning things apply equally to falconers learning things. Sometimes the hawk trains the falconer faster than the falconer trains the hawk.

## 4.21  Mental maturation and the orientation toward quarry

Field research on wild peregrines by Dr. Steve Sherrod and by others has clarified the stages through which young falcons go during their development. These are:
a) Newly hatched chick is offered food by parent.
b) Downy chick begs food from parent.
c) Newly fledged chick chases parent for food. When satiated, it plays and chases objects resembling prey, but does not catch live prey.
d) Chick physically attacks parents for food.
e) Parent drops dead prey for chick who chases it and catches it. Chick's search image reorientates from the parent to the prey.
f) Parent drops live prey which reinforces connection of pursuit with food.
g) Chick has increasing difficulty in obtaining food from its parents and is left unattended for longer periods. It becomes more successful in catching its own live prey and begins to stray away from the nest area, selfhunting.
h) Chick is completely weaned to independence.

During the course of captive management and falconry, we interfere with or alter this progression according to our own needs. For example, most falconry birds are now domestically bred and many falconers wish to use their birds for breeding during the spring and summer when the hawking season is over and the birds are molting. This usually entails having the chick reared by natural parents in the breeding pen so that it develops with natural imprinting and is accustomed to being in an aviary. The chick is then usually removed around stages d) or e) for falconry training.

In the wild, the aim of the parent falcon is to make the chick become a successful hunter, independent of its parents, ie stage h). In falconry, the aim of the falconer is to make the falcon a successful hunter of wild prey but to remain still partially dependent on or manageable by the falconer. The problem with the wild-caught falcon is that she tends to be too independent spatially and is insufficiently orientated toward the falconer. She too easily wanders off selfhunting, looking outward for opportunities instead of inward toward the falconer for game. Although she may have a number of drawbacks in her prey preferences, her strong point is that she is a superb hunter, better than most falconers could make her in several seasons' flying. It is the falconer's task to make the wild-caught falcon's life more pleasant and productive than she experienced in the wild, so that she wants to stay with him as a hunting partner, and does not see him as a potential predator, such as a coyote. Another factor to be considered is that it is now virtually impossible to obtain such a bird in Britain and here at least the discussion is now purely academic. The would-be falconer is left with his young domestic falcon endeavoring to bring her to perfection in a hostile world.

Young black gyr/Altai saker 'Black Jack' preening.

# 5 # Training

Figure 5.13.1 This fit, young, male peregrine looks bright, alert, and eager to fly.

# and Conditioning

## 5.1 The training program

The training program has to consider two aspects side by side. First is the actual mental training using the systems already discussed. Second is the physical management of the bird, making sure that it has a good appetite to be responsive to your training efforts and developing the physical condition of the bird so that it is fit and strong.

The training of a wild-caught accipiter differs in some ways from that of a young domestic falcon and therefore it would be pointless to give a potted recipe for training. Different birds must be brought on at different rates according to their responses. The skilled falconer will bring on a bird in such a way that he doesn't make it stale with needless repetition and yet doesn't venture out onto the thin ice of risk. The fastest bird I ever trained was a hacked New Zealand falcon called Sally. From feeding her on the fist for the first time to stooping loose to the lure took twenty minutes. Marvelous. On the other hand, I had a haggard hawk-eagle called Gorgon who never flew loose, despite all my efforts. He was a very, very slow, deeply suspicious bird. He seldom bated, he just looked at me with an unchanging, impenetrable trancelike stare.

Although there are these differences, the falconer should have a fairly shrewd idea of his own schedule. If his hawking is planned to start on a certain date, he should work forward from that date and plan out his program with certain targets to aim for along the way. Part of my job is to train 20–25 crow falcons each season. Each bird goes through a preplanned program of training and, allowing for bad weather and individual differences, is ready by a set date. I tend to be very jealous of the bird's intellectual virginity. It is a lot easier to take a young bird and train it right first time, straight through. Its training goes bang, bang, bang,—finished. On the other hand, if someone has messed it up in some way, made it hoodshy perhaps, then everything is on stop while this is sorted out and it might take more time and effort to rectify than the rest of the entire training.

For the crow falcons, my program goes like this:

Day 1–5—hatched in incubator and hand reared.
Day 5–10—reared by imprint falcon until ring stays on.
Day 10–40—reared in big pen by a natural pair of falcons.
Day 40–45—in the hack box.
Day 45–60—flying at hack.
Day 60–80—loose in a large free-flight pen with other hacked falcons.
Day 80—measured, fitted with anklets, jesses, and tailmount, taken up hooded.
Day 81–85—hooded, or secluded weathering while weight is slowly reduced.
Day 85–99—taken in hand, trained to fist and lure, jumped to fist for exercise and flown loose.
Day 99–105—stooped to lure and jumped to fist for exercise.
Day 105–110—long-lured over 500 meters and introduced to dragged dead crow.
Day 110—entered at a crow and kept to one kill a day until at least ten kills. Not flown at quarry the day after a strenuous flight.
Day 120—ready for ringers!

Some readers would see this and think that my training schedule starts when the falcon is 85 days old. This is not so. The training program starts on the day the egg hatches and the falcon goes through a very careful process of imprinting, learning, developing physical skills and mentally maturing. The daily food association with man is only introduced at day 85; by this time the falcon has already graduated through several major stages in its training.

It is important that the falconer works out a simple program for his individual bird and takes the training through in a positive, progressive manner. Young hawks are tremendously receptive and to dither with a half-trained bird is to invite problems. There is a whole myriad of problems waiting to beset birds which are not taken through training at their natural rate: screaming, aggression, carrying, "moodiness," difficulties in entering at quarry. The experienced falconer must learn to anticipate and side-step all of these.

As a breeder, I send out many young hawks each year to their new owners, and inevitably, every year some of them don't turn out well. This is almost always due to the falconer who does not have the ability to do the bird justice and who is not prepared to take responsibility for it. Instead, he blames it on the bird. On the other hand, all the birds which stay behind with us turn out well, because we put extra attention and work into any developing problems, in order to overcome them.

Therefore, assuming you are soon to take delivery of a new bird, work out two schedules for yourself: the first schedule is your calendar, showing target dates through to catching quarry regularly. Your second is a list of attributes you wish your hawk to have. At present you are at point A: early summer with an untrained, unfit, hawk. You have to get to point B: early autumn with a trained, fit bird. Maybe you are getting a Harris hawk, then here are some possible targets:

— The hawk should be in top class health and feather condition.
— She should hood well, and have a well-fitting hood.
— She should be good mannered on the fist and never try to foot you.
— She should come immediately 200 meters to the fist without reward.
— She should be fit and capable of 150 high jumps in one session.
— She should be experienced in wind and hilly terrain and should wait on in suitable areas.
— She should work well with your dog and the dog with her.
— She should work well from the lofting pole.
— She should follow you well and choose suitable high perches for overlooking the terrain.
— She should take rabbits well and also have experience with feathered quarries.
— She should not scream.
— She should work with other Harris hawks to which she has been properly introduced.
— She should be pleasant to handle on the kill and throughout the day.

During the course of this section I will be looking at some of the aspects you will need to cover when going with your hawk from point A to point B.

## 5.2    The wild hack

Much has been written about how to hack birds of prey, systems of hack management and their pros and cons. Stevens (1955) and Sherrod (1981) cover the main points quite adequately. My own experiences have been limited to buzzards, kestrels, merlins, sakers, peregrines, gyrs, various hybrids, and New Zealand falcons. I have hacked the latter extensively both as juveniles and as adults and have even had them nesting at hack. Each year we wild hack 20–30 big saker/gyr/peregrine type falcons in Wales and in Northumberland.

A hard-penned youngster is not safe to put out at hack immediately because it can already fly and might become lost. Also, if hacked from its original home it may well interfere with other breeding pairs on the premises or on the weathering lawn. Hacking out high-spirited falcons intended for serious falconry is a different matter again from having a few cuddly kestrels or buzzards lurking around the yard. Big falcons can potentially cover considerable distances, paying particular attention to such magnets as pigeon lofts. In most of Britain they are thus exposed to unacceptable danger. Apart from human persecution and shooting, the falcons have to run the gauntlet of busy traffic and a landscape festooned with wires. The hack site must be chosen so that there are none of these hazards, no gamekeepers, no rivers, lakes, or water-troughs in which the hawk might drown and the minimum of barbed wire fences. Standing crops are taboo because if a young hawk lands in one it can't relaunch itself, the same can apply to dense forestry plantations. Inquisitive, stampeding cattle are to be avoided. In short, you need to be able to control the landuse over the immediate 100 hectares (200 acres) or so around the hack box. Some stock and foxes can be excluded temporarily with electric sheep netting.

To get them to fly well, the box should be on a slope with plenty of hill-lift in all the main wind directions. This will draw them like a magnet and will encourage them to get into the air. It is hours in the air in strong wind which really does the good.

There can be no doubt that, if the falcon survives, it is improved physically by hacking. Its wind and muscles are better, it foots better and, most of all, it flies better. It begins to resemble the passage falcons, now no longer available to most falconers. But what does it do to the falcon mentally?

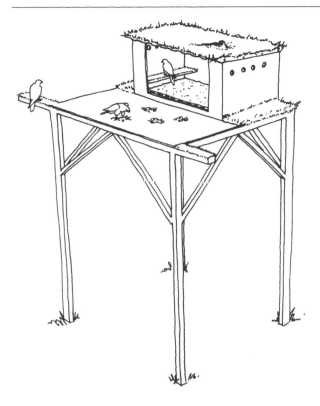

Figure 5.2.1 Tower hack box for young falcons.

A naturally imprinted falcon, even though captive bred, has a fear response of man and does not regard the falconer as a parent figure. Flying wild at hack (in contrast to tame hack) does not encourage a bond between falconer and bird and so this has to be forged later. The hack falcon may learn to wander and selfhunt, both attributes which we avoid by not extending the hack too long. When it comes to tackling quarry the young bird is constantly disappointed and without the falconer's assistance may give up on some species such as rooks and crows and be difficult to enter to them again. While in theory hack is supposed to teach the falcon that it cannot catch pigeons, in my experience it is more likely to teach them they can catch pigeons, especially if they tear around the countryside and develop the right tactics. None of these selfhunting problems arise in the first two weeks of hack.

Falcons which are intended for game hawking with waiting-on flights, are required to centralize over the falconer in expectation of invisible game being flushed out. Wandering off, chasing non-game species, landing on the ground or undertaking attack styles other than the stoop, are considered faults. Therefore on balance the potential game hawk may learn more bad habits during

hack than it gains in terms of physical fitness, flying skills and footing ability. Such skills are probably best learned by an initial intensive training to a swung lure, followed by training in waiting on (see section 5.18) and then by consistently being served with real game to induce an almost mechanical routine of going up, waiting on and stooping. A strong bond of faith in the falconer serving game is the essential key to all this.

Falcons intended for flights out of the hood at rooks, crows, seagulls, houbara, stone curlews, magpies, larks, and so on are required to undertake a much wider variety of techniques ranging from direct flying attacks to ringing flights, shepherding, stooping, and tail-chasing. Their footing too has to be considerably better than the average game falcon's. The falcon needs a knowledge of quarry, of the elements and of tactics which can be learned only through experience of real situations. There is no short cut to producing such maturity. A period at hack benefits such a falcon, especially if it is a slow-maturing clumsy bird such as young sakers and gyrs. We have occasionally had to train some unhacked ones due to having too many birds for the hack site capacity. The difference in their pursuit flights are immediately noticeable.

The first two or three months of a falcon's life are critical. If the bird is not entered and thoroughly wedded to its intended quarry it may orientate itself more toward the falconer as a parent figure, become lure bound, start to scream and in some cases (particularly malimprints) start to attack him.

Most of the above is fairly standard teaching and, as far as it goes, is perfectly true. However, since we have been hacking large falcons on a regular basis we have been able to experiment with the finer points of the procedure. This is what we've evolved: first of all one must breed sufficient birds to make up same-age cohorts, this means 2–6 falcons all hatched within about five days of each other. These are placed in the hack box overlooking a broad landscape. The hack box is well ventilated with a food hatch at the back and an open vertically barred door at the front, facing north or east. Branches or perches around the hack box enable the youngsters to clamber out and to return easily. The fledglings are placed in the box one week before they are capable of upward flight and transmitters are placed on their legs (see figure 3.9.3). This gives them enough time to imprint on their surroundings. During this week I kill or drive away as many foxes in the hack area as I can. Mammalian predators are very quick to catch young falcons at this stage, even in the middle of the day. The transmitters are all hermetically sealed, painted in individual colors (including the antenna) and have a life of 60 days. At dawn the next day, sufficient food is tied to the hackboard in front of the window to last the branching falcons for three days. The window is then opened from below using draw-cords. The behavior of the young falcons is monitored by radio and field-glasses from 300 meters or so.

We have found that the best hack period is about 14 or so days. This is long enough for them to become hard-penned and to build muscle and generally develop the sturdy frame which is the hallmark of a hacked bird. Because there are several of them they get flying experience by playing and chasing each other. Also they pull leaves from the tops of trees. But they don't wander far, seldom more than 1–2 kilometers and they don't do much chasing of prey. Occasionally a bird will kill early, in a week or ten days, but normally there is no serious chasing in the first three weeks so the hawks don't get disappointed or too orientated toward selfhunting. But after three weeks the situation can change almost overnight and it is not safe to leave them out. I cannot understand how people reckon to manage 4–5 week hacks. By this time my birds are away almost all the time and although they may come back every day or two they seldom come in at all to the hackboard. I know this because sometimes we put wild peregrine chicks out with ours to be returned to the wild following some incident with their own nests. We always pinpoint all hack birds at dawn, and again once or twice during the day, and again at dusk, making sure that they are roosting up off the ground away from foxes and cats. After two weeks of good flying at hack they have gained most of the flying skills they need, but still need 2–3 weeks to mature mentally. They do not need to be loose at hack during this period, because of the risk that they will disperse; they just need time, untouched by humans, to grow up mentally.

When the birds come in from hack their transmitters and hack bells are removed. These hack bells are just light bells to help us locate the birds and to identify the falcons as domestic ones in case somebody should be tempted to shoot them. We then turn them away into a big flight pen for a further 2–3 weeks in groups of up to 20 falcons.

This completes the mental maturation process; when they come out they are mentally ready for hunting for their own food and no longer have the juvenile urge of looking for a parent figure. They never scream at humans.

On catching up from the big pen, a tailmount and anklets are fitted and each bird is then made to the hood, fist, and lure, being back on the wing after ten to twelve days, depending on the weather. We prefer to fly them free first at the hack ground. Then, if any of them have a "technical hitch" they are on their home ground and won't go far. As soon as another bird is put up, the wanderer returns. After about ten days on the wing generally getting fitter and more reliable in the routine of trained birds, they are ready for entering at crows or rooks.

Hacking can be used to teach a falcon to home and some of them pick this up very quickly. All of my New Zealanders have been homers but now that we have telemetry to aid us homing tends to be more of a nuisance than a blessing. A falcon on the loose at home can cause a lot of damage before you can get there.

Accipiters are best not hacked except in extreme cases of aggression. Hacking reduces the bond with the falconer which is the last thing one wants to happen with accipiters. Buzzards do not benefit very much from hack; some become confirmed wormeaters and camp scroungers.

I enjoy hacking time. I like to be up at dawn watching the youngsters waking up and tipping over in the wind trying to scratch the last fluff off. Then one by one they launch uncertainly into the wind, mounting higher and higher on different levels before turning downwind with panic written all over their faces. A few short days later they are full of confidence, scything around the sky, sneaking between the air molecules as they pierce the wind which before had battered them back down. Even a biologist is allowed a romantic streak.

## 5.3   Imprinting and the tame hack

Once the imprinting process is broadly understood (see section 4.7), then it is possible to produce a bird imprinted on humans in some ways and not in others, as discussed in 4.17. This is normally achieved by hand-rearing birds from hatching onwards, either alone or in groups. As soon as the chick is capable of picking up its own minced food from a bowl, hand feeding is discontinued. From then on, the aim is to familiarize and imprint the bird on all aspects to do with humans except feeding. We wish to discourage the idea that humans are parents and encourage the youngster to mature mentally and not remain in permanent adolescence, screaming for food from a parent figure rather than catching its own. We put the young bird in a large, clear-sided imprinting box. Taped on the floor and lower sides is disposable brown paper to catch the worst of the mutes. The chick itself is placed on a shallow box or tray of pea-gravel with its dish of food. In this way the chick can see what is going on and be in the center of human activity, without risk of being trodden on or expelled by a house-proud spouse. It is taken out of the box frequently for handling, sitting on laps and so on, and hooded with a large hood. It is never openly offered food; it is always dumped near a dish of food ready waiting. Once it can pull for itself it is fed always on the lure and soon learns to run across the lawn for the lure, taking care that a long line is used so that the human is out of the picture.

As the chick grows older, it is fitted with anklets (see 3.2) and a leg transmitter (figure 3.9.1). Soon it is almost ready to fly. It is clear of fluff except a few "last stars of childhood" on its head. We leave the imprints on the long staffroom windowsill upstairs overlooking the valley and they eventually fledge from there. Each night, if they haven't come back in, we either retrieve them with a lure, or make sure they are safe and leave them until the morning. Our birds usually go and join in with others at wild hack, this improves their flying. Otherwise they need to be hacked for 3–4 weeks to become as proficient as the wild hacked ones are in half that time. The reason for this is that the imprints are slower to mature mentally and tend to fly with their brakes on. They have to get properly through this stage until they are flying boldly "out of their shoulders." Our hack sites are all very windy, and this is essential for the birds to learn to cope with stormy weather. Calm, sheltered hack sites achieve little.

Other falconers hack their imprints from a vehicle or for a shorter period, such as two hours per day. Obviously one has to use a system which fits the individual circumstances. It may not be safe to hack from home. Birds which are intended solely for breeding do not need to be hacked. I prefer to hack them and fly them at least to the lure for their first autumn. It develops their physique and character and enables me to check that they are really

A1 physically. It also means they can be flown again later in life if needed, whereas a bird which has not been flown in its first season seldom flies well if trained later.

From being hooded, lured, and hacked, it is just a short step in the youngster's education to start catching game. For falcons destined for pursuit flights, it is fun to rear several together so that they can be flown incasts. It is a lot of work to achieve a good lot of quiet, well-mannered, easy-hooding, skilled flyers, but once they are entered one starts to harvest the reward.

## 5.4 Kitting out and taking in hand

When taken in hand, the bird is fitted out with simple anklets and a tailbell. New Zealanders and accipiters are quite hard on their gear and therefore we usually attach the tailmount to the two feathers next to the two deck feathers, one on each side, taking care that the tail can fan fully. This means the weight is spread over four feathers (see 3.2 and 3.5). We normally put a sleeve or tape on the tail for the first two weeks until she has settled down.

When the hawk iscast we also measure and photograph her properly (see 2.4), check her identification and take a blood sample. This is split, labelled, and stored (see 2.29) for future use as a DNA source. The bird is also checked over to be sure she is in full health. Training and handling will inevitably put her under some physical and mental pressure which could fan the flames of a disease. During measuring, the head width can be used as a basis for selecting a hood, either by making one up from Slijper's Canon or by using a blocked hood of that size (see Appendix 2).

Provided that she cancast through the hood, and is fat and in good health, she is best left hooded quietly for 48 hours. The least traumatic way to man her is to tie her to a perch in a quiet part of the garden where nothing can go behind her and where she can see what is going on from a distance. Most of the day will be spent on the ground, picking at jesses and generally getting used to everything. Go past her (not toward her) every hour or so, putting a tidbit on the block as quietly as you can, and then retire. If she sprawls, or ignores the tidbit, or flicks it away, she is probably still too high to do anything with. If she hops up onto the block and eats it, you are on your way. In the evening, preferably once it is dark, make in as gently as you can, hood her up and put her in her night quarters. Repeat this

Putting youngsters out together at time hack helps to teach them the social graces.

Old birds at tame hack may spend hours dozing and preening rather than flying about.

the next day and the next until she anticipates your approach with a positive attitude and starts to take food from your hand. At the same time, stay nearer as she feeds. You can start her on a few tirings, such as a juicy pigeon wing, which she can pull at by her block with you lying near her giving her extra tidbits from the glove. She will then come naturally to feeding on the fist and stepping onto the fist. You have sneaked into her life without

confrontation. If, on the other hand, you attempt the old-fashioned approach to manning by putting her on your fist and carrying her about you will give her a lot of negative conditioning at the start which will take further work to cancel out. You also risk injuring her leg and hip joints, her leg scales, and her feathers. Remember, the ends of her long bones are not yet fully fused; she is still very delicate at this stage.

If she had been on her own in her pen you could have reduced her weight gently for a few days before catching her up. But then you would not have known her fat weight or been able to check her health first.

## 5.5   Manning and basic training

When the hawk was young, she gradually developed a fear response to all unfamiliar objects which were not part of her family routine (see 4.10). This blanket of fear excluded man and all his works from her world. Manning is the process whereby the handler sneaks himself inside this blanket to join the hawk in her world. He may bring some aspects of his own world along with him. Of course, if the hawk was raised in such a way that she has no fear of man (see 5.3) then no manning is needed. Accipiters are among the most fearful of hawks and stress for them in captivity can lead to diabetes, aspergillosis and other ailments. Social imprinting is often the best solution for this group.

Until this barrier of fear between hawk and man is removed, she will not be receptive to further training.

Traditional manning was an exercise in overcoming the fear response by using habituation. The hawk was carried around day after day on somebody's fist until it ignored stimuli which at first had scared it. Many trainers didn't even link the habituation with positive reinforcement or appetite motivation. The result was a system which worked but was extremely inefficient both in effort put in and in the quality of the trained bird. It was also needlessly stressful for the bird. Such birds often needed an hour of manning before being flown at quarry and, if lost in the field, were often unapproachable within 24 hours. Modern manning relies less on habituation and more on the creation and reinforcement of pleasant associations of the falconer with food. This system is faster and more positive than habituation which simply teaches the hawk to tolerate situations.

Skilled breeders are able to produce domestic hawks tailormade for their future use, whether for natural breeding or hunting. By the careful use of imprint foster-parents they produce youngsters which grow up naturally imprinted but without fear of everyday sights and sounds. Such birds are thus "naturally" tame, stress free, and a pleasure to be with. They don't need manning, they breed well and they are very resistant to disease.

Around a hawk, or indeed any individual, there is an invisible personal territory or no-go area. You can see it operating on the London Underground in the rush hour; despite the crowding, everybody tries to keep slightly away from each other and, to avoid giving threatening signals, they avert their gaze. Staring is hostile. Appeasement displays are frequent: "Whoops! So sorry!"—"Not at all. Clumsy of me."

So it is with manning. If you force yourself into a hawk's personal territory by tying it to your fist it will feel uncomfortable, if not downright afraid (figure 5.6.1) In the wild such intimacy between top predatory hawks (as distinct from kites, vultures and so on) is only tolerated between bonded birds—either a mated pair or parents and offspring. The Harris hawk which is sociable in its own hunting group is one of the few exceptions to this.

So the falconer's first task is to get himself accepted and established in some sort of bond, preferably as a hunting partner and not as a parent which can lead to all sorts of problems. He must give no threat displays, no staring (including camera lenses), no towering over the hawk, no sudden attacklike movements. He must give appeasement signals—offering food. He must take care not to let himself be associated with any nasty experience

Figure 5.5.1 Top: A shy, wild hawk has a big personal space and avoids man. Below: A tame hawk is happy to share its space with its trainer.

for the hawk. Often rather than go into immediate close confrontation he starts off by keeping mainly at a short distance or by coming up to the hawk momentarily to offer it a tidbit and then withdrawing. In this way he works himself naturally and gradually into the hawk's life and trust, forming a bond much stronger than mere habituated familiarity.

Such a hawk will recognize its trainer. It may tolerate any familiarity with him but hate at the approach of strangers. You can tell a person who doesn't understand hawks by the way he walks around the weathering lawn. Insensitive to the hawk's signals of unease at his approach, he comes too close and makes the hawk bate. He is like the dreadful person at a party who insists on pushing up to you and mouthing bad breath all over you. You react in the same way as the hawk does—by trying to escape!

The main use of the hood is to prevent the hawk from getting an unwanted experience or lesson. If you can cut out the bad, negative lessons and give the hawk only good ones, it will train in a very short time. There is no point in having a marvelous training session if the hawk bates itself to bits on the way home afterward. If you just pop the hood on at the end of the lesson you can carry it home without fuss and leave it in its familiar quarters in tranquility until it is ready for its next lesson.

Normally I start a hawk's training by hooding it, unless the bird is imprinted on humans. Hand-raised birds need to be made to the hood while they are still growing; once they are hardpenned they can be very awkward to start to the hood. As soon as the hood is on, I assess it very carefully for fit and if it doesn't fit exactly I make another that does—particularly with respect for comfort for the hawk and for not coming off. The hood must NOT be able to come off. The falconer should of course learn to hood on a made bird, preferably a falcon, not on an untrained bird. If a bird is suspicious of the hood then, whenever you walk up to it with a tidbit, serve it in an old hood. Every little bit of positive reinforcement helps.

Many authors deem it unnecessary to hood hawks and to some extent they are right. But there is quite a lot of difference between having a single Harris hawk or display bird and managing an accipiter or a team of pursuit falcons. These latter birds are hot stuff and cannot be tied near one another or flown in the sight of one another with-

out causing them to bate. A little effort early on to make the hawk to the hood well pays back later in speed of training, ease of transporting and general reduction in stress. I have driven for thousands of miles with falcons fast asleep in their hoods, even when untrained. If they had been unhooded they would have been physical and mental wrecks. Of course if the falconer is no good at hooding, he can cause a lot of damage, but we are talking here about the hawk's needs, not the falconer's inadequacies.

After about a week she should be feeding moderately well on the fist. Her hooding will probably be not very good. Many hawks only accept the hood when a juicy tiring is poking up through the beak hole. Some are awkward to hood when being taken up but accept it more graciously after hawking at the end of the day. If this is your first hawk and you are not a good hooder you may prefer not to hood at all but use a traveling box. At about this stage we usually take the bird for a long walk, hooding or using tirings when necessary, taking the dogs along and getting out into fresh ground. Prior to this her lessons had only lasted a few minutes or as long as one could spin out her meal. This afternoon or two of traditional manning is only done when she is ready for it. After this, it should be downhill all the way. In the space of two or three days she should "click" and be transformed from accipiter-type behavior, all nerves and bates, to cuddly merlin-type behavior, running round you and landing on your shoulder.

Falconers forget that the hawk is getting nasty experiences as well as "official" lessons. Most falconers cannot carry a hawk in the field without giving it a rough ride on the fist and the bird thus associates the fist with an unpleasant experience and does not perform so well with fist work. Often the green beginner is better than the blasé, "experienced" falconer in this respect. Unless you can really float your fist so that the hawk never stirs a wing, not even when you jump over a fence or ditch, you will have to fight that much harder to overcome the perpetual negative experience the hawk is getting. If you have a problem with carriage, your first "hawk" should be a cup full of water. A comfortable hawk will preen on the fist or put a foot up, sometimes while you're still moving along, and a hooded hawk may go to sleep with its head in its scapulars after a couple of hours walking.

She is ready now for the lure. I usually start

Figure 5.5.2 The hawk overflies the lure because she is not keen enough.

with a dead quail on a line. Thrown out on the ground in front of her she should plonk straight on it from a few meters, called off an assistant's fist. I lie down beside her and let her break in, offering tidbits. When she has eaten about half her ration on the quail, I use a small separate pick-up piece to lift her off the quail (covering the remainder with hand, grass, or bag). As I get back to the mews door she should be finishing the last mouthful of the pick-up piece, which comprises the other half of her ration. I have taken nothing away from her. She has only to clean her beak as I put her down, then she is left in peace.

The next day I call her a few times from fence posts in different places (if an accipiter) or from an assistant's fist (if a falcon) to the fist for small bits of meat, about ten to twenty meters. This is a proper flight, not a glorified hop, but not far enough away for her to start thinking about sheering off. I finish off with a call to the lure which consists of the artificial lure (in the case of a crow-hawk, a tuft of shredded black inner tube) garnished with a good-size chunk of feathery quail, a whole leg for example.

Normally I do most of the creance work to the lure. It is easier to judge the hawk's condition to the lure than to the fist. If the hawk starts toward a lure on the ground 5 meters out from you at 90 degrees and then overflies, she is almost certainly not keen enough (figure 5.5.2). But if she overflies the fist you can't be certain that the fear response isn't keeping her from you. The other reason for introducing the lure early is for safety. Once she

"knows" what the lure is (see 4.19), you have some prospect of getting her back if you have a disaster and lose her half-trained.

The creance is attached using a sheetbend and two falconer's knots direct to the jesses (figure 5.5.3). If you don't use the sheetbend the line can cut the jesses like cheese-wire, and if you leave the swivel on it will constantly catch and tangle on the smallest thing.

I try to do as little creance work as possible. The emphasis in training should always be speed of response, not distance. Repeated high-jumping to the fist indoors will quickly hammer home the

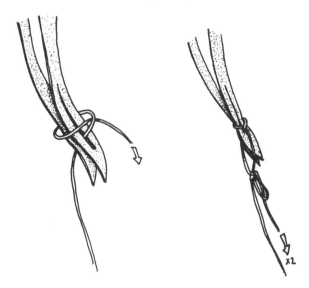

Figure 5.5.3 Attaching the creance to the jesses using a sheet-bend and a double falconer's knot.

lesson of a fast confident return to the fist and it is better to get this well learned and then only need three or four days with the creance. I usually fly the falcons loose once they immediately come a full 50 meter creance length and a few years ago I started to wonder why I was training my hawks so quickly. Then I discovered that people had been cutting bits off the creances for other jobs and the creances were getting shorter and shorter! So much for progress.

A typical lesson at this stage would be 2 meters to the fist, 10, 20, 30 meters to the lure, getting a small amount each time, $\frac{1}{10}$ crop on last lure call, $\frac{2}{10}$ picked up on the fist, hood up, take home, $\frac{1}{10}$ crop as she is put away on her perch. She can now stay unhooded when not being trained, if she hoods well and if she stands quietly when unhooded.

Once an accipiter is coming promptly 50 m to the lure, swing the lure onto the fist and she will come to that too. I make all species of accipiter, buteo, and falcon to both fist and lure. The falcons are taught to take the lure in the air, using a thin stick to hold the lure up if necessary for the initial lesson. Later they are exercised to the lure to improve their footing, maneuverability, and fitness. Still later the game falcons can be taught to wait on using the lure. Accipiters also get plenty of lurework, giving them valuable experience of being picked up off the "kill." It is, of course, possible to fly an accipiter without using a lure, just as it is to ride a horse without a saddle, if you are a masochist. To reach the full potential of an accipiter's attack strategies entails starting some attacks from perches other than the fist and you need a lure then to keep control. To fly an accipiter solely from the fist is to miss most of her potential as a hunting bird.

The next day I put a transmitter on. If I can't get 50 meters away from the hawk before she comes, I fly her free there and then. The best place to fly an accipiter free is on open ground with no trees for at least 500 meters in any direction. Teach her to take off and land on the ground and she will do that instead of flying a long distance to reach a perch every time she misses. Put her on the ground or on a stone and call her. Give her 15–20 short (10 meter) calls until you have to run to get away from her. Call her at oblique angles along walls and fences (figure 5.5.4). Teach her to fly from the fist to a perch you show her a few meters away. Vary the terrain but only introduce high perches that you can't reach when the hawk has proved her reliability. A couple of evenings on fence work should teach her to keep up with you and move on to order. Later on this lesson is used when hunting through woodland, but first teach it in a situation where you have good control.

In one respect hawks and horses are very similar. There are some people who, when they ride a horse or work a hawk, somehow put it on its toes; they "energize it." That animal will become like a coiled spring, poised to do its master's bidding. It is happy, alert, attentive. When the person asks it to do something, the animal goes into action with vigor. Ten to one that rider doesn't carry a stick and that falconer doesn't need a bag of tidbits. Other people have the opposite effect. The horse becomes a slug, dragging its feet, it gets nappy and needs a stick or spurs to provide any temporary semblance of impulsion. The hawk becomes "moody" and can only be tempted back with an assortment of bits and pieces accompanied by much whistling, hallowing, and general pandering. I'm sure that a lot of this is due to differences in actual training and handling methods. But also, behind that, I think the animals can detect the person's natural energy and respond to it.

Figure 5.5.4 Calling the hawk obliquely along a fenceline.

Most of the hawk's obedience training has been achieved by fast-response high jumps rather than long calls. The outdoor work has been done in a variety of places so that she is accustomed to novelty. There should not be a lot of tedious line work in a "training field." Using one place for training can induce superstitious behavior (see 4.17) and lead to a confused response in unfamiliar surroundings later on.

The moment you are confident that you can get her back it is time to prepare for entering. Many falcons are ruined at this stage because people overtrain them. Some raptors are very intelligent and it only takes a couple of lessons for them to learn that you are the Great Provider, the source of all free handouts. They will quickly train you to provide these free meals and will soon train you to come to them. Do not fall into this trap! It happens most when hawks are trained while still in their juvenile dependency stage.

Once entered, instead of just tolerating the dog by habituation, the hawk now gets positive conditioning as she links the dog with the point and the flush of game. The falconer must retain the positive link between himself and food and with "hot" attacking species, such as goshawks and merlins, he may have to stop flying quarry periodically to reinforce this link. Species which are less keen on their quarry must not get too linked with the trainer and the maximum effort has to be made to condition the hawk toward quarry. All raptors notice very clearly if the falconer and dog are making a big effort to find and reflush game, and the falconer who wanders round the fields nattering to a friend and expecting the quarry to come out with its hands up will soon have a hawk with no interest in killing for itself.

But we are rushing ahead. There are a lot of aspects to consider before the hawk is ready for serious hawking.

## 5.6   Motivation

Now we're getting into training, you are probably discovering that all this discussion is fine but the reality is that the trainee is not responding as well as it should. Maybe the hawk has gone on strike completely.
It is time to look at motivation and at training techniques.

You can't train an animal to do something until it is motivated to do it. You can't reward the hawk for flying to the fist unless it wants to do it in the first place. Calling to the fist or lure is actually just a simplified version of the Direct flying attack (see 6.10) as far as the hawk is concerned. The reasons why a hawk flies to your fist are basically the same reasons why it flies at a rabbit.

Motivation comes initially from inside the animal, whereas training is the outside world working on the animal. The hawk's brain receives messages from its body through nerve signals, chemicals, or hormones. These trigger it into making decisions (figure 5.6.1). Receptors in the crop stomach, intestine, and liver monitor what quantity and quality of food is in the digestive tract and the levels of substances in the blood stream. As these levels fluctuate, so the brain is motivated toward the desire to eat and to hunt for food, or, later, to relax after a heavy meal. These pathways are complex and it is not a simple matter of the hungrier it is, the more it wants to hunt. Far from it, a starving bird is likely to be apathetic. Also linked to the hawk's internal drives are external ones, such as the sight of others feeding, or the presence of tempting easy prey, or having a hungry family to feed. Some male Mauritius kestrels we radiotracked spent up to 95 percent of daylight hours actively hunting when they had young to feed. They themselves weren't necessarily hungry, they were driven by their reproductive instincts to forage for their young. The racing pigeon fraternity use this drive to motivate pigeons using the Widower System.

The neural pathways for hunting for food and for eating are separate. Just because an animal wants to eat, does not mean it wants to hunt. And just because it doesn't want to eat, doesn't mean it doesn't want to hunt. There are many examples of predators, including raptors, which kill more than they want to eat, or which kill something and then hide it without eating it. Although in most everyday examples hunting and eating are linked, this is achieved by separate neural pathways. Therefore, if you want an animal to do something, you have to try to maximize its motivation and this may require some careful thought and analysis.

When you introduce external training methods, motivation becomes a balance between pleasure and pain. Pain includes punishment and also negative reinforcement, the two are not the same. Punishment is given after the unwanted behavior and tends to decrease bad behavior. Negative reinforcement tends to increase good behavior or decrease bad behavior, thus the horse increases its effort to avoid the whip. But it only does enough to avoid it, it doesn't give more. An animal which is trained through positive reinforcement on the other hand, will strive to give even more because of the possibility of getting even more reward. This is essentially how we train a hawk; it does something because it wants to, not because it is forced to.

So the hawk gets first turn at the dialogue. She must tell you how she feels, what her internal

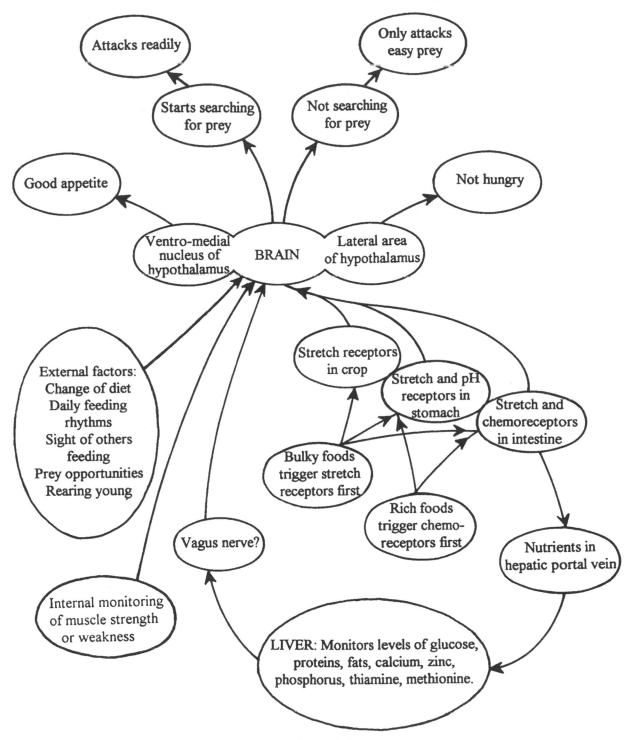

Figure 5.6.1 The pathways linking food intake, appetite, and hunting behavior.

Only bonded birds allow one another within their personal territory.

motivation is. So you must be receptive and ask the hawk. Only then can you tell her anything, because your message must be tailored to her needs. Be clear in your own mind what your message is. If you are not clear, how can you expect her to be? Each day have specific goals laid on the firm foundation of previous progress. Reach each goal in small steps and get each step right before moving on. Ask yourself—how can I make it simpler for her? The better you get at this question and answer game, the better communication you will have and the hawk will seem to get more intelligent.

Try not to ask her questions that will result in incorrect answers. If you ask and the hawk doesn't do it, either she hasn't understood, or she is saying "No, I don't have to." This is establishing a pattern of refusal, which is in fact a form of training, but not for what you want. You must make it easy for her to say "Yes" and only work from the last point where you got a consistent "Yes."

The hawk will know when you have lost control, just as a child or dog does. The skilled trainer works right up at the cliff-edge of losing control, but stays in command. The unskilled trainer cannot easily see where the edge of control is; he constantly goes over it, resulting in behavioral problems to be overcome or, worse still, the loss of

the hawk.

To progress further in training we need to look more closely at motivation and the internal factors which drive the hawk, and the symptoms which enable you to read them.

## 5.7    Physical condition

So far in training we have assumed the hawk is responsive and in the right physical condition for training. To bring a raptor into condition is the key to successful falconry and requires a good understanding of how the digestive system works in practice and how the hawk metabolizes energy.

Starting perhaps with a fat youngster, or a newly molted hawk, the object is to achieve a bird which has plenty of muscle, little or no fat, a good appetite and which is free of disease. Such a hawk

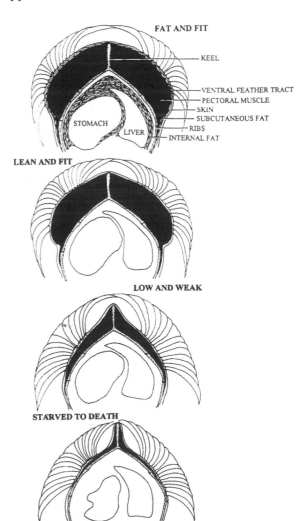

Figure 5.7.1 A section of the chest of a falcon to show the pectoral muscles and fat stores.

will fly keenly, strongly, and predictably.

There are three ways of judging condition: by feeling the hawk's muscles, by weighing it and by watching its behavior. The traditional way of feeling the hawk's pectoral muscles is unreliable in that most of a hawk's fat is stored inside the body cavity around the internal organs, over the scapulars and around the sacrum, lower abdomen, and tail. Only the weighing machine can detect it. Although some fat is stored in the pectoral muscles and in a thin subcutaneous layer over them it can happen that an unfit hawk will have wasted breast muscles and yet be very fat. Another hawk may be fit and well-muscled and have no fat at all (see Figure 5.7.1). Thus you can feel the muscle mass but not the fat. If you can actually feel that your hawk is thin then you have reduced it too much. How can it give of its best if its muscles are wasted?

Weighing the hawk and keeping a progress

| Species | | | | Sex | Ring number | Name |
|---|---|---|---|---|---|---|
| SAKER | | | | ♀ | 10320W | JEDRAN |

| Date | Time | Weight | Crop | |
|---|---|---|---|---|
| 22/7/95 | 2300 | 1210 | 0 | Taken out of pen, measured, tail belled, anklets hood etc fitted after dark |
| 23 Sun | 20 00 | 1190 | 0 | Hooded all day. |
| 24 | 20 00 | 1177 | 0 | Hooded all day. |
| 25 | 0900 | 1155 | 1/10 Rabbit | Unhooded on quiet corner of lawn. Took a few titbits. |
| 26 Weds | 0900 | 1140 | 1/10 Rabbit. | Sitting up on block well and not bating off when approached with titbit. |
| 27 | 0930 | 1130 | 2/10 Rabbit | Fed on rabbit leg on block with me sitting next to her. Left her to tire on the foot. |
| 28 | 0900 | 1125 | 3/10 Rabbit. | Ate some rabbit on fist indoors. Bit bouncy but not too bad. Good with titbits on lawn. |
| 29 | 0830 | 1130 | 3/10 Rabbit | Busy all day. Fed on fist around campfire in the evening. Hooding well. |
| 30 Sun | 1100 | 1125 | 3/10 Rab | Stepping up on to fist well + feeding freely. Took her out riding (hooded) for 2 hrs in pm. |
| 31 | 1030 | 1120 | 3/10 Rab | 18 fast jumps to fist. Introduced lure. Doesn't want to bath! |
| 1 Aug. Tues. | 0930 | 1118 | 4/10 Rab | 27 fast jumps to fist. 10 metres to lure. |
| 2 | 0900 | 1130 | 3/10 Rab | 30 jumps but patchy. 10 metres to lure. Needs to be down a bit. |
| 3 | 0830 | 1120 | 3/10 Rab | 45 good jumps. 25 metres to lure. Travelled overnight to Northumberland. |
| 4 Fri | 1430 | 1115 | 3/10 Rab | Bit strange for her up here! 30 jumps + 20 metres to lure. Weathering in cold wind. |
| 5 | 0930 | 1105 | 4/10 Rab | Flew loose. One straight 20 metres to lure, 1 call + turn. 40 jumps in mews. |
| 6 | 0900 | 1115 | 4/10 Rab | 7 stoops to lure in 3 bouts. Took lure in air on last attempt. 40 jumps. |
| 7 Mon | 0900 | 1120 | 4/10 Rab | 22 stoops in 2 bouts. Got a bit wet so gave 40 jumps after dark. |
| 8 | 0930 | 1125 | 4/10 Rab | 35 stoops. 45 jumps. |
| 9 | 1430 | 1125 | 3/10 Rab | Rained all day. 65 jumps. |
| 10 | 1400 | 1120 | 3/10 Rab | Long luring – 500 metres. 30 stoops. Finished with 100 m call to dragged dead crow. |
| 11 Fri | 1430 | 1117 | 3/10 Rab | About 35 stoops to lures in a cast with Hagar. No problems. Thrown a dead crow. |
| 12 Sat | 1500 | 1115 | 6/10 Crow | Watch Hill. Hagar took crow in rush patch. Jedran joined flight. No crabbing on kill. Split crow for them |
| | | | | |

Figure 5.7.2 A training progress chart. See appendix 3 for blank charts.

chart is a much more reliable method provided that weights are properly understood, recorded, and checked with behavior on a progress chart (figure 5.7.2). A good counterbalance scales or checked electronic scales should be used; spring balances are untrustworthy. Keep a 500 gram weight to check the scales each day. Working in grams, once you are used to it, is infinitely easier than in ounces and one tends to work more accurately too. For a hawk of about 900 grams (2 lbs.) I weigh to an accuracy of one gram and pay attention to differences of 5 grams, which is $\frac{5}{28}$ or just under 0.18 ounces. This is about the weight of one mute. A difference of 5 grams will normally show a detectable difference in behavior in a bird of this size, depending on factors we'll examine in the next section.

## 5.8   The components of weight

Let's look at the hawk's weight in more detail. It consists of five components:

a) Base weight. This is the base weight below which the hawk will die. This starvation weight depends on species, sex, age, air temperature, humidity, and on the speed of starvation. A starving Red-shouldered hawk was found by Kendeigh in 1945 to have a base weight of 60 percent of its fat weight. See also figure 1.1.1.

b) Stored fat. This can contribute up to 30 percent of the fat bodyweight.

c) Muscle. The muscles throughout the body can vary by 20 percent of the fat bodyweight depending on whether the hawk is fit or starving.

d) Gut contents. The maximum weight of the gut contents can add a further 20 percent to a hawk's fat weight and this is why, ideally, a hawk should be empty to obtain a proper weight record. A fresh goshawk pellet weighs 10–12 grams.

e) Equipment. The hood, anklets, bells, and so on should be taken into account and subtracted before calculating percentages but can be left in the total on a daily basis.

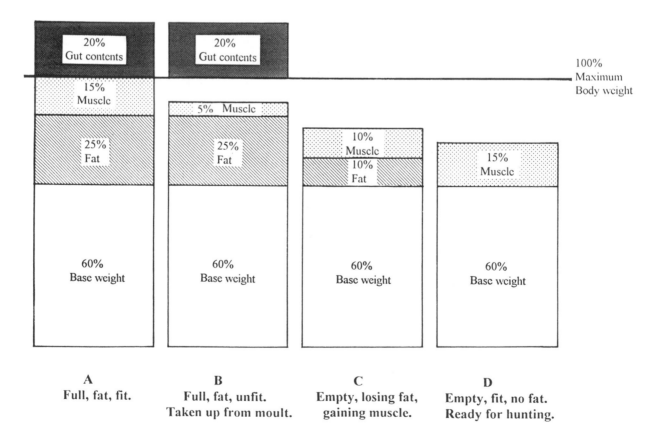

Figure 5.8.1 The components of weight.

These weight components all vary independently from one another and therefore just because a hawk is at a certain weight does not necessarily mean it is ready to fly. The components also vary considerably between individual birds and between species, particularly between large hawks and small ones. No generalized figures can be given but Figure 5.8.1 gives some idea of the variation.

During reclaiming after the molt, the falconer aims to remove all stored fat from his bird and build up the muscles to their full capacity. If fat is left on the bird during the hawking season it will buffer the effect of dieting and appetite controls, resulting in unpredictable behavior, rather like loose steering on a car. As the fat is lost, there is a reduction in weight and, as muscle is formed, there is a gain in weight. The two processes should be simultaneous and usually result in a net loss in weight because more fat is lost than is replaced by muscle, depending on what type of hawking will be done. Jack Mavrogordato in *A Hawk for the Bush* gives 10 percent as a rough guide and this has become known as the 10 percent rule. It's not a hard and fast rule by any means but it's a start.

The exchange of fat for muscle is done by reducing the intake of energy to below the amount of energy used up. So it is wise first of all to check for internal parasites and treat these before cutting the weight down. The plan is not to eliminate fat (by food reduction) and then build up muscle, but rather to burn off the fat using increasing exercise which at the same time builds up the muscles. Therefore, we need some idea of what energy is being lost and what is being gained.

## 5.9   Energy losses

The raptor uses its energy in three ways: for its basal metabolism, its existence metabolism, and its productive metabolism. The basal metabolism is the energy needed simply to keep the body functioning and the heart beating. It is proportional to body size; small hawks, such as sparrowhawks and merlins, have a much higher basal metabolism than do large buzzards and eagles. Some individuals and some species, such as the desert falcons, need far less to eat than others of equivalent size, such as peregrines. In survival terms, the energy demands of the central nervous system, the brain and brain stem, take priority. It can only use energy in the form of glucose. The other systems can use energy in other forms.

The existence metabolism is the extra energy needed for the raptor to cope with the physiological effects of temperature changes, wind, rain and so on. Depending on climate some species need about 15 percent more food in winter than in summer, or if moved to a cold district from a warm one. Every autumn when the frosts come, one hears of trained sparrowhawks dying from low blood sugar fits because their trainers have not made allowance for the effects of the bad weather. As the season progresses the falconer should aim to increase the hawk's weight by at least 5 percent of the early season flying weight. This goes into filling out with extra muscle. Also, by the winter, the hawk should know its business and a little extra weight, especially for the delicate species, is a wise insurance policy. A friend who had cut his sparrowhawk rather finely and then, neglected to give it its second feed on Christmas day because he was celebrating, was horrified to find the next morning that it had lost thirty grams and was in a state of collapse. Only by tube feeding and assiduous nursing was the hawk saved and two weeks were lost before the hawk regained its strength. In such a situation the hawk should not be fed solid food because it won't have the strength to put it over into the stomach; the food will remain undigested in the crop. If this happens the soured crop contents must be flushed out and the crop irrigated with warm water, or, better still "Reglin" which helps promote motility in the gut. Then it should be tube fed warm electrolyte fluids at the rate of about 20 ml/kg. If available it can also be given steroids, B vitamins, iron, and if necessary, antibiotics. It should be kept slightly warm and undisturbed. Once it is perking up, the first meals should be very fine and nutritious, such as bird liver with a little fat, put through a blender.

Conversely, sakers flown in the desert almost live on air. Just the brain, tongue, and liver from a hare is enough to keep them steady; any more and they pile on weight and become unmanageable.

The productive metabolism is the energy required for activities such as hunting, courtship, nesting, and so on. In racing pigeons the energy used during flight is about eight times that for basal metabolism. This is why, if a sparrowhawk is allowed to get low in fat and muscle, an afternoon's flying in cold weather can reduce the blood sugars to a fatally low level. When the body needs energy, the liver converts stored glycogen from a recent meal into glucose in the bloodstream. When the level of glycogen in the liver gets low then stored fat is converted into energy. Unfortunately, in small species with a high basal metabolism, the body cannot convert fat into energy fast enough for the metabolic demand. This is why it is possible for a small hawk to show symptoms of temporary lowness even though it is not near the bottom of its weight range. This lowness can occur in half an hour if the metabolic demands are high and the remedy is to minimize the existence and productive metabolic demands and to supply an easily assimilated form of energy such as glucose or lean meat. As long ago as the sixteenth century the anonymous author of *A Perfect Booke for Kepinge of Sparhawkes or Goshawkes* advised that leaving a sparrowhawk empty in the morning after she hascast makes her poor; a small feed then is necessary to keep her "lusty"

After eating a meal, the digestion takes about six hours and so for this period energy is being converted directly from the food. This is called dietary energy. Further energy is stored as glycogen in the liver. This supply can be reconverted to energy and will keep the hawk going a further six hours or so. The remaining food is converted into fat and muscle, and some of this fat will promptly be needed to convert back into energy to last the bird for the remaining 24 less 6 (from food), less 6 (from the liver) = 12 hours. So there is a constant ebb and flow of nutrients and energy in the bird's body.

In the absence of fat, hawks can convert their own muscle, which is protein, into energy. Proteins are the building blocks of the body and their amino acids are broken down by gluconeogenesis to glucose. Protein yields only about one quarter as much energy as fat and so if a bird depends on burning up its own muscle it loses weight and condition rapidly. This is why, if a raptor is gradually cut down in weight over a two or three week period after the molt, there is a steady weight loss followed by a sudden drop. During the early stages the bird is metabolizing fat into energy and water, which presumably is why the mutes are so watery at this stage, but once the fat is gone, protein is metabolized and four times as much is needed for the same amount of energy. This means you have gone too far and you must boost the meals so that the weight returns to slightly above that at which the sudden drop occurred. The aim is not to remove all the fat but to use it to build up muscle,

and the balance, especially in small species, is a knife-edge. Attempts to control the behavior of an unresponsive intermewed bird, which may have forgotten its conditioned responses, by lowering its weight further, should be resisted. Such a bird does not need starving, it needs training.

It actually takes time and energy to break down protein into energy, so much so that a small accipiter, in low condition, may not have sufficient blood sugar levels to convert its muscles into useable energy and will become a victim of temporary lowness or hypoglycemia. This is even more extreme than if it had had some fat reserves to call on. Also of course, the last thing you want a hawk to do is burn off muscle tissue. It needs it for flying about with.

Muscles also store large quantities of glycogen which is intended for anaerobic muscle activity. Once this is used up during a sprint, then the muscles need glycogen brought to them rapidly by the blood supply from the liver, as well as having the breakdown products, carbon dioxide, and lactic acid removed.

Another point to bear in mind, especially as it is often the hottest time of the year when hawks are taken up from the molt, is dehydration. Birds adapted to a temperate climate need, very roughly, sixteen times as much water for evaporation to keep cool at 44 degrees centigrade than at 1 degrees centigrade. When a hawk is burning energy in flying or bating, it is heating itself up and has to pant to cool down and this loses water through the surfaces of the airsacs. Some lose a lot of water during car journeys or other possible stress situations and even if water is available some may be too wild or stressed to drink. Deep freezing has a tendency to dry out the food and therefore warm tapwater is often better for thawing food than a slow, drying heat. In hot weather, a bath should always be available and the hawk should be kept out of direct sunlight. In cold weather, the hawk should be fed a little extra fat, especially after a lot of flying.

This constant interchange of nutrients for energy is a perpetual process and should be stimulated. It acts at three levels, physiological, physical and mental. Whenever you get the chance, oscillate the energy reserves of the hawk. Don't maintain her at flying weight constantly for two or three weeks at a time. Whenever a day appears when, due to bad weather or other commitments, she will not be flown, tank her right up. Then ease her

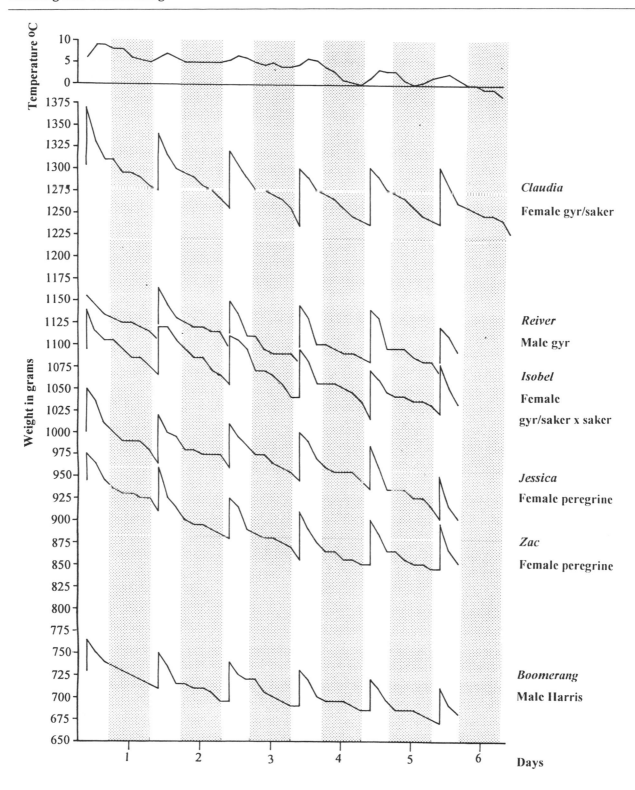

**Shaded area = night time**

Figure 5.9.1 Changes in weight for six raptors being cut down over six days.

down just before her next hunting day. This encourages her physiological systems to function rapidly in their task of energy conversion. A good bulging crop will keep her gut in good physical

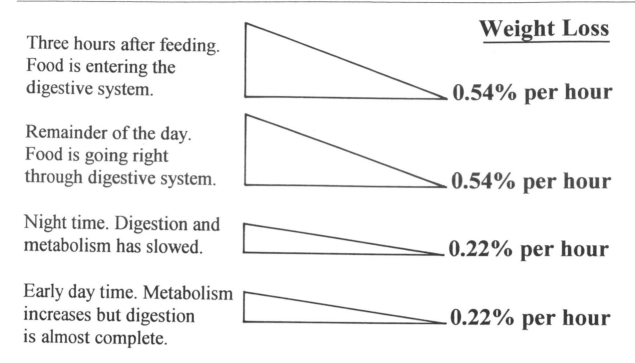

Three hours after feeding. Food is entering the digestive system.

**Weight Loss**

0.54% per hour

Remainder of the day. Food is going right through digestive system.

0.54% per hour

Night time. Digestion and metabolism has slowed.

0.22% per hour

Early day time. Metabolism increases but digestion is almost complete.

0.22% per hour

Figure 5.9.2 Mean weight changes for the six raptors in 5.9.1.

shape and pull at those stretch receptors. And at a mental level she will have more sparkle too. Even with the breeding birds we follow the same principle; raising and lowering their weight stops them getting stale and lethargic and makes them much more active and interactive.

Just keeping a hawk awake speeds up its digestive processes and increases its existence metabolism. The Persian author of the *Baz-nama-yi Nasi* in 1868 noted that a hawk when carried would mute three times for every two mutes when left unattended. By weighing a hawk periodically throughout the 24 hour cycle it is easy to quantify this. Figure 5.9.1. shows the weight fluctuations of six raptors over six days and nights. The shaded areas indicate the hours of darkness and the top graph records the temperature. The birds were left undisturbed on perches without exercise and were not heavily fat. They were fed at 10 A.M. and their weights recorded before and after the meal and then every three hours. The amount of food given was not enough to maintain a steady weight and so they gradually lost weight over the six days in the same way as when a hawk is reduced in weight for hawking. Figure 5.9.2 shows the mean values for each hawk for the six days expressed as percentage of body weight.

For the first two hours after feeding the food is passing along the digestive system and weight is

not lost very quickly, but by the third hour it has traveled the whole length of the gut. Once the first food is fully digested, the hawk is muting frequently, and during daylight it has a rapid metabolism. During this period it loses weight more quickly. On average, weight is lost at 0.54 percent of total body weight every hour. Once darkness comes, the hawk goes to sleep and digestion continues at a slower rate, usually with fewer, but larger, mutes. There is not much food left in the gut and weight is lost at half the speed as before: only 0.22 percent of total body weight per hour. By morning the hawk is almost empty and does not lose much weight from muting. It is obtaining energy by metabolizing the last of its fat stores or by metabolizing protein from muscles. Thus the weight loss throughout the 24 hours is by no means a straight line loss, but rather it falls at different rates according to what energy stores are being used at the time and the speed of metabolism.

When the hawks are at steady or increasing weights, these differences become more marked (figures 5.9.3 and 4). The volume and activity of the gut is greater. The food does not travel through much more quickly, but in greater amounts, so weight is lost more rapidly, at up to 1.17 percent of body weight per hour. By nightfall the pressure in the gut decreases, as does digestive activity and also the metabolism. But some food is still present

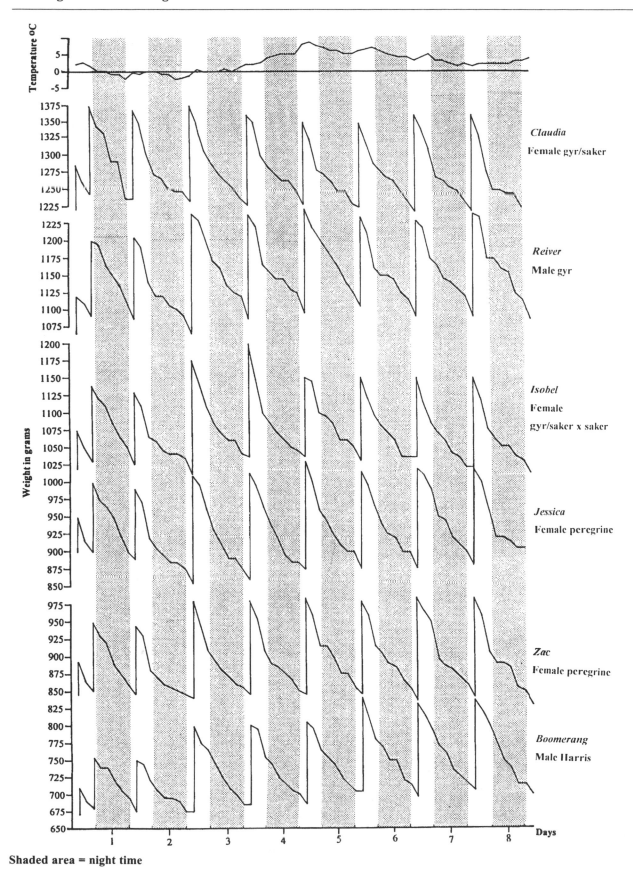

Figure 5.9.3 Changes in weight for six raptors being raised in weight over eight days.

**Shaded area = night time**

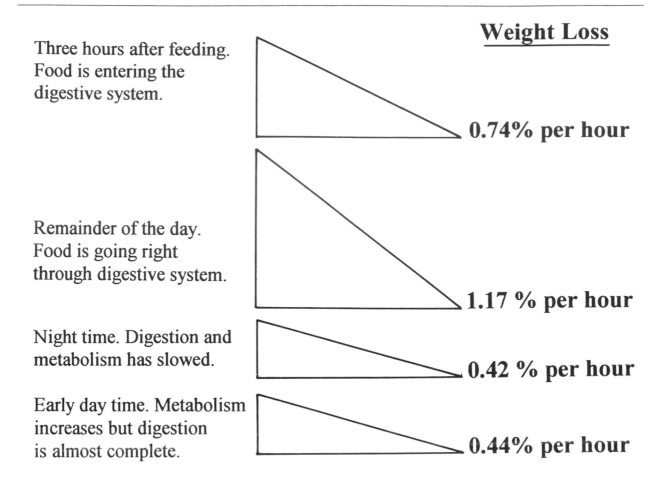

# Weight Loss

Three hours after feeding. Food is entering the digestive system.

**0.74% per hour**

Remainder of the day. Food is going right through digestive system.

**1.17 % per hour**

Night time. Digestion and metabolism has slowed.

**0.42 % per hour**

Early day time. Metabolism increases but digestion is almost complete.

**0.44% per hour**

Figure 5.9.4 Mean weight changes for the six raptors in 5.9.3.

and weight is lost at 0.42 percent of body weight per hour—still almost double what happened when the hawk was decreasing overall weight. In the morning, the metabolism and digestion picks up slightly and weight is lost at 0.44 percent of body weight per hour.

Hooding in a quiet place has a similar effect to natural darkness and if a hawk is left hooded on a full crop it sometimes happens that the next morning she still has half a crop left and is not fit to fly.

The way in which a hawk is reduced after the molt needs to be done carefully. The old writers recommended keeping a fat peregrine or goshawk hooded for the first six or seven days lest in her breathless bating she be struck down by an apoplectic fit. If the hawk is on her own in a flight pen it is a simple matter to lower her by giving her a reduced ration for a week or ten days before taking her out. As soon as she is at all civilized it is best then to push ahead with exercise. Not only will the work burn off the fat more rapidly, it will also convert it into muscle. It is much better and safer

to build up muscle this way than to strip her down almost to base weight and then to try to build up muscle through feeding. The best way to do this with an accipiter is to give her high jumps (see 5.15) which not only gives her measurable controlled hard exercise but also sharpens her up mentally and produces a snappy response.

Once the hawk has used up all her fat and is enseamed, the good falconer feeds her up well and flies her hard. The more work she does the more food she burns up, the bigger her appetite, the more toned up her system and the stronger she gets. Being strong and keen she will be obedient and eager to fly. Inexperienced falconers are often astonished at the crops a fit falcon can take. "Aren't you going to fly her tomorrow?" is the query on seeing the bulging crop. But the next morning there she is, bright-eyed, winnowing her wings, bursting to carve the sky to pieces over your head.

## 5.10 Energy gains

It is much easier to strip weight off a hawk than to put it on again. The quantities and qualities of food are so hard to judge that inexperienced falconers suffer constantly from their own mistakes.

Different foods have different energy values which can be measured either directly by calorimetry or indirectly by measuring the effects on the hawk's weight. Some values for common foods are listed below:

|  | Kcal/g | Grams equivalent to 100 g mouse |
|---|---|---|
| Mouse | 1.57 | 100 |
| Small birds | 1.31 | 120 |
| Hare meat | 1.19 | 132 |
| Day-old chicks | 1.08 | 145 |
| Whole rabbit | 1.01 | 155 |
| Beef heart | 1.01 | 155 |

Thus a hawk which required 100 grams of mouse to keep a steady weight would need about 145 grams of day-old chick. Warm, fresh food has a higher energy content than cold or thawed food. Fat in any food puts up its energy value tremendously. If while feeding up your hawk, you stand proudly discussing her performance with a friend and fail to notice that gobbet of fat she bolts down, you will be in for a shock the next morning. We've all done it. Bird fat from ducks, moorhens, winter migrants, poultry heads and so on may put your hawk out of condition for several days—a good supplement perhaps during the molt but not during the hawking season.

Different parts of an animal have different food values. The front part of a rabbit is red meat, almost as good as hare, whereas the white meat from the back and hind legs is very poor, almost as bad as washed beef. Small hawks such as sparrowhawks need high energy food and if fed on rabbit they cannot digest the food fast enough to maintain weight.

The common diets fed to hawks are dead day-old cockerels, rats, mice, coturnix quail, rabbits, hares, butcher's meat, and assorted small birds and game birds caught by the hawk. Of these only rats, mice, quail, and adult birds provide a complete, balanced diet. Some, such as butcher's meat, are extremely unbalanced and should be fed for only very short periods and never to young hawks. Day-old chicks, rabbits, and hares are subsistence diets and the latter two are not adequate to keep small hawks alive. Subsistence diets require supple-

mentary vitamins and minerals to balance them.

Adult large falconry species, if they regularly receive good feeds of pheasant, ducks, or other fresh kills out hawking, will survive on one of the subsistence diets. But breeders and growing youngsters need a full balanced diet if they are to do well. Many of the hatching problems which have dogged merlin breeders have been traced to diet rather than to technical procedures.

We do not know exactly what the nutrient needs of each species of bird of prey are, nor can one design a perfect supplement because this also depends on the composition of the basic diet. But one should be aware of the different roles of vitamins and minerals in the diet and the problems which can arise if they are over or under supplied (see 2.10).

The quantity of food to be fed depends on its energy content. Also smaller hawks with their faster metabolism need proportionately more food than do larger ones. Sharp-shinned hawks need to consume up to about 25 percent of their own bodyweight in food daily. Medium-sized raptors need about 8–15 percent and golden eagles only 5–6 percent. But of course these figures vary widely depending on the type of food and on the metabolic demands the hawk may have to meet.

A golden eagle can eat about 1500 grams of food in one meal, about six times its daily requirement. Smaller hawks, needing relatively more food, have to eat more often. This means that small hawks, such as sparrowhawks and merlins, can be flown on "appetite" rather than on weight, if flown daily. (See 5.12.)

How does one measure the quantity of food a hawk eats? It is all very well to weigh the food or to weigh the hawk before and after feeding but this is hardly practical out hawking. The solution is to measure the crop size. This is the system I use:
- Empty crop—nothing can be felt in the crop and the mutes show no pressure or are green with bile.
- $\frac{1}{10}$ crop—nothing can be felt in the crop but you have fed her a certain amount which has gone straight down into the stomach for digestion.
- $\frac{2}{10}$ crop—food can be felt in the crop but nothing is visible.
- $\frac{3}{10}$ crop—a slight displacement of the feathers makes the food visible.
- $\frac{4}{10}$ crop—there is a definite small rounded

crop visible.
- $^5/_{10}$ crop—the crop is larger and more pointed at the base.
- $^6/_{10}$ crop—the crop is wider but is still pointed at the base.
- $^7/_{10}$ crop—the crop is now flattened at the base.
- $^8/_{10}$ crop—the crop is now becoming asymmetrical, building up more on the bird's right side.
- $^9/_{10}$ crop—the crop is even larger but is not quite tight and the feathers are able to cover it.
- Full crop—the hawk refuses more and seems uncomfortable. Bare skin may show on the front and either side of the crop. The tip of the bird's beak may touch the crop when at rest. Bird may not tuck its head into its scapulars until some of the crop has been put over.

It is fruitless trying to photograph these crop sizes; there is no substitute for looking carefully and feeling gently with finger and thumb. It is very helpful now and then to cut up the hawk's food into 10 gram rations and feed it bit by bit, noting what the crop looks like with each known weight consumed. It may seem difficult at first but a skilled falconer can keep his hawk within 1–2 grams of a predetermined weight day after day. Until he is able to feed reliably he will never get on top of the problems which arise from poor conditioning. Also, by trying to train or fly a hawk when it is not fully responsive, disobedience or poor attitudes to quarry can arise and can be hard to eradicate later. Thus the problems pile up.

## 5.11 Enseaming or preparing the stomach

To get a hawk into flying condition is not just a matter of getting the fat off and the muscle on, although many modern falconers seem to think so. It is also a question of toning up the digestive system.

It is easy to fly a falcon to the lure or an accipiter to the fist. It is not hard to catch things in a mediocre sort of way. But to make a hawk really strong and bold, to take her into the field at the height of her courage, that is the mark of the skilled falconer. Unfortunately it is not so easily achieved or even explained. Inexperienced falconers cannot even recognize it. Certainly the ancients understood it much better than we do.

First, attention at all times should be paid to

the tone of the whole digestive system. Good tone is best achieved by plenty of bulk going through the system. Hunger or appetite seems to be controlled by the hypothalamus via stretch receptors in the crop and stomach and by pH sensors in the stomach. Feeding small crops for long periods seems to allow the crop to shrink, reducing the appetite. On the other hand, a hawk that is frequently fed large crops, even if the food quality is low, will be hungry after only a small crop.

In terms of bulk, casting material such as feathers or fur is of little use because it is returned from the stomach and does not enter the intestine at all. Best then at least once a week to give a good "blow-out" of rabbit or even, if necessary, of washed meat; anything that will fill her right up without putting her out of yarak.

It is noticeable that goshawks tend to maintain their drive to hunt possibly for an hour after they have taken a full crop. This may be because they are more impulsive attackers than falcons or it may be because it is not until food reaches the goshawk's intestine that hunting is inhibited. Peregrines on the other hand tend to be keen to hunt almost in proportion to the size of their crops. If one's peregrine is overkeen its condition can be adjusted quite well by giving an appropriate small feed.

Second, one must attend to the lining of the gut. If the gut is lined with mucus or grease it cannot function properly and the appetite will be poor. Additionally, the cuticle or koilin lining of the gizzard (see section 1.4) is shed periodically, either as a whole or in pieces. Its function is to protect the stomach from digesting itself with its own acids and it is continuously sloughing off and being replaced by new material. If too thick a layer accumulates it can be cleaned off either chemically with "scourings" or mechanically with rangle and castings.

Typical medieval scourings consisted of pellets made from clarified butter and sugar with a variety of additives such as powdered cloves, saffron, rue, rosemary, aloe, nutmeg, and celandine root to make the effect milder or more severe according to need. These recipes used properly had a pronounced effect on the appetite and were not placebos by any means. Saffron for example contains colchicine which is used in the treatment of gout. Eastern falconers still use ammonium chloride or sal ammoniac to loosen and strip off the excess cuticle in the gizzard. This drastic procedure is now fortunately less common; it has killed many hawks.

The more natural way of cleaning the stomach is through the use of rangle stones andcastings. Wild hawks use rangle and I have found it used by Common, Mauritius and Nankeen kestrels, by merlins, New Zealand falcons, at least three sub-species of peregrine, sakers, and gyrfalcons (see figure 5.11.1). I have also found one sample from a wild common buzzard in Scotland and from a wild golden eagle in Utah. There are no records that I know of from accipiters although it would be difficult to find with these woodland species. The author of *The Skoole for a Young Ostringer of Faulkener* considered that rangle is harmful to ac-cipiters and could kill them, but other authors do not agree with him, indeed Bert (1619:78) recom-mended giving a goshawk stones together with knots of thread from the weaver. It would be sur-prising if accipiters do not use rangle when buz-zards and eagles do. Many other species such as crocodiles, seals, sea-lions, cormorants, divers, fulmars, and petrels also use rangle, some even more extensively than raptors do. The only com-mon denominator appears to be a diet of meat, often with a high fat content.

Wild falcons normally take five to twelve stones, preferably rounded but with a slightly tex-tured surface. They fly down to a stream or gravel area where the stones are water-worn and carefully select the size required. This is about 12–16 mm maximum diameter for a 1 kg (36 oz.) falcon, 10–14 mm for a 500 g (18 oz.) falcon and 4–8 mm for a 250 g (9 oz.) falcon. This was determined from several hundred stones. The eight buzzard stones were relatively small at 6–15 mm (mean 8.2 mm) diameter. The eagle stone was 31 X 12 mm. One female peregrine here, deprived of rangle for a month, swallowed 35 stones as soon as she was offered them.

We do not know exactly how often wild fal-cons use rangle, but field studies and experiments with aviary birds show that some falcons take ran-gle approximately once per week, others once per month. Some individuals may use it more often, others seldom, if at all. They pick it up at any time during the day and usually retain it overnight. It is taken separately fromcasting material and the stones arecast up the following day in a group, before eating a meal. Sometimes the stones are covered with a thin film of mucus but usually they are fairly clean. I have seldom found rangle in a

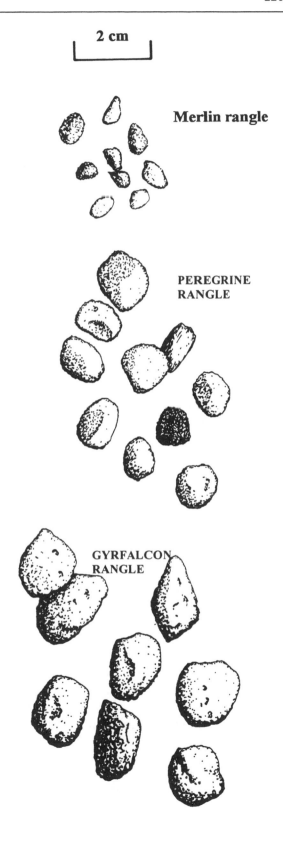

Figure 5.11.1 Merlin rangle, peregrine rangle, and gyrfalcon rangle.

pellet. When stones appear in the pellets they are usually the gizzard stones of a prey animal such as a quail or pigeon and are noticeably smaller and sharper than rangle.

The best way to give rangle is last thing at night once the afternoon's casting-free crop has been put over. The stones should all be thrown up the next morning. If the hawk will not take the stones voluntarily it is a simple matter to pop them into her throat one by one while she is hooded. In practice, the aviary falcons take all theirs voluntarily but the trained birds are given rangle overhand so that I have control over what is going on.

The best time to give rangle is when the hawk has lost a lot of body fat and is perhaps ready for the creance. Stones can be given every night then for a week or ten days, after which give her good-castings. The stones tend to stir up the mucus in the stomach and abrade off any excess cuticle and all this passes on down through the intestine. The castings too will tend to soak up the mucus, but only once the stones have loosened it. Later in the season if the hawk has had a lot of rich feeding and has a sluggish digestion a further course of stones will not come amiss.

The preparation of the stomach is neatly summarized in the following rhyme:

> Washed meat and stones will cause a hawk to
> fly;
> Long fasting and greatcasting will cause a
> hawk to die.

This whole subject of the stomach is poorly understood by many modern falconers who often blame a poor performance on their birds rather than on their own management. The way in which a hawk flies, assuming it is fit, depends on its inner motivation which depends on the management of its stomach and appetite. The prairie falcon, for example, has a tough constitution and ability to survive when necessary on short and poor quality rations. This makes the management of its appetite that much more difficult and has earned it a reputation among those accustomed to the easier peregrine as being an erratic performer. The prairie is a fairly quick-tempered bird which will not tolerate sloppy handling in the same way that a peregrine will and its stomach needs careful attention. In these two attributes it demands more skill from the falconer than a peregrine.

Whereas the goshawk will perform adequately despite quite varied treatment, the less rapacious hawks such as the buzzard and the kestrel need very careful management if they are to chase with any enthusiasm. Unfortunately most of the beginners who handle these species do not understand this aspect well enough to realize their hawk's full potential and often find the experience rather frustrating and disappointing.

I have spoken to many vets over the years about rangle and they have pooh-poohed the concept of enseaming. However, I have also studied the wild birds carefully and seen the changes in my own birds and prefer to believe the birds rather than the vets!

## 5.12  Appetite and weight control

As we have already seen, small hawks need a reasonable crop of food every day. They cannot go without food for several days as eagles can. This means that, even if they are fairly fat, they become hungry at some time each day for their meal and this daily hunger is used in the "appetite" system as motivation for the bird to fly in falconry. It is not a question of starving the hawk, but simply of ensuring that the time of day when she is hungry and ready for her meal coincides with the time at which you intend to fly her.

Under a given set of conditions, a merlin may need $3/10$ crop free of casting material in the morning and $9/10$ in the afternoon in order to maintain a steady weight. Because productive metabolism is greatest during the day, most of the energy drain occurs then. On a time basis one can calculate that $1/10$ crop provides for only just over one hour. Thus if given $4/10$ crop instead of $3/10$ crop the merlin will be in optimal hunting order about one hour later than it was on the previous day, or, if fed $2/10$ crop one hour earlier, all other variables staying the same. This is the "appetite" system of conditioning. It works well, but only within strict limits. The bird must be near its "fit not fat" weight, and if the meal is delayed for more than two hours or so the bird's hunger and responsiveness may decrease.

To be successful with the appetite system one must be clear about the time at which the hawk is fed up. When food is fed to a hawk it is stored first in the crop from whence it is transferred or "put over" bit by bit into the stomach for digestion and from there to the intestine for absorption. A goshawk or peregrine with an empty gut, with no pressure in the mutes and often with green bile present, will put the first food right through in 2–3 hours and produce a good high pressure mute. Now if you hawk all afternoon and start giving odd bits of food at 2 P.M., finally feeding up at 6 P.M., the effective time of feeding was 2 P.M. If altogether you gave $^5/_{10}$ crop it doesn't matter much whether you give $^1/_{10}$ at 2 P.M. and $^4/_{10}$ at 6 P.M., or the whole $^5/_{10}$ at 2 P.M. The extra $^4/_{10}$ will only be stored in the crop while the bird is digesting the first portions. If, on the other hand, you start flying at 2 P.M. but the hawk gets no real feed until 6 P.M. then obviously feeding-up time was 6 P.M. The late feed-up time means that the hawk will have lost more or gained less than it would have done and yet will have less keen an appetite at 2 P.M. the next day. This is the falconer's eternal dilemma. On afternoons when it is pouring with rain one hangs around wondering whether to feed up now, so that the hawk will be ready the following day or to wait, hoping the rain will clear up in time for a brief excursion before dark, even at the risk of a poorer performance the following day.

Larger hawks are usually flown on a combined appetite-weight system. More attention is paid to the weight of the bird than to its appetite. Thus a goshawk may take hares at a certain weight but refuse them if she weighs 50 grams more. A similar situation applies to peregrines and rooks.

## 5.13 Symptoms of high and low condition

Watching falconers with their birds, it is quite obvious that many are unable to tell with any certainty what condition their birds are in. They are insensitive to or unaware of the signals which the hawk is giving them. More than one falconer has starved a hawk to death because he has believed a faulty weighing machine rather than the symptoms before his very eyes. Also it often happens that by the time a hawk is first weighed after being taken up for training it has already lost quite a bit of weight and so the falconer has no fat weight on which to base calculations for an approximate flying weight. It is crucial therefore to be able to see from a bird's behavior what its condition is despite wildness or imprinted tameness which may mislead you.

When a hawk is fat and fit it is very strong, and may well fight hard when cast in the hand. It easily gets breathless and in the field it may be lethargic and unresponsive, or it may fly off a long distance without stopping. It may ignore quarry and, if the lure is thrown out to it, it may overfly it. It may refuse to feed on the fist or take a bite or two and flick the meat away contemptuously. It will bate strongly, bouncing back up afterward and glaring at the falconer with hot breath, or it may even refuse to stand on the fist at all.

A fit hawk is strong to fly but does not easily get breathless. A really fit goshawk should be able to take pheasants in the air in their first flight and should seldom give up the pursuit of a rabbit or pheasant while it can still see it. If grounded it will get up and have another go. Unless poorly manned, the fit accipiter will come to the fist and bind but not overfly it. Similarly a fit falcon may, through ebullience, overfly the lure once or twice but still take it seriously and soon hit it hard. The fit falcon in still weather should manage 60–70 stoops to the lure in two bouts of 30–35 without resting on its wings, looking away, perching, or panting. At home it should perch with one foot up and feathers slightly fluffed, both eyes open, and watchful. It may winnow its wings for exercise and when resting the wing-tips will be over, not under, the tail. When feeding it will tear up its food strongly and impatiently.

A low falcon will not fly so strongly and may give up when flying quarry after one or two hundred meters. The pectoral muscles will be noticeably wasted. It may not be particularly responsive in the field but when it does come it will not overfly the fist or lure. Some birds may be maniacally keen and aggressive. Young birds may start to scream, mantle, attack the handler or dogs, and drag food away in a mantling shuffle. However, after one or two greedy bites, the low bird may be slow or reluctant to feed, standing jealously over the food but not actually pulling at it. On the perch the feathers are more fluffed out, the eyes are oval and although one foot may be lifted it may still rest on a knuckle. The wings may droop below the tail. Bating is weak and moth-like.

A very low hawk, just before it dies, will be fluffed out, standing on both feet, wings and undertail coverts drooping. Eyes are semiclosed and sunken, and one of them may close completely occasionally. The bird appears unusually tame and dozy and when offered food may refuse to eat or may pick at it a little without swallowing. It cannot be relied on to feed itself and will need tube-feeding. It has difficulties recovering from a bate and is reluctant or unable to fly. As its blood sugar levels drop further it may lack co-ordination, have fits and finally die.

Of course such a hawk may well be suffering from some disease and so, together with these general signs of lowness, there may be symptoms of the disease, such as digestive, respiratory or parasitic disorders. If there is the slightest question mark over the bird's health the very first rule of good management is to *get the bird's condition up* and stop flying it. A strong hawk can often fight its

way through disease even if untreated, but a low hawk, even with the latest medicines, may quickly slip beyond hope of recovery.

## 5.14 Factors which can mask condition

Although a hawk may have been carefully brought to the optimum physical condition, there are vari-

Figure 5.13.2 A keen, strong European sparrowhawk.

ous factors which can offset these efforts. Obviously if there is high level of an undiagnosed parasite or a disease, such as aspergillosis, the hawk will be unable to do its best. So if for some reason the hawk seems below par, its health should be checked. A bird well-gone with aspergillosis for example may show no symptoms at all except a lack of stamina; while it is functioning anaerobically it is fine, but after an initial effort it is unable to continue aerobically.

Physical or mental stress can mask conditions. A newly imported hawk which is not acclimatized may require extra rations and careful treatment. Wild-caught hawks which are insufficiently manned may be too stressed to perform properly although in the right physical condition. Even tame hawks get spooked in a strange place or with unfamiliar sights.

Biological urges such as migration, territorial disputes or homing may put a raptor right off hunting. If things aren't going too well my New Zealand falcons fly off home in disgust!

Malimprinting can cause a hawk to show deceptive behavior. A mantling, screaming imprint can put on such display that one is convinced that she is at death's door. It can be very difficult to judge the condition of such hawks accurately; they can quickly go from one extreme to the other.

One afternoon I took five sparrows with a slightly malimprinted New Zealand falcon who broke the neck of each one of them then flew off and cached its corpse, returning after a few minutes to continue hunting. Similarly with goshawks; often when a river has separated me from my hawk on its quarry I have called the hawk off the prey back to the fist or lure. On one occasion the quarry, a moorhen, flew off unharmed. On two other occasions my goshawks have taken one prey in each foot. These experiences occur because the behavior centers for hunting and for eating are separate. We don't know yet what part of the brain triggers searching and attacking behavior, but the appetite is controlled through the hypothalamus. Thus it is possible for a hawk to be keen to hunt but not to eat, as for example when a parent bird has young to feed. On several occasions I have found kills of wild falcons and harriers with a casting beside them, indicating that the kill was made before the hawk had cast. This dissociation of hunting and feeding is relevant to multiple kills. Once a hawk is thoroughly made, after fifty kills or so, I often do not feed any of the kill at all if the flight was an easy one.

Wild hawks have daily cycles for hunting and trained hawks behave similarly. Most perform well in the early morning, less well during the middle of the day and best at the last half hour before dark, especially in winter. Sometimes the change of behavior can be quite dramatic.

Hawks, and dogs for that matter, seem to work better after being kept home for one or two days. Bert (1619:41) recognized this and Harry McElroy calls it "frustrational conditioning." Thus if one is planning to fly at a field meet, rather than flying the hawk every spare minute beforehand, it is usually best to rest her on the day before the meet starts and feed up early in the day. Also if one is wanting to introduce the hawk to an unfamiliar species of quarry the best time to try it is during the first week of the hawking season after the molt. That is when she is at her most open-minded.

Some old intermewed game hawks, who have flown with mechanical precision for several seasons, will go well almost regardless of what condition they are in. Then you can relax and enjoy yourself!

## 5.15 Fitness training

What do we mean by fit? Fitness implies suitability for a job. Thus a well-muscled body builder might be fit for weight-lifting but be hopeless at the marathon, and the super-fit marathon runner would be pathetic on the weights. The top endurance horses are gaunt, lean-looking brutes, far removed from the sleek well-muscled show-jumpers. The best pursuit falcons are the endurance birds, while the game hawks are the rounded, heavily muscled ones. Feathers may hide her body but you have to learn to undress her with your eyes.

In order to function, muscle needs glycogen (for energy) and oxygen brought to it by the blood, and lactic acid, carbon dioxide, and heat removed from it. During exercise the blood can increase its transporting capacity by up to sixty times. There are two main types of skeletal muscle fibre: red muscle which is good for endurance work and has a high capacity for using oxygen, and white muscle which is associated with power and sprinting and has a low capacity for using oxygen. Within these broad groups are further types of muscle fibre, not all of which come into use every time the whole muscle contracts. Of these there are two main types: the slow-twitch muscle fibers which have a slow contraction time and a good capacity for using oxygen; they can therefore work continuously without fatigue. The second is the fast-twitch muscle fibers which have a fast contraction time. These are the ones most involved in performance work. Some of them have a high capacity for using oxygen and can manage sustained work over long periods, the others have a low oxidative capacity and fatigue rapidly but are capable of the most strenuous fast work.

Thus for most of the daily activities, the hawk uses mainly her slow-twitch fibers. When she sets off on a long flight, perhaps a hunting patrol, she uses mainly the high oxidative fast-twitch fibers, and when she bursts into an attack on prey she uses her low oxidative fast-twitch fibers.

All these fibers are scattered throughout the muscles in varying proportions. Harriers and short-eared owls for example, are likely to have a high proportion of high oxidative fast-twitch muscles to sustain them while they quarter up and down, assiduously searching for prey. Accipiters, which depend on a powerful sprint, are likely to have a high ratio of low oxidative fast-twitch fibers. Although the ratio of fibre types depends on the species and the ways they hunt, fitness training can increase the oxygen-using capacity of the fibers, enabling them to avoid fatigue longer.

Fatigue is when the muscle can no longer continue at peak performance due to one of the factors becoming limiting. It may not have enough glycogen, or enough oxygen, or it may not be able to get rid of surplus lactic acid or surplus heat. It may also get dehydrated.

When the hawk is not flying hard, the blood can bring sufficient oxygen for the muscles to work aerobically, using the glycogen stored in the muscles themselves as an energy source. If this stored glycogen is exhausted, it will take her 1–3 days to replace it. Thus, if she has done a hard day's fast flying she must be given one or two very quiet days before being again asked for peak performance. If you try to get her to fly to the point of exhaustion two days in a row, she will not manage much at all on the second day.

When the hawk has to fly really hard, she will be using her fast-twitch fibers and soon the blood cannot bring enough oxygen for the muscles to work aerobically. They go into oxygen-debt and function anaerobically, resulting in a build-up of lactic acid. The acid eventually will cause the muscles to seize up. If there is not too much acid, a little rest or gentle exercise is sufficient to clear it and the hawk can continue again until its glycogen runs out. Anaerobic respiration is only about $\frac{1}{12}$ as efficient an energy-user as aerobic respiration. It is crisis management. Thus, lactic acid build-up limits the fast performance of the hawk's muscles in the short term causing fatigue, whereas glycogen depletion causes longer-term exhaustion.

Fitness training aims at encouraging more mitochondria to improve glycogen utilization and at increasing the blood supply to speed up the transport of materials and delay the onset of anaerobic respiration and the resulting build-up of lactic acid. It also improves the capacity and blood supply of the lungs, giving better oxygen uptake. The improved blood circulation also helps dissipate excess heat, which is a limiting factor for gyrfalcons flying in warm climates.

To do this requires exercise which must be of the same type as the performance ultimately required of the hawk in hunting. Thus the accipiter needs fast, hard exercise which will increase the power of its muscles, resulting in more thrust and more speed, and which will increase the distance it can sprint before fatigue sets in. The crow-falcon, on the other hand requires hard, sustained work so that it can keep going at peak performance for ten or more minutes. Fitness is not so critical for waiting-on flights, but exercise is needed to improve internal motivation which will maintain discipline in responses. Without it, the game falcon becomes a fat, lazy prima donna. Harris hawks need to improve both their general fitness and their sprint, obviously a gentle country walk does nothing to improve sprinting.

You need to be able to measure how much exercise the hawk does, and what effects it is having on the bird. This is not easy. On the one hand, the hawk is motivated to fly by hunger, or the desire to chase and so on, on the other hand it is limited by the pain of fatigue. Hawks tend to govern their own intensity of training, but the best ones will overwork themselves. Although it is possible to monitor heart rate, respiration rate, body temperature, and blood lactic acid levels under research conditions, this is not feasible for the average person with a free-flying raptor. Instead you can only "read" her behavior, watch for her beak starting to open, and see how well she performs in a given amount of exercise.

As in any animal, youngsters become fit more

quickly than old ones, especially old ones which have never been properly fit before. Interval training gets hawks fit more quickly without overworking them. In this way you can exercise two or three falcons at a time like union workers ( one working, two resting). You can go round and round the cadge, exercising each bird in turn, then resting her while you do the others, then another bout, and so on. This gives her time to clear any lactic acid, reducing fatigue but increasing the amount of exercise. She should be only partially recovered before the next exercise period. As soon as her breathing returns to normal, she is ready again.

There are six ways to exercise raptors: calling off and long-luring which are good for the slow-twitch muscles, trailing, which is good for both types of muscle fibers, high-jumping and exercise luring which are good for the fast-twitch muscles, and flying at quarry which uses the fibers which the hawk actually needs for hunting.

Calling off from posts or trees is a common way of getting an accipiter or buteo fit; unfortunately this can be very time consuming. It is certainly a good way of getting the falconer fit! I think the best time for this is for the first two or three days after flying an accipiter loose for the first time. It helps build confidence in both hawk and falconer. Much more than this risks orientating the hawk too much toward the falconer and not enough toward quarry. It does nothing for the fast-twitch fibers which the hawk will need for its first attempts at quarry. To show much effect, the hawk needs to go a good distance, for example, if you take a Harris out on a horse for a five-mile ride, throwing it off and calling it in all the way, it will start to improve in general fitness. A slow putter from tree to tree for a mile or two is really neither here nor there.

Pursuit falcons are often trained by long-luring, that is, called to a lure from about 500–1000 meters in a straight line. The hawk flies at its own speed, which is not top speed. Although this does help get them fit to some extent, the main reason for doing this is a mental one. It is teaching the falcon that when the hood is removed, she should look out and be ready to start at something a long way off. Secondly, it teaches her to come in to the lure from a distance. Long-luring does not improve flying and footing skills in the same way that the exercise lure does.

Trailing is a progression from calling-off and long-luring. Basically the falcon is called to a lure

held by a falconer sitting in the back of a vehicle. The lure is trailed on a long line from a strong fishing pole. As the hawk comes in, the vehicle starts to move, the lure speeds up and becomes airborne, held out to the side of the vehicle away from the slipstream and dust. The line is wound in until the lure is only a few feet from the rod with the hawk close to catching it. The vehicle can then proceed at a steady, fast speed so that the falcon is compelled to use her fast-twitch muscles in order to keep up. The trail can go for a measured distance at a measured speed and thus the falcon's performance can be monitored until it reaches a peak. It is better to use a sandflat for this in the desert, rather than an English country lane! This method does not improve flying skills but is good for experienced birds. Written records should be scrupulously maintained so that none of the falcons are worked over their performance limit, otherwise they will be set back several days.

In the early stages, or when daylight time is short, the hawk can be given high jumps indoors. The hawk is placed on a low perch (not its normal block) and called steeply upward to the fist for a tidbit. Seventy to a hundred of these jumps can do a peregrine a lot of good because she finds it quite hard but an accipiter can do it almost without using its wings at all. They can manage 200 jumps or more. Buteos are easily disgusted with it and may refuse to cooperate unless the trainer uses special techniques. The problem is that if you give the hawk a tidbit every time she jumps, she gets more and more tired and less and less hungry. As she gets fitter and has to do a lot of jumps, then all those tidbits soon amount to a full crop.

Steve Layman has developed a good system for the high-jumping technique. First you need a safe room, free of obstructions and perches, with the window covered over. On the floor is a deflated basketball stuck to a meter square of carpet. The hawk can land on this safely without damaging feet or feathers and learns to center on it as part of the routine. The hawk is taken up as for hawking, weighed, brought into the jumping room and allowed to settle down until she is relaxed. The initial plan is to shape the behavior we want. Once a firm foundation of routine has been established then high numbers of jumps will become possible later on.

So to start with, the hawk is placed on the ball and then asked simply to jump up onto the fist for a tidbit which is hidden in the glove. She cannot see it from the ball. She must jump up, as an act of faith, and then see and eat the tidbit. Then she can be placed back on the ball. Get a rapid repetitive up and down behavior established. Sometimes, as she is eating the tidbit on the glove, place another tidbit on the ball. She will quickly turn around and fly back down onto the ball. Soon she is flying fast up to the fist and down to the ball. If she misses the ball and lands on the floor, wait a moment until she regains the ball before calling her to the fist. As she comes to the fist, raise it high above your head.

It may take several days to establish this behavioral routine. Psychologically this is an attack sequence and she must be encouraged to use energy and commitment. Just use sequences of 5–6 calls to start with. Do not attempt prolonged sequences and risk refusals. Quit before she starts to lose interest. By the time she is doing about 75 good fast jumps on a 1:1 ratio, i.e. being rewarded every jump, start to skip regarding her now and then. As you have not been showing her the tidbit, she never knows until she has arrived, whether there is one there or not. You are now on a variable ratio of reward. Gradually reduce the numbers of regards until you reach the point where she is getting about three rewards for 10 jumps, but these are on a random basis. Sometimes she gets two in a row. Sometimes she has to do six jumps for nothing. It is the same for her in the wild and she is mentally prepared for disappointment. If you have managed to shape her behavior well, instead of becoming disappointed she will be inspired into maximum effort. She will start to get really fast and aggressive in her approach and, as you get into high numbers, you will need to raise her flying weight sometimes by 10 to 20 percent. You can also relate food quality to performance. Have two tubs of food, one of washed rabbit, one of quail. When she is slow, give her rabbit. When she is fast, give her quail. Don't try for maximum numbers every session; sometimes finish early and feed all the remaining tidbits at once. Thus she is encouraged to make maximum effort immediately and cannot outguess what will happen next.

We have now mechanized this system to make it even more effective and linked with the hawk's natural instincts and abilities. We use shelves which slide in and out of the pen wall, instead of a human fist. This reduces the risk of the hawk becoming man-orientated. For accipiters the room can contain plastic netting screens, or soft branches. Thus, just as if she was in a wood and

saw an small bird briefly, the accipiter has to quickly launch and attack while the "prey" is exposed.

High jumps have long been used by eastern falconers and are increasingly being used in the west. The system has many advantages. It does not lower a game-falcon's pitch. It can be used indoors, in the dark, and in the rain. A few high jumps are a good way to warm a hawk up before proper flying. Jumps can easily be quantified and used as part of a controlled fitness program. Goshawks, for example, are not fit to hunt until they can manage 80–90 jumps. I used to high jump my birds over twenty years ago, but gave up because I could never get much beyond 40–50 jumps. But when Steve showed me the technique of rewarding on a variable schedule then 200–400 jumps became possible. This has a tremendous psychological impact on the bird and helps to build up stamina and endurance.

The exercise lure for a falcon is an excellent way to give her a good pipe-opener and can be used on all nonhawking days except when it may cause her to lower her pitch or to become lure-bound. However, an unfit falcon will not reach or hold a good pitch for long so one is on the horns of a dilemma here. Personally, I find that a good workout to the lure (about 50 stoops in two lots of 25) in her home exercise field, does not lower a game-hawk's pitch out in the hawking area. Also, it does make her more responsive to the lure. I have seen game falcons in some countries which would ignore the lure and only come down to live game. Such a bird is half trained and half lost. The crow falcons are given a lot of exercise to the lure and also we try to get them fit in a different way. They have to be capable of very enduring flights, they need plenty of red muscle but nothing surplus. They need to be able to go on and on and on. And then when you finally think they will have to give up, they've got to find that little bit more and finish the job. Game falcons, on the other hand are more like body builders, they need plenty of weight on board to strike a devastating blow. Fitness is important but not so critical. So as far as possible they are flown at maximum weight, but not to the extent that they become disobedient.

Hard flying at quarry every day will eventually bring the accipiter to the peak of fitness. But to attempt this before the bird is at least half fit will overface it and lead to other problems, such as lack of confidence. In Britain I would say that only about one in fifty goshawks are flown fully fit. If a hawk is flown less than three days a week of good, hard flights at quarry, she will not be fully fit and supplementary fitness training will be needed. For a goshawk, a hard flight is one of at least 100 meters. Pheasant flights of 200–300 meters will force the gos into lactic acid production and will gradually improve her fitness, whereas a 20 meter dash at a rabbit doesn't tax her system to its limit at all. Accipiters flown only at weekends do best with about a 100 high jumps on nonflying days.

Buteos and Harris hawks do not even have the explosive anaerobic sprint of the accipiter and for them fitness training is essential. Because of the mental attitude of the Harris, the falconer flying it tends to have the same, laid back, casual approach. This is a pity because it is possible to get a much better performance with the Harris than most people seem to be content with.

Before a hawk is flown loose, whether for falconry or for rehabilitation, she must be got fit. It is not a clever position to be in, when a hawk is:
   a) on her first flights loose
   b) at her lowest weight
   c) unfit
   d) unentered.

How long will she survive if you lose her? Careful consideration should always be given to hawks which have not learned to fend for themselves.

She may be sound in wind, but is she sound in limb? A rehab bird especially may have received an incapacitating injury and it is vital to find out if she is fully fit again before hacking her out. There are two easy ways to assess her soundness. First she must be exercised until she is quite tired; only then will a weakness become apparent. Then, just like trotting up a lame horse, she should be flown in a straight, level flight directly toward and away from an observer filming with a video camera. The film is then played back on slow speed or freeze frame. Look closely at the wing beats. Are both wings exactly in unison? Do they beat to the same depth? Are they level? If one wing is working slightly harder than the other it will skew the mid-line of the body, causing her to yaw. The hawk will try to compensate for this by tilting her tail slightly. Can you see the tail out of line?

The second way is to return the tired hawk to a quiet pen and watch her without her being aware of your presence. Preferably use closed circuit television. Does she droop her wings, and does she

do so evenly? While it may be acceptable to release to the wild an unsound buteo or other "searching" hawk (see part 6), any species, such as accipiters and falcons, which rely on their flying ability to attack agile prey need to be 100 percent fit. No compromises.

## 5.16 Lures and lure theory

In the late fourteenth century Chaucer wrote "With empty hand men may none hawks lure." But the lure has more uses than simply for calling the hawk back. It follows therefore that the lure takes a variety of forms and is used in different ways and circumstances.

The main reasons for using a lure are these:
   a) to call the hawk back
   b) to exercise her
   c) to improve her footing ability
   e) as a dress rehearsal for quarry
   f) to call her back when she is afraid of you
   g) as a more visible way of calling her back from a distance
   h) some falcons prefer to hit a lure rather than to land on the fist
   i) to make an aggressive hawk less orientated toward the falconer
   j) to give flying displays for the public.

   a) To call the hawk back is the commonest use for the lure. I normally introduce the lure as soon as the hawk is coming a meter or so to the fist. Some hawks are reluctant to come any distance to the fist and they can often be induced to overcome this by calling to the lure. Soon the lure can be raised up to the glove and the hawk begins to come to the fist with no difficulty. The lure should be garnished with food to start with and this should be firmly attached. By the time the hawk has been flying free for a week or two I no longer garnish the lure except in particular circumstances. Garnishing it is a tedious chore and can lead to problems in the field.

   Some people do not use the lure for accipiters or buteos, regarding them as birds of the fist. I do not follow this line of thinking, the lure is far too useful to leave at home. Newly trained goshawks are usually good to the fist and even return to it after a miss. But it is not long before such perfection fades and very often in the course of the season there will be times when the lure gets you out of a scrape. My goshawks have not always been models of obedience to the fist, but with the lure to help me I have never had to wait for more than a few minutes at most and I expect them to come in from a good distance. An accipiter is best given some reward whenever it comes a distance whereas the Harris, at the other end of the spectrum, can usually be flown without lure or reward.

Sometimes, in an emergency, it is impossible to find a clear area of ground where the lure would be visible and approachable. Therefore falcons should be taught to take the lure in the air before they are trusted loose. This is done by winding the lure line spirally along a stick so the lure is either at the end, like a feather duster, or on a short length of line, as on a fishing rod. In this way the lure can either be held static in the air, just off the ground, or it can be trailed about a bit. Falcons normally get the idea after one or two lessons. When calling a hawk back to the lure from a distance never twitch it away at the last minute. She may fly straight on or next time refuse it. Lose her trust and you lose her.

When calling in a hawk the lure should be presented so that it is easy for the hawk to take, the glide path should not be too steep and the ground should be clear. If the hawk does not come promptly do not keep calling it, you are simply teaching her not to come. Nor go toward her otherwise she is teaching you to come. Failing to come is almost never a physical problem; she should easily be capable of flying the distance. Rather the problem is that she lacks motivation. She doesn't want to come sufficiently to fly the distance. On the other hand, as with a shy dog, if you start to walk away and leave her behind she may come twice the distance without being called at all. The more you pander to her whims the worse she will get.

Never forget the use of time. Often if the hawk is disobedient, it pays to use the politician's approach and do nothing at all. Rather than lay out your wares of assorted lures, just ignore her. Just let time do its work. After a while she will get restless and you will have the upper hand again. Young hawks, for all their waywardness, are extremely dependent on the falconer. Almost every incident of disobedience or "moodiness" in a hawk is traceable to poor technique on the part of the falconer. Although it takes some patience and forbearance there are times in the training of hawks, and of horses too, when the implacable disregard of time can have a profound effect. The difference is that while the minutes or even hours tick away, by not calling the hawk at all she is made to wait for you. You call the tune. She is the one who is waiting, not you. She begins to realize that if she does not come promptly she may have a considerable wait before she has another chance, just as she would with real quarry. Thus the falconer tames the shrew.

Once the hawk is fully trained, the recall or retrieve lure can be used. It is a simple lure with about four feet (3.2 m) of line and no stick (figure 3.10.1). In olden days it was carried looped over the shoulder like a climbing rope, and we still do this sometimes when crow-hawking. When needed, you simply unhook it, swing it until the falcon approaches and then throw it out. Alternatively it is worth training her to come right in and land on the lure on the glove. This saves you dismounting.

b)  Falcons can be exercised to the lure by a variety of methods. The technique commonly used in Britain works well and has been passed down from generation to generation. It is described in detail in the next section. The exercise lure should be capable of being struck hard without injury to the hawk. There should be no metal on or near it and it should weigh about one third of the weight of the hawk. For large falcons a lure made up of car rubber inner tube cut into strips (Figure 3.10.3) is hygienic, safe, and relatively indestructible. The falcon makes a stoop and pass attack at it. For accipiters, buteos, and eagles a stuffed synthetic rabbit or fox skin dragged along serves well (figure 5.16.1) but in a wet climate needs frequent changing. They tail chase and make a direct flying attack, rather than a stoop and pass. For exercise purposes they can easily be trained to use a rubber lure.

c)  The falcon's flying and footing ability can be improved by luring especially with the pole lure. An unhacked young falcon, newly hard-penned, on first being flown, will be incapa-

Figure 5.16.1 Dragging a rabbit lure for a young Harris.

ble of landing properly let alone hitting any prey accurately. A week or ten days lure flying will improve fitness and teach the falcon the use of its wings and feet; a prerequisite of serious hawking. Without it a falcon used for waiting-on flights at game may take a long time to develop good footing ability and will seldom fly like a wild bird. A good falcon needs only to get near prey to bind to it whereas an inexperienced falcon seems to bungle even easy shots. Some indeed are incapable of catching dead birds thrown up to them.

Like so many things, more of it is not necessarily better. A poor hawk will soon become lure bound if overlured. After ten days or so the hawk should be entered at quarry without further delay. The rook or crow hawk can continue to be exercised to the lure on days in between hawking quarry. Care is needed to maintain the balance of attractiveness between quarry and the lure. The best falcons get too quarry orientated and the poor ones too lure bound; both faults must be remedied as soon as noticed. If a falcon shows signs of becoming lure bound, then fitness can be maintained by high-jumping until she is catching quarry better.

Accipiters do not improve their footing much with lure work and they certainly do not appreciate being made to miss the lure. It is best to get straight into real hawking with them.

d) Teaching the falcon to wait on using the thrown lure (figure 3.10.1) is described in section 5.18. Careful and imaginative use of the thrown lure can teach a falcon a great deal toward waiting on. Poor use of the lure, when the falconer does not understand clearly what he is trying to achieve, will soon ruin the falcon.

e) Often the young hawk needs to know what the quarry looks like. It needs to develop a "search image." By placing a dead rabbit in some rushes and then twitching it out on a 70 meter creance the young buzzard or goshawk can be taught to start at rabbits. After a brief chase it can be allowed to "kill" it and eat some of it. After a couple of dress rehearsals, as realistic as possible, the hawk is ready for the real thing.

Falcons intended for game seldom need a dress rehearsal; most game species are virtually irresistible to them. Pursuit falcons may need more careful entering and we will look at this in the next three sections.

f) Sometimes hawks, especially accipiters, get jumpy and are reluctant to return to the fist. Throwing out the lure may bring her down; the falconer may even have to move away. If the situation has deteriorated to this extent the falconer must analyze the problem and remedy it because such a hawk is half lost.

g) All raptors usually come much further to the lure than to the fist. Also a swung lure is much more visible than a raised fist. A trained falcon can see and come in to a swung lure from 3–4 kilometers. Remember that a lure swung slowly and in a twitching fashion is much more enticing than one swirled at high speed, however anxious one may be. In some countries, people still use live lures. The ethics of this is discussed in section 8.9. A flapping clockwork pigeon (figure 3.10.4) is just as effective in attracting a lost hawk, with none of the ethical problems associated with live lures.

h) The fast-flying aerial falcons, particularly peregrines, are reluctant to come in to the fist once they have got speed up. They prefer to truss the lure in the air and flutter down with it further on. Failing a lure, a cloth cap on a string, or anything similar, will often bring her down. This trait of falcons is probably the reason why the lure was originally invented.

i) The way in which the lure can be used to reduce aggression by making the hawk less falconer orientated is described in section 5.23.

j) The exercise lure is commonly used to give flying displays for the public at centers or at regional summer shows. There is probably scope here for some of Frank Beebe's ingenious mechanical lures which tow a dummy along a zigzag route, like a jinking rabbit. We are also experimenting with replica prey made as radio controlled aircraft.

The actual construction of the lure depends on its use. The best lure for attracting a hawk or for a dress rehearsal is a dead quarry on a string or a flapping clockwork dummy. Such lures are not suitable for every day use and indeed are not always desirable. If the hawk refuses it then you are in the proverbial cactus—you have nothing left to offer. For everyday use, I prefer a simple light-weight rubber lure which, although similar in many respects to the quarry, is still quite obviously a lure. The hawk is familiar with it and responds to it. If, for some reason, she is a bit uppity or jumpy and refuses the lure, I can still use dead prey or a flapping dummy as a last resort.

Lures made of dried wings do not do well in our British climate. Left in the hawking bag by neglectful falconers, they soon smell and become prime sources of bacterial infection. Bumblefoot and enteritis are just around the corner.

Some falconers advocate the use of a heavy lure to prevent carrying. I tried this quite thoroughly when I was young with two sparrowhawks and a merlin and it made no perceptible difference. To prevent carrying requires a more fundamental approach to the problem than this (see section 5.21). Hawks easily distinguish between light and heavy quarry and act accordingly.

There is one further kind of luring which is used in the waiting-on flight. This is when the falconer waves his glove or hand to a falcon raking away from the point. Both he and the falcon need to be quite clear that the meaning of this signal is for the falcon to center over the falconer, not to come down to the falconer. Try to keep this signal unambiguous, for example, whistle or call differently and perhaps wave or swing your glove in a different movement to luring.

Whatever you do, don't lure her or you will lower her pitch, or in the old words, she will "abate her gate."

## 5.17  Training for pursuit flights

The initial training of a pursuit falcon is the same as for any other type, but once she is flying free she must be brought to a peak of fitness and appetite. She can be exercised by a mixture of high jump-ing, lure flying to the exercise lure, long luring, and trailing (see 5.15).

Lure flying to the exercise lure takes some skill. The falconer must be able to place the lure in the air in the right position at the right moment, and this takes coordination. He must also be able to "read" the falcon as she flies, to judge how motivated she is and how tired she is, and he must be clear in his mind what he is trying to teach or to achieve.

The exercise lure we use is a simple bundle of rubber car inner tube cut so that it hangs like a handful of seaweed. It is held together by some creance cord threaded through it and knotted. It does not have a top side or a bottom side, it is the same all the way round. There are two cords at the head end for tying on meat in the early stages and a sliding plastic toggle is a good way to secure it. This meat is thus visible everytime the lure lands on the ground. The meat should be a good joint of rabbit or similar, strong so that it will not come off, and not too much, so that if it did come off, she would not get a full crop from it. Never use day-old chicks on the lure; either they come off, or they spray yolk, leaving you looking like a politician after a bad campaign.

The lure is attached with a small Sampo ball-bearing swivel which spins very freely. This is important to prevent the line twisting. The line is soft cotton which does not cut your fingers as does nylon or terylene. It is about 12 feet (4 m) or so long and wound on a short white lure stick in the fashion shown in figure 3.10.2. You should prac-tice winding up the lure in this way, using only your right hand. It is very quick, you can wind a line at slow walking speed.

There are two basic moves in exercise luring. Other moves are just variations on these. They are the left turn and the right turn, the left being faster and easier.

First wind up the lure line until only a short length is left. Hold the stick at all times in your gloved left hand (assuming you are right handed). Hold out the lure in your right hand as in figure 5.17.1. This is how much line you need. Now hold it as in 5.17.2. Hold out your hands as though you were holding a tray of food, elbows loosely in at your sides, but without being stiff. The line should slide over your right hand like a pulley when you move your hands apart. When your hands are to-gether, the lure should just clear the ground. When they are apart, it should come up near to your right

Figure 5.17.1 Measuring out the right length of line for the exercise lure.

Figure 5.17.3 Put your right foot forward and shoot the lure out onto the ground with your hands coming together. Then pull it back.

Figure 5.17.2 As your left hand pulls away, the line should run through your right hand as if on a pulley.

hand. When you need to, you can use your thumb on the line as a brake.

Now start to swing the lure so that it comes forward, underarm past your ankles and then backwards over the top past your head, in the vertical plane. Swing it smoothly and as slowly as you can, but keeping the line straight at the top of the circle. Practice this for a while and walk around swinging it until you are thoroughly at home with the movement.

Next put your right foot forward as in figure 5.17.3, and slide the lure out in front of you as far as you can, letting your hands come together as you do so, to give maximum reach. Do this many times until you can shoot the lure out and land it exactly on a target spot, like a fly fishermancasting for a rise. The line should stay straight at all times.

There should be no slack and no bounce back or jerk.

When you're getting slick at this, it is time to practice the left turn itself. Shoot the lure out onto the ground and then pull it back, low, just above the ground. Turn left as you pull, and bring your hands apart, sliding the line through your right hand. This gives the lure extra speed as in figure 5.17.4. This movement is shown again from the side in 5.17.5 and 6. Keep turning and bring your right foot round until you face the opposite direction (figure 5.17.7 and 8). Keep the lure swinging and you are now facing the other way with the lure rotating at your right side, as in your original exercise. The falcon of course would have gone past and you are looking up watching her as she climbs away from you. Pretend you are watching her go up; she turns on a wingtip, and starts to come back in toward you. You have to prepare to turn left again. So put your right foot forward as before, and shoot out the lure. This time be confident, don't hesitate, before the lure has had a chance to hit the ground (figure 5.17.9 and 10), pull it back and turn left as before. Keep practicing. Swing the lure a few times, then right foot forward, shoot out the lure, then turn left. Keep going until it becomes smooth, controlled, and second nature. When you do it with a falcon you will not have time to be thinking about arms and legs. You must constantly

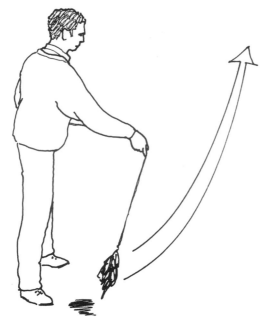

Figure 5.17.4 As you pull it back, pull your hands apart, letting the line pulley through your right hand.

Figure 5.17.5 The same movement as 5.17.3. seen from the side.

Figure 5.17.6 The same movement as 5.17.4 seen from the side.

Figure 5.17.7 As you turn left, bring your right foot forward and follow through with the lure.

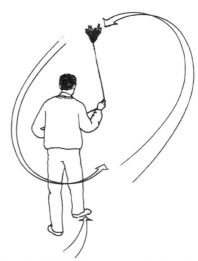

Figure 5.17.8 The lure comes backward over your head, circling on your right side. You are watching the falcon on her outrun.

watch the falcon. You have to time it so that at the exact moment she comes in, you shoot out the lure in front of her beak, then pull it back, keeping it no more than four finger widths in front of her as she goes past. If you do it well, her legs will come forward trying to catch the lure. This means she believes she almost has it. If you misjudge it, either the lure will be too far ahead of her, in which case she will go through the motions but will start to slacken. Or she will catch it and you will have to let her down with it.

When you are happy with your left turn, try the right turn. This time have your left foot forward as in figure 5.17.11. Shoot out the lure, then pull it back, sweeping it along low down, turn right and separate your hands all at the same time (figure 5.17.12). Again, you should end up facing the

Figure 5.17.9 The same movement at 5.17.3, but faster so that the lure does not touch the ground. This is what the approaching falcon sees.

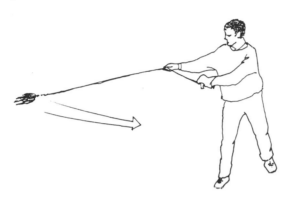

Figure 5.17.10 The same as 5.17.9 seen from the side. This is a fast version of 5.17.5.

other way with the lure swinging at your right side as before. You may have a spot of bother with this. The trick is to keep the lure below the level of your right hand as you turn, then, as you start to swing it, it will naturally circle in the right direction. When you've got the hang of it, speed up until you are able to present it to an imaginary falcon coming toward you at Mach 3.

Now get a friend to stand in front of you. His hand is the approaching falcon. Get him to hold it high, low, left, or right. When you shoot out your lure, you should be spot on target. The friend now calls out "left" or "right" and you should be able to turn either way without strangling yourself or getting a black eye.

You will notice that when you turn left as in figure 5.17.6, the line, as it pulleys through your right hand, does not do so at a sharp angle, so your right index finger does not get so sore. But when you turn right, as in figure 5.17.12, it almost cuts your finger in half. This limits the speed with

Figure 5.17.11 The right turn. The left foot starts off forward and swings round as you turn.

which you can turn right.

When you exercise a slow falcon, such as a lanner, saker, or kestrel, you have plenty of time and can easily turn right or left. But when you fly a big fast falcon such as a gyr or gyr hybrid, when she is hunting fit, she is traveling too fast for a right turn. Also, you must indicate to her in advance, which way you plan to turn, otherwise, if you dither, she may hit you and knock one or both of you out. It is the difference between a racing car and a family runabout.

Also with slow falcons you can start doing fancy twiddles and high passes. This is not wise

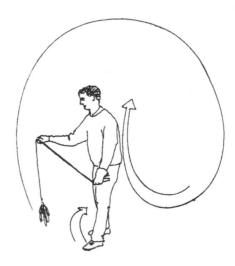

Figure 5.17.12 Turn right round with the falcon and you will end up back in position 5.17.8.

with a fast bird; she will carve you up. Keep these for displays.

To make a falcon exercise hard she must be keen to catch the lure and must believe in her own abilities. If the lure is twitched away no matter how hard or well the falcon tries, she will tend to be half-hearted, waiting for the falconer to throw up the lure signaling the end of the exercise. The falconer must make her believe that if she tries harder she can catch it. If the falconer lets the bird "best" him now and then in a good effort, and finishes in such a way, the falcon will work hard and improve. It is the same variable schedule of rewards as that used for high-jumping or for calling off. Without this incentive many falcons make large shallow circuits and rest in between stoops. This gives them time to clear lactic acid. The falcon should be encouraged to work well in the vertical plane, stoop steeply and downwind and to circle tightly keeping up the pressure. Failure to achieve this will show in its poor performance in the field, especially against crows. The best ones stoop like yo-yos. Most of the gyrs come over your head and then stoop vertically on you, a move which is hard to evade and liable to leave you sitting in a cow-pat.

The young falcon will not fly at top speed because she is frightened of crashing. At the bottom of the attack she has to pull out and this puts a tremendous strain on her pectoral muscles, and it is hard for her to judge her windspeed, groundspeed and margin for error. We have had gyrs hit the deck and somersault five meters (15 ft.). Soft ground and thick grass is handy! She must gradually be given more and more confidence and higher levels of difficulty and she will start to fly faster and faster until, as the Americans say, she's really cruising. Gradually you can introduce crosswind stoops and down-wind stoops. Always let her beat the lure on a good effort. You can increase her accuracy and steepness by flying her in clearings in trees or amongst trees, but again, make sure the trees have soft branches. Never fly her with your brain in neutral and always concentrate on what she needs to achieve next. Low wing-loaded falcons cannot stoop hard down wind because the strain on them is too great at the pullout. These are the sort which have to circle to climb. The powerful falcons can naturally stoop hard down wind and always stand on their tails to climb. This is in their breeding.

Thus the exercise luring has elements of teaching flying skills, developing obedience and reliability, and of physical fitness training.

So far she has looked inward to you for dead food. You must teach her to look outward for live prey. Obtain some dead prey, such as a crow which you've been keeping in the freezer for just such an occasion. Attach a 30 centimeters cord to its legs, with a little toggle like a dog retrieving dummy. Break both wings so they flap freely and attach some good food securely to the neck. Go out to a strange place and give her a quick call to the ungarnished fist so that she realizes she is free. As you approach a blind hedge or a bit of cover the crow will flush out from the other side and fall on short grass. She should flip over the top and nail it. All this happened because you had a hidden friend following your instructions who lobbed out the crow when he heard your signal whistle. He stays hidden until you reach the falcon on the crow, where you make a fuss of her, preferably for about half an hour. It does no harm to tweak the cord a bit when you first arrive, to make the crow appear alive. You can repeat this a couple of times in completely different places.

Once she has had a dead crow in her foot and is confident enough to start at it without hesitation, she is ready for a dragged crow. We attach the crow to a 100 meter creance and hide it in a tussock. The lure man is on a horse or in a vehicle. The falconer is 100–200 meters away from the lure at right angles to the direction of drag. When all is ready there is an agreed signal, the falconer unhoods the falcon and holds her up. The "crow" then flushes from its tussock. The falcon starts after the crow, cutting across the corner so that it always sees a slightly side view of the crow, not just a straight-away view. The horse or vehicle is now moving fast so that the lure bounces 2–3 meters into the air as it goes along. The falcon comes up into a tail chase and binds to the crow, and the lure man drops the other end of the lure line to prevent the falcon being dragged. He slows down and comes back, picking up the end of the lure line for a while, jerking it as if the crow was still alive. This makes the falcon hang on tight and teaches her to go in strongly, not timidly. She is now ready for entering.

For desert hawking at houbara and stone curlew, the falcons can be got fit with exercise luring or by trailing, taking care to do enough, but not too much.

## 5.18 Teaching a falcon to wait on

Those species which search for prey naturally from waiting on are much easier to teach than those which do so less frequently. Of the large falcons the peregrine and the black falcon are the most aerial. The desert falcons: gyr, saker, prairie, lanner, and lugger are not usually quite so aerial and may be more difficult, but many take to it very well and are easily equal to a good peregrine. The New Zealand falcon will wait on but tends to be like an indignant wrestler who can't wait until the bell goes before running over and tackling his opponent. Any prey at all from a frog to a hare will cause her to dive. The common and American kestrels hover well and are probably the easiest of all to teach to wait on.

The red-headed falcon and the merlin prefer to zoom around, power flying. Although they will come overhead for brief periods, they are not very keen on actually waiting overhead and need to be served promptly.

Individual birds vary greatly in their tendencies to go up. Some go up immediately and can hardly be tempted down. Others can hardly be induced to go above head height. The easy ones are no problem but the difficult ones require careful treatment to get them steady and to keep them steady. What follows is intended for those with a difficult bird.

The first problem is to teach the bird to go up and the second is to teach it to wait there, in position. The third problem is to teach it what to do when it comes down. We teach the answers in reverse order. Compared to some of the other species such as the prairie falcon and the New Zealander, and especially to the accipiters, the peregrine tends to be a poor footer. It is exasperating to see a peregrine wait on and stoop beautifully only to lose the quarry through poor footing.

Therefore the first thing to attend to is the falcon's wind, flying ability, and footing ability. Hacking or taking a passage bird largely solves these problems, but let's assume we are dealing with a newly fledged unhacked captive-bred bird. Once the falcon is flying loose, I normally give her about a week of stooping to the exercise lure (see 5.17). Soon she will be making 6 or 7 passes at the lure. If she starts to pant or to set her wings or looks as if she might land, I let her catch the lure. This is done as far as possible by me being a little too slow so that the falcon believes she caught it

through her own efforts. After she has had a few bites on the lure she is coaxed on to the fist with a pick-up piece and the lure very carefully and discreetly removed and stowed in the hawking bag. The pick-up piece is then removed into the palm of the gloved hand until only a small bit is left showing. This makes the falcon believe that she herself has consumed the meal, not that it is being taken from her. When this final bite has gone, the remainder is removed carefully without her seeing it and she is put on the post orcast off, ready for another session. Some falconers do not use posts because the falcon may develop a habit of landing on them, in which case an assistant is needed.

Soon she will manage say 60 stoops in two sessions of 30 each at the ungarnished lure. Apart from teaching her to fly and getting her fit, this improves her footing and her picking up from the kill. It also improves her discipline and, importantly, teaches her to look inward to the falconer for quarry rather than outward. It also gives you an idea of what kind of hawk she will be. The best go up and down like yo-yo's with a good hard down wind stoop and a minimal interval between stoops. Low flying, up wind passes and big circuits are faults. I do not regard cutting the lure on the ground without binding to it as a sign of style. Rather it is a fault, particularly of unhacked peregrines, which will result in the loss of downed quarry unless it is cured. Flying the falcon in a small field with trees around it makes her stoop more steeply and forces her into tighter, more controlled, circuits. By letting her catch the lure only on good driving downwind stoops a lot can be done to improve her style. Once she knows she can do it she will repeat it, but to start with a lot of youngsters are a little afraid of hurling themselves about too much.

Many falconers believe stooping to the lure will lower her pitch and if you continue to do so once hawking has started this may occur. But a week or two during her early development is a good investment for the future. In many ways it equates with the days when the young falcons chased their parents until food is dropped for them to catch.

Once the falcon is fit and tackling the exercise lure well, go on immediately to the next stage. cast her off but let her circle two or three times before showing the lure. Then take her up in the usual way. This is teaching her to wait in expectation of her quarry. Don't overdo it. This teaches her to *look in*, to *hold position*, and *to wait*. This is just as important as height.

Next, change the lure to a thrown lure (figure 3. 10. 1). Instead of having a 3 or 4 meter line and lure stick, the thrown lure has the line reduced to 30 centimeters with a short plastic or horn toggle 3 centimeters long at the end. With a quick swing it can be thrown out like a flushed partridge about 50–80 meters. It can be identical to the exercise lure but is ungarnished. It should be safe for the falcon to hit violently. If the falcon carries it any distance she can pull at it to her heart's content but will gain no satisfaction until you arrive. Soon she will eagerly hop from it to the garnished fist and jealousy of being robbed, the prime motivator of carrying, is thus foiled.

After some seasons with a sliding weight lure I abandoned it in favor of the simple thrown lure because of the risk of the weight bouncing on the ground and striking the falcon. A lure fired by bungee cord, like launching a glider, can also be used, but this requires preplanning, which is not so good. Alternatively, hitting tennis balls out into cover is good practice. A dog is used to find the uncaptured balls. When garnishing the tennis ball to start with, a small slit is made and this grips the meat.

Cast the falcon off and when she has done a couple of circuits and is coming over down wind, shout "Ho!" and flick out the thrown lure so that she diverts and binds to it in the air.

The next step is to teach the falcon to go up. This is done after her basic training. There is no point, indeed it is dangerous, to get the falcon up high without her having a clear idea of why she is there and what she has to do next. Waiting-on needs operant conditioning. First we have to get her up in the air before we can reward her to encourage her. Although the best young falcons will go up in a flat calm, it is much easier to get the young falcon up in rising air. Where can we find such air?

In the warmer parts of the world, the morning sun heats the bare ground so that mushroom-shaped bubbles of warm air (thermals) start to rise up. These are exploited by the soaring raptors such as vultures and eagles. Thermals occur here in Britain on good warming days but they are seldom frequent enough or strong enough to be relied on. The more usual source of rising air is to look for a place where horizontal wind is diverted upwards. Wherever there are hills or obstacles the windward

side will have rising air. I prefer to use hill lift rather than thermals for two reasons: with hill lift you can predict exactly where it will be even before you leave home and you can clearly define the shape of the lifting air and its ceiling. By looking at your falcon's position you know what lift she is experiencing and, if she goes too high, she will go beyond the lift and come down. She will thus automatically tend to take the easy option and hold position. Thermals, on the other hand are not easy to predict before leaving home, or to locate, and often their ceiling is very high indeed. There is a real danger that the young falcon will be sucked up out of sight and control, coming down in a hazardous place some distance away, without actually learning the specific lesson that you were trying to reinforce.

A little care in selecting the right place makes a world of difference. A windy field with a thick hedge or line of trees is a good place to start (figure 5.18.1).cast off the falcon into the lifting air on the windward side of the trees. Soon she should be up over the trees and, as previously trained, be looking in toward you. She should cruise around above the trees breasting the wind expecting the lure. Now walk downwind without showing the lure. She should swing out and come over at about two tree heights like flying a kite. If she does not come over, wave your arm, or take off your hawking glove and swing it briefly to encourage her over. Be consistent so that she learns your arm signals. Don't use the lure to bring her overhead unless she rakes off badly and gets out of control. As soon as she comes over and is in position shout "Ho!" and throw out the lure down- or across-wind. She should turn on one wing, strike the lure and either bind to it or turn sharply and land on it on the ground. If you throw the lure into the wind she will hit it slowly and with the lift of wind in her face it is an invitation to carry the lure.

In my experience peregrines accomplish all this fairly easily and soon learn to stoop when you shout "Ho." This means that you can wait before you throw the lure out until the falcon is far enough down her stoop to hit the lure before it hits the ground. Remember the use of the *bridge* in reinforcement techniques (4.17)? A consistent pitch of 100–200 feet with good positioning can be achieved in this way together with stooping to order. The falcon is then ready for hawking live game and the transition should be made as soon as the falcon is ready, without delay. In America,

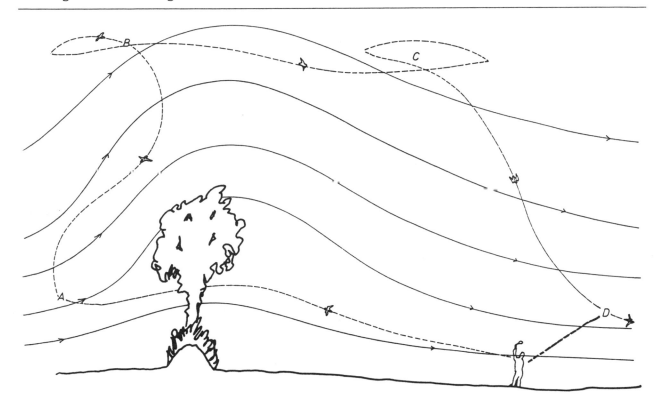

Figure 5.18.1 Early lessons in waiting on using lift over a line of trees.

bagged pigeons are used, but in Britain bagged game is illegal. Some falcons, particularly the non-peregrine species, quickly get wise to the thrown lure. They simply slow their descent so that they take the lure when it hits the ground. If your dog retrieves dummies you can foil this by throwing the dummy into cover so that the falcon has to catch it in the air. However, this is seldom satisfactory, many young falcons will go into cover after

it. Better then to go straight on to live game.

If the falcon is being used for partridges it is a wise investment to breed and put out partridges in fields with suitable holding cover and a good prevailing wind direction. Leave a pen of call birds to stop the others straying. Using a pointer, it is then possible to get reasonably reliable set-ups for your falcon in the early part of the season and during this tricky stage in her development.

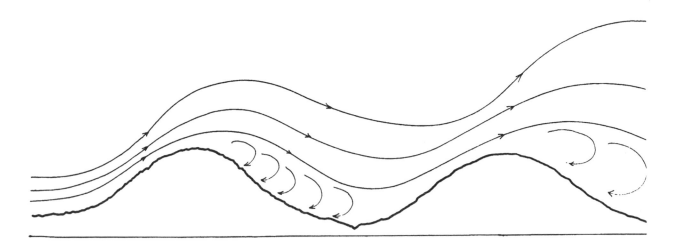

Figure 5.18.2 Lift and sink areas in the hills.

If the transfer is being made direct to grouse then you must find grouse on a slope with some lift (figure 5.18.2). Do not even bother to run the dog in areas of no lift or in a lee; if you find a grouse there you can't fly your hawk so leave those areas for another day when the wind is in a different quarter or for a more experienced falcon. To fly a young falcon on a lee slope at this stage is inviting trouble. I checked out the air on my usual training slope in an ultralight. On a normal day the lift was 600–800 feet per minute (180–240 m/min.). Just by opening her wings for one minute, the falcon would reach 500 feet. On the lee slope behind, it was dangerous. The air was descending at the same rate, which is faster than the ultralight could climb. If we flew into that area we would inevitably be driven into the ground, and so would a young falcon.

Where wind hits the hill it will tend to flow around and channel up the side valleys. But if the hill presents a broad front, or is at the head of a basin, the wind will be forced over the top, giving excellent orographic lift. A hawk is almost bound to go up here, indeed there may well be several wild hawks already up there. On the lee slope the air is moving downward and may be turbulent, the hawk is forced to the ground. If quarry is found in this place (as it often is, sheltering from the wind) the hawk must either struggle through the lowering air or reach a windward slope and come back over. With an inexperienced hawk it is better to carry her to a lifting place before unhooding then, once she is well up, run back to the point keeping the hawk above the lowering air.

Falcons are as lazy as humans. They do not use the stairs if the elevator is working. Anybody who has studied wild falcons knows that they have their lift spots—usually windy gullies or faces. They simply glide across to the lift and go straight up, either like an air bubble in water or in tight lazy spirals. Then off they go hunting.

If you fly your falcon often in the same place, she will soon learn the lift spots and go and use them even if this means going some distance away. Let her go. When she has got enough height she will come back over. Don't try to impose your own earthbound mentality onto her concept of aerodynamic space. Only when there is no lift will the falcon slog upwards in powered flight. It is tiring and cannot be maintained for long. You are asking a lot of a young bird in those conditions.

Having got the falcon in position over a point

on a windward slope the grouse must be flushed uphill and downwind—straight into the dog's face. There is some advantage here if the dog will lie or "set" right down. Come around the point making a big circuit until you are facing the dog. Early in the season provided the falcon has over-flown the grouse and is approximately in position, the grouse should hold unless cover is sparse. You can make some small noise to let the grouse know your position. As the falcon comes overhead, preferably slightly up wind, rush into the grouse. I use a light stick to help beat the heather patches. As the grouse rise, or just before if you are confident of an immediate flush, shout "Ho!" The falcon will start to turn and stoop, lining up on the grouse. If you have served her well the grouse will be flying uphill, downwind and the falcon will have a downwind stoop. Most probably the grouse, if not hit cleanly, will hit the ground to evade the falcon. A good falcon will turn and take it on impact, or will go back up waiting to be re-served. What you don't want happening is for the grouse to put in and for the falcon to land on the ground nearby. Otherwise the grouse will spring off again leaving the falcon (and you) with a slogging tail chase.

If the grouse and falcon are both down on the ground separately, do not approach because you may spring the grouse. Lure the falcon out and once she is in the air hide the lure so that she goes up. If she is blown and won't go up and you think the grouse is an old one and likely to flush at any moment, then you must keep the pressure on and not waste time. If the falcon is near the grouse run in to about 50 meters from the grouse. Then lure the falcon but make her miss the lure so that she turns to come in again. As she throws up and begins to come back in run on with dog at heel and flush the grouse. Either the falcon will hit it, or she will tail-chase it or she will put it in again. It depends on the position and height of the falcon, the timing and direction of the reflush and the heart of the grouse. Alternatively, the grouse may not flush at all in which case you know it is fairly thoroughly intimidated. If you try to flush it the dog will catch it. If you pick it up in your hand and throw it, it will tumble to the ground and hide rather than fly.

In such a situation the best solution perhaps is to leave the grouse. Failing that, one can hood up the falcon and wait for 10 or 15 minutes after which time the falcon may go up well and the grouse flush cleanly. With a young bird, without bagged game, you have to decide whether to stick to a very strict discipline of only going for a kill from a perfect set-up, or of getting her a kill so that she understands the reason for the whole exercise and appreciates the limits of her killing cone (see 6.14). Probably the best compromise is to achieve a few kills to start with, in the best style you can, and then gradually tighten up the discipline until she is only allowed one stoop at each grouse and if she fails, is taken down with no reward. The ultimate aim is to establish a pattern of stereotyped behavior.

Often the young falcon will miss the first grouse, tail chase for a while then return at a good height. Now is the time to flush a second grouse from the covey under her. If all goes disastrously wrong and you are left with the falcon faithfully waiting on but no game to serve her either run the dog on looking for fresh grouse or, especially if the hawk is young, shout "Ho" and throw out the thrown lure.

Purists will say "This hill lift is all very well, but I want my falcon to learn to mount in dead air over flat ground." In operant conditioning you have to get the bird to *do* something first, then reward her. In other words you train her, link by link, from the end result, forward. First you get her flying, footing, centering, and stooping to the thrown lure organized. Then you build forward from this. You get her to go up and appreciate the advantage of this position. Then she will *want* to go up. Then you take her to a less lifting place where she has to work harder to get up. Until in the end she will mount in a powered climb, knowing it will bring its reward. What you mustn't do is take her to some dead air and expect her to climb for no reason. She *may* do so, in which case you are lucky. But if she skims around low down, you are establishing a pattern of refusal. You are actually training her *not* to mount. The skilled falconer is measured not by his best bird, but by what he can achieve with the worst ones.

Another line of approach is to use a balloon to raise a lure into the air so that the falcon learns to go higher and higher to get the lure. This is explained in the latest edition of Beebe and Webster. You should be teaching the falcon to climb above expected game so she is in a position of advantage (the high search 6.4). With the balloon, you are teaching her to make a direct flying attack (see 6.10) on exposed "quarry" in a high position. Yes, it gets her to go up, but psychologically she has

different intentions. From her point of view she has succeeded in catching her prey by attacking it from below, not by climbing above it.

Later in the season it may well be hard to find the time, the good weather and the quarry to continue with waiting-on flights at game and the falcon gets unfit and goes to pieces. Some falconers stoop their falcons to the lure for exercise at home in between hawking days. This works for some falcons but lowers the pitch of others and the latter will have to be grounded until next season. Very few falconers have the time and quarry to continue all season with waiting-on flights. For most, it is an addictive holiday.

Buteos, eagles, and even accipiters can be trained to wait on. Buteos, Harris hawks and most eagles learn it easily because it is part of their natural search methods (see 6.4). The training of these species is not complete until they hunt well from waiting on. Most buteos and eagles are poor in the tail chase, whereas in the dive from high up they are really spectacular. The principles of teaching them to go up are the same as described for falcons, although of course they will not stoop to a swung lure.

## 5.19  Entering

Game falcons and accipiters do not normally need any entering. But some of the less rapacious buzzard species and pursuit falcons which have to chase quite challenging prey such as crows, gulls or houbara may need a gradual introduction to their quarry.

When entering, you must first get the hawk properly fit, with a good digestion and appetite. She will have been introduced to dragged or thrown dead quarry in a dress rehearsal so already has the makings of a "search image." She knows what to look for. The moment that you judge she is ready for entering, feed her a small ration early in the day so that the next day she has a 28 hour hunger and has lost a little weight (perhaps 10 grams on a 900 gram bird). She should not be low, but this is the lowest weight that you will ever fly her at. You must achieve maximum motivation without losing strength. Take her out and try to give her some really good easy slips or flushes. If you have a problem with this, take her to an area where her prey is common, such as a rookery or a rabbit warren (depending on the hawk) and put her in a tree or on a vantage point. Sit down in a quiet place one or two hundred meters away and let her start selfhunting. If she flies away, don't call her back. Follow her, if necessary using the radio. Keep going until dark. The moment she kills, run in and help her. Make sure the quarry is dead, secure the hawk with a cord through one of her anklets tied to your hawking bag. Open up the brain and neck and then sit down about twenty meters away for about an hour, she may want more, possibly the rest of the afternoon. Don't rush her. Every moment that she sits with her own kill a little voice is saying to itself in her brain "Brilliant! So this is what life is all about! I must do this again!" If she is getting stuck up with feathers or fur, open up the carcass. Don't let her pig-out, let her have just enough so that she is flyable again the next day. Don't use a pick-up piece; cut off a wing or leg and walk her home with that.

If it is getting dark and she still hasn't killed, throw out your dead prey from behind a screen and try to make the best of a bad job.

Once she is entered, do the same the next day, but it should all come quicker and easier. Soon you will be able to start slipping her at things, with reasonable confidence that she will go for them.

It is important that you think positive at this time and make sure that one way or another your hawk is successful. We try for hours to find a crow which looks as if it is blind in one eye with a wooden leg. You must find any off-peak quarry which will just give the hawk an extra chance. The hawk too will sense if you are really trying. Most hawks are willing to make a number of attempts to catch prey, but if they are unsuccessful, then they lose heart and refuse. They must kill long before this, otherwise they will be half-hearted for a long time before becoming properly wedded. We try to enter the bird either on the first day, or at latest, the second. She will get special treatment for at least the first five kills and won't be pushed to make doubles until she has killed 10–30 singles, depending on her commitment. If possible the first five kills should be made without a miss. After that, the level of difficulty can gradually be increased.

In some countries, bagged quarry is used or misused. The ethics of this are discussed in 8.9. Bagged quarry is a short cut which often makes falconers lazy. When rehabilitating a bird which has no selfconfidence, it may be necessary to arrange easy prey for it to get started. Without it the bird could never manage to become independent in the wild. But the skilled falconer makes every effort to get his bird hunting genuine quarry without the need for substituting bagged game.

## 5.20  The diagnosis and treatment of vices

Vice is unwanted behavior and as such it has the same roots as other behavior, ie inherited, imprinted, or learned. First identify the unwanted behavior, then work out its root. If it is inherited or imprinted it may be a lot harder to eradicate than if it has been learned. For example your goshawk may take crows and gulls well but may always tail off if they go up more than 30–40 meters (100 ft.). This is a common inherited limitation of goshawks. Or the bird may scream because it is imprinted on you as a parent figure. You can't change its imprinting but you can change the parent figure—give the bird to another falconer (you may have to pay him to take it!). You can also negatively condition the hawk on you as the food source by flying the hawk at hack or at quarry and minimizing calls to the fist, but this makes falconry difficult. Finally, if the hawk doesn't learn not to scream you will at least have taught yourself not to create a screaming hawk in the first place.

We'll look at some common vices, carrying, hoodshyness, and aggression and screaming, in the next three sections and analyze them in terms of behavioral origin and in ways of training to reduce them.

## 5.21  Carrying quarry

Carrying quarry is a vice which can have a variety of roots and is therefore hard to diagnose and cure. Some of the smaller attacking hawks, such a merlins and sparrowhawks, have a strong inherited tendency to carry as a protection against piracy by

Figure 5.21.1 When she carries she is so expressive. And so are you.

other predators. Some species, such as New Zealand falcons, instinctively want to cache food and may carry it away and hide it before coming back to the falconer and carrying on hunting. Raptors that have been reared with jealous siblings soon learn to carry food (figure 5.21.1). Small, well-advanced males carry to escape from less-agile, bullying sisters. "Learned" carriers are easier to cure then "inherited" carriers and it is important to remember that carrying prey to a safe place has survival value both for wild hawks and for trained ones.

The first steps in preventing carrying are made early on in training. When she is at home on the perch cut yourself a little bowl of bechins—small pieces of meat as tidbits. Every half an hour or so come round the corner into the weathering area and quietly approach her and give her a bechin. Always whistle or make a noise before you come round a corner onto a hawk so that she is forewarned. (I do this with my staff as well.) Soon you should be able to appear and walk openly up to the hawk and give her a bechin in her beak quite boldly, with her showing every sign of eagerness and anticipation. When out lure training, you walk around her and approach from all angles with a bechin. If the garnishing on the lure was only small, she will quickly consume everything on the lure and be left standing on a food-less lure with you wandering around with tidbits. You become the focus of attention. Soon she will bate from the lure back onto your fist as soon as you approach. This should be the pattern for the rest of her days. I do not expect to have to bend right down to a trained hawk to take her up off the lure; she should jump up off it at my approach and I just pull up the lure by its cord and put it away. High jumping too, strongly reinforces this behavior and quickly gets a wary passage hawk changing into friendly behavior.

As well as preventive training, it is important to prevent carrying happening and thus reinforcing itself. Don't start getting up to all sorts of strange and rather alarming antics like crawling up to the hawk. Just wander up in a series of oblique diagonals, talking to yourself and not staring or standing high above the hawk (figure 5.21.2). Give her the right signals. She knows you're there. If you crawl up to her you are like a predator creeping up on its prey. Be open about it and show that you are a nonthreatening companion. Beat her at her own game. The hawk is on her hard-earned prey. She

Figure 5.21.2 Do not approach a nervous hawk directly. Come in at an angle with eyes cast down.

sees you as a sister or another predator coming to rob her of prey. First show her that there is no way you want her prey because you've already caught your own—a nice juicy lure or pick-up piece. What's more, your kill is more attractive because you've already plucked yours and there is lots of red meat showing, just ready for eating. Pull a few bits off. Instead of jealousy at your approach, envy takes over. Let the hawk have some of the tidbits and finally let her rob you of your kill before she has broken into her own. Using the links prey/ pick-up piece, or if necessary prey/lure/pick-up piece, let the hawk step onto the fist and quietly remove the kill and lure out of sight into the hawking bag, or cover it with grass or sand. Keep the fist on the ground at the kill spot and let the hawk feed there awhile. Once she is thoroughly settled, walk well away from the kill spot before finishing off. Some hawks, especially Harris hawks, will bate back for the kill spot otherwise, to check. NEVER lift the hawk with her kill off the ground (figure 5.21.3). This sows the seeds of carrying and of attacking the trainer. It is about the shortest cut to disaster.

If she is newly entered, thread one glove cord

Figure 5.21.3 Sowing the seeds of vice.

through one anklet and tie the other cord to something heavy, such as the hawking bag. Settle with her and let her eat her kill, helping her with it and giving her tidbits. I try to spin this out for at least half an hour with a young hawk. Every minute you spend doing this is like putting money into the bank. She is associating you with her success.

In some countries, particularly the Middle East, it is not customary to use a pick-up piece, a piece of meat large enough to be held in the glove to tempt the hawk off her prey or lure onto the glove. It is good psychology to use one, especially with new passage hawks, and helps reinforce the bond and prevent carrying.

If the hawk carries a lot, don't let her break into any of the kills without you being there—you wish to reduce the link kill/food and reinforce the link falconer/food. If the fear of robbery is so great that you can't get near the hawk, then throw the hawk the lure by tying the lure on a 50 meter line and throwing it close to the hawk (figure 5.21.3). Then walk round in a half-circle and tow the lure

back to the hawk. If you still can't do it you must have a hard case because I've caught even wild hawks that way, just winding the hawk up with the line before making in. Obviously if you know you've got a difficult one, don't fly her at quarry until you've remedied it. Give yourself a chance to cure the habit on chosen terrain. Otherwise the hawk may come down with the quarry in an awkward place, such as a barbed-wire fence or a corn field, where it is hard to give the lesson properly. This trick is also useful for any hawk which comes down with prey onto thin ice or quaking bog where it is unsafe for the falconer to approach. She can be tempted to grab the lure and then towed gently in to safety.

Anticarrying treatment can be very effective and it is possible to teach a hawk to "retrieve" her kills this way, or to abandon them to come to you, so that the quarry flies away unharmed. This is handy if you are hawking a river which is deep and cold, with the hawk down on quarry on the other side. It is also useful to get the hawk to show herself if on quarry in thick cover. Instead of lying low, waiting for you to pass, the accipiter can be called out or at least made to ring a bell and reveal her position.

## 5.22  Hoodshyness

Another common vice is hoodshyness. Putting the hood on is a neutral-to-unpleasant experience for the hawk and, unless done adeptly from the start, can give negative conditioning. It is hard too, to link it with positive reinforcement and, if persevered with, the negative conditioning links with all aspects of being handled and the whole relationship is destroyed. Most hawks, a few days after starting, get awkward to hood but settle again after a week or two more. This awkward period is due to the hawk becoming less afraid of the falconer than of the hood and so she starts to resist.

Usually a hawk which is bad to hood is due to bad technique on the part of the falconer. So blame yourself. Then look at your technique and improve it. Behind every skilled act is a lot of experience and practice and too many falconers think they can run before they can walk. Be prepared to look critically at yourself and improve.

My approach is to put the hood on, come what may. If the hawk shows signs of standing for it, then I do it as calmly as possible. On the other hand, if the hawk doesn't show much sign of stay-

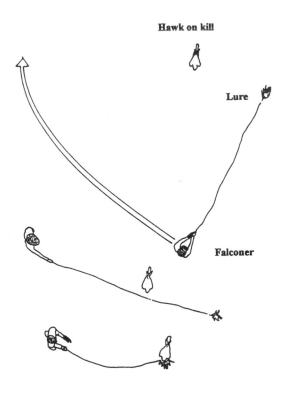

**Hawk on kill**

**Lure**

**Falconer**

Figure 5.21.4 Top: When a nervous hawk is on her kill, throw a lure out to the side of her. Center: Move quietly round in a semicircle until the lure line is near the hawk, then tow the lure in until the hawk grabs it. Bottom: Approach the hawk gently, walking alone the lure-line to keep it secured and low.

ing upright, after two or three bates I slip the hood on while the hawk is upside down, rather than persist in attempts to get it on the conventional way and reinforce the negative conditioning. This is easily and quickly done: the hawk is already held by fairly short jesses so that her feet are secured. I then raise my left knee so she is draped over it safely. Never let a hawk hang upside down for a moment; it is bad for her back, her leg joints, and her mind. Laid on my knee she may try to bite, but it is easy to hook the chinstrap under her beak and flip the hood over her head. The procedure takes no more than a second or two and is much better than entering a confrontation. If the falconer finally quits without getting the hood on the bird, she learns that if she resists enough she can evade the hood and then you've really made yourself a problem. During early training the hawk is hooded most of the time and gets very comfortable, sleeping quietly and having a peaceful time. The training periods are positive but still stressful and so the hood is a welcome relief. But the hood must be comfortable and it must be put off and on gently and easily, without a lot of menacing waving about. Just roll the hood over its chinstrap onto the hawk's head, using the rotation of your wrist. Your wrists and arms should be held as if you were driving a screw into the hawk's left wing, not in the frontal, sit-up-and-beg position, as if you were placing a pot on a high shelf. This is jerky. I normally close the hood with my right hand as soon as it is on (figure 5.22.1). Then I use my teeth to close the second brace a few moments later.

If the hawk is chronically, traumatically hood-shy as a result of abuse, there are two weapons—habituation and positive reinforcement. Suspend hoods near the hawk on her perch. Soon she stops

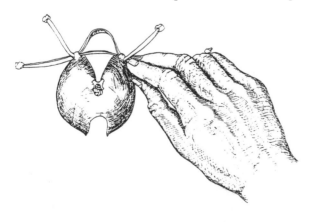

Figure 5.22.1 Closing the hood braces with one hand.

reacting to the sight of them without associating the unpleasant hood with you. Use your cupped hand, or a huge hood that she can see out of. Let her feed from food inside the hood and stroke her back with your hand. Gradually stroke the back of her head as she feeds, then cup her head with your hand, then come over the front of her head with your cupped hand, then have a big hood in your cupped hand, the plume between your thumb and base of index finger so that it nestles in your palm. These lessons are repeated and become associated with food. When you stop to think about it, there are usually graduations to an activity so that you don't have to do it in one desperate hop. A cutaway mouth opening allows the hawk to see out and is easier to put on. As her tolerance improves, a tighter hood can be used. Positive reinforcement can be given by feeding the hawk tidbits inside the hood and by feeding the hawk while the big, open hood is on, so that she links hooding with food. The hawk can be left hooded at night so that she doesn't link wearing the hood with food, and hence constantly pull at the glove while hooded. You want to link putting on the hood with food.

With really bad hooders, the hawk bates and works herself into a frenzy so that she gives herself no chance to realize that hooding is not too bad after all. The hood becomes a bogey man. The simplest remedy is to put the hawk in a sleeve with her head showing, or sometimes I walk around just carrying the hawk tucked under my arm. Then put the hood on and off many times until you see the nictitating membrane cross the eye as the hood approaches. While she is still sleeved or brailed you can feed her tidbits from the hood, then gradually revert to normal procedures. I find this method more effective and preferable to the alternative of soaking the hawk with water. Spraying with water quietens hawks down and makes them reluctant to bate. It is a useful method especially in a hot climate as it also cools the hawk down.

Some hawks, such as gyrs and New Zealand falcons are intelligent and hate being hooded at certain times. They often resent it when first being taken up to be weighed and loaded for hawking. After hawking, with a good crop they take the hood as sweet as pie. They look at you and say "Okay, you can put it on now." These hawks are not hoodshy, they just have times when they want to stay unhooded. I usually give them a tiring on the fist, then fit the hood beak-opening over the tiring, then they put their head inside and hood themselves. We all know it is an old trick, but dignity has been maintained.

## 5.23   Aggression and screaming

Aggression toward people and screaming both arise from the same root cause and are commonest in raptors imprinted on humans, which have no fear response toward the trainer. In a situation of jealousy, such as on the kill, there is nothing holding back such a hawk from flying at the falconer to drive him away. Another situation is when an entered hawk becomes frustrated from not being served with game and flies at the falconer or his dog. Aggression in the hawk is usually a sign that the falconer has mishandled the relationship somewhere along the line.

The commonest species to become a problem through aggression are red-tails, goshawks and Cooper's hawks. They are large enough to cause real damage and if one attacks a dog or person the victim may be put off hawks for life. We have a female common buzzard, now 16 years old, who was brought to us by the police for attacking little old ladies in woods. Probably taken illegally as a nestling and malimprinted, she attacks selected people and ignores others. Out on loan, she chased someone up the garden path. He ran indoors and she flew straight through the window pane of the kitchen door to get him! This same bird was once cast by a young friend called Tom, years ago. In a different place, two years later out hawking, she saw Tom again and flew through a group of five people to nail him. Tom now has a complex.

As shown in section 4.21, young hawks go through a phase in their development when they become aggressive toward their parents, "bullying" them to provide food. Normally this wears off as the bird starts to kill for itself and becomes independent. Young falconry birds, particularly malimprints, may turn this onto their handler who acts as a parent figure. Anything which produces food, including the hawking dog, may trigger it. As the red-tail is often in inexperienced hands, the young falconer spends longer than normal handling and training the bird (reinforcing the parental bond) and is less successful at producing quarry (diminishing the hawk's independence). As autumn slips by, the hawk begins to orientate inward toward the handler rather than outward toward killing for itself. Aggressive instincts to foot and grab are diverted from the prey to the falconer.

In large hawks, such as the big eagles, this semidependent stage is necessarily a long one and it seems that young eagles respond to a certain amount of discipline. Japanese and Asian methods of training eagles usually include some discipline, either physical or social. For example, the falconer holding the eagle is treated with subservience by other people present to demonstrate to the eagle that the falconer is a dominant figure and thus to be respected. Physical methods used with eagles to maintain respect and hence one's own personal safety are based on dominance behavior in the wild. I will not detail them here because of the risk of misunderstandings and abuse.

So what can be done about an aggressive or screaming hawk? Basically she must be encouraged to grow up, to progress through the next stages of development to "independent" adulthood. First the falconer can reduce the parental bond; he must aim to be a hunting partner, not a parent. Stop flying the hawk from and to the fist. Fly her at quarry and find her plenty of opportunities. Encourage selfhunting. Call her in to the lure, not to the fist, and don't pick her up until she has had almost a full ration. Do not arrange matters so that the hawk is kept tethered but not flown at quarry. Handling her by putting her out to weather each day means that you are returning her to dependence. Once the hawking season is over put the hawk in a good-sized molting pen with a member of the opposite sex (both birds naturally imprinted of course). Let them see people, but not as food providers; food reaches them through a chute or hatch. Provide a nest. If, being young, they don't breed, it doesn't matter. The object of the exercise is to get them to interact as mature adults, possibly even forming a pair bond. More ferocious individuals, such as goshawks and Cooper's hawks, may need to be kept physically separated for their own safety, as do raptors imprinted on humans. But they can still be provided with a nest and allowed to go at least partway through the breeding cycle.

We are seeing in recent years a phenomenon in which naturally imprinted birds, domestic-raised by their parents, are falling into the hand of inexperienced people and are becoming screamers. These birds are not malimprints. They have had their development arrested at puberty by handlers who have failed to develop their hunting skills and independence. The hawks have simply transferred their allegiance from the natural parents to the handlers. If possible it is better to have left such birds with their parents for an extra month after being hard penned and then to get them going at quarry reasonably quickly. It helps too to keep them in daily contact with another hawk, failing that even a mirror may work, to help the hawk retain its identity as a hawk. On the other hand, if the hawk is left in the pen for too long in the autumn it will be past the best period for learning and quarry and conditions generally will be more difficult. Although hawking books tell you not to hurry training, in cases such as this there is a lot to be said for pushing through it fairly rapidly with more emphasis on lure-work than on the fist. Dependence should not be confused with obedience. The worst thing that can happen to a young hawk is to be stuck with a falconer who messes about with it all the time, keeps calling it unnecessarily to the fist and fails to expose it frequently and regularly to catchable wild game. The hawk is like a shooter who, unable to find real game, becomes frustrated and shoots up road signs instead.

Harris hawks start to imprint at around day 5 and if they are hand-fed for any longer than this, they are liable to scream. Even totally parent-reared Harris hawks often scream during their first autumn, because of their naturally long dependence period. As they become mature hunters, they quieten down, but, being group hunters, they are naturally communicative. Accipiters, on the other hand, become independent very suddenly, about three weeks or so after fledging, and thereafter go about their own business through the woods, silently.

Probably the main reason why so few falconers do well with buzzards, including often the red-tail and sometimes even the Harris, is that they misunderstand the nature of their aggression and the ways they prefer to hunt. They treat them as second-class goshawks not realizing that the buzzards are completely different physically and mentally. Whereas goshawks have hair-trigger reactions, an explosive takeoff, good acceleration and a rapacious disposition, buzzards are slow, calculating and incapable of rapid, powered flight (see 1.16). Any form of taxing tail chase is impossible for them. Their hunting is based on searching and their preferred attacks are the dive and the glide attack. Pitted against agile prey, their only hope for success is from a height advantage, preferably with the benefit of surprise. Although experienced common buzzards will take rabbits well,

they need to do so on their own terms and will often glide over seemingly vulnerable rabbits to smash into the one selected as the best bet—usually young, sick or unsuspecting.

Once one accepts the buzzard for what it is and helps it to do its own thing, instead of trying to force it into the goshawk mould, then success will come. The successful hawk will be less frustrated and less likely to attack people.

The above applies to a lesser extent to the red-tail and to the young Harris. Older and more experienced birds should be capable of more "classy" flying, but when they get really experienced some start to show their limitations and refuse flights which they would have taken on in their hot-blooded youth. Don't we all?

## 5.24 Bad practices

While writing this book I talked to a number of vets, falconers, and breeders about practices in handling birds of prey which have caused death or injury and which are avoidable. Dear, oh dear! What a catalogue of disasters! Many of them have been incorporated into the relevant section of the book, but some of them are worth repeating as a warning. You may like to add further examples from your own experience.

Many accidents arise from tethering. Tethering raptors is not a good idea generally, unless there is a specific reason for doing so. It should never be done as a convenience for the falconer. Think of it in the same way as tying up a dog or a horse; you would not tie them up for more than short periods, and certainly not day after day.

Many tragedies have occurred because perches have been faulty. Bad welding, perches not secured properly so that the bird escapes or attacks an adjacent bird (figure 5.24.1), birds tied to unbarbed staples hammered into wood, perches light enough for the bird to drag and kill another, these are common bad mistakes. Then there are poorly designed perches. Some of these designs are still recommended in current books. These perches allow the bird to get tangled up, causing feather damage, sprained joints, or broken limbs. Some, such as the screen perch and the pole perch, cause death overnight on a regular and frequent basis (figure 5.24.2). Rope bound around perches comes slack, causing claws to get caught and wrenched off. Other perches kill by slow attrition, causing bumblefoot to the victim. These include

Figure 5.24.1 An unsecured perch allows one hawk to reach and kill another.

Figure 5.24.3 A molting falcon escapes with leash trailing.

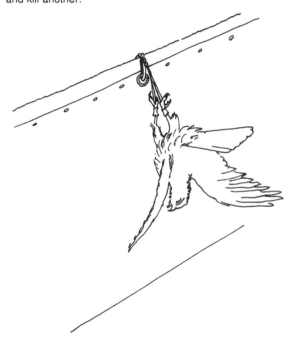

Figure 5.24.2 The screen perch in use.

smooth, flat-topped blocks and filthy perches. If you have any of this faulty equipment, go out, smash it up, and bin it. Don't give it to young friends. Don't wait for the accident to happen. Get rid of it. Get rid of it in your mind as well. Don't hang on to old "traditions." This gear is dangerous. Give your birds the best available, in the end it is the cheapest.

The falconer's knot and leash are another voracious killer. Every year, dozens of hawks are lost with leashes trailing because someone has tied them up with the falconer's knot (figure 5.24.3). Sooner or later it will come undone. Falconers

know this, so they tie two in a row! Never leave a hawk unattended when tied up with a falconer's knot. I have watched a falcon undo a double falconer's knot in less than 20 minutes. Keep the falconer's knot for tying the hawk to your glove or for tying up your horse. Otherwise use a safe alternative such as a loop leash (figure 3.4.2).

Never carry a hawk on the glove unless it is properly secured with a knot. If you wind the leash around your fingers in the "traditional" manner (figure 5.24.4), you will sooner or later let go of the hawk. Either you will trip over or the hawk will bate suddenly and be off. When we used to run course, we found beginners would let go of everything about 2–3 times in one week. There are plenty of safe ways of securing a bird to the glove quickly and easily without tangling problems.

Another common abuse is to fail to tie up a hawk while it is hooded. Hawks will bate while hooded and can easily fly off. Never leave a hooded hawk unsecured or able to reach a neighbor. They can easily crab and quickly cause a bad injury. Hungry hawks hooded on a cadge easily bite out blindly, and often the first thing they find is the carpal joint of an adjacent falcon. One bite on this joint can cripple a bird for life. If a hawk bates with its hood on it will fly high up into the sky until exhausted. In that state it is an ideal decoy for a passing eagle. Also hooded hawks can bate

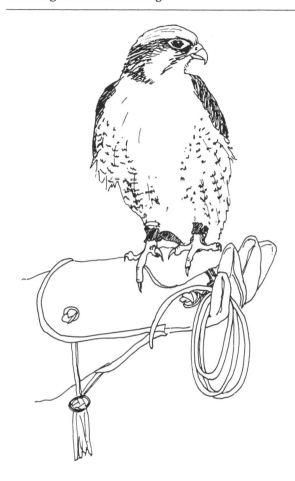

Figure 5.24.4 The traditional way of securing a falcon to the glove. If you trip, you don't just lose your balance.

unexpectedly, the result being a broken wing, shut in a car door. Another problem with hoods is the use of patterns which constrict the mouth opening and hence can choke a hawk to death if it needs tocast or vomit. Dutch and Bahreini hoods with traditional small beak openings are unsafe (figure 5.24.5).

Vets and rehabilitators can unwittingly stress a bird by failing to hood it adequately. Some vets have treated hawks without using a hood and caused the bird to become neurotically afraid of humans. Others have crammed on hoods which are too small, causing eye infections.

Hawks on cadges in cars should always be physically separated and attended. Boxes or partitions are a better solution and also discourage interference from the public. Boxes should be kept clean and dry and free from mold or ammonia fumes. Hawks on cadges should never be left unattended; they may crab. One person went grouse-hawking on his own and forgot where he left his cadge on the moor. He spent the rest of the day

frantically searching for it. Hawks should never be tethered in the open when other hawks are being flown; this is common at public displays and meetings. Sooner or later a free hawk will bind to a tethered one and small accipiters and falcons rarely survive this.

Clips and fastenings are common hazards and frequently cause death or injury. Avoid any clip which has a leaf or coiled spring. They all can fail. Americans are at present very fond of clips, but they can cause loss or injury just as easily as knots. Also avoid any clip which includes a key-ring. Key-rings are very good for keeping keys. Recently a friend tethered his peregrine/saker using a key-ring. She got free and killed his female Finnish goshawk tied nearby. Even on the lure, key-rings are a hazard. They can wrench apart allowing your falcon to fly off with the lure. Cable-ties have caused a number of injuries when hawks have got beaks or claws caught under them. Poor cable-ties will also fail unexpectedly, allowing transmitters to come off.

Badly designed lures containing lead shot, or metal, kill or maim falcons when a stoop is misjudged. Splintered bone ends on dried wings can cause foot injuries. Poor lure technique can cause the line to tear the propatagial membrane. Unhygienic lures can cause foot or gut infections.

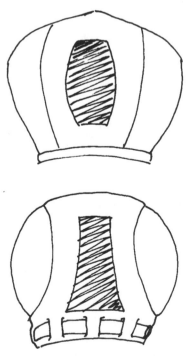

Figure 5.24.5 The dutch style hood and the Bahreini style hood have narrow beak openings which can kill.

Flying hawks wearing jesses with slits caused death or injury to many (figure 5.24.6). There is no excuse for perpetuating this mistake. Another dangerous practice is to reverse the mews jesses so that the slit is at the anklet and the knot trails, waiting to trap the hawk in a Y-shaped branch. There have even be examples of really stupid falconers flying their hawks with the swivel still on the jesses!

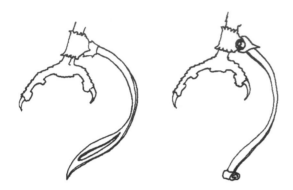

Figure 5.24.6 The traditional slitted jess and the reversed mews jess can hang the hawk in a tree.

Creances are another source of injuries. Hawks suffer sprained joints or a broken tibiotarsus when pulled up too abruptly. Hawks get tangled up in trees and strangle themselves or cut themselves with the thin line running over their legs or wings. Hawks escape with the swivel on when the creance has been badly tied to the swivel, not to the jesses. There are even people still using unsecured dragged creances. One peregrine flew off with a 50 meter creance, never to be seen again in this life!

Big hawks which are a hazard to people or property should be flown only very circumspectly in uninhabited areas, if at all. An eagle which attacks dogs, can just as easily attack children. Red-tails and Harrises, if managed wrongly, may also attack children. Harrises which have been fed on fluffy, yellow day-old chicks may attack yellow pom-poms on children's hats. These birds must all be grounded.

Other accidents relate to the way hawks are kept. Every year in hot climates, hawks are killed because a careless owner has left them in the sun, or where they can get into the sun, or where the sun comes round even though the hawk was in shadow to start with. A sequel to this, common in the Middle East, is to place the hooded falcon on its perch, close to the car in the narrow shadow.

Someone then backs the car over it or opens the door on it. All hawks need proper protection from extremes of weather.

The opposite is to leave the hawk tethered near the ground at night in cold weather. The hawk then gets frosted and develops dry gangrene in its toes or manus. Alternatively it is left in a damp place with moldy material nearby in the shape of moldy orchard fruit, hay, straw, lawn clippings, mushroom manure, shredded wood bark, or old sacks. Never use a barn or stable which has had hay in it, or take a hawk into a room which smells musty. The result can be aspergillosis.

Protection from predators is also necessary while weathering. Accidents include hawks killed by rats, cats, jackdaws and crows, a black eagle killed and swallowed at night by a python, a goshawk killed by a genet cat, right down to the commonest mistake of all—tethering hawks too close together. Many a hawk placed under a shady tree has been killed by a falling branch. Often, when on hawking trips, hawk are put out to weather on unprotected lawns; in this case take some electric sheep netting with a small power pack, to keep off strange dogs and unwelcome visitors.

The worst predator of hawks is the ferret. Ferrets are notorious escapologists and if they get out of their traveling box in the car, or out of their hutch at night, they will quickly kill even a large goshawk. If ferrets are kept at the same establishment as hawks, there should be a fail-safe system of keeping them apart.

Wrong feeding has caused many deaths. Examples include feeding food which has "gone off," food which contains lead shot, and food which is lacking in essential nutrients with a result that the young chicks get rickets. Or food high in fat leading to high blood cholesterol causing arteriosclerosis. These is common in breeding females and is preventable by using a low-fat diet and giving some exercise. Even the way the food is fed causes accidents: food tossed to a hawk on a high perch, the hawk drops it and bates itself to death trying to get at it. Or food thrown to a hawk in view of another bird, causing mass bating and feather damage. Or food pulled away from a hawk so that it punctures the sole of its foot with a hind claw. Or food fed to a chick which has not yet put over its previous meal, thus leading to sour crop. Or food with long or sharp bones in it, causing a perforated crop or a blocked gizzard.

Chemicals can cause a problem. One hawk

was deloused with a proprietary insecticide and then offered a bath. It drank some of the water and died. Another person cleared an infestation of ants with an insecticide but his owl then ate some of the ants and died.

Poor aviaries result in lost or dead hawks, usually through taking short cuts with materials. Non-reinforced corrugated plastic roofing sheet gets brittle and easily breaks in a storm. All main structures should be reinforced with steel strapping; most aviaries are prone to wind damage. Lapboard warps and soon lets in rats. Knots in the wood drop out, allowing hawks in adjacent pens to foot each other through the holes. A lack of double doors has caused the loss of many hawks. Food chutes and access points should be properly made to prevent escapes. Food drawers are better than chutes so that uneaten food can be removed. Netting should be checked regularly to detect holes or damage. Loose string netting can tangle a hawk. Sharp netting should never be used. Dense foliage, such as nettles, should be removed, young hawks land in it and can't get out, or chill and die of pneumonia. Predators on the roof, especially cats at night, can keep hawks off their eggs, or kill them through the wire. They should be prevented with an electric wire.

Molting hawks should be checked carefully and not neglected. Changes in food intake or behavior should be acted upon. Tight anklets should be removed. Many nonspecialist vets think that hawks have feathers like a pigeon's; never let anyone pull damaged feathers out. If one does get pulled out, plug the socket with a stub of quill for several days to keep it open and in shape.

Traveling is a source of stress and kills many hawks. Hawks should not be put into socks or sleeves except for very short periods under supervision. We heard of one case in Pakistan where falcons were transported in sleeves for three days. Unable to mute properly, they got kidney failure and died. Boxes should be strong enough to keep hawks in and tea-breaking airport staff out. Musty hawk boxes are a major source of *Aspergillus* infection When traveling by car, hawks should not be placed in the boot (trunk) where they can succumb to petrol or exhaust fumes at much lower levels than those tolerated by dogs or humans. Nor should a mews or aviary be sited next to a garage where fumes can reach the hawk. Hawks can easily overheat or dehydrate in the back of a car, even when the driver himself is pleasantly cool.

Apart from injuries to the hawk, there is also a risk to humans. Imprints with a record of attacking people should not be flown loose, particularly not near children. Learn how to catch and handle hawks without either party being clawed, and if you do get clawed, soak the injured part in hot water with disinfectant as soon as possible. This often prevents an infection developing. Gentlemen should also take precautions when relieving themselves near a hungry hawk; one's pride and joy is another's pick-up piece, and I believe the record for this type of injury is eight stitches.

Most of the blunders mentioned above are avoidable. Learn from other people's mistakes. There are plenty of accidents which can befall hawks (electrocution for example) without doing something which you know has caused death or injury before. You have been warned!

# 6  Hunting Strategies

Figure 6.10.2 A New Zealand falcon makes a direct flying attack on a bellbird *(Anthornis melanura melanura)*.

# of Wild Raptors

## 6.1    The components of the hunt

We have now reached the stage at which the hawk is ready to be taken into the field to hunt wild quarry. She is healthy and mentally and physically ready for action. But what can we expect from the bird and will our standard falconry techniques let her realize her full potential? To find this out we need to look in detail at the ways in which our falconry birds go about taking prey in the wild, unaided and unhindered by the falconer.

In any hunt for prey there are two basic parts: the search and the attack. In the attack itself there are often two parts: the first part in which the prey is still unaware that it is being attacked and therefore makes no effort to escape and the second part when the element of surprise has been lost and the predator and prey must contest for supremacy.

The information in this section is based on existing scientific literature and on my own observations of approximately 2,900 hunts by 45 raptor species. Some of these hunts were by wild birds, either casual observations or radiotracking studies, some were by birds at hack, a large number were by trained birds being radiotracked and allowed to do whatever they wished, and a smaller number were by trained falconry birds under more controlled conditions. Of the five methods of study, radiotracking tame birds gives the most complete understanding of each situation, while other methods tend to be more fragmentary or artificial.

Obviously there is a big jump between observing what happens to attempting to interpret it, and from the scientific viewpoint one must be very cautious before venturing an interpretation. However, most readers of this book, who are faced with the day to day reality of interacting with a real live raptor, cannot afford the luxury of reserving judgement, as can the behavioral scientist. Every day, we have to act on what we see, just as we also do with human relationships. Probably the complex situations described in this section will never be fully amenable to proper scientific observation and interpretation because they are so varied and unrepeatable. We just have to try to understand them as best we can and venture where behaviorist angels fear to tread. On the other hand, perhaps some of the insights expressed in this section will trigger some young scientist to look more closely at a particular aspect, or help to link up, by cause and effect, observations from completely different disciplines, such as anatomy, ecology, and ethology.

Hunting occurs whenever a predator searches for, or attacks, prey. During the searching phase the raptor is attempting either to locate prey which already is, or could become, vulnerable, or it is attempting to place itself in an attack situation in anticipation of prey becoming vulnerable. An attack may be opportunistic and not preceded by any searching. Both search and attack may use more than one strategy.

The main hunting methods used by birds of prey include:

Search strategies
   a)  Still-hunting.
   b)  Fast contour-hugging flight.
   c)  High searching—hovering, poising, prospecting, and soaring.
   d)  Slow quartering.
   e)  Stalking.
   f)  Listening.
   g)  Flushing from cover.
   h)  False attack.

Attack strategies
   a)  Direct flying attack.
   b)  Indirect flying attack.
   c)  Tail-chase.
   d)  Glide attack.
   e)  The drop, the dive, and the stoop.
   f)  Deception flights.

The many species of raptor which catch prey show a broad spectrum of hunting methods. At one end of the spectrum are the "searching" hawks, such as the vultures, kites, harriers, many buzzards and owls, and kestrels. These tend to concentrate on prey species such as small rodents, reptiles, amphibians, and invertebrates which are relatively helpless, widespread, easily captured, and which make little or no attempt to escape when attacked. Most of the prey are found singly but if in flocks, such as of termites, they still make little or no attempt to escape. This means that the searching hawks themselves tend to need smaller hunting ranges relative to their size than "attacking" hawks and can exist at greater densities. Some are heavily dependent on one or two staple prey species, such as voles, and their own breeding performance follows the numbers of the prey. The extreme searchers, such as the carrion feeders, do not need to make an attack at all, because their prey is already dead.

The attacks of the searchers tend to be simple and short—a mean distance of 15 meters for small hawks and about 25 meters for larger ones. Their most frequent forms of attack are the direct flying attack, the drop, and the dive. If they tail-chase at all it is only for short distances. Because prey are small, attacks tend to be more frequent and have a higher success rate than those of attacking hawks although the biomass captured per unit time is proportionately similar. The wing-loading of searchers is relatively low, enabling a slow, careful flight, emphasizing the importance of the searching phase of the hunt rather than the attacking phase. The size difference between the sexes is small. In general males are about 75–105 percent of the weight of the females.

Between the searchers and the attackers are a variety of intermediate forms, such as the red-tailed hawk. Some of these intermediate species tend to behave more like searching hawks for the first year or so of life but gradually become more active in their attack strategies, particularly during the breeding season.

At the other end of the spectrum are the "attacking" hawks. These include most of the accipiters, most of the falcons except the kestrels, the Micrastur forest falcons, the hawk-eagles, and some of the eagles. A high proportion of the attacks by juveniles include tail-chases but adults more often use less energy-expensive surprise attacks, such as the indirect flying attack and the glide attack. Attacking species make more complex attacks and the mean attack distance, although proportional to the size of the raptor, tends to be longer than those of searchers. Sometimes in falcons and eagles it exceeds 4 kilometers. The quarry are usually alert, agile, and relatively large vertebrates, sometimes larger than the raptor itself. Prey normally shows active escape behavior and

may live in flocks which aid the detection of predators (see 7.4). The wing-loading of the attackers is relatively high and the sexual dimorphism is pronounced. Males are only 50–70 percent of the weight of the females. This is discussed more fully in Cade (1982).

The main physical advantage of the accipiters, hawk-eagles and micrasturs, all of which hunt in or near forests, is the sprint. Small accipiters can sprint only 50–100 meters but are very agile and dexterous. Large accipiters can sprint for about three times this distance if they have to. Their attack strategies are designed to place the hawk within sprinting distance before the prey starts to escape.

The main attack strategies of the typical long-winged falcon are the stoop and the tail-chase. The attacks are designed to place the victim inside the killing cone (see section 6.14) for a dive or stoop. Failing this, many species such as the merlin, saker, and the gyrfalcon, can manage an arduous tail-chase.

Buzzards and harriers are not very effective at sprinting, stooping or tail-chasing and therefore, as searching hawks, concentrate on less agile prey which are more easily caught. The emphasis which different raptor species place on each hunting strategy is examined more closely in section 6.17.

## 6.2   Still-hunting

Still-hunting is probably the most universal type of searching used by birds of prey because it requires the least effort. There are two sub-categories: "perch and search" and "waiting in ambush." In the former the hawk perches for a time at a suitable vantage point and looks and listens for prey. Small accipiters and owls usually search a radius of only 10–100 meters but large falcons and eagles can detect and attack prey over 4 kilometers away. Should the hawk fail to spot any vulnerable prey it may fly to another perch to examine a fresh area. Ideal perches for still-hunting have a good view of an area holding vulnerable prey and some concealment for the hawk either in the form of foliage or a disruptive background or simply sufficient height distance from the prey for the hawk to remain unnoticed.

As the hawk gets hungrier it becomes more active and tends to change perches more frequently—every two minutes or so. It may also launch attacks at poorer opportunities. More aerial species, such as falcons and harriers, usually abandon still-hunting as they get hungrier and use more energetic search methods, still-hunting intermittently while resting. On windless days, kestrels and buzzards which would otherwise be hovering or high searching (see 6.4), often find it easier, in energy terms, to hunt from a perch, even though this may restrict the area they can cover.

Forest species, such as accipiters, hawk-eagles and probably the Micrastur forest falcons, sometimes deliberately wait in ambush in a concealed position near places such as waterholes and food sources where prey congregate and become exposed. When the prey moves into a vulnerable position the hawk bursts from concealment, taking the prey by surprise. Such hawks seem fully aware of the importance of concealment and I have at times watched a New Zealand falcon deliberately keeping behind a tree limb to remain hidden until the best moment, watching intently with just half its head showing round the side of the trunk.

Peregrines too will wait persistently overlooking gorges where racing pigeons and migratory birds habitually pass. Some individuals have gained a reputation for seeming to know the pigeon racing schedules! Because the attacks launched by the large falcons and eagles are often very long—over one kilometer—the field observer tends to underestimate the importance of still-hunting in these species. The falcon that stoops from 200 meters like a bolt from the blue may have actually started the attack from a perch 2 kilometers away. It may also have deliberately waited for the quarry to reach a certain vulnerable point before intercepting.

## 6.3    The fast contour-hugging flight

In this kind of searching, the hawk flies rapidly 1–2 meters above the ground, forest canopy or water, or along hedgerows and wood edges, to take prey by surprise. Speeds of over 55 kilometers per hour are achieved, usually by flapping flight, although eagles in hilly country can glide round the contours on fixed wings. It is expensive in energy demands but the gain in surprise offsets this.

The substrates hunted over vary considerably, from moorland and tundra hunted by merlins and gyrfalcons, or to hedgerows hunted by sparrowhawks. Several genera hunt this way for birds or insects just above the forest canopy and accipiters hunt in a similar fashion below the canopy in open forest.

Birds are the commonest prey taken in the fast contour-hugging flight; flushing too late, they are snatched in the air. Small mammals are usually overlooked and in any case the hawk is traveling too fast to stop safely. This type of search is used primarily by diurnal raptors with high wing-loadings; it is presumably too hazardous for nocturnal species. I have twice seen young New Zealand falcons whose total flying experience to date I have known, break into a complete 200 meter contour-hugging sequence without any apparent in-

Figure 6.3.1 A European sparrowhawk hunts a hedge row for small birds using a fast, contour-hugging flight.

itial learning attempts. They did it quite spontaneously, so presumably it is instinctive.

It is difficult to interpret attacks launched from this kind of search because often a failed attack consists of only a slight deviation from the raptor's already erratic path. Many attacks are aborted. Also, if the hawk already knew the prey was there, then the flight was not a contour-hugging search but an indirect flying attack (see 6.11). Both can look the same unless you have been tracking the hawk for some time beforehand and have seen the full sequence.

## 6.4   High searching

When high searching, raptors use a variety of flight styles to maintain height in order to search the air and ground below. These styles include hovering, poising, prospecting and soaring.

Hovering is most commonly used by kestrels, some kites, and occasionally, some buteos; these species usually have long or forked tails to give added lift and control. Many species which have difficulty in hovering, such as large falcons and some buteos, sometimes poise, momentarily hanging in an upcurrent to pinpoint prey.

When prospecting, the raptor flies steadily at a height of 10-100 meters on a basically direct course. Although it has not actually located prey at this stage it may be aware of the presence or approximate location, or probable presence of prey on its flightline, perhaps because it has found prey there before, or in similar areas. If the prey is detected, the patrolling hawk may attack immediately or it may overfly and then return with a low surprise attack from cover. Accipiters usually make short 100-1000 meter prospecting flights whereas large falcons often make long patrols covering a lot of country, sometimes using cloud as cover.

Soaring searching is commonly used by vultures, eagles, buteos, kites, and some falcons, particularly in habitats where the air is warm and lifting. Indeed, the geographical distribution of

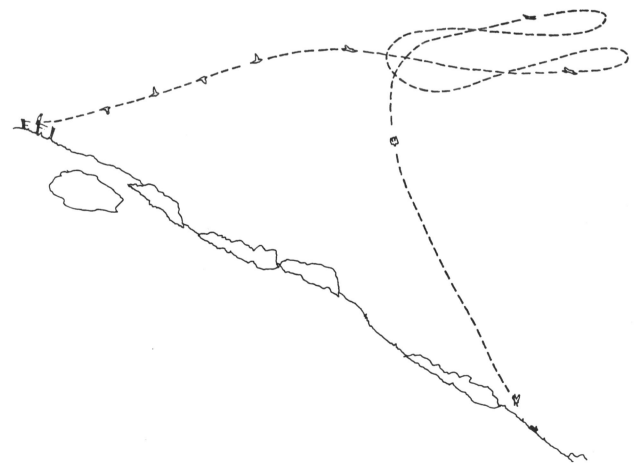

Figure 6.4.1 A goshawk soars using hill lift to search some rough ground. She spots a rabbit and dives into an attack.

most of the vultures is dictated by the presence of lifting air for a major part of the day throughout the year. The soaring bird covers a roughly circular path on open wings but may use flapping flight for short periods when moving from one thermal to another. Falcons and eagles sometimes hunt co-operatively, one bird flying low shepherding up prey which succumbs to an attack from the partner soaring above. Groups of soaring Eleonora's falcons form a curtain ambush above migrating passerines running the gauntlet on sea crossings between the Mediterranean islands. Raptors will also soar above flushing agents such as herds of game or stock, ground predators, other raptors, fires, shooting parties, trains, cars, agricultural machinery, and motor boats. It is this instinct that falconers harness for waiting-on flights.

High searching allows a raptor to examine thoroughly an area which, due to an absence of perches, could not be searched by still-hunting. In the wild it is often less successful than still-hunting because there is less element of surprise. Also the more strenuous forms are very energy expensive.

Figure 6.4.1 shows a hunt by a goshawk in a rough hilly area which she has hunted many times before. She knows that there are usually rabbits out feeding among the scattered bushes and bracken but she can't see them from her low perch on a fence post. There is a little breeze coming up a slope so she flies up until she has caught the wind, then slope soars effortlessly for a few turns, while scanning the clearings below. She sees a rabbit which hesitates a moment too long and in a steep fast dive she takes it, just outside its hole.

## 6.5    Slow quartering

This is most often used by raptors with low wing-loadings such as harriers and short-eared owls. The bird beats along slowly at ground speeds usually below 35 kph (22 mph), 2–10 meters high, with prolonged steady flapping flight, looking and listening for prey. The ground is searched carefully for small mammals, invertebrates, carrion, nests, and the young or incapacitated of more active species. Most prey are caught on or near the ground by a simple direct attack.

Hawks with high wing-loadings are incapable

Figure 6.5.1 A harrier hunts reed beds by slow quartering.

of slow quartering. They cannot fly slowly enough without stalling except in hilly terrain where up-currents make slow, low flights feasible. As shown in 1.14, juveniles of some species have lower wing-loadings than adults, allowing them to quarter to some extent.

## 6.6    Stalking

Strictly defined, stalking is a search strategy only if the raptor is unaware of the location of the prey. In practice the hawk usually seems to know or suspect the prey is present but seems unsure of its exact location. For example, a kestrel may notice a movement in a tussock and fly down to make a more detailed search on foot. Or the hawk may be seeking out prey which it has just chased into cover and lost.

Many species of accipiter, buteo, and other genera stalk prey on foot, particularly when invertebrate prey is abundant. Wakely found that a male ferruginous hawk made 18 percent of its hunts entirely on the ground and some individual buzzards in Britain become earthworm specialists. Juveniles often eke out a subsistence living this way

until they learn to catch more active quarry. David Hancock reports nesting bald eagles walking the exposed mudflats and eel grass, poking with bill or feet to attack invertebrates and small stranded fish.

When the prey is small and relatively helpless, this is perhaps better called "gleaning," whereas true stalking is a way to approach alert, elusive prey.

Forest-living accipiters and falcons make aerial stalks, flitting quietly from tree to tree preparing to attack a crowing pheasant or a quacking duck. Male gamebirds displaying in the forest often lure in more than they bargain for! In contrast to the indirect flying attack, the aerial stalk consists of slow moves calculated to pinpoint the prey's position without the hawk itself being detected; the hawk can then unobtrusively move into a position ready to launch an attack. The stalk is therefore a search strategy. Figure 6.6.1 shows a stalk made by a young male goshawk called "Tom." It was in pretelemetry days and he wore three bells. We were in a forestry plantation when in the distance we heard some mallard quacking. Tom moved softly and inconspicuously through the denser parts of the wood, avoiding the clear-

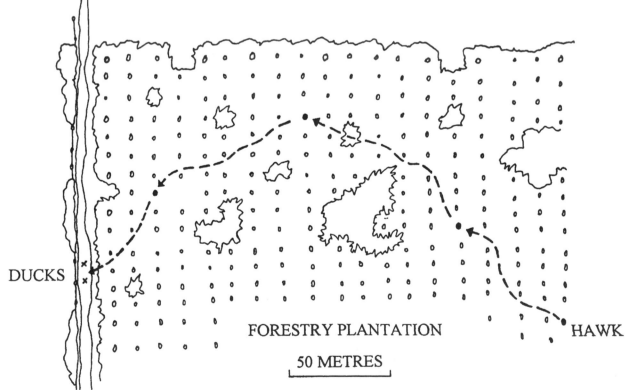

DUCKS

FORESTRY PLANTATION                    HAWK

50 METRES

Figure 6.6.1 A goshawk hears some ducks in a distant stream. He flies quietly from tree to tree. When he has pinpointed the ducks, he attacks.

ings. I ran quietly below him on the thick pine needles. Somehow he managed to fly and land without making more than a few chinks from his bells. He stopped three times to get his bearings, waiting for the quacking to resume. From his last perch, 50 meters from the ducks, he could tell exactly where they were. He burst out from the trees in a direct flying attack (see 6.10) and bound to a duck before it had got a meter into the air.

I have seen the same pattern of behavior in changeable hawk-eagles *(Spizaetus cirrhatus)* and Humayun Taher reports almost identical behavior in India of changeable hawk-eagles successfully stalking junglefowl.

## 6.7  Listening

Listening is usually used in conjunction with the more leisurely search methods such as still-hunting, slow quartering, and stalking. Owls of course are specialists at this, but diurnal raptors have excellent hearing too and will locate prey by sound alone. While studying spruce grouse and blue grouse, Hancock has several times had goshawks appear overhead when he was holding young grouse chicks giving distress calls.

One of our New Zealand falcons at hack discovered a sparrow's nest by the cheeping of the chicks inside: it tore the nest to pieces and ate the contents. Several times I have seen New Zealand falcons attempt to attack twigs or wire fences squeaking in the wind. Result: one very puzzled falcon!

## 6.8  Flushing from cover

This is a search strategy because the aim is to move the prey into a vulnerable situation rather than to attack immediately. Often a hawk will flit around in the branches of a tree attempting to push quarry out into the open where it can be attacked. Accipiters chasing woodland birds often "bounce" bushes trying to flush the quarry. They slam into the side of the bush and then immediately fly up, ready to pounce if the prey flushes from the other side. Sometimes they get quite frustrated.

Large falcons, having seen or driven prey into cover, also often swoop violently over the spot attempting to flush the quarry out in panic. Sometimes they will work in pairs; Humayan Taher reports a male red-headed merlin in India flying low and flushing small birds and doves which were then actually attacked by the female.

## 6.9  False attack

The false attack is not easy to identify in the field. Usually it takes the form of one or more rushes which are not pressed home but which search out the more vulnerable individuals in a flock of birds such as pigeons, gulls, ducks or crows. Once such an individual has been singled out the attack begins in earnest.

False attacks are also used to scatter groups or to shepherd prey away from cover. Once driven into a vulnerable position the real strike is launched.

I saw a flight by a New Zealand falcon in Britain at a scattered group of crows about 600 meters below us. The falcon was in very strong condition and slightly overweight for crows. After watching them in full view from a fence post for several minutes, she launched into a glide attack (see 6.13) off the side of a hill slope. She came in on them at such a terrific speed that she could hardly have stopped if she had tried. She shot over their heads and "bounced" them all up off the open pasture into the air, thoroughly alarmed and intimidated. Immediately she threw right up and winged over straight down onto the nearest crow which was then in a totally vulnerable position—a meter or two off the ground and struggling to get air-borne. The first pass was a false attack, a shadow punch to be followed by the real body blow.

Similarly, the experienced falcons flown at crows already in the air, often put in a devastating first stoop before throwing up high above the prey. Such a show of power takes a lot of the fight out of the prey, making it easier for the falcon. In this sense one could say that the prey has been mentally "wounded" even though not physically touched.

The difference between flushing from cover and a false attack is that in the former, the hawk is physically unable to launch an attack until the prey is exposed, whereas in the false attack the prey is exposed but the hawk wants to do some more work on it before actually attacking. It is difficult to distinguish sometimes between false attacks and play. Often a falcon will stoop at prey but not actually hit it, although it obviously could have done so. The reasons for holding back may be because the falcon is young and playful, or not very hungry, or because the prey seemed a little too strong for it, or because the prey was with

Figure 6.9.1 A peregrine stoops straight through some rooks in a false attack to search out weaklings.

protective companions. The prey too will sometimes seek to play with the falcons. We have a flock of racing pigeons at home which every year, when the hack falcons across the valley have been flying for about a week, fly over within about 50 meters of the soaring falcons, as if tempting them to chase. Perhaps they know that the falcons are still young and that they are safe for a week or two yet.

## 6.10  Attack strategies: the direct flying attack

This is the simplest form of attack and the first to be attempted by the young hawk. It flies directly toward the prey in an attempt to catch it. Alert prey may promptly start to flee so that the attack then merges into a tail-chase.

Invertebrates and less agile prey are normally taken in a simple direct flying attack and this is commonly used by owls, harriers, buteos, and kites. It is also used when contour-hugging. Of necessity it is a short attack when launched against

agile prey, a quick burst of sprinting. It is the commonest attack to be seen by people flying trained accipiters from the fist at flushed game.

The direct flying attack has four usual outcomes: either the prey is caught, or it flees and the hawk tail-chases, or it escapes to cover, or the hawk abandons the attack. It takes many attacks for the young hawk to learn the maximum distance at which it is feasible to launch a direct flying attack at each particular species of prey. While a moorhen out in the open is extremely vulnerable to a direct flying attack by a goshawk, wood pigeons can seldom be taken on such attacks longer than 50 meters. Because there is no surprise element, the prey normally starts to flee immediately, and then it is a question of whether or not the hawk can fly it down. The longest direct flying attack I have seen by a goshawk was by a female at an escaping lesser black-backed gull 400 meters away: she outflew it after a further 200 meters. Falcons of course attack at much longer distances, although the attack generally becomes more complicated rather than a direct flying attack.

Figure 6.10.1 A goshawk makes a direct flying attack at a pigeon passing below its tree.

Only when the young hawk learns the abilities of the various prey species, the significance of cover and of concealment, and its own limitations in the direct flying attack, does it start to avoid chases where the chances of success are small and attempt more advanced strategies.

Figure 6.10.1 shows a wood pigeon which has

Figure 6.10.3 A northern goshawk makes a direct flying attack on a pheasant.

Wild adult female New Zealand falcon confuses the prey by twisting over before striking.

the misfortune to fly past a tree containing a goshawk. The hawk, without hesitating, launches a direct flying attack, hits the pigeon but fails to bind because so many feathers come out. The pigeon struggles to regain momentum but the goshawk piles back into the attack and, after a tail-chase of just a few wingbeats, successfully catches the pigeon.

In figure 6.10.3 a pheasant creeps into some secure cover but is spotted by a goshawk. Wings pumping, the gos is triggered into action and strikes the pheasant with sufficient power to disarm any reaction.

## 6.11  The indirect flying attack

This is a surprise attack and can be very effective. Before starting, the raptor knows exactly where the prey is, not just its approximate location as in aerial stalking. The hawk makes use of cover or irregularities in the ground to conceal the initial part of the attack and thus the route is indirect. The whole flight is made at speed, with vigor. Figure 6.11.1 shows a goshawk making a ground-skimming attack on a covey of partridges out on some winter wheat. The hawk manages to get within about 10 meters before the partridges detect it and explode into action.

In the open the hawk may skim the ground, wingtips brushing the surface. To the uninitiated this may look like a direct flying attack but this is not so; using the small undulations of the ground, the hawk often succeeds in getting right into an unwary flock and this makes all the difference. A direct flying attack would have flushed the quarry off right from the start and would have faced the hawk with a hopeless tail-chase. Watching such an attack out in a clean open field one can hardly believe that the prey cannot see the approaching hawk but if you put your head down flat against the ground at pigeon's eye level, differences of elevation of just of few centimeters suddenly become significant. Dr. Steve Sherrod has even seen peregrines and bald eagles using the ocean swell to conceal these surprise attacks.

This ground-skimming attack was recognized in old falconry when it was called flying to the "querre," probably from the old french "curee," a flat skin or hide. The original "quarry," from the same derivation, was parts of a deer's offal laid out on the flat skin for the hounds.

The longest ground-skimming attack I have seen by a goshawk was 1100 meters at herring gulls *Larus argentatus* on Dornoch Links in Scotland. She reached within 50 meters before they flushed and she spurted straight up into them. The longest I have seen by a falcon was about 300 meters by a New Zealand falcon at a magpie. Indirect attacks using obstacles as cover are often much longer; 600–700 meter attacks are quite

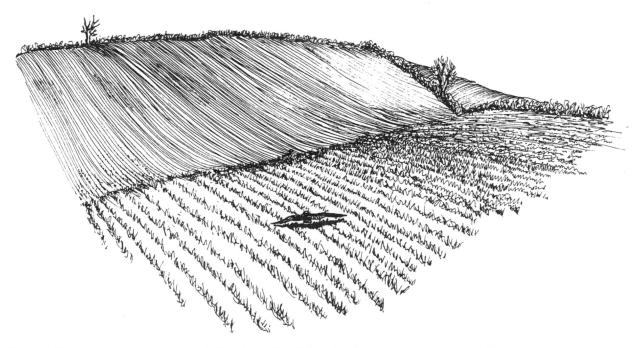

Figure 6.11.1 A goshawk makes a ground skimming indirect flying attack on some partridges in a field of winter wheat.

Figure 6.11.2 A goshawk makes an indirect flying attack by using the river for concealment to attack moorhens feeding out in the open.

common for New Zealand falcons.

Maybe the hawk will use a bush to hide its approach, or a sunken lane or a riverbed. This low flight along a river was known as flying "at the raundon or randan," possibly after the light boat of that name which used to skim along rapidly. Figure 6.11.2 shows a male goshawk which has spotted some moorhens feeding out on some grass on the opposite bank of the River Eden in Scotland. Any obvious move would have sent the moorhens scuttling for the riverside cover, so instead, the hawk drops quietly from the fist and skims along the surface of the river. When he reaches the point where the moorhens are, he twists quickly up and over the top of the bank, giving them a nasty surprise.

Indirect attacks seldom diverge more than about 45 degrees from the direct route and use a fast flapping flight from the start. Aerial stalking, on the other hand, may diverge 180 degrees and is an unhurried, stealthy approach, seeking to pinpoint the prey first. In the indirect attack the raptor relies on its original estimation of the prey's position and if the prey has moved a few meters, or if the hawk has misjudged, then the attack may be too far off target for the hawk to make good the error in the final sprint in the open. Hawks use the indirect flying attack once they have learned to recognize when certain prey are too far away or too near cover for a direct flying attack to succeed.

Page and Whitacre (1975) found that 81 percent of 343 attacks by merlins hunting shorebirds were either ground-skimming or glide attacks which gave the advantage of surprise. Only 14 percent were at birds already on the wing and none of the aerial stooping tail-chases they watched were successful. They noticed that even kestrels were successful in catching shorebirds by ground skimming.

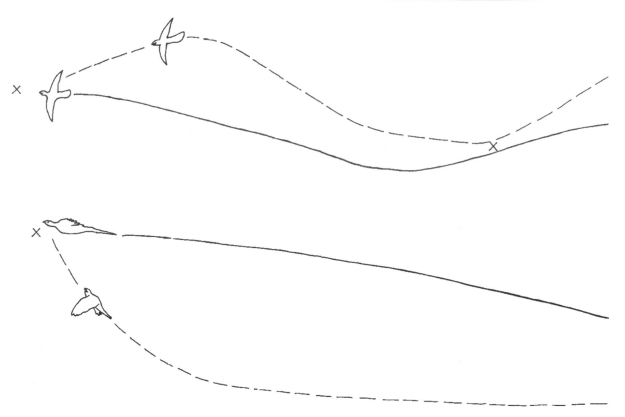

Figure 6.12.1 Top: The falcon tail chases in a series of shallow attacks. Below: The accipiter follows below and approaches from the blind spot.

## 6.12   The tail-chase

Tail chasing is when a raptor pursues a fleeing prey and attempts to catch up with it. Accipiters usually follow on a bird's blind spot, below and behind, then swing upwards in a short burst of acceleration to truss the quarry (figure 6.12.1). But styles of tail-chasing vary tremendously and the most that can be said is that the more experienced hawks tend to throw up high if their attempt to grab the prey fails whereas young hawks usually make a total commitment and if this fails, give up.

If the quarry flies up high into the air goshawks usually abandon the chase: young hawks at about 10 meters and experienced ones at about 30 meters up. However, fit, determined hawks occasionally far exceed this, especially in pursuit of favorite quarry. A male goshawk of mine once made a glide attack from about 300 meters at a flock of 40 mallard on a barley stubble. They flushed as he closed and he went up chasing them over a river valley to a height of about 100 meters and about 800 meters from me. At this point I was unable to distinguish which bird was the hawk until a duck dropped out and dived for the river

Figure 6.12.2 A New Zealand falcon tail-chasing a New Zealand fantail.

Figure 6.12.3. A jack merlin tail-chases a pipit.

with the hawk close behind it. The duck found sanctuary in the river and the hawk had caught a moorhen by the time I arrived. Such flights, unfortunately, are the exception.

In the tail chase, the prey has some control and may attempt to ring up, that is to stay above the raptor and outfly it. Low wing-loaded birds which can climb easily use this strategy: skylarks, rooks, gulls, herons, short-eared owls, even hoopoes, and there are undoubtedly many others. In the struggle for height supremacy strict tail chasing may be abandoned and the two contestants may circle up in opposite directions, seemingly unrelated to each

Figure 6.12.4 A Cooper's hawk tail-chases a woodcock.

other. If the falcon succeeds in getting above the prey this must then dive for cover as quickly as possible and risks being taken either high in the air or on the descent. Such ringing flights are very energy-expensive and have a low success rate; falcons often seem to start them just to try the quarry out. After about 100 meters any weakness in the quarry will show but if it should be strong and buoyant most falcons, sensibly, abandon it.

Old falconers used to say that merlins fly "cunning" in their second season. All this means is that the merlin has had sufficient experience of grueling tail-chases to learn that there are easier ways to catch prey, such as the glide attack and the indirect flying attack.

## 6.13  Glide attack

The raptor usually launches into a glide attack from a perch and attempts to reach the prey unforewarned. Although a few initial flaps may be made to clear foliage, the raptor more often slips off the perch without a single wingbeat and then glides in a fairly flat, less than 30 degree angle, toward the prelocated prey. As airspeed increases, the hawk slowly closes its wings until the last few meters, then suddenly opens its wings and tail to reduce airspeed. It may also rock from side to side either to baffle the prey or perhaps due to the difficulties of rapid braking. The raptor then slams into the prey on the ground or after a brief tail-chase. Using slow-motion film of goshawks, Goslow showed that, on striking, the feet were thrown forward so that they struck at a speed 15 percent faster than the pelvis.

The glide attack is fundamentally different from stooping or diving and even when the entire attack is not observed it is usually possible to identify it. The glide attack is launched at initially nonfleeing, unaware, agile prey. Whereas a high overhead direct flying attack might suffice for a hare sitting in its form, a rabbit out feeding near a hedge is more likely to bolt for cover on detecting the hawk, and this is where the glide attack meets with success (figure 6.13.1). It is a surprise attack, relying on the inconspicuousness of the head-on profile to prevent detection, rather than using any natural cover for concealment. Some speed is sacrificed in order to maintain this small profile and most of the distance is covered at speeds less than the hawk's flapping flight speed at that flight angle. If the hawk is detected in the later stages of the

glide, it may accelerate using a few pumping wingbeats into a direct flying attack. Usually the hawk is not noticed until it is a few meters away and making braking movements. At this speed of approach the hawk is committed to attacking a small area and the prey may react quickly enough to dodge out of the danger zone. One rabbit so attacked by a female goshawk of mine did a backward somersault one meter in the air, the hawk passing harmlessly underneath. One of us was surprised, one was frustrated, and one smiled.

Unbelled hawks have a relatively high success rate against agile prey by using the glide attack. It is seldom used by young hawks, possibly for three reasons: they tend not to recognize immobile prey as living but require a trigger, such as a sound or movement, to stimulate an attack. Second, young birds seldom have the selfconfidence to attempt attacks at relatively long distances. Thirdly, young hawks have yet to realize the significance of selfconcealment.

Glide attacks by falcons can be very long indeed. A peregrine that scores across the sky from one side of your field of vision to the other may be making a glide attack. Over distance of up to 2–4 kilometers, even at a shallow angle of only 5–10 degrees, the falcon is able to build up tremendous speeds and even though the quarry, such as pigeons or waders, takes flight well ahead, the falcon is hard to evade.

Some experienced falcons learn to combine this technique with other methods. The hunt may be started from a crag or high point at quarry on the ground 2–4 kilometers away. The falcon pumps out high for the first 500 meters or so, climbing hard, then sets its wings into a glide attack. Within 500 meters of the quarry, having approached thus far undetected, the falcon has probably reached its terminal velocity and, instead of going straight in at the prey and risking it flying out ahead, it may shoot out over the prey so that within seconds the prey is covered by the falcon's killing cone (see 6.14) and is set up for a stoop.

As well as having a high success rate, the glide attack is very energy-effective. It is used a great deal by experienced birds of prey, more than was realized before the advent of radiotracking.

Because the glide attack is in the open and yet is a surprise attack, it does not work as well on flocks as on singletons. Outlying members of a flock see more of a side view of the approaching hawk and are more likely to detect it and give the

Figure 6.13.1 A common buzzard makes a glide attack on an unwary rabbit.

alarm. On flocks, the hawk is better off with a concealed approach such as an indirect flying attack or, in the case of a falcon, by coming overhead and getting the flock within its killing cone. Page and Whitacre (1975) found that when merlins performed glide attacks and ground skimming indirect flying attacks on shorebirds 25.6 percent of 343 hunts were successful when the prey was alone. But on flocks of 2–10 birds only 6.9 percent were successful. As flock size increased the shorebirds got more confused and on flocks of 11–49 birds, 8.3 percent of attacks succeeded. On flocks of fifty or more, 21.4 percent of attacks succeeded. Overall, a singleton was 3.2 times more likely to be caught than one in a flock.

Large raptors weighing over 300 grams tend to use glide attacks more than small hawks do. This is because they have heavier wing-loadings and launch attacks at longer distances. Smaller hawks do not build up sufficient speed over their short attack distances. During a radio-tracking study of wild Mauritius kestrels, which have an average attack distance of 13 meters, only two out of 63 attacks were glide attacks and their mean distance was 25 meters, easily the longest attacks attempted. In a comparable study of wild New Zealand falcons 15 percent of all attacks were glide attacks. In the three species, Mauritius kestrel, New Zealand falcon and northern goshawk of which I have studied the hunting behavior quantitatively, the glide attack always had the highest success rate.

## 6.14   The drop, the dive, and the stoop

These three attacks are all launched from above at an angle steeper than 30 degrees to the horizontal.

The drop, or parachute, is used for short distances; in a big downward hop, the hawk simply opens its wings and drops from a post or low branch onto easy prey. During the whole descent, normally no more than 2–3 meters, the head and wings are held back and the legs are thrust forward ready to catch the prey (figure 6.14.1).

The dive is longer than the drop; usually between five and thirty meters. The dive of the kestrel or of the osprey is typical. During the descent the head leads, as in the stoop, but before impact the head goes back and the feet come forward to grasp the prey. Although the dive looks like a stoop there are three main differences: first, the

bird is not traveling as fast as it can. On impact it must stop, or almost stop, and so it descends only at a rate at which it can seize the prey without injuring itself. Often it will hesitate during the dive and realign itself. Secondly, on impact the diving bird's head is behind its feet, out of the way of damage. Thirdly, on hitting the prey, the hawk attempts to bind to it and to maintain its hold (figure 6.14.2).

The stoop, on the other hand, is usually executed with all the speed that the hawk can muster in the circumstances; nothing is held back. During impact, the falcon's head is leading and the feet are held open on each side of the keel. The strike is made with the claws and the undersides of the open feet, the semifolded legs cushioning the shock, shoot out at the last moment to extend the falcon's reach if the stoop is slightly wide of the mark. I had this well-drummed into me during fieldwork on wild New Zealand falcons who struck me some hundreds of times on the head and back during nest visits. Analysis of slow motion film by a number of workers has confirmed it and when one considers the falcon's anatomy there is no other part of the body capable of striking such

Figure 6.14.1 A red-tail drops straight onto a snake.

Figure 6.14.2 A common kestrel dives onto a vole.

Figure 6.14.3 A peregrine stoops onto a red grouse.

a blow. The upper surface of the toes shows bruising after quite a slight blow and could not be used offensively.

A male peregrine which I flew one season, a rather reckless hard-flying bird, bruised both his hind toes on the ground in a mistimed stoop. He then started to "miss" his grouse, shooting straight through the coveys without hitting a bird. It only slowly dawned on me that he was "pulling his punches" and after about three weeks, as his feet improved, his stoops started to connect again.

The stooping falcon is not attempting to bind to the prey but to kill or disable it with a glancing blow and then to continue on its flight, turning to recover the prey afterward. Occasionally a large falcon hitting small prey will simply gather it up and keep on going. I have a vivid recollection of my wife's male prairie falcon flown from a pitch at larks. Having put a lark back in after a short sharp flight, we reflushed it for him. He stooped past my shoulder, smacked it hard right in front of me, and just left behind him an empty space. The lark seemed to have disappeared into a time warp! The falcon landed some distance further on to consume his meal.

When the quarry is nearly as large as the falcon, the stooping bird cannot bind to the quarry; it could not survive the impact. However, if the stoop is a shallow one and the prey is flying away at a good pace, and particularly when the falcon has to avoid dropping the prey into water or forest below, it will often do its best to bind.

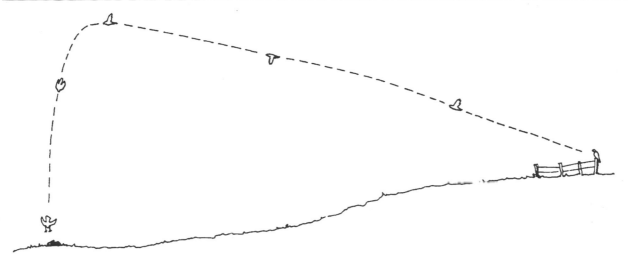

Figure 6.15.1 A changeable hawk-eagle spots a squatting hare, launches out high and lazily, then dives into an attack.

Each falcon has a slightly different style of stoop, some have shallow scything stoops, some have steep yo-yo stoops; the most dazzling perhaps is the flickering corkscrew stoop or canceleer. One cannot hope to cover all the permutations, instead I will discuss what happens in simple, straight-forward stoops.

Estimates of a falcon's speed in level flight and in the stoop vary but Ratcliffe's (1980) and Cade's (1982) estimates of 104 kph (65 mph) in level flight, 320 kph (200 mph) for a good average stoop and 368 kph (230 mph) for terminal velocity in a long stoop are probably near the mark for the peregrine. Other authors such as Orton (1980) have estimated level flight speeds for peregrines of 144–192 kph (90–120 mph) achieved in 90 meters (100 yards) from cruising and Jacek Strek got similar results flying his gyrfalcon behind a snowmobile on frozen lakes.

Of course speeds vary between individuals, the larger sexes and species traveling faster. With some stooping falcons one can almost hold a conversation as the bird is falling, other falcons seem to slip down through the air in the blink of an eye, as if all air resistance had momentarily disappeared.

The stoop is examined more closely in section 7.9 on waiting-on flights.

## 6.15 Deception flights

Some people believe that one can tell when a raptor is making a serious attack. This is not always true.

Sometimes an experienced hawk, seeing prey out in the open with no cover around and knowing that a direct or indirect flying attack, or even a glide attack, is not feasible, may make a deception flight in full view of the prey. Usually the prey is already aware of the hawk's presence so there is no point in the hawk concealing itself. All it can conceal is its intentions. Even to the experienced observer, unless he knows the hawk, this is undetectable until the end. I have had two hawks which made several of these attacks. Essentially it is a question of either getting the victim inside the killing cone or within sprinting range.

The first hawk was a wild-caught adult female changeable hawk-eagle which I flew at brown hares in the big open fields of Fife in Scotland in 1970. A typical example: I carried "Oddjob" to the edge of a field and let her scan it for squatting hares, too well concealed for me to see. After a few moments she took off and started to climb in a rather stately way until she had reached about 70 meters (200 ft). I thought she was heading back to India. Suddenly she flicked over and dived hard. As she did so, a hare bolted from its form. Before it had gone five meters, the hawk-eagle hit it in a vertical dive which left the hare unconscious and the bird shaken on the ground nearby. During the season she repeated this performance several times and it was quite clear that both she and the hares had been aware of each other throughout. Although she would sometimes catch hares by outflying them she preferred to use this technique and make life easier for herself.

Another hawk was a New Zealand falcon called "Rebel." In her first season after about thirty kills she became adept at killing crows. On several occasions I showed her crows out in the open in full view with no height disadvantage 500–800 meters away. There was no way she could get near them using a "conventional" attack, they would have made off ahead of her and reached cover or at least given her a long and strenuous flight. So instead she would launch out 45–90 degrees from the crows steadily gaining height until she was 70–120 meters up. Then, almost casually, she would drift over the crows which always stayed on the ground unless she had tried it on them before. Once she had them in her killing cone it was a simple matter for her to make a hooked or corkscrew dive, binding to one on or near the ground. As an example or energy-effective predation in the face of apparently uncatchable quarry, it was hard to beat.

Such flights remind me of how, as boys, we used to catch hares and rabbits by walking past them in their seats and casually spiral in on them until within striking distance. The victim is never approached head-on and never has a break-point where it makes a decision to bolt. It seems to think you are not attacking—until it is too late.

## 6.16   Hunting in groups

Some raptors join forces to hunt. This may just be a loose aggregation of mixed raptor species cashing in on a temporary abundance of prey, such as near a fire. This "group foraging" occurs among many of the "searchers." Some, such as the zone-tailed hawk *(Buteo albonotatus)* are wolves in sheep's clothing and mimic turkey vultures *(Cathartes aura)* to disguise their approach to prey. Or it may involve several individuals competing for the same prey, such as when Eleonora's falcons all go after the same passing passerine over the sea. Or it may involve actual cooperation between individuals. In this case they are usually related in some way—they may be a mated pair or family group and in Harrises they may also be cousins or "helpers." In this case the prey is normally shared between participants.

Cooperative hunting helps the participants to catch prey which they could not so easily catch on their own. Dean Hector founds that aplomado falcons killed in 45 percent of their joint hunts but only 21 percent when solo. When it is a family group hunting together, the gain may be not so much in food, but in knowledge. It is part of the training process for the young birds.

## 6.17   The ways in which experienced raptors hunt

Young birds of prey have many or all of their hunting patterns genetically implanted in them. They can instinctively undertake a complete hunting sequence although they have never been in such a situation before. But this is only a part of the story. Just as the young bird can fly instinctively and yet needs experience and practice before it becomes a skilled flyer, so also does it need experience of actual hunting for its abilities to develop fully. Thus, in the first year of life, 60 percent or more of the young birds may die, largely through factors related to poor hunting success. Yet experienced adults in the same period may suffer a mortality of only 5–20 percent.

Looking at these figures, some falconers have suggested keeping wild-taken raptors in captivity for their first year and then hacking them out to the wild, thus circumventing the high juvenile mortality. This of course fails to take into account the underlying reason for the mortality which is not lack of age, but lack of experience.

An experienced adult can survive in an area where prey availability is perhaps only 25 percent of that needed to support a young bird. We know this from flying both experienced and inexperienced birds in the same area. The inexperienced bird tends to search a smaller area, be less able to detect and assess attack opportunities, and has poorer flying skills to be successful in the attack. When he has a mate and chicks to feed, an adult male may have to provide for three or four times his own needs and may spend 95 percent of his daylight hours during the breeding season actively hunting. The juvenile raptor faces a hazardous apprenticeship before it can reach this level of achievement. A wild peregrine, by twelve months old, may have experienced 1000–2000 hunts; a falconry bird would be doing well to achieve this in five years.

As hawks get older they diversify their strategies and often switch from one method to another. They learn to judge accurately the reactions and escape distances of their prey and learn to recognize quickly when a quarry is vulnerable to an attack. Different species emphasize some hunting patterns more than others. It will be a long time before we can quantify these strategies for all species but figure 6.17.1 is an approximate outline for a few selected, mainly falconry species. The morphological adaptations for different flying abilities are discussed in section 1.18.

| | Still-hunting | Contour-hugging | Hover/poise | Prospecting | Soaring | Slow quartering | Stalking | Listening | Flushing from coulee | Direct flying attack | Indirect flying attack | Tail chase | Glide attack | Stoop and pass | Dive and bind | Attack static ground quarry | Pursue into cover | Continue pursuit inside cover | High aerial chase | Hunt cooperatively |
|---|---|---|---|---|---|---|---|---|---|---|---|---|---|---|---|---|---|---|---|---|
| Peregrine | C | R | N | O | C | N | N | N | R | C | O | C | R | C | C | R | O | N | C | C |
| Gyrfalcon | C | C | O | C | C | R | O | ? | O | C | C | C | O | C | C | C | C | R | C | O |
| Saker | C | C | O | C | C | R | R | ? | O | C | C | C | C | C | C | C | C | N | C | O |
| Prairie falcon | C | O | O | C | C | R | R | ? | O | C | C | C | C | C | C | C | C | N | C | O |
| Lanner | C | C | O | C | C | R | R | ? | O | C | C | C | C | C | C | C | C | N | C | C |
| Lugger | C | O | O | C | C | R | R | ? | O | C | C | C | C | C | C | C | C | N | C | C |
| New Zealand falcon | C | C | O | C | C | N | O | C | C | C | C | C | C | C | C | C | C | C | C | O |
| Red-headed Merlin | C | C | O | O | O | N | R | ? | C | C | C | C | R | C | C | C | C | R | C | C |
| Merlin | C | C | N | R | R | N | R | ? | C | C | C | C | R | O | C | C | C | R | C | O |
| European hobby | C | R | R | R | C | N | N | N | N | C | R | C | R | O | C | R | N | N | C | O |
| Common kestrel | C | R | C | R | C | N | O | O | R | C | R | O | C | R | C | C | C | N | R | R |
| Sharpshin | C | C | R | C | O | N | C | C | C | C | C | C | O | R | C | C | C | C | N | N |
| European sparrowhawk | C | C | R | C | O | R | C | C | C | C | C | C | O | R | C | C | C | C | N | N |
| Cooper's hawk | C | C | R | C | O | R | C | C | C | C | C | C | C | R | C | C | C | C | N | N |
| Black Sparrowhawk | C | C | R | C | O | R | C | C | C | C | C | C | C | R | C | C | C | C | N | N |
| Northern goshawk | C | O | R | C | O | R | C | C | C | C | C | C | C | R | C | C | C | C | N | N |
| Changeable hawk-eagle | C | O | N | C | O | R | C | C | C | C | C | C | C | R | C | C | C | C | N | N |
| Common buzzard | C | R | C | O | C | R | O | R | R | C | R | O | C | R | C | C | C | O | N | R |
| Red-tailed hawk | C | R | R | O | C | R | O | R | R | C | R | O | C | R | C | C | C | O | N | R |
| Ferruginous hawk | C | R | R | C | C | O | O | R | R | C | R | O | C | R | C | C | C | O | N | R |
| Harris hawk | C | R | R | O | C | R | O | R | C | C | R | C | C | R | C | C | C | C | N | C |
| Golden eagle | C | C | R | O | C | R | R | R | R | C | O | C | C | R | C | C | C | N | N | R |

Figure 6.17.1 The hunting strategies of various raptors. C=common, O=occasional, R=rare, N=never.

# 7 Hawking in

# the Field

## 7.1   Introduction

In section six we looked at the different ways in which birds of prey hunt in the wild and the potential that each species has. Now we can look in a practical way at how these abilities can be harnessed in the course of falconry.

Some of the methods, such as stooping, are visually more exciting than others, such as dropping onto a dead sheep. Also, some species lend themselves better to a partnership with an earthbound falconer than do others. For example a goshawk sitting quietly on a branch and then dashing out 50 meters after a rabbit is easily transferable to a falconry situation whereas a harrier patrolling perhaps a kilometer of moorland to dive onto a mouse would tax the patience and fitness of the keenest falconer. Therefore many or most of the species of birds of prey eliminate themselves from the falconer's mews because their natural hunting methods are too unexciting or impractical.

The falconer may have some preferences over the kind of flights he is interested in. He may be so obsessed with the stoop that he regards any subsequent tail-chase if the stoop misses, as a vice. Or he may want a hawk to fly solely from his fist and kill prey in a short sprint, rather like using a shotgun. He may prefer to do all the searching for the hawk himself, only slipping the hawk when quarry is actually located, or he may require the hawk to search for the prey as well as to attack it.

The hunting behavior of raptors is geared to the terrain they inhabit, as is the escape behavior of the prey. To expect a raptor to function well in the wrong terrain, for example a peregrine in a wood, is to handicap it. Similarly to find prey in the wrong terrain, such as a duck over land, is to make it vulnerable.

Some hawks, such as accipiters, red-tails, Harris hawks and New Zealand falcons, take a wide variety of prey in a wide variety of habitats. It is obvious therefore that these are more likely to be successful hawking birds for the "common man." Waiting-on flights at game such as partridges or grouse are much more specialized and therefore much less easy to accomplish. Access to suitably stocked land is limited and often expensive and the campaign needs to be fairly intensive if the falcons are to stay on form and not lower their pitch. If grouse or partridges are scarce or uncooperative, the game hawker is doomed to disappointment. He may spend all afternoon trying to get a proper "set-up" for his falcon: a firm point and a clean flush in the open. Most of the quarry seen during the course of the day will remain unflown at. The goshawker on the other hand if partridges are scarce looks for rabbits or pheasants, woodcock, ducks, yes, even waterhens....

Provided the ingredients are all present and correct, waiting-on flights at game are not too difficult; success rates of 90 percent or more have been achieved by experienced teams although 50 percent is more normal. But when one or more of the ingredients are wrong, nothing the falconer can do will bring success; it is an intractable problem. With a goshawk if game is scarce or cover is thick one can hobble along one way or another, but unless a game falcon is served day after day with quarry the whole scenario is a failure.

It has been my experience that the most effective falconers are those from a shooting background. They have a knowledge of the quarry species which is invaluable in the field. Others, with no previous experience of fieldsports, progress nicely until it comes to entering the hawk at quarry; then they hit a brick wall. Many falconry books are reticent on this, often only one chapter is devoted to actual hawking. There are some people who can almost go out with a hawk which is blind in one eye and with a wooden leg and yet come home with something in the bag. Somehow the quarry always flushes in their direction, they happen to be in the right place at the right time. It is not a matter of luck, although at first it may seem so. It is a question of field experience and persistence. Others can go out with the fanciest hawk they can buy and the most they ever catch is a cold. They are not tuned in to the hawk or the quarry, or the relationship between the two.

Other authors, far more experienced than I will ever be, have described how to undertake classic flights with falcons and hawks. Many more people than ever before have access to peregrines and other powerful raptors, but do not have the lifestyle or the finances to achieve those flights which so delight the purist. The result is considerable dissatisfaction and frustration. Probably nine out of ten of the peregrines taken up for training by would-be falconers fail to take a dozen head of quarry and such people are quick to receive the derision of those in a more fortunate position. This is sad. So many flights, easy to describe in their theory, fail to work out in practice, at least on a repeatable basis.

What I would like to do in this section is first of all show how, by using its potential more advantageously, the hawk can successfully take quarry in situations often thought of as impossible and second to enhance the falconer's appreciation of his bird and its abilities. There are many falconers, experienced ones too, who have never seen for example a glide attack or an indirect flying attack, who cannot recognize the field conditions which make them appropriate and who have never attempted deliberately to achieve them. This reduces both their effectiveness in the field and the variety of flights for them to enjoy. To maintain a falcon for waiting-on flights, its hunting behavior must be carefully conditioned to remain stereotyped. But in almost all other types of hawking a hawk cannot be considered accomplished unless it is capable of taking a wide range of quarry species under a variety of field conditions and by a full repertoire of strategies.

## 7.2    The hawking year

Hopes and dreams—they are what falconry is built on. I'm a dreadful dreamer. Spring is the worst time, when I'm making plans for the forthcoming season and watching those embryos grow. I think to myself: "I'll hawk larks in the mornings with a merlin, grouse in the afternoons and take the goshawk for a quick look around before it gets dark." I've done it too—for about three days! But I can't keep it up, and once the holiday is over and the working week rules, it is hard enough just keeping one hawk going.

Old falconers warn about this and young would-be falconers disbelieve them until they've tried it themselves.

Perhaps the best way to show how hawking works out in practice, is to give figures based on my hawking records and the experiences of other falconers. Falconry should not be undertaken in a spirit of competition but at the same time, before taking on a hawk, or attempting a particular type of quarry, the falconer needs a realistic idea of what it entails in terms of personal commitment and access to hawking grounds.

Table 7.2.1 is based on hawking in Britain and will obviously vary from country to country. It is instructive to jot down a few figures for your own hawking expectations and then review them again at the end of the season.

A\B. Starting dates for larks and gamebirds are dictated by the quarry and their legal seasons. An August start benefits from the long days, good weather and inexperienced quarry and early finish gives the hawks a good settling in period for breeding or molting. In arable country it may not be possible to start much before Christmas owing to problems of access on land. In Britain, lark hawking licenses do not start until 1, September, at the moment.

C. When lark or grouse hawking the falcon is normally flown on every day legally possible for a short season. With rook hawks, goshawks, and sparrowhawks, one may achieve 6 or 7 days per week early in the season but only 1–2 later in the season owing to short days or bad weather. Rook hawks require stooping to the lure on nonhawking days. Buteos and Harris hawks need more flying than accipiters to maintain fitness. Once the dark evenings draw in and prevent week-day hawking, these hawks need high-jumping to maintain fitness.

D. Quite often the hawking season will be reduced owing to a variety of hazards—prolonged bad weather, injuries, mother-in-law visits, etc. One is lucky to have a full season.

E. The first figure is a minimum for successful hawking. Beyond the second figure the hawk is possibly being overworked.

F. The first figure is for an inexperienced bird. If the hawk averages worse than this something is seriously wrong and the hawk may start refusing quarry. You should analyze your whole set-up. The second figure represents a good skilled bird. If the hawk aver-

Table 7.2.1 The hawking year—expectations.

## THE HAWKING YEAR—EXPECTATIONS

|  |  | Merlin at larks | Falcon at grouse game | Falcon at rooks/ crows | Goshawk at mixed game | Sparrow hawk | Red-tail/ common buzzard | Harris hawk |
|---|---|---|---|---|---|---|---|---|
| A. | Start hawking | 1 Aug. | 12 Aug. | 10 Aug. | 10 Aug. | 10 Aug. | 10 Aug. | 10 Aug. |
| B. | Finish hawking | 15 Sep. | 10 Dec. | 10 Jan. | 30 Jan. | 30 Jan. | 30 Jan. | 30 sJan. |
| C. | Number hawking days/week | 7 | 6 | 3–7 | 3–7 | 3–7 | 5–7 | 2–7 |
| D. | Number hawking days/season | 46 | 23 | 66 | 75 | 75 | 125 | 125 |
| E. | Flights/day | 1–5 | 1–5 | 2–3 | 2–10 | 2–10 | 0.5–5 | 1–10 |
| F. | Flights/kill | 9–1.5 | 8–1.5 | 5–2 | 10–2 | 10–4 | 6–2 | 6–2 |
| G. | Kills/season | 5–40 | 5–40 | 15–70 | 30–150 | 15–100 | 10–80 | 30–150 |
| H. | Acres required | 500+ | 3000+ | 10000 per month | 1000 | 500 | 1000 | 1000 |
| I. | Types of ground | Open downland. Stubbles. Close-cropped moorland | Dogging grouse moorland | Very open arable or grazing land | Almost anywhere | Same as goshawk | Same as goshawk | Same as goshawk |
| J. | Dogs required | Pointer optional | Pointer essential | None | Pointer or spaniel desirable | Flushing dog desirable | Pointer or spaniel desirable | Pointer or spaniel desirable |

ages better than this you have setup the quarry so that it is overmatched; a happy position to be in, but is it sporting?

G. The first figure is for an inexperienced bird or handler who has had enough success to build on for the future. Below this figure for a full season one or more factors are significantly wrong. The second figure represents a good hawk well flown. In some countries there are bag limits eg. for larks and blackbirds. Taken on average throughout the season the hawk's flights: kills ratio and total score is a fairly good indication of the quality of sport enjoyed. A consistent stylish performer will be nearer the right hand category than the left.

H. The areas quoted are for each bird flown and vary tremendously according to its game capacity and quality. With lark hawks and sparrowhawks it is best not to work an area more than twice a week, grouse hawks not more than once a week, partridge hawks, rook hawks, goshawks, buteos, and Harris hawks not more than once a fortnight. Six or seven kills by a rook hawk on a thousand-acre patch will so educate the rooks that the falcon can no longer get near them and they are virtually unhawkable, crows are even less cooperative. A rabbit-warren ferreted more than once a month or twice a season will start to show poor results. But where there is a temporary glut of game it may be best to hawk more frequently while the going is good. By November most game populations show a marked reduction—other predators have been taking their toll. In the game-rich areas of Britain, particularly in the east, scores ten times larger than in the more desolate areas can be achieved. Where quarry numbers are too low to achieve the minimum number of flights in column E, hawking will be unsuccessful.

## 7.3    What the hawks can do

The whole essence of falconry lies in establishing the right balance between predator and prey. In this it is simply a mirror of the balance of nature, honed by millions of years of evolution acting on the players of this endless game. Weight the balance too much in favor of the hawk and it would kill too much and soon wipe out its prey resource and itself. Weight it too much in favor of the prey and the hawk would be unable to kill and would die of starvation. The prey numbers, no longer dampened by predation, would be controlled primarily by food supply and would tend to become very cyclical with population explosions followed by drastic starve-outs, some of them possibly terminal to the gene pool.

In falconry we examine this balance between predator and prey, between hawk and quarry, very precisely indeed. This is one of the things which makes falconry so fascinating, and curiously, it is an aspect which seems to be scarcely covered at all in the ornithological literature.

When a man goes out with a gun, all he has to do is to get his quarry to expose itself within the range of his gun for long enough for him to fire the shot. The shot, whether bullet or bird shot, travels faster than the speed of sound and the prey literally does not know what has hit it. Thus all the survival skills obtained by instinct and experience to avoid predators are of little avail. How can you avoid a missile traveling so fast? Therefore the gun-hunter, who might imagine he understands a lot about his prey, only actually appreciates half the story. He is at the same level as the man with a camera or field-glasses.

The situation which to the gun-hunter is the end of the hunt (the view and the shot) is to the falconer actually the start of the hunt. This is the point when the hawk sees its prey and starts off in pursuit, matching its own abilities with those of its prey. The prey is exposed to predators all the time and it has plenty of ways of escaping. If it is sick, handicapped, or unlucky, it may be killed. If not, it has a good chance of surviving completely unscathed and back feeding in the same familiar area a few minutes later. The chances of it escaping injured are probably less than 0.1 percent.

In order to understand this very fine balance, first we will examine the ways some particular species of raptors hunt using the methods described in part six. Then we'll look at the ways

some of the prey escape. Of course we cannot cover all hawks and all prey but just sufficient to give an idea of what goes on and enough to get you thinking about your own particular bird and its prey. Once we've painted this picture with a fairly broad brush, we'll go into some of the flights in more detail and show how they have become traditional flights because of this very fine tuning between hawk and quarry.

The Tables 7.3.1. and 2. show approximately how the more common species of falconry birds perform at various quarry species. Don't think that just because a particular quarry is abundant in your area, then that is the best quarry to hawk. The prey may not be available to the raptor because the terrain may be unsuitable for its hunting methods.

In chapter six, I outlined the different basic techniques commonly used by wild raptors to find and attack prey. Some of the techniques, such as the slow steady quartering of harriers, do not lend themselves to falconry. Others, such as the sprinting direct attack of the accipiter, are suitable for hawking in all sorts of situations. It is best if the falconer asks his trained hawk to do as similar a flight in falconry as it would in the wild. For example, if you want a really good pointing dog, train a pointer, not a terrier. You want an animal with the right build and the right instincts for the task.

Following from this have been the traditional divisions of falconry into different types of flight. On the one hand are the high flights with falcons, and on the other, the low flights with accipiters and accipitrid hawks. Both of these are pursuit flights; the sustained pursuits of the falcons are usually aerobic flights whereas the shorter sprints of the accipiters tend to be anaerobic. The third type of flight is the waiting-on flight undertaken by many falcon, buzzard, and eagle species. This is the high search followed by a stoop or dive.

Of all the flights in falconry, the traditional classic flight is the high pursuit flight, culminating at its best in the ringing flight or *la haute volée*. In days gone by, the quarry included kites, herons, some owls, and cranes. Nowadays the classical flights are obtained principally with corvids, houbara, and gulls flown by large falcons, and with larks flown by merlins. Many of these flights, and also those at some of the smaller quarry such as pigeons, stone curlew and jackdaws, tend to be long, twisting tail-chases in which the prey attempts to stay in the air and avoid the falcon with-

Table 7.3.1 Falcons and their prey.

W = Waiting on   D = Direct pursuit   E = Excellent   M = Moderate   O = Occasional   P = Poor

| | Peregrine falcon ♂ | Peregrine falcon ♀ | Gyr falcon ♂ | Gyr falcon ♀ | Saker falcon ♂ | Saker falcon ♀ | Prairie falcon ♂ | Prairie falcon ♀ | Lanner falcon ♂ | Lanner falcon ♀ | Lugger ♂ | Lugger ♀ | New Zealand falcon ♂ | New Zealand falcon ♀ | Red headed Merlin ♂ | Red headed Merlin ♀ | Merlin ♂ | Merlin ♀ | Kestrel ♂ | Kestrel ♀ |
|---|---|---|---|---|---|---|---|---|---|---|---|---|---|---|---|---|---|---|---|---|
| Partridge | WE | WE | WDE | WDE | WM | WM | WE | WE | WE | WE | WM | WM | WDE | WDE | - | WDO | - | - | - | - |
| Red grouse / Sharp tailed grouse | WE | WE | WDE | WDE | WM | WM | WO | WE | - | WO | - | - | | WDM | - | - | - | - | - | - |
| Sage grouse | WP | WE | WE | WE | WP | WM | - | WE | - | WP | - | - | - | - | - | - | - | - | - | - |
| Pheasant | WO | WE | WDE | WDE | WO | WM | WP | WM | - | WO | - | WO | - | WDM | - | - | - | - | - | - |
| Mallard | WO | WDE | WDE | WDE | WO | WM | WP | WE | - | WO | - | WP | - | WDE | - | - | - | - | - | - |
| Teal | WE | WDE | WDE | WDE | WM | WM | WE | WE | WE | WE | WO | WO | WDO | WDE | - | - | - | - | - | - |
| Woodcock/ Snipe | WE | WM | WDO | WDO | WO | WO | WE | WE | WM | WM | WP | WP | WDO | WDM | DO | DO | DO | DO | - | - |
| Stone curlew | DE | DM | DM | DO | DE | DE | DE | DE | DO | DM | DO | DO | DO | DE | - | - | - | - | - | - |
| Houbara | DP | DE | DM | DM | DO | DE | - | DE | - | DO | - | - | - | - | - | - | - | - | - | - |
| Magpies | WDE | WDM | WP | WP | WDM | WP | WDM | WDM | WDM | WDM | WDM | WDM | DO | DE | WDP | WDO | - | - | - | - |
| Crows / Rooks | DM | DE | DE | DE | DE | DE | - | DE | - | DO | - | DO | DP | DE | - | - | - | - | - | - |
| Gulls | DE | DE | DE | DE | DE | DE | - | DE | - | DO | - | DP | - | DE | - | - | - | - | - | - |
| Skylarks | - | - | - | - | - | - | WE | WO | WE | WO | WO | WO | WDM | WDM | DM | DM | DE | DE | WO | WO |
| Hedgerow birds | WP | - | - | - | WO | - | WE | WO | WE | WE | WM | WM | WDE | WDM | WDM | WDM | DM | DM | WO | WO |
| Starlings | DE | DP | - | - | - | - | WE | WO | WE | WO | WO | WO | WDM | WDM | DM | DM | DM | DM | - | - |
| Rabbit | - | WP | WDO | WDO | DP | DO | - | DO | - | DO | - | DO | - | DM | - | - | - | - | - | - |
| Hares | - | WDP | WDE | WDE | - | WDE | - | DM | - | DO | - | DO | - | DO | - | - | - | - | - | - |
| Mice / Voles | - | - | WDO | WDO | WDE | WDE | WDE | WDE | WDE | WDE | WDE | WDE | WDE | WDE | - | - | - | - | WE | WE |

out seeking cover and without necessarily climbing for height. On a windy day, this is the norm. On a still day, a crow or gull is not sufficiently fast or agile to escape the falcon and therefore seeks refuge in climbing for height. The stage is then set for a ringing flight.

In the waiting-on flight the hawk is first allowed to climb to a pitch above the falconer (high searching). The falconer then flushes the quarry within the killing cone of the hawk. The hawk is thus in an overwhelmingly dominating position and able to put in a stoop at the prey which has been "served" to her. Buteos and eagles also like to use the high search and this is one of the most

spectacular ways of flying them in falconry.

The low flights of accipitrid hawks consist mainly of direct and indirect flying attacks and perhaps some glide attacks. Whereas falcons are normally wedded to just a few, similar, prey species, the accipitrid hawks are best flown at a wide variety of species in varying circumstances. Thus, although flights may be brief, no two are alike.

## 7.4   What the quarry can do

When they are attacked by a raptor, the prey respond in different ways. First of all, they can normally recognize if the raptor is attacking rather

Table 7.3.2 Accipitrid hawks and their prey.

E = Excellent    M = Moderate    O = Occasional    P = Poor

| | Harris Hawk | | Redtail | | Common Buzzard | | Ferruginous Hawk | | Goshawk | | Black Sparrowhawk | | Coopers Hawk | | Sparrow-hawk | | Shikra | |
|---|---|---|---|---|---|---|---|---|---|---|---|---|---|---|---|---|---|---|
| | ♂ | ♀ | ♂ | ♀ | ♂ | ♀ | ♂ | ♀ | ♂ | ♀ | ♂ | ♀ | ♂ | ♀ | ♂ | ♀ | ♂ | ♀ |
| Quail | M | M | O | O | - | - | P | P | E | M | E | E | E | E | O | E | - | O |
| Partridge | M | M | O | O | P | P | P | P | E | E | E | E | E | E | P | O | - | P |
| Red/Sharp tailed grouse | P | P | P | P | P | P | P | P | E | E | E | E | - | E | - | - | - | - |
| Sage grouse | - | - | - | - | - | - | - | - | - | O | - | - | - | - | - | - | - | - |
| Pheasant | O | M | O | O | P | P | P | P | E | E | O | E | P | M | - | P | - | - |
| Mallard | O | O | O | O | - | - | - | - | E | E | O | E | P | E | - | - | - | - |
| Teal | P | P | - | - | - | - | - | - | E | E | E | E | E | E | - | O | - | - |
| Snipe | P | P | - | - | - | - | - | - | P | P | P | P | O | O | - | O | - | O |
| Woodcock | O | O | - | - | - | - | - | - | M | O | M | M | E | E | - | O | - | - |
| Moorhen | E | E | M | M | M | M | M | M | E | E | E | E | E | E | - | E | - | O |
| Magpie | P | P | - | - | - | - | - | - | O | O | O | O | O | O | - | O | - | - |
| Rook / Crow | O | O | - | - | - | - | - | - | O | O | - | O | - | O | - | - | - | - |
| Gulls | P | P | - | - | - | - | - | - | E | E | M | E | M | M | - | M | - | - |
| Wood-pigeons | P | P | - | - | - | - | - | - | O | O | O | O | O | O | - | O | - | - |
| Doves | P | P | - | - | - | - | - | - | M | O | E | E | E | E | P | E | - | O |
| Larks etc. | P | - | - | - | - | - | - | - | O | - | O | O | O | O | M | M | O | O |
| Hedge-row birds | O | - | - | - | - | - | - | - | O | - | M | O | M | O | E | E | M | M |
| Squirrel | E | E | O | O | - | - | - | - | E | E | - | E | - | M | - | - | - | - |
| Rabbit | E | E | M | M | O | O | M | M | E | E | - | M | - | M | - | - | - | - |
| Hare | - | - | M | E | - | - | M | M | - | E | - | M | - | M | - | - | - | - |

than just flying past. Then they can usually tell at least what genus the raptor is and take appropriate evasive action. If a buzzard flies over a flock of feeding pigeons, they usually flush and stay circling in the air until it has gone. If a peregrine comes over, they are more likely to stay on the ground and keep watching. If a goshawk comes over, they flush quickly and leave the vicinity or climb high. If the hawk catches one and is down on the ground eating it, the others may resume feeding unconcernedly.

Crows react in a similar way, but in addition, they will harass the raptor and rob it of any element of surprise, forcing it to quit. Even if a victim is caught, they usually gang up on the hawk and may succeed in driving it off and rescuing their companion.

Problems arise with the New Zealand falcon which sometimes looks and behaves like a falcon, and at others like an accipiter. If the crow or pigeon stays on the ground it may be caught where it stands. On the other hand, if it tries to fly off, it may be pursued aerobically and quickly beaten in the air. Thus escape tactics which are suitable for specialized raptors, may prove deficient against a versatile one, even if it does not have the peak performance of the specialist.

Table 7.4.1. shows the commoner escape tactics of various prey species. How do your own common prey species compare? To most experienced falconers, this table is fairly straightforward; they recognize common patterns and remember many examples. Surprisingly though, this information is not generally known among ornithologists and scientists and there is not very much published about it. Don't expect these tables to be 100 percent accurate; there are always exceptions. The main aim is to get you thinking.

Most prey will seek cover if they can, either to avoid detection or to escape from attack. Game birds, rabbits and hares, and some others, will also freeze, that is, squat absolutely motionless, even away from cover, relying on cryptic coloration. This initial "freezing" only continues as long as the victim "thinks" it has not been detected. The moment it believes that the predator has noticed it, the prey animal will bolt. Thus it is different from tonic immobility, in which the prey has been attacked, and has either been captured or very intimidated by the predator, and "plays dead." Others, such as the water birds, will skulk or keep a low profile, in cover at the water's edge, but not actually remain "frozen."

When they flee, some prey, such as the gamebirds, rely on rapid acceleration to outsprint the predator, rather than on agility. Gamebirds and ducks usually manage a jink or two, seldom more than a 45 degree deviation from their flight path, whereas corvids and squirrels concentrate more on dodging than on getting away. The small gamebirds rely on anaerobic sprinting flight and soon have to land again, but the larger gamebirds can actually keep flying long enough to deter many raptors from continuing pursuit. The corvids and many small birds also use their powers of flight one way or another to exhaust or discourage their pursuers. Although the gamebirds often do things which seem intelligent, most of their escape is usually instinctive or reactive; they are also often intimidated into losing heart or into tonic immobility. Corvids, and many other birds on the other hand, are strategists and will think up tricks as they go along, even helping one another and decoying the raptor away from the victim. These species are less easily intimidated and, even when caught, may still be rescued by their companions. Some of the species such as some corvids, starlings, and some waders for example, form tight-knit defensive aerial flocks to intimidate or baffle an attacking raptor. This is a different type of flocking to ground flocking, such as in gamebird coveys and pigeon flocks. These feeding flocks usually have sentinel birds which reduce the risk of surprise, but once they are attacked, the flock may scatter as part of the escape strategy, rather than bunch up.

Some of the bigger gamebirds, corvids, gulls, and mammals, either by their size and strength, or by their biting or kicking, or by fluffing out their feathers, may either fight off the raptor or intimidate it so that it loses courage. Finally, when all else seems lost, many prey species have loose feathers so that the raptor is left with a footfull of feathers and the prey escapes unscathed. Often the raptor is distracted for several critical seconds by the feathers, before it realizes that what it has caught is worthless and the real meal has gone. Pigeons and doves, which are favorite prey for many raptors, have loose feathers all over, whereas the gamebirds tend to have a loose pad of feathers on the rump. Lizards shed their tails too, and falcons have been recorded with several lizard tails in their stomachs, but no whole lizards, an arrangement which seems to be a working compromise for both predator and prey!

## 7.5  Hawking grounds and quarry populations

If something costs you nothing, you don't value it so much. If you have a long-term commitment to something, you will look after it better. These truisms apply to many things in life, from marriage to land.

In some parts of the world there are large tracts of government land where anyone can hawk, provided he has obtained the necessary permits. The land is managed on a broad sustainable basis, but otherwise the hunting is a free-for-all. Long may

Table 7.4.1 Prey response chart.

C=Common   O=Occasional   N=Never   Y=Yes

| QUARRY | Seeks cover | Seeks water for cover | Freezes | Attempts to escape by dodging | Sprinter | Out-flies or out-runs | Intelligent | Defensive aerial flocks | Easily intimidated | Dangerously armed | Loose feathered |
|---|---|---|---|---|---|---|---|---|---|---|---|
| Quail | C | N | Y | O | C | N | O | N | Y | N | Y |
| Redleg Partridge | C | N | Y | O | C | N | O | N | Y | N | Y |
| Grey Partridge | C | N | Y | O | C | N | O | N | Y | N | Y |
| Red/Sharp-tail grouse | C | O | Y | O | C | O | O | N | Y | N | Y |
| Sage grouse | C | N | Y | O | C | C | O | N | N | O | Y |
| Pheasant | C | N | Y | O | C | O | O | N | Y | O | Y |
| Mallard | C | C | N | O | C | C | O | Y | Y | N | N |
| Teal | C | C | N | O | C | C | O | Y | Y | N | N |
| Snipe | C | N | Y | C | C | C | O | N | Y | N | N |
| Woodcock | C | N | Y | C | C | C | O | N | N | N | Y |
| Moorhen | C | C | N | O | N | N | C | N | N | N | N |
| Stone Curlew | C | N | Y | C | O | C | O | N | O | N | N |
| Houbara | C | N | Y | C | N | C | O | N | N | Y | N |
| Magpie | C | N | N | C | N | O | C | N | N | Y | N |
| Jackdaw | C | N | N | C | C | C | C | Y | N | Y | N |
| Rook | C | N | N | C | O | C | C | Y | N | Y | N |
| Crow | C | N | N | C | O | C | C | Y | N | Y | N |
| Gulls | N | C | N | C | N | C | O | Y | O | Y | N |
| Pigeon/Doves | C | O | N | C | C | C | O | N | O | N | Y |
| Pipits | C | O | Y | C | C | C | C | N | Y | N | N |
| Larks | O | O | Y | C | C | C | C | N | Y | N | N |
| Blackbirds | C | N | N | C | C | O | C | N | Y | N | Y |
| Starlings | C | N | N | C | C | C | C | Y | N | N | N |
| Rat | C | O | N | O | N | N | C | - | N | Y | - |
| Squirrel | C | N | N | C | N | N | C | - | N | Y | - |
| Rabbit | C | N | Y | C | C | O | O | - | N | O | - |
| Hare | O | N | Y | C | C | C | O | - | N | Y | - |

this continue!

For the falconer, this gives a nice sense of freedom, but it doesn't encourage a sense of responsibility. The same applies to some of the houbara hawking grounds. Often the feeling is: if the quarry is there, go for it now before someone else does. This is fine provided that everything is on an extensive basis and harvests are within yield limits. Falconry is normally selflimiting, so that falconers can seldom be accused of overhunting, especially not in North America. On the houbara-hawking grounds in North Africa and Asia, there are still some falconers who are too keen and over-hunt. It is up to the more responsible and senior Arab falconers to encourage hawking on a sustainable basis so that there will always be quarry available for future generations.

Throughout most of Europe and eastern North America, hunting grounds are either private or more controlled. The would-be falconer first has to identify land which is suitable for his needs and then seek access to it. Alternatively, he may get access to some land and then have to train a hawk suitable for that terrain. Obtaining access may be a simple as knocking on the door and asking permission. Or it may entail signing contracts on sporting rights or leases, or in passing hunting exams. You should also comply with the local regulations on game seasons, bag limits, display of hunting permits, and so on.

Once you have obtained permission to hawk on a particular area, the first thing to do is to buy a detailed map and mark in the exact boundaries with a colored pen. Then you should go over the land and become acquainted with it so you can work out how best to hawk it, what hazards there are, and where the boundaries are on the ground. You should also find out if there are any other people hunting on it, possibly for different quarry. For example you might have permission to hawk rabbits, another person may release and shoot pheasants, another person may stalk the deer with a rifle, and the local hunt may draw the woods for foxes. You may have to make sure that you are not in the wrong place at the wrong time, even though you have permission.

If you are paying for the hawking on a commercial agreement, all well and good. On the other hand, if you simply have permission, then it is good manners to at least offer a small gift by way of thanks. This may be a bottle of something at Christmas, or some of the game you have taken, or

a hand with some of the farming chores, such as hay-making. Our crow-hawking land extends to about 50,000 acres, forming a straggling mosaic of farms, so during the season we hold a barbecue for all our landowners and their families. This gives them a chance to see the falcons and talk about things at leisure, as well as an opportunity to have a good chat and knees-up with their neighbors from other isolated farms. The British Falconers' Club invite all their landowners to a dinner at the end of their major meets, and, although this is not cheap, it is a worthwhile investment in goodwill supporting the continuation of hawking in the area.

If you are just hawking pest species, such as rabbits or corvids, then the landowner is usually happy for you to kill as many as you can. But if you have taken the full sporting rights and are hawking pheasants, partridges, grouse, or ducks, then you may get involved in game management. This might entail managing the woodlands, releasing gamebirds, controlling predators or improving ponds, in other words, turning gamekeeper throughout the nonhawking season. This can be a great source of satisfaction, as admirably portrayed by Dan Cover in America. The greedy person who catches as much as he can, and then leaves the place desolate at the end of the season, is obviously not popular. Particularly for people who live in a town, without roots in the country, it can be a rewarding experience to get involved with some land and follow it throughout the seasons, rather than just appearing occasionally, hawking, and then going away again. It is also a good way to get the younger generation involved and understanding the practical aspects of land management and ecology.

## 7.6 Rabbit hawking

Most young falconers all over the world start their hawking careers on their local version of the rabbit. The rabbit and its slightly smaller American cousin, the cottontail, have furnished sport since the beginning of hawking and no one surely can call himself an experienced falconer until he has put a few hundred in the bag.

The finest rabbit hawking I have ever enjoyed was with a goshawk and a pointing lurcher (like a small rough-haired greyhound), called Tess. The lurcher would point the rabbits lying out in frosted bracken or rough grass. On seeing the point the goshawk would fly over to the dog and Tess, on hearing the gos's bells approaching, would flush the rabbit which would come out at a fairly high rate of knots. The goshawk would turn into the attack, often killing immediately. But if she missed first shot, the rabbit would continue at a torrid pace with Tess on its heels spraying snow on the turns, busting it from any cover. The hawk would throw upward briefly, look for a clear shot and smash back in. The dog's tail would come up as she braked, then she'd kill the rabbit with a quick nip and, like "wild dog dingo" (grinning like a horse collar), she'd lie down beside the hawk. Such flights are the fastest thing you will see in hawking short of the quarry getting airborne. Such a powerful team should be reserved for good, strong winter hill rabbits, summer rabbits are overmatched and are mopped up unceremoniously.

Where rabbits are found out in the open, there is scope for waiting-on flights with a Harris or red-tail, even in ideal circumstances, with goshawks. Achieving such a set-up requires as rigorous attention to detail as waiting-on flights with falcons. Groups of Harris hawks, with the males staying high and acting as spotters, and the females lower down, are probably the best form of flying Harrises are capable of. They can certainly kill a lot of rabbits this way.

Ferreting is a sport for the young and the hopeful. The ideal size of party is one or at most two. If there are two of you, then BE QUIET. Don't stamp around; communicate with signals. Otherwise, not surprisingly, the rabbits will be sticky to flush and the ferret will kill them below ground. Take two ferrets, preferably small white ones, individually marked. They should be fit and active, and given a small feed before starting. A big fat roley-poley, bleary-eyed ferret which is too dozy to get out of the carrying box is no use; you will regret using it. When you open the carrying box the ferrets should pop up like jack-in-the-boxes, and when placed at the entrance to the hole give a quick shake and beetle straight in. A good light traveling box can be made from half a plastic 5 gallon container with a strip of rubber inner tube for a shoulder strap. Remember you will have a lot of carrying to do; heavy wooden boxes are a penance. The box opening should be 10 cm square so that you can replace a ferret one-handed without the other ferret getting out as you do so. The box door should bolt firmly and there should be NO WAY the ferrets can escape. If the ferret gets out of the box in the car when you are not there it will almost certainly kill

your hawk if the latter is hooded or if the car is dark. For this reason, many falconers will not keep hawks and ferrets on the same premises.

On arrival at the warren, set down the box a little way away, quietly take out one ferret and place it in the bottom hole so that it works upwards through the tunnels. Softly walk round to above the warren so the hawk has a downhill slip and so that a rabbit hesitating in the mouth of the hole cannot see you. Otherwise it may well go back in, face the ferret and get killed. Particularly if the hawk is a good one, keep about 20 meters back. The rabbit should clear the warren and not double back into another hole. If the ferret sticks, put the second one in to rustle it up. If the warren is quite large you will need to work both ferrets to confuse the rabbits. If the warren is very big, leave it alone.

If the rabbits normally bolt toward a nearby set of holes it is often worth blocking them up beforehand with balls of dry grass. This can cause a hotly pursued rabbit some embarrassment. If a hardflown rabbit escapes down a hole—leave it. If you try to ferret it again, it will usually face the ferret rather then bolt.

Most of the time the ferret will come out when called or if left for half an hour to sleep off its feed. If the ferret stays down, call at all the holes, thump the ground with your hand and rattle a dead rabbit in the hole. Don't let go of the rabbit. I remember on one occasion after half an hour in freezing conditions the ferret was still down. I wiggled my dead rabbit. Silence. I went over to look in another hole and when I came back my one and only rabbit had gone! Only after stowing it in the bowels of the earth did my muddy, bloody ferret emerge. If all else fails, tie a rabbit to the creance through a hole in its hock and put it down a hole, then stamp, yell, and rattle all over the warren. The shaking earth coming from the tunnel roof will usually stir the ferret, and when he takes the bait you can pull him out like an eel. A ferret locator and spade should ensure that you never lose a ferret, but it is all more equipment to carry.

There are a few danger situations when ferreting that you need to be aware of. One of these of course, is if the hawk nails the ferret. Get in fast and hold the ferret's jaws with your gloved hand. Pull out a dead rabbit and try to get the hawk on to that. Above all, get control of the ferret. It is incredible what mistreatment a ferret can take without injury. After such an incident put the ferret away, it will be extremely annoyed and will stink.

Another danger is when a good hawk nails a rabbit the moment it leaves the hole because the falconer was too close. The ferret comes out after the rabbit and promptly joins in. Rabbit holes are often associated with fences—which means barbed wire and netting. Sooner or later your hawk will hit it hard, so it is worth training your hawk to it. Call it to the fist or lure so that it is likely to hit the fence at a slow speed. It must realize that wire is solid (unlike twigs) and it must learn either to go over the top or through a hole or at least put on the brakes rather than hit full tilt. A wire barb can scalp a hawk easily.

Although it is possible to ferret in open simple places in late summer, most warrens contain litters of young quite late and it is best to wait until October before starting. Avoid any warrens with extensive vegetation masking the holes; ferrets can walk a hundred meters away leaving you calling pathetically at the original hole.

Ferreting is definitely an informal activity. One soon amasses a wealth of hysterical anecdotes which would lower the tone of this book. Like Phil, whose driving amazed the traffic on the dual-carriageway outside Edinburgh when a ferret got out of its traveling box and attached itself to his earlobe. Or Simon, who, while wearing his best suit, managed to get a strong-willed ferret suspended from his nose. Bleeding like a stuck pig all down his tuxedo, he was rescued by his girlfriend who led him round the kitchen table by pulling on the ferret, and then threw a bucket of water at him.

Flying the hawk at rabbits or hares after dark using a spotlight is a relatively modern development and not one, I think, to be encouraged, except as a method of pest control. Eagle owls, goshawks, and Harris hawks can be flown in this way, indeed the eagle owl can be flown with the lamp switched off, but then one doesn't see anything. An eagle owl coming in to the fist in complete darkness is an eerie and unnerving experience.

The best that can be said for lamping is that it enables rabbits to be flown in places where they seldom come out in the daytime. But the lamp beam arouses suspicion and many farmers dislike it. A well-dazzled rabbit often hardly moves before the hawk hits it, but where they have been lamped before they usually move to cover as soon as the beam hits them. As hedges and wood edges often have barbed wire fences this exposes the hawk to a high risk of injury. Although some hawks adapt quite well to flying down a lamp

beam, one needs to be fairly desperate to risk a valuable hawk in this way, particularly as the flights themselves are often poor or hard to see.

## 7.7 Hare hawking

In Britain, brown and blue hares are taken by trained hawks. In North America the alternatives are the black-tailed and white-tailed jack rabbits and snowshoe hares. In the Middle East, the "rabbit" is in fact a desert hare or, in Arabic, *errneb.*

Hares are a sporting proposition only if tackled in certain ways, otherwise they can be disappointing. If a big goshawk or a red-tail, or even an eagle, is slipped from the fist at a hare on flat ground, the result is usually a slogging chase ending in a twisting turn. At this point the hawk either takes the hare or gets grounded. She may get up again and have another go, but generally as a spectacle, it is poor. If the hawk is inexperienced, the hare, instead of running fast, jinks whenever the hawk gets close and the young hawk, discouraged, gives up. An experienced hawk, on the other hand, often takes them with as little difficulty as taking the lure. Many hares are taken in Germany and eastern Europe in this way by lines of falconers with eagles or goshawks.

These flights are improved if a dog such as a slow lurcher, saluki, or similar is used. This speeds up the whole event by quite a few frames per second and keeps the hare moving if there is cover to hand. If the hawk catches the hare, the dog is close behind and is able to kill it quickly, preventing injury to the hawk which could kill her or put her off hares. I have used a lurcher and various pointers and spaniels for this job with good results; either the hare escapes or it is killed promptly. The dog then stands or lies nearby, panting and guarding the hawk. Frederick II gave detailed instructions for training the dogs in this role and it is a pity more falconers do not support their hawks in this way.

In Arabia the desert hare or *errneb* is hunted in two ways. One of the most skilled ways is to track it in the sand. After a windy night in the Empty Quarter, the sand has moved and it is possible to pick up tracks which are only an hour or two old. Alternatively, the trackers get up at about 4 A.M. and drive around the hunting area, towing a bush behind the car. Then, at dawn, we go out again and, picking out the fresh car tracks by the bush marks, we follow until we find hare tracks over the tire prints. Then we know that we have the tracks of a hare which was ready to find a seat for the day. We follow this trail, seeing where the hare has fed, and judging how long ago by the hardness of the droppings. When the foot prints are in pairs, very close together and soft, the hare is near its chosen seat. History is written in the sand. The braces of the falcon's hood are loosened and the last string jess or *sabook*, previously attached by a sheetbend bow to the leash or *mursel*, is untied. Eyes strain to spot the motionless hare crouching under a low camel-browsed bush. Then the cry goes up "*Dornuk*! *Dornuk*!" (Between us!), the hood is whipped off and the saker held high. A moment's hesitation and she is off, with the hare disappearing like a pixie through the scrub, bouncing against its shadow across the open ground. Its route is marked by the stoops of the falcon and the cries of the falconers. Just as the hare, the falcon, and their two shadows all converge at once, the hare throws itself up in the air like a rag doll, the falcon passing harmlessly through the gap between the hare and its shadow. Sometimes it looks as though it will be caught for sure, but a skidding turn sprays sand as it scoots into a bush. As the falcon turns over to dive in, out comes the *errneb* throwing her out of position and making her pant in the overpowering heat. The hare's course describes a large circle but the falcon is fit and a stoop in some open ground tumbles it. In a moment all is over and the falconer runs up and kills it with his knife, murmuring the prayer *Bis'm Allah* (In the name of God). Thus it is rendered fit for our meal and we cook it with vegetables on a bed of rice and eat it with our hands. The saker gets the tongue, brain and liver; she maintains a steady weight on this ration in this climate. Curiously, she needs to be sharper for hares than for houbara, even though the *errneb* is small, like a cottontail with big ears.

Alternatively, the Arabs use salukis to go steadily through the scrub, checking likely bushes by scent. Often the hare, on hearing the approaching falconers, sneaks away and moves quietly ahead (*insellet*) so that you cannot come up to it by tracking. The saluki overcomes this problem. Once the hare is roused, the chase is on and the dog keeps the hare moving, working in partnership with the falcon. At the end of the flight the dog guards the falcon from eagles until we arrive. This is a harsh land with death always just round the corner for the unwary or unlucky.

Another exciting way of taking hares and hill rabbits is to use a waiting-on flight. I have done this with goshawks, a changeable hawkeagle, a red-tail, and Harrises, but Ferruginous hawks and other large buteos and assorted eagles are possibly even more successful. Unfortunately, most of those flying Harris hawks and red-tails have not got experience of training falcons for waiting-on flights and seldom attempt it with their hare-hawks. This is a pity because these large hawks wait on naturally and are most effective from this position. To see a golden eagle flown in this way is really impressive and a stark contrast to flights from the fist.

Blue hares are not difficult. Possibly a record best "first" was by Cathy Blakey who, when she was working for us, slipped a female Harris out of the front door of our grouse-hawking cottage in Sutherland. Cathy was actually having a hot bath when the hawk took its first blue hare.

## 7.8 Mixed game in hedges and farmland

Let us look at strategies for hawking mixed game such as rabbits, pheasants, partridges and blackbirds in a hedgerow where vegetation is at least shoulder high, but without trees. In many parts of Europe and eastern North America such hedges and strips form a major proportion of holding cover for game. Assume there is one falconer carrying an accipiter, a buteo or a Harris. His dog will usually be some kind of spaniel, German short-haired pointer or German wire-haired pointer. Once you start thinking about the position of the falconer, dog, and hawk, while hunting a hedgeline, then you can start to apply the same principles to other irregular patches of cover.

Figure 7.8.1 shows the arrangement when the wind is in any part of the quadrant shown. For the other three quadrants, reverse the direction of beat or the sides of the hedge accordingly. The falconer and his dog work along the hedge into or across the wind. The falconer may stand in any of the numbered positions shown according to circumstance.

1. A good position for steady progress along the hedge. Staying 10 meters out and walking quietly, one can detect game running ahead or back and see the game beginning to flush before it actually clears cover—this gives the hawk a good start. Keeping a little off the hedge encourages the game to flush cleanly rather than run along the hedgebottom and

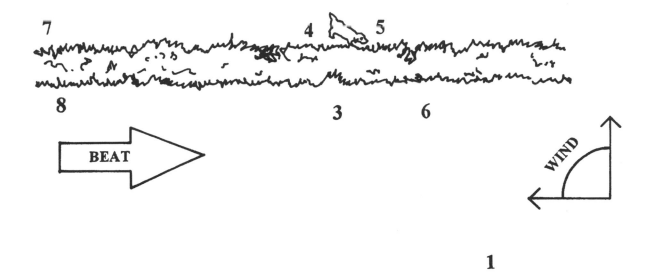

Figure 7.8.1 Hawking a hedgerow.

also makes it more likely to come your way. Game flushing upwind has to come toward you, game going downwind presents a nice slip. The hawk can more easily see game leaving the blind side and can more easily get over the hedge. But it is harder to see and to control the dog from this position so it needs to be reliable.

2. A good position if the dog is unreliable but one must be resigned to losing game on the blindside or long tail chases due to poor starts. If the dog points, or starts feathering, one can move quickly to position 4. or 5., hold the hawk up high and pray. The Harris hawk and the New Zealand falcon quickly learn to perch on a stick handle, especially if you push a hawking glove onto the stick the first few times. Then you can loft the bird high above the hedge before sending the dog in to flush.

3. A poor position for visibility as you walk along, but not a bad one to adopt if you get a firm pheasant point, or if the dog is hard to control or see.

4. You may have to adopt this position if the scent is tricky and the dog needs more careful handling, but it is not so good for the hawk.

5. From this position, the game is most likely to go out on the blind side and the hawk will be faced with a stiff climb to get over the hedge before pursuing. Some game will double back down the hedge.

6. This is a bad position because it pinches the game between the dog and the falconer. Rather than flush out cleanly, it will most likely keep to cover and go along the hedge, or even in some cases, get taken by the dog.

7/8. The falconer is too far behind so that dog and game are out of control. The hawk is faced with all slips being upwind and has a poor view of the game flushing. From position 7. most game will also be on the blind side.

If there are trees in the hedge, the best place for the hawk is in the one just ahead of the dog, upwind. The falconer can then move into the side of the hedge opposite the dog and beat toward the hawk. Once he has gone past the tree, he can signal the hawk to move on to the next tree; most learn this very quickly.

Some falconers advocate flying the hawk only from the fist. I disagree with this for several reasons. First of all, the hawk in the tree has a much better advantage and will detect and kill more game. Secondly, the hawk can intimidate the game more easily, forcing it to put in nearer the falconer so that there are fewer hopeless long tail-chases which can easily cause a lost hawk. Thirdly, being no longer a hawk perch, the falconer is able actively to beat and participate in flushing the game so that effectively the quarry now has three adversaries rather than just two. Fourthly, flights which start from the fist show predominantly a tail view of the action, you get a poor idea of the speed of the hawk closing the gap, whereas the viewpoint when the hawk flies from a tree is usually more varied and interesting. Fifthly, a hawk flying up and down trees gets more exercise than one kept on the fist and does not face such frustrations as the falconer failing to release the jesses in time. The argument that flying a hawk from trees makes it independent simply doesn't hold water. Throughout the day, one is constantly having to move the hawk from tree to tree or call it down for one reason or another and this reinforces discipline rather than the reverse. With the slower hawks, especially the buteos, you will be lucky to catch much at all if you don't use trees.

Should she miss the quarry in an open district, she should either return to the fist or land on the ground. This is achieved by calling her from the ground during training. It is maddening if she flies off 500 meters each time, looking for a perch.

When you are hawking in the woods, the hawk should be in the trees just ahead, not lagging behind. It is surprising how much game runs or flits quietly ahead unseen by the falconer. A hawk, well-placed just in front, spots this game and either attacks it or intimidates it so that it stays put and is pointed properly, rather than running out ahead and escaping.

If you are flying the hawk from the fist, you can either let it go in its own time, orcast it off, or in the case of sparrowhawks, physically throw it at the quarry. Throwing orcasting off the hawk seldom helps and often hinders; the reaction time of an accipiter is so much faster than a human's that they usually do better by themselves. Throwing the hawk is a common method for catching quail in Turkey, where a halsband is used.

Inexperienced falconers often carry on beating

without reference to the hawk. If the hawk is out of position, or not ready, then STOP. Any game flushed will otherwise be wasted. Constantly check on the hawk and always endeavor to flush the game in the best way for the hawk. Similarly you must pay attention; it is no time for conversation or daydreaming. Serving the hawk is the most serious responsibility of the falconer in the field and is the hallmark of a good falconer and the key to a good hawk. If for some reason you cannot serve your hawk regularly and well, all sorts of problems will develop. Potentially good hawks will start selfhunting, inexperienced ones will get fist or lure bound and may start to show undesirable aggression toward the falconer or his dog.

If the hawk does start selfhunting, cutting her weight down will not necessarily cure it; in fact it often makes it worse. Bert (1619:55) was adamant on this point. The remedy is to get the hawk more orientated toward the falconer and less to looking outward for quarry. The falconer must be the source of the quarry, and there must be little available elsewhere, so that the hawk has more hopes of obtaining quarry or food with the falconer and is less confident of its chances elsewhere. In bad cases a few days off game, simply working to fist and lure for discipline, is a good antidote. In the case of a crow-hawk I do not regard selfhunting as a fault. A good crow-hawk is expected to go out on slips of several hundred meters tackling awkward quarry unaided. If, on returning unsuccessful, she spots a few crows in a vulnerable situation, I would be worried if she ignored them.

When beating out a thick hedge or strip of woodland, game will run out ahead—pheasants and red-legged partridges may be sneaking out up to 200 meters ahead. Flying the hawk from trees or standing out a little from the hedge often allows the hawk to spot such quarry. Otherwise efforts must be made to stop off the hedge. If you believe an old pheasant is giving you the slip, do a "P loop." Head out from the hedge and run forwards, coming in again a 100 meters or more further on. With any luck, you have then pinched the pheasant between you and the dog and it will be forced to flush out. Where a hedge runs into a wood it is best to do this as a matter of course.

A good goshawk, when thoroughly fit, can take both partridges and pheasants in the air in the first flight. But to achieve this level of fitness it must be flown at least six days per week with a lot of tree work and hard flights. If you fly only three days a week (as Sebright did), and fly only from the fist, you will find goshawks as disappointing as he did. Then is the time to give high jumps on nonhawking days (see 5.15). Goshawks improve immensely with experience, certainly for three or four seasons. A young bird's first season or 100 head are its apprenticeship for the future.

Woodcocks come into Britain from Scandinavia normally in late November when the moon is full and the north is freezing up. During December and January, particularly when snow is on the ground, they can be found in the woods and damp scrubby corners where there is unfrozen mud or water. Often, during the daytime, they shelter in the bramble or sallow bushes around small springs in the woods. Here they can be flushed out by dogs and chased by a Cooper's hawk or goshawk waiting in a tree nearby. However, woodcocks flush out strongly and once they clear the canopy, they can outstrip an accipiter. Occasionally, when the weather is very cold for several days, the woodcocks lie very close and put in again after a hundred meters or more and in those circumstances a well-placed, strong goshawk can kill them. In North America, woodcock are found only in the east and the same methods of hunting them apply as in Europe.

Dogs point woodcock well, but pointers are difficult to work in thick cover, and it is often a question of pushing on as best one can. Also woodcock do not hold reliably before a point even with a hawk overhead. Even though the dog is steady, the woodcock may jump spontaneously after a few moments and time cannot be wasted when getting the hawk placed.

It is very seldom indeed that woodcock can be pointed in an open enough place to fly a falcon at them from waiting on. Given such a set-up, a very sporting flight results. However, I have flown them a few times with New Zealanders starting from trees over a point and then going into a long tail-chase. So far I have always been left too far behind, stuck in a bog, to reach the falcon after she has put the woodcock in. One day I will do so, and I think in the second flight the falcon will call the tune. Modern falconers have neglected the woodcock, which is a pity. It is a fine challenging quarry.

Rats and squirrels are sometimes taken during mixed hawking. Rats can be flushed with a dog, stick, ferret, or waterhose and are easily captured. However, the quality of the flight is usually poor, and the risk of being bitten is high, so rats are best avoided. An old common buzzard which is not of much use for anything else can show some good chaotic fun in a granary after rats. I remember a male gos of mine in Scotland out duck-hawking flying across the river and picking a swimming rat out of the water like a cherry off a cake. But generally speaking rats are best left well alone.

Gray squirrels provide a modicum of sport for Harris hawks, goshawks, red-tails and, occasionally, Cooper's. Squirrels not only have a very nasty bite, but also a thick skin and a very elusive way of handling themselves. Some hawks develop a very good eye for squirrels and hunt them assiduously and effectively. Indeed at some of the goshawk nests I have visited in Sweden and Finland, red squirrels were a staple. Generally the best help the falconer can give is to keep the squirrel moving with a stick and well-aimed stones (mind the hawk with the ricochets). When the hawk catches one, unless you can quickly kill the squirrel, leave it to the hawk. Don't stand nearby distracting the hawk which may promptly get bitten. Wide protective jesses can be of some use although the bites are usually on the toes. Slitted jesses are definitely taboo. Do not hawk squirrels unless you are prepared to carry home a crippled hawk. If you do fly them, only use a hawk which is experienced at rabbits and which goes for the head. A fumble-footed youngster is bound to get bitten.

Mallard and teal, and to a varying extent a wide range of duck species, can be taken by an accipiter in the first 30 meters or so before they have reached full speed. The hawk flashes from the fist and binds to the duck pulling it back down. This is how most ducks are taken in Britain. This was called hawking at the "crepe" or creep. The usual way of doing this is to use the "P-loop" method. First you walk to the river and then carefully scan up and downstream, marking the ducks. Then you walk away from the river in a loop and approach the marked ducks quietly. The reason for this is that the goshawk needs a short surprise slip to be successful at ducks. Also, the idea is that the ducks are flushed suddenly and cleanly and are properly in the air before they realize that the hawk is after them, otherwise they will dump back down, dive, and refuse to reflush.

Where ducks are on small isolated ponds or marl-pits, the simplest method is to let the hawk fly quietly into an overhanging tree while you are still some way off. This will alarm the ducks and hold them down. You then rush the pond with dogs and people together to get a sudden surprise and a quick flush. Of course, if it turns out no ducks are there, then you are the one who is surprised and flushed.

The flight with a small accipiter at hedgerow birds is very deceptive. Areas which before seemed full of birds become deserted when you appear with a sparrowhawk or sharpshin. Hedgerows which you so confidently expected would produce plenty of flights provide nothing, and amid the luxuriance of late summer suddenly seem dauntingly large, dense, and hopeless.

The young falconer, perhaps with his first "serious" hawk looking for quarry for the first time, begins to realize there is more to this hawking business than teaching the bird to come back. Much more.

While it helps of course to have a good knowledge of the basic habits of the prey, the way prey behaves when hunted by a hawk can only really be discovered by experience.

For most small accipiter work, the assistance of a beater is really handy, indeed often a necessity. Even with a dog, a single falconer cannot work a hedgerow for small birds. They all fly out on the blind side or well ahead. But with a beater armed with a stick, working five meters ahead on the other side, a good proportion will come out and be flown by the hawk. Of course, after a few days, the beater will get fed up of bashing away, being yelled at, not seeing anything and then being told afterward what he missed. He will probably go on strike. But this is all good leadership training for the young falconer.

Having reached this far he starts to find that although the hawk chases the quarry, most potential prey quickly get back into cover and refuse to cooperate further. The simple answer is that big hedges are hard in winter and impossible in summer. The falconer must look for small hedges, small isolated patches of cover, farmyards, and a hundred and one little places where birds can be found where the hawk can get a proper chance. Rushy fields, patches of stinging nettles or thistles, animal feed troughs, small ditches and streams; a bird in one of those is worth many in a big bush.

Most small birds are protected in most countries and in Britain you will need a license to fly them. Sparrows, which are common in summer, disappear from a lot of places in the autumn and as the leaves fall, blackbirds and thrushes become

more of a proposition. After a season at blackbirds you will be older, wiser and much more respectful of them as a quarry. If you've caught a few and still got a healthy hawk you have done well.

Small accipiters are frail, and in addition to being fully conversant with Mavrogordato's *A Hawk for the Bush* and Harry McElroy's *Desert Hawking*, remember the advice of the anonymous author of *The Perfect Boke for Keeping Sparrowhawks and Goshawks*. Namely, not to let the hawk stand empty in the morning after she hascast but to feed her a little to keep her "lusty." Especially once the frosts start, you must guard against her blood sugar levels getting low and keep her weight up. She should fly in October about 15 grams or half an ounce heavier than she did in August.

Although I flew several sparrowhawks and a shikra in my student days and acknowledge the skill required to keep such birds in flying order, I would not want to fly one now. The flights are so short and brief, the best hardly better than a poor merlin flight, and the hawks are so delicate, that I suppose I am too lazy or too spoiled to attempt it. That they have their place in falconry and provide an excellent grounding (if severe one), there can be no doubt, and certainly no falconer can consider his education complete until he has flown at least one small accipiter successfully. One of the sad aspects that occurs nowadays is that the tyro falconer soon obtains a Harris hawk. Although these are marvelous birds, they are in many ways just too easy. The falconer quickly learns bad habits and slack practices. He abandons the hood, is slack about handling the bird, and is careless around its feet and in tying knots. Out hawking, he is inattentive to the hawk's whereabouts and, when the hawk chases quarry, the falconer strolls casually after it without a care in the world. He starts to believe he knows a thing or two about hawking! But when he tries this blasé approach on an accipiter, his life suddenly becomes a nightmare in which even walking through a doorway requires careful consideration. An apprenticeship on a small accipiter helps to develop good habits and a sensitivity which are a necessity for the skilled falconer.

## 7.9    Waiting-on flights with falcons

Gamebirds, such as red grouse, willow grouse, ptarmigan, sharp-tailed grouse, sage grouse, prairie chickens, pheasants, red-legged partridges, chukar, Hungarian or gray partridges, francolin, and various species of quail, are commonly taken in a waiting-on flight by falcons, although many of the smaller species which seldom fly far from cover, are more usually flown by accipiters. In addition, many species of duck are flown in the same manner by falcons, where they can be flushed cleanly in open country.

The basic elements of game hawking are the same the world over. The falcon must go up into her "high search" position (see 6.4). She has a natural instinct to do this, and is encouraged by the falconer's training. She understands from previous experience that the falconer below is a flushing agent who might disturb prey. She keeps him in her killing cone. It is his job, as part of this act of faith, to produce the quarry. Once it is flushed, the falcon stoops and has a good chance of killing the quarry outright. This pattern of hunting technique is repeated time and time again without variation, so that the falcon becomes "set" in this habit. All the gamebirds fly in approximately the same way: they have a good acceleration when flushed, sprint mainly anaerobically, and then have to land. Their flight is direct, making a direct hit not too difficult, compared to agile prey such as lapwings, which seldom sustain the full impact of a stoop. Within this broad framework there are many permutations; cock sage grouse for example fly so fast and so far, and are so heavy and tough, that only the strongest falcons can kill them, and even then, only after they have reviewed their ideas on speed! The medium-sized gamebirds, from partridges and red- and sharp-tailed grouse through to pheasants, are tempting targets for most falcons in the 700–1200 grams (25–43 oz.) range, as are the ducks. Further down the size range, quail, teal, and snipe tend to be too nippy and agile for large falcons and this is where many male falcons come into their own.

Let's look at the stoop more closely. I will assume that the level flight speed of a red grouse when chased by a falcon is 88 kilometers per hour (55 mph). Grouse, sensibly, fly a lot faster when pursued by a falcon than when casually flushed. From these data, and from watching the relative performances of the birds in action, an approximate graph of the acceleration curves are shown in Figure 7.9.1. The grouse is the first to get its speed up and in level flight the peregrine can only catch up with it after several hundred meters.

As a falcon circles in the air, it has below it a "killing cone" in which it can stoop (figure 7.9.2).

Any quarry inside this airspace is vulnerable to a stoop from above. Outside this 45 degree cone is a wider 30 degree cone in which the falcon could make a shallower, less powerful stoop. Outside the 30 degree cone the falcon would more or less have to tail-chase a grouse in an angled wing-beating direct attack.

Obviously the parameters vary tremendously and independently. We are trying here to understand the principles of what is happening rather than to arrive at exact predications. Transferring the acceleration curves into vertical and horizontal distances one reaches figure 7.9.3. The falcon, waiting on, is at position 0 at the top of the figure. Below it is its killing cone in which it can stoop at quarry. If the falcon is 100 meters up it can cover a 200 meter diameter of ground (ie 100 meter radius) below, inside its 45 degree killing cone. Take a piece of paper and lay it across the graph at the 100 meter line. You will see that in a 45 degree stoop she will travel down 100 meters and across 100 meters and take just over five seconds.

Vertically below the falcon is a grouse at position 0 which flushes right-handed across the graph. Its position each second is plotted by vertical bars. The falcon starts its stoop and its position each second is shown by the radiating ripples. The points at which the falcon would actually contact the grouse are shown by the "contact" curve. At 100 meters elevation the actual strike would be at about 95 horizontal meters in a stoop slightly steeper than 45 degrees.

Take another example. If the falcon started from the ground ie at zero initial altitude, (top line of graph) a tailchase would ensue, the contact point being more than 500 meters away from the start, off the edge of the graph. If the falcon started from 50 meters (165 ft.) up and made a shallow stoop or tail-chase it might reach the grouse after seven seconds, about 135 meters (445 ft.) horizontally from the start. Rather like somebody peddling downhill on a bicycle, the long-winged high-geared peregrine can continue to build speed by wing-beating after the point at which a shorter-winged, low-geared hawk would have had to set its wings in a shallow stoop.

If the falcon starts from only 50 meters up, surely this is all the more reason for it to stoop vertically? If you follow the line down the vertical axis, you will see that it would take about 3.6 seconds for a falcon to stoop vertically in a nose dive straight into the ground. During those 3.6

seconds the grouse will have traveled about 60 meters horizontally. Therefore, from 50 meters the earliest point at which the falcon could hit the grouse is after seven seconds at a stoop angle of about 20 degrees, which isn't really a stoop at all. If the falcon had not set this course right from the start, there would be further delay and the whole thing would quickly degenerate into a tail-chase. Similarly, if the grouse had started, not from the center of the killing cone but a bit nearer the edge, a tail-chase would have been inevitable. If the fal-

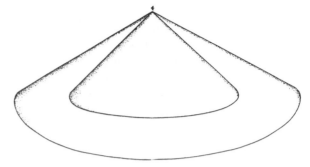

Figure 7.9.2 The 30 degrees and 45 degrees killing cones.

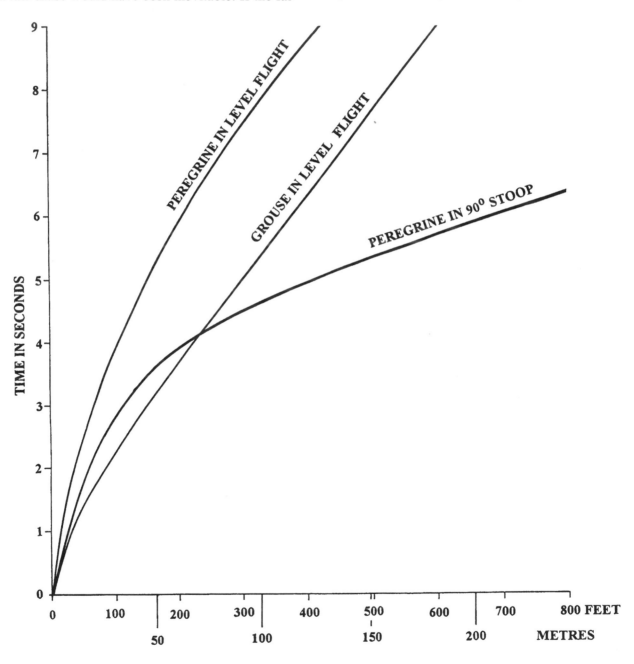

Figure 7.9.1 The speeds of red grouse and peregrines.

coner could manage to flush the grouse from the outside of the killing cone inward, under the falcon, then the situation might be saved, but the grouse probably has its own ideas about this.

What if the falcon goes to a higher pitch, say 200 meters? The dashed line showing the contact point indicates that the falcon and grouse would converge after 6.2 seconds. The stoop would be about 60 degrees and the grouse would only have traveled about 120 meters horizontally. Classic stuff. And look, the grouse could have been 75 meters off center and still been hit with a 45 degree stoop, no problem.

This looks great, let's get that falcon up a bit

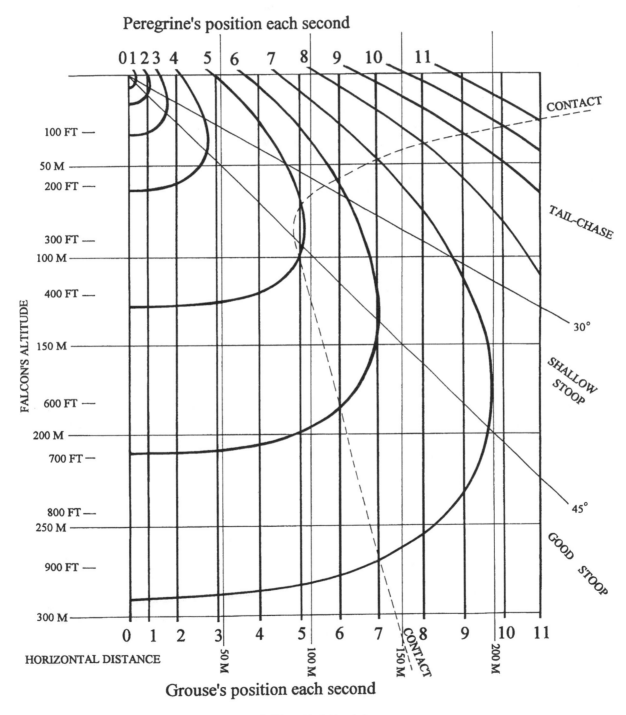

Figure 7.9.3. The movements of falcon and grouse and different heights of stoop.

higher! What if it stoops from 300 meters? This time it takes 7.3 seconds, the grouse covers about 145 horizontal meters, the stoop is about 64 degrees and the grouse could have been 150 meters off center and still been hit in a 45 degree stoop.

The stoop itself of course will probably be steeper at first, then flatten out. Because grouse skim along close to the ground the falcon is forced to flatten out and so a vertical stoop is not truly vertical but hooked or spiralled. When faced with quarry high in the air, the falcon still normally flattens out before or at contact in order to throw up high and regain dominance. One seldom sees a falcon continue in a downward trajectory below the quarry after the strike. So figure 7.9.3 is very much idealized. But what can be learned from it?

First of all, if you count 45 degrees or steeper as a true stoop, then the first contacts inside the 45 degree cone only come once the falcon is about 100 meters or more up. Less than this and it can only manage a shallow stoop or a tail-chase. There are only a few ways around this basic problem. One is to flush the grouse from the outside of the killing cone toward the center. Another way is to slow the grouse down. You could do this by turning it into a partridge or a pheasant perhaps. Or you could tilt the ground level so that the grouse has to fly uphill. This slows down the grouse, makes the journey for the falcon shorter, and makes the grouse easier to hit. But no selfrespecting grouse will put up with this for more than a few wingbeats! Round it goes and away down hill. Now there's trouble. The tables are turned completely. The grouse hurtles away gaining speed rapidly. Wide valleys open before it. There are limitless options for escape. The falcon meanwhile is condemned to a steep tail-chase with the grouse controlling the flight. No longer so intimidated, the grouse leads the falcon a merry dance out of sight. The good news is, when the falcon gives up and comes back. The bad news is when the falcon catches the grouse a long way off and is itself killed by an eagle.

Let's say we are hawking partridges in a fairly enclosed agricultural district. Really the falcon has to get onto them quickly before they reach cover. The birds will be holding fairly tight and can be flushed with reasonably accurate timing and direction. We need a falcon which waits on closely, in position and at a pitch of about 100–150 meters. From there she has a chance of stooping and killing within a horizontal distance of 100 meters or

so. The partridges will be so under control that they will not have opportunity to dream up spoiling tactics and with a bit of luck the falcon will kill one stone dead. From a lesser pitch, the partridges will make the hedge. Also, from a lesser pitch, the falcon is not really waiting on at all; she is zooming round in circles. This means that the falconer is running round the field tripping over God-knows-what, with his head in the air, trying to watch the falcon and time his flush for the split second when she is facing the right way. He is probably also shouting instructions to his dogs and companions, instructions which will be misunderstood and acted on five seconds too late, by which time a further diatribe of contradictory yells is already issuing forth. A very genteel partridge might die from shock at the bad language, but this is probably the limit of its risk.

So then it's the prima donna's turn to fly. Just back from the open grouse moors, his falcon mounts beautifully to 300 meters or more. From this height she can make a 30 degree stoop at anything within a 1100 meter circle, and—oh look!—by drifting over this way a bit there's an interesting flock of pigeons! But wait, someone's waving his glove and whistling pathetically. The falcon comes back over to see what he wants and then *Brrrr* up go the partridges. *Ssssss-ump* down comes the falcon. What a stoop! But too late, they're already in the hedge 100 meters away. The falcon was just too high up. But what a bird, back she goes to her original pitch. Panic below. The dogs are being "helped" by a falconer who is trying to detach his crutch from a barbed wire fence. I'll tell you what, those pigeons really do look irresistible....

Let's leave the enclosed country and head for the wide open spaces: the grouse moors of Scotland, or the endless dry stubbles of a coto in Andalucia with red partridges running in the far distance. Or the American sage brush country where you're happy to come home with your dog, let alone a grouse as well. By dog or by car, one way or another, the game is marked. Off comes the hood, a gentle shake of feathers and away up goes the falcon. The game is held down and we pause for a moment to consider our position. A dog or a visitor is warned to keep back. We spread out, ready to run in for the flush. Has anyone seen the falcon? She is so high that we can't see her. In Scotland she's in cloud, in Spain she's a small peregrine in a big sky, and in Wyoming she's a

The prairie falcon needs careful handling but can be a very capable performer. This little male at 470 grams (1 lb. ½ oz.) would kill red grouse or larks, whichever were pointed, with equal enthusiasm.

white gyr in a sky lightened by reflections from the snow. One way or another her presence becomes a rumor. But she's a good bird. She knows the score. Let's get in and serve her. *Brrrr!* Up go the birds. And another. And another. Off they go, disappearing into the distance. Nothing happens. Then... "Wow! Did you see that?" Some keen-eyed enthusiast with field-glasses reckons the falcon came out of nowhere and may have hit one but he can't be sure. The younger members of the party start to run. The geriatrics trudge off to their vehicles and set off in belated pursuit. A dog, still pointing a straggler in a hollow, gets fed up of waiting, flushes its bird and then starts cruising around wondering where everyone has gone. The falcon is now no longer a rumor. She has become a conjecture. She is not my bird. I have to decide what to do. In Scotland, I trudge to a high point, looking for a signal, trying to keep the drizzle off the electronics. In Spain, I lie down and doze in the sun, letting the rise and fall of excited Spanish conversation waft over me. In Wyoming, it's 15 degrees below outside so I bucket along in a station wagon

the size of a cowshed, trying to reach companions on a crackling radio. Unflown falcons huddle patiently in the back. Eventually order is restored. I think deep thoughts about the meaning of life.

And it doesn't stop there. We haven't even started to talk about wind yet. Falcons, particularly young or unfit ones, prefer to stoop upwind because they have more control and can stoop more steeply knowing they can pull out afterward more easily. The oncoming wind and the wind shear effect help lift them up away from the ground at the time of most strain on the pectoral muscles. They dislike stooping downwind because they have a faster ground speed which on low-flying quarry is hazardous. Occasionally young falcons misjudge the downwind stoop and, being unable to pull out, smash into the ground.

When both falcon and quarry are up in the air near together, such as in a tail-chase, wind speed is irrelevant. They are both in the same body of moving air and are thus unaffected in relation to each other, like two swimmers drifting down a river. Only their ground speed is changed by the wind direction.

But when falcon and prey are in the air and apart then they may be experiencing different wind speeds. Wind tends to be stronger higher up than near the ground. The grouse that skims off into a 20 kilometers per hour wind may make its pursuer at 150 meters (500 ft.) face a 50 kilometers per hour wind. This wind shear effect can thus aid the quarry on an upwind flight and the falcon on a downwind flight. This is why many game falconers try for a downwind flush. The benefits come only when there is significant wind shear. In some situations, such as on windward slopes, there is a reverse wind shear; the wind low down being stronger than at height.

Going back to the graph, if the falcon is low—only 80 meters (260 ft.)—and directly above a grouse flushed into a 20 kilometer per hour (12.5 mph) wind, what happens? Even under still air conditions the falcon could have achieved only a 30 degree stoop and contact 80 meters (460 ft.) from the start point. With a stronger headwind than the grouse has, and at such a shallow angle, the falcon is driven back in relation to the grouse so that its attack angle becomes even shallower—nearer 20 degrees—and a tail-chase is inevitable because at a 20 degree angle the falcon's acceleration is drastically reduced. Conversely, had the grouse flown downwind, the stronger tailwind at altitude would have helped the falcon get into its speed and would have kept the stoop steeper than 30 degrees.

The effects on the killing cone of a steady wind, and wind shear are shown in figures 7.9.4 and 7.9.5. Once a falcon becomes experienced, it learns to use the wind instead of fighting it. Take a windy day with a 50 kilometers per hour wind at 150 meters (500 ft.) and a 30 kilometers per hour wind at ground level. The falcon is placed 100 meters upwind and the grouse is flushed upwind

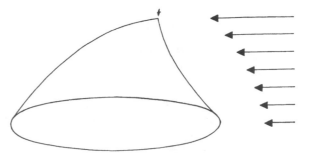

Figure 7.9.5 The effect of wind shear on the killing cone.

into its killing cone. The experienced falcon will start into a downwind stoop, taking advantage of the wind strength. Halfway down it twists into an upwind tack for a better controlled upwind strike. The grouse meanwhile, forging into a 30 kilometers per hour wind, has a ground speed of only 58 kilometers per hour (36 mph) and is almost a sitting target.

The lessons to be learned from this are if your falcon normally holds a pitch of 150 meters (500 ft.) it does not matter much which direction the grouse flushes in, provided that it flushes within 100 meters (330 ft.) of the center of the 45 degree cone. If on the other hand the falcon has a low pitch of only 60 meters (200 ft.) the grouse is best flushed downwind, or alternatively the falcon must be placed slightly upwind. Grouse prefer to fly upwind and downhill. Most of all they have their eyes cocked to monitor the position of the falcon and will use whichever option takes them out of the killing cone most rapidly. The skilled falconer anticipates what action the grouse are most likely to take, or can be persuaded to take, and tries to place his falcon in such a position that there is no way the grouse can get outside the killing cone before the strike.

These graphs and diagrams are a bit complicated and theoretical and can't be used in real life situations. But I hope that if you are stuck indoors, with falcons on all the chair backs, waiting for the weather to clear for a quick flight before dark, that they will set you to arguing the finer points with your companions, and convincing yourselves that I have got it all completely wrong.

It is only by understanding the stoop itself properly, as an aerodynamic maneuver with its attack angles and acceleration curves, that one can appreciate the situation that the falcon is faced with. Only when all the factors are right can the falcon use the stoop and both the falcon and its

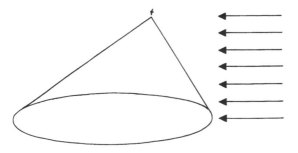

Figure 7.9.4 The effect of an even cross wind on the killing cone.

prey may go through a variety of tactical moves to achieve or to avoid these factors coming together. The falcon's use of interception, shepherding, and of terrain hostile to the prey to prevent it seeking cover, all form a series of complicated moves easily misinterpreted by the ground observer, particularly if only an incomplete sequence is seen.

Usually falconers team up and hawk in pairs or trios. Where grouse are scarce and three or four hawks are to be flown, it is futile to have everybody trailing along behind one dog. Better to form a line with a dog handler at each end and two pointers running at a time working independently. Depending on the terrain each dog will take a beat 200–500 meters wide. When one gets a point, this is signaled across to the other handler who drops his dog and takes it in. The grouse are then flown. In this way everyone walks half as far and sees twice as much hawking.

In hilly terrain, the lie of the land becomes of more importance than the wind. Flushing the grouse up the slope puts them at a grave disadvantage regardless of wind direction. Grouse flushed downhill can get speed up and cover a lot of ground very quickly. On flattish land, when the wind is slight, it is a waste of time heading the point, ie for the falconer to make a circuit until he is approaching the dog head on, trying for a downwind flush. On calm days it is best to flush the grouse straight out, it is quicker, less likely to go wrong, the flush is more controlled and you have a better chance of flushing birds singly and thus getting several flights from one covey. This is particularly important for a low-flying young falcon which needs a carefully timed flush. Also, the young hawk, coming back high after losing the first grouse, really benefits from having a second flush under her as she comes over. A few such occasions make all the difference at a critical time in a hawk's career.

One advantage of heading the point, especially when hawking alone, is that it is easier to control the dog when it is facing you. If you are behind the dog it may, in its enthusiasm, when told to flush, run through the whole covey and spring the lot. When you face the dog, once it has flushed the first bird or birds, it is easier to drop the dog leaving you free to concentrate on the falcon.

Provided the essential ingredients are there, red grouse hawking is one of the easier forms of falconry. A well-made grouse falcon enjoys a high success rate. By and large, one is free of the con-

stant problems found hawking partridges in more enclosed areas—no power lines, roads, people, pigeons, and so on. The grouse too is a naturally tempting quarry, very predictable and incapable of serious evasive tactics in the air. On the ground it seldom reaches insuperable cover (except where bracken encroaches) or shows the intelligence of a magpie. The dogs love its scent. The whole scenario is eminently repeatable and this is the ideal way to build up the stereotyped behavior of a good game hawk.

Black grouse, if found on a moor, are very similar to red grouse. Ptarmigan and chukar are difficult due to the hilly terrain they inhabit. With the former it is cold, wet, and windy and with the latter, too hot for the dogs to work after mid-morning.

Of the partridges, the gray or Hungarian partridge is preferable for hawking as it flushes well whereas the red leg and Chukar partridges run and run. No falconer who has hawked grouse or pheasants should find partridges difficult. The problems mainly arise, not from the quarry, but from the distracting influences such as other potential prey and the presence of thick cover. If there is a lot of cover you will find, as Sebright did, that nine out of ten of the partridges taken are killed by the dogs.

Although partridges themselves are not difficult, keeping a partridge falcon in work is. To find her a couple of flights a day for any length of time requires access to a lot of partridges, often in areas where game rents are at a premium. The rich coveys of September soon become scattered and unapproachable. Stubbles soon give way to bare plough. By December most partridge falcons have been grounded. In Spain, where I have the good fortune to hawk redlegs with the Royal Spanish Falconry Club, the coto or hawking ground, is very open and partridges have to be spotted a long way off from a vehicle. I detest cars and try to convince my Spanish friends to use horses, which are still used on the coto for hare coursing, but they roll their eyeballs, murmur "Mad Ingleesh" and take me for another little snack of chopped squid! In America, a car is needed, not only to cover such large areas of ground, but to keep the falcon and falconer from freezing up in the process.

Quail can vary from very easy, if found in cultivated or arid land, to impossible where cover is thick. Harry McElroy's Desert Hawking II is still the best source of advice on them. Quail in an open landscape can be taken with a smallish falcon

Figure 7.9.6 Red grouse.

waiting-on. But quail love cover and a more versatile hawk is usually needed. I used to hawk California Quail with New Zealand falcons, which were once known as "Quail-hawks." They would disappear inside thick areas of cover to get to the quail.

Various species of duck can be flushed under a large falcon waiting-on and killed in the stoop. This has been brought to perfection in parts of America where suitable ponds are available for consistent flights. Good conditions are rare for this flight in Britain; the main places are the tiny lochans of Caithness and Sutherland where one often finds a teal or two while out grouse-hawking. These little ducks know very well the distance to the next safe pool and, just when you think your falcon will be rewarded with a successful stoop, the duck disappears, showering the falcon with water. It can keep up this game until both falconer and falcon are exhausted and wet, having just completed a whistle-stop tour of these tiny, hidden lochans which sprinkle the moors like jewels.

Once well on the wing, ducks leave accipiters behind, but can be flown down by a persistent falcon. The ease with which this is done depends on what water is available down below for succor. With water below, the duck will come down, but if no water is to be had, it will make a determined effort to outfly the falcon and head for distant water, making a flight of several kilometers. A big, fast falcon and a young falconer are needed for this flight. These flights usually arise when a falcon is slipped from the fist at a duck which is trading past.

Occasionally, in wetland areas, high shepherding flights can be undertaken at ducks with large falcons. Beebe (1992) describes these in some detail. In Spain there is good duck-hawking in many areas, before the land dries out too much, and high flights are possible, on a rather haphazard basis.

Snipe, larks, and pipits can be flown successfully by small falcons waiting-on. This is an advanced flight. Snipe are not as easily intimidated as gamebirds, and are fast and agile. Usually they evade the first stoop and may then proceed to ring up rapidly, leaving the falcon behind. A merlin, or male prairie falcon, may succeed in putting in the snipe only to lose it on the ground. The falcon will then be reluctant to go up again, wanting to keep a close eye on proceedings. The solution is to fly the falcon in an adaptation of the old method of flying at the "view" or "toll." On pointing the snipe, the merlin is cast off and the falconer then produces his lure and begins to exercise the falcon in the normal way. After two or three stoops, the falcon will be warmed up and will be coming in hard and steep. Its passing overhead makes the snipe reluctant to rise. Just as the falcon turns to come in again, the falconer or dog flushes the snipe and the flight is underway, in top gear right from the start. If the snipe gets well into the air it will probably be safe.

## 7.10  Pursuit flights with falcons

Pursuit flights with a falcon start off as a direct flying attack and then turn to a tail-chase or pursuit as the quarry flees. The quarry has three choices: to get into cover where the falcon cannot reach it, to evade the falcon in the air using superior agility or speed, or to stay above the falcon. If the falcon is slipped in such a way that she can easily climb above the prey, then no high aerial flight will result; the prey has been dominated right from the start. It is left with only two options, and, if there is no cover nearby, it will probably be caught. The falconer may try to arrange such a situation for a young falcon to encourage her, but then will gradually make it harder and harder for the falcon, maintaining a careful balance between confidence and challenge.

Some species, such as most of the big falcons, can be trained for both waiting-on or pursuit flights, whereas some of the others, such as merlins, are better at pursuit. By and large, saker, gyr, New Zealand falcon, or merlin genes give persistence; gyr, peregrine, or merlin genes give speed; gyr, saker, New Zealand, or merlin genes give intelligence and courage; New Zealand or merlin give agility; and peregrine genes often make the bird more aerial and given to climbing above the quarry before pressing the attack. Saker and lanner genes makes the bird slower, although there is a tremendous difference in speed between different forms of saker.

The quarry needs to be of a species suited to this type of escape behavior (see 7.4) and matched to the falcon. Larks for example, often go for height when pursued by a merlin, whereas pipits tend to try a low escape and put into cover, and are thus more easily caught. Starlings tend to be less approachable and have sorted out their escape before the merlin can get there. The starlings work in groups and use sentinels. When a falcon approaches, they either shelter in dense cover or take to the air in a tight flock, staying high. They can therefore pose a considerable strategic challenge.

For the larger falcons, gulls, and houbara have many similarities. It is difficult to hawk gulls regularly because they are in a different place every day and this makes it difficult to locate them and obtain permission. The other problem is that they are often in large flocks and a good falcon quickly gets in among them and takes one without much contest. It is best where they are in low numbers so that a one-to-one flight ensues. The same comment applies to rooks and crows. Houbara tend to be flown as singles but often prefer to face the falcon on the ground rather than in the air. If they can be got well up before slipping the falcon, there is a prospect of a long aerial chase which can last several minutes and go long distances. In Morocco, where houbara live near people, they can be approached more closely and may be dominated from the start, whereas in Pakistan they are more flighty and often produce quality flights.

Crow-hawking, first to last, is an exercise in risk management. Crow or rook-hawking on horseback must be the most exciting form of falconry available anywhere in the western world today. It is heavily addictive to those who try it! Three seasons ago, for example, an old friend, Tony Owens rode out with us. He has flown goshawks for thirty years and dabbled with grousehawking with peregrines. After three days hawking, his horse went down in full gallop during a flight and Tony was sent home with a suspected broken neck. The next day he was back out with his neck bound up in a neck support having arranged a new home for his seven-year-old gos over

the telephone! Last season, Peter Owens went down, man and beast, during a flight and nobody went to look for the pieces until afterward. Liam O'Broin found himself on the boat back to Ireland with three broken ribs, a broken shoulder blade and a broken collar-bone.

In pretelemetry days, rook hawking was a tricky business because it was so easy to lose the falcon. After some successes, I gave it up through nervous and physical exhaustion, fortunately before losing my peregrine. Strict rules of procedure for rook hawkers, outlined by Jack Mavrogordato in *A Falcon in the Field*, while ostensibly aimed at producing quality flights, were mainly necessary to reduce the losses of trained falcons. Telemetry has had more effect on this type of hawking than on any other. Modern technology has helped overcome some of the hazards in modern falconry. We use telemetry and walkie-talkies to enhance the sport, to reduce the risk of losing a falcon, and to save the horses from needless exertion. Nobody enjoys the misery of a hawk left out, or of a long hack home on a horse which has already given of its best and which will be going out again the next day.

We are very privileged because we fly falcons at crows in Britain for two months as preparation for houbara hawking in the Middle East. This means we have twenty or more young hacked falcons to get going between August and October. Every year is a new challenge and a valuable insight into the way individual falcons progress. We work as a team, using 8–10 falconers to manage this number of birds.

Anyone who has trained and entered a young hawk or falcon knows the work this entails. When you have a whole team of birds to get going, the problems are immense. We judge our birds not by the best ones, but by the worst. It is easy to have a couple of star performers and the rest nowhere. The rule is quite simple—and this applies to game hawks and dog teams just as much—*worst first*. Always take the worst bird up and fly her first. If time runs short, the "Ace" may not be flown. But she will not be too much the worse for it, whereas the bad bird will have improved. Of course there will be times when you have to break this rule; these are when flying conditions or quarry are too difficult for the bad hawk but bearable for the good one, or when there are visitors out and you wish to guarantee sport. Many falconers put themselves under too much pressure at the beginning of the season by inviting lots of people out when the young hawks are not ready. So the old trusty ones get an airing and the youngsters get short shrift. A little willpower is required.

The system we now use has been developed in stages over the last fifteen seasons or so and it works. As in so many things in falconry, it is the details which are all important for success. We do not use bagged quarry, so we use dummy crow lures and fly falcons incasts so that they learn from each other. Once a few youngsters are killing well, they quickly teach the rest.

The first step is to prepare the land. Few people realize just how open the land needs to be until they have been out rook or crow hawking properly. Most people who hawk rooks use a vehicle and make do with land which is substandard. The alternative is to hawk on foot. Using a vehicle, the usual method is to cruise along the farm roads until some rooks are spotted, then to drive or walk to a suitable place from which to slip, if possible. Once the hawk has been slipped, one stands there like a potted plant, watching the flight in the fieldglasses and then run or drive to pick up the bits. This is as near to classical hawking as a car follower gets to foxhunting. Only half the experience is there.

To hawk from horses, the land, first of all, needs to be both hawkable and ridable. This means open, with a minimum of 500 meters between cover. Cover includes any woodland more than a single straggly tree or bush, bracken beds, or any crop over about 50 centimeters high. Wire fences, stone walls, flocks of sheep, rushes, or bracken will ruin it for an unhacked peregrine but most hybrids will not be deterred. Crows usually need to be bettered in the air before they bale out for cover, so you may well still get a good flight. The land should preferably be gently undulating so that you are constantly exposing new vistas. Flat ground may be marvelous for the first flight but then there's a long way to go before fresh ground. If the land is at all hilly, large basins are best as they hold the flights inward. Convex domes going down to blind valleys, as in many of the Welsh hills, are disastrous. The flights always slide off into bad ground.

There are parts of Europe open enough for rook and crow hawking, including Poland, Hungary, and Spain. Some of these areas depend on wintering rooks and offer ideal country for the flights. In North America, there is plenty of open country, but only sparse numbers of corvids, and the falconer would have to drive a lot. It remains to be seen if North American falconry will develop classical ringing flights with large falcons; the problem is suitable legal quarry.

The land must hold sufficient quarry; but not too many. Our land runs from grouse moorland and high fells along the ridges. This has very low densities of crows and is difficult riding but acts as a good buffer zone of open country. The middle belt of "white ground" is the best. This has a scattering of strong moor crows, the bane of the shepherd and of the gamekeeper. This white ground is permanent rough grazing for sheep and cattle. In Wales, most of the white ground is poor riding because it is either boggy, rocky, too steep or all three. In the north, the going is a lot better and in many places it can be ridden at speed. You often have to cover a fair bit of ground to find crows but the scenery is enjoyable and, when you finally come up to some crows, you have a good chance of a sporting flight, a gallop and a kill. White ground runs down to more intensively managed country; smaller enclosures cut for hay or silage, and often of reseeded leys which are easily damaged by horses. However, they tend to hold a lot of crows and rooks. They are also more heavily interspersed with cover. The farmers will not thank you for taking a lot of horses across this land and therefore we tend to keep it for entering young falcons at the rooks, which are much easier than crows, or for days when the wind is too high to fly the higher, more exposed, ground or for days when there are only two or three horses out, and even then the falconer will usually dismount and run over sensitive ground to the kill. The fastest action occurs on the low ground if one can arrange access. The ground can be ridden at speed and there is plenty of quarry; sometimes too much.

In terms of land area, we use about 10,000 acres in Wales and about 30,000 acres in the north. I believe Roger Upton, who hawks rooks in Wiltshire, uses about 14,000 acres for his team of falcons. The ground is really of not much use at all if it is in blocks of less than 2,000 acres. Obviously it depends on the density of quarry, but we find that if we move off at 2 P.M. and get back to the horse boxes around 6 P.M., having ridden 10–15 miles, the very least we cover is 2,000 acres and it is often double this. To keep visits down to no more than once every ten days means that 30,000 acres is about our minimum. Hawking the area more often educates the quarry and is not fair on the farmer. Because a significant proportion of every property is unhawkable for one reason or another—steadings, woodlands, bad ground, and so on—to obtain 30,000 acres of hawkable ground means obtaining permission on about 50,000 acres altogether. Therefore we manage our ground like a hunt country. It takes an hour to box across to the far end. For this reason during the season we move some of the horses to another farm and keep them there for several days while we do a more concentrated campaign in that area. To get this amount of ground requires a great deal of liaison with the farmers and a lot of work to obtain their goodwill. We therefore hawk in an organized group under the control of the Master Falconer and sometimes also, a Field Master. Green coats are worn by the members so that both the Field and the farmers can identify who is responsible for what. Except for certain meets, Fields are restricted to six horses or less, with no foot followers and no cars except the hawking van. From the farmers' point of view, our aim is to kill as many crows as possible with the minimum damage to land or stock. From my point of view I have to get all my young falcons killing well in preparation for hawking later at houbara. From the Field's point of view, they of course want to see high class sport, good country, good flights, and good gallops.

When you realize how much work is entailed in obtaining suitable land it is quite obvious that classical mounted crow and rook hawking, as practiced by the Old Hawking Club, is not feasible except for a limited number of falconers with the time, opportunity and finance. It is a major logistical exercise. The individual falconer can have a lot of fun with just one or two falcons at very little expense, provided he has some land and transport.

The next piece of this jigsaw puzzle is to arrange suitable hawks. The Old Hawking Club preferred passage peregrines for rook-hawking but these are not obtainable in Britain and, anyway, purebred peregrines are not first choice for crow-hawking. This is because they are aerial specialists. Some of our best performers have been peregrine/sakers and saker/peregrines, gyr/peregrines, gyr/sakers and gyr/saker/sakers, but occasionally, peregrines and gyrs. We need a falcon which climbs straight up without ringing, is a persistent chaser which will not give up, and which can still take the crow on the ground in light cover. Last week I slipped Black Jack, a young black gyr/Altai saker, at some rooks about 800 meters

($\frac{1}{2}$ mi.) away, downwind. He climbed straight out and beat his rooks, killing one first stoop. The climb was 3.2 kilometers (2 mi.) from slip to stoop. All conditions have to be just right for a flight like that.

One of the annoying traits of peregrines, unlike the desert falcons, is that often they will not start at crows on the ground. This means that you either have to slip at a crow in flight which can entail some fairly fast thinking and some haphazard results, or you can flush the crows yourself, which immediately puts your falcon at a disadvantage. A good crow hawk is acutely selfaware and knows the importance of surprise as well as height. Often the falcon, once she is slipped, will fly steadily in toward the crows, keeping in close alongside the cantering horses to mask her approach, before sprinting forward into the attack.

For the basic approach to hawking we use a similar system to that described so ably by Roger Upton in his book *Falconry: Principles and Practice*. Of the hawks, those with saker or gyr are much more nimble on the ground or in the air than straight peregrines, and hacked birds are far superior to unhacked birds. Unhacked birds, for some reason, seldom come on with their footing or flying as well as the hacked birds, despite much extra work put into them. It seems experience lost at that critical age is hard to make up. Very large falcons, birds weighing over a kilogram, can be too intimidating for rooks and crows (not to mention grouse), so that the quarry flies low or seeks cover, thus ruining the flight. Ringing flights are more frequent with smaller, less intimidating, falcons.

Strong winds are no longer quite the hazard they used to be in pretelemetry days. The more a falcon is flown in the wind, the better she gets, until by the time she has forty or fifty head to her credit she exploits the wind as much as the crows do. When the clouds are scudding by and conversation is reduced to the utilitarian, real hawking is to be had. Slipped from a windy slope, the falcon opens her wings and without moving a feather simply shrinks up into the sky. Climbing along under the cloudbase over the crows, her attack—a convex hook—is effortless and uninhibited by the nearness of the ground. The straggling crows are scythed and fall about in confusion. The falcon turns and blows into one with an economy of effort that marks her as a bird worth riding your heart out for.

Strong wind magnifies everything out crow

hawking. The successes etch on the memory, the failures are more disastrous, the runs more gut-busting. A good crow hawk is really spectacular in strong wind, possibly the best hawking modern falconry has to offer. But an indifferent performer may get disheartened and will certainly cause a lot of grief. To fly crows in the stormy hills in winter in a Buchanesque landscape is to experience hope, uncertainty and despair, desperation, elation, and physical exhaustion, a privileged insight into the life and mind of a matchless falcon and her ancestral struggle for survival.

Although crows are often taken because they seem to fail to realize that they are being attacked and are killed unceremoniously where they stand, once hard pressed, they do not intimidate easily and they keep their heads. Frequently they will stoop at or gang up on the falcon. Crows are seldom killed stone dead in the air, normally the falcon binds to the crow and, on landing, breaks its neck with a bite. Peregrines are very fumble-footed on the ground and crows frequently escape from them. If they do escape, the peregrine can seldom fly them down again. The falcon must quickly learn to take the crow by the head and kill it immediately. If it flaps around for several minutes in the open it will soon be covered by a heap of angry crows and may well be damaged or put off crows. My New Zealander normally kills the crow in the first 30 seconds and once the victim is dead, the rest of the flock don't get so agitated and keep their distance. Then she drags the crow to the nearest hedge or cover, even a hoofprint will do. A falcon in the open on a crow is really vulnerable and many a good bird has been killed by passing humans. Our falcons are frequently attacked by other raptors especially, in Britain, by buzzards.

Falcons usually like crow meat provided it is still warm, once cold, they find it unappetizing; some few falcons will eat it then but goshawks are reluctant. Fat hawks in aviaries normally leave cold crows. It is good policy to give crow meat to young eyasses in the breeding pens occasionally so they learn to accept it.

Rooks are more adroit than crows but do not have as much heart. Smaller falcons are better for them than big ones. When rooks billow up in great clouds, they can bewilder a young falcon, but an experienced falcon takes a rook out of a flock very easily.

Jackdaws are a more difficult proposition. It is hard to get a falcon above them, they are so wary and buoyant. In the air, peregrines are usually too clumsy to hit one. My New Zealander, if she gets above them, can kill them by putting in a cork-screw stoop. This is a hard move to evade. My best falcon for jackdaws is a half New Zealand falcon, $\frac{1}{4}$ gyr, $\frac{1}{4}$ Peales, called Cocktail. When he tail-chases them, they both jink together across the sky, as if hit by an electric shock.

Magpie-hawking is a completely different flight to crows because the magpie has no speed and has to resort to subterfuge. Magpies are flown using falcons constantly in a position of aerial dominance, and the country needs just the right type and amount of cover, not too much, not too little. There are some ideal places in North America and in Spain. A magpie will not stay in the air with a falcon unless it really has to, so there are no long tail-chases or rings. To hawk magpies well you need to be young, fit, on foot and prepared to hear quite a lot of colorful language.

We use horses to follow the crow flights and take out only as many falcons as there are falconers to carry them. The remaining falcons stay in the hawking van and are changed when convenient. In August and September the weather can be hot and you can reach the bottom of a falcon in a strenuous flight. When this happens it is better to feed her well and skip a day, which effectively means that two teams of falcons are flown on alternating days. Also, with a big falcon, it is possible to hawk crows without the more critical weight control necessary for smaller falcons. This is useful, especially in the second flight when she may have some food on board from a kill in the first flight. Although we use a lot of young falcons because we are training them for houbara hawking, if I just hawked crows for my own pleasure I would use two teams of about three birds each, with none over 900 grams (32 oz.).

When hawking on horseback, ringing flights are valued as a source of a good gallop, similar to a good run with hounds. Indeed, heron plumes were occasionally presented to those first in at the kill. When hawking on foot, one is left with the option of standing still and watching through fieldglasses or running like mad, missing the spectacle and probably resorting to telemetry to determine the outcome. What action there is, occurs so high and far away that the birds, if visible, are just tiny specks. Seldom does the kill occur close at hand, and a falcon giving up on such a high flight can be tempted by fresh quarry over a very big area. Therefore to enjoy (and survive) good ringing or high flights a hawking pony is essential. Of all the classical flights of traditional falconry, this is the most exciting.

Judging the distance of a falcon in the air, either waiting on, or during a flight, is very tricky and estimates are seldom worth the paper they are printed on. The contestants usually seem much further away than they really are. Often a flight high in the air seems a long way away, but as the birds come down to the horizon and eventually near the ground against features which are measurable on a map, it turns out that they are nearer than expected. In our terrain, with 7X or 8X fieldglasses, the details of a crow flight get hard to follow at more than 1000 m once it drops below the skyline. With better fieldglasses, in good light, with a clean background, one would do better. Usually what happens is: while the falcon is in the sky and beating her wings, she is just about visible, but when she folds up and stoops, she completely disappears. If she misses and throws up, a wing may glint briefly before the second stoop and the other crows will indicate a kill. A miss at this stage almost always requires telemetry because it is hard to spot the falcon again once unsighted and in a few moments she could be anywhere. When mounted, as a rough guide, a high flight with a few rings, followed by a race for cover, usually travels about twice as fast as one can gallop. It is an amazing sensation when you get a high flight, and you gallop like mad, to have the falcon float down with her prey right in front of you.

In my experience there are two types of high flight: the ringing flight and the straight climb. Birds with a low wing-loading such as the heron ($0.37$ g/cm$^2$), red kite ($0.31$ g/cm$^2$), and to some extent, the rook ($0.31$ g/cm$^2$) climb most rapidly and easily in rings of about 50–100 meters diameter. The same applies to the lower wing-loaded falcons such as the saker types at about $0.60$ g/cm$^2$. On the other hand, the crow which is more powerful than the rook, and at $0.42$ g/cm$^2$, heavily wing-loaded for its size, is capable of standing on its tail and flying directly upwards in a steep climb. The result looks desperate and ungainly as the bird flaps hard, thrusting itself up almost vertically with hardly any horizontal travel. It will only do it when pressed by a falcon of similar capabilities, such as the peregrine/saker at $0.69$ g/cm$^2$. Such a falcon will go up with the crow, staying only a meter or two behind. The crow cannot go down,

nor can it go sideways. If it went sideways it would momentarily lose height in relation to the falcon and be immediately attacked. It can only go up. The experienced falcon will keep climbing until it is about a meter above the crow. Then it will turn over and lunge at the crow which will dive and roll to avoid the outstretched feet of the falcon. Both swoop and throw up together and the aerial contest is resumed. The purpose of this little maneuver is to test out the crow; will its nerve break and will it dive for the ground? Has it got the strength to avoid the falcon and the willpower to renew the upward climb? The falcon has a better measure of its prey and resolutely struggles on upwards. This time it climbs higher and higher above the crow. Two meters, three meters, five meters.... The point is reached at which both the crow and the falcon realize that the situation is now untenable. Simultaneously, both dive in a corkscrew stoop. Both are by now several hundred feet up and may even be in cloud. Down they come in the canceleer, the life or death spiral stoop. Below them the falconers are cantering gently, trying to anticipate the outcome, ready to burst into a gallop if needed, willing the falcon to bind. The two dots in free fall suddenly come together. She has him! Everyone yells and waves, the horses mill about, momentarily forgotten. Abruptly, the descent is slowed like a parachute opening. The falcon and her prey float down and drift to the ground like a sycamore seed. The riders converge from different directions, anxious to be there when she lands. On the ground, the crow contests the falcon with hoarse croaking and the falconer slips from his horse and quickly kills it, offering the brain to the breathless falcon. The horses, flanks heaving, jostle and toss their heads, their riders excitedly relive their version of the flight. The falcon, too exhausted to feed, is intent on breaking the neck of the long-dead crow, her face buried in the shiny black feathers, holding on grimly like a ferret and twisting and jerking with her beak. Finally convinced the crow is dead, she eats the brain and sets to plucking the body. The fluffy crow feathers stick to her eyes and she wipes them impatiently on her shoulder. The falconer's horse has set to grazing and it is time for a dram.

Not all flights have such a happy conclusion. The crow, by twisting and rolling in the descent, may manage to make it all the way down without being caught. Both birds then have to lose speed rapidly and they flatten out just above the ground. The crow has been desperately seeking any refuge.

If there is none then he is surely taken; on the ground, in the open with a peregrine/saker above him, his options are severely limited. But he may find a tussock or a sheep, or even a falconer's horse. If the falconers are near enough, they can rouse out the crow by riding up, shouting, and cracking whips. If the cover is small, the falcon can probably rouse out the crow herself, chasing it from sheep to sheep until finally the crow's luck runs out. But if the crow has made it to a plantation, then the flight is over; he is safe for another day. He will sulk in there, regaining his breath, his dignity, and finally his cockiness. The falcon, frustrated, is taken down to the lure, hooded up and rested while another falcon is prepared. Not until the party is well gone and all is quiet does the crow emerge, wiser but unharmed.

A high flight like this may take five to ten minutes. If there is little or no wind and the flight starts in open ground there is a good chance of a high flight without the crow reaching cover. This is achieved by the falconer standing off from the crow by 200 meters or so. The falcon is unhooded and slipped, either when the crow is in the air (in which case timing is critical), or at a crow on the ground. As soon as the falcon starts, the falconer shouts *"Au volée!"* to alert the other members of the Field and to flush the crow so that it can start its climb. Of course it may not climb, but go for some nearby unforeseen escape route or it may try to outmaneuver the falcon. In these cases, in still air, with an experienced falcon, his outlook is bleak. But if he is a strong crow who is not so confident that he thinks he can outface the falcon on the ground (as he could a wild peregrine) or too intimidated because the falcon is too large, he will take to the air, and the falconer will immediately ride underneath to persuade him that he has taken the best option. If, on the other hand, the falconer slips the falcon in such a way that the falcon is above the crow when it reaches it, no high flight will ensue. The crow, dominated from the outset, will easily be overpowered. Thus the game falcon, given to checking at crows when waiting-on, knows that she can easily master them from such a height advantage, they are like moorhens then.

So, to obtain the high flight, the falconer is trying to slip his falcon in such a way that, when they come together, the falcon is below the crow, cutting it off from the ground and forcing it into an aerial contest. If such a contest lasts five minutes and the day is windy, the flight will drift. In a 12

kilometers per hour wind the flight will go a kilometer, in a 12 miles per hour wind, a mile. Without even trying, the crow thus has access to a kilometer or two of downwind ground. If this is completely open, all well and good. But few of us are fortunate enough to have such plain ground and it is more likely that somewhere in this distance, perhaps slightly to the side, is some sanctuary for the crow. The crow will keep his head. He knows his ground intimately. Although too busy avoiding the falcon to have time to look around him, he knows where he is and he calculates his chances. When he sees his moment, he begins his dive for safety, flinging himself about wildly to avoid the last desperate attempt of the falcon. The experienced falcon too is not stupid. She knows his game. She will keep herself between the crow and the cover, shepherding him away and anticipating his moves. When he does make a break for it she will exert all her energy into one final effort, scything down to skim him off the fringe of the trees. And as she bears him down to some safe spot she will hear above the noise of the trees the cries of the Field which have turned from despair to triumph.

In late summer there are days when a breezy day goes quiet toward evening. The falconer keeps back a strong climber and some good land for this time in the hope of setting up a good ringing flight. Each season we get just a few really high classic flights that none of us will ever forget.

On a windy day where there really is no cover, the flight will go on and on. Because of the buffeting wind, the falcon will time and time again beat the crow in the air, only for it to roll away from her in the stoop, making use of its wind-induced agility. Higher and higher they go. The wind up there is perhaps twice as strong as at ground level. They drift faster and faster. Below them the riders are in problems. They have ridden hell for leather, devil take the hindmost. Eyes streaming, watching the clouds, some have already got stuck in ditches or bogs. Now there is a hold-up, an impassable wall, a mad scramble for a hunting gate, jumping into the muddy gateway, wrestling with rusty barbed wire, pulling the horse through (mind the stirrup on the gatelatch), a fumbling for the saddle, swinging on somehow, a shout of "Gate!" to an appearing rider, then bucketing on, feeling for the off stirrup, trying to balance the horse. No time, a big ditch coming, sit down and don't interfere with the horse, he makes it with his front feet but goes down in the back, heaves up, struggles back into his stride, a chance to catch the stirrup, get organized, look for some good going, go on at a hand gallop, eyes in the sky, looking for the contestants. Nothing. A cold clamp. Hold up hard and pull out the field glasses. Trying to make the horse go from a gallop one moment to stockstill the next. Horse! Stop breathing! Please! Small field glasses, fine for searching for crows, but not for following a flight. Oh, for the Zeiss! Still nothing. Let's go on. Go on! Twisting on through the rushes, reading the ground for bogs. Another ditch. Come on Peter, you can make it! Big jump! Damn! The far side is soft. Peter is in to his belly, winded, all four legs stuck fast. I take the reins over his head, covered in peat. Leave him be for a moment to recover himself. He won't panic, he knows what to do. Where is the hawk? Where are the others? Have they seen anything? There comes a chestnut Arab. "Barbro! Where are they?"

"Don't know! I've lost them!"

I take out the lure and swing it a few times. If she's still going, she'll ignore it. If she's broken off and can see me she'll come in. Either way, no harm done. Still nothing. "Here! Keep swinging!"

I roll up the lure and throw it across to Barbro who unravels it and starts to swing it, taking care not to tangle the horse's legs. I switch on the telemetry receiver. The body aerial in my bag strap picks up no signal, the flight has gone on. Peter has got his wind back "Come on old friend! You can do it!" He turns to sniff his shoulder, then throws his head back against the ground, rolling himself on to one side with a massive heave. His offside legs pull clear of the soft ground and he paws out his front legs feeling for traction. I stand back, holding the reins and martingale clear of his flaying leg. He hesitates, rocks himself back upright and then, with a groan, makes a big effort and scrambles to his feet. He is muddy to his saddle flaps, but unharmed. I check him over and slip the reins back. Wiping my hand on my breeches, I'm back in the saddle and we go on, heading for the ridge about half a mile ahead. I take out the walkie talkie on the saddle. "Are you there? Over."

"I can hear you, over." It is David in the hawking van.

"They've gone on over the top. Can you go up by Watty Bell's Cairn and try for a signal. Over."

"I'm on my way, over."

We're making good speed now along a sheep track on firm going. But it's all uphill and there are some free horses coming to challenge us. This is no time for a kicking match. We shout and wave and they frisk about, prancing and dancing, but we press on and make it to a gate. Once through, I unfold a yaggi and try again. Still no signal. Either they have gone on over the ridge downwind, or they are down in some dead ground, in a "slack" as they say here. The rest of the Field are coming. I can hear their hooves on the road. The hawking van comes up. "No signal here. Go on up to Crow Rock and try from there. We'll cut across here on the horses."

We push on, but trotting now on the rough bits. No sense in knocking up the horses. A few minutes either way can't be helped at this juncture. "Signal on that face to your right in line with that patch of bracken, over."

"We'll go and see, over."

We canter on, threading through the boggy bits more circumspectly, heading to the side of the bracken in order to get a cross-bearing. There is a good signal. She's up there somewhere. Spread out and listen for her tailbell. And don't tread on her. "There she is!"

The crow is well dead. Lilah is plucking it contemptuously and the feathers gust away downwind like smoke from a faltering fire. She looks at us, gathered round, flanks heaving, splattered with mud, legs like jelly. She looks at us with the superior gaze of someone who is the sole person in the party who knows the whole story.

When you try for a high flight in a wind, you live dangerously.

## 7.11 Field meets

Whenever two or more falconers hawk together, they need to agree certain ground rules. This will ensure the safety of their hawks, the success of the day's sport, and the longevity of their friendships. Field meets thus vary from an informal mini-meet, to an international meeting lasting several days. The British Falconers' Club International Field Meeting, held every four years, lasts four days and organizes 67 hawking parties over 240,000 acres. To achieve this requires major organization by dedicated local falconers approaching landowners, mapping boundaries, arranging dates and meeting places, which falconers will be coming, with what hawks, dogs, and visitors, inviting honored guests, arranging control of Press coverage, accommodating all participants, arranging evening entertainment, and providing a formal Landowners' Dinner.

NAFA's annual meet usually attracts 350 or more falconers, not to mention visitors and families. Again, all arrangements have to be made, although the hawking grounds have to be sorted out by the individual falconers. This can mean that small groups go off and do their own thing, whereas in Europe the groups are more organized.

If you plan to attend such a meet, then it is up to you to ensure that you have organized yourself properly. All legal details and permits should be attended to well in advance, as well as travel plans and room bookings. Your hawk should be an experienced hunter, not a raw novice, fit, and in good flying order. An accipiter which is liable to be unsettled by the change of scene will need to be on the sharp side of its flying weight, but with enough condition to stay strong despite long days in bad weather. Your gear, from your transmitter mount to your car tool kit, should be clean, checked, and in good order and you should have with you whatever you need to cope with eventualities, including a detailed map of the area.

Most organized field meets have a Field Master who is a senior falconer who knows the ground and is responsible for the whole group's activities for the day. You should report to him and do what you are told. If you follow in convoy, then help the car behind to keep in touch. I remember once in Britain, after hawking, we were a convoy of about 16 cars trying to find our way back to the hotel in the dark. We drove and drove down more and more tortuous country lanes, and ended up all blocked into a dead-end farm track. It turned out the leading car was a young couple trying to find a quiet place for a cuddle, and extremely embarrassed to find a whole convoy of muddy falconers crowding round wondering what was going on up front.

A few simple rules are needed when hawking in groups: keep spectators together and away from the hawks and game. Post markers in blind areas to mark flights. Shout "Hawk free," "Hawk secure" when flying accipiters. Agree who is to slip next. If you slip out of turn and catch someone else's hawk then don't expect much sympathy. If you are hawking in a line then stay in line and keep an eye on everyone else. The object is to go slowly and find game, not to race to the other end. The best treatment for a persistent "racer" is to load him down with dead hares and rabbits to carry.

If there are slow hawks, such as buzzards, present, the easy slips, such as moorhens, will be reserved for them. Field Masters should aim to give every hawk opportunities within their capabilities so that everyone gets a kill or a good flight. When a falcon is waiting-on and the cover is thick, such as a big field of crops, don't leave the falconer and his dog on their own pathetically running round trying to flush game for the tiring falcon, get in there and help him serve her. While some senior visitors and ladies may be permitted to watch "from the gallery" and even be excused for a little "coffee-housing," able-bodied people should do their best to help.

Falconers should declare the state of their hawk beforehand to the Field Master. Tell him if your hawk is poor on feather, good on fur; a bit high, better flown later; flies free but has never taken quarry before, takes other people's hawks off the fist and so on. Similarly, they should declare their dogs. Big field meets are not a place for training or even for birds which are not "spot on." It is infuriating to work hard for a good flush for a bird, only to be told afterward by the falconer that his bird has only ever been flown to the lure before. It is also amazing how many falconers go to field meets without dogs and tag along, expecting you to find all their slips for them. What do they do at home? When you eventually serve their hawk, they muff the flight and then blame it on the dog frightening their bird. One's smile becomes glassy.

A nonhawking member of the field should be allocated to assist each falconer by marking his hawk and accompanying him on long flights, so that if the hawk is lost he can relay back for more help. One soon gets to recognize certain individuals whose birds spend a lot of time Away Without Leave. If they don't return within about quarter of an hour, then carry on hawking, but try to ensure that the next bird slipped is as big or bigger than the missing one. Some Harris hawks are very crabby with strange birds, even on the fist. When faced with bad behavior, the Field Master may send the miscreant home or cross him off the list for subsequent days. He may then be unable to find any party prepared to take him.

Similar escorts should be provided for visiting guests and overseas visitors as a matter of courtesy and hospitality. We always appreciate visitors, and making return visits to them, and this is one of the charms and attractions of big meets. Similar efforts should be made for young and inexperienced participants, so that they feel welcome and not cold-shouldered. Many are too shy or intimidated to approach people, and it is up to everyone to ensure that they are not left out. Otherwise first impressions become last impressions.

Where telemetry is in use all falconers present should check their transmitters to avoid duplication of signals, and receivers should be carried in the field, if not by the falconer, then by an assistant. Losing a hawk on strange ground at a field meet is not good for relations with landowners, and at the very least wastes everyone else's precious hawking time. Transmitters should be switched off when not in use, particularly at the meet site, otherwise a lost hawk is hard to recognize from all the other signals.

If a flight takes the falconer away from his party, it is permissible for him to attempt an immediate reflush of game which the hawk has put in, but not to seek fresh game. He should rejoin the party as soon as possible and not go hawking on his own. Permission from the landowner will have been obtained for that specific group on that specific day. *Under no circumstance should a falconer return later and hawk the ground.* This will arouse the wrath of the landowners and of the local falconers and will jeopardize future hawking in that area.

Field Masters should do their best to avoid random flushes caused by uncontrolled dogs or beaters. Random flushes increase the chances of two hawks being slipped and crabbing and also cause long unsuccessful tail-chases which disrupt the party and delay the hawking. Beaters or people working dogs should say to themselves "If I flush quarry now, what hawk is there in a position to have a good chance of catching it?"

Some quarry such as pheasants, partridges, grouse and quail, will run ahead of the flush when they hear a party approaching. Field Masters should ensure that a falcon is put into the air or a hawk into the trees ahead to hold the quarry down or, if this is not feasible, to work the quarry away from holding cover so that it runs into a flush point rather than thick cover.

Field Masters should warn falconers of prohibited areas or dangers such as hidden roads, electricity lines, deep water, swamps, or other impassable places. There are four main classes of water that interests the falconer: water that is too shallow for quarry to dive into and escape, water that can be waded in or across, water that is clear to swim, and water that is clogged with floating weed, swamp, or ice which will support a hawk on a kill and yet which is impassable to falconer or dog. This last water is the most dangerous. If the kill is out of reach of branches or poles, it may be possible to hold a creance across the area with a weight on it, so that it forms a V. By walking around the pond one can sometimes wind up or snag the hawk or its kill sufficiently to drag it to the bank or to make it lift off with the kill. Alternatively, if an opened previous kill is attached to the middle of a creance, by walking around the pool, it can be dragged to the hawk who may be coaxed to transfer its attention to it and then be slowly dragged ashore.

While clubs in some countries impose a semi-formal bag limit of four per hawk per day, the bag really depends on a variety of circumstances, ranging from prey density and ease of capture, to the experience and fitness of the hawk and to future hawking plans. What is inexcusable is to waste quarry that has been killed; almost all quarry is suitable for consumption by hawks or humans. In European countries, the best of the quarry is normally donated back to the host landowner. If you live in a state where there is a "let lie" clause on some quarry, such as waterfowl, you must ask yourself whether the wastage of game justifies multiple kills.

Falconry is an exercise in cooperation between hawk, man, and dog. Field meets are no place for a competitive spirit; there is no need to give a prize to the person whose hawk caught the most or flew the highest. A good falconer who has served his hawk successfully will stop flying to help those in the party who have been less fortunate.

Since the advent of Harris hawks in falconry we now have the phenomenon of "gang-hawking"—several hawks being flown loose together. Under most circumstances, more than two hawks are not very sporting. First the quarry is too heavily overmatched, secondly the hawk and the falconer lose initiative. The same applies to the use of sight-hunting dogs (gaze-hounds).

## 7.12 Hawking dogs

Over many thousands of years in association with man, dogs have been bred for different tasks. Of the hunting dogs, we have flushing dogs, such as spaniels and terriers, pointing dogs, coursing dogs or gazehounds, and scenting hounds. For sheep and cattle, we have eyedogs, heading dogs and huntaways. For guarding, we have Alsatians and mastiffs. There are also of course companion dogs, fighting dogs, hairless hot-water bottle dogs and edible dogs, of which no more needs be said!

Of the hunting dogs, the gazehounds and scenting hounds were bred to catch and kill the quarry themselves, the flushing dogs were bred to find and flush game for men armed with bows, nets, spears, clubs, slings, or hawks. In recent years guns have been added to the list of weapons and it has become fashionable to refer to the pointing and flushing dogs as "gun" dogs. But do not let the dictates of vile saltpeter blinker your thinking.

My own experience of dog work includes springer, cocker and Brittany spaniels, German short-haired and wire-haired pointers, English pointers, Irish setters, lurchers, greyhounds, and salukis; scenting hounds for hares, foxes, coyotes, and deer, and huntaways, heading and eye dogs for stockwork. Normally we have 2–4 working dogs here at any one time. Through days shared with friends one gets to see other breeds and other handlers working and there is always plenty new to learn in this complex and, by falconers, often neglected subject.

Although a few flights, such as crow hawking, do not require a dog, dog work is important for most types of falconry. Even if you are lucky enough to live in an area so rich in game that you can get slips regularly without a dog, you will not easily be able to serve your hawk " in the retrieve" (ie refind game which she has flown in and flush it for her to kill on the second flight, a common occurrence in pheasant and partridge hawking).

I remember my first springer, "Smokey," whom I trained "by the book." He would drop to flushed game, retrieve from the other sides of rivers—everything. But I soon found that when you're hawking with a goshawk the last thing you concentrate on when a pheasant flushes is the dog—and he knows it. He'll follow the bells to the end of the earth and between him and the goshawk the pheasant will have a hard time. I soon learned that a dog sitting on its backside is not a very useful piece of apparatus and that while we were going through the gundog rule book together, the pheasant would be legging it for the nearest rabbit hole.... So nowadays I expect my dog, on flushing game, to be there with the hawk. On the few occasions when I want a careful flush, such as when flushing a covey of grouse one bird at a time, with

a pointer, I drop the dog verbally or by whistle or eye, and, if the dog is in its first season or two, put on a checkcord for the flush.

You need to be clear in your own mind what your policy is with ground game. When the dog is young you must be able to stop him and this can be linked in with his steadying to sheep, for which we use an electric collar. But it is a mistake to be too firm with a dog on rabbits. How can the dog be expected to divine that moment between legitimately working a rabbit and what you consider to be rioting? One of the critical things in hawking is the timing of the flush. When the dog is on point and you say "Get him up!" you want the dog to go in with conviction and flush immediately, not in fifteen seconds' time. A dog that prissies about instead of flushing cleanly (which it will start to do if you keep checking it) can quickly ruin a young falcon or even cause it to drift away and be lost. Secondly, when hawking rabbits, few flushing dogs can move faster than a hawk. I prefer it if the dog stays hot on the rabbit and keeps it moving. When the hawk catches the rabbit, the dog should lie down beside the hawk and honor her. If the hawk is having trouble with the quarry the dog should quickly kill it by nipping the back end and then leave it for the hawk. The dog shouldn't shake the quarry or disturb the hawk. When the hawk is down on a kill, especially on bird flights which finish some way from the falconer, the dog should stay beside the hawk and guard it from interference by wild predators, especially eagles and buzzards, and, in farming areas, curious cattle. All this requires that the dog should be reared with hawks and be taught to treat them with total respect as an extension of you, the falconer. I have trained springers, wirehairs, and a lurcher in this way, working with goshawks and various falcons. For further details see Frederick II:267.

When using a pointer for grouse, it is often possible to get several flights at the same covey, if the dog continues to hold the point during each flight. However, if you live in a place like Wyoming, which Bob Berry tells me holds many thousands of golden eagles in winter, you may well prefer to train your dog to run and find the falcon and stay guarding her.

Usually, toward the end of its life, a spaniel develops the habit of coming out from the cover and running round the blind side to see if the quarry has flushed yet. This is annoying and should be stopped. Always shout "Ho!" clearly when the quarry flushes and rate the dog if he comes out before the shout. Of course there are times when he has to come out as the quarry may not be in there after all—but then it's up to you to read the situation right. The shout of "Ho!" should be his signal, not the sound of hawk-bells.

The hawking dog's main role is to find game, mark and flush it to order. For waiting-on flights this usually entails a pointer or setter quartering the ground and holding point. If you have enough work to warrant such a specialist dog, an English pointer is hard to beat. If, on the other hand, you expect waiting-on flights for only 3 or 4 weeks and have more varied terrain to cover later in the season, a GWP or GSP is a better all-round choice. Whatever it is, it should get well out, at least 200 meters each side of you, more if the visibility is good. Under good conditions the dog may cover up to 800 meters (about ½ mi.) between turns and so the falconer needs to walk only slowly. If a car is being used, the dog can be allowed to range out further but a telemetry collar is sensible. A dog lost in American sagebrush country runs the risk of coyote and mountain lion traps, quite apart from natural hazards. Under good scenting conditions, the dog may draw scent from birds up to 200 meters upwind, but in calm weather, he may be able to detect the birds from a few meters only. In good conditions then, the dog may take in 200 meters at each sweep and range well out, but in poor conditions he will need to work more closely and carefully for fear of missing or bumping birds. The birds themselves vary in their reactions. On some days they may be very wild and run ahead and flush off before the dog can get near enough for a solid point, on other days they will often flush spontaneously after a minute or two and it is easy to think it is the dog's fault when it isn't; best to put the falcon overhead without delay when the birds are getting wild or cover is sparse.

It is a pity that many falconers tend to train their dogs according to shooting field trials precepts rather than to their own needs in the hawking field. We don't have field trials for hawking dogs, mainly because no two falconers can agree on what their dogs should or should not do. Long may it continue! For my own part I expect a minimum of handling. Once the dog is more than a few meters away from me I use a whistle or hand signals. Nothing frightens game more, or ruins my afternoon so quickly, as someone who roars at his dog for some minor or imagined misdemeanor.

The mark of good dog handling is calmness and unhurriedness and enough relaxation to be able also to concentrate on the hawk, the quarry and on appreciating the scenery. Foresight, preparation, and avoidance will prevent many problems in dog handling together with the clear understanding that one is hawking for ENJOYMENT, not for peak efficiency. I do not expect the dog to work every single scrap of ground, to sit every time I stop for a pee, or to quarter like a metronome. I hawk to escape the rat race, not to create a new one. If your top priority is to kill game you may as well use a heat-seeking missile or a good pesticide.

There are however, a few times in falconry when the dog needs to do the right thing. One of these is when obtaining a good point for a waiting-on falcon, one is when working with an accipiter which is frightened of the dog and one is when working ferrets and the dog must sit quietly. A dog should be trained and prepared methodically beforehand. Never expect to train a dog when you are working a hawk; train the dog first and then work them together.

The kingpin of dog training is the "drop." Over long distances I use one long blast on the whistle; close to, I click my fingers quietly. If you can drop your dog any time, any place, then at least you can "switch it off" and sort out whatever disaster has occurred. Get this one command certain and the rest is just icing. The drop is a positive command, whereas "No" is an open-ended command which leaves the dog in limbo.

A plea here to those with pointers on the moor. Train your dogs to heel and walk on a lead properly. It is no fun for a member of the field (often of the fair sex) to be towed around a hot grouse moor by a headstrong dog while you swan ahead in the distance.

Where there is heavy cover, a general purpose pointer is of more use, particularly if it has a good coat, as has a GWP or a Brittany spaniel. It is better, in my experience, to have one or two dogs that you know well, to do a variety of jobs rather than have several specialists. A wirehair may not be as suitable for grouse hawking as an English pointer, but you can get more solid points over a good wirehair than an overeager English pointer with no brakes.

Often one finds that while the initial point was in the open, such as stubble or a root crop the quarry puts in to such thick cover that a thin-skinned pointer cannot evict it at the "retrieve"

A good dog represents a lot of work, a lot of help and a lot of friendship. This one of our wirehairs "Ratty," grouse hawking at Kinlochewe.

and dances around on the outside. In these circumstances you need a dog with a dense coat and a certain amount of railway train in its breeding.

Dogs soon learn to alter tactics according to the situation and will benefit greatly from the extra experience and from the rapport that you have with it. I don't think it is possible to overemphasize the importance of frequent and regular work for both hawk and dogs. Behind every good performer is a background of solid work.

For very dense cover there is nothing to beat a good English springer. They will go through the brambles like a dose of salts and if they give a couple of barks when the scent gets red-hot, I regard that as no fault; it sets the goshawk up wonderfully. The cocker is good too but he cannot take full days for long and maintain condition. Teams of 6–8 spaniels used to be worked in the woods with a goshawk and such an arrangement has terrific flushing power. Even two or three dogs will confuse and flush game which would give one dog the run around. For really dense cover and holes, a terrier or wirehaired dachshund is useful but they cannot keep up if you have a lot of running, and they are easily unsighted in long cover.

Some recommend using spaniels to flush game for pointers. I think grouse-hawking is tense enough without introducing a spaniel into the focal point. I prefer to flush the grouse myself with a stick, sending it back over the pointer, rather than use a spaniel which can make a pointer as unsteady

through jealousy as it might become through flushing the game itself. With a stick, one can flush the grouse with better timing and better directionality than with a spaniel, particularly if you can read your pointer well. If you hawk rabbits or hares a lot in fairly open country, then a lurcher will improve the quality of the sport. A rough-haired greyhound/collie cross, about 22 inches high, is large enough for both quarries and has plenty of brains. A good lurcher can be taught to point and, when unsighted, can follow by scent at a fairly useful pace. Only one running dog should be slipped with a hawk, otherwise the quarry is overmatched and the hawk risks being injured through jealousy. This type of hawking has a long history in the Middle East, Asia and parts of Europe but has been neglected by many falconers, particularly in America where it has great potential.

To work well, dogs need to be fit, preferably with plenty of roadwork behind a horse, bicycle, or slow car. Our pointers get at least five kilometers at 20 kilometers per hour most days of the year except work days. This keeps their pads hard and their muscles firm. It also extends their working lives, often by two or three seasons, and remember, an extra season at the end of a wise, experienced dog's life, is worth much more than trying to cram in work too early in a young dog's life, through impatience. At home, our dogs are kept "at hack" on the farm, guarding the place and keeping an eye on things. Attempts to wander off rabbiting are controlled by means of supervised exercise coupled with discipline by means of an electric collar and telemetry in extreme cases. If you let a dog wander off down the woods rabbiting and then creep up on him with an electric shock and a roar, it's amazing what a psychological effect it has. For the rest of his life the dog believes you have God-like powers. Of course, there will be times when the dogs must be confined in soundly made pens. But these, like stables for horses and blocks for tethering falcons, are necessary evils for the benefit and convenience of the owner. No animal is improved by being confined for long periods. When you are working with a lot of animals, ones which need to be able to "read" you and you to "read" them, at a subliminal level, one of the hardest things is to maximize contact time, just being together.

When choosing a dog, first see plenty of specimens of the breed actually working and also check on similar breeds which may have more potential.

Then see one or preferably both parents working, with particular attention to physical conformation and well-being, intelligence, drive, and nose. Do not bother too much about the parent's training—this is nonhereditary! Having bred several litters of pups myself and followed their progress, some to be champions, some to be straight workers, I know that most, if not all, have the potential to be champions, but it depends whose hands they fall into. The ones with that extra, are often the least likely to shine in field trials.

Also for slow developers, such as the wirehairs and those breeds required for multipurpose work, it is essential to build a firm foundation of discipline and fieldwork. Few are ready for serious work before three years old and should certainly be kept steady until about four years old. Never, at your peril, put a wirehair loose in a car, always use a dog box. A wirehair can remove the seats, side panels, roof lining, trim, sun visors, and all handles in fifteen minutes. Or less.

I had a cocker spaniel called "Sue" in New Zealand whom I used for hawking California quail. The quail, on putting in, would flutter up inside the "Bush Lawyers" a particularly nasty type of three dimensional crucifix. Sue would struggle to climb up after them in the thorns. Once she climbed about 25 feet up a Macrocarpa tree after a possum. But, with her short legs she'd get tired on long days, and I taught her to jump against the side of the horse so that I could pull her up to travel home in front of the saddle. Like many spaniels, Sue was virtually impervious to punishment (I'd received her as an old dog) and I never succeeded in devising a treatment which had any effect on her, short of causing actual bodily harm.

Nothing cements the bond of companionship more than the hunt, and one's dog is the ultimate companion, always eager when you reach for the hawking bag, always cheerful when you're low, never asking questions. Many a man who treats his dog sternly in public is soft as fudge when they're alone. A certain president of the Irish Hawking Club had one of our pups, and I remember hearing his voice change when he thought nobody was listening. Yes, a hawking dog is something special.

Young male goshawk.

# 8 Raptors and

Figure 8.2.1 This is Old Aralditey. Hacked back in 1984 at a ruined castle, she bred next season.

# Man

## 8.1 The international contribution of falconers to raptor conservation and welfare

Man's first personal contact with raptors came through falconry and religion sometime in prehistory. In some countries, raptors were worshipped as gods, such as Horus in Egypt; in others they were esteemed, more prosaically, as hunting companions. Falconry probably originated in Asia, reaching Japan by 247 A.D. and Europe and North Africa by the fourth century. Although North and South American Indians revered raptors, falconry itself was introduced there by Europeans.

Falconers have traditionally conserved raptors in the wild as a sustainable source of hunting birds. In 501, in Burgundy anyone stealing a hawk was heavily fined, or if unable to pay, six ounces of flesh was cut from his breast and fed to the bird. In Britain, during Henry III's reign, anyone stealing a hawk from a nest was imprisoned for a year and a day. If he stole another person's hawk, he was executed. It was common in Britain to turn hawks free at the end of the season. Merlins were released in late autumn in the same way that sakers and peregrines are still released now in the Middle East. Goshawks were often turned out into a local wood to nest, to supply young for the next season.

Falconry became deeply entwined in the cultures of nations, and people wanted to learn more about the birds. Frederick II's 1250 *The Art of Hunting with Birds* examined all aspects of raptor biology and on some topics is still unrivalled today. In 1379, Henri de Ferrières wrote in a French manuscript: "He who wishes to learn falconry must possess three qualities: he must be very fond of birds, must be interested in them, and be good and kind to them."

So falconry, right from the start, grew up with the basic premise that wildlife is a renewable resource, sustainable indefinitely if managed carefully. Surprisingly, even as I write now, in the mid-1990s, there are still many people and organizations who cannot or will not grasp this funda-

mental fact. This is what lies at the root of many of today's wildlife problems.

As firearms become widespread, people could kill animals more quickly and easily and falconry fell from favor. This is the way with technology. Children now play war games on their computers without even leaving their rooms. Wildlife was given a human morality. There were the good guys—game animals, and the bad guys—vermin and pests. The former were preserved for hunting, and the vermin were eliminated. Gradually the big mammalian predators were exterminated in areas populated by humans. Raptors, without a role in falconry, were now seen as competitors for game and therefore vermin. Massive campaigns in Europe (documented by M. Bijleveld) eradicated whole populations, and migrating raptors were shot for sport, as they still are in Malta. The Victorian era was a century of shame for raptors in Britain, with systematic slaughter from gamekeepers and greedy exploitation from egg collectors. Fortunately for raptors, the two World Wars put an end to the "golden era" of game shooting. With the reduction of income from the British Empire, the big estates went into recession, and most of the keepers went to the Front, never to return. Raptor populations had a respite and a recovery. But for some it was too late: the goshawk had been exterminated, as had the white-tailed sea-eagle and osprey. The red kite had just a few pairs left in Wales, and the common buzzard and golden eagle hung on in places with few gamekeepers. Similar scenes occurred in Europe, and in North America, where it is even now legally easier to obtain a gun than a hawk, people were still busy winning the West and shooting every raptor they saw on sight.

After the Second World War many farmers returned to the land, and chemicals were seen as a way of improving productivity by winning the struggle against those pests. DDT was the wonder chemical, to be used on crops, in orchards, on livestock and around the home. The sad impact on raptors was unraveled by Derek Ratcliffe in Britain, followed by a spate of further investigations throughout the world. Whole ecosystems were poisoned and even on remote places like the Auckland Islands, 1000 kilometers south of New Zealand toward Antarctica, the New Zealand falcons were contaminated through feeding on fish-eating petrels.

The Americans, always ready to do everything bigger and better than everyone else, almost wiped out their peregrines completely before discovering the folly of pesticides. In Germany and Poland, the tree-nesting populations of peregrines were exterminated. Raptors were in big trouble and, as biological indicators, became the flagship species for clean-up campaigns. Suddenly, they were endangered national heritages. Anything which might threaten them was stamped on hard, and falconers overnight became "bad guys."

A few simple facts were overlooked. Falconers have never, in any country at any period in human history, endangered any population of raptors or any other species. The same cannot be said for agriculture, pesticides, shooters, or domestic cats, all of which have exterminated species completely. Wherever falconry has become popular, falconers have organized systems of selfcontrol either in law or through codes of conduct, recognizing their dependency on sustainable use. And falconers, with their millennia of experience of hands-on contact with raptors have pioneered their welfare and breeding in the wild and in captivity. Finally, falconers are sitting targets for new-found protectionists. The falconer does not want to kill raptors; he tends his few birds alive and thus is easily detected and targeted. The shooter who kills or poisons raptors is almost undetectable, as is the farmer using pesticides. We have had gamekeepers in Wales who, on their own admission, kill over a hundred raptors a year. Nothing comes to court. The effort by protectionists fell disproportionately on falconers as "soft" targets, rather than on those who made a significant impact. In the U.S.A., where raptors are heavily regulated for falconry, they are still frequently shot illegally and few North American Falconry Association field meets go by without one of the falconers' birds being shot at by casual shooters.

Although falconers were prosecuted for keeping hawks, to my knowledge, no chemical companies in Britain or Europe were ever prosecuted for poisoning them. Indeed, pressure from large companies resulted, not in the chemicals being outlawed but in a voluntary ban, a gentlemen's agreement. This enabled them to continue exporting these chemicals to Third World countries which, despite knowing their ecological impact, had become dependent on them.

In Britain, sufficient peregrines survived in nonagricultural areas to make a slow unaided recovery. But in North America and parts of Europe, they were virtually extirpated. Other bird-eating raptors were similarly affected. What was to be done? In North America, Britain and West Germany, some of the prominent falconers pooled their resources and placed their own peregrines into joint breeding programs. On both sides of the Atlantic major milestone successes were made in breeding raptors in captivity. As the feasibility and potential were realized, public funds were raised and some of the projects became formalized. In the U.S.A., The Peregrine Fund was set-up under the astute leadership of a falconer-biologist, Prof. Tom Cade, heading a team of a new breed of applied biologists pioneering breeding techniques, undertaking field research, and then reintroducing young peregrines back into their former haunts.

In Canada, Richard Fyfe's team at Edmonton and David Bird in Montreal set up programs, while in Europe, the Deutscher Falkenorden under Prof. Christian Saar and Dr. Trommer set up their breed and release scheme for peregrines. The British Falconers' Club meanwhile concentrated on the goshawk and reintroduced it back to Britain in a quiet success which has restored it once more as an integral part of the British fauna.

Falconers have always been determined individualists, and when they applied themselves to restoring raptors a whole night sky of individual stars started to twinkle around the globe. Experienced old-timers like John and Frank Craighead and Fran and Frederick Hamerstrom set a powerful example of what could be achieved when the practical skills of falconry were linked to the discipline of the biological sciences. This inspired further generations of up and coming falconer-biologists, myself amongst them. Gradually they became more organized, and the Raptor Research Foundation was formed in North America, and the Hawk and Owl Trust in U.K.

Nowadays, there are raptor biologists working all over the globe. Wherever there is hands-on work to be done you will find that the biologist either has a falconry background, or is using techniques developed by someone else who has. It is all very well shouting about the plight of raptors, but when it comes actually to doing something about it, then falconry, through the dedication of hundreds of individuals, has made the international contribution which has turned the tide.

In honor of the achievements of falconers to raptor conservation we have established a database as a record for future generations. This list of contributions is given in Appendix 1, and I welcome hearing of further contributions as the list is far from complete.

Falconers learned from all this. With the increasing human pressure and modern technology it is obvious that few species of wildlife will ever again be secure. Any international event could wipe out a species very quickly. The future of falconry as a field sport would be jeopardized if it relied totally on the sustainability of wild populations. Activated by the alarm of pesticides, they set up breeding projects to become selfsufficient in falconry birds, and in Britain, Germany, and North America they achieved this aim in a few short years. This is documented in detail in 8.5.

Falconry continues all over the world, bringing with it a back-to-basics missing from the crazed modern urban lifestyle. In North America, there is a large number of regional clubs all under the umbrella of NAFA, the North American Falconers' Association. Founded in 1961, it now has a number of "senior statesmen" and this growing maturity shines through in their publications such as *A Bond with the Wild*. In Mexico, falconry is popular although, with a few exceptions, the standard is not high. In South America, there are numerous small groups of falconers scattered in different places. In Britain, there are at present about 8,500 people keeping diurnal raptors in a plethora of clubs which are jointly represented by the Hawk Board. The main club, the British Falconers' Club, traces its origins back through the Old Hawking Club to the heydays of falconry, and this history is admirably documented in Roger Upton's two books.

In Europe, there are clubs in Ireland, Britain, Denmark, France, Belgium, Holland, Germany, Switzerland, Austria, Italy, Spain, Portugal, Hungary, Czechoslovakia, Poland, and across to Russia, Georgia, Kazakhstan, and central Asia. There are also clubs flourishing in Japan, India, Tunisia, Zimbabwe, and South Africa. In the Middle Eastern countries there are no clubs as such because falconry is still an integral part of society in most of the Arabian countries. In many other countries there are small clubs and groups of individuals, some relatively new, and some who have hawked for many generations.

Most of these clubs are represented internationally by the IAF, the International Association of Falconry. Founded originally by Jack Mavrogordato, its current President is Mr. Christian de Coune in Belgium. The IAF fights for falconry on international issues, promotes the international Code of Conduct and helps maintain contacts between the clubs to the benefit of the sport and of the birds themselves.

## 8.2   The ethics of rehabilitation

There are three elements we have to consider in rehabilitation: the individual bird itself, the state of its wild population, and the situation of the person giving aid.

Surprisingly, little effort is made by welfare societies to *prevent* the main causes of wildlife casualties, thus reducing the need for rehabilitation. Changes in the design of roads, cars, electricity poles and wires, and the lay-out of windows, and the control of cats (see 8.8), would do far more for wildlife than all the rehabilitation programs. Although a proportion of animals come in for treatment as a result of starvation in the autumn, the majority of animals needing treatment appear to result from man-made causes, rather than from natural selection. Even as I write this, one of my best gyr/peregrines has just broken his wing on a wire while chasing a crow, and his sister last year was killed by a wind generator while chasing a crow. Possibly the main use of rehabilitation is simply to document and amass data on wildlife injuries with a view to preventing them, along the lines of the pioneer work on electricity pole design by Morlan Nelson.

When a bird comes into human hands it may be in the form of an egg, or as a chick, or as an older bird which has been through legal procedures and is now ready for return to the wild. All of this group have originated in the wild and are potentially physically and mentally healthy, but are naive about survival in the wild. From the legal point of view they belong in the wild, not in captivity, even if this requirement over-rules biological considerations. Some of these may have been hand reared and imprinted on man (see 4.7) rendering them unsuitable for release.

The second group of birds includes those

which come into human hands because, although they are physically uninjured, they have been unable to survive in the wild. These are mainly starving young birds in the autumn and winter which are part of natural attrition and selection. They are the failed surplus population which has been lucky enough to be found before actually dying. It is possible to fatten them up, get them fit again, and give them a second chance in the spring.

The third group is those which have been physically injured, often through man-made hazards, but which, with proper care, could potentially make a full recovery and return to an independent life in the wild.

The fourth group includes the injured ones which will obviously never be able to return to the wild but which could still live in captivity with a reasonable quality of life. Such a life would need to be moderately low in stress, and might include a "useful" element such as breeding or educational purposes which could justify the cost of keeping it. This group includes psychologically damaged birds (malimprints) as well as physically injured ones. Unfortunately, many of these crippled birds are still kept alive with no real quality of life because the rehabilitator does not want to face the issue.

The fifth group are the injured which will not recover sufficiently to join the previous group. These have poor prospects. Even badly injured birds can contribute in that they provide veterinary information and experience on wild birds. This may give insights into disease aspects of the wild populations and may enable treatments to be developed which help other birds in the future.

So the first step is to assess the bird carefully and assign it to one of these groups. This may require the services of a vet and in many cases will only gradually emerge as the success of treatment becomes apparent. In the case of "attacking" species (see 1.18 and chapter 6) it is essential that they achieve full function and fitness (see chapter 5) before return to the wild.

So far, so good. But now we have to consider this bird as it relates to its wild population. The bird is two things: it is an individual animal with resource needs, and it is a parcel of genes which will survive only if passed on to another generation before the bird dies. The wild population too is a quantity of individual animals with collective resource requirements. The individuals need a prey base, hunting areas, nest sites and territories,

and so on. The resources available to the wild population are finite and limit the size of the population. Every year a healthy population outstrips its resources and is cut back to its original size when the resources become tighter during the winter. A healthy population is controlled by *mortality,* not by *productivity.* Thus, if a population is healthy, adding further individuals to it will not improve its health, or its numbers; it will only add to its mortality. Either the added individuals will die, or they will compete with others who will die instead. The only way to increase a healthy population is to increase its resources by increasing the carrying capacity of the habitat in one way or another.

Therefore, before releasing a bird into a wild population, one must know whether or not the population is already at the limit of its resources. We will examine simple population dynamics in 8.3. and criteria for reintroductions in 8.6. There are examples of productivity-limited populations below carrying capacity, such as the red kite and the sea-eagle in Britain, but they are not common.

The wild population is also a gene pool which includes a variety of genes (see 2.3 and 8.6). In the case of a common, widespread species in genetic contact with neighboring populations, such as the common kestrel in Europe, there is a wide variety of genes in the pool and thus a high degree of unrelatedness. On the other hand, if the population has been reduced in numbers, such as with the Californian condor and the Mauritius kestrel, the variety of genes is also reduced. In a case like this, imagine there are ten original birds left in the wild and that the genes are evenly spread between them (unlikely, but bear with me). Each of these ten carries 10 percent of the quantitative responsibility for the population and also 10 percent of the genetic responsibility. Along comes a conservationist and traps two of the birds (20 percent of the genetic responsibility) and breeds 90 young ones. Meanwhile none of the birds die (you can tell this is a model and not real life!). We now have a population of 100 birds. In quantitative terms the population is now ten times better off. In genetic terms it cannot be better off, in so far that, although the existing genes and their alleles can recombine into different variations, no new genes are created (for practical purposes). But are the birds genetically equally responsible? No. Eight birds carry 80 percent of the genetic responsibility and 92 birds carry 20 percent of the genetic responsibility. The population is now genetically unbalanced. Can you see where we're going? What if one of the first eight birds fell ill? It would be important to save it and get some genes out of it and into further individuals. Thus by keeping it alive you have not actually "saved" it. Only once the genes have been transferred to others is it saved and, bearing in mind that it only gives a random 50 percent of its genes to each offspring then, if it only has one chick you have only genetically saved half of it (see 2.3). It would need to have at least five young ones in order to save about 97 percent of the genes.

All of this applies to any genetically isolated population. It might be the last few birds in the whole world, or it may be an isolated population like the Welsh red kite which had become inbred but which is now getting a genetic shot in the arm from European gene pools. It also applies to genetically isolated captive populations.

Thus rehabilitation to the wild of individual birds may have a negative or a positive effect on the wild population both in terms of competition for resources, and in terms of genes. You can assess for yourself when the impact is likely to be negative and when it is likely to be positive. It is quite clear that for the vast majority of species which are already numerically common and genetically varied, the effect on the wild population is deleterious. This is all quite apart from the risk of introducing disease into the wild population. Thus, most of the releases are futile.

This can be a bitter pill to swallow. The law, which is based on only a primitive understanding and application of population dynamics, assumes that the more birds go back to the wild the better. The law is geared to prevent uncontrolled taking from the wild and automatically assumes that, if a bird has come from the wild, the best thing to do is put it back there. In this it is often wrong.

We are gradually moving away from the protectionist viewpoint toward a conservationist viewpoint. This means that populations must be managed both quantitatively and genetically on a sustainable basis. There is a better understanding of how habitat limits populations and that healthy populations produce excess young for their habitat, a surplus which is harvestable on a sustainable basis if the species has some value as a resource to man. Many of the common raptors fall into this classification, as do game birds and mammals, trees and so on. The problem with pest species takes us one step further; with these, man has first

to kill off all the annual harvestable surplus and then get stuck into the breeding population before he can hope to reduce the population below the carrying capacity of the habitat. Thus with pests, it is a never-ending battle to suppress populations and a good insight into the effect of selfregulating mechanisms of populations. Unfortunately, because raptors were hit so badly by pesticides, they became subjects of a massive media campaign which gradually changed public attitudes, and which resulted in overlegislation. Everyone viewed raptors as endangered and rare. Now that many populations have recovered, people have difficulty in readjusting their attitudes and in targeting their conservation effort into aspects giving genuine benefit.

So finally we come back to people. Most people rehabilitating raptors are private individuals or small groups. Most big organizations do not do it because it is of little conservation benefit, which is their main criterion. Others do it by obtaining funding from nonspecialist sources who believe that it does have conservation benefit or who wish to be associated with what they see as the moral high ground. The global economic recession and the increasing raptor numbers are gradually reducing this support. Meanwhile, the public expect to be able to bring these casualties to someone, somewhere, who will care for them.

In Britain, thousands of orphaned or injured raptors and owls each year are tended by hawkkeepers who actually have to pay to register many of the species. In 1990, the 230 Licensed Rehabilitation Keepers in U.K. tended 1230 raptors of which 580 (47 percent) were released back to the wild. Many of these had been referred to them by the Royal Society for the Protection of Birds or the Royal Society for the Prevention of Cruelty to Animals. Some have to be euthanased, some are nursed back to health and are returned to the wild, and some live to old age in retirement aviaries, some even becoming parents. Unfortunately, many of these birds are kept alive in unsuitable conditions by people who mean well, when euthanAsia would have been more appropriate. There are over 2,000 permanently disabled diurnal raptors in Britain. It is not necessary to be an LRK to rehabilitate raptors and we estimate that a further 1500 are treated each year by ordinary falconers. I normally receive about 3–6 birds per year from the RSPCA or the police and we are not a public center, or an LRK.

Most people rehabilitate animals for humanitarian reasons. They might just as quickly come to the aid of a little old lady who fell down in the street. This is genuine altruism which commands respect. It is all very well to look at cold scientific reasoning, as I have done above, or to comply with laws which are often nonsensical. It is something else to go out of your way to help a fellow creature in need. People often denigrate rehabilitators on the grounds that it is a waste of time. Critics fail to appreciate that, while *they* may consider it to be a waste of time, others obviously don't. It depends by what criteria you run your life. Rehabilitation work evidently gives some people a sense of satisfaction and achievement, and this in itself is worthwhile. The hypocrisy I would point out is the different morality expressed toward old or injured humans compared to the other life forms. With humans the prevailing morality seems to be "keep them alive at all costs" (although many old people would not agree), with other species it seems to be "if it has no breeding future, kill it." My own personal view is that first; decisions have to take into account the resources available, and second, if a human or any other animal is terminally ill, *and does not want to carry on*, we should try to allow it to die painlessly and with dignity. With terminally ill animals, we obviously cannot ask them, we can only do our best to assess the situation and reach a decision based on the animal's needs, rather than our own sentiments.

The humanitarian reaction springs from the heart rather than from the mind, and often the resource implications are neglected. To look after injured animals takes time, skill, facilities, and funds. If these are overlooked, animals will suffer. These aspects must be considered and be properly attended to, and some rehabilitation organizations have codes of conduct and support systems for this. Also there is a great deal of difference in commitment between *rescuing* an animal, often with attendant media publicity, and *rehabilitation* which may tie up resources for months. Often it takes one organization to rescue, another to rehabilitate and a third to assess habitat and supervise the return to the wild.

Often rehabilitation is used as a justification for hands-on contact with wild animals. There should be no need for this justification because there is no reason why many wild animals should not be kept as pets. This is a perfectly valid and sound recreational use of a resource, provided that welfare issues are attended to. There is a growing attitude amongst hard-line protectionists that the only justification for hands-on contact with wild animals should be for the conservation benefit of wild populations. I disagree with this approach, and I cringe at some of the misunderstandings which arise as a result of it. Much of my understanding of wild animals comes, not from science, but from being myself brought up in constant contact with animals. My approach to them is not anthropomorphic, but it is not strictly scientific either, because science is an inadequate tool.

I don't want to go into the finer details of assessing habitat, preparations for and release into the wild and postrelease monitoring. Most of the raptor handling techniques have already been covered in detail in this book. Having myself surveyed habitat and monitored its use by wild Mauritius kestrels in detail, I believe that a human can reach only a very gross assessment of habitat. Prey *availability* (and I mean that in its full technical sense), is a very hard parameter to predict, bearing in mind that it is dependent on the hunting skills of the release candidate. For all practical purposes it is a question of trying it and seeing what happens. I used to spend days trailing around west Wales looking for a place with no resident peregrines. As soon as I put my release bird on the wing a resident falcon would show up. My own assessment was futile; the birds told me the answer.

When one investigates rehabilitation, one of the first things to become apparent is the lack of data on "success," whether measured in terms of survival of released individuals, or as positive impact on wild populations or some other way, such as the effect on the person doing it. These parameters are very difficult to assess to a scientific level of satisfaction. The result is a lot of claims and counterclaims, all of which are inconclusive. Only when you have analyzed all the *real* reasons for rehabilitation can the real criteria for success be evaluated.

Isn't there a paradox that a falconer might spend all afternoon trying to catch a prey animal with his hawk and then all evening tending to some poor injured bird? Or that he might go out to kill a rabbit in order to feed the injured bird? Life is seldom straightforward. I think if you are fundamentally against killing, you must stay well away from the world of animals because it is a mayhem of births and deaths with no individual justice. Best to hide your head in the sand and pretend that by eating plants you are not competing with other life forms for resources.

## 8.3 The effects of falconry on wild raptor populations

In most countries where falconry is practiced, falconers are "consumers" of hawks. Britain and Germany are exceptions in that they are now probably selfsustaining in domestic raptors. Most other countries rely on taking a "harvest" of hawks from the wild each year. Many of these birds are returned to the wild the following spring. Within limits, the yield is sustainable long term and this can be demonstrated both on a scientific basis and on a historical basis. To understand why this is so requires a brief excursion into population biology.

Using Ian Newton's excellent data in his monograph on the sparrowhawk as an example, we can visualize the survival of sparrowhawks as in figure 8.3.1. Of a sample of a hundred juveniles, only about 40 percent survive after their first year. This is because many fail to become skilled independent hunters in their first few weeks of life and die. After their first year the hawks do better; about 68 percent survive each year. Only the occasional individual survives more than nine years.

Put this cohort together with successive years and we get figure 8.3.2. You can see that each year

the population, on average, is made up of diminishing proportions of successive age groups. Of these groups, those between the numbers 25 and 75 on the vertical axis are the most effective breeders. One way or another, only about half the adults produce the year's crop of youngsters. By the third year, only about 26 of the original hundred are left alive to breed. In other words, it takes about four juveniles to fledge to produce one breeding adult. So if a falconer comes along and traps an adult, he is having about the same impact as if he had trapped four juveniles. This is why conscientious falconers restrict themselves to trapping passage birds (juveniles in their first autumn). In terms of minimizing the impact of a harvest, the earlier in the life cycle the birds are taken, the less effect it has.

Now let's throw a few more variables into the basic model. Imagine what the figure would look like for a peregrine, or for an eagle. The eagle has a longer immature period, a longer adult life, a lower productivity rate and a lower mortality rate. Some of the eagles might still be alive after forty years and the whole figure would stretch across four pages of this book.

When we look at productivity, many different factors can affect how many young are produced. For example, there may not be enough nest sites available for all the adults to breed. They are

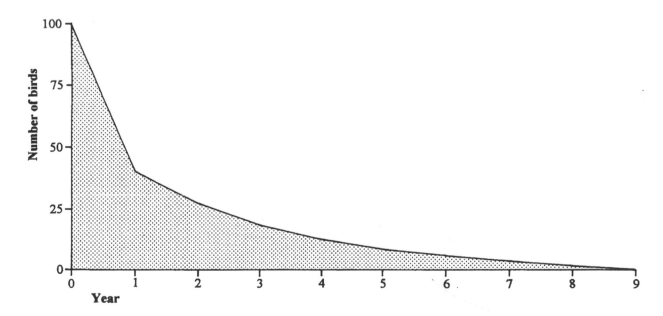

Figure 8.3.1 The average survival for a cohort of a hundred juvenile European sparrowhawks.

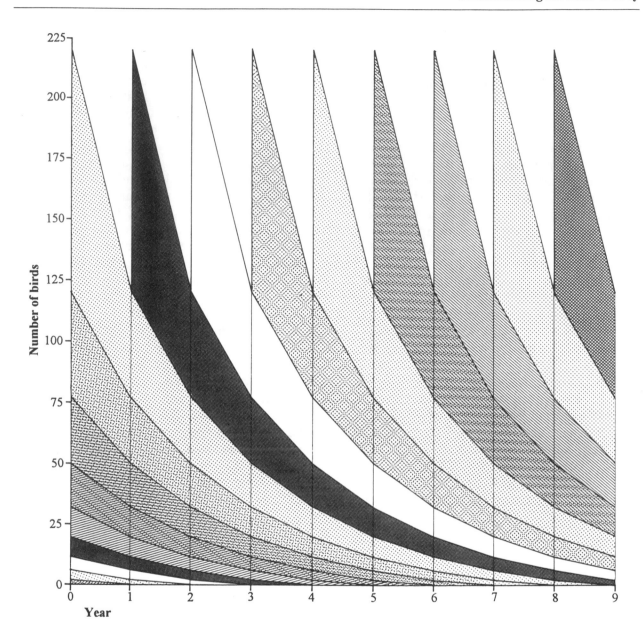

Figure 8.3.2 The age structure of a population of European sparrowhawks.

forced to play musical chairs. Peregrines in Britain, kestrels in Holland and Wisconsin, sakers on the plains of Asia; many populations are restricted by availability of nest sites. When artificial nest sites were provided, the populations increased to new levels. When nest sites are in short supply, only a proportion of the available adults can breed. If one of the nesting adults is killed, its place may be taken by a newcomer within hours. There have even been cases in which both parents have been shot and the young ones have ended up being reared by replacement parents. This is a sure indication that nest sites are limiting and that surplus adults are present which are unable to breed through lack of a nesting territory. Another indication is to look at a map of all the nests (figure 8.3.3). A nice even distribution indicates that breeders have spaced themselves out away from their neighbors. A clumpy and irregular distribution tends to point to a shortage of nest sites, or of birds. Falcons often show this distribution, whereas species which build their own nests are able to take a more constructive approach to the problem and make a nest where it suits them.

Prey is a common limiting factor. In early spring, if the male cannot provide enough food, the

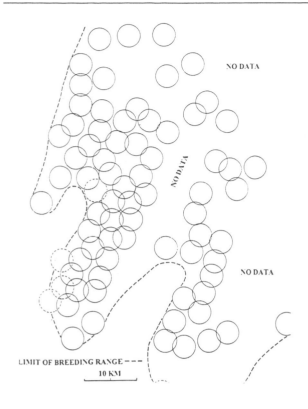

NO DATA

NO DATA

NO DATA

LIMIT OF BREEDING RANGE - - -
10 KM

Figure 8.3.3 Evenly spaced pairs of New Zealand falcons.

female may not lay. If she does, she may rear less young. And the young themselves will have difficulty surviving and more will die off. The hawks themselves have to compete for the available prey. Imagine hacking out extra birds into this situation. Even more would die. Conversely, removing some of the young may actually increase the number of survivors. Thus, what we might subjectively perceive as "good" (hacking out extra birds) or "bad" (trapping up surplus birds), may objectively be the opposite of what was expected. Prey availability thus affects both productivity and mortality. Prey availability is not the same as prey density, although it may depend on it.

Although raptors can locally affect prey numbers (goshawks can wreak havoc on concentrated pheasant areas), by and large it is the prey numbers which control the raptor numbers. This is most obvious with raptors which specialize on mammals, such as voles and susliks, which cannot travel far. Once the voles have eaten all the local food, their numbers crash. The vegetation regrows, and the mammals slowly increase again. Thus there are cyclical "vole years" and the population graph is like saw-teeth. The predators which rely

on these voles tend also to be cyclical, following the prey cycle. It is a different matter for avian prey. If food gets short, they can fly somewhere else. The hawks too can fly somewhere else. This is why after a vole or hare crash in the Arctic, numbers of goshawks, gyrfalcons, and owls head south. These raptors are surplus and most are doomed. Removing them from the wild population will have minimal effects on future numbers.

When you consider that birds have been taken from the wild for falconry for thousands of years, coupled with the fact that falconry has never contributed to the extinction or near extinction of any raptor or its prey, it seems extraordinary how unbalanced the pressure has been on falconry by protectionists, compared to the pressure on the major factors in the fluctuations of raptor populations. Shooting by game preservers, for example, has exterminated raptors in some countries, and yet it is allowed in all the countries where falconry is banned. The use of pesticides known to affect raptors is permitted in most countries where falconry is banned. One has to look further for the real reasons behind the differing attitudes to the use of raptors as a resource, and we will do that in some of the following sections.

## 8.4    The ethics of hybrids

First of all what is a hybrid? A hybrid is a cross between different species. It is not a standard commodity. Some hybrids are very outcrossed, such as crosses between separate genera, for example redtail X Harris, or Cooper's hawk X Harris. Some of these species and genera have completely different chromosome complements, and their hybrids are probably infertile. The genus *Falco,* as we know it today, has in the past been split into separate genera or subgenera such as the peregrine group *(Rhyncodon)* and the great or desert falcons *(Hierofalco).* Hybrids between these subgenera are more outcrossed and usually less productive than hybrids within each subgenus. Thus a saker X peregrine is more outcrossed than say, a saker X gyr or a shaheen X peregrine. Research is still continuing on the relationships within the gyr/saker complex, and it is likely that genetically they are a single "superspecies." They are fully fertile over several generations. It is thus debatable whether or not these could be termed hybrids at all.

Are hybrids likely to interbreed with wild raptors and thus alter their genetic structure? Again, there is no blanket answer. There are two aspects : *could* they breed (are they sufficiently genetically compatible) and *would* they pair up (would they recognize a wild raptor as a potential mate)? For example, the only large falcon in Britain is the peregrine. A shaheen/peregrine hybrid might breed normally with a wild peregrine, but a peregrine X desert falcon hybrid paired to a peregrine (in captivity at least) shows a reduced hatchability. A desert falcon X desert falcon hybrid, such as a gyr/saker, would be no more likely to breed with a peregrine in Britain than would a pure desert falcon such as a gyr, saker, or lanner. Lanners have been flown and lost in falconry in Britain since the Middle Ages without a single report even of a pairing with peregrines. The reasons why individual birds pair or fail to pair have already been discussed in 2.6 and 4.11 and there is growing evidence from falcons, and from some nonraptorial species, that imprinting on the parents critically affects future mate selection. Thus, for example, a saker reared by a peregrine may be more likely to pair up with a wild peregrine than would a peregrine reared by a saker. Even here there is a natural block because, although the saker might try to pair with a wild peregrine, the wild peregrine would repel its advances, recognizing it as an alien species. The implication for managing hybrid raptors is either to imprint them on man, or on a species which is not found in the wild in the country where the bird will be flown. Precocial and social species, such as ducks, have different systems of imprinting and mate selection and we cannot make valid comparisons between them and solitary, altricial raptors.

The only example in Britain in which there is a serious risk of crossing is not a hybrid at all but red-tail X common buzzard. Even here there has been no known successful interbreeding in the wild. But in the event that that happened on a sufficient scale to warrant concern, we would have to sterilize or malimprint the red-tails, but there would be no need to stop flying other exotics, such as Harrises.

Basically the problem is not one of hybrids, as such, but one of genetic pollution of a wild gene pool. This is happening all over the world and with increased movements of plants and animals is likely to continue. In Britain for example, the domestic cat has polluted the Scottish wild cat, the ferret has polluted the polecat, and examples among the ducks and pigeons are rife. To argue

that wild gene pools must remain pristine is nice, but it implies also the habitat for that population also remains pristine so that the two remain well adapted in evolutionary terms. This is not so easy. Most of the species are living in very different and fast-changing habitats to those in which they originally evolved. Those which can adapt in the space of a few generations have a chance to survive. The specialists go. In replacing the *anatum* peregrine in North America, The Peregrine Fund released several races of peregrine, on the principle that natural selection would gradually choose the best-adapted birds for modern conditions.

Curiously, our attitude to this problem is very dichotomous. With plants and animals other than man, the moral high ground is to maintain original gene pools. On the other hand, with the human races, the morality is against discrimination and pro introductions of nonindigenous genetic races. Morality is a wonderful thing.

The wild gene pool is seldom what one thinks it is. Studies by Dr. Wink and others have shown that the falcon species share most of their genetic material, just as man has about 95 percent of his genetic material in common with the other apes. Our whole concept of species is changing, and taxonomic edifices are tumbling. So it is foolish to jump to conclusions. But as a rough and ready guideline the most likely individuals to interbreed with a wild population are subspecies or very close relatives, nonindigenous to the area, for example, Peales peregrines, shaheens or barbaries flown in central U.S.A. or Europe. In the Middle East, where gyr/saker hybrids are flown, the National Avian Research Center in Abu Dhabi has formed a Middle East Falcon Research Group which includes all the falcon veterinarians. One of the aims is to assess genetic pollution and to develop the best techniques for sterilizing hybrids or birds likely to pollute wild stock.

Genetic pollution is not necessarily a bad thing, in fact the very term is a misnomer. The introduction of a few genes from a related gene pool can inject some vigor into ailing or maladapted populations. The red kite in Wales, which has now been studied genetically by Dr. David Parkin's team, probably received genes from a stray German red kite several generations back, which seems to have given the population a much needed kick in the genetic pants. Some of these local populations which have recently become genetically isolated from the main population may benefit from a flow of genes to prevent them becoming inbred.

If lost, could hybrids survive in the wild? Certainly the hybrids between gyrs, sakers, or peregrines kill quarry in falconry as well or better than their purebred counterparts, and one must therefore assume that they would continue to do so in the wild. Thus, they could survive as individuals for their lifetime, even though their genes might die out. Unentered falconry birds of whatever parentage have a poor chance of surviving in the wild, and it is essential that the falconer takes all possible precautions to prevent the loss of an unentered bird.

There is a last point on the "con" side of the argument, and that is that hybrids are in some way unnatural or unsporting. I cannot see that hybrids are less "natural" than say flying a nonindigenous species, or using telemetry, or transporting hawks in cars with hoods on their heads, or keeping a hawk in a city. On the point about being unsporting, we have already discussed in 7.4 the balance between predator and prey, and it is up to the falconer to maintain this balance.

The trained peregrine is only suitable for certain types of land. In Britain, these are grouse moors and in certain very limited lowland areas. Most falconers do not have legal access to suitable land in lowland Britain to fly a peregrine. Does this stop them? No, instead they try to hawk land which is unsuitable for peregrines, and they come unstuck. The peregrine is a superb aerial specialist and in the right situation, such as a grouse moor, can scarcely be more than equalled. But it has three faults which make it unsuitable for pursuit flights in most of lowland Britain: first, it chases in a series of stoops, a method which although spectacular to watch, means the flight tends to cover a lot of distance, and most prey can reach cover first. Secondly, the peregrine is seldom willing to enter the flimsiest of cover. If the prey just lands on the ground, or under a sheep, the peregrine will stoop ineffectually and then, if not taken down promptly, is likely to drift away and get into mischief. Thirdly the peregrine tends to lack persistence; if things aren't exactly to its liking it often refuses or checks at something easier. Peregrine/sakers on the other hand get onto prey more quickly than a peregrine and, even when stooping, do not go so wide that the prey has so much time to make toward cover. They can kill in thin trees which means that large areas are not rendered unhawk-able by walls, fences, sheep and so on, as they are for a peregrine. Finally, on the ground, they have the confidence and determination to kill a crow quickly, whereas a peregrine, although physically capable of doing so, often hesitates or refuses. Thus, for hawking with trained birds in managed habitats, hybrids are sometimes better adapted than purebreds.

It may well be that some hybrids, such as those between red-tails, Harrises and ferruginous hawks, have no significant advantages, in which case their production will soon be abandoned. So-called "developed" countries are suffering increasing obstacle pollution in the form of roads and traffic, barbed wired, and overhead cables. This has had a major impact on wildlife and closed up huge areas of country to all but the most basic types of hawking. If some designer hybrids enable falconry to adapt and continue despite these massive changes then they will have a role to play in the future.

## 8.5 The past and future of domestic breeding

Although lanners at least were probably bred in captivity in Britain in Elizabethan times, there were few serious attempts to breed hawks because it was easier to obtain them from the wild. Strict laws were passed to protect the nesting falcons and often goshawks were put out at the end of the season to nest in a local wood. Their youngsters were then available later for hawking.

When hawking went out of favor, raptors had a very hard time at the hands of shooters, and in Britain some became extinct. In North America, and in many other countries, hawks were often shot on sight. Then came organochlorine pesticides. Hawk numbers crashed. Suddenly raptors became "magnificent, rare, and endangered." Many falconers were prosecuted or persecuted just for keeping a live hawk. While falconers were hounded and blamed for the demise of raptors the pesticide producers and users, which had a much bigger impact, were persuaded to limit their activities voluntarily over a period of thirty years.

In Britain, falconry was stuck between a rock and a hard place. On the one hand it was getting almost impossible to obtain licenses to take hawks from the wild in any significant numbers owing to the population declines. On the other, there was a burgeoning interest in raptors and in people who wanted to take up falconry. Despite the gloomy predictions of some old-timers and the loudly voiced skepticism of most protectionists, some falconers had made their first tentative attempts to breed hawks in captivity. It wasn't easy, but success followed success, and a body of expertise was established. In America, Tom Cade, backed by many prominent NAFA members, set up The Peregrine Fund in order to restore U.S. peregrine numbers through captive breeding. It was a long haul, but it was an outstanding success and a monument to what can be achieved by hard work and dedication, pioneering techniques of breeding and reintroduction. In Britain, the British Falconers' Club held breeding seminars and conferences. Many projects sprang up in Europe. More details of all these achievements are listed in Appendix 1.

By the late 1970s, although the screws were being tightened on the supplies of wild hawks, we gradually realized that falconry had a future if it could be entirely selfsustaining by breeding its own birds. Not only did it have a future, but also it could control its supply, and escape from the yoke of legislation surrounding wild birds. In 1981, Britain implemented the Wildlife and Countryside Act in response to the EC Birds Directive. During the same period CITES, controlling international trade in endangered species, started to come into operation. These were new and far-ranging controls aimed at protecting wild birds. Because few raptors were being bred in captivity, the legislation was worded confusing wild-source birds with domestic ones. Domestic bred raptors had to be registered and ringed. The Department of the Environment computer followed the fortunes of the captive birds.

By 1994, there were around 16,000 diurnal raptors registered to about 8,000 hawk-keepers in Britain. Domestic raptor production was booming—and so were wild raptors. Much of the legislation was now unnecessary and no longer cost-effective. With free trade throughout a growing European Community it was impossible to maintain such high levels of regulation out of step with the other countries. So now falconry has access to as many birds as it wants and there is virtually no limit to its potential growth.

Of course during this period, some wild raptors were taken illegally by egg collectors, game preservers, pigeon racing enthusiasts, falconers and people posing as breeders. I do not have reliable data on the total illegal take of each species, however it was insufficient to stem the increase in most of the raptor populations, some of which are now at saturation. These illegal birds probably were significant in boosting the captive population sizes of some indigenous species during the early years of domestic breeding. However, the domestic productivity rates of indigenous and nonindigenous species are very similar and therefore it is probably safe to assume that most of the declared breeding is genuine. The main exception to this is the goshawk, which is difficult to breed, is a desirable falconry bird, and is under great pressure from game preservers who often try to persuade falconers to take them rather than kill them illegally.

During the period 1981–1993 when full registration was in force, it was possible to get statistics which can never be repeated. During 1980–1991, 23,804 diurnal raptors were registered as bred in captivity in U.K. alone, including 16 species to the second generation. By 1992, the following species had been bred worldwide for two generations in captivity ie F2, and have internationally recognized domestic populations, many of which are numerically and genetically selfsustaining:

| | |
|---|---|
| *Vultur gryphus* | Andean condor |
| *Milvus migrans* | Black kite |
| *Milvus milvus* | Red kite |
| *Haliaeetus albicilla* | White-tailed sea eagle |
| *Gyps bengalensis* | Indian White-backed vulture |
| *Gyps fulvus* | Griffon vulture |
| *Accipiter gentilis* | Northern goshawk |
| *Ayccipiter nisus* | European sparrowhawk |
| *Accipiter cooperii* | Cooper's hawk |
| *Parabuteo unicinctus* | Harris hawk |
| *Buteo jamaicensis* | Red-tailed hawk |
| *Buteo buteo* | Common buzzard |
| *Buteo regalis* | Ferruginous hawk |
| *Aquila chrysaetos* | Golden eagle |
| *Aquila rapax* | Tawny or steppe eagle |
| *Polihierax semitorquatus* | African pygmy falcon |
| *Falco sparverius* | American kestrel |
| *Falco tinnunculus* | Common kestrel |
| *Falco punctatus* | Mauritius kestrel |
| *Falco chicquera* | Red-headed falcon |
| *Falco columbarius* | Merlin |
| *Falco novaeseelandiae* | New Zealand falcon |
| *Falco subbuteo* | European hobby |
| *Falco biarmicus* | Lanner falcon |
| *Falco mexicanus* | Prairie falcon |
| *Falco jugger* | Lugger falcon |

| *Falco cherrug* | Saker falcon |
| *Falco rusticolus* | Gyr falcon |
| *Falco peregrinus* | Peregrine falcon |
| *Falco pelegrinoides* | Barbary falcon |

The process continues. The British data show what happened:

In the 1970s, falconers already kept numbers of indigenous species because they had been able to obtain them under license, and many were rehabilitating injured hawks. It was easy too, without quarantine and without CITES, to import raptors. By 1980, these initial populations were already being bred in small numbers. Everyone was excited about captive breeding, and every available bird was paired up. As a result the commoner species, such as the kestrel, sparrowhawk, and buzzard, increased exponentially in captivity (figure 8.5.1). In 1987, over 1000 young kestrels were produced. Suddenly nobody wanted them. They were hardly worth the cost of registration. Pairs were separated or died, and production fell drastically within three years. By 1993, it was half of peak level and still falling. In 1988, sparrowhawk production peaked, followed the next year by buzzards. These three species were only in limited demand by serious falconers, and nobody was prepared to pay high prices for them. People began to realize that it costs money to breed hawks, and kestrels do not pay the bills.

Falconers, on the other hand, were prepared to pay for the species which were the backbone of the sport: peregrine and merlin, Harris hawk, goshawk, and red-tail. These in 1980 were in lower numbers and also were slower to come to breed (figure 8.5.2). The goshawk and the merlin posed difficulties to breeders. By 1985 their production was increasing slightly. People who had gained experience on kestrels now set their sights on more expensive birds. Everybody wanted a pair or two for breeding. Prices rocketed. In 1987, Harrises reached a peak price of 1,600 pounds ($2,560) for a female. The falconry demand was totally swamped by the demands for breeding stock. Three years later this generation came into production; output soared. Britain meanwhile went into a deep economic recession. Prices halved. The demand for breeding stock fell back, leaving falconers as the main market. But the Harris gained popularity, being tough and undemanding, and easily flown near towns, it does not have the divorce-making propensities of the goshawk. It is also easy and cost-effective to breed and will no doubt dominate the falconry world in Britain for the foreseeable future.

The peregrine, red-tail, goshawk, and merlin similarly increased, but output will never reach the same levels as the Harris, because they do not have the same market volume potential as the Harris and are not so cheap to breed. The peregrine suffered from a lot of price hype, the worst of which is promulgated by protectionists in sensationalist media. Prices of more than 10,000 to 15,000 pounds ($16,000–$24,000) were still being quoted in 1993. In reality, peregrine prices in U.K. peaked in 1988 when the best birds fetched up to 1,200 pounds ($1,920). In 1993, similar birds fetched 500–600 pounds ($800–$960). In 1994, the German protectionists claimed that sakers cost 30,000 pounds ($48,000), whereas adverts by saker breeders in U.K.'s *Cage and Aviary* newspaper averaged around 400 pounds ($640) for a female saker. The value generator for big falcons has always been the Middle East falconers who traditionally buy passage sakers and peregrines, usually at a ratio of about 10:1. The commonest peregrines are *calidus* (nebli), trapped on autumn passage. Many of these falcons are released in March of the following year so they have a chance to return to the breeding grounds. One of our current projects at the National Avian Research Center in Abu Dhabi marks sakers at nests in Asia using microchips. Some of these birds are later trapped and find their way to falconers in the Middle East. We have organized the falcon hospitals so that when a falcon is brought in for health checks the microchip is detected and recorded on our central computer. Similarly, all released birds are chipped and some are detected back on the nesting grounds. Additionally, a proportion carry either conventional radio tags or satellite tags which enable biologists to trace their migration routes. We are thus slowly building up a picture of the turnover and sustainability of falcons in Arab falconry.

Unfortunately, many protectionists do not understand that there is a world of difference between a young aviary-bred peregrine or saker and a big passage falcon which is already a proven hunter. As already discussed in earlier parts of this book, there is a lot of skilled work, and attrition, in bringing on a young domestic falcon to the standard of a passage falcon. Thus falcons, like horses, can have very different values. Two animals which might, to the untutored eye, look alike, but one animal might be worth ten times more than the

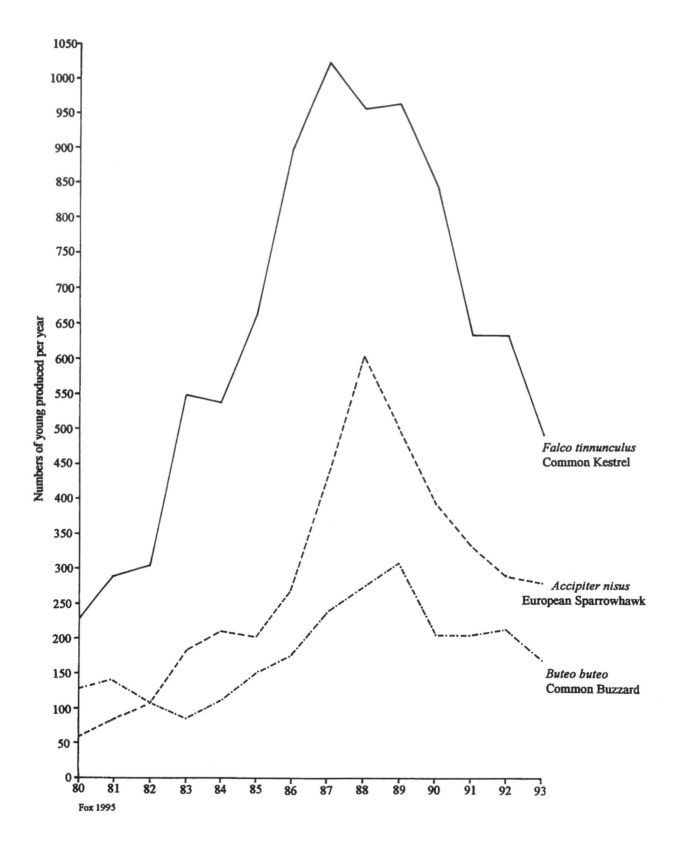

Fox 1995

Figure 8.5.1 The production of aviary-bred common kestrels, European sparrowhawks, and common buzzards in the U.K. 1980–1993. From the Department of the Environment statistics.

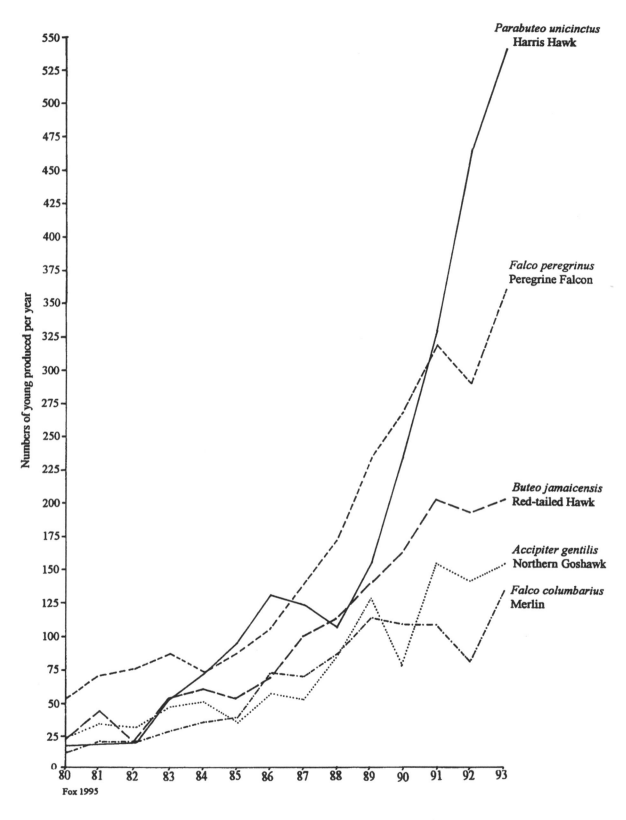

Figure 8.5.2. The production of aviary-bred Harris hawks, peregrines, red-tails, northern goshawks, and merlins in the U.K. 1980–1993. From the Department of the Environment statistics.

other. Many breeders have been swept up in the idea of breeding falcons for the Middle East market, only to find that their birds were either physically or mentally unsuitable for this market, or that their prospective buyers did not know how to manage them, as they were only used to passage birds. Having now bred, hacked, and trained falcons for the Middle East for eight years, I know that it can be done on a repeatable basis and that there is a prospect that Arab falconry could survive on domestic falcons if the wild falcons face problems on their nesting grounds. There is plenty of scope in this situation for education—of breeders, of falconers and of protectionists.

Looking now at the production of lanners, sakers, and luggers (figure 8.5.3), these species started from a lower base and do not have such a good market price. Some, particularly lanners, are used for flying displays, but for field falconry in U.K. conditions they are inferior to peregrines. Nevertheless, they breed well in aviaries, and their numbers are climbing steadily. I hope that breeders will maintain and increase the captive lugger population; this species is not in the front rank for falconry, but it is now on Appendix I and we have now started working in the Punjab.

The British have always had a liking for variety and in the late 1960s and early 1970s imported many different species of raptors. Some of these became sustainable through domestic breeding; others were imported later from other collections. As a result, there are quite a lot of species producing under 30 or so young per year, the prairie falcon and American kestrel being typical. Many of these species are held by just a few breeders who are slowly breeding them up. Over the last ten years, the ferruginous hawk has slowly increased to the point where it is ready to double or treble output quickly. But for many of these species, the demand (reflected in prices) is not there. Therefore many of the birds are not actually paired for breeding and it is likely that, although they may increase slowly, they are probably at market saturation below 50 birds per year.

The big danger with these small populations is inbreeding and a population crash. The black sparrowhawk, the red-headed merlin, and the New Zealand falcon have all started from very limited gene pools in Britain. The black sparrowhawk has been bred successfully by Jemima Parry-Jones, but it only takes the deaths of a few key birds in these small projects to endanger the future of the whole captive population. With the New Zealand falcon, of which all the birds in the world outside New Zealand derive from my original stock of six individuals, we have kept back or loaned out almost all the progeny to breeding projects so that numbers can be built up. We really need to see an annual production of about 50 birds per year.

Other species, not shown on the graphs, are even less fortunate. Many of these are poor or slow breeders, such as eagles, and many are represented by just a few individuals. They are not sustainable long term at these levels.

Thus in Britain, falconry is now selfsustaining for all the main falconry species and quite a few fringe species as well. If one pieces together the different figures shown, starting with the small output species and going through to the peak ones, it is possible to discern a general pattern. Imagine starting with say, two pairs of a medium-sized raptor which breeds at two or three years old and which breeds tolerably well. In the first few years, the loss of any of these four birds could be critical. Slowly numbers increase, but they may be all of one sex, or all from one pair. Gradually further pairs are made up. Genetics then become a major headache, and maybe a few more unrelated birds are obtained to make further outcrosses. From that point it could take 10–15 years to reach an output of 15 birds a year. Once this point is reached the species should start a steady climb, potentially going exponential. This could take 10–15 more years. This climb will flatten out as market saturation is reached, which could be at 50 birds or could be 500 birds.

Although this model gives an idea of the timescale, reality is seldom this straightforward. In practice there are other little twists and turns. For example, the founder stock may be owned by four different people, none of whom are speaking to each other. To try to overcome this problem and maximize production from these small populations, zoos have organized TAGs (Taxon Advisory Groups). Breeders specializing in a particular taxon get together to breed on a co-operative and planned basis. This is a very sensible approach.

The British populations are not of course totally genetically isolated. It is easier now to move birds around Europe and to obtain birds from North America. Weird, CITES-inspired regulations come and go every few years. What is government policy in one country is illegal in another and vice-versa. The nub of the matter which gov-

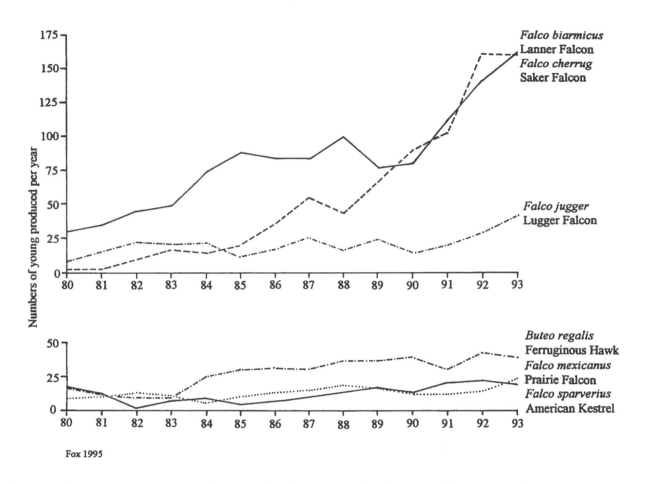

Fox 1995

Figure 8.5.3 The production of aviary-bred lanners, sakers, luggers, ferruginous hawks, prairie falcons, and American kestrels in the U.K. 1980–1993. From the Department of the Environment statistics.

ernments are having to come to terms with is the clear differentiation in law between domestic birds and wild-source ones.

What does "domestic" mean? Many of our domestic animals can and do interbreed with wild ones. For how many generations do you have to breed an animal for it to become domestic? Should it be genetically or physically distinguishable from the wild-type? Should it show "tame" rather than "wild" behavior? Should it have some sort of agricultural connection? Should it not have an existing wild-type?

None of these questions really get to the point of domestication. Legislators tie themselves into knots without solving the problem. A classic example in the British law is *Columba livia*, the rock pigeon, feral town pigeon, racing pigeon, fancy pigeon, and edible pigeon. All are one single species. In law, as a feral pigeon, it may be killed or sold dead by authorized people at all times. As a

rock dove, it is fully protected. As a racing pigeon, it is not included under Schedule 3 allowing it to be sold alive. Otherwise, it is regarded as domestic poultry and thus escaping the strictures of wildlife law. A footnote below each schedule mentions that common names are for guidance only, the law being based on scientific species. The law, as they say, is an ass!

The British 1981 Wildlife and Countryside Act was intended to help preserve *wild* life forms, which, in fairness, it does quite well. It does not really come to terms with the question of domesticated forms. It is based on the premise that certain species are "wild" and certain other ones are "domestic poultry." Birds, such as pigeons, which didn't fit this mould, are fudged. Since then, among raptor breeders alone, we have bred about 50,000 hawks in captivity. The law didn't plan on this happening. It has been an unprecedented and successful large-scale domestication of wildlife.

You may have noticed that I've still avoided defining "domestic." In reality I think the word defies definition and is not really helpful. It has so many connotations. But for legal and management reasons one has to come to a working definition.CITESfor some time regarded life forms which were second generation captive bred onwards as different from wild-source life forms. But this leaves a huge group of the most contentious animals, the first generation and the half generations, in a legal limbo. With this definition you could actually breed a wild animal from a domestic one. Therefore I think that in legal terms the only clean definitive cut-off point is the first generation. In other words either something was born (or laid, not hatched) in the wild, or it was born in captivity. This leaves us two clear groups: wild-source animals and captive-source domestic ones. No other "definition" is definitive. Laws in many different countries are now being challenged and changed in line with this. Once there is a clear international acceptance of "wild" and "domestic" and an appreciation that the law refers not to a whole species but to the individual animal in contention, then it is possible to make progress. The full weight of international law can be brought to bear to help *wild* life forms and separate legislation can cover domestic ones.

A further aspect of domestic breedingwhich is still under scrutiny in several countries is that of ownership. In some countries wild animals are owned by the state. If you shoot a wild bird (legally) then usually, you own the body. You may or may not be allowed to sell it. I'm not too sure what happens if you eat it and then the state claims it back! If you trap the bird alive under a permit, you may be allowed to possess it, but the state may own it. If you breed it, the state may still claim ownership of the youngsters. Or you may own them. The state may control the sale. The state may also give you a permit to export the bird. This means that the bird will pass into another jurisdiction. The new possessor will almost certainly legally own it. Can you see what a jungle we've got into? If the new possessor sends it, or its progeny, back to you, that is a personal ownership transaction. You have thus obtained ownership from the state. Of course you did not need to export it to another person in the first place. You could export it to yourself. Many people own birds in several different countries. This whole question is an international mess. Again, the only solution can be

that animals born in captivity are privately owned.

The final area of confusion is the definition of "trade." Some legislators regard trade as a movement across a frontier. So if you take a couple of falcons hawking for a week or two in a neighboring country and then come home, the official statistics show that four falcons have been traded. It's amazing what you can do with statistics! Other legislators include some financial element. This may be a "value for trade" as defined by Customs and Excise; this figure is usually a work of fiction in itself. You may take your home-bred hawk abroad hawking only to be charged import tax in each direction on a notional value which the Customs official has just established by telephoning a protectionist organization which has given him an astronomical figure. Other regulators distinguish somehow between commercial and noncommercial trade. The idea is that price equals production costs plus profit margin. Some regulators allow commercial trade but not noncommercial trade. If you keep birds in two separate countries and move them regularly, as we do, you find yourself faced with all sorts of fees and taxes which are completely unwarranted, and with laws designed for wild birds which are entirely inappropriate and achieve nothing in conservation terms.

Breeders who are trying to set up and run a program are faced with all these issues. I'm not trying to be mischievous; I have had personal experience with every single point mentioned in this section, and my peer reviewers think I have understated the problems!

## 8.6   Breeding for conservation and gene banks

Having looked at the progress of projects motivated primarily by falconry, let's move on to projects intended primarily for the conservation of species in the wild.

The first point to consider is money. Most people consider it last. They run out of funds and their project goes to the wall. You have to look at ways in which money can be brought into a project. Bills have to be met. In the case of birds which have a falconry interest it is possible to sell surplus young and cover costs. Some birds can earn their keep in displays at zoos and centers. Others, with a reputation for being endangered, such as the Mauritius kestrel, can help swell the gate and people tend to dip into their pockets if they feel it will help save a species in some way. Rarity is always a crowd puller even if the object of attention has no other special features. Rarity itself is a marketable commodity, even without any birds being involved. Paradoxically, many conservationist organizations rely on certain species remaining "endangered" or "threatened" in order to attract funds. This often results in major inconsistencies between true, biological endangerment, and perceived endangerment reported to the public.

Some projects have sponsors, some have endowments, some run on the backs of more lucrative projects. All projects require stability, long-term commitment and financial security. If a project is under-capitalized the birds will suffer. To provide this continuity usually requires more than a private individual can supply; it needs a team effort of many individuals and organizations.

The next question to consider is what exactly is the object of the project? The best projects last no more than a day and don't involve any breeding, just a translocation. This is how long it takes to move eggs from one wild nest to another. Egg manipulation is the quickest and most cost-effective way of boosting a raptor population. The next step on from this is to take threatened eggs, hatch them out, and then return older chicks to nests in the wild, as we have done with red kites in Wales. The next step is a much bigger commitment, to maintain a gene bank for a protracted period.

Given that egg and chick manipulation is by far the simplest and most cost-effective way of increasing wild raptor populations and, once a policy decision has been taken, can be achieved on a somewhat opportunistic basis, I will leave it on one side. The techniques are reasonably straightforward.

If a "breed for release" scheme is contemplated, then there needs first to be a clear management decision. Will the progeny be used to supplement an existing population? If so what are the factors causing the population to be below capacity? Are these factors known? Have they been addressed? Are they tractable—will they respond to remedial treatment? Are they essentially irreversible? If the factors are not known, a release scheme may be useful as a method of investigating them. If you put out all your young birds with radiotags or some other identification and, for example, you find that they all get poisoned, you then have a pretty clear idea why the original population died back. In other words the release scheme was not intended to boost the wild numbers but was being used as an investigative method. The next stage is to address the factors causing the attrition and reverse them. The wild population may well then reassert itself unaided.

For these reasons, releasing stock into an existing population is seldom necessary. Two circumstances spring to mind where supplementation can be useful. One is where a population has died back and now only occupies a small part of its former range and, although the historical factors causing the decline no longer exist, the remnant population has failed to expand geographically. This is what happened to the red kite population in Britain; it needed a little push to encourage it to expand its breeding range. Another reason for supplementation is when a population has died back in numbers right across its range, leaving scattered pairs which are no longer in contact with one another. This happened with the *anatum* peregrine in North America. The subspecies was extirpated by pesticides over most of the continent, but a few scattered, poorly reproductive pairs and individuals hung on. The Peregrine Fund's strategy was to release captive-bred young to support these local foci and maintain traditions of use. These then rebuilt local populations which gradually linked up again.

The other reason for breed and release is for reintroductions. There are seven well-recognized criteria for reintroductions:

a) There should be good historical evidence of former natural occurrence.

b) There should be a clear understanding of why the species was lost to the area. In general, only those lost through human agency and unlikely to recolonize naturally should be regarded as suitable candidates for reintroduction.

c) The factors causing extinction should have been rectified.

d) There should be sufficient suitable habitat available.

e) The released individuals should be as close as possible genetically to the original population. I think this criterion will change over the next decade. Because habitat is changing so rapidly, what most populations need is a wider variation in genetic variation, rather than genetic "purity." Wider variation gives more chance of surviving fast-changing selection pressures.

f) Obtaining individuals for a release program should not prejudice the survival of the donor population.

g) There will be increasing examples in the future of original range being no longer suitable, so that the only option if the species is to survive in the wild, is an introduction or transplant to a completely new area, as distinct from a reintroduction. The impact the introduced species may have on the new ecosystem may well outweigh any advantages gained for the species itself, so this course requires very careful consideration. A gene bank in captivity may be the only prudent alternative.

In practice, however much field data are gathered and however much theoretical modeling takes place, there is always an element of trial and error. Ask the birds; often they come up with some surprises. When red kites were reintroduced by hacking, into England and Scotland, the survivability was phenomenal—about 80–90 percent. Obviously the habitat was crying out for colonization but the Welsh population was simply not producing sufficient excess to spread into England. Similar results occurred with the reintroductions of peregrines in Germany.

These are the cold, clinical management considerations to be assessed before a release scheme is contemplated. They are often overlooked by amateurs who are so keen to get involved in an active conservation project that they fail to see an overall perspective. Professionals quite rightly-castigate them for rushing in "where angels fear to tread." At best the professionals consider it a waste of resources.

On the other hand, professionals can be curiously blinkered in their approach to wildlife management. In many countries they assume proprietorial rights over wildlife which are not theirs and for which they cannot actually handle the responsibility. Most wildlife managers nowadays are tightly restricted on budget and yet do not appreciate that an action plan which for them might be a waste of resources, for some dedicated amateurs is a good use for resources which are not transferable anyway to another action plan. The typical clash is when amateurs are told "not to breed a species in captivity, that it is a waste of time, that what is needed is more field work." The fact that the amateur may have a job, 2.4 kids and

be agoraphobic, escapes the professional. The professional too easily just sees the immediate wildlife problem and is unable to handle the people problem and the people resources. The result is a stalemate. The professional doesn't get his fieldwork done because he hasn't got the funds. The amateur is prevented or opposed in his contribution because the professional thinks it is a waste of time.

On a national scale this leads to friction and frustration. On an international scale it amounts to neglect. In many Third World countries there are many species crying out for active conservation work. Local and expatriate professional biologists do not have the resources to do anything significant. Specimens could have been collected for captive breeding as a gene bank or as a source of study material. This is resisted by professionals invoking CITES. The situation is thus left to deteriorate further until the population becomes "endangered." This puts it in a position where a professional has some prospect of raising sponsorship money for fieldwork. He does a survey. He thinks that is "conservation." It isn't, it's just studying the animal. The animal is no better off; in fact it may be worse off carrying various transmitters and other research detritus. The actual conservation only starts with management, as far as the animal is concerned. Management requires different skills and different thinking to those employed by most field biologists. Many field researchers actually resent management because it devalues their datasets! Eventually the crisis point is reached, as it was with the Californian condor and the Mauritius kestrel. Captive breeding becomes the last available option. But by then the gene pool is into a severe bottle neck, and the person or organization designated to breed the remnant birds is under grim pressure to be successful. In North America, hard-line protectionists actually wanted the California condor to become extinct "with dignity" rather than be taken into captivity and bred up for reintroduction.

This is not the way to tackle these situations. Specimens should be made available to dedicated amateur breeders much earlier on in the process. Without depriving field-scientists of resources, they can then develop breeding techniques for the species and establish a captive breeding population on a broad and representative genetic base. The field scientist should spend some time studying the captive birds so that he starts to understand what makes the species "tick" and so that he can pose questions to the breeder which may require several breeding seasons to answer. The captive birds can also be used for filming and publicity campaigns to inform people about the total project and to raise further funds. During this process the qualified scientist will start to gain some respect for the experienced aviculturalist and vice versa. I am quite sure that the experience I have gained in breeding and handling captive raptors is easily equivalent to the nine years of university degrees and to the fieldwork I have done. I also know many qualified biologists whom I would not trust to so much as open the door of an incubator.

When immediate release of progeny is not contemplated, the breeding project takes on the complexion of a gene bank. Genes can either be stored as whole live birds, or as frozen semen (see 2.15). Whole birds have a nasty habit of dying and so it is necessary to keep breeding, generation after generation. The important thing to concentrate on is the genes, not the birds.

The first step is to establish the extent of genetic variation in the wild population. This is what we have been doing with the New Zealand falcons. We trapped falcons and obtained blood samples from as many birds from different places as possible. We achieved about 35 birds. By DNA profiling it is possible to assess the coefficients of relatedness (see 2.2). The founder birds should reflect this full range of genetic and geographic variation. A minimum of about eight "unrelated" birds should represent about 90 percent of the total current genetic variation. I put "unrelated" in apostrophes because just because two birds came from the wild doesn't mean that they are unrelated, far from it. We have trapped two resident falcons 300 kilometers apart and found that their coefficient of relatedness was over 50 percent. In other words, they were as close genetically as brother and sister or mother and child. Obviously all populations are related to some extent and each has its own characteristic background relatedness. A species, such as the Mauritius kestrel, which has been through at least one severe genetic bottleneck, will be highly inbred and may show a background coefficient of relatedness of 40 percent. This is not necessarily a bad thing. Deleterious genes will also have been heavily weeded out during this process; if they hadn't, the bird would not be here now. Other species, such as the peregrine, found all over the world in big and varied populations with lots of

forms or subspecies, intrinsically show more genetic variation and thus a background relatedness of perhaps only 15 percent. We don't know these figures yet; we've also started on the saker and gyrfalcons, but it will be some years before we can put everything together.

Assuming the founder birds carry 90 percent of the genetic variation, the next task is to preserve all these genes as long as is anticipated. For all practical purposes, no new genes are created. But genetic variation can be lost. Every time you breed, you risk losing genetic variation. If you don't breed, you risk losing birds *and* their genes. So the trick is to increase the interval between generations. If your generation interval is four years, ten generations will only last forty years. Therefore, as breeding stock for the next generation, you pick birds which were the last to be produced by the previous generation. Youngsters produced earlier by those birds can be used for other purposes.

All of this requires meticulous record keeping and tactful organizing between breeders. This is what the TAGs set out to achieve.

As well as making efforts to preserve genes, it is important to be ever on the scrounge for additional genetic material. CITES has been a major barrier to sources of breeding stock. Sad to say there are many extremist conservationists who would rather see a crippled animal killed than used for breeding.

Unfortunately, conservation is seen as a luxury. When a country's economy goes down, conservation is marginalized. It is very important not to separate ordinary people from hands-on work with real wildlife. Time and time again, the committed amateur achieves more than teams of paid professionals who, when they stop getting paid, stop working. It is simply not safe to rely entirely on professionals, nor is it safe to have a public whose interest in wildlife has been obtained solely through television rather than real life. People who have been reared on an edited view of reality are not in a position to make judgements on wildlife issues; they have become puppets of the media men.

TAG groups on the other hand, can easily become introverted. Many participants may not have even seen their study animal in the wild. It is important for them to build a symbiotic relationship with field workers. Field workers also often have access to wild genes in the form of deserted eggs, or injured birds which would be invaluable to a breeding project and which would otherwise be wasted. Most breeders, by the nature of their work, are rooted to one particular location. They would like to contribute to the conservation of species in the wild, but they have to stay at home. Far from being avaricious for birds for themselves, many dream about providing animals for reintroduction projects. Most of these projects are impractical and do not fulfill the biological criteria, but some do. The barn owl situation in Britain is a classic example of an animal hyped up as threatened, followed by an amazing response from people thus motivated to "do" something about it. The owl's real problems, such as habitat, are rather intractable, but people felt they could breed them up and release them. And they did. Thousands upon thousands were bred, released, and died. Protectionists then turned on these people and castigated them for their well-intentioned efforts. The point to come out of the whole fiasco is that there are many ordinary people who, pressured by tales of endangered wildlife, want to do something practical to help. They feel that they can't preserve a rain forest in their back garden, but they can breed owls.

Now they are realizing that this approach was simplistic. Proper research, guidance, and coordination is essential. But this is not to deny that there is an amazing human resource there if only it could be tapped. Perhaps over the next decade, some of these TAG groups will be able to set up gene banks for threatened endemics in a coordinated program with field workers. It may not be particularly glamorous or high profile, but then the best work is often steady and low-key.

## 8.7   Lawyers, politicians, and civil servants

Lawyers, politicians, and civil servants, for all their faults, have a job to do. Most of them are not specialists in wildlife biology, and few have any real personal freedom of decision. Their decisions are often made for them by panels of "experts" and by pressure groups. As a result, national and international laws concerning wildlife show little underlying logic or science, they merely reflect popular levels of concern on different issues. Therefore they are not coordinated, and hypocrisy is rife.

I don't want to list a catalogue of criticism.

This would be easy, but is a negative and polarizing approach. But I'll give a few examples to show you the kind of galloping hypocrisy we are talking about.

In Britain, the Wildlife and Countryside Act 1981, Part I: 8 (1) strays onto welfare issues and makes it illegal to confine any bird in a cage too small for it to stretch its wings freely. The very next subsection promptly exempts poultry! Thus a falconer who leaves his hawk in its car box overnight when away from home (a very safe and comfortable arrangement for all concerned) is liable to prosecution entailing a fine of up to 1000 pounds and a ban on keeping registrable birds for five years. The chicken farmer meanwhile, who is cramming millions of birds into cages, gets away with it. How is this? Simply due to pressure from the agricultural lobby on politicians on "economic" grounds.

Another classic example which permeates legislation in America, Europe and internationally through CITES, is the failure to differentiate between three different categories. The first category is the *species*. This encompasses all individuals genetically included in an internationally recognized taxon, the species (including all *subspecies*), whatever their immediate origins. Obviously, if a species is not internationally agreed, then it can have no legal definition. Similarly subspecies are taxa which cannot be perfectly differentiated and therefore cannot be subjected to separate legislation. If one could clearly differentiate between all individuals of two subspecies then they could be classed as two full species. It is the very fact that there is a gray area which means they are given subspecies status. Geographical origin is not a valid criterion in legislation because it is seldom known with certainty.

The second category is the differentiation between *wild* and *domestic*. We have already discussed this in sections 8.5 and 8.6. International legislation has to take into account the substantial populations of animals which, although genetically and physically identical to free-living wild animals, are of domestic origin. These populations are going to increase in the future and will be traded and moved internationally more and more. Legislation needs to identify these and cater for them. Many species are now more numerous in domesticity than in the wild, and in the long-term many species will depend on domestic populations for survival as a gene pool.

The third category is the differentiation between *species* and *individuals*. Many laws are framed to encompass whole species, whereas when the law is actually applied, the item in court is not a species but an individual animal. This individual animal may have been born in the wild, or in captivity. This has ownership implications which have been discussed in 8.5. For example, the Mauritius government claims ownership of all Mauritius kestrels. Individuals shipped abroad still "belong" to the Mauritius government although now outside its jurisdiction and subject to the laws of their new host country. As these individuals breed, the breeders consider that they own the progeny. Birds may be sold or exchanged with other collections. Everytime birds are shipped somebody has to pay import taxes on a "value" for customs. The whole thing is a mess.

Protectionist organizations are not slow to cash in on this confusion. For example, the Royal Society for the Protection of Birds recently launched a very commendable campaign to stop the international trade in wild birds. This trade is undesirable if it is an unsustainable drain on wild populations (see 8.2 and 8.3) or if there are welfare implications with birds suffering or dying in transit. But because the documentation on bird movements does not include the source of the birds, the monitoring organizations count all movements of nonfarmyard domestic birds as "trade in wild birds." Thus I found at the top of their list of 637 species which are "near threatened and which are currently traded," the New Zealand falcon. As it happened, only six birds have been exported from New Zealand, all to me. The trade referred to was based entirely on movements of my domestic-bred progeny from these founder birds. Nor were most of the birds sold, most were sent to reputable breeders to establish a gene bank. But again, monitoring records do not cover monetary matters; all movements between two parties are automatically recorded as commercial trade. Given that the whole thrust of the protectionist argument is to reduce supplies of wild-caught birds in favor of domestic ones, it hardly promotes goodwill and understanding by using domestic birds as scapegoats.

Anyone involved with wildlife knows that CITES has been a disaster in that it has failed to protect wild populations, failed to cater properly for the requirements of domestic populations, failed to design a system that is internationally workable, and left the door open for the crook at the expense of law-abiding people. Although the overall aims of CITES are commendable, it has suffered at the hands of idealists and theorists with insufficient experience or understanding of real-life situations. There is so much disparity between the priorities of the different nations, and imbalance in their representation, that I despair that CITES will ever achieve its goals.

Gradually though, we are seeing a change of attitude away from old-fashioned, total protectionism toward sustainable management. While it is obviously essential to maintain wildlife habitat, particularly in critical areas, there is a growing awareness that man and wildlife have to live *together,* not apart. All the best areas of the world for living things are dominated by man. For wildlife to survive there, it can only be by careful management. This cannot be by total protectionism (except in very limited cases) but by balancing the needs of species with resources. Wildlife is itself a resource, whether in a managed "wild" or in closer association with man. Decisions have to be made on aspects such as carrying capacity, overproduction, culls, harvestable surpluses, funding habitat maintenance, and so on. Some of these decisions are hard. The approach has to be pragmatic rather than idealistic. We need balanced international legislation to support sustained management. And organizations need to depolarize and bring their members toward realistic attitudes for the survival and welfare of all life forms. Some of these attitudes toward the relationship between man and raptors are described in the next three sections.

## 8.8  Antifalconry issues

There are people who are against falconry on the grounds that it is either bad for the hawks, or for their prey, or for the people doing it.

Is falconry bad for the hawks? If so, is it bad for their wild populations or for the captive raptors? They, like most life forms, are a renewable resource which can be managed on a sustainable basis. Thus, although falconers can be seen as consumers of hawks, this does not mean that falconry decreases the breeding population of hawks any more than consuming soya beans decreases the acreage of soya. Consumers of both commodities have an interest in their sustainable management. The detailed issues concerning wild and domestic raptors and their welfare have already been covered in sections 8.1-8.6. so let's go straight on to the possible bad effects on the prey species.

Falconry is the taking of quarry in its wild state using trained birds of prey. We will deal with issues concerning sky trials and bagged game in 8.9. and ecological effects on prey populations in 8.10.

Is falconry cruel?

This requires further clarification: does falconry inflict unnecessary suffering on the prey, and do falconers delight in any suffering of the prey?

Physical pain is part of nature's warning system to protect ourselves from serious injury. If you could not feel pain, you might not suffer, but you might easily burn your fingers off. The only way to avoid pain is to be dead, and the only way to avoid dying is not to be born. I don't think any of us would prefer a lifeless planet. So we are not talking about avoiding pain, but about minimizing it. But time after time experiments which have set out to reduce pain on the "spare the rod" principle, have ended up "spoiling the child." Pain is part of nature's reward and punishment system, and by eliminating pain in one incident, we do not necessarily reduce the total pain on this planet. For example, if I kill a crow with my falcon, I might cause the crow pain but save countless other small birds and lambs the pain which the crow would have inflicted. Of course this is simplistic; the logical sequel to this would be to eliminate (painlessly) all animals on the planet which kill other animals. This would then totally destabilize the herbivore populations which would be controlled solely by food supply and thus suffer periodic mass starvation. Pain is a fact of life, and we are part of life.

Nor can one judge quality of life solely by absence of pain. Some people become vegetarians because they disapprove of killing animals. They would like a utopia in which animals are born each year and live a carefree existence, but somehow never get killed. This can't be done. From the farming point of view, if we don't eat meat then we don't have farm animals. So the vegetarian, in wishing to prevent the death of existing animals, would preclude the lives of future generations of animals. These are not the actions of real animal-lovers.

For all our high opinions of ourselves, we humans are, and always will be, inextricably bound up in the web of life systems on this planet. We cannot exist without these life systems. The system depends on energy from the sun, combined with nutrients from the Earth, being constantly recycled and recombined. Some of the life forms, such as plants, can harness the sun's energy directly and can therefore exist without eating any other life forms. Others, such as all the animals, cannot use energy from the sun and are totally dependent on eating those which can. Some, such as herbivores, are directly dependent, others, such as carnivores, cannot even eat plants and must eat other animals. Regardless of what one's views may be on God or on the origin of our universe, these are the basic facts of life on Planet Earth.

People who have been raised in towns without first-hand contact with the natural world often have an ignorance of the facts of life which border on the obscene. We have had people come to our farm who are frightened of baby lambs, who think fields and hedgerows are a "wild" landscape, or who in wet and muddy Wales have reached middle-age without ever owning a pair of gumboots. They cannot begin to understand the problems faced by the farmer whose task it is to translate the sunlight falling on his patch of ground into human food. They do not realize that for all their isolation from nature, they are animals which depend on it. A starving Third World child knows more about the facts of life than many of our urban adults.

From the human species' point of view, in our current evolutionary state, we are hunter/gatherers. Humans, especially young adult males, have

David Hancock gives school children a real life encounter with a young Peale's falcon.

the physical and mental abilities, and instincts, to hunt in small cooperative groups. This is less developed in females who tend to be better gatherers. This pattern repeats itself again and again in different human populations. Although we can subsist for extensive periods on either an exclusive meat diet or an exclusive plant diet, we are essentially omnivorous.

There is no particular merit or demerit in your diet type. Humans are capable of adapting, but many other species can't. Cows cannot eat meat. Hawks cannot eat grass. It is not a question of morality, these are the facts of life. The only option for a hawk is to eat meat, and the only way it can obtain meat is by using the combination of physical and mental attributes which we have already examined in this book. Killing by a hawk cannot therefore be said to be cruel. It is natural, and it is a condition of existence on this planet. The "trained" hawks of falconry differ only in that they have been "trained" to tolerate the presence of man. They have not been trained to be cruel or to do something which they do not already do in the wild (see chapter 6).

The question remains that while it may not be cruel for a wild hawk to go about its daily business, surely it is cruel for a falconer to keep hawks for unnecessary hunting? The problem here is the word "necessary." Nothing is really necessary. It is not necessary for the falconer to hunt with a hawk, or to eat meat, or to have a car, or to have children or even to be born. From the point of view of other life forms, this planet would probably be better off without humans. Thus, in practical terms, the only good conservationist is a dead conservationist! How you prioritize your values is a matter of personal choice, not of necessity. One person may prefer to drive a car and cover the world in tarmac. Another may prefer to walk and hawk. The first is a new choice, the second is an old one.

Whether we kill animals for sport, for money, through ignorance or for pest control is not relevant to the argument about necessity. Pests are just life-forms we do not currently want.

We all have our instinctive urges which we try to satisfy, but these instincts vary according to our age and gender. No amount of moralizing or Sex Discrimination legislation can release us from our biological roots. For example, the majority of people in prison are male. The majority of people caring for babies are female. These are statistics

which are common through history and around the globe. We are what we are. Young men like to roam around in small groups, hunting either prey, or other humans, or basketballs, or money. Young women have other goals, and these differences can be clearly seen in the magazines in a newsstand. Most young women don't like violent games, and most young men don't like decorating the house by pulling the reproductive organs off plants, their flowers.

It is not a big step from not wanting to do something, to being against it. For example, not only do I feel no urge to pick flowers, I would rather people didn't. But insofar that picking flowers is done sustainably, I am content not to object to something which obviously gives others enjoyment. I expect the same tolerance in return, providing that I do not interfere with other people's lives, for example, by keeping a noisy hawk in the suburbs. More than this, in a democratic society, I would not expect my activities to be limited only to those which have majority approval; otherwise our lives would soon be confined in a straitjacket of antilegislation. This is a slippery slope which has no end.

You will notice that although I believe that falconry, along with all of man's other activities, is unnecessary, I have not claimed that it is undesirable. In this section I am discussing arguments against falconry. Pro-arguments are covered in 8.10, 8.11 and 8.14.

So we've looked at the question of "unnecessary suffering" from the hawk's and the falconer's viewpoint. What about the suffering from the prey's viewpoint? Given that the prey is born, then it must die. It can meet its death in various ways, some of which are more painful than others. It can also suffer and survive. Any assessment of this suffering should include:

a) The ability of each species to feel mental or physical pain.
b) Short-term mental suffering during actual pursuit or attack.
c) Long-term mental suffering, for example, while caught in a trap or cage for some hours, unable to escape.
d) Short-term physical pain, for example, while actually being attacked and killed. There are data for many species from many sources that the ability to feel pain is much reduced at this time.
e) Long-term physical pain, for example, being

caught by a limb in a trap, or being injured and only killed later. This pain includes shock and its physiological aftermath.

f) Escaping wounded to survive or die later.

g) Natural selectivity: whether the method tends to cull animals which are already old, sick, diseased, or injured from another cause, and therefore tends to curtail other suffering.

h) Suffering of nontarget species such as in systems of agriculture, industry, water, energy, communications, and transport which incidentally, and sometimes avoidably, cause suffering to animals, for example by the misuse of sprays and poisons, fishnets which catch seals, lack of provision for mammal movements in the design of roads and fences, ingestion of lead shot by waterfowl, and so on. The very inadequate data available indicate that about 220 million vertebrates are killed or maimed by British drivers every year, a toll on wildlife which is new this century. In Germany, more game is killed by drivers than by shooters.

Without in any way wishing to dismiss it as irrelevant, let's leave on one side the incidental effects on nontarget animals and other, "natural" causes of death such as disease and starvation. Let's look more closely at the methods man uses to kill wild animals deliberately. (For the sake of brevity I am excluding fish, but you might like to make your own estimates for fishing with hooks and with nets). We need to define our terms:

— *Natural selectivity:* Natural selectivity indicates that weak or infirm individuals are more likely to be caught than healthy strong ones. No selectivity indicates that prey animals are captured in about the same proportion as represented in the locality.

— *Legal selectivity:* 100 percent selectivity indicates that only certain legally unprotected target species are captured (but not necessarily killed). 0 percent selectivity indicates that species are caught in about the same ratio as available in the locality.

— *Human supervision of control method:* Whether or not the activity is supervised by a human, or, in the case of traps, the time interval between checking.

— *Precapture pursuit interval:* The length of time from the start of evasive action by the prey, to its capture or escape.

— *Catch-to-kill interval:* The length of time be-

tween initial physical contact between predator (or weapon) and prey, and the death of the prey. The time span shown indicates approximately 90 percent of the distribution curve but excludes prey which survive the attack.

— *Abandonment of maimed prey:* Prey which have been significantly injured (ie more than losing a few feathers) and which are not killed by the predator. These animals may or may not survive.

— *Approximate annual volume:* The figures given are for England, Wales, and Scotland and, except for scent hounds, cats and birds of prey (for which supportive data exist) are very much estimates based on expert opinion; factual information at present being unavailable. The figures therefore indicate only the order of magnitude.

— *Gaze hounds:* Dogs such as greyhounds, salukis, lurchers and whippets which hunt by sight and kill in a sprint. They are usually used singly or in pairs, sometimes at night, catching hares and rabbits.

— *Scenting hounds:* Dogs such as fox hounds, stag hounds, harriers, and beagles which hunt by scent, usually in a pack. There are about 314 registered packs in England, Wales, and Scotland. Scenting hounds catch foxes, red deer, brown hares, and mink. The deer are not normally killed by the hounds themselves but brought to bay and shot by the huntsman. Many of the foxes ascribed to fox hounds are not killed above ground by hounds but are shot below ground.

— *Terriers:* Dogs used to tackle prey, such as foxes, underground (excluding their use above ground for rats etc).

— *Cats: Felis catus,* the domestic cat. Used to control small mammals on farms and industrial sites, kept widely as pets with a major impact on small vertebrates near areas of housing.

— *Ferrets:* A domestic form of the polecat, *Mustela putorius.* Normally used to bolt rabbits or rats into nets or to guns or hawks, but occasionally killing prey underground.

— *Birds of prey:* Trained raptors commonly of the genera *Falco, Accipiter, Buteo, Parabuteo* and *Aquila.*

— *Gassing:* Government-approved gases (eg. "Cymag") used to kill mammals, such as rabbits, in their tunnels.

— *Poison:* Government-approved substances (eg. "Warfarin," "Klerat" [brodifacoum], "Ratak" [difenacoum], "Storm" [flocoumafen]), used to kill mammals such as rats, mice, and moles.

— *Dead traps:* Government-approved spring traps, such as break-back mouse and rat traps, pliers type mole traps and "Fenn" type tunnel traps, intended to kill any creature triggering them.

— *Snares:* Wire loop traps of government-approved specification and method of use, designed to hold the prey alive until released.

— *Live traps:* Government-approved traps, usually a wire cage or box, designed to capture animals alive and physically uninjured.

— *Shotgun:* A smooth-bore gun firing many small pellets in a spread pattern, used to kill birds and medium-sized mammals, usually while moving.

— *Rifle:* A rifled-barrel gun firing a single bullet, used mainly to kill static, medium-sized to large mammals.

— *Angling:* Fishing using hooks for fresh or salt-water fish.

— *Net-fishing:* Fishing using nets for fresh or salt-water fish.

A comparison of the methods:

A simple table can be made (table 8.8.1 and figure 8.8.1), based on data gleaned where possible from published information but primarily from a consensus of expert opinion. More detailed research into these parameters is needed.

In examining this table you could apply addi-

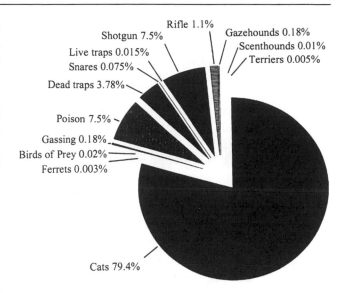

Figure 8.8.1 Estimated proportions of wild birds and mammals killed by man and his animals in Britain 1995, excluding road deaths and pollution.

tional criteria and you could apply different weighing to the seven criteria used here. It is not easy to quantify these things; we can only assess them comparatively as best we can. Obviously the values given are indicative rather than absolute. Only two methods score well on all points: gazehounds and raptors. They are both naturally and legally selective, supervised, quick in pursuit, quick to kill and leave no wounded. Scent hounds follow close behind with good scores on five criteria. Guns fall down on their high incidence of wounding and maiming. The use of terriers and ferrets down holes has difficulties in supervising and intervening if there is a problem. Cats and traps score badly

Table 8-8-1 Killing Methods

| | Natural Selectivity | Legal Selectivity | Precapture Human Supervision | Pursuit Inverval | Catch-to-kill Interval | Maiming | Approx U.K. Annual Volume |
|---|---|---|---|---|---|---|---|
| Gaze hounds | Yes | 99% | Yes | <2 mins | 0–5 secs | 0 | 500,000 |
| Scent hounds | Yes | 99% | Yes | >2 mins | 0–5 secs | 0 | 35,000 |
| Terriers | No | 70% | Yes | >2 mins | 2–30 mins | ? | 15,000 |
| Cats | Yes | 0% | No | <30 secs | 0–30 min | 20%? | 210,000,000 |
| Ferrets | No | 95% | Yes | <5 mins | 0–15 mins | 10% | 10,000 |
| Birds of prey | Yes | 95% | Yes | <2 mins | 0–5 mins | 0 | 60,000 |
| Gassing | No | 70%? | Yes | N/A | 0–30 mins | 1% | 500,000 |
| Poison | No | 80%? | Yes | N/A | 0–2 days | ? | 20,000,000 |
| Dead traps | No | 60% | 24 hrs | N/A | 0–24 hrs | 5% | 10,000,000 |
| Snares | No | 70% | 24 hrs | N/A | 0–24 hrs | 10% | 200,000 |
| Live traps | No | 70% | 24 hrs | N/A | 0–24 hrs | 0 | 40,000 |
| Shotgun | No | 99% | Yes | <2 mins | 0–15 mins | 30% | 20,000,000 |
| Rifle | Yes | 100% | Yes | 0 | 0–15 mins | 10% | 3,000,000 |
| Angling | | | | | | | |
| Net-fishing | | | | | | | |

in comparative terms. In addition, some of the methods, such as poisons, are liable to misuse, or to poaching. Surprisingly, there is no legal control on the use of cats and these are the major killers of protected species.

As well as the suffering caused to individual prey animals, it is relevant to look at the scale. There are about 2,000 active falconers in Britain each taking about 30 head of legal quarry per year, a total of about 60,000 prey. The 314 registered hunts and unregistered packs in Britain kill around 35,000 foxes, hares, or deer. In contrast, the 7.5 million cats in Britain are estimated to kill at least 75 million birds and 135 million mammals annually. In other words, for every head of prey taken by someone's raptor, the cats take 3,500 prey and for every fox killed by hounds, cats kill about 6,000 creatures. Not only this, but cats do it in such a slow way that they have been selected as the model animal for studies of aggressive predatory behavior. Cats also put into perspective the 3.2 million experiments on laboratory animals each year in Britain and the four million migratory birds killed in Malta each year.

It would be nice to have firmer figures for these parameters, but meanwhile it is possible to make some simple broad-brush analyses. For example, cats are responsible for about 79 percent of all kills. If you look at the parameter that you are interested in, such as the catch-to-kill interval, and multiply it by the volume, you can see quite quickly where the major sources of suffering really exist.

In attempting to reduce animal suffering as represented above, one must take into account the consequences of eliminating these methods. What would happen if rats and mice were allowed to proliferate unchecked? What would happen if deer and rabbits could not be controlled on farm land? What efforts would landowners make to maintain and improve habitat benefitting all wildlife if they obtained no sporting return? Would the alternative deaths awaiting the prey animals be preferable to the ones they have now?

Unfortunately, few people attempt to evaluate these issues in any logical or scientific way, preferring to win hearts emotively rather than minds. The result is massive inconsistency and hypocrisy. The RSPCA, which funds many research projects into the alleviation of animal cruelty, has sadly neglected the cruelty aspect of cat keeping because a major proportion of its income derives from cat

keepers. In recent years the RSPCA membership has become increasingly political and this is backing it into an untenable position in a moral corner. The RSPB is also heavily supported by cat lovers and has, as far as possible, avoided research on the impact of cats on wildlife. But it has at the same time remained neutral on fieldsports, a position which seems wise considering the RSPB's increasing land ownership and its real requirement to manage unwanted wildlife on its land. The British Association on Shooting and Conservation, for its part, does not appear to have researched the extent of suffering involved in shooting and is reluctant to provide information on this. Therefore most of the major organizations have their own reasons for not wanting to investigate some aspect of this issue and so at present it is impossible to conduct an informed debate owing to sheer lack of factual information.

The activities to change the status quo have largely been confrontational rather than research. Most attempts at "education" by both antifieldsports and profieldsports are very short on facts and rely heavily on emotion. The major thrust by the antifieldsports lobby has been to push for legislation against fieldsports, and to do this it has of necessity concentrated on numerically small fieldsports which it might have some prospect of banning. Paradoxically therefore, the legal efforts would have insignificant benefit to wildlife. For example the recent legal efforts in Britain have been the MacNamara Bill 1993 and the McFall Bill 1995 which were essentially attempts to ban hunting of mammals with dogs. Considering that, of all mammals killed by cats and dogs in Britain, dogs only kill 0.4 percent, to exclude cats from the issue seems somewhat one-sided, particularly as a proposed safety clause would have removed rabbits and rodents from the Act.

Animals are usually killed because they are pests, food, or a recreational resource, or combinations of these. The rabbit, for example, is all three. Some, such as foxes, can be a recreational resource in one locality and a pest in another. It can be difficult to agree on what is and what is not a "pest." At present it seems to be more socially acceptable to kill some pests (such as rats) with dogs than to kill other pests (such as foxes) with dogs. Rats and foxes have equally developed nervous systems and presumably experience similar levels of pain. The movement against fox hunting therefore must hinge, not on biological grounds, but on a perception that the hunters enjoy hunting. Many of the antihunting organizations are funded by cat keepers who believe that because they do not enjoy watching their cats mauling little birds, they are therefore eliminated from the charge of cruelty. This is not a source of consolation to the cats' victims. The question of human enjoyment is not relevant to the suffering animal.

Given that one of the legitimate reasons for killing wild animals is as a recreational resource and that the enjoyment is derived from the total hunting experience rather than from the kill itself (see 8.14), it seems logical to maximize the experience benefit and minimize the numbers of kills. This is a cost-analysis approach. Thus in hunting with hounds, or in falconry, many man-hours of leisure enjoyment are obtained per kill. One fox killed could represent about 100 people/days of hunting, not to mention ancillary activities. Shooting with a shotgun is intermediate, ranging from cost-effective activities such as rough-shooting or wildfowling, to more killing-dependent activities such as driven game shooting. Keeping pet cats is the most cost expensive activity. Many millions of deaths produce no enjoyment, rather the reverse. Unlike working cats, the enjoyment of pet cats is not dependent on killing at all.

For a variety of valid reasons, we are unlikely ever to cease killing wild animals in Britain. Whatever our reasons for killing wildlife, we must try to do it humanely, and that means minimizing suffering as outlined above. We must minimize the amount of pain to each individual, and we must minimize the numbers of individuals caused pain. Where wildlife is a pest or a food source, killing is obviously a prime consideration. Where wildlife is a recreational resource, priority should be given to maximizing the hours of leisure enjoyment and minimizing unnecessary killing. The only area in which there is *wanton* killing without any concomitant enjoyment is in the practice of allowing pet cats to range freely, killing protected wildlife at random. Legislation and research focussed on this would provide the largest single reduction in wild animal suffering. Simply reducing predation by cats during the sensitive breeding months of April to July could reduce wildlife deaths by 100 million per year, the equivalent in one year of banning all hunting with dogs until the year 2,200 A.D.

## 8.9   Sky trials and bagged game

In this section I want to tackle the ethics of using prey animals which have been previously held or captured by man. *This of course is not falconry, which is the taking of wild prey in its natural state by means of trained hawks,* but it is legal in many countries with Britain, Germany, and the Netherlands as notable exceptions.

What do we mean by "bagged?" The commonest bagged game is a domestic pigeon which is handled and released in the same way as when releasing pigeons in a pigeon race. Another way is to use the same method as that employed by dog-trainers, namely to "dizzy" the pigeon and place it on the ground in rough grass. It will stay there for up to half an hour, allowing the person to come back with a dog and obtain a point, which presents a realistic set-up for a young falcon learning to wait on. "Dizzying" is just a form of predator-induced tonic immobility. A further way is to use a commercial spring trap beloved of the American shooters. This can be triggered from a distance and will throw birds up to pheasant size into the air.

Less innocuous forms of release include handicapping the animal in some way, for example by trimming the primaries, or by attaching a string to it. Thus, quite apart from the hawk, the use of bagged game in itself may entail some degree of suffering or discomfort.

Bagged game is used under these circumstances:

a) To enter a young raptor, in the same way that its parents do in the wild.
b) To help teach a falcon to wait on.
c) To exercise a falcon.
d) To make competitive sky trials for falcons.
e) To call a bird back with, for example, a live pigeon on a string.

a) The use of captured game to teach youngsters to hunt is widespread in wild raptors and in many mammalian predators too, such as the cat family. New Zealand falcons tend first to fly away from the pursuing youngster and then drop dead prey for it to catch (see 5.19) and then later, as the youngster gets more proficient, to release live prey high in the air where the young falcon has a good chance of catching it. To this extent bagged game is natural. There are alternative methods for falconers using towed dead prey or clockwork ones, and these have been described in chapter 5. In the right circumstances, these obviate the need for bagged game.

There are some ethical dilemmas in entering young raptors. The first is the practice of flying raptors which are unentered. This is common (for very good reasons) among display birds and among people who keep raptors as pets rather than for hawking. If an unentered raptor becomes lost, it has only a small chance to learn to catch prey in the few days before it becomes too weak to fly. This is especially true for older birds which have passed their youthful learning period and become "lure bound." For the hawk's benefit therefore, if not for the falconer's, it is desirable that the hawk should have at least taken one or two prey for itself so that it knows that prey mean food. Then, if it gets lost and gets hungry, it will at least try to catch its own food. Otherwise it is likely to starve to death without so much as launching an attack on prey which may be right in front of it.

Rehabilitators are often faced with the task of returning raptors which have never hunted before back to the wild. We have had to do a number of peregrines like this. Usually they have been taken from a nest illegally and then been the subject of a court case. By the time the legal procedures are finished it is well into the autumn. The bird has to become proficient at flying, and become fit, at a time of short winter days, bad weather and low prey numbers. Being a single, older bird, it cannot be hacked properly because it would quickly wander off. It cannot be allowed to stray too far because of the risk of losing it in an unentered state. To get such a bird, at such a late stage, to catch prey reliably, without using bagged game, is at best a major work commitment, at worst, impossible. The current healthy state of wild peregrine populations in U.K. no longer justifies such an expenditure of resources; indeed, releasing such a bird is probably counter-productive (see 8.2). In such a scenario it is definitely more ethical to flush some dizzied pigeons under such a bird than to release it unentered to almost certain starvation. Alternatively, if one is against killing, it would be better to kill the peregrine and thereby save the lives of its future prey.

b), Training to wait on, exercise, and sky trials,
c), can all be lumped together. Essentially the
and falcon is taught to wait on, as it does in the
d) wild (see 6.4) and a racing pigeon is released. The falcon then stoops at the pigeon and may or may not catch it. The method is described in Beebe and Webster in detail. This is a common practice in the Americas, Spain, Italy, and the Middle East. Most pigeons escape. This is not a particularly cruel practice but it is the lazy falconer's way of training and exercising his bird. When time is short, it is obviously easier to give your falcon a flight at a pigeon than to go hawking. Many falconers in North America stoutly maintain that it is impossible to train a high mounting falcon without using pigeons. They are wrong! Certainly it is a lot easier to use pigeons, but it is disappointing when experienced falconers find themselves unable to cope without pigeons. It is one thing to use some pigeons to teach a young falcon how to hunt, another when the falconer relies on using pigeons on a regular basis for the rest of the falcon's career.

Sky trials are when several falconers meet to fly their falcons at pigeons on a competitive basis. The method has been described by Gerald Richards in *Game Hawking...at its very best.* Only nine out of 202 pigeons were killed. Thus, in itself, it is no more cruel than falconry. My objections to it are that it debases falconry into a competition between people rather than a hunting experience. To me, when you hawk together, you all work as a team to help the hawk, whoever's it is. It is sad to see a fine old sport like falconry reduced to a slick televised competition.

And this brings me onto my second objection. Once you hold a sky trials, impressionable youngsters attend and go away with the idea that this is falconry. Worse still, the media will be there (in Spain they are actively promoted) and before long it all appears on television. The public then think that this is falconry and a bad image is created. In Spain, where attitudes to animals are different, falconers find my comments bewildering. But when videotapes of sky trials are sold abroad, the damage is done.

e) The use of a pigeon on a string to call a falcon

back is still prevalent in the countries mentioned above. Again, it is a sign of a lazy or inexperienced falconer. Many game falcons are flown in such a high condition that they won't come down to a dead lure and the falconer has become slack on his discipline and weight control. The clockwork lure-pigeon (figure 3.10.4) works just as well as a real pigeon, so there is really no excuse for this archaic practice.

Thus, with a few exceptions, I condemn the use of bagged game. Most of it is unnecessary to the sport of falconry and brings it into disrepute. In most cases, with a little thought, there are humane alternatives.

## 8.10 Falconry as a "green" field sport

Falconry has got to be the most environmentally friendly fieldsport and method of pest control. In recent years there has been an astonishing revolution in falconry. At least 37 species of diurnal birds of prey have now been bred domestically for two or more generations and thirty of these are available on a sustainable basis. This has almost been like condensing about 10,000 years of domesticating farm animals into just twenty years. The significance for falconers has been immense because at last their hunting birds are available on a secure long-term basis.

No raptors have been taken under license from the wild for falconry in Britain since 1988. British falconry is now selfsufficient for birds of prey and has no negative direct impact at all on wild raptors. Over 2,500 injured wild raptors are tended by hawk-keepers in U.K. every year, and about half of these birds are returned to the wild (admittedly with unknown success), so the only impact falconry has on wild populations is a positive one (see 8.2).

But what is true falconry? Falconry is the hunting of wild quarry in its natural state by means of trained birds of prey. As such it is really just a controlled form of natural predation. This is what I find so fascinating about it. I remember on one occasion radiotracking a wild Mauritius kestrel in a last remnant of the forest there. I ran along behind it in the trees while it searched for and attacked tree geckos. At the end of the day it went back to its nest area. If it had been a falconry bird I would have taken it home safe to its mews, but

this was the only difference; otherwise it could well have just been a sequence in a normal day's hawking.

This close intimacy enables the falconer to see at first hand the way in which predators function and also to understand just how closely the prey have adapted to this predation. Hawks are remarkably quick at identifying weakness in a prey. Any animal which is weak, molting, diseased, pricked by shot, or simply an odd color, is immediately targeted. I would say, from watching goshawks attacking flushing wood pigeons and ducks, that an experienced hawk recognizes a weak bird in a group within the first half a second of them rising. By the time the birds are at waist height any odd bird has been singled out, and the goshawk will fly it with much more conviction, almost as if it knows the outcome is inevitable.

This rabbit was easily taken by my male gos. The right lower incisor had an abcess and had broken off. The other teeth had nothing to wear against and kept growing. The rabbit was starving.

Falcons, such as peregrines, tend to be much less impulsive. They like to be in control of the situation. But studies by Rudebeck in Sweden and by German falconers hawking corvids, have shown that falcons too are selective. Initial attacks at flocks are often feints, designed to try out the prey and reveal any weakness (see 6.9). If the whole flock is strong the falcon may well lose interest, but if one of the individuals appears slower than the rest, or loses its nerve, then the falcon attacks in earnest. Of course raptors are not selective all the time; they are perfectly capable of taking healthy prey. But studies reveal that the proportion of weak or handicapped prey in their tally is considerably higher than the proportion in a shot sample.

By watching the way in which a raptor hunts its prey one comes to a much deeper understanding of the prey themselves, their cryptic coloring, the way they go about their daily business, always alert, always near an escape route or in flocks with sentinels, their whole way of life finely tuned to predators. But when the predator actually arrives, a whole new kaleidoscope of behavior is revealed, and one suddenly realizes the prey have got a lot more tricks up their sleeves than at first appeared (see 7.4). The falconer and his bird together discover that in certain situations prey are safe from attack and, as they get more experienced, they learn to recognize situations where an attack could be successful. This breeds a respect for the prey to the extent that an animal, such as the crow, which to others may be regarded as a pest to be killed at every opportunity, to a falconer poses intriguing intellectual possibilities and a physical challenge. To hawk it successfully may entail the use of four-wheel drive vehicles or horses, radiotracking, specially bred and trained falcons, and access to large areas of open terrain, together with a daily commitment for several weeks. Not (you might say) the most cost-effective way of going about killing crows. Quite possibly not! But wait a minute, what are we actually trying to catch in a fieldsport? Not, as a superficial look might suggest, the quarry. That is a necessary adjunct. No, our real quarry is a much more elusive customer. His name is enjoyment. Just when you think you've got him, he slips away. And then, in a quiet moment, you suddenly realized you've glimpsed him again. This is what falconry is all about.

I remember a day a few years ago. A falconer called Graham was working for me and it was his first day out hawking red grouse. We were hawking in Sutherland in Scotland with important guests. Graham had helped hack and train the young falcon, called "Snake," and when my dog locked on point in a broad basin, Graham was told it was his flight. He unhooded Snake, and with a shake of her bell she climbed effortlessly to a good pitch above us. I faced the dog and with a quick rush flushed a single grouse under the falcon. She dipped a moment and then ignored it. Unbelievable! What could be up with this bird? And then we realized. Twice as high as Snake, in an unmarked sky, appeared the searing crossbow-shape of a wild peregrine. In tight rings Snake caught an updraft and climbed to do battle. Not daring to take our glasses off them for fear of losing them, we watched the aerial dogfight, silenced by distance. Alternately stooping and locking talons, they

drifted out of sight over the hill. I could hear the radio signal fade as Snake disappeared over the ridge. Graham ran uphill through the long heather, whistling and swinging his lure. After ten minutes he was almost exhausted, and we lost sight of him too. We were left, actors in an unresolved drama, waiting for a prompter.

Then I heard some very soft bleeps on the radio. Like the faint pulse on a recovering heart victim, we sensed that Snake was returning, coming back on stage. Graham, suddenly recharged with energy, came bounding down the hill, stumbling and sprawling with fatigue. We were ready. The pointer, after twenty minutes, was still absolutely motionless on the remainder of the covey, which in turn had stayed tight due to the falcons overhead. Snake came back over and resumed her position of authority. The moment we were in her killing cone I flushed the grouse back up the hill over the dog's back. Like a dark bee, one skimmed up toward the burn. Snake peeled over and hooked down and as the two dots merged they disappeared from view into a small gully. The falcon did not come up again, and I knew she had got it. When I arrived I found Graham lying beside the falcon under a bank. Steve Frank took a photo of them. Graham's first grouse had left him totally physically and emotionally drained. He'd gone from the heights to the depths and back again and was now being eaten alive by midges. Such is falconry!

The point of this story is not to show how inefficient falconry is, but to show how *efficient* it is. Many, many man-hours of interest, involvement and enjoyment are obtained per head of game taken. Indeed some falconers go several years before they manage to catch anything at all, so absorbing is the sport.

This is not to say that falconry cannot be effective at killing game. Many professional falconers are engaged in pest control, particularly in places, such as in towns and parks, airfields, and rubbish dumps, where to discharge a gun would be dangerous. Goshawks and Harris hawks are quite capable of accounting for a dozen rabbits in an afternoon without making a lot of noise or endangering anybody. Hawks and falcons used in pest control are also used, not primarily to kill the pest, but to frighten it off. And as it doesn't pollute the environment. It is a very "green" method of pest control.

Finally, as well as being selfsustaining, selective, natural, and nonpolluting, falconry seldom leaves prey injured. Normally it is either caught or it escapes unscathed. The kill, especially by experienced falcons, is often absolutely instantaneous. Hawks on the other hand often hold their prey until the falconer arrives. He may then decide to kill it humanely or to release it. But whatever happens the falconer leaves the field with a clear conscience that no animals are left behind wounded and that the prey have faced only a situation to which they are naturally adapted.

In the old days falconry had a huge following across Europe and Asia. Now, at the end of the second millennium, with increasing urbanization and huge pressures on the countryside, it is a splendid way to renew contact with nature and to come to understand how natural systems work. In Britain 83 percent of people live in towns. Many now have a very distorted view of nature from being reared on "Bambi" TV programs. There is a big taboo on death. But many strive, consciously or unconsciously, to renew their links with nature. Maybe they take up rambling or birdwatching. But others feel that this is more like voyeurism and want to be actually involved in nature. Many people, especially boys and men, still feel a strong instinct to hunt. Some play computer games or football, but others want to be out hunting real quarry, not an artificial one. Falconry enables people to get out into the fresh air and hunt real quarry without having a major impact on the environment.

A falconer can hunt through a path of countryside and leave no trace. No bangs, no empty cartridges, no wounded game, no risk to other people. He doesn't need to modify the countryside by building sports grounds or golf course, or by killing vermin, rearing large numbers of game birds, and restricting public access. His demands on prey populations are small; his bag for the whole season is often less than a shooter's bag in one day, and his prized quarry is often a pest species.

Thus falconry is a natural, low-impact fieldsport, selfsustaining and well suited to the needs of modern man. It helps us to understand natural ecosystems and to realize that we are part of them.

## 8.11 Ways to learn falconry and hawk-keeping

When I was a boy I hawked for three seasons before I ever met another living falconer. The books available then were few to someone of my limited means. Jack Mavrogordato had published his first book *A Hawk for the Bush* and Michael Woodford had just published *A Manual of Falconry*. Most of the other books were too historical to have much relevance for me. Growing up in the country, without others to help, my attitude has always been "Ask the birds." They will tell you what they need.

This is a very hard, slow way to learn something as unforgiving as falconry. I treasure those years very much. They were simple, natural years when I hacked my birds without really being aware of the deep intellectual pool of knowledge whose surface I was swimming on. In factual terms I could probably teach somebody in a couple of days all the information I learned during my childhood, how to put on jesses and all that kind of thing. But I could never easily teach someone how to read a hawk's mind, how to interpret the glance of a hawk which betrays what it is thinking.

When I started meeting and corresponding with other falconers, all the complications of modern falconry started. In the twenty years after the war the small groups of falconers started to come to a focus. Pesticides decimated the hawks which suddenly had special status. Rumors circulated that hawks could be bred in captivity.....

More and more people wanted to learn falconry and to meet this demand Philip Glasier started to run course. In return for working at his center in the summer it opened, he taught me to block hoods, to exercise falcons, and a host of other practical things which cannot easily be picked up from books. Many of these details had been passed on, person to person, from the Old Hawking Club and back into the mists of time.

In 1971, I was approached to run three course under contract during the summer. Although I had only taken my first head of game scarcely five years earlier, I took the opportunity and all went well. For the first time I realized what a diversity of approaches there are to falconry. The British Falconers' Club's attitude to beginners then was that you would not be accepted into the Club until you were taking quarry regularly with a trained hawk. This rather left beginners out in the cold; by the time they were taking quarry regularly many of them had lost all desire to join!

The North American Falconers' Association and some of the clubs in other countries have their own apprenticeship schemes. This is an admirable way of getting beginners off on the right foot. Of course it depends how good the tutor is, both at falconry and at teaching, but it is the next best thing to actually being reared in hawking. In Zimbabwe, Ron Hartley, runs a club at Falcon College which not only gets the youngsters off on the right foot in falconry but also instills in them a deep ethos of responsibility toward raptor conservation. As a result, Zimbabwe is one of the few African countries with established local interested people caring for their raptors.

The problem was that up until the 1980s, hawks were in short supply. Tyros were discouraged because they represented future competition for scarce birds. This is not so any longer. Beginners now do not represent competition for hawks but they do represent competition for hawking grounds and, worse still, they represent an increasing threat to the future of falconry through potentially bringing the sport into disrepute by doing something stupid. When there were only a hundred falconers in Britain keeping a low profile, there was no problem. Now that there are perhaps ten thousand hawk-keepers in Britain alone, many in populated areas and many actively seeking publicity, then there is great potential for a bad press.

Through the early eighties we taught course for three or four weeks in the summer and learned more about the process of learning. The first thing we learned was the amazing capacity of the human race for messing people about. The person who could book a course, send a deposit, arrive on time without bringing their dog/ferret/mother/children, without losing their flight ticket/hearing aid, able to both speak and write English, capable of getting up in the mornings and eating normal meals was a rare gem.

Apart from their idiosyncrasies, the beginners fell into three groups: those who had no natural aptitude or empathy with hawks and who should not be allowed anywhere near a live one. These we weaned off the idea by whatever means we could. The second group really wanted a summer break doing something special, a taster. They had no serious intention of continuing, but supported falconry and enjoyed actively participating for a few days. We tried to make their week enjoyable, to show them some of the fascination of falconry and we didn't worry too much if they didn't take in all the technical details. The third group were the ones who meant business. We were more fussy with them, picking them up on small errors which could have been fatal to a bird. At the end of the three

weeks we lent them the buzzards which had been used on the course. They took them away for a year. Some caught quite a lot of rabbits with them, some gave up falconry when they sent the bird back. But they had had a chance to get started without great expense using birds that were tough enough to weather callow treatment. With dogs, horses and hawks I find it is always better if one of the partnership is already trained.

We found that the best course consisted of four to six people. This made the group "gel" with fertile discussions and a happy atmosphere. You can only teach intensively in short bursts, then there has to be time to consolidate. Then coursers can talk among themselves and discuss different viewpoints. There's always a wise guy who wants to show the others how to fit hood braces! In the mornings we covered theory and indoor practical work such as fitting anklets and repairing feathers. In the afternoons we did outdoor practical work such as calling off hawks and, on the advanced course, hawking, either crow or magpie hawking or rabbit-hawking.

When people first arrived on their course, on their first morning, I would ask them one question—"Why are you here?" Few of them had thought about this and we would return to the point several times during the course. Everyone has different motives for taking up hawk-keeping and/or falconry. Some of these motives are not even conscious. We tried to get people to come to terms with their real motives and to act on them, either to give up or to go forward.

One of the main problems is that most of the people coming in to falconry have urban backgrounds. They have not been brought up in the country and do not understand it. They do not understand farming or farmers' problems. They do not understand how country folk live and work. And most of all they do not have the field craft skills necessary to produce good slips for their birds. Usually they have come into it through a fascination with a hawk on the fist. Thus we found that some of the keen roughshooters who came on a beginners' summer course had taken over fifty head by Christmas whereas many with no country background caught nothing within three years. These are the kind of people who become "muddlers" who never really get it together. A lot of people never really get it together in falconry.

More and more course have sprung up. There are also now "taster" days, corporate entertainment days, weekends, and hunting days. These are situations in which falconry interfaces with the public on very intimate terms. Anyone can ring up and go on one of these days. They can take a camera or video. That material could be used in the media against falconry. It is thus important to ensure that all of these activities are properly conducted and do not bring falconry into disrepute. It is also important that beginners are properly taught and receive value for money. Course can help avoid many of the elementary pitfalls. They are almost always better than nothing at all. But they are only a very small beginning down a very long and interesting path. The good falconer, when he hits a problem, will not immediately go running for advice. He will try to puzzle it out for himself, he will ask his bird, and he may come up with some very original solutions.

Much better than a course is to become a working pupil for several months or a year. There are various establishments involved professionally in some aspect of hawk-keeping, such as commercial and private breeding projects, some research and conservation institutions, zoos and "falconry" display centers, rehabilitation centers, pest destruction and clearance contractors and genuine falconers. Anyone hoping to be involved with hawks as a career would do well to work at one of these places on a voluntary or semivoluntary basis in order to get a grounding in the subject and to get a realistic view of it as a potential career. Most find the work harder than they had expected, and less glamorous. Unfortunately there are very few openings for genuine professional falconers. Most falconers nowadays are amateurs; those who do employ a professional look for a good man and are understandably reluctant to let an inexperienced person anywhere near their precious hawks. Having said that, it is often better to bring on a young inexperienced person and teach them good habits from the start than to employ someone who has flown hawks for a few years and reckons he knows it all.

In North America and Germany there are falconry tests, linked to possession licensing. Some of the questions in the multiple-choice tests have several possible answers and raise a smile or two, but in the main they are a genuine attempt to ensure that beginners have a basic grounding before they obtain a hawk. In Germany, they have a practical exam, and a verbal test, on raptor biology, falconry and management, hawking dogs, and

wildlife law, and 30–50 percent fail. In Britain, where anyone can buy a hawk, ignorance is widespread and humility is rare. But a balance has to be struck in this, as in all things. You don't have to pass any tests to have a baby human, and a child is a much greater commitment and responsibility.

Many young people nowadays are not good readers and find it hard to learn from books. Videos are a good way of teaching these people some aspects and more and more films of variable quality are becoming available. They can demonstrate things which cannot easily be described in books, on the other hand they can encourage an "instant expert" attitude based on a very shallow approach. We use in-house videos for training our staff and find them very useful. We make very basic ones which take only half a day to complete and have never been nominated for an Oscar. Our quail-breeding video for example lasts an hour and goes through every little detail the technician needs to know when operating our particular quail facility. The technician can have a rerun at any time without plaguing me with questions and, whenever we take on other technicians, even temporary ones, the film gives them a good grounding before they get started. Sometimes I think I have taught someone a particular point when in reality I taught it to somebody else (I easily get confused nowadays); the staff-training videos help eliminate this problem.

It is important to achieve and maintain certain standards, not just for the beginner, but also for experienced hawk-keepers. The Hawk Board in Britain has produced guidelines on hawk-keeping covering the welfare of both hawks and quarry, and intending to prevent disreputable activities. In Britain, Germany, and North America standards of welfare are among the highest in the world. Part of the intent of this book is to help maintain those standards and to encourage them elsewhere.

## 8.12  The philosophy of the falconer

Throughout the course of history, and recurring in many cultures, falconry has been seen as a training for princes, leaders, and gentlemen. It is the most senior of the hunting sports because it is the most difficult and the most challenging. Falconry teaches humility and fortitude, it enhances the spirit, it improves fine judgement and gives the falconer a sense of oneness with nature.

The falcon is a solitary animal, not a social

one. She has no instincts to obey a leader, to follow the commands of a society. She cannot therefore be punished or ordered to obey; she can only be asked and rewarded. Pauper or prince, she treats all men as equals and there are times when even princes crawl on their knees before a falcon. She is never servile or sycophantic. To a man accustomed to being obeyed, this is a lesson in humility. His horses, salukis, and people may obey his commands but to his falcon he is just a hunting partner.

And what a poor one! Weak of eyesight and slow of foot, the falconer is more a hindrance than a help to his falcon. He has to resort to cars and radios to help him keep up with and find his falcon. The nerves at the bases of her feathers enable her to feel the air with the sensitivity of a concert pianist's fingers. Her world is an interplay of wind, gravity, and speed. She sees the plodding falconer on his flat earth below and it is only the invisible bond between hunting partners which stops her raking off downwind to prey on fortune—alone.

Because he is such a poor hunting partner, the falconer must learn fortitude. When he wakes in the morning he must think of his falcon's well-being before his own. Out hunting he must be prepared to go through great physical hardship, trying to find prey for his falcon, following her flight, helping her when things go wrong, searching for her when she is lost. Sometimes his body will be aching with fatigue but his spirit will be soaring in the clouds with her, willing her success in the flight. A moment later an eagle may appear and the falconer's emotions turn to anxiety and desperation. Forgetting his tiredness he will make every effort to save his falcon. If all goes well he will end the day contented, his falcon beside him on her perch with a good crop. But if she is still out there in the dark, lost, he can think of nothing else. He does not notice what he is eating. He gets no sleep.

His heart is out there with his falcon. Where is she? Is she safe? What plan can he make to find her again?

This is the difference between the falconer and a man with a gun. At the end of the day the gun is cleaned and put away, a mere machine, a tool. The falconer never puts away his falcon. She is always in his thoughts. As His Highness Sheikh Mohamed Bin Zayed Al Nayhan said recently, "We value our sakers like our children."

When the falconer flies his falcon, part of his heart flies with her. All the time and effort he has spent on her have forged a bond in his heart. When she does well his heart almost bursts with joy. When she does badly, he is disappointed and sad. But he must learn not to show it, to bear his sadness without burdening it onto others. Although his emotions are taken on a roller-coaster ride by his falcon, and although his body may be brought to the limit of physical endurance, the falconer must cope with it all with fortitude. If he is not prepared to do this, if he is not prepared for the downside as well as the upside, he should never have flown his falcon. He should have stayed at home.

When he takes out his falcon, and slips her, he does not know what fate has in store. But he is prepared for it. He will have prepared in advance as best he can and he is ready to meet the challenge. He is ready for life.

The wise falconer can feel the spirit of a falcon, like an aura. The spirit of a horse or dog is different. They are social animals with a desire to please. They are dominated by man. The spirit of the falcon is independent, selfreliant and usually stronger than man's. Daily contact with such spirit enhances, inspires, and strengthens our own, through example.

Is this why we admire the falcon so much? She may be frightened of you, she may be angry at you, she may be pleased to see you. She will never lie to you, although you may not understand her. She has no selfpity and, even on the point of death from some consuming disease, her spirit is unbroken. It is a privilege to be in the presence of such a spirit, to draw strength from it and to learn from it. The gaze of a dying falcon is the distillation of life and a denial of triviality.

The wise man learns to listen when no words are spoken. How does he do that? He learns from his falcon who communicates with more subtle signs than mere words. These signs are the truth. The falconer learns judgement.

Sometimes out hawking the falconer finds a set-up that looks perfect. Wide open terrain, quarry well placed, wind direction right. Everything fine except for one bush out in the middle. That one bush is sufficient to alter the course of the whole flight. Instead of trying to outfly the falcon in aerial combat, the quarry makes an extra effort for the bush. It is the falconer's job to know his ground in advance. He should know about that bush and be prepared for it. Perhaps he will be able to maneuver the quarry far enough away from the bush to get a fair flight. Or perhaps he will select a falcon which can take quarry inside such a bush. He has to use his judgement and balance the risks. And so it is in the boardroom. A strategy may look perfect, but the good tactician will look for that small bush and will evaluate the risks in just the same way as he does out hawking.

Similarly, the falcon teaches us the importance of time and timing. When we are breeding falcons we are carefully considering plans up to five years ahead, trying to predict our needs and envisage all the factors. When we are training the falcon we are making preparations for hawking trips some weeks or months ahead, carefully ensuring that when the date comes everything will be ready. The falcons must be fit and keen and in good health. They are not machines; if something is wrong you can't get a mechanic to fit a replacement part. And out hawking there will be moments when two seconds will make the difference between success and failure. A brief fumbling with the hood is all it takes to delay the falcon long enough for the quarry to become badly placed and the whole flight ruined. Particularly when the quarry is on passage and the falconer is trying to judge the right moment to slip his falcon, timing is everything. And so the falconer learns to manage time and to handle timing. He learns to treat time almost as a physical entity. You can't see it, like distance. You can't touch it, like food. But nevertheless it is a major factor and taskmaster. A falcon which seems dull now, may simply with the passage of two hours of time, fly like an arrow. In politics and in everyday life, time and timing are crucial.

A good falconer is measured not by his best bird, but by his worst one. It is not hard to have one or two top class birds, but not easy to make a whole team of good ones. If there are only one or two good ones and they are flown first, then they get better and better but perhaps become overworked and too exposed to accident or disaster. If something happens to them the falconer is left with a very poor team, unable to show sport. But by bringing on his other birds he can work from strength and if some cannot be flown he still has others he can rely on. It is just the same in life. The most effective team has all its members consistently and reliably good, not one or two good people carrying too much load and the rest a poor lot.

Everyone looks for excitement. But it has to be balanced according to each person's needs. When we are young we risk our necks. As we grow older and the body begins to fail, we value our health

more and turn more to mental challenges and risks. The businessman gets excitement from making big business decisions. Others just gamble at cards or get secondhand excitement through films. Falconry offers a blend of physical hardship with risk management. Falconry is such a deep intellectual pool that you can never reach the bottom of it. People looking at falconry from the outside think that it is all about killing things, pitting one animal against another. This is not so. The quarry which the falconer is actually hunting is enjoyment. And that, as everyone knows, is a most elusive prey. Enjoyment cannot be bought, bottled, organized, or preserved. Often you don't appreciate it is there until it has gone. It comes in all shapes and forms from a long contentment, to a fleeting glimpse, to a surging thrill. The falconer realizes this and understands that all the ingredients must be there for it to work. This is why falconers are keen conservationists for their falcons, their quarry, and their hunting grounds. What use is the most prized falcon if she has no quarry to match her powers? Yes, the falconer wishes to catch his quarry, because falconry is about life and death. But he wishes to pursue the quarry in a way which enables it to use all its own natural abilities.

The prey has no natural defense against a gun. The bullet or pellets travel too fast for it to react. It may fly up into the air, be hit, and fall into a crumpled heap. With the falcon it is different. Millions of years of evolution and a lifetime of experience has taught the prey to deal with this eventuality. Some fly high, some fly low. Some creep and hide. Some disappear down a hole. Some twist and turn and outfly the falcon. The strong are more likely to survive than the weak. None escape injured to die later. The falconer thus gets an insight into natural systems. He knows how each species has different tactics to escape. He works out his own strategy with this in mind. And he has respect for his quarry, not as a mere target for a shot, but as a worthy opponent for his falcon.

The man who has no personal contact with animals is like a man who has lived all his life in the same village, unaware of the wide world outside. The man whose only contact with animals is at a distance, such as at a zoo or through television, is like a traveler in a foreign country who never gets to speak to the inhabitants. When people say "animals should be left in the wild" they are saying: "keep them separate from us, we are of a different world." Falconry is an interface between humans and the wild, a chance to be involved in the wild and not just a voyeur. You are not just looking in the window; you are actually in the party.

When you have understood, whether we like it or not, that we are all in this together, man, animals, plants, all stuck on Planet Earth, all dependent on one another, you become less arrogant and less confident of man's ability to control everything around him. We have not begun properly to understand complex natural systems yet. We cannot even predict the weather or earthquakes. We are using up finite resources. We call it all progress. But we are running in the dark, faster and faster. We may just be hastening toward a cliff when we should be quietly feeling our way along, step be step. Falconry is a way of feeling our way along, of comprehending the complex life systems which we depend on and are part of, and falconry is a preparation and training for life.

Golden eagle.

# Appendix 1

Some falconers who have made significant contributions to the conservation of birds of prey:

Note: This list is far from complete, there are many more people involved. Please send details if you have further information or corrections. Some of these people have now died but their contributions live on.

Barea, Laurence. - Ecological studies of New Zealand falcons.

Barton, Dr. Nigel. - contributions to veterinary aspects of raptors in the Middle East.

Bednarek, Dr. Walter. - Studies of captive breeding and of goshawk ecology.

Beebe, Frank. - Important studies on birds of prey in British Columbia, especially Peale's falcon on Langara Island. Important early efforts to develop captive breeding of falcons.

Berry, Robert B. - Director of the Peregrine Fund Inc., developed technique for cooperative insemination of human-imprinted raptors, active in legislative aspects of raptor conservation, breeding, and falconry.

Bodington, G. - Has done considerable field work of peregrine and Taita falcons including DDT impact.

Bond, Frank M. - Attorney at Santa Fe and Director of Peregrine Fund Inc., has been active in legal and legislative aspects of raptor conservation at state and national levels; serves as legal counsel for NAFA.

Bond, Richard M. - Soil Conservation Service (student of G. E. Hutchinson at Yale). Early peregrine population study in western North America (condor 1946), plus several popular articles on raptor conservation and falconry. Deceased.

Brosset, Professor Andre. - Work on prey selection and breeding biology.

Brull, Dr. Heinz. - Pioneering work and many-time author on ecology of central European raptors.

Burnham, Dr. William A. - The Peregrine Fund Inc., major contribution to captive breeding, and reintroduction of peregrine falcon in the Rocky Mountain region, plus extensive field studies of Arctic raptors and development of numerous international raptor conservation efforts around the world.

Cade, Professor Tom J. - Founder of the Peregrine Fund Inc. and prime mover for the successful restoration of the peregrine to North America. Initiator of many other studies on raptors in numerous countries.

Callejo, Dr. Jesus Rodriguez. - Promoter of raptor conservation in Central Spain through field studies and film making.

Condy, Dr. J. B. - As first President of the Zimbabwe Falconers' Club, he ensured that falconry was written into the Parks and Wildlife Act of 1975, and so the progressive conservation-based falconry policy was facilitated, which has led to the symbiotic relationship between the Department of National Parks and Wildlife Management of Zimbabwe and the Zimbabwe Falconers' Club.

Cooper, John, DTVM. - Author of many papers on raptor veterinary medicine and pathology.

Craighead, Drs. John and Frank. - Pioneering authors of *Hawks, Owls and Wildlife* and many other studies of predator-prey relationships and population ecology.

Dunkley, Dr. A. S. - Has contributed to the research on peregrine and Taita falcons. coauthor of book on Taita falcon. Helped to guide breeding program in Zimbabwe and contributed to vet care of raptors.

Ellis, Dr. David H. - Extensive raptor fieldwork in Alaska, U.S.A., Central and South America, Siberia, Russia, and Mongolia.

Enderson, Dr. James H. - Colorado College, major contributions to captive breeding, and reintroduction of peregrine falcon, plus eyrie monitoring in Colorado.

Fentzloff, Claus. - Contributions to the breeding and reintroduction of the sea-eagle in Europe.

Fowler, Jim. - Popularizer of raptor conservation, etc. via the Merlin Perkins Wild Kingdom TV show and other TV and radio programs, as well as lectures.

Fox, Dr. Nick. - Conservation work on New Zealand falcons, red kites, Mauritius kestrels, and sakers. Founder of the Raptor Association of New Zealand and of the Middle East Falcon Research Group.

de la Fuente, Dr. Felix Rodriguez. - Author and film maker, pioneer of wildlife conservation in Spain with a continuing impact long after his tragic death.

Fuller, Dr. Mark. - Pioneering radio tracking of raptors. Director of Raptor Research and Technical Assistance Center.

Fyfe, Richard. - Canadian Wildlife Service. Broadscale actions on many fronts to conserve Canadian raptors, especially the peregrine falcon—pesticides studies, captive breeding and reintroduction, field management techniques.

Giesswein, R. - Has made substantial contributions to the captive breeding and release of the peregrine.

Glasier, Philip. - Founder of the Hawk and Owl Trust, U.K.

Greaves, N. - Has led research work on falcons in Matopos National Park and environs, as part of the famous Black Eagle Survey Group, helped Ron Hartley in Falcon College.

Groenwald, A. - Has done considerable fieldwork on the peregrine and Taita falcons including DDT impact.

Hahn, Dr. Eddie. - Studies of environmental contamination of raptors.

Hamerstrom, Dr. Fran. - Many studies of raptors, especially harriers, prolific author, and an inspiration to many young people who have gone on to make their own contributions.

Hartley, Ron. - Started the Raptor Conservation Fund and Falcon College, important raptor studies and conservation initiatives in Zimbabwe, especially in conjunction with the training of school boys at Falco College.

Hunter, Don. - Founded a major raptor study and conservation organization: The Raptor Research Foundation, Inc. Active in captive breeding of falcons.

Hurrell, Dr. Leonard. - Pioneered captive breeding methods, especially of merlins and sparrowhawks.

Hyde, Noel. - Field studies and diet studies of New Zealand falcons.

Jameson, Dr. E. W. - Historical and cultural works on raptors.

Jenny, J. Peter. - Vice-President, The Peregrine Fund Inc., captive breeding and reintroduction of raptors, especially aplomado falcon, and major initiative in raptor conservation in Latin America, Guatemala, Ecuador, etc.

Jones, Carl. - Jersey Wildlife Preservations Trust, captive breeding and restoration of Mauritius kestrel and other conservation initiatives in the Mascarene Islands.

Kenward, Dr. R. E. - Studies of raptor behavior and ecology, with pioneering population models from radio tracking of goshawks, buzzards, and saker falcons.

Lincer, Dr. Geoffrey. - Studies of environmental contamination of raptors.

Link, Dr. Helmut. - Studies of goshawk ecology.

Martin, Steve. - Important popularizer of raptors and birds of prey conservation via nationwide "Birds of Prey Show" performed at various zoos and other venues in North America.

Mavrogordato, Jack. - Studies of wild and captive raptors.

Mebs, Dr. Theodore. - Early work on buzzard and peregrine populations in Germany.

Meng, Dr. Heinz. - Early breeding and release of peregrines in the United States.

Mundy, Dr. P. J. - Principal Ecologist and Ornithologist, Department of National Parks and Wildlife Management of Zimbabwe. Member of Zimbabwe Falconers' Club Raptor Research Unit, done surveys on Matopos falcon and peregrine and lanner falcons, etc.

Nelson, Morlan W. - Soil Conservation Service, retired, major popularizer of raptor conservation, especially in Idaho and the intermountain west, responsible for establishment of the Snake River Birds of Prey National Conservation Area, photographer for Disney nature films, etc.

Nicholls, Dr. M. - Studies of raptor genetics and pioneer of raptor education programs.

Nye, Alva G. Jr. - Great popularizer of appreciation of raptors—"discovered" Assateague Island peregrine migration route—active at state and federal levels in passage of protective legislation, etc. Deceased.

Olendorff, Dr. Richard. - Bureau of Land Management—raptor conservation and federal land management policies, also promoted federal aid for work on species such as the peregrine falcon, bald eagle, osprey, ferruginous hawk, etc. Deceased.

Osman, S. M. - Wildlife Preservation Society of India, studies of peregrine falcon migration and navigation.

Parry-Jones, Jemima. - Contributions to developments in breeding raptors and to education on raptor conservation. Author.

Pfeffer, Ralf. - Studies of the ecology of sakers and shahins in Kazakhstan.

Pielowski, Dr. Zygmunt. - Pioneering work on raptor behavior and ecology in Poland.

Potapov, Dr. Eugene. - Studies of rough-legged buzzards and peregrines in Russia.

Querl, R. - Contributed to the Raptor Research Programme directly and by way of his students at the Peterhouse School Falconry Club.

Redig, Pat, DVM, University of Minnesota. - Major contributions to raptor vet care, rehabilitation, and reintroduction of peregrine falcon.

Remple, David. DVM. - Major vet hospital and vet program for trained falcons in Dubai, many publications on falcon veterinary studies.

Rice, Jim. - Detailed history of peregrine population decline in Pennsylvania (in Hickey 1969).

Riddle, Ken, DVM. - Major vet hospital and vet program for trained falcons in Abu Dhabi, many publications on falcon veterinary studies.

Saar, Professor Christian. - Hamburg, captive breeding and the reintroduction of the peregrine falcon in Germany.

Sherrod, Dr. Steve. - Sutton Avian Research Center, Oklahoma, captive breeding and reintroduction of peregrine falcon, also translocation and restoration of southern bald eagle in the Southeastern United States, and numerous other research and conservation efforts associated with the Sutton Center.

Spofford, Dr. Walter R. - Upstate Medical School, Syracuse, NY. Popular articles and numerous lectures on raptor conservation. Major study for National Audubon society on golden eagle populations, especially in relation to sheep predation and aerial shooting in western states.

Temple, Stanley A. - Department of Wildlife and Ecology, University of Wisconsin, involved in early efforts to breed and release peregrine falcons, developed techniques for reintroduc-

tion of Andean and California condors, numerous field studies of raptors, has developed a major graduate studies center for conservation at University of Wisconsin.

Terrasse, Jean-Francoise. - Cofounder of Fonds d'Intervention pour les Rapaces, raptor release projects.

Thomsett, Simon. - Nairobi, raptor conservationist and rehabilitator, currently supported in several raptor conservation and education projects by the Peregrine Fund Inc.

Thomson, W. R. - As the first government Falconry Coordinator, he was instrumental in developing the progressive government falconry regulations in 1976 in Zimbabwe. He also institutionalized the data base on raptors from Zimbabwe Falconry Club Members, started research on DDT impact on raptors and started the successful Zimbabwe Falconry Club falcon breeding project mainly for peregrines. He has published and lectured widely.

Timimi, Dr. Faris. - Contributions to veterinary aspects of raptors in the Middle East.

Trommer, Dr. Gunter. - Veterinary studies and work on peregrine breeding and release in Germany and in Poland.

Walton, Brian J. - University of California, Santa Cruz, major contribution to captive breeding and reintroduction of peregrine falcon in California, plus other management work with California condor, elf owl, Harris hawk, and other raptors.

Weaver, James D. - The Peregrine Fund Inc., retired, major contribution to captive breeding and reintroduction of peregrine falcon plus extensive field studies of falcons in the Arctic.

White, Professor Clayton M. - Environmental impact studies on North American raptors and Editor of the journal *Raptor Research* for many years.

Zimbabwe Falconers' Club Members. - Monitoring Verreaux eagles, birds of prey sightings in national parks and nests, captive breeding of Taita and peregrine falcons and research into breeding of Verreaux eagles, training center for foreign students, and teaching conservation methods to the public and falconers.

# Appendix 2

| Common name | Species | Sex | Ring size (UK) | Internal ring diameter (mm) | Head width (mm) |
|---|---|---|---|---|---|
| American kestrel | *Falco sparverius* | M | R | 7 | 24-27 |
| | | F | R | 7 | 25-28 |
| European kestrel | *Falco tinnunculus* | M | S | 7.5 | 27-29 |
| | | F | S | 7.5 | 27-30 |
| European merlin | *Falco columbarius* | M | P | 6 | 26-28 |
| | | F | R | 7 | 26.5-29 |
| Red-headed merlin | *Falco chiquera* | M | S | 7.5 | 26-27.5 |
| | | F | S | 7.5 | 28-30 |
| European hobby | *Falco subbuteo* | M | R | 7 | 26-27.5 |
| | | F | S | 7.5 | 28-30 |
| Little falcon | *Falco longipennis* | M | R | 7 | 28-29 |
| | | F | S | 7.5 | 29-32 |
| Eleonora's falcon | *Falco eleonorae* | M | S | 7.5 | 31-33 |
| | | F | T | 8.7 | 33-35 |
| Bat falcon | *Falco rufigularis* | M | P | 6 | 25-26 |
| | | F | R | 7 | 28-30 |
| Aplomado falcon | *Falco femoralis* | M | S | 7.5 | 30-31 |
| | | F | T | 8.7 | 31-33 |
| Orange-breasted falcon | *Falco deiroleucos* | M | T | 8.7 | 31-35 |
| | | F | U | 9.5 | 34-39 |
| New Zealand falcon | *Falco novaeseelandiae* | M | U | 9.5 | 33-34 |
| | | F | V | 11.5 | 36-39 |
| Brown falcon | *Falco berigora* | M | V | 11.5 | 34-44 |
| | | F | W | 12.75 | 40-47 |
| Black falcon | *Falco subniger* | M | V | 11.5 | 38-40 |
| | | F | W | 12.75 | 40-42 |
| Grey falcon | *Falco hypoleucos* | M | V | 11.5 | 36-38 |
| | | F | W | 12.75 | 40-43 |
| Lugger falcon | *Falco jugger* | M | W | 12.75 | 36-38 |
| | | F | W | 12.75 | 38-42 |
| Lanner falcon | *Falco biarmicus* | M | W | 12.75 | 36-38 |
| | | F | W | 12.75 | 38-42 |
| Prairie falcon | *Falco mexicanus* | M | W | 12.75 | 39-43 |
| | | F | W | 12.75 | 40-47 |
| Saker falcon | *Falco cherrug* | M | W | 12.75 | 40-44 |
| | | F | W | 12.75 | 43-48 |
| Gyrfalcon | *Falco rusticolus* | M | W | 12.75 | 43-49 |
| | | F | X | 14 | 45-50 |
| Barbary falcon | *Falco pelegrinoides* | M | V | 11.5 | 36-37 |

| | | | | | |
|---|---|---|---|---|---|
| | | F | W | 12.75 | 38-40 |
| Black shaheen | *Falco peregrinator* | M | V | 11.5 | 36-37 |
| | | F | W | 12.75 | 38-40 |
| Spanish peregrine | *Falco peregrinus brookei* | M | V | 11.5 | 37-38 |
| | | F | W | 12.75 | 38-42 |
| Peregrine falcon | *Falco peregrinus peregrinus* | M | V | 11.5 | 38-42 |
| | | F | W | 12.75 | 43-45 |
| Peale's peregrine | *Falco peregrinus pealei* | M | V | 11.5 | 39-43 |
| | | F | W | 12.75 | 44-46 |
| | | | | | |
| Sharp-shinned hawk | *Accipiter striatus* | M | N | 5 | 20-25 |
| | | F | P | 6 | 26-29 |
| Shikra | *Accipiter badius* | M | N | 5 | 21-24 |
| | | F | P | 6 | 24-27 |
| European sparrowhawk | *Accipiter nisus* | M | P | 6 | 23-26 |
| | | F | R | 7 | 26.5-29.5 |
| Collared sparrowhawk | *Accipiter cirrocephalus* | M | P | 6 | 22-27 |
| | | F | R | 7 | 26-30 |
| Cooper's hawk | *Accipiter cooperii* | M | U | 9. 5 | 30-32 |
| | | F | V | 11.5 | 33-36 |
| Black sparrowhawk | *Accipiter melanoleucos* | M | U | 9.5 | 34-38 |
| | | F | V | 11.5 | 39-42 |
| Brown sparrowhawk | *Accipiter fasciatus* | M | U | 9.5 | 34-38 |
| | | F | V | 11.5 | 39-41 |
| White sparrowhawk | *Accipiter novaehollandiae* | M | U | 9.5 | 34-39 |
| | | F | V | 11.5 | 39-43 |
| Northern goshawk | *Accipiter gentilis gentilis* | M | V | 11.5 | 37-42 |
| | | F | W | 12.75 | 44-47 |
| | | | | | |
| Harris hawk | *Parabuteo unicinctus* | M | W | 12.75 | 40-44 |
| | | F | W | 12.75 | 42-47 |
| | | | | | |
| Common buzzard | *Buteo buteo* | M | W | 12.75 | 42-44 |
| | | F | W | 12.75 | 43-45 |
| Red-tailed hawk | *Buteo jamaicensis* | M | X | 14 | 44-46 |
| | | F | Y | 16 | 46-51 |
| Ferruginous hawk | *Buteo regalis* | M | X | 14 | 46-50 |
| | | F | Y | 16 | 48-52 |
| | | | | | |
| Golden eagle | *Aquila chrysaetos* | M | ZA | 25 | 62-66 |
| | | F | ZA | 25 | 65-68 |
| Wedge-tailed eagle | *Aquila audax* | M | ZA | 25 | 62-66 |
| | | F | ZA | 25 | 65-68 |
| | | | | | |
| Australasian harrier | *Circus aeruginosus gouldi* | M | W | 12.75 | 41-43 |
| | | F | W | 12.75 | 42-45 |

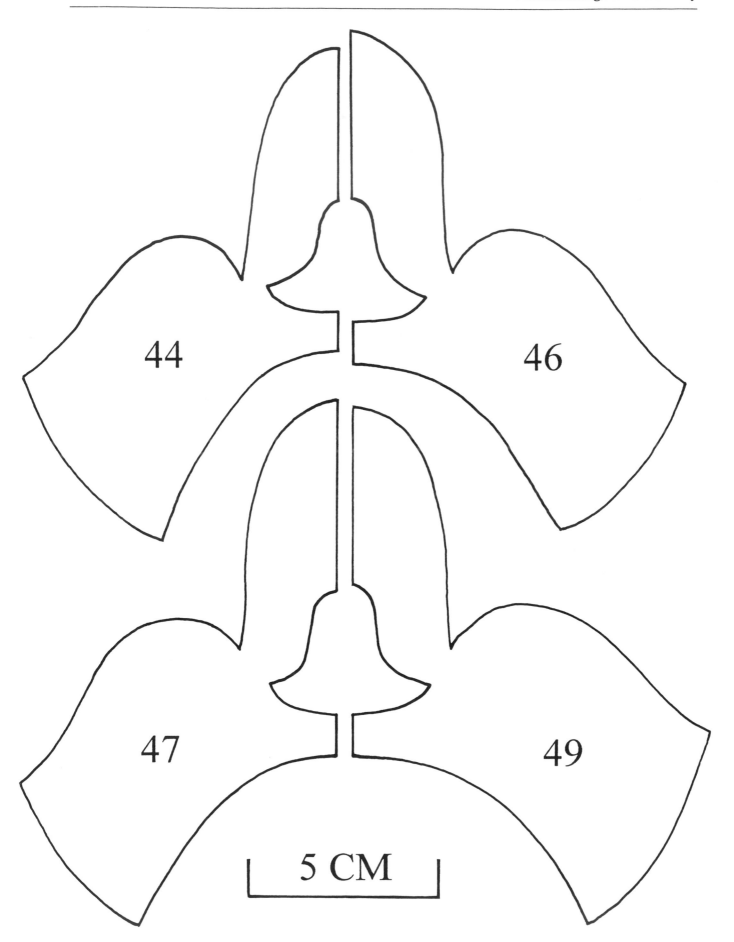

5 CM

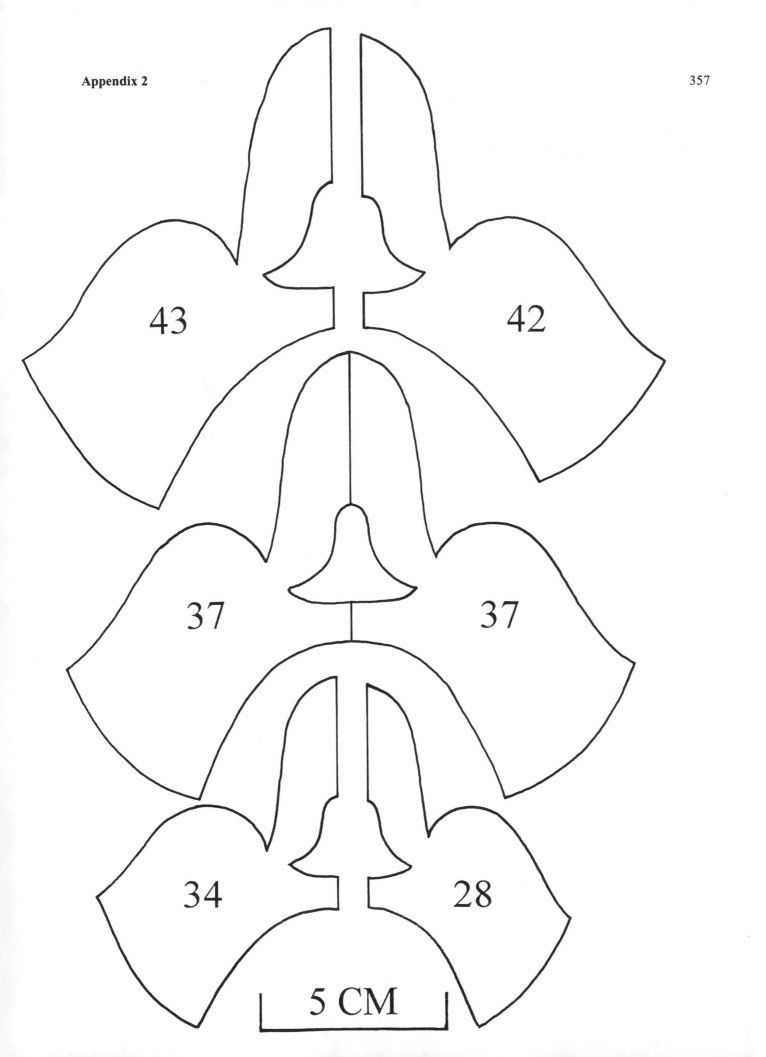

43

42

37

37

34

28

5 CM

# Appendix 3

**EGG CHART**     **EGG ID MARK**

| LAID | | | | MOTHER | |
|---|---|---|---|---|---|
| SET | | | | FATHER | |
| PIPPED | | | | CHICK RING No. | |
| HATCHED | | | | HATCH WT g | |
| LENGTH mm | | BREADTH mm | | FRESH WT g | PIP WT g |

Fox 1995

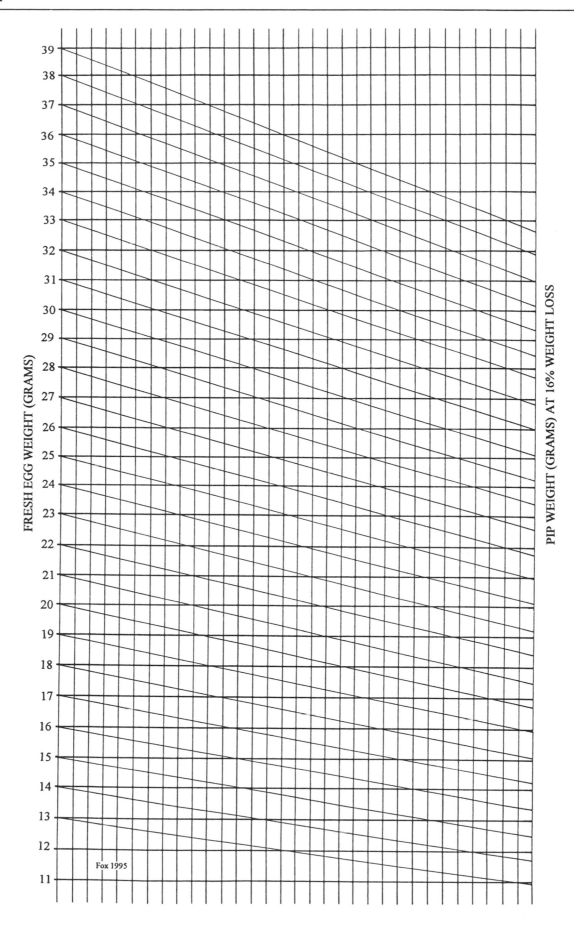

FRESH EGG WEIGHT (GRAMS)

PIP WEIGHT (GRAMS) AT 16% WEIGHT LOSS

Fox 1995

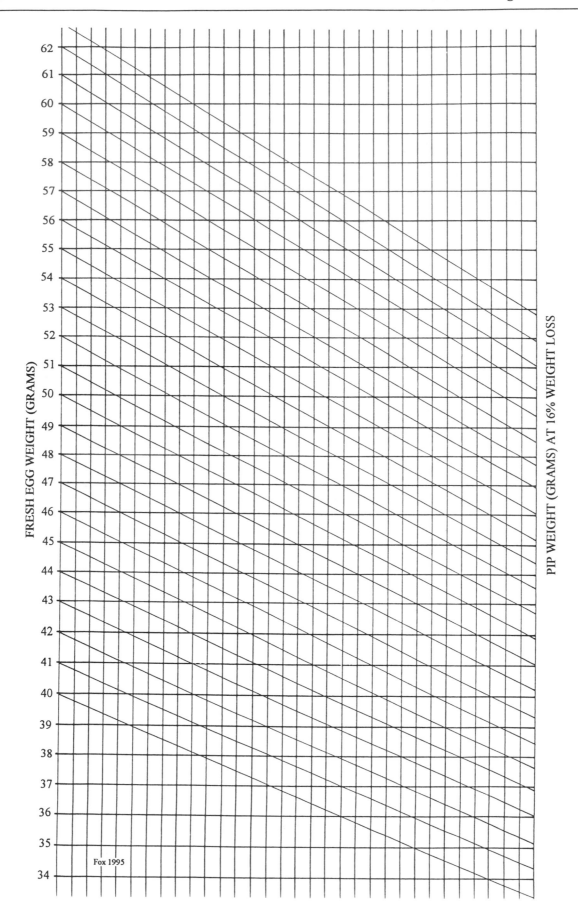

FRESH EGG WEIGHT (GRAMS)

PIP WEIGHT (GRAMS) AT 16% WEIGHT LOSS

Fox 1995

## GROWTH RATES AND FOOD CONSUMPTION

SPECIES:                                          SEX:                                          EGG No:

BAND No (left leg):                         (right leg):

PARENTS (female):                         (male):

HATCH DATE:                                 FOSTERED TO:

| | Wt empty    Wt fed    Wt food | | | | |
|---|---|---|---|---|---|
| 1 | | | | | |
| 2 | | | | | |
| 3 | | | | | |
| 4 | | | | | |
| 5 | | | | | |
| 6 | | | | | |
| 7 | | | | | |

Fox 1995

| Species | | | | Sex | Ring number | Name |
|---|---|---|---|---|---|---|
| Date | Time | Weight | Crop | | | |
| | | | | | | |
| | | | | | | |
| | | | | | | |
| | | | | | | |
| | | | | | | |
| | | | | | | |
| | | | | | | |
| | | | | | | |
| | | | | | | |
| | | | | | | |
| | | | | | | |
| | | | | | | |
| | | | | | | |
| | | | | | | |
| | | | | | | |
| | | | | | | |
| | | | | | | |
| | | | | | | |
| | | | | | | |
| | | | | | | |
| | | | | | | |
| | | | | | | |
| | | | | | | |
| | | | | | | |
| | | | | | | |
| | | | | | | |
| | | | | | | |
| | | | | | | |

# Further Reading

## Chapter 1

Baumel, J. J. (ed). 1979. *Handbook of Avian Anatomy: Nomina Anatomica Avium.* Academic Press, London. ISBN 0-12-083150-3.

Brown, L. H. 1976. *Birds of Prey: their Biology and Ecology.* Hamlyn. ISBN 0600-313-069.

Brown, L. H. and D. Amadon. 1968. *Eagles, Hawks and Falcons of the World.* Country Life.

Burton, R. 1990. *Bird Flight.* Facts on File, Oxford. ISBN 0-8160-2410-3.

Cade, T. J. 1982. *Falcons of the World.* Cornell University Press. ISBN 0-8014-1454-7.

Campbell, T. W. 1988. *Avian Hematology and Cytology.* Iowa State University Press. ISBN 0-8138-0064-1.

Cooper, J. E. 1978. *Veterinary aspects of captive birds of prey.* Standfast Press. Glos. ISBN 0904-602-044.

Cramp, S and K. E. L. Simmons. 1980. *The Birds of the Western Palearctic* vol. II. Oxford University Press. ISBN 0-19-857505X.

Farner, D. S. and J. R. King. 1974. *Avian Biology.* Academic Press, New York.

George, J. C. and A. J. Berger. 1966. *Avian Myology.* Academic Press.

Hildebrand, M., D. M. Bramble, K. F. Liem, D. B. Wake (eds.) 1985. *Functional Vertebrate Morphology.* Harvard University Press, Cambridge, Massachusetts.

Kermode, A. C. 1970. *Flight without Formulae.* Pitman. ISBN 0-273-41680-4.

King, A. S. and J. McLelland (eds.). 1979 & 1981. *Form and Function in Birds,* vols. 1 & 2. Academic Press, London.

A. S. King and J. McLelland. 1984. *Birds: Their Structure and Function.* Bailliere Tindall, London. ISBN 0-7020-0872-9.

Marshall, A. J. 1961. *Biology and Comparative Physiology of Birds.* Academic Press, New York.

McLelland, J. 1990. *A Colour Atlas of Avian Anatomy.* Wolfe Publishing. ISBN 0-7234-1575-7.

O'Connor, R. J. 1984. *The Growth and Development of Birds.* John Wiley and Sons. ISBN 0-471-90345-0.

Pendleton, B. A. G., B. A. Millsap, K. W. Cline, and D. M. Bird (eds.). 1987. *Raptor Management Techniques Manual.* National Wildlife Federation scientific and technical series, no. 10. Washington, DC. ISBN 0-912186-82-8.

Pennycuick, C. J. 1972. *Animal flight. Studies in Biology 33.* Edward Arnold, London.

———— 1989. *Bird Flight Performance, A Practical Calculation Manual.* Oxford University Press. ISBN 0-19-857721-4.

Pennycuick, C. J. and A. Lock. 1976. "Elastic energy storage in primary feather shafts." *J. Exp. Biol.* 64: 677-689.

Piggott, D. 1977. *Understanding gliding: the principles of soaring flight.* A. & C. Black. ISBN 0-7-136-1640-7.

Rayner, J. M. V. "Form and function in avian flight." In Johnston, R. F. (ed). *Current Ornithology,* vol. 5. Plenum Press, New York.

Skutch, A. F. 1976 . *Parent birds and their young.* University of Texas Press. Austin & London. ISBN 0-292-76424-3.

Snyder, N. F. R. and J. W. Wiley. 1976. *Sexual size dimorphism in Hawks and Owls of North America.* Ornithological monographs no. 20. American Ornithologists' Union.

Spedding, G. R. 1982. *The Vortex Wake of Birds: An experimental Investigation.* PhD thesis, University of Bristol, U.K.

Sturkie, P. D. 1965. *Avian Physiology.* Comstock Publishing Associates, Ithaca, New York.

Tucker, V. A. and C. Heine. 1990. "Aerodynamics of gliding flight in a Harris Hawk, Parabuteo unicinctus." *J. Exp. Biol.* 149: 469-489.

Voitkevich, A. A. 1966. *The feathers and plumage of birds.* Sidgwick & Jackson, London.

Wattel, J. 1973. "Geographic Differentiation in the Genus *Accipiter.*" *Nuttall Ornithological Club* 13:1:231.

Welty, J. C. 1975. *The Life of Birds.* W. B. Saunders Co. ISBN 0-7216-9231-1.

Wu, T. Y. T., C. J. Brokaw, and C. Brennen (eds.). 1975. *Swimming and Flying in Nature.* Plenum Press, New York.

Zeigler, H. P. and H. J. Bischof. (eds.) 1993. *Vision, Brain, and Behavior in Birds.* MIT Press, Cambridge, Massachusetts. ISBN 0-262-24036.

## Chapter 2

Anderson Brown, A. F. 1979. *The Incubation Book.* Saiga Publishing Co. ISBN 0-904558-70-3.

Carter, T. C. and B. M. Freeman, (eds.). 1969. *The Fertility and Hatchability of the Hen's Egg.* Oliver & Boyd, Edinburgh.

Cooke, F., and P. A. Buckley. 1987. *Avian genetics: A population and ecological approach.* Academic Press. ISBN 0-12-187570-9.

Cunningham, F. J., P. E. Lake and D. Hewitt, (eds.). 1984. "Reproductive Biology of Poultry." *British Poultry Science.* Longmans Ltd.

Deeming, D. C. and M. W. J. Ferguson, (eds.). 1991. *Egg Incubation: Its effect on embryonic development in birds and reptiles.* Cambridge University Press. ISBN 0-521-39071-0.

Drent, R. 1973. "The Natural History of Incubation." In D.

S. Farner and J. R. King (eds.). *Avian Biology*. vol. 5. Academic Press, New York.

Freeman, B. M. and M. A. Vince. 1974. *Development of the Avian Embryo*. Chapman and Hall, London. ISBN 0-412-11520-4.

Gee, G. F., C. A. Morrell, J. C. Franson and O. H. Pattee. 1993. "Cryopreservation of American Kestrel Semen with Dimethylsulfoxide." *Raptor Research* 27 (1): 21-25.

Grant, G. S. 1982. "Avian incubation: egg temperature, nest humidity, and behavioral thermoregulation in a hot environment." *Ornithological Monographs* no. 30. The American Ornithologists' Union, Washington, DC.

Haak, B. A. 1992. *The Hunting Falcon*. Hancock House, Surrey, BC. ISBN 0-88839-292-3.

Harvey, R. 1993. *Practical Incubation*. Hancock House, Surrey, BC. ISBN 0-88839-310-5.

Johnson, A. D. and C. W. Foley (eds.) 1974. *The Oviduct and its Functions*. Academic Press.

Moore, H. D. M., W. V. Holt, and G. M. Mace. 1992. *Biotechnology and the conservation of genetic diversity*. Oxford Science Publications. ISBN 0-19-854030-2.

North, M. O. and D. D. Bell. 1990. *Commercial chicken production manual*. AVI. Van Nostrand Reinhold. ISBN 0-442-31882-2.

O'Connor, R. J. 1985. *The Growth and Development of Birds*. John Wiley and Sons. ISBN 0 471 90345 0.

Parry-Jones, J. 1991. *Falconry: Care, captive breeding and conservation*. David and Charles. ISBN 0-7153-8914-9.

Slack, J. M. W. 1991. *From Egg to Embryo*. Cambridge University Press.

Schwartz, A., J. D. Weaver, N. R. Scott and T. J. Cade. 1977. "Measuring the temperature of eggs during incubation under captive falcons." *Journal of Wildlife Management* 41 (1):12-17.

Thear, K. 1987. *Keeping quail: a guide to domestic and commercial management*. Broad Leys Publishing Co. ISBN 0-906137-15-2.

Tullet, S. G. (ed). 1990. "Avian Incubation." *Poultry Science Symposium* 22. Butterworth-Heinemann, London. ISBN 0-7506-1002-6.

Van Vleck, L. D. 1983. *Notes on the theory and application of selection principles for the genetic improvement of animals*. Department of Animal Science, Cornell University, Ithaca, NY.

Van Vleck, L. D, Pollack and Ollenacee. 1987. *Genetics for the Animal Sciences*.

Watson, P. F. 1978. "Artificial Breeding of Non-Domestic Animals." *Symposia of the Zoological Society of London* 43. Academic Press.

Weaver, J. D. and T. J. Cade. 1983. *Falcon Propagation: a manual on captive breeding*. The Peregrine Fund Inc., Ithaca, NY, U.S.A.

Woodard, A., P. Vohra, and V. Denton. 1993. *Commercial and Ornamental Gamebird Breeders Handbook*. Hancock House, Surrey, BC. ISBN 0-88839-311-3.

## Chapter 3

Beebe, F. L. and H. M. Webster. 1994. *North American Falconry and Hunting Hawks* 7th edition. Denver, CO.

Beebe, F. L. 1992. *The Compleat Falconer*. Hancock House, Surrey, BC. ISBN 0-88839-253-2.

British Falconers' Club: *Journals* 1937 -.

Ford, E. 1992. *Falconry, Art and Practice*. Blandford, London. ISBN 0-7137-2248-7.

Glasier, P. 1978. *Falconry and Hawking*. Batsford. ISBN 0-7134-0232-6.

Kimsey, B. A. and J. Hodge. 1992. *Falconry Equipment*. Kimsey/Hodge Publications, Houston, TX.

McElroy, H. 1977. *Desert Hawking II*. Privately printed.

North American Falconer's Association: *Journal* 1961 -.

Parry-Jones, J. 1994. *Training Birds of Prey*. David and Charles, Devon. ISBN 0-7153-0142-X.

Upton, R. 1991. *Falconry, Principles and Practice*. A. & C. Black. ISBN 0-7136-3262-3.

## Chapter 4

Bolles, R. C. 1975. *Theory of Motivation*. Harper and Row, New York.

Dawkins, M. S. 1985. *Unravelling animal behaviour*. Longman.

Halliday, T. R. and P. J. B. Slater. 1983. *Animal Behaviour*. Blackwells Scientific Publications, Oxford.

Hess, E. H. 1973. *Imprinting*. D. Van Nostrand Co. ISBN 0-442-23393-0.

Krebs, J. R. and N. B. Davies. *Behavioural ecology*. Blackwell Scientific Publications, Oxford.

Lorenz, K. 1965. *Evolution and modification of behaviour*. University of Chicago Press.

Martin, S. 1994. *The Positive Approach to Parrots as Pets: Videotape 1. Understanding Bird Behavior. 2. Training through Positive Reinforcement*. Natural Encounters Inc. P. O. Box 68666, Indianapolis, IN 46268.

——— "New Training Thoughts for Falconry Birds." *Hawk Chalk* XXXIII, no. 2: 44-54.

McFarland, D. 1981. *The Oxford Companion to Animal Behaviour*. Oxford University Press. ISBN 0-19-86610-7.

Pryor, K. 1985. *Don't Shoot the Dog!* Bantam Books. New York. ISBN 0-553-25388-3.

Sherrod, S. K., W. R. Heinrich, W. A. Burnham, J. H. Barclay, and T. J. Cade. 1981. *Hacking: a method for releasing peregrine falcons and other birds of prey*. Peregrine Fund Inc., Cornell University.

Sherrod, S. K. 1983. *Behaviour of fledgling peregrines*. The Peregrine Fund Inc., Ithaca, NY.

Skutch, A. F. 1976. *Parent birds and their young*. University of Texas Press. ISBN 0-292-76424-3.

Stevens, R. 1955. *Observations on Modern Falconry*. Privately printed.

Tinbergen, N. 1951. *The Study of Instinct*. Oxford University Press.

Weiskrantz, L. (ed.) 1988. *Thought without Language*. Clarendon Press, Oxford.

## Chapter 5

Abs, M. (ed) 1983. *Physiology and Behaviour of the Pigeon*. Academic Press, New York.

Aschoff, J. (ed.) 1981. *Handbook of Behavioural Neurobiology*. Plenum, London.

Beebe, F. L. 1992. *The Compleat Falconer*. Hancock House, Surrey, BC. ISBN 0-88839-253-2.

Beebe, F. L. and H. M. Webster. 1994. *North American Falconry and Hunting Hawks* 7th edition. Denver, CO.

Bert, E. 1619. *An Approved Treatise of Hawkes and Hawking*. Richard Moore, London.

Bolles, R. C. 1975. *Theory of motivation*. Harper and Row, New York.

Boni, B. 1994. *A Tale of Two Passagers: A Treatise on the Passage Red-tailed Hawk and Passage Female Copper's Hawk*. Privately printed. Tucson, Arizona.

Bower, G. H. (ed.) 1980. *The Psychology of Learning and Motivation*. Academic Press, New York.

Dewsbury, D. A. 1978. *Comparative Animal Behaviour*. McGraw-Hill, New York.

Edmunds, M. 1974. *Defence in Animals*. Longmans.

Ewart, J. P. and D. J. Ingle. (eds.) 1983. *Advances in Vertebrate Neuroethology*. Plenum, New York.

Farner, D. S. and J. R. King. (eds.) 1974. *Avian Biology*. Academic Press, New York.

Ferster, C. B. and B. F. Skinner. 1957. *Schedules of Reinforcement*. Appleton-Century-Crofts, New York.

Fitzsimons, J. T. 1979. "The Physiology of Thirst and Sodium Appetite." *Monographs of the Physiological Society*, no. 35. Cambridge University Press.

Garatinni, S. and E. B. Sigg. (eds.) 1969. *Aggressive Behaviour*. Excerpta Medica, Amsterdam.

Halliday, T. R. and P, J. B. Slater. (eds.) 1983. *Animal Behaviour*. Blackwell Scientific Publications, Oxford.

Hinde, R. A. 1970. *Animal Behaviour*. McGraw-Hill, New York.

Hinde, R. A. (ed). 1972. *Non-verbal communication*. Cambridge University Press.

Huber, F. and H. Markl. 1983. *Neuroethology and Behavioural Physiology*. Springer-Verlag, Berlin.

King, A. S. and J. McLelland. (eds.) 1981. *Form and Function in Birds*. Academic Press, London.

Krebs, J. R. and N. B. Davies (eds.). 1984. *Behavioural Ecology* (2nd Edition). Blackwell Scientific Publications.

Lorenz, K. 1965. *Evolution and modification of behaviour*. University of Chicago Press.

Marler, P. R. and W. J. Hamilton. 1966. *Mechanisms of Animal Behaviour*. John Wiley and Sons.

Marler, P. R. and J. G. Vandenburgh. (eds.). 1979. *Handbook of Behavioural Neurobiology*. Plenum, New York.

Marshall, A. J. (ed.) 1960. *Biology and Comparative Physiology of Birds*. Academic Press, New York.

Martin, S. 1994. *The Positive Approach to Parrots as Pets*: Videotape 1. *Understanding Bird Behavior*. 2. *Training through Positive Reinforcement*. Natural Encounters Inc. PO Box 68666, Indianapolis, IN 46268.

Martin, S. 1994. "New Training Thoughts for Falconry Birds" *Hawk Chalk* XXXIII, no. 2: 44-54

Mavrogordato, J. G. 1960. *A Hawk for the Bush*. H. F. and G. Witherby, London.

McElroy, H. 1977. *Desert Hawking II*. Privately printed.

Oakes, W. C. 1993. *The Falconer's Apprentice: A Guide to Training the Passage Red-tailed Hawk*. Eaglewing Publishing, Roy, UT. ISBN 1-885054-01-7.

Parry-Jones, J. 1994. *Training Birds of Prey*. David and Charles, Devon. ISBN 07153-0142-X.

Pedley, T. J. (ed.) 1977. *Scale Effects of Animal Locomotion*. Academic Press, London.

Phillips, J. G., P. J. Butler, and P. J. Sharp. 1985. *Physiological Strategies in Avian Biology*. Blackie: Glasgow and London. ISBN 0-216-91780-8.

Pryor, K. 1985. *Don't Shoot the Dog!* Bantam Books. New York. ISBN 0-553-25388-3.

Rosser, B. W. C. and George, J. C. 1986. "The avian pectoralis: histochemical characterization and distribution of muscle fiber types." *Can. J. Zool.* 64: 1174-1185.

Stein, B. E. and M. A. Meredith. 1993. *The Merging of the Senses*. MIT Press, Cambridge, MA. ISBN 0-262-24036-X.

Stevens, R. 1955. *Observations on Modern Falconry*. Privately printed.

Tsukada, Y. and B. W. Agranoff (eds.) 1980. *Neurobiological Basis for Learning and Memory*. John Wiley, New York.

Upton, R. 1990. *Falconry: Principles and Practice*. A. & C. Black, London. ISBN 0-7136-3262-3.

Weiskrantz, L. (ed.) 1985. *Animal Intelligence*. Clarendon, Oxford.

## Chapter 6

Note: The great majority of references on this topic are in short notes and papers rather than in books.

Cade, T. J. 1982. *Falcons of the World*. Cornell University Press. ISBN 0-8014-1454-7.

Cramp, S. and K. E. L. Simmons 1980. *The Birds of the Western Palearctic*. vol. II. Oxford University Press. ISBN 0-19-857505-X.

Cureo, E. 1976. *The Ethology of Predation*. Springer-Verlag, New York.

Hamerstrom, F. 1986. *Harrier: Hawk of the Marshes. The hawk that is ruled by a mouse*. Smithsonian Institution Press. ISBN 0-87474-538-1.

Newton, I. 1986. *The Sparrowhawk*. T. & A. D. Poyser Ltd. ISBN 0-85661-041-0.

Orton, D. A. 1989. *The Hawkwatcher: Adventures among Birds of Prey in the Wild*. Unwin Hyman, London. ISBN 0-04-440140-X.

Page, G. and D. F. Whitacre. 1975. "Raptor predation on wintering shorebirds." *Condor* 77:73-83.

Ratcliffe, D. 1980. *The Peregrine Falcon*. T. & A. D. Poyser Ltd. ISBN 0-85661-026-7.

Schipper, W. J. A. 1973. "A comparison of prey selection in sympatric Harriers (*Circus*) in Western Europe." *Le Gerfaut* 63: 17-120.

Village, A. 1990. *The Kestrel*. T. & A. D. Poyser Ltd. ISBN 0-85661-054-2.

Treleaven, R. B. 1977. *Peregrine*. Headland Publications, Penzance.

Walter, H. 1979. *Eleonora's Falcon: Adaptations to Prey and Habitat in a Social Raptor*. University of Chicago Press, Chicago.

## Chapter 7

Allen, M. 1980. Falconry in Arabia. Orbis, London.

Anon. 15—. *A Perfect Booke for Kepinge of Sparhawkes or Goshawkes.* Quaritch 1886.

Beebe, F. L. and H. M. Webster. 1994. *North American Falconry and Hunting Hawks* 7th edition. Denver, CO.

Beebe, F. L. 1992. *The Compleat Falconer.* Hancock House, Surrey, BC. ISBN 0-88839-253-2.

Bert, Edmund. 1619. *An Approved Treatise of Hawkes and Hawking.*

Blaine, G. 1936. *Falconry.* 1970 Reprint, Neville, Spearman Ltd. ISBN 84435-320-8.

Brander, M. 1963. *Gundogs: their care and training.* A. & C. Black. London.

British Falconers' Club: *Journals.* 1937 -.

Brodie, I. 1978. *Ferrets and ferreting.* Blandford Press, Poole. ISBN 0-7137-0903-0.

Carlisle, G. L. 1983. *Grouse and gun.* Stanley Paul, London. ISBN 0-09-153360-0.

Cummins, J. 1988. *The Hound and the Hawk: the art of medieval hunting.* Weidenfield and Nicolson, London. ISBN 0-297-79459-0.

Davis, H. P. 1970. *Training and Hunting your own Bird Dog.* G. P. Putnam's Sons.

De Chamerlat, C. A. 1987. *Falconry and Art.* Sotheby's, London. ISBN 0-85667-338-2.

De La Fuente, F. R. 1970. *El Arte de Cetreria.* Libreria Noriega, Mexico. ISBN 968-18-2226-9.

Durman-Walters, D. 1994. *The Modern Falconer.* Swan Hill Press, Shrewsbury, England. ISBN 1-85310-368-3.

Ford, E. 1992. *Falconry, Art and Practice.* Blandford, London. ISBN 0-7137-2248-7.

Frederick II, 1248. *De Arte Venandi cum Avibus.* 1943 translation by C.A. Wood and F.M. Fyfe. Stanford University Press.

Freeman, G. E. 1869. *Practical Falconry.* Horace Cox, London.

Glasier, P. 1978. *Falconry and Hawking.* Batsford. ISBN 0-7134-0232-6.

Haak, B. A. 1992. *The Hunting Falcon.* Hancock House, Surrey, BC. ISBN 0-88839-292-3.

Harting, J. E. 1898. *The Rabbit.* Longmans, London.

Hollinshead, M. 1993. *Hawking Ground Quarry.* Hancock House, Surrey, BC. ISBN 0-88839-320-2.

Humphreys, J. 1990. *The Complete Gundog.* David and Charles, Newton Abbot. ISBN 0-7153-9412-6.

Irving, J. 1983. *Gundogs - Their learning chain.* Loreburn, Dumfries. ISBN 0-9506670-1-3.

Jackson, T. 1989. *Hunter, Pointer, Retriever.* Ashford, Southampton. ISBN 1-85253-189-4.

Jameson, E. W., Jr. 1962. *The Hawking of Japan.* Privately Printed, Davis, California.

—— 1993. *Shortwinged Hawks: A review of Ancient and Modern Hawking.* Privately Printed, Davis, California.

Latham, Symon, 1615. *Latham's Faulconry, or The Faulcon's Lure and Cure.*

Latham, Symon, 1618. *Latham's New and Second Booke of Faulconry.*

Martin, B. P. 1990. *The Glorious Grouse.* David and Charles, Newton Abbot. ISBN 0-7153-9237-9.

Mavrogordato, J. G. 1960. *A Hawk for the Bush.* H. F. & G. Witherby Ltd.

Mavrogordato, J. G. 1966. *A Falcon in the Field.* Knightly Vernon Ltd.

McKelvie, C. L. 1990. *The Book of the Woodcock.* Swan Hill Press, Shrewsbury. ISBN 1-85310-113-3.

McElroy, H. 1977. *Desert Hawking II.* Privately printed.

Michell, E. B. 1900. *The Art and Practice of Hawking.* 1959 Edition, Holland Press.

Mirza, Taymur. 1868. *The Baz-Nama-Yi Nasiri.* Translated by D. C. Phillott, 1908, Bernard Quaritch, London.

Moxon, P. R. A. 1967. *Gundogs: training and fieldtrials.* Popular Dogs, London. ISBN 09-029762-8.

North American Falconer's Association: *Journal* 1961 -.

O'Broin, L. 1992. *A Manual for Hawking.* Privately printed.

Parry-Jones, J. 1994. *Training Birds of Prey.* David and Charles, Devon. ISBN 0-7153-0142-X.

Remple, D. and C. Gross. 1993. *Falconry and Birds of Prey in the Gulf.* Motivate Publishing, Dubai. ISBN 1-873544-39-1.

Sebright, J. S. 1826. *Observations upon Hawking.* J. Harding, London.

Stevens, R. 1957. *Observations on Modern Falconry.* Privately Printed.

Timimi, F. A. 1987. *Falcons and Falconry in Qatar.* Privately printed, Doha.

Turner, R, and A. Haslen. 1991. *Gamehawk.* Gallery Press, Lavenham.

Upton, R. 1980. *A Bird in the Hand.* Debrett.

Upton, R. 1987. *O, for a falconer's voice.* The Crowood Press, Marlborough. ISBN 1-85223-015-0.

Upton, R. 1991. *Falconry, Principles and Practice.* A. & C. Black ISBN 0-7136-3262-3.

Van de Wall, J. W. M. 1986. *De Valkerij Op Het Loo. The Royal Loo Hawking Club 1839-1855.* Joh Enschedé en Zonen. Haarlem. ISBN 90-70024-42X

Waller, R. 1987. *Der Wilde Falk ist mein Gesell.* J. Neumann-Neudamm, Melsungen.

Webster, H. M. 1988. *Gamehawking at its very best.* Windsong Press, Denver. ISBN 0-912510-04-X.

Woodford, M. 1966. *A Manual of Falconry.* A. & C. Black. ISBN 0-7136-0736X.

## Chapter 8

Arnall, L. and I. F. Keymer. 1975. *Bird diseases.* TFH Publications Inc., New Jersey. ISBN 0-87666-950-X.

Beebe, F. L. and H. M. Webster. 1994. *North American Falconry and Hunting Hawks* 7th edition. Denver, CO.

Bijleveld, M. 1974. *Birds of Prey in Europe.* MacMillan, London.

Bradshaw, J. W. S. 1992. *The Behaviour of the Domestic Cat.* C. A. B. International, U.K. ISBN 0-85198-715-X.

Burr, E. W. 1987. *Companion Bird Medicine.* Iowa State University Press. ISBN 0-8138-0362-4.

Cade, T. T., J. H. Enderson, C. G. Thelander, and C. M. White. 1988. *Peregrine Falcon Populations : Their Man-*

*agement and Recovery.* The Peregrine Fund Inc. ISBN 0-9619839-0-6.

Cavé, A. J. 1968. "The breeding of the Kestrel *Falco tinnunculus L.*, in the reclaimed area Oostelijk Flevoland." *Netherlands Journal of Zoology* 18 (30): 313-407.

de Chamerlat, C. A. 1987. *Falconry and Art.* Sotheby's Publications, ACR Edition Internationale. ISBN 0-85667-338-2.

Coles, B. H. 1985. *Avian Medicine and Surgery.* Blackwell Scientific Publications, Oxford. ISBN 0-632-01403-2.

Cooper, J. E. and J. T. Eley. 1979. *First aid and care of wild birds.* David and Charles, London. ISBN 0-7153-7664-0.

Cooper, J. E. and A. G. Greenwood (eds.). 1981. *Recent Advances in the Study of Raptor Diseases.* Chiron Publications, Keighley, England. ISBN 0-9507716-0-0.

Craighead, J. J. and F. C. Craighead. 1969. *Hawks, Owls and Wildlife.* Dover Publications. ISBN 486-22137-7.

Davis, J. W., R. C. Anderson, L. Karstad, and D. O. Trainer. (eds.). 1971. *Infectious and parasitic diseases of wild birds.* Iowa State University Press.

Dawkins, R. 1989. *The Selfish Gene.* Oxford University Press. 0-19-286092-5.

Fenech, N. 1992. *Fatal flight: the Maltese obsession with killing birds.* Quiller Press, London. ISBN 1870948-53-X.

Filkins, K (ed). 1993. *A Bond with the Wild: A Celebration of American Falconry.* North American Falconers' Association. LCCCN 93-85241.

Forbes, N. A. and G. N. Simpson. 1994. *Emergencies and First Aid: A course for rehabilitators and falconers.* Clockhouse Veterinary Hospital, Wallbridge, Stroud U.K.

Freeman, G. A. and F. H. Salvin. 1859. *Falconry: Its Claims, History and Practice.* Longmans, London.

Hallet, G. 1988. *Land and housing policies in Europe and the USA.* Routhledge, London.

HMSO. 1981. *The Wildlife and Countryside Act 1981.* Her Majesty's Stationery Office, London. ISBN 0-10-546981-5.

Harrison, G. J. and L. R. Harrison. 1986. *Clinical Avian Medicine and Surgery, including aviculture.* W. B. Saunders Co, Philadelphia. ISBN 0-7216-1241-5.

Knecht, C. D., A. R. Allen, D. J. Williams, and J. H. Johnson. 1987. *Fundamental techniques in Veterinary Surgery.* W. B. Saunders Co. Philadelphia. ISBN 0-7216-1397-7.

Lacy, R. 1988. "A report on population genetics in conservation." *Conservation Biology* 2 (3):245-247.

Lack, D. 1954. *The natural regulation of animal numbers.* Oxford University Press.

Lack, D. 1966. *Population studies of birds.* Oxford University Press. ISBN 0-19-857335-0.

Llewellyn, P. J. and Brain, P. F. 1983. "Guidelines for the re-habilitation of injured raptors." In Olney, P. J. (ed). *International Zoo Yearbook* 23: 121-125. Zoological Society of London.

Lovegrove, R. 1990. *The Kite's Tale: The story of the Red Kite in Wales.* RSPB, U.K. ISBN 0-903138-37-9.

Mace, G. 1986. "Genetic management of small populations." *International Zoo Year Book* 24/25: 167-174.

Medway, Lord. 1980. *Report of the Panel of Enquiry into Shooting and Angling (1976-79).* c/o The Causeway, Hor-

sham RH12 1HG, U.K.

Meijer, T. 1988. *Reproductive decisions in the Kestrel: a study in physiological ecology.* Drukkererij Van Denderen B. V., Groningen.

Newton, I. 1979. *Population Ecology of Raptors.* T. & A. D. Poyser Ltd. ISBN 0-85661-023-2.

Newton, I. 1986. *The Sparrowhawk.* T. & A. D. Poyser Ltd. ISBN 0-85661-0410.

New York State Department of Environmental Conservation. Undated. *New York State Falconry Examination Manual.* New York State Department of Environmental Conservation, 50 Wolf Rd., Albany, NY 12233.

Oakes, W. C. 1993. *Topical Index of North American Falconry: The 1940's, 1950's, 1970's, 1980's.* Eaglewing Publishing. Roy, UT.

Olney, P. 1990. Proceedings of a Raptor Rehabilitation Workshop, London Zoo 1990. The Falconry Centre, Newent, England.

Page, R. 1977. *The Hunter and the Hunted.* Readers' Union, Devon.

Potter, C. (ed.). 1991. "The Impact of cats on Native Wildlife." Proceedings of a Workshop 8-9 May 1991, The Endangered Species Unit, Australian National Parks and Wildlife Service.

Ratcliffe, D. 1980. *The Peregrine Falcon.* T. & A. D. Poyser Ltd. ISBN 0-85661-026-7.

Redig, P. T. 1993. *Medical Management of Birds of Prey.* 2nd Edition. The Raptor Center, University of Minnesota.

Redig, P. T., J. E. Cooper, J. D. Remple, and D. B. Hunter (eds.). 1993. *Raptor Biomedicine.* Chiron Publications Ltd, Keighley, U.K.

Ryman, N. and L. Laikre. 1991. "Effects of supportive breeding on the genetically effective population size." *Conservation Biology* 5 (3): 325-328.

Royal Society for the Protection of Birds. 1992. *The International Trade in Wild Birds.* RSPB, The Lodge, Sandy, Beds, U.K.

Smith, J. A. and K. M. Boyd (eds.). 1991. *Lives in the Balance.* Oxford University Press.

Travis, A. S. (ed.) 1980. *Angling in Britain 1980: Report of the Travis Commission.* The Angling Foundation.

Tubbs, C. R. 1974. *The Buzzard.* David & Charles, London. ISBN 0-7153-6323-9.

Turner, D. and P. Bateson (eds.). 1988. *The Domestic Cat: the Biology of its Behaviour.* Cambridge University Press.

Upton, R. 1980. *A Bird in the Hand.* Debrett's Peerage Ltd. U.K. ISBN 0-905649-34-6.

Upton, R. 1987. *O for a Falconer's Voice.* Crowood Press, Marlborough, Wilts. ISBN 1-85223-015-0.

Village, A. 1990. *The Kestrel.* T. & A. D. Poyser Ltd. ISBN 0-85661-054-2.

Walter, H. 1979. *Eleonora's Falcon.* University of Chicago Press. ISBN 0-226-87229-7.

Watson, J. N. P. 1991. *A Green Guide to Country Sports.* The Sportsman's Press, London. ISBN 0-948253-525.

Webster, H. M. and J. Enderson. 1988. *Game Hawking...at its very best.* Windsong Press. ISBN 0-912510-04-X.

# Index